This is a refreshing and timely book on finance law, which has been written with students in mind. Its expert author employs various tools to assist understanding of a complicated area of law. He adopts an impressive multi-faceted approach incorporating theory, practice and doctrine (including private law underpinnings), with reference to domestic and international corporate finance spheres.

—**Dr Alisdair MacPherson**, *University of Aberdeen, UK*

Connelly's masterful exposition of the English private law principles that underpin financial transactions fills a genuine gap in the market. It is precise, theoretically informed and user-friendly, containing valuable pedagogic elements – most prominently, case studies, diagrams and extensive extracts from leading cases.

—**Dr Andreas Kokkinis**, *Associate Professor, Birmingham Law School, UK*

Finance Law

For the student who wishes to understand law as it is practised in a modern financial context, *Finance Law* offers the only up-to-date university-level textbook which explains legal principles as they are applied in today's advanced financial transactions.

Essential for any student or researcher seeking an introduction to this complex and fast-moving world, this text:

- is based on the author's extensive teaching experience in finance law
- covers the modern form of credit facilities agreements, security, syndication, securities and securitization, derivatives, and payment and clearing systems
- is packed with interesting case studies, including the Mozambique Tuna Bond Scandal, the takeover of Manchester Utd plc, and the securitization of student loans
- motivates study with theoretical discussions and historical contextualization
- explains key transaction structures, such as investment grade lending to groups, intercreditor agreements, interest rate swaps, and multilateral payment systems
- grants insight into key legal principles and structuring applicable to trillion-dollar deals across the globe
- is written by a structured finance practitioner and academic with extensive post-qualification experience of advising lenders, corporate borrowers, and sovereigns on international finance.

Designed for final-year undergraduates and LLM students, *Finance Law* is not only the perfect accompaniment to any finance module but can support any advanced programme on insolvency law, mergers and acquisitions (M&A), corporate governance, international economic law, and more.

Stephen Connelly is Reader in Law at the University of Warwick, UK.

Finance Law

Stephen Connelly

Routledge
Taylor & Francis Group
LONDON AND NEW YORK

Designed cover image: Seekershadow / Getty Images ®

First published 2025
by Routledge
4 Park Square, Milton Park, Abingdon, Oxon OX14 4RN

and by Routledge
605 Third Avenue, New York, NY 10158

Routledge is an imprint of the Taylor & Francis Group, an informa business

British Library Cataloguing-in-Publication Data
A catalogue record for this book is available from the British Library

Library of Congress Cataloging-in-Publication Data
Names: Connelly, Stephen, author.
Title: Finance law / Stephen Connelly is Reader in Law at the University of Warwick, UK.
Description: New York : Routledge, 2025. | Includes bibliographical references and index.
Identifiers: LCCN 2024061971 | ISBN 9781032600307 (hardback) | ISBN 9781032600222 (paperback) | ISBN 9781003457220 (ebook)
Subjects: LCSH: Financial institutions—Law and legislation. | International finance—Law and legislation. | Corporations—Finance—Law and legislation. | Commercial loans—Law and legislation. | Finance—Law and legislation. | Credit—Law and legislation. | Security (Law)
Classification: LCC K1066 .C656 2025 | DDC 346/.08—dc23/eng/20241231
LC record available at https://lccn.loc.gov/2024061971

ISBN: 978-1-032-60030-7 (hbk)
ISBN: 978-1-032-60022-2 (pbk)
ISBN: 978-1-003-45722-0 (ebk)

DOI: 10.4324/9781003457220

Typeset in Joanna
by Apex CoVantage, LLC

For Samuel

Contents

Detailed contents

Preface

This book is designed as a textbook for a one-semester course on the English law of finance as used in contracts across the world. It is aimed at graduates but can be and has been taught to finalist undergraduates. It focuses on private law and on the transactions which deploy and are affected by that private law. As such, the regulation of finance is pushed to the background, giving way to a focus on fundamental legal principles. After all, it does not seem prudent to study the second-order regulation of finance if one does not understand the first-order rules of finance set out in private law and how they operate in private financial transactions.

Finance law, as this book conceives it, is not a sui generis legal framework like obligations or property but stands in relation to them as engineering stands in relation to physics. Finance law is an *applied* law—the law of obligations, property, companies, and equity, as applied and giving publicly recognized form to social relations of indebtedness.

Finance law is also, in practice, inherently international in scope. 'International' here means the cross-border use of English finance law and practice, not public international law. Not only is it possible for a Nicaraguan borrower and Chinese lender to enter into a loan contract governed by English law, but they do, and they might secure it with mortgages of Liberian and Maltese-flag ships docked in Lisbon, held by a Singaporean bank. Even if the various contracts and instruments of this relationship are not governed by English law, the structuring will likely follow the practice developed in the City of London and New York, and the student of finance law will still be able to understand these transactions, subject to local counsel's advice. As Philip Wood has noted, England and Wales has developed a creditor-friendly private legal system, with the result that lenders, who will not lend unless their standard contractual terms are used, very often adopt English law as the law of the contract, even if no party or asset ever comes near the British Isles.

The topics have been selected in line with three principles: (1) where possible, the topics build on the student's foundational legal knowledge; (2) the topics build on each other, with key legal concepts being explored and then encountered again and again through the text; and (3) the topics provide motivation, both in terms of reflecting actual financial practice and also key areas of policy concern in the world today. A great deal of the law of finance is very difficult in the abstract; yet it makes some sense, at least, once one understands *why* financiers are doing what they do. To use a cliché, finance is the dog that wags the legal tail, and trying to make the tail wag the dog, or worse pretending there is no dog and only learning legal rules, will be a waste of everyone's time. This contextual approach reflects my teaching of finance law, company law and advanced contract law at the University of Warwick and at Birkbeck College, University of London. There is no chapter which has not been before students in some form at some point in the last decade. It is also worth disclosing that the topics drawn on my experience at the Frankfurt office of what was then Allen & Overy, where I specialized in European syndicated finance.

The following chart sets out the interrelationship of the various chapters and topics, the main thread of development, after Chapter 1, running through Chapters 2, 6, 8, 9, and 10. The chapters on sovereign debt (insofar as governed by CFAs) and leveraged buyouts (LBOs) may be regarded as optional topics. The two chapters on security could be taken as standalone, yet engaging with them as intended, directly after Chapter 2, will considerably deepen one's appreciation of the material in the main thread of the textbook.

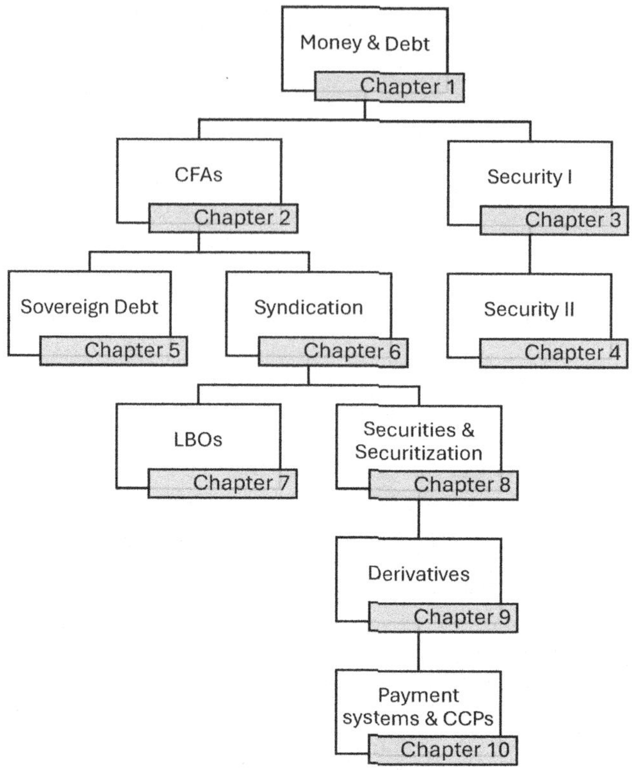

Figure FM-0 Plan of the work

Prerequisites

This book is designed for students possessing what was traditionally called 'foundational legal knowledge,' and the text constantly refers back to things law students are likely to have encountered at undergraduate level, from unilateral contracts to legal and equitable interests in property. While I have endeavoured to review key knowledge, it would be impractical to rehearse the absolute basics such as contract formation or vitiating factors. Non-law students have taken this course when taught and have gained something from it, but they were expected to catch up on the basic legal principles and thus had a much higher workload than their peers.

The essential **prerequisites** for this textbook are:

- Contract law
- Property law (ideally, law of moveable property)

Desirable prerequisites include:

- Company law
- Commercial law (if the course covered e.g. title to goods, payment, security)

Some knowledge of company law—separate corporate personality, limited liability, the freely transferable share—is highly desirable. Company law might be regarded as essential for the study of leveraged buyouts (LBOs) in optional Chapter 7. Some basic knowledge of tort and equity and trusts is also welcome, but I have not singled these out because often sufficient exposure to them for our purposes is garnered from contract (misrepresentation) and property (equitable interests and trusts of land).

In terms of optional **corequisites**, this textbook may be usefully studied alongside several courses offered at the finalist and graduate level, including:

- Banking law
- Financial services regulation
- Mergers and acquisitions (especially Chapter 7)
- Corporate finance (Chapters 4, 6–8)
- Corporate governance (provided the course acknowledges how important creditors are to governing a company)
- International economic law (Chapter 4 on commercial sovereign debt, and Chapter 10 on payment systems)
- LLM dissertation

In short, the textbook and course offer a useful complement to any LLM centred around corporate and financial law.

Topics

With reference to the diagram outline above, the chapters cover the following topics:

Chapter 1: This chapter is very different from the others; it contains almost no positive law. Rather, it aims to situate finance law in its social context. The reason for this is that finance law can feel to the student a niche, advanced subject far from the everyday concerns of crimes and delicts. Finance is something that happens in the City of London and New York, and could quite happily be avoided. Chapter 1 is designed to show that finance is grounded in money and debt, and these 'things' are central to our socio-economic lives. The nature of money (possibly theorized as debt) is an exceptionally deep topic on which, JM Keynes once intoned, we should meditate once a day. As an opener to any course, this chapter calls into question the very nature of something we would otherwise simply assume in such a course: what is it to *pay* someone? To this end, the chapter contrasts English law's nominalist theory of money with two other theoretical accounts—one I term 'realism,' which regards money as a debt relationship, and one I term conceptualism, which groups together several theories which regard money as representing some more complex problematic, such a primordial debt to goods or the structure of the economic system itself.

Chapter 2 introduces the core transaction of this textbook: a kind of standardized loan contract called a credit facilities agreement (**CFA**). It discusses not only the relationship created between lender and borrower, but how the money lent under the agreement is itself borrowed in the money markets, and how the credit facilities agreement is designed to operate in tandem with those money markets. The CFA is based on the London Form which is used worldwide, meaning that the lessons learned and examples given in this chapter are useful for interpreting any loan agreement that follows the London Form.

Chapter 3 examines how lenders under CFAs mitigate risk by taking security over a borrower's assets. The focus here is on the basic principles of the English law of consensual security. The chapter then turns to consider the four kinds of consensual fixed security recognized in England and Wales.

Chapter 4 continues directly from Chapter 3 by investigating the floating charge (or 'debenture') which forms a key feature of any secured financing transaction to a corporate. It looks at the problem of taking security over book debts to illustrate the limits of the floating charge. The two chapters conclude with a more general discussion of how the principles of security are applied in real secured transactions, and as part of this there is an account of guarantees and indemnities.

Chapter 5 is an optional study of the growing use by sovereign borrowers of loans governed by credit facilities agreements normally used by corporates. What follows is a detailed case study of the growth of such lending and the risks that have arisen, exemplified by the Tuna Bond Scandal which struck Mozambique in 2017–18. The pedagogic aim here is to show by doing: to demonstrate to students who are no doubt thinking of topics for a dissertation, how they might go about tackling questions at the intersection of international economic law and private finance law. The chapter discusses how to obtain quantitative financial data to back claims, and how to combine this with a critical legal methodology, to derive transformative policy recommendations.

Chapter 6 introduces syndication. It begins by examining the law and history of a problematic idea: that a creditor may sell a personal obligation of a debtor to pay to a third party—i.e. one may sell debt. It traces the evolution from prohibition to permission, with an excursion into champerty (which has recently become relevant again in New York). We then turn to selling debt in the context of syndicating a credit facilities agreement, discussing how and why this is achieved, and residual legal doubts concerning whether transfers of debt should bind other parties to a credit facilities agreement. The final part of this chapter is all but essential to the remaining topics. It investigates an advanced form of syndication called structured finance, in which the lenders contractually alter the default provisions of insolvency law to benefit certain lenders over others—a process called subordination. The chapter looks at how this is achieved and how the courts have struggled with the perceived conflict between freedom of contract and public insolvency policy.

Chapter 7 is an optional account of leveraged buyouts—the financing of the acquisition of 100% of the shares of a target company. These complicated transactions not only engage a further 'structural' form of subordination additional to the mechanisms analysed in Chapter 6, but also offer an opportunity to examine in some detail the company law topic of capital maintenance. Chapter 7 is certainly worth the effort given the transaction techniques it explains, but as additional motivation it takes the form of a detailed case study of the leveraged buyout of Manchester United plc.

Chapter 8 offers an introduction to securities (debt instruments). It focuses on (promissory) notes and their role in public securities issuance by corporates seeking debt capital. This leads to a discussion of the modern forms of debt securities issuance in which a global note is issued to a single holder, who holds on behalf of all investors. We examine the legal nature of these investors rights versus the noteholder, adopting Benjamin's 'interests in securities' account. The chapter the adds this knowledge back into what we learnt in Chapter 6 to introduce the financial technique called securitization. To motivate this discussion, our case study is the securitization of student loans.

Chapter 9 introduces derivatives. This topic merits a course of its own, so we have focused on two key issues: (1) explaining to students just what a derivative contract is by what it does, and (2) close-out netting. Close-out netting has been chosen for analysis because it raises many of the questions already examined in Chapter 6 in particular, and because it feeds into our discussion of CCPs in Chapter 10.

Chapter 10 brings us full circle to the nature of money, now armed with eight chapters of detailed financial law knowledge. We look at the nature of payment using bank money and cheques, providing historical legal context for the development of modern payment systems and highlighting once more how the legal principles of Chapter 6 inflect the systems we encounter today. Modern payment systems are then compared with securities clearing systems, and we make no bones about illustrating the genetic link between central bank payment clearing and the clearing of securities and derivatives using a Central Counterparty (CCP). The discussion of payment includes an account of cryptocurrencies. The chapter culminates in a case study of the near collapse of one securities exchange in Norway, and its legal and regulatory significance for the regulation of payment and other clearing systems.

These may look like distinct practical topics, linked by a small number of key legal principles, but the truth is these topics are also linked within the financial system itself. In any given project financing, LBO, or securitization (all encountered in the text) you will find subsidiary features and transactions detailed in the remaining chapters. An LBO, for example, will involve CFAs, security, structured finance techniques, the issuance and clearing of securities, and the hedging of risk with derivatives. The interrelation of the elements of this work parallels the reality of advanced finance transactions.

Evidently, not every possible financial topic is or could be covered. There was no room for a discussion of (secured) receivables financing, for example, or investment funds in any great detail. Other topics, such as set-off and netting, are integrated into the main thread of the text, though I appreciate they could just as well merit their own chapter. Then of course there are topics such as insolvency law and banking law which, while in class I would talk to when opportune, I have only gestured towards given that these matters are properly covered in other courses and works.

As noted above, rather than simply cover every bit of law, the preference has been to expend effort contextualizing law in real financial practice, and thereby to link student study to what some of those students will experience in practising finance law or researching the effects of finance in a given field.

Acknowledgements

Many people have been involved in the development of this book, often long before the book itself was conceived. In practical terms, my knowledge of finance law comes from all that I learnt at Allen & Overy—a firm which made an especial effort to ensure its trainees and associates learned the law of financial transactions. Philip Wood and Steven Schuit provided excellent teaching at various stages, and at a more practical level I learnt a great deal from Cathy Bell-Walker, Peter Hoegen, Clare Gibbons, and the absolute *mensch* that is Chris Jahnke. A special nod goes to Hugh Maule, of Lawrence Graham, who trained me in corporate finance.

Warwick Law School, with its famous contextual approach, is the chief inspiration behind this book's approach. I studied as an undergraduate there, learning contract and commercial law from the exceptional Hugh Beale, and now have the honour of teaching his contract module at the School. Everyone at the School has helped me along the way, and I risk missing so many people out of this paragraph. If we restrict things to those directly involved with this book, I give thanks to the amazing Rosie Woodhouse, who helped prepared the final manuscript, Christian Twigg-Flesner and Chris Mills who convened contract modules with me which covered some of this material (for letting me do so)l; Celine Tan and Karina Patricio Ferreira Lima (of Leeds) for our close collaboration on sovereign debt (Chapter 5); Andrea Kokkinis (now Birmingham) and Sheharyar Hamid (now LUMs) for working with me on law of business organizations, finance law, and corporate finance; Serena Natile for her work on mobile money (highlighted in Chapter 2); Dal Singh for our discussions of banking regulation; and Laura Lammasniemi for her pedagogic advice. I should also acknowledge Stewart Motha, who suggested I convene an intensive version of my finance law module at Birkbeck College. Thank you also to the many students who have joined me in the study of finance law and appreciated my approach and been willing to join me in going beyond traditional topics to study finance law as it is practised today. Of these, special mention to Dr Saveethika 'View' Leesurakarn, who worked with me on the bail-in of centrally cleared derivatives while she pursued her own research on non-performing loans. As ever, any errors remain entirely my own responsibility.

Finally, thank you to my family, for you are perfect.

Stephen Connelly
Le Pitarrot
August 2024

Table of cases

C

D

E

F

G

H

I

J

K

L

M

N

O

P

R

S

T

V

W

Y

Z

Australia

Canada

France

Hong Kong

USA

Table of statutes

G

I

J

L

M

P

S

T

Table of statutory instruments and rules

U

U

Other

Non-UK legal instruments

European Union

France

Norway

Spain

United States, Federal and State level

Chapter 1

Money and debt

Some theoretical considerations

Chapter contents

DOI: 10.4324/9781003457220-1

1.1 Introduction

It is common in legal studies that money be taken for granted. Students will discuss the rules of contract law using examples in which a monetary value is deemed consideration for the delivery of commodities, yet this money will be treated as just another widget to be exchanged.[1] Damages for torts and breach of contract will be assessed in monetary terms, but the values discussed will not be critiqued. The capital invested in and employed by a corporation will be regarded formalistically in company. The situation becomes particularly troublesome for students subjected to 'law and economics' approaches, where they are invited for example to calculate when someone should accept the risk and cost of breaching a contract using monetary values that are as immutable as the numbers used to represent them. To use money uncritically in this way (and for that matter mathematics) is to deprive oneself and others of a great deal of understanding.

What is the relationship between law and money? To explore this question in a brief and introductory manner, it seems useful to explore three classes of theory about what money is: let us call them the realist or credit theory, the nominalist theory, and the conceptualist theory.

A naïve version of *realism* is this: that there is a correspondence between the material entities of the world and the ideas the mind has of them, and that universal ideas such as 'cat' or 'value' correspond to universal aspects of the material object under consideration (and its relationship to the cat species). In particular, a realist might argue that a table is made up of legs and a top, and bits of wood and nails. All these components are things, but their relationship as a table is something as well. Once you see that, you notice that all things can be broken down into relationships of constituent parts which are themselves relations, and so on. Identifying what a thing is now reduces to understanding relations. In monetary terms the realist might notice that people are economically related by contracts, property rights, debts and credits, and argues that these relations are 'real.' Money is just such a real relation.

Nominalism holds that ideas have no such import; the *only* entities are the material things 'out there' and our ideas are mere fictions—the names we define for the matter we encounter. In money terms, money's significance is a fiction created by humans, and monetary value is what is agreed (conventionally) by humans. Why though should we believe one fiction rather than another? Why should some stamped metal be money and not, say, a seashell? Nominalists tend to supplement their doctrine with a theory of command: the determinant of what is true/good/money from amongst the fictions is the command that it be so by someone with authority (God/state). In simple terms: if a king says sticks are money, then sticks *are* money because the king said it.

Conceptualism holds that the universal ideas are entities but that they do not need our minds to be—concepts are also entities that subsist independently of individual minds. An idealist might say that a square table expresses the idea of a square which subsists somewhere, even when there are no squares in existence. We are more interested in various materialist accounts, which for example might argue that a human symbol expresses some complex social structure or process. Indeed, the social structure or process may well have generated the symbol. Money is a classic example of this: conceptualists (as we are calling them) regard money as a symbolic expression of a complex social structure (the actually existing state) or process (capitalism), whether we are conscious of them or not.

This threefold classification may be usefully compared to Michel Aglietta's 'Régulation Approach' to money.[2] 'Régulation' here does not mean technical rules issued by an authority, such

1 A version of this chapter first appeared in Illan rua Wall, Freya Middleton and Sahar Shah (eds), *The Critical Legal Pocketbook* (Counterpress 2021) and is reproduced with permission.

2 Michel Aglietta, *Money: 5,000 Years of Debt and Power* (Verso 2018). For an introduction to Aglietta on money, see J Grahl, 'Review Essay Money as Sovereignty: The Economics of Michel Aglietta' (2000) 5 New Political Economy 291. On the *régulation approach*, see

as 'financial regulation.' Rather it means the way an economic system is ordered, drawing on the sense of 'regular.' The Régulation Approach is interested in the way an economic system is ordered during particular historical periods, and particularly how it manages to sustain itself in the face of crises. Over the last 40 years Aglietta has developed this classification of monetary systems:

(1) *Centralized*: this corresponds to my 'nominalism.' Under a centralized system the only money is issued by the central authority, and it amounts to a debt owed by that authority. In its pure form, individuals cannot incur debts; they can either only transfer goods, services, or the centralized form of money.
   (a) This system is very stable, but it means that a person can only buy an asset if they have assets or money of equivalent value *now* to exchange. No one can buy 'on credit.'
   (b) The only debtor is the central authority, and if it cannot pay, then the whole system collapses very quickly.

(2) *Système fractionné* (fractionated system): corresponds to realism and is the opposite of the centralized system. Here anyone can be debtor and creditor, and while central money may exist, the primary means of exchange are 'money equivalents' which are nothing other than debt obligations, i.e. I pay you by transferring to you a debt owed by a third party.
   (a) Individuals can buy on credit, both because they can owe a particular seller and because that seller can 'sell' the credit to a third party.
   (b) This system is intrinsically unstable because (i) the value of the debt varies with the particular debtor and the speculative beliefs of any transferee and (ii) debts fall due at particular times—a debt owner may be required to pay others now, but only hold debt no one wants and which is due only in the future.

(3) *Système hierarchisé* (hierarchical system): is not conceptualist but a mixture of the above and corresponds most closely to today's financial systems. Here the centralized authority issues money, but also (i) permits the creation of private, negotiable debts and (ii) operates a 'mesoeconomic' system that mediates between the two, usually through a set of banks which have a direct credit line with the central authority and which themselves 'create' money for their customers.

In what follows we will encounter nominalist, realist, and some conceptualist accounts of money. We will see that English law adopts a nominalist approach—an approach which has the effect of occluding money's deep relation both with debt and with the society in which it operates. The aim is to place the narrow law of money within its political economic context.

1.2 English law's nominalism

Aristotle sought to define money by listing the functions which people have suggested it performs. F.A. Mann modernizes this,[3] suggesting that money is:

(1) a medium of exchange;
(2) a measure of the value or as a standard for contractual obligations;
(3) a store of wealth; and
(4) a unit of account.

Bob Jessop and Ngai-Ling Sum, 'Pre-Disciplinary and Post-Disciplinary Perspectives in Political Economy' (2001) 6 New Political Economy 89; Alain Lipietz, *The Enchanted World* (Verso 1985). The approach has its roots in Althusser's structuralist Marxism. I have not engaged with Marx's account of money here due to restrictions on space, but see the opening chapters of Karl Marx, *Capital: A Critique of Political Economy*, vol 1 (Ben Fowkes tr, Penguin 2004).

3 Charles Proctor (ed), *Mann on the Legal Aspect of Money* (6th edn, OUP 2005) ch 1. Subsequent editions of *Mann* have unfortunately moved away from the sociological theorizing that underpinned Mann's original approach.

He argues that generally (1) is regarded as money's key feature, but I think it is not so difficult to run at least (1), (2), and (4) together in English law as aspects of the same function, namely that of being 'a fixed and unvarying "price" in terms of a unit of account that is generally accepted within a given society for payment of debt or for goods and services rendered.'[4]

For English law's view, here first is Dicey and Morris' definition of the nominalist theory of money:

> A debt expressed in the currency of another country involves an obligation to pay the nominal amount of the debt in whatever is the legal tender at the time of payment according to the law of the country in whose currency the debt is expressed (*lex monetae*) irrespective of any fluctuations which may have occurred in the value of that currency in terms of sterling or any other currency, of gold, or any commodities between the time the debt was incurred and the time of payment.[5]

This is nominalist because we do not look to the real meaning or value of GBP100 (in, say, gold, or even subjectively) to establish whether someone who pays GBP100 has satisfied their obligation so to do. Rather, GBP100 has been given a final, if fictional, definition by the state of issuance (the UK). GBP100 is a name. If GBP100 is stated (i.e. paid), its value is the value of its statement.[6]

In this way the nominalist theory is closely linked to the command of the sovereign. A sovereign defines GBP100 as 100 units of 'money,' and this definition is *objectively* true because its truth value is commanded by the state.

Ludwig von Mises captures the 'flatness' of legal nominalism when he distinguishes the legal from the economic definitions of money thus:

> The fact that the law regards money only as a means of cancelling outstanding obligations has important consequences for the legal definition of money. What the law understands by money is in fact not the common medium of exchange but the legal medium of payment. It does not come within the scope of the legislator or jurist to define the economic concept of money.[7]

It is interesting to compare this with Aglietta's classifications of money. The UK monetary system is not centralized but hierarchical, yet English law proceeds as if it were only centralized: there is only one kind of money, and it is what the state says is money.

When the English court has been asked to define money, rather than the obligation to pay, it discloses once again the need to refer to, but rule out, the role of debt in providing meaning:

> [money is] that which passes freely from hand to hand throughout the community in final discharge of debts and full payment of commodities, being accepted equally without reference to the character or credit of the person who offers it and without the intention of the person who receives it to consume it.[8]

---

4 Frederic Mishkin, *The Economics of Money, Banking and Financial Markets* (Addison Wesley 1986) 8–9.

5 Dicey & Morris, *Conflict of Laws* (13th edn, Sweet & Maxwell Ltd. 1999) Rule 206. The rule also extends to judgment debts: *Miliangos v George Frank (Textiles) Ltd.* [1976] AC 443 (HL), particularly Lord Cross' opinion (though the innocent party may elect for enforcement in sterling if payment is not forthcoming).

6 See also *Davis Contractors Ltd. v Fareham Urban District Council* [1956] UKHL 3, [1956] AC 696, a contract is not frustrated just because it is a bad bargain or costs have increased; cf *WJ Alan & Co Ltd. v El Nasr Export & Import Co* [1972] 2 WLR 800. Here a party accepted payment by means of letter of credit priced in an alternative currency (GBP not Kenyan shillings). The party was then estopped from demanding payment in Kenyan shillings.

7 Ludwig Von Mises, *The Theory of Money and Credit* (first published 1912, HE Batson tr, Jonathan Cape 1934) 69.

8 *Moss v Hancock* [1899] 2 QB 111, 116.

In searching for meaning it suggests, but dismisses, the idea that money is a kind of debt obligation. To understand these dicta, we must examine the conflicting proposal—that money has everything to do with creditworthiness and debt.

1.3 Mitchell-Innes' realist account of money

The nominalist theory regards money as a neutral factor in relations. We can imagine a sort of capitalist end-of-days scenario to grasp this, where all economic relations were wound up, and all the money in the world was 'cleared.' This would essentially mean that when all transactions are complete, everyone holds some real value (a commodity) and no one holds money. The nominalist theory would see no difference when money drops from the relations. The credit theory of money, on the other hand, seeks to show that money is not neutral but is itself a separate tradeable commodity with its own value. When we regard money as tradeable, the realist holds, we call it 'debt,' but in fact all money is debt, and debt and money are just two sides of the same coin.

Modern English law is not blind to the fact that debt is tradeable (although this was not always the case). It is just that English law holds, as we have seen, that money is something other than debt and is used to discharge debt. Consequently, we must hold two legal frameworks in our minds simultaneously: the nominalist interpretation of money, and the law's view of debt as a special kind of property. It is only certain theorists who regard the two legal frames as equivalent.

Alfred Mitchell-Innes has no link to the Régulation Approach but his account provides a very approachable illustration of one of Aglietta's *systémes fractionnés*.

The value in question is *debt*. Money is defined as a (negotiable) debt obligation. In 1913, Mitchell-Innes proposed a thought experiment in which a simple economic grouping—a village—uses debt as a means of payment. Imagine that Desyn is a villager and a cobbler.[9] He makes some shoes and offers them for sale to Angie, Bertie, and Charlie. Angie is a farmer, Bertie is a thatcher, Charlie is a blacksmith, and they all want new shoes. Now, in a non-monetary system it seems that they only way Desyn will part with his shoes is in exchange for goods he wants (this is called barter), and if he does not want Bertie's roofing expertise just now then Bertie will not obtain new shoes. The classical economic account would have it that at this point the village economy will fail unless money is invented. But the anthropological evidence supports Mitchell-Innes' argument that this non-fit of interests is no problem at all. At the very least, Desyn will want thatching for his roof at some point in the future, and so he accepts from Bertie a promise to provide thatching when Desyn needs it. This promise is recorded, perhaps on paper, perhaps carved onto a stick, into clay, or some other medium. Desyn accepts similar promised from Angie and Charlie, and all receive their shoes.

Think about why Desyn accepted these promises. He must *believe* that Angie, Bertie, and Charlie will perform their obligation when asked to do so, and it helps that he knows them personally, given that they all grew up in the same village, or at least are related to people who did. The Latin for believe is *credere*, and 'he believes' is *credit*. Hence, we call Desyn's assessment that Bertie and the others will keep their promises in the future as credit, and the attribute of being so credible as *creditworthiness*.

Presently, Desyn requires goods for his own purposes, and so he goes to Ephraim, Farhad, and Gethin, who respectively produce chicken eggs, wine, and hats. Again, Desyn could exchange shoes for these commodities, but if the sellers do not want shoes, he now has two possible solutions: (a) he can promise to each of E, F and G that he will provide shoes when demanded; or (b) he could

9 Alfred Mitchell-Innes, 'What Is Money?' (1913) 30 Banking LJ 377, which he followed up in 'The Credit Theory of Money' (1914) 31 Banking LJ 151.

transfer to them the promises of A, B, and C to provide goods or services. For example, if Farhad needs his roof fixed, then he may accept Bertie's promise to Desyn that he fix a roof, that promise now being transferred to Farhad. In effect, Desyn has paid for wine using a promise of a third party; in other words, Mitchell-Innes argues, the promise has become money.

We can make certain comments about what has happened here:

(1) A legal point: that while the debt is a contractual obligation to deliver goods or services, we are not interested in the promise as an obligation but rather as some property capable of being transferred to someone else. Just observe that contract law and property law are two distinct methodologies or discourses for judging a state of affairs (and it matters not as between themselves that they be in contradiction).
(2) A political economic point: that in this system money arises as the set of promissory relationships within the village. It arises from below, so to speak, and because money is said to originate in relations, the credit theory of money could also be called a realist theory, in the sense that reality is defined as all the relationships between things.
(3) A political theoretic point: that this model of promissory relations bears comparison with Hobbes' social contract theory.

Returning to the village, Mitchell-Innes now introduces the moneychanger into the equation such that all participants come to regard this new person's obligations to pay as most creditworthy, again by reference to moneychanger's ability to pay but also acceptability to any villager as a promisor. Why? Well, whereas the villagers all specialized in their various trades, the moneychanger specializes in this: the assessment of creditworthiness. If Desyn holds an Angie debt, he could loan this to moneychanger and moneychanger will promise to 'repay.' This is particularly useful if no one trusts Angie but the moneychanger. The moneychanger potentially accepts debt that no one else would. Now Desyn has moneychanger debt and he can buy goods in exchange for it. The moneychanger debt will be accepted if people regard moneychanger as creditworthy, and the fact that moneychanger now may hold significant amounts of other debts deposited with him would suggest that he is capable of meeting his obligations.

So, for example, Desyn deposits Angie's debt with moneychanger, and in exchange Desyn now holds moneychanger debt. He purchases goods from Ephraim in exchange for a promise by Desyn to deliver some service. Ephraim then deposits this debt with moneychanger, who issues new moneychanger debt to Ephraim. At the close of the day, moneychanger looks at his table and sees that he owes Desyn, but that thanks to Ephraim's deposit he has a debt now owed to him by Desyn. So, what does he do? He simply 'sets off' the debt Desyn owes to him against the debt he owes to Desyn. If we assume that the two cancel each other out, we are left with a debt owed by Angie to moneychanger, and a debt owed by the moneychanger to Ephraim. The moneychanger will set off many such debts at the end of each business day in a process called *clearing*.

Observe now what the medieval moneychanger is doing. He acts as a kind of translator of creditworthiness between people who do not have enough information about each other or do not otherwise trust each other sufficiently. By acting in this way, the villagers need not stop at the bounds of their immediate community but may deposit with the moneychanger debts owed by persons from other villages, and even towns and cities far away. Medieval moneychangers developed networks of bankers to assess local creditworthiness and clear debts in distantly spread trade networks. Suddenly, individual, highly specific communities of social indebtedness become bound together by these trans-community debt relations mediated through the language of early finance. And it was finance, for nothing required the moneychanger to wait for deposits in order to issue bank debt; the moneychanger could initiate the whole process by issuing the bank debt to someone like Desyn in exchange for a promise by Desyn to repay—the making of a loan.

As David Graeber has noted, the anthropological evidence for these practices are widespread and go back to Sumerian times.[10] Furthermore, the things people used to record these debts were remarkably varied, from shells, to annotated wage slips, to tally sticks, to dried fish—all cases in which money in the legal, nominalist sense was simply not present. Yet law, or at least normativity, was present. Modern law regards these debts as obligations but refuses to regard them as money. So be it. But by doing so the law blinds itself to the functional equivalence of state-issued monies and the variety of real money relations constituted as between people, more often than not today via the mediation of private banks. That is why economists will speak of bank money. After all, that is what you pay with when you use your contactless debit card.

We should not, though, be so quick to jump from our ideal village to modern bank money. Of the greatest interest is the origin of the real money in the community of obligation, in a kind of morality of indebtedness linked to whether someone is credible. On the one hand, you might think that someone like Angie who does not repay would be morally condemned by everyone in her community for breaking her promise. Yet there is just as much evidence that in some communities, repayment of a debt is an insult: being bound to someone enhances community ties, whereas repayment is the clearest statement that one wishes to end a communal relationship.[11] You should ask yourself: in the history of debt, what effect did the invention of bank money have on these communal relationships?

1.4 Some conceptualist theories

Broadly, what unites conceptualist theories is an account of money which regards the money form as an expression or appearance of some underlying process. Of these theories, some could be said to tend to idealism in that they regard money not unlike a religious symbol that signifies an incommensurable ideal entity, be it ancestors, gods or *the* God, or the state or nation. Others tend to be materialistic, regarding money as an expression of concrete economic processes and our valuation of them.

1.4.1 The violence of money

By way of example, Aglietta and André Orléans use the theologico-literary theory of René Girard to argue that money arises from an originary violence to become the bearer of all our desires and indeed hates.[12] In a mirror-image of Hobbes, Girard argues that where a person desires the other, it is but a short series of steps from failing to obtain this object of desire to, first, seeking to emulate that person and, second, desiring those objects which the other desires. For Aglietta and Orléans this leads to a conflict over attainment of the desired object, to violence and possibly death. Simply agreeing not to fight as per a social contract will not do; rather, the monarch emerges to perform two functions: (1) as with Hobbes, the Leviathan-monarch is capable of a sovereign violence with which the individual cannot hope to contend; but more fundamentally (2) the Leviathan-monarch is the desirable other par excellence—a desirability accentuated by the excess of its incontestable power. Again, we find the individual seeking to emulate the desired other by seeking that which the other desires: wealth. Aglietta and Orléans argue that with the issuance of sovereign coin, and the demand of its return through taxation, money becomes the desired object of all. This process has the advantage of deferring all particular struggles between persons away from individual objects

---

10 David Graeber, *Debt: The First 5,000 Years* (Melville House 2011) 90. For a foundational sociological account of money, see Georg Simmel, *The Philosophy of Money* (Routledge 1990).

11 See for example Graeber (n 10) 100.

12 Michel Aglietta and André Orléans, *La violence de la monnaie* (PUF 1982).

and onto a generic object of desire which maintains this status precisely because sovereign violence is all but insurmountable.

In the third stage identified by Aglietta and Orléans, money escapes the control of the sovereign as mercantile trade develops across borders, and both coin and credit monies circulate. Money is abstracted from the body of the sovereign and now circulates as a symbolic bearer of an ideal sovereign power representative of the circulating 'wealth of nations' as a whole. Money in a sense becomes attainable; the original conflict between particular persons for an individual object is taken up as a generalized conflict between all persons for an object characterized as having no intrinsic value save that it be the object desired by everyone else. Speculation is now understood as a modern instantiation of originary violence in which financiers, seeking to imitate each other, battle for control of the object of desire, and its speculative 'value' reflects nothing other than this desirability.

1.4.2 Primordial debts

Aglietta has subsequently sought to play down the more poetic aspects of this theory of money's violence,[13] but members of the *Régulationist School* finessed some of these findings into what is known as 'Primordial Debt Theory.' The core of the theory is that monetary policy and social policy are the same thing because money and society are linked through debt. This sounds similar then to the credit theory of money, but whereas a realist argues for the reality of common ideas as intrinsic parts of entities (a particular debt relation between persons is part of each unit of money), Primordial Debt Theory adopts the conceptualist stance that these debts become abstracted from real relations and are transferred to a notional creditor such as the ancestors, gods, or the community as a whole. Money then expresses this incommensurate debt relation that each person owes to this abstract entity. Bruno Théret qualifies this by claiming that that which is expressed is the state.[14]

Théret draws on the idea, due to Feuerbach, that humanity creates its own gods. He writes:

> At the origin of money we have a 'relation of representation' of death as an invisible world, before and beyond life—a representation that is the product of the symbolic function proper to the human species and which envisages birth as an original debt incurred by all men, a debt owing to the cosmic powers from which humanity emerged.[15]

Payment of this debt, which can however never be settled on Earth because its full reimbursement is out of reach—takes the form of sacrifices which, by replenishing the credit of the living, make it possible to prolong life and even in certain cases to achieve eternity by joining the gods. But this initial belief-claim is also associated with the emergence of sovereign powers whose legitimacy resides in their ability to represent the entire original cosmos. And it is these powers that invented money as a means of settling debts—a means whose abstraction makes it possible to resolve the sacrificial paradox, by which putting to death becomes the permanent means of protecting life. Through this institution, belief is in turn transferred to a currency stamped with the effigy of the sovereign—a money put in circulation but whose return is organized by this other institution which is the tax/settlement of the life debt. So, money also takes on the function of a means of payment.

Théret draws on Auguste Comte and French revolutionary tradition to argue that the state is the secular God that occupies the place of the originary creditor, granting us security, health, and learning. The state, however, is to be understood not as the sum of public institutions but the product of living

13 Michel Aglietta, *Money: 5,000 Years of Debt and Power* (Verso 2018).

14 Bruno Théret, 'The Socio-Political Dimensions of the Currency: Implications for the Transition to the Euro' (1999) 22 Journal of Consumer Policy 51.

15 ibid.

social-economic relations. Théret envisages a currency like the euro both symbolically representing the European Union *and* actively fostering the further social communality of European citizens.

A number of arguments can be adduced against Primordial Debt Theory:

(1) As with Hobbes' State of Nature, Primordial Debt Theory largely rests on a pseudohistorical fiction.
(2) The concept of state debt is never fully identified, and one might say that Primordial Debt Theory proponents are not describing a social datum but construing various sub-facts to fit their theory.
(3) Credit theory identifies a relationship between persons. Primordial Debt Theory supposes a 'relationship' between each person and some ineffable which arguably includes that same person, being a taxpayer. Whether this structure is sound or not, it no longer describes a debt relationship (I cannot owe myself).
(4) Théret places considerable weight on the role of the euro as a unifying currency. It is questionable whether the euro has had the predicted effect of uniting the EU socially.

Yet what Primordial Debt Theory allows us to do is appreciate the flatness and paucity of law's understanding of money. When we are invited to reduce matters of law, particularly contract law, to a comparative analysis of price, the appearance of arithmetic neutrality amounts to nothing more than a comfort blanket against the deep social issues at play behind the money form.

1.4.3 Imperialism

As a final example of a conceptualist theory, we might consider an account inspired by the speculative hypothesis of RM Cook as to how the Athenians invented coinage.[16] Athens pursued a policy of expansion, but the conquest of other city states generated a common problem for the Athenian military—overlong supply chains. A force that remained unfed due to delay in delivery of supplies, or broken supply chains, could become mutinous. The Athenians needed an efficient, just-in-time way to feed troops, and the answer involved the invention of money.

Consider a small Greek town, and for argument's sake it has three factors of production: a smith, a tanner, and a farmer. The farmer acquires just enough leather clothes and shoes from the tanner and just enough tools (like a plough) from the smith, and in exchange he provides the tanner with animal hides and food, and the smith with food. The smith (who we pretend is happy to repair and sharpen existing tools) supplies these to the farmer and the tanner, and he also receives clothes, an apron, and shoes from the tanner. The tanner, duly supplied by farmer and smith, gives them just what they need. The key here is that everything that is consumed in this town is produced by this town. It is *autarkic*—there is no additional demand that it produce more, nor any internal shortfall, and it does not produce a surplus.

On conquering such a town, a representative of Athens would proclaim this law: that every year each person must pay a tax. This was not original; people had to pay tithes of corn or hides before. What was new was that this tax was to be paid in Athenian coin. All very well, but 'where,' asked the new subjects, 'were they to find coin? It doesn't grow on trees.' The clever response was that the coin was to be found in the pockets of the soldiers, who were paid with it. Clearly, the subjects could not rob the soldiers; to obtain the coin they had to trade for it—meet the demand of the soldiers (food, wine, 'entertainment,' etc.). The result was twofold: not only did the soldiers receive their much-needed supplies at the point of need, but in order to meet the tax requirement the subjects reconfigured their economic activity to meet the soldiers' demand. An autarkic town (a town that could feed itself) suddenly had to feed an army and pay tax, in addition to feeding itself.

---

16 I owe this reference to Graeber (n 10) ch 9.

Thus newly conquered regions were integrated economically within the Greek military apparatus. Autarkic towns were now subjected to an external demand which could only be met by a reconfiguration of the mode of production in those towns. On the due date, taxes were collected and the coin was taken back to Athens. For what purpose? To be sent out again as pay for conquering soldiers, thus reinitiating the whole military economic cycle and sustaining a new social reality we can call the state, or even a kind of imperialism.

Graeber gives a modern example of this from imperial colonialism.[17] General Gallieni deployed a *taxe moralisateur* in Madagascar for precisely this purpose—the duty to pay tax would cause the Malagasy to move from subsistence farming to growing cash crops to feed metropolitan France. This was because only cash crops could be sold for francs, delivery of which was a requirement of tax policy. The Malagasy resisted this for some time; even when they were made to harvest sugar cane, there are reports that the cane would be burnt in great bonfires in village centres, depriving the French of the commodity. Ultimately, the weight of war's economic force won through.

By relating nominal money and real debt relations to a third term—the singular power of a sovereign to impose a tax—I claim we have slightly better understanding of the conceptual nexus that drives money in the general sense. The concept is the process constituted by these three terms: the particularity of the money name, the general relations of indebtedness in the economy in question, and the specificity of the sovereign imposition.

1.5 Conclusion

We seem to have travelled far from law's judgment that money is just whatever the state declares it to be. Yet law has been with us all the way. The realist theory is not pure economics; as debt relations break away from personal knowledge of the debtor to abstract bank monies, law steps in to recognize that an obligation is itself properly capable of alienation and enforcement. The law does not call these obligations money, but these obligations serve a monetary function *and* law likewise serves that function in recognizing the obligations as enforceable, even when alienated to third parties. At this stage, however, law feels subordinated to the real and is arguably a supplementary feature of the realist account. With conceptualist theories, however, law is reintegrated into the money form because particular debt obligations cease to be the signified of a given debt obligation or money token. Money now is the expression or, if you will, *appearing* of a god, state, or concrete economic relations as a whole. The abstract legal fiction (be it money, debt obligation, share, security), shorn of any particular relation, functions as a symbolic differentiator. On the one hand it reveals the incommensurable by signifying sovereign, state, god, economic system; on the other it draws a veil over the violence of money by distracting our attention towards that symbolic abstraction. We must appreciate therefore that 'rules and legal institutions . . . are not merely cover for pre-existing economic relations; they in fact enable their conception and development.'[18]

This is, from a legal perspective, an almost entirely naïve account of what is going on in finance law. In the next nine chapters we are going to learn about the law that governs, even constitutes, money and debt. This will allow us, in Chapter 10, to return at a more advanced level of knowledge to the question of money. For now, you just need to appreciate that 'money' is not to be taken for granted, that you must problematize it, and that at the very least each coin and note symbolically represents a vast and complex financial-legal system at work.

---

17 ibid ch 3.

18 Antoine Lyon-Caen and Antoine Jeammaud, *Droit du travail, démocratie et crise* (Actes Sud 1986) 9.

Chapter 2

Credit facilities agreements

Chapter contents

DOI: 10.4324/9781003457220-2

2.1 Introduction

This chapter links our theoretical analysis of money to the London Form of credit facilities agreement (CFA). CFAs are loan contracts that regularly run to 80 or more pages of tightly drafted interlocking terms and extensive definitions. Yet a loan is fundamentally a very simple thing: a delivery of a commodity called money in exchange for a repayment of an equivalent amount at a specified time. In all likelihood, the borrower will also promise to pay an extra sum representing, so to speak, the 'absolute rent' paid by the borrower for having the use of the money for that time. This extra sum, as you are no doubt aware, is called **interest**.

The loan (and corresponding debt) is one of those legal relationships which is so 'obvious' and embedded in English law that transactions and most court cases proceed without ever asking the question what it is as a matter of law. The next section will do just that, but if you feel comfortable with what a loan is, jump ahead to section 2.3 where we start tackling the CFA.

2.2 Some fundamentals: debts, loans, instruments

2.2.1 Debt as a special kind of obligation

The notion of a debt is basic in English law, and a loan is one of the legally significant acts that gives rise to a debt. As we saw in the last chapter, the word 'debt' derives from *debitum* (what is owed). This suggests that debt is a kind of obligation like a contractual promise or duty of care, but it is a special, 'stronger' kind of obligation because it traditionally conferred greater procedural rights on the obligee (the person owed the obligation) than, say, that conferred by an obligation of a promisor to perform work or pay damages for breach of contract. The core of that stronger procedural right is that when a creditor is owed a debt, they are entitled to demand immediate payment and, if unpaid, move directly to enforcement.

As the following case illustrates, the procedural advantage of suing on a debt compared to suing for breach of contract was formally removed in the 1870s. As we will see, however, suing on a debt is still preferable procedurally, despite this simplification of the rules of court.

MOSCHI v LEP AIR SERVICES LTD [1973] AC 331 (HL)

Moschi was managing director of company which owed a debt to Lep. Moschi had guaranteed to the creditor, Lep, that the debtor would pay what it owed. Obiter, Lord Diplock considered whether, on its true construction, the contract of guarantee under consideration was a promise to pay a sum of money if the debtor did not (and so a debt), or a promise to make sure the company paid its debt (breach of which sounded in damages).

Per Lord Diplock at 347 A–F:

> Each promise that a promisor makes to a promisee by entering into a contract with him creates an obligation to perform it owed by the promisor as obligor to the promisee as obligee. If he does not do so voluntarily there are two kinds of remedies which the court can grant to the promisee. It can compel the obligor to pay to the obligee a sum of money to compensate him for the loss that he has sustained as a result of the obligee's failure to perform his obligation. This is the remedy at common law in damages for breach of contract. But there are some kinds of obligation which the court is able to compel the obligor actually to perform. In some cases, such as obligations to transfer title or possession of property to the obligee or to refrain from doing something

to the detriment of the obligee, a remedy to compel performance by a decree of specific performance or by injunction is also available. It was formerly obtainable only in a court of equity. In these cases it was an alternative remedy to that of damages for breach of contract obtainable only in a court of common law. But, since a court of common law could make and enforce orders for payment of a sum of money, where the obligation was itself an obligation to pay a sum of money, even a court of common law could compel the obligor to perform it. Historically this was the only remedy which the court would grant at common law when an obligor failed to perform this kind of obligation. The remedy of damages for non-performance of the obligation was not available as an alternative.

It ceased to be important to identify an obligation which the obligor had failed to perform as being an obligation to pay a sum of money after the Judicature Act of 1875 had abolished the necessity for a plaintiff to select the form of action appropriate to his claim. But before the Common Law Procedure Acts 1852 to 1860 there were important procedural differences between an action brought to compel performance of the obligation arising from a promise to pay a sum of money (for which the form of action was *indebitatus assumpsit*), and an action brought to recover compensation for the loss sustained as a result of the obligor's failure to perform any other kind of obligation arising out of contractual promises—for which the form of action was a special assumpsit.

Held on this point: the contract of guarantee in question contained a promise to ensure the debtor paid, and so Moschi must pay to Lep damages resulting from his breach, not repay a debt.[1]

As Lord Diplock notes, the procedural advantage of suing on a debt as opposed to other kinds of obligation back in the 1850s was that exceptionally, and unlike for any other broken contractual promise, the courts which heard contract claims could compel the defendant to perform the contract by paying the certain sum of money. The claimant just had to file the correct writ and convince the court that the matter related to a debt, not another sort of breach of contract. Lord Diplock also notes that this procedural distinction was abolished. This begs the question: why should we continue to separate out debt from all the other kinds of obligation that may arise? It feels like 'debt' is a hangover from legal history.

The central reason for still isolating debt as something special, legally, is that despite the Judicature Act 1875, every practising lawyer knows there remain procedural advantages in claiming for a debt over claiming for any other breach of contract. Michael Bridge has enumerated the following:[2]

(1) A debt claimant bears a significantly lighter burden in gathering evidence and, moreover, is able to recover a summary judgment in an appropriate case.[3]
(2) Consequently, the onus is on the debtor to prove the debt is not due.

1 cf *McGuinness v Norwich and Peterborough Building Society* [2011] EWCA Civ 1286, [2012] 2 All ER (Comm) 265, which cited Lord Diplock's dicta with approval but interpreted the guarantee in the instant case as a promise to pay which gave rise to a debt claim.

2 Michael Bridge, 'Debt Instead of Damages in the Common Law' in LA DiMatteo and C Lei (eds), *Chinese Contract Law: Civil and Common Law Perspectives* (CUP 2017) 423, 425.

3 Civil Procedure Rules, part 24.

(3) Traditionally, a court would not award post-judgment interest on a damages claim, only a debt claim. While statute has changed this,[4] the interest rate on certain debt claims is higher.[5]

(4) Because a debt is a primary obligation to pay, the rule on penalties does not apply, for that rule only polices secondary obligations to pay money if a primary obligation is not performed.

(5) The classical rules on mitigation and remoteness do not apply to a debt claim.[6] To illustrate this last point, we need only refer to an anticipatory breach case with which you are likely familiar.

WHITE & CARTER (COUNCILS) LTD v MCGREGOR [1962] AC 413 (HL Scot)[7]

McGregor, a garage owner, had paid for adverts to be displayed on bins operated by the council. After McGregor had inadvertently renewed the contract for a further three years, he sought to repudiate it. As you know, the House of Lords held that the innocent party had a right to accept the repudiation and sue for damages for breach *or* to affirm the contract and demand payment of the price (i.e. a debt) for the whole forthcoming three years.

At this point in your studies, you may have baulked at the lack of commercial sense making McGregor pay for three years of adverts. Surely the council could have sold the advertising space to a third party. McGregor thought the same, and argued that the council ought to have mitigated its future losses by seeking a replacement advertiser (McGregor only paying for the hiatus while that replacement was found).

Held: A debtor cannot plead mitigation in a debt claim; the creditor was entitled to repayment of the whole debt come what may.

Perhaps the primary practical procedural advantage of claiming for a debt derives from the Insolvency Acts, which grant special enforcement powers to those owed certain sums of money that have fallen due. For example, if the creditor demands payment in the statutory form, they can move to bankrupt the debtor within 21 days if the debtor fails to pay (a *statutory demand*).[8] Compare this to a breach of contract giving rise to damages. As a matter of common law, the precise quantum of damages is open to dispute;[9] the parties will need a judge to declare the precise sum of damages payable, and so lengthy court proceedings must be pursued. Only when the judge has determined the damages owed will the innocent party be able to enforce the resulting *judgment* debt. The great thing about an obligation to pay a certain sum created by a loan is that it has already attained the status of a debt, and so has already reached the enforceability stage. In principle, the creditor should be able to enforce it forthwith, and the debtor will need to find some other argument than quantum

4 Eight per cent. Senior Courts Act 1981, s 35A, as amended, but the claimant must expressly claim this interest.

5 Eight per cent *over* Bank of England base rate. See the Late Payment of Commercial Debts (Rate of Interest) (No.3) Order 2002, SI 2002/1675. As at the time of writing, this is some five per cent higher than the judgment rate for damages.

6 See most recently, *Thai Airways International Public Company Ltd. v KI Holdings Co Ltd. & Anor* [2015] EWHC 1250 (Comm).

7 Discussed as a fine example by Bridge (n 2) 436.

8 For demands against companies, see sections 123(1)(a) or 222(1)(a) of the Insolvency Act 1986; against natural persons, section 268 of that Act.

9 *Robinson v Harman* (1848) 1 Ex 850, 154 ER 363.

to prevent enforcement.[10] In practical terms, the ability to enforce in this way, backed by the threat of bankruptcy, is extremely effective.

ESSENTIAL DEFINITIONS: DEBT, LOAN

A **debt** is a species of obligation conferring additional procedural advantages on the obligee (the creditor). It is an obligation by one person (the debtor) to pay the creditor a certain ('liquidated') sum of money on a given date and time. The creditor has a right to demand, receive, and enforce payment without further adjudication as to quantum.

A debt can be created by a number of mechanisms, including by statute or procedure laid down by statute,[11] or in court proceedings e.g. as a judgment debt. The mechanism with which you will be most familiar is by contract, either by:

(i) Specialty contract, constituted by deed or covenant;12 or
(ii) Simple contract, under which creditor agrees to transfer money to debtor in consideration of debtor promising to repay an amount equal to that sum at a later date, and we call such a contractual arrangement a (contract for) **loan**.

Debts constituted by simple contracts in this technical legal sense will very much occupy us in this book. As we shall see, these modern contracts are not simple in the financial sense.

2.2.2 A debt is not a property right in specific money

It is important to disabuse yourself of one misconception at this early stage: when a creditor advances money to a debtor with an obligation to repay, the law does not require the debtor to retransfer exactly that money which the creditor had advanced. The law requires the debtor to pay an **amount equal to the sum advanced**. This is because the creditor is not interested in the property in the money; he has transferred title to that property and is quite happy to receive different money back, as long as it is at least the same nominal value as the money he had advanced. A little thought will confirm why this is the case. Imagine creditor has advanced consecutively numbered GBP50 notes in aggregate value of GBP10,000 to debtor with a proviso for repayment of just those notes and no other. What is the debtor supposed to do with these notes? If he pays them into a bank or uses them in any exchange, he will lose the notes and more than likely never find them again in the financial system. So, the only option open to debtor is to hold on to the notes. There is no practical use in 'borrowing' the GBP10,000; all debtor has done is accept the risk he may lose those notes, e.g. to fire or theft. Evidently, for a loan to work financially, the law must accommodate a transaction in which creditor sells money to debtor in consideration of debtor 'repaying' what is in property terms different money, but which in contractual terms is the same nominal value of money. Permitting that allows the debtor to use the borrowed money for some purpose which will generate sufficient return at least to repay the creditor with other money. The impractical scenario of requiring retransfer of

10 E.g. the alleged debtor was never indebted (*numquam indebitatus*); the debt is not due and payable; that it has already been paid; that the alleged loan was actually a gift; that the liability is limited and so forth. On *numquam indebitatus* and limitation, see *Mathew v Blackmore* (1857) 1 H & N 762, 156 ER 1409, 26 LJ Ex 150.

11 See the discussion of debt instruments in Chapter 8.

12 The distinction between specialty and simple debt contracts is archaic save in one practically important respect: the limitation period for simple contract debts is six years from when the payment falls due; under specialty contracts it is 12 years (ss 5, 8(1) Limitation Act 1980).

the exact notes provided is not legally impossible, but it is not a loan. Rather, it is what is called a bailment—an arrangement, broadly speaking, in which a bailor asks a bailee to look after specific property, perhaps by holding it in a vault or bonded warehouse.

HISTORICAL EXCURSUS: THE GOLDSMITH BANKERS[13]

Above we drew a distinction between a loan contract and a contract of bailment. It turns out these two contracts are more intimately linked in financial history than you might have guessed. Back in the seventeenth century in London, wealthy people like Samuel Pepys carried their gold and cash about with them, but that left them open to robbery. Another group of Londoners also faced a problem with protecting their gold and coin: the goldsmiths who worked the metal and who (like today's diamond carvers) were under constant threat of burglary. These goldsmiths built themselves heavily fortified workshops with vaults beneath to protect their gold and that of their customers. It must have proved successful, because the customers started to leave their gold, and then cash, with the goldsmiths, who acted as bailees of the property and charged a fee.

This did create a problem with payment. To pay someone, a Mr Pepys would need to go to his goldsmith, a Mr Hoare, say, withdraw the required cash and gold, and then journey back to west London to effect payment, all the time risking robbery. To avoid this risk, the practice developed whereby Mr Pepys would write an instruction to Mr Hoare, ordering him to pay the gold or cash directly to the person named in the instruction. Mr Pepys would then sign the instruction and hand it to the payee, who would present the instruction to Mr Hoare for payment. This documentary instruction is the forerunner of the **cheque**. To avoid fraud, Mr Hoare soon standardized the instruction form and issued the forms to his clients.

Subsequently, goldsmiths like Hoare realized that only about 10% of the gold and cash would ever need to be paid out on any given day; the remaining 90% simply sat there, at best holding value. This observation, combined one suspects with clients being short of funds to honour cheques, combined with the practise of moneylenders long known in the City. Mr Hoare and other goldsmith-bailees started lending out the cash which was not being drawn. This was only possible if, when a given client sought to withdraw his funds, the client himself was no longer characterized as a bailor of specific property (this cash), but a lender of money to be refunded in an *amount equal to the sum* deposited. On that basis, it did not matter if the particular notes deposited had gone to a third party, as long as the client's debt owed by the bank was paid. The clients were apparently happy with this change of relationship from bailment to deposit (loan)—after all, Mr Hoare charged his debtors interest on the loans he made to them, and he passed through a portion of that interest to his own depositors (the interest you receive on your bank account).

It was good business. Mr Hoare's descendants still operate their bank in Fleet Street, London. If you are permitted to visit, you can still see the notes and cheques Hoare & Co. created to facilitate payment in the seventeenth century, including ones drawn on Samuel Pepys' account. You may also visit the house they built with the profits at Stourhead, Wiltshire.

---

13 See further: 'Goldsmith Banks' in Peter Temin and Hans-Joachim Voth, *Prometheus Shackled: Goldsmith Banks and England's Financial Revolution after 1700* (OUP 2013) ch 3.

2.2.3 A further important distinction: the relationship between contract and debt instrument

A loan is a simple enough thing to create. One need only transfer money to someone on the objective understanding it will be repaid at some point in the future.[14] Often the courts will impute a contract post hoc, the parties having never really thought specifically about making an express contract to lend. More likely, the parties will record what has already happened—a creditor lent money to a debtor on the understanding it be repaid—in documentary form:

> **RECORDING A SIMPLE LOAN: THE IOU (literally: 'i owe you')**
>
> I, John Smith of 1 Broomfield Rd, Coventry, acknowledge that I have received today from Kate Liddle of 2 Sovereign Rd, Coventry, the sum of £1,000 by way of loan bearing interest at 5 (five) % per year payable half yearly on 1 March and 1 September in each year which I undertake to repay to Kate Liddle on demand.
>
> Dated [*date*]
> [*John Smith*]

Is this document a contract? Look closely—has the lender promised to do something? Has the borrower promised to do something if the lender performs some action? In both cases the answer is 'no,' because the lender has already done all that might have been required of her. There is no offer of a promise in consideration of a reciprocal promise or future action, and so neither a bilateral contract nor a unilateral contract subsists here.

Is this then a gift? Evidently, the borrower is not promising to pay over money gratuitously; he only promises to do so because the lender has lent money to him. Intuitively, this document feels like it really does create an enforceable debt claim against the borrower.[15]

So, what is going on? You might have felt this was a contract because it is difficult to imagine how the borrower should agree to indebtedness without the lender advancing credit, and how the lender would have agreed to lend without the borrower promising to repay. And indeed, the IOU seems to record as much. Some nuance is required, however. There *could be* a contract, but the IOU is not it. The IOU has arisen to record a state of affairs resulting possibly from a contract or other arrangement where indebtedness has been incurred, such as an advance of monies for some purpose. It may be that K (Kate) orally offered to lend J (John) GBP1000 in consideration of J promising to repay plus interest. J accepted this offer, and let us assume intention to create legal relations is present in this context. *That* is your contract. In fact, things may not have happened in that way—there may have been no explicit offer and acceptance—but it seems the court will review what did happen and impute a simple loan contract. What is essential is the objective voluntary transfer of money and a promise to repay.

K delivered GBP1,000 to J. When she did so, she wanted some written proof that J owed K the money, plus interest. Therefore, she asked J to write the IOU as proof that she had acquired a new

---

14 *Volpi and another v Volpi* [2022] EWCA Civ 464, [2002] 4 WLR 48. There remains in English law a rebuttable presumption that an advancement of money from parent to child is a gift, not a loan, but in this case it was rebutted because an agreement, signed by the adult child, expressly provided for repayment of the CHF6m the father had advanced.

15 A simple transfer of money does not automatically create a loan: *Cary v Gerrish* (1801) 4 Esp 9, 170 ER 624; *Aubert v Walsh* (1812) 4 Taunt 293; *Welch v Seaborn* (1816) 1 Stark 474; *Pearce v Davis* (1834) 1 Mood & R 365, 174 ER 125; *Graham v Cox* (1848) 2 Car & Kir 702, 175 ER 293. However, there is a presumption that the money ought to be repaid, which the transferee must rebut: *Seldon v Davidson* [1968] 2 All ER 755, [1968] 1 WLR 1083 (CA). This thought links back to the doctrine of resulting trusts.

kind of asset, namely a claim for the debt. The claim is *clear* and *unconditional*,[16] for K is not obliged to do anything more for the money to be due, and there is no basis on which J can dispute the claim, for K has performed in full. Moreover, the IOU is written so that K can transfer the document to third parties, who can use it to claim the debt from J. The document is evidence of K's title (or the title of any transferee of the IOU) to that unconditional claim for repayment. Its reason for subsisting may be due to an underlying part-performed contract, but the document is not itself a contract. The contract is a creature of the law of obligations; the IOU is a title born of the law merchant and now governed by the Bills of Exchange Act 1882. Under section 3(4)(b) of that Act, the IOU is valid notwithstanding its failure to 'specify the value given, or that any value has been given therefor.' Questions of consideration and intention to create legal relations are simply irrelevant when it comes to the enforceability of an IOU.

An IOU is documentary evidence of the lender's transferable title to the debt owed by the borrower. This genus of document is called in law an **instrument** (which includes bonds, cheques, documentary credits, bills of exchange) Specifically, as this is a document manifesting a promise to pay, it is what statute calls a **promissory note**.[17]

We could simplify this document even further, for example by removing the name of the creditor. In such a case, the court will interpret the creditor to be the person holding the document at the time the demand to repay is asserted.[18] This ability for any bearer to step into the shoes of the creditor is not as radical as one might expect. One special feature of instruments such as promissory notes is that even if made out to a named creditor, they can be transferred to a new creditor by simply writing the name of the transferee creditor and date onto the promissory note and delivering it to them.[19] This writing is called **indorsement**, and the attribute of documents of being transferable in this way, combined with their enforceability irrespective of proof of whether value has been given, is called **negotiability**.[20] These are not attributes of the underlying contract. If we want to transfer rights and obligations under a loan contract, we will need to do something more complicated, which we will examine in Chapter 6.

In the above IOU, the date for repayment under the underlying contract is recorded to be 'on demand' rather than a specified date. This means that Kate Liddle, the creditor, can ask for repayment ('call (in)' the loan) at any time she sees fit. Another possible simplification is to remove reference to any interest payable, but doing this is likely to create trouble later for reasons with which you are familiar: the creditor may later seek to argue that an interest term is implied into a contract to lend money.

We will not spend much time discussing promissory notes per se until Chapter 8, but rather the loan contracts that may give rise to them. Thus we are focused, from now through to Chapter 7, on contracts creating obligations of indebtedness, of which the primary example is the CFA. Having simply flagged that the financial world is also full of things called 'debt instruments,' you are asked to reserve mental space for those things until Chapter 8.

---

16 It must be a self-contained promise to pay. Any words which would be mysterious to any person who does not know the full circumstances renders the document non-negotiable within the meaning of the 1882 Act: *Wirth v Weigel Leygonie & Co Ltd.* [1939] 3 All ER 712 (quoted by Colin Bamford, *Principles of International Financial Law* (OUP 2019) 684).

17 Section 83(1) Bills of Exchange Act 1882: 'A promissory note is an unconditional promise in writing made by one person to another signed by the maker, engaging to pay, on demand or at a fixed or determinable future time, a sum certain in money, to, or to the order of, a specified person or to bearer.'

18 *Curtis v Rickards* (1840) 1 Man & G 46, 133 ER 241.

19 Words to the contrary will negate this, but then the document ceases to be a promissory note within the meaning of the Bills of Exchange Act 1882, s 83(1).

20 Bills of Exchange Act 1882 ss 2, 73. *Crouch v Crédit Foncier of England* (1872–73) LR 8 QB 374, 381 (Blackburn J), citing with approval *Miller v Race* (1758) 1 Burr 452, 97 ER 398. It is no longer possible to indorse a cheque: Cheques Act 1992.

2.2.4 Loans and credit facilities

The CFA is, as its name suggests, a special kind of loan agreement called a facility agreement. In essence, a **facility** amounts to a lender's promise or option to make available funds on a loan basis, such that the borrower then may use this facility to borrow some, all, or none of the funds available. It is 'facility' in the sense of 'capacity to do or use.' In some cases, the borrower may even repay and reborrow funds from the same facility.

The traditional way in which a facility works is that an account is set up with a zero balance between a lender and borrower (to be). The terms of that account,[21] as specified in a facility agreement, are such that the borrower may incur indebtedness on that account with respect to the lender.[22] Normally, that indebtedness is limited in amount to a pre-agreed sum called a **commitment**. The borrower incurs this indebtedness by submitting a request to utilize the facility in a specified amount, and when funds are advanced, the borrower is said to **draw down** the funds. The borrower may then use these funds for the purposes specified in the facility agreement. Some example contract drafting is provided below.

SAMPLE CLAUSE: A FACILITIES CLAUSE

2.1 The Facilities

Subject to the terms of this Agreement, the Lenders make available to the Borrowers:

(a) a sterling term loan facility in an aggregate amount equal to the Total Facility A Commitments;
(b) a multicurrency revolving loan facility in an aggregate amount equal to the Total Facility B Commitments;
(c) a multicurrency term loan facility in an aggregate amount equal to the Total Capex Facility Commitments.

[*The next clause is just as important*]

7. REPAYMENT

7.1 Repayment of Term Loans

(a) Each Borrower must repay the Term Loans made to it in full on the Final Maturity Date.
(b) No Borrower may reborrow any part of a Term Loan which is repaid.

7.2 Repayment of Facility B Loans

(a) Each Borrower which has drawn a Facility B Loan shall repay the loan on the last day of its Interest Period.
(b) [*Detailed terms providing for rollover, explained below*]

The facilities clause makes available three different facilities. The names of these facilities are selected for convenience, not legal import, with 'Capex Facility' simply being a reference to the fact

21 In a standard corporate facility agreement, the existence of this account is often implicit in the contract. In asset finance, by contrast, the accounts are expressly provided for.

22 For a legislative definition in the context of building societies, see Building Societies (Limited Credit Facilities) Order 1987 SI 1987/1975, art 3.

that the purpose[23] of that facility (as stated elsewhere in the contract) is to fund *capital expenditure* (i.e. purchase of things like land and machinery). A facility is more often offered in a single currency, but this contract also offers a multicurrency option, which means the borrower can select which currency it wishes to borrow from predetermined subset (usually USD, euro, and GBP).

All these facilities are **committed**. This means that the lender is obligated to disburse funds when the borrower requests them provided that pre-agreed conditions precedent are met. Thus the borrower has a corresponding enforceable right to draw down those funds subject to meeting the conditions. By contrast, an **uncommitted** facility is one where disbursing funds is entirely at the option of the lender: the borrower may request, but the lender has the right to refuse disbursement for any reason or none. To the extent the lender is committed, the market practice is for the lender to charge a commitment fee. This is *not* interest, for no money has yet been borrowed; it is a fee in consideration of the lender standing ready to lend when requested by the borrower.

Facility A and the Capex Facility are **term** facilities: a committed loan for a pre-agreed period (the term) and amount, which is to be repaid according to an agreed schedule e.g.:

(1) A 'bullet'—the loan must be repaid in full on maturity of the term.
(2) 'Amortizing'—the loan is repaid in equal instalments over the term.
(3) A 'balloon'—as amortizing, but greater amounts are repaid towards the end of the term.

Once a Term facility is drawn down (e.g. by GBP10m), the facility is reduced accordingly. Even if the GBP10m is repaid, it cannot be redrawn. Term facilities are designed to mirror the long-term capital requirements of Borrower (e.g. the financing of plant and machinery, or of real estate).

Facility B is stated to be a revolving credit facility (**RCF** or **revolver**). This is a committed loan for periods and amounts to be selected by the Borrower, subject to conditions.

(1) Borrower selects one-month, three-month, or six-month Interest Periods for such sums as it requires being agreed multiples of GBP1m.
(2) At the end of the Interest Period the loan is repaid, *but* it may be borrowed again multiple times (see cl 7.2 above).
(3) As a matter of law, Borrower must repay each loan, but in practice (provided there is no Default occurring) Borrower and Facility Agent agree that rather than borrow new money each time, Borrower may keep the existing money, redenominated as a new loan. This is called a **rollover**.

RCFs are designed to mirror the short-term liquidity requirements of corporates (e.g. stock in trade, wage bills), but that uncertainty also means RCFs likely charge a higher commitment fee compared to term facilities. RCFs also come with a sting in their tail. It is very easy for corporates to develop a habit of rolling over loans (say of GBP3m) every month or three months, effectively treating the sum as borrowed from a loan facility. The risk the borrower runs is masked because of the rollover: the borrower need not find GBP3m and deliver this to the lender, only for the lender to find another GBP3m to deliver to the borrower. All that is no problem *until* the lender refuses to lend. As with term loans, RCFs are subject to conditions precedent, and if these are not met on a rollover date, the borrower may not roll over the loan, for the lender is entitled to refuse to lend. Such a condition precedent may be that there are no Events of Default (see below) outstanding. Yet the borrower must still repay the GBP3m previously borrowed, and must immediately find a vast amount of cash it is unlikely to have to hand. During times of economic stress, RCFs might be regarded as key drivers of instability due to the frequency of rollovers (every

23 The purpose of loans such as this potentially raises the issue of a *Quistclose* trust (see *Barclays Bank Ltd. v Quistclose Investments Ltd.* [1968] UKHL 4, [1970] AC 567).

month, three months, etc). On each rollover date the borrower faces a significant illiquidity problem unless the lender agrees to waive any unmet conditions precedent and relend. That option of the lender becomes a powerful negotiating lever where a borrower is in financial trouble and a workout is being considered.

Some other common types of facilities include the following:

Guarantee facilities: a guarantee is a promise to *ensure* that some principal will perform an obligation. Non-performance permits the beneficiary of the guarantee to pursue the guarantor should the guaranteed performance fail to occur. It may be that the beneficiary must demand performance or payment from the primary obligor first, and only if performance is not forthcoming may it have recourse to the guarantor (a secondary guarantee). Or the guarantee may provide that it is given on a 'first demand' basis—the beneficiary may go straight to the guarantor and demand performance/payment. A guarantee is structured like a normal credit facility, save that on drawdown the finance party does not lend funds, rather it issues a guarantee. The issuance of the guarantee in a certain amount creates a contingent debt obligation from the 'borrower' under the guarantee facility. Should the guarantee be called—the finance party-guarantor pays out—the 'borrower' will owe an equivalent amount in debt to the finance party.

RE SSSL REALISATIONS (2002) LTD [2006] EWCA Civ 7

The legal principle for which this case is authority is discussed in Chapter 6. *The facts illustrate a special kind of guarantee facility in action.*

Members of the Save Group of companies, including SSSL, operated petrol stations (one company per petrol station). Like any goods subject to excise duty, those who deal in petrol are only permitted to do so by the UK Government if they effectively guarantee a large sum payable to HMRC (the fiscal authority) representing the duty payable on the petrol. In this context the guarantee is called a bond, which as a personal surety is much closer in sense to the term's original meaning. The purpose of the bond is to ensure HMRC are paid duty, placing the risk of smuggling and theft on the dealers of petrol.

It is very difficult for any trading company to take on such a large bond itself. Instead, it will approach a finance house to provide a bond by means of a guarantee facility. In this case, Save Group contracted for such a facility with AIG Europe—with AIG Europe guaranteeing duty payments by each group company.

The bond created corresponding (contingent) debts of each group member. The group companies had also made various loans, creating corresponding debts, between themselves. In view of this, it was a term of the guarantee facility that should any Save Group company become insolvent (as SSSL did), no other group company would claim repayment of its intragroup loan *until* AIG Europe's guarantee facility debt was repaid in full.

Letter of Credit (LC) facilities: in one sense an LC is like the debt instruments used as payment in Mitchell-Innes' fictional village. An LC is a negotiable document issued by a bank which, when presented with conforming documents to a second bank, will cause that second bank to release funds to the presenter without question. The second bank will then revert to the issuing bank for reimbursement. The facility here operates like a guarantee facility—it is a right of the borrower to cause the bank to issue a debt instrument. The issuance creates a contractual repayment obligation equal in amount to the value of the debt instrument issued. For further discussion of the use of debt instruments as modes of payment, see Chapters 8 and 10, as well as any textbook on international sales using documentary credits.

2.2.5 Towards the CFA

This brief discussion of debt, loan contracts, and IOUs serves to demonstrate how simple a loan agreement need be. One requires no more than a few lines of legally enforceable drafting. Why, then, is a CFA so long and technical? The CFA is so complicated because it is doing three things at once:

(1) Ensuring the creditor can obtain and repay capital it, the creditor, will then on-lend to the borrower.
(2) Establishing an ongoing debt relationship between creditor and borrower (this is the core 'contract for loan' bit).
(3) Ensuring the creditor can sell its title to the debt of the borrower to third parties, but also transfer other rights and obligations under the loan contract.

If you look at a standard form Loan Market Association CFA, it will broadly have this tripartite structure. Element (2) elaborates the simple loan agreement we encountered in this section, adding in many more terms to ensure the creditor does lend when asked and the debtor does repay when required. Elements (1) and (3), on the other hand, are all about the how the lender-borrower relationship at the heart of the contract interacts with the rest of the financial system. A CFA ought not to be taken as an isolated bilateral agreement, but as something that 'plugs into' that financial system and so requires the legal drafting that permits the interaction.

We will first focus on (1): the terms of the contract which cover how the creditor will find the money it will need to lend to the borrower. This requires us to understand why banks do not necessarily possess that money to begin with, and to understand that, we must look again at the modern nature of money.

2.3 Funding: the interbank market and the central bank

The essential idea of this subsection is in modern banking: banks do not sit on great vaults of cash waiting to lend it but borrow just the money they need just when they need it for lending. Traditionally, banks borrowed this money from other banks. Since the Global Financial Crisis (GFC), banks have been much more reliant in borrowing directly from central banks such as the Bank of England or European Central Bank. Whatever the source of funds, the lender bank is taking a risk in promising to deliver money to the borrower when requested, simply because when it makes the promise, it does not own that money. Later, we will examine how the bank mitigates the risk that it will (1) struggle to source those funds when it needs to lend them and (2) be unable to repay those funds if its borrower does not repay. First, we explain just what we mean when we say banks borrow money from each other.

2.3.1 Cash and cash equivalents

It is important to realize that money no longer means, as in Aristotle's thought, the physical metal stamped with value and mark of the issuing ruler. Money is not coin; coin is just one type of money. In fact, this observation is not that new, for historically the role of money seems to have been played by a much wider set of instruments than cash; even in Akkadian times the physical holder of value (e.g.

gold) did not itself enter circulation but remained in the temple. Grain traders conducted clay-tablet transfers by reference to temple holdings. Think back to our IOU. It recorded that the lender lent cash, but the recording—the instrument—represents a title to that debt, a right to be paid. As such, it is the next best thing to money and can be used as such. Grain traders passed around these instruments as if they were cash, using them for payment. Modern money is for the most part titles to debt, not cash.

The advantage of cash is that in principle, anyone willing to sell something will accept a certain amount of cash in exchange. Bob may wish to sell his car: he will not barter it for a painting because let us assume (1) he does not want a painting, (2) nor does anyone else who Bob can identify. Rather, Bob will accept cash, because with cash he can exchange it for anything he does want of equal nominal value, provided it is available. This ability to use cash immediately in exchange earns it the epithet *liquid*—it can change into any form at a moment's notice. Hopefully, these observations are unsurprising, but they can be enhanced looking at other things which behave very much like cash: **cash equivalents**. All we need to do is identify assets which either can become cash very quickly and without restriction, or which can be used in a cash-like manner i.e. the market actors will accept the asset in exchange without question and themselves use it as payment. Almost certainly, you make most of your payments using cash equivalents, because you pay not with cash but with a debit card or banking app. In short, you transfer, and the seller of goods or services takes transfer of, your title to a debt owed by a bank. The realist theory of money predicts as much. When we speak of **money**, what we really mean is not just cash but cash *and* certain cash equivalents.

How 'equivalent' should a cash equivalent be? Macroeconomists distinguish money by relative liquidity, that is, by how quickly non-cash can be turned into cash. A standard macroeconomic textbook might define different the expanding spheres of money as follows:[24]

Circulating currency

M0 = circulating currency (cash) + bank reserves of currency with central bank (no longer published in UK)
M1 = currency in circulation + sight bank deposits
M2 = M1 + time (or savings) deposits at banks with unrestricted access
M3 = M2 + larger, fixed term deposits + accounts at non-bank institutions

Here, from IMF statistics, is how much these types of 'money' there are in the UK and Eurozone as a percentage of GDP as of 2007:

Table 2.1 Circulating UK and Eurozone currency as a percentage of GDP

	Currency	M0	M1	M2	M3
UK	2.6	3.0	63.5	107.7	124.6[25]
Eurozone	6.8	12.3	43.0	78.1	91.8

The UK is an extreme case here, but the general trend in Europe, for example, is that most money is not cash but data on bank accounting systems, and that the money supply increased up to the Credit Crunch. Indeed, the biggest growth category was M1 (sight deposits as European Central

24 Michael C Burda and Charles Wyplosz, *Macroeconomics: A European Text* (5th edn, OUP 2009) 209.

25 The BoE actually uses M4, which is cash outside banks (i.e. in circulation with the public and non-bank firms) + private-sector retail bank and building society deposits + private-sector wholesale bank and building society deposits and certificates of deposit (Bank of England, 'Further Details About M4 Data' (31 January 2023) <www.bankofengland.co.uk/statistics/details/further-details-about-m4-data> accessed 14 September 2024). In 2010, the total money supply (M4) measure in the UK was GBP2.2 trillion while the actual notes and coins in circulation was only GBP47 billion, 2.1% of the actual money supply: see Richard Lipsey and Alec Chrystal, *Economics* (OUP 2011) 455.

Bank data from 2008 shows). Realizing this helps understand the rise of cryptocurrency. In the Global South, payment by mobile phone has exploded. In Kenya alone, 70% of the population use M-Pesa for payments.[26]

MOBILE MONEY AND GENDER INEQUALITY

Serena Natile has examined the growth of mobile money in Sub-Saharan Africa and its effect on gender dynamics of financial inclusion. She writes of mobile money and other digital financial technology that facilitates payment and credit:

> Digital financial technology, or fintech, facilitates access to financial services for those excluded from mainstream finance. Digital financial inclusion has become a central policy tool to achieve the UN Sustainable Development Goals (SDGs), including gender equality (SDG 5). Access to digital financial services is said to provide women living in poverty or on a low income with autonomy, safety, and entrepreneurial opportunities. While these services have included more female users in the formal financial system, they perpetuate the gendered structural causes of financial exclusion and can create additional vulnerabilities, especially for women at the lower end of the global income distribution.
>
> [For example, in] digital finance, resources are not redistributed within the community as in informal finance: fees that were paid to members of the community are now paid to providers (often linked to Western transnational corporations).
>
> Providers argue that this is a reasonable price to pay for the improved security, safety and traceability, however the proliferation of financial products and services risks reducing already limited resources available to more vulnerable communities (limiting access to basic needs such as food) with generational impact.

For a detailed analysis, see Serena Natile, *The Exclusionary Politics of Digital Financial Inclusion: Mobile Money, Gendered Walls* (Routledge, 2020).

In CFAs you will find a related notion of **Cash and Cash Equivalents**, which are defined terms. Cash Equivalents will extend to easily convertible, or liquid, assets such as exchange-traded securities, precious metals, and so forth. This is similar to the economic category **MZM**, or **money with zero maturity**, which includes financial assets immediately redeemable at par on demand. In the CFA context, this definition is used in part also to assess the liquidity of the borrower by reference to its ability to convert its assets quickly into cash. A borrower holding only real estate will be very illiquid because it takes weeks to realize a land-sale; a borrower holding bonds and gold will be much more liquid and will be able to meet calls for payment fairly quickly.

The key points this section is trying to hammer home are that money is not limited to cash, and that when banks are lending each other money, or lending to non-banks, truckloads of cash are not leaving the bank and travelling across the City. Everything can be done on computer by reference to reserves of cash (and gold), which remain in situ, often held at a central bank.

---

26 Simone di Castri and Lara Gidvani, 'The Kenyan Journey to Digital Financial Inclusion' (2013) GSMA Working Paper No. 15 <www.gsma.com/mobilefordevelopment/wp-content/uploads/2013/07/> accessed 5 May 2024. Cited in Serena Natile, *The Exclusionary Politics of Digital Financial Inclusion: Mobile Money, Gendered Walls* (Routledge 2020) 1.

2.3.2 Money multiplication

When one borrows, one promises to repay. When a bank receives a deposit, it effectively borrows the deposit and promises to repay it, for example on demand. If one is financially conservative, one will only make such a promise to repay on demand if one has the cash ready to hand, for example sitting in a vault. Yet one can be much more speculative by promising to pay using cash one does not yet have but which one believes one can obtain when payment is demanded. Why might a bank take this risk? Because assets sitting in a vault might at best retain value, may well depreciate in value, and are earning no income at all for bank or depositor. That already motivates immediately lending out deposited capital to generate income. Yet banks quickly noticed that a depositor tends not to withdraw all their money at once, and that if the bank times things correctly, it could loan out money worth more than the capital it needed to keep in reserve to pay to its depositor on any given day.

Remember, when someone promises to (re)pay, they are not promising to transfer title to a specific numbered set of coins or notes; they are promising to (re)pay using any money they can acquire at the relevant time. Thus, when bank A takes in GBP100 cash from a depositor, the depositor does not have a call on that exact GBP100, but a claim on the bank for some GBP100. When depositor uses her debit card to pay, she transfers part of her claim on the bank to the payee. The GBP100 cash is economically underpinning this transaction but legally is not the object of it; the debt claim is the object being transferred. This separation of money and cash permits something rather surprising: money multiplication.

First, we observe that when a bank accepts a cash (or gold) deposit from a customer, it does not put the money in its vault but immediately lends it out again; this is how it not only makes money but also funds the price it pays the depositor (the interest) for using its money. If the depositor wants her money back immediately, as a matter of prudence the bank should hold some reserves 'in its vault' for just this eventuality. If we estimate that every bank should hold back 10% of every amount it would otherwise lend, then what we have is a sequence of loans and reservations that converges on zero.

For example, depositor injects new money into an economy by depositing an equivalent of, say, GBP1000 in Swiss francs with Bank I, which reserves GBP100 and lends GBP900, which is taken by the borrower and deposited with Bank II (for ease of argument); Bank II reserves GBP90 and lends on GBP810, and so on until the money is exhausted.

We do not simply have a single GBP1,000 *being spread very thinly* because Depositor thinks she owns GBP1,000 at Bank I, and while Bank I thinks it owes GBP1,000+interest to Depositor and owns >GBP1,000 (reserve plus credit + more interest), the first borrower, Bank II, also owns GBP900 now, and will have to pay GBP900 +interest later, and so on down the line. The essential aspect of this process is that if the commercial banks get this multiplier right collectively, the initial GBP1,000 M0 'currency' stands as a collective reserve in the banking system that is backing (or collateralizing) a bet that a further sum of GBP9,000 loans (sight deposits) will come good. Thus, we have GBP10,000 of M1.

This money multiplication is more formally called *fractional reserve banking*. The greatest concern with this arrangement is just what happens when one of the banks fails to repay its loan, and so breaks the chain of loans multiplying the same reserve. Imagine, for example, that Bank III defaults because it has collapsed into insolvency for other reasons. Bank II will try to recover what it lent—GBP900—but that may prove extremely difficult for a number of reasons:

- Bank II's claim is for some money; it has no proprietary claim on specific monies held by Bank III or any third party. It will have to prove what is owed in the insolvency proceedings and is highly likely to recover less that was lent.

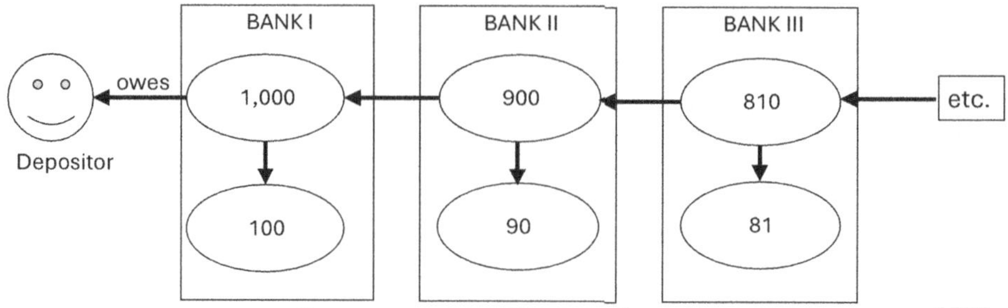

$$If\ p = proportion\ lent\ then\ \sum p = 1{,}000p + 1{,}000p^2 + 1{,}000p^3 \ldots = 1{,}000p(1 + p + p^2 + \cdots) = \frac{1{,}000p}{1-p} = 9{,}000$$

It's just 90% of 90% of 1,000 etc. — Sum of infinite geometric series

Figure 2.1 Money multiplication

- Bank III's reserve is only a tenth of what it borrowed; other recoveries will need to come from recouping lending to third parties (and those loans may only be repayable several years hence). Moreover, Bank II has no greater right over that reserve than any other unsecured creditor, so it must share it with them.
- Even in the unlikely event that Bank II is repaid in full, receipt of funds is likely to occur *after* Bank II's own debt to Bank I falls due, given the length of insolvency proceedings.

As such, Bank II is likely to face a liquidity mismatch: it needs to pay Bank I at some point but only has GBP90 in its reserve to meet that debt. Bank II will thus need to find that money from somewhere else. This poses no problem if we are talking about GBP900, but what if we are talking about GBP900m or more? Being owed such huge amounts is not improbable, for we are speaking here of a closed set of major banks, which will be multiplying money at every opportunity with every deposit. If Bank III has defaulted on one payment, it is likely to default on all of them, it being insolvent. And this will not only affect the Bank III/Bank II relationship; it will affect Bank III's relationship with every other bank from which it has borrowed funds. One result of this is that when Bank II looks around to borrow the missing GBP810 in order to pay Bank I, all the other banks are in the same position as Bank II—they do not want to lend money; they are looking to borrow. Bank II, lacking credit, faces defaulting on its loan from Bank I, replicating the problems faced by Bank III. Money multiplication can feel like an overstretched elastic band, which may contract suddenly and violently, or even worse, simply snap. When that happens, multiple banks find themselves unable to borrow money to repay lenders and depositors, we have, broadly speaking, a **credit crunch**.

The collapse of Bank III has left Bank II and other banks hunting around for money to repay creditors (including depositors) as these debts fall due. Where no bank will lend because they all desperately need cash, the situation is systemically critical for the banking system. Every bank is technically insolvent. In such a situation, the banks need emergency funding from a lender that is capable of finding money to lend no matter how dire the macroeconomic situation. This **lender of last resort** is the central bank, for it may, if necessary, create new money to meet the needs of struggling banks.

Naturally, central banks do not wish to leave things until disaster strikes before they intervene. Central banks work together globally to reduce the risk that commercial banks will not meet their borrowing commitments to each other. One mechanism, following the Basel Accords, is to develop bankers' own estimations of how much of deposit they need to keep in reserve into a formal standard: a capital adequacy requirement. The risk-weighting the commercial banks put on deposits to calculate how much they hold in reserve is mandated by central banks as part of their prudential oversight role. In our example, we could say that the 10% retention is actually central bank policy (it is more complicated than this). Hopefully, you can see that if the central bank suddenly doubled the reserve requirement to 20%, then the brakes would go on the money multiplier as commercial banks scrambled to comply, and future deposits would not stretch quite as far. This is how central banks control money supply in the system—something far different from minting coins, which as we saw above, would only affect money at about 2.6% of GDP and ca. 1.9% of M3 in circulation.

Through money multiplication (fractional reserve banking), we see that banks very often lend money to each other to ensure they are maximizing the value of deposited funds. Since the Credit Crunch of the Global Financial Crisis, commercial banks have been much more reliant on the central bank for this kind of bank lending. In either case, we now understand that when a commercial bank wishes to lend to a corporate borrower, the commercial bank will itself be borrowing that money from other commercial banks or from the central bank.

2.3.3 The interbank market for money and central bank lending

As the money multiplier discussion illustrated, banks and central banks are interconnected as a financial system. Let us now examine how these connections work in detail by developing some key financial terminology. Imagine if (1) Bank I can find no borrower for the GBP900 and (b) Bank II wants to lend GBP810 to borrower but does not have the capital (deposits). In this case, Bank II contracts to borrow GBP900 from Bank I at a certain price (interest) and on-lends this capital to borrower for the price of interest + a bit more interest (**margin**).

Lending of money between banks is so standardized that this market for money is called the **InterBank market**, and it operates in London through the Bank of England infrastructure. The InterBank market was much more significant before the GFC; these days the central banks play a greater role. For ease of explanation, let us first follow through this transaction as if it were being conducted on the InterBank market on the kind of terms applicable around 2010 (and which you may still find in older loan agreements).

The CFA is built around this basic structure: that there are always at least two loans in play: (1) one from lender (Bank II above) to borrower, and (2) one to the lender (Bank II) from a third-party bank (Bank I above). Bank II will pay interest to Bank I, but it will expect borrower to pay at least the same interest to it, which it will pass through to the Bank I *and* that additional margin (interest) which is Bank II's profit. This 'price' of money is called the **cost of funds**. It is the cost Bank II is charging the borrower for obtaining those funds in the market. Given the size of the amounts owing and subtleties of variation, the cost of funds can vary in very small increments and so tend to be quoted not in percentage points but basis points.

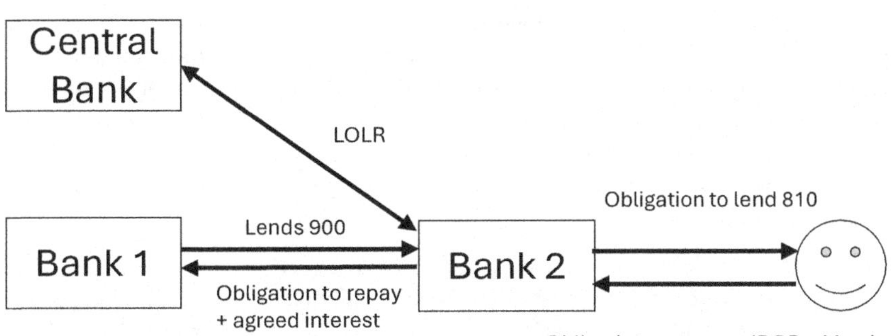

Figure 2.2 Interbank lending

> **ESSENTIAL DEFINITION: BPS**
>
> 1 basis point (bp) = 1 hundredth of a percentage point
>
> To put it another way, 100 bps = 1%. Margin is sometimes expressed in bps because this is a finer, more convenient scale for finance, where 1% of EUR3bn would be an unwieldy EUR30m.

Things are slightly more complicated than this, however. One would expect Bank II to charge the borrower at least an amount equal to the interest payable to Bank I, yet it does not. The reason for this is a matter of financial secrecy. The interest rate Bank I charges Bank II reflects the risk Bank I is taking lending to just that person (as with any interest rate). If one knows the various rates banks are charging each other, one has a fairly good signal that the bank being charged on average the highest rate among them may well be perceived as the riskiest bet for lending, whereas the bank paying on average the least interest between them will be considered the safest. The last thing Bank II wants anyone to know is that it is, for argument's sake, regarded as the riskiest bank in the market by the other banks. That would reinforce those concerns, exacerbate the perception of risk, and potentially result in no one wishing to lend to Bank II anymore. For this reason, banks do not charge corporate borrowers an amount equal to the exact price they paid to borrower funds from a given other bank; instead, they use an accepted market index rate which reflects the average banks are being charged in the interbank market. This effectively hides the rate charged to Bank II in amongst the mean of all the rates being charged between all the relevant banks. This seemed acceptable to borrowers because the rate seemed standardized between all possible bank lenders and objectively determined by a neutral rate setter.

Until fairly recently, the index of the cost of funds in an InterBank market was called the **InterBank Offered Rate (IBOR)**. You may still encounter it in older CFAs. In particular:

- The quoted IBOR relates to a particular market. Thus the rate quoted in London is called the London IBOR or **LIBOR**. The rate quoted in Paris or Frankfurt at the European Central Bank is called EURIBOR. The rate in Tokyo is TIBOR and so on.
- Note that the United States uses the Effective Federal Funds Rate.
- The locus of the IBOR *tells us nothing* about the currency being offered. Thus in London one can borrow inter alia sterling, USD, euro, renminbi, and so on. To specify the currency borrowed we write e.g. USD LIBOR.
- We also need to specify for how long the currency is being borrowed. Three-month GBP LIBOR means the quoted offering rate for borrowing sterling for three months. The term of borrowing can be from overnight to 1 year; the time value of money implies that normally the cost expands with the term of the loan.
- The LIBOR rate is *not* the cost of funds a bank actually pays. It is an index of the cost (offering rate) a number (now 18) of reference banks *claim* they would charge a notional bank for the borrowing of some currency.

This difference between the claimed cost of funds and reality was dramatically exposed during the GFC of 2008. As Willem Buiter said, LIBOR was 'the rate at which banks don't lend to each other,' and he called for its replacement.[27] This was partly because the reference banks were afraid that if they quoted a high cost of funds to the then LIBOR administrator, the British Bankers' Association (BBA), this would leak out and other banks would believe that the reason for the high quotation was that the reference bank itself could not borrow funds in the money markets and/or had limited capital, an assertion which would initiate a Lehman Bros' style crisis of confidence in that bank's liquidity.

Following the LIBOR scandal, the administration of LIBOR was contracted out to ICE LIBOR, a New York outfit. But in the last decade a new index is being introduced, called **SONIA**—or the **Sterling OverNight Index Average**. SONIA has been administered by the Wholesale Markets Brokers' Association since 1997 and is the weighted average of actual unsecured overnight sterling transactions exceeding GBP25m. Importantly, the focus is on overnight deposits of funds by commercial banks with the central bank, and not as with IBOR transactions purely between commercial banks.

In late 2019 the Loan Market Association provided an 'exposure draft' (i.e. not yet recommended) of a revolving CFA with new interest clauses taking into account the sterling **RFR** (Risk-Free Rate) SONIA, and its USD and Eurozone RFR equivalents, being **SOFR** and **€STR**, respectively.[28] The drafting reflected key differences in the new mechanism:[29]

- Unlike LIBOR, which is set for a term (e.g. three months), SONIA is simply an overnight rate: it changes daily.

  LIBOR is forward-looking: it sets a rate for a coming term e.g. three months. SONIA-based drafting is backward-looking: it requires the Facility Agent to integrate the rates backwards from the Interest Payment Date on a compounding basis. That means on day 1, the agent must calculate the interest on the principal, then for day 2 add interest and principal and calculate the new interest on that, for each day of the relevant period and each RFR applicable on that day.
- This makes it difficult for the Obligor to calculate what its Interest will be in advance. The Exposure Draft thus includes an idea of 'lag,' e.g. an estimate can be determined for a three-month term by taking the historic data for three months from the date of estimation, on a rolling basis. This presents problems if the borrower wants to prepay a loan (repay it earlier than envisaged). For this reason the London market favours a non-cumulative compounded rate which can be determined at any moment during an interest period, not just at the end and looking backwards (which date may not even have been reached).
- Overnight rates are typically lower than LIBOR, and the difference can be significant between long-term LIBOR rates and an overnight. The shortfall can be dealt with either by:

  (1) increased Margin; or
  (2) an adjustment spread for this purpose, in addition to Margin.
- The concept of Reference Bank is discarded. The fallback now is the Central Bank as Lender of Last Resort, not other banks in the money market. There is an option to fall back to actual Cost of Funds. There is an RFR for each of the main currencies, as shown in Table 2.2.

The aim was to have this drafting in use by 2021, but beyond sterling it did not gain wide traction, and lenders were still using US dollar LIBOR as late as Q4 2024. Revised wording, especially

27 Alistair Osborne, 'Former MPC Man Calls for Libor to Be Replaced' *The Daily Telegraph* (London, 11 September 2008).

28 Euro Short Term Rate.

29 For the calculations ('exposure draft version') see Hanif Virji, 'LIBOR Transition: Demystifying the Interest Calculations in the LMA Exposure Draft' (2021) 4 JIBFL 263.

Table 2.2 The principal Risk-Free Rates

Jurisdiction	Currency	Risk-Free Rate
United States	USD	Secured Overnight Financing Rate (SOFR)
United Kingdom	GBP	Sterling Overnight Index Average (SONIA)
Switzerland	CHF	Swiss Average Rate Overnight (SARON)
Japan	JPY	Tokyo Overnight Average Rate (TONA)
European Union	EUR	Euro Short-Term Rate (€STR)

for SOFR, was circulated in 2023, with €STR drafting in the pipeline. You will still find the 'classic' LIBOR drafting in longer-term loan agreements which are still live.[30]

2.4 Funding in a CFA

A loan document need only be one page: a promise to repay money lent. Yet the CFA can be over 150 pages long. The reason, as trailed, is partly because a bank does not necessarily have the capital available to lend; it must borrow it in the InterBank market or from a central bank.

Evidently, if a bank is obligated to lend a certain amount of sterling and it cannot do so, then it is in breach of contract and—worse—it is unable to pay a money debt as it has fallen due. It is, technically, insolvent. The CFA focuses on ensuring that the bank can obtain the funds to lend, and, correspondingly, it will be in a position to return those funds to the market when due.

2.4.1 Cost of funds in the CFA

CFA EXAMPLE CLAUSE: CALCULATION OF INTEREST

The following drafting is from an older (2008) clause, chosen because it permits illustration of several points.

Calculation of interest

The rate of interest on each Loan for each Interest Period is the percentage rate per annum which is the aggregate of the applicable:

(a) Margin;
(b) LIBOR or, in relation to any Loan in euro, EURIBOR; and
(c) Mandatory Cost, if any.

30 For more, see Toby Mann and Katie Hoyle, 'Loan Documentation and Risk-Free Reference Rates: Current Overview' (2023) 2 JIBFL 85.

The clause tells us that the rate of interest is constituted by three separate elements:

(1) Margin;
(2) LIBOR or an RFR (or for euro Loans, EURIBOR or €STR); and
(3) Mandatory Cost, if any.

The core cost of funds here is item (2): LIBOR (or its RFR equivalent when adopted). Again, this *not* the actual rate at which Lender borrows the money in the InterBank market but the market reference rate. Because LIBOR is stated here, the rate is floating i.e. it varies with the changes of LIBOR over time. Were a constant rate to be specified (e.g. 100bps), then the rate is called fixed. Notice how this allocates risk:

(1) A floating rate varies the price Borrower pays, and so puts Borrower at risk. The Lender does not completely avoid risk because the lender does not necessarily pay LIBOR to the bank from which it sourced the funds. The lender will hope its actual interest rate is at LIBOR or very close to it; if the actual cost of funds is much higher, the lender will start losing margin (its profit) and then capital, too. This latter scenario happened frequently in the Credit Crunch of 2008.
(2) A fixed rate means that the borrower will pay the same interest rate plus margin come what may, whereas the lender takes the risk of its cost of funds varying in the market.
(3) If Borrower takes a floating rate, it may wish to hedge this with an interest rate swap for a fixed rate (see Chapter 9). If the borrower takes a fixed rate, leaving the lender with the risk, the lender may enter into its own interest rate swap.

In the example clause, given that euro LIBOR exists, why is EURIBOR referred to as an alternative reference rate for euro? Why not borrow euro in the London money market? The reason is practical. The sample clause comes from an of this agreement in which the Frankfurt branches of banks are lending, and so the continental banks simply prefer to borrow their euro in Frankfurt.

The Mandatory Cost element is now *optional* and largely obsolete—it is included in the CFA here because it is pre-2013. The idea behind Mandatory Cost is that it was designed to pass on the Lender's costs of supervision by central banks. More particularly, you will remember that central banks set the reserves banks must hold with the Central Bank as part of money multiplication. The Mandatory Cost aims to reflect the difference between the interest on depositing with central bank and lending to borrower. The Mandatory Cost formula was very complicated, which was why it was abandoned in late 2013.

For completion, here is more modern drafting reflecting the use of one of the RFRs, namely SONIA (the sterling RFR).

CFA EXAMPLE CLAUSE: CALCULATION OF INTEREST (SONIA)

Calculation of interest

(a) The rate of interest on each Loan for any day during an Interest Period is the percentage rate per annum which is the aggregate of the applicable:
  (i) Margin; and
  (ii) Compounded Reference Rate for that day.
(b) If any day during an Interest Period for a Loan is not an RFR Banking Day, the rate of interest on that Loan for that day will be the rate applicable to the immediately preceding RFR Banking Day.

Notice (a)(ii) is now doing the work of LIBOR, while Mandatory cost has been jettisoned. The following definitions are excerpted which explain the method by which SONIA, an overnight rate, is converted into a rate applicable to, say, three months or whatever is required.

Compounded Reference Rate means, in relation to any RFR Banking Day during the Interest Period of a Loan, the percentage rate per annum which is the Daily Non-Cumulative Compounded RFR Rate for that RFR Banking Day

Daily Non-Cumulative Compounded RFR Rate means, in relation to any RFR Banking Day during an Interest Period for a Loan, the percentage rate per annum determined by the Agent (or by any other Finance Party which agrees to determine that rate in place of the Agent) in accordance with the methodology set out in the Schedule (*Daily Non-Cumulative Compounded RFR Rate*) or in any relevant Compounding Methodology Supplement.

RFR is the SONIA (sterling overnight index average) reference rate displayed on the relevant screen of any authorised distributor of that reference rate.

Certainly, do not worry about the precise calculations; this is a job for the facility agent or bank. Our concern is to simply observe that a CFA is not isolated from the InterBank market and overnight rates offered by central banks—that these rates feed directly into the *price* clause of the CFA. Notice how risk is allocated between lender and borrower as a result.

Anyone using a Loan Market Association (LMA) form of CFA will be prompted to detail the terms of repayment of capital and payment of interest, all linked to the lender's need itself to obtain the funds in the money markets. Even if finance parties are in the middle of a credit boom and, being impatient to wait for lawyers to draft a full CFA, lend on a term-sheet basis, the term-sheet's 'heads of terms' will still at least specify repayment and interest payment terms. Yet on the margins of finance, loan contracts do arise where even the most basic terms are missing, and implication may be necessary.

AL JABER v AL IBRAHIM [2018] EWCA Civ 1690, [2019] 1 WLR 885

AJ agreed orally to lend USD30m to AI to fund an Arabic-language broadcast station. There was no evidence of a discussion of interest. The loan was given and went unpaid for several years. Eventually AJ demanded repayment of the USD30m and payment of interest in the additional sum of USD32m. When AI refused to pay, AJ sued and claimed that an interest term should be implied into the oral contract.

Held: You should be able to tackle this already, given your study of implication of terms in contract law. Think through what you would do before reading the answer below.

You will remember the judgment of Lord Neuberger PSC in *Marks and Spencer plc v BNP Paribas Securities Services Co (Jersey) Ltd* [2015] UKSC 72, [2016] AC 742 [14]–[21]. It partly explains why this case is so recent, for the question of implying an interest term has arisen many times before but needs to be reconsidered in light of the current law on implication. In *M&S*, Lord Neuberger noted the term that is to be implied must either be necessary in order to give business effect to the contract or it must be obvious in the sense that 'it goes without saying.' In most cases, it will be both (see [21]).

> Is an interest term necessary in a loan agreement? Interest-free loans are not particularly unusual—your permitted overdraft on your bank account is such a loan (the bank is lending you money so that you can pay third parties). So no, one can think of a loan agreement without an interest term, it is not necessary, and so will not be implied.
>
> Is an interest term 'so obvious it goes without saying'? Had an officious bystander raised the possibility of interest, it may well be that the parties would have said 'of course,' but this test is more subtle than that. It is one thing to say there must be some kind of term; it is another to say what that term should be. What is the interest rate—1%, 10%, floating? Which one of these would the parties say 'of course' to? It cannot be determined, so this test is not satisfied, either.
>
> In short, it was held that in the absence of contextual evidence that both parties objectively understood a definite interest term was to be part of this agreement, the court would not imply it for them. The loan was interest-free.

The takeaway from *Al Jaber* should not be that a court will *never* imply an interest term—ultimately, implication by fact is by its nature determined by the context of any given contract. Given the detail and complexity of the modern CFA and its negotiation, it would be difficult to argue that an absent interest term ought to be implied. Yet one can imagine questions arising when term-sheet funding occurs during credit booms, that is, where financiers prepare one-page heads of terms and proceed to fund, leaving actual drafting of the contract to later.

There are equitable exceptions to contract law's general wariness when it comes to implying terms.[31] The most relevant for our purposes is the equitable rule that where a charge of land (see Chapter 3) securing debt is silent as to interest, equity will imply a right to recover interest (normally at a rate of around 4%–5%).[32] In such a case the parties must *expressly exclude* a right to interest in the loan and/or charge documentation.[33]

2.4.2 Match funding

A related area of risk, even if the bank can borrower the money it needs to lend, is that it bears the risks that it will (1) only be able to obtain funds early, after which it must hold the funds without them earning interest from the borrower until lent; (2) only obtain funds at greater than the reference rate; and (3) not be able to repay those funds into the market when due (a risk with respect to the counterparty bank). To minimize this risk, Lender always aims to borrow funds that mirror the loan to be made to Borrower e.g.

(1) if Borrower is to borrow GBP10m, GBP10m is obtained from the InterBank market;
(2) if Borrower seeks GBP10m, it is GBP which is obtained (not USD or any other currency) and in an appropriate market; and
(3) if Borrower seeks to borrow in three days' time and for three months, Lender should obtain funds in three days' time and for three months.

This principle of mirroring is called **match funding**, and this is reflected in the CFA's drafting,

31 See further *Halsbury's Laws* (2021) vol 49, para 62.

32 *Mendl v Smith* (1943) 112 LJ Ch 279.

33 *Al-Wazir v Islamic Press Agency Inc.* [2001] EWCA Civ 1276, [2002] 1 Lloyd's Rep. 410.

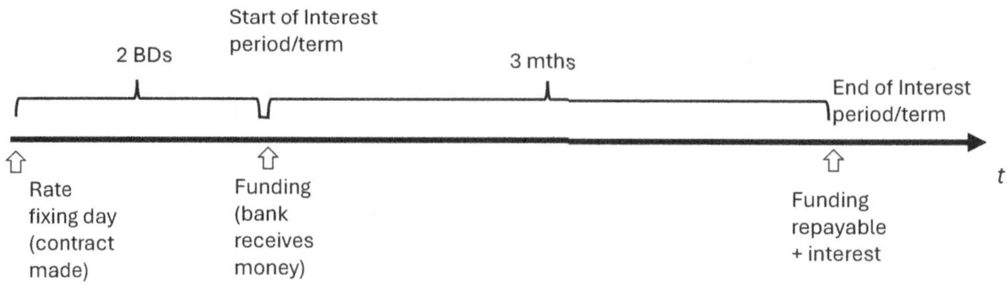

Figure 2.3 Utilization timetable

From the perspective of the InterBank market what occurs revolves around a funding contract. As a basic example, consider the following time frame.

The three months is called the Interest Period and matches the selection made by the Borrower.

By way of example, here is a Utilization clause from a pound sterling CFA, which will be supported by Schedules containing the form of Utilization Request and a timetable to be followed.

CFA Example Clause: Utilization

5.1 Delivery of a Utilization Request

A Borrower may utilize a Facility by delivery to the Agent of a duly completed Utilization Request not later than the Specified Time [i.e. 3 working days prior].

5.2 Completion of a Utilization Request

(a) Each Utilization Request is irrevocable and will not be regarded as having been duly completed unless: (i) it identifies the Facility to be utilized; (ii) the proposed Utilization Date is a Business Day within the applicable Availability Period; and (iii) the currency and amount of the Utilization comply with clause 5.3 (*Currency and amount*).

(b) Only one Loan may be requested in each Utilization Request.

5.3 Currency and amount

(a) The currency specified in a Utilization Request must be sterling.

(b) The amount of the proposed Loan must be an amount which is not more than the Available Facility and which is a minimum of £25,000,000 or, if less, the Available Facility.

You can see that Borrower must send a Utilization Request to borrow (we say **draw down**) a facility three days before the date of drawdown. This gives the Facility Agent time to notify the Lenders of the need to obtain, and for them to obtain, a funding contract.

2.4.3 Prepayment and breakage costs

It is a common misconception that banks would prefer to be repaid early (we call this **prepayment**, reserving **repayment** for payment of the Loans on the due date), a misconception enhanced in lawyers' minds by the rule in *Pinnel's Case*.[34] The nature of InterBank lending should tell you why this is in fact not desirable.

- E.g. Borrower borrows GBP30m for 12 months from Lender (in this paragraph, the **Loan**). Lender matches this with a 12-month InterBank loan from Y Bank. Borrower prepays the Loan after three months, leaving Lender with GBP30m just sitting on its balance sheet and for which it must find another home which will produce returns on capital. This is extremely inefficient from a Return on Invested Capital perspective.

A standard CFA is thus strict about *voluntary* prepayment, specifying the need for advanced notice, prepayment in multiples, and only permitting prepayment of term loans after the Availability Period has expired.

As discussed in the above example, Lender will have received prepayment of capital which *ought to have earned* an agreed Interest Rate for the period from prepayment to the next Interest Payment Date (**IPD**), if different (note Interest Periods are selected on utilization). The loss of this Margin is called a **breakage cost** to Lender—a cost due to Borrower breaking the agreed Interest Period of the Loan early.

You might think that if a borrower breaks without lender consent, causing the lender loss, the Lender cannot receive prepayment earlier than an IPD and then just sit on its hands. Rather it must reasonably attempt to find a new home for the capital and so mitigate its loss.[35] Yet we already saw in section 2.1 that the mitigation is not applicable to debt claims, that the lender may demand payment in full. One might object that in the case of prepayment the borrower has indeed paid in full and in advance, and any further losses pertain not to the debt in itself but are a consequence of not following the other terms of the contract around time of repayment. On that view, one might say that losses caused by a break occasion contractual damages, not a simple debt claim, and thus mitigation applies. Such a view, however, ignores that the loss is a loss of interest payable (and so a debt). The lender is not claiming the loss of possible interest it could have obtained in the market, but only that interest the borrower was contractually obliged to pay. As such, mitigation does not apply to the loss of that interest debt.

The CFA does not rely on the common law but covers these matters in a 'break costs' clause. This clause deploys a definition of 'Break Costs,' which does integrate a limited contractual presumption of mitigation. The clause assumes the lender will place—but does not require it to—the prepaid funds in a deposit account with a leading bank, thus earning at least some interest, and the borrower need only pay the difference between that interest and the interest that would have been payable under the CFA for the relevant period. This may by no means be a small amount. From the lender's perspective, it has protection against a borrower failing to respect the lender's goal of match funding.

2.4.4 Margin protection, market disruption, and lender discretion

Given the margin is the profit a lender makes on provision of money, the lender will go to some lengths to prevent risk to this amount, such as:

(1) Putting the cost of expenses onto the Borrower (a fees clause).
(2) Building in Mandatory Cost clause (rarely now).

---

34 That early payment can be valuable consideration for a variation of contract: *Pinnel's Case* [1602] 5 Co Rep 117a, 77 ER 237.

35 *British Westinghouse Electric and Manufacturing Co Ltd. v Underground Electric Railways Co Ltd.* (No.2) [1912] AC 673.

(3) Deploying an increased costs clause to cover any 'Increased Cost' incurred by a change in regulation or law or compliance with such law or regulation, particularly with the reserve requirements central banks place on banks.[36] These are very widely defined, and it is difficult to stipulate a scenario in which the clause would apply and be enforceable. In recent years, the breadth of the clause has been partially circumscribed by making explicit references to laws concerning reserve requirements.

(4) Providing for a tax gross-up to ensure Borrower pays or repays the gross of any required tax deduction—remember, that money is matched to the market.

(5) Assigning risk where there is market disruption.

Let us look at this final measure in more detail.

Given the CFA's close linkage to the money markets, especially where a loan is subject to a floating rate, it is quite possible that the reference interest rate be unexpectedly altered by circumstances beyond the parties' control and not simply as a result of market dynamics. Imagine, for example, that the world's IT systems fail and on a given interest calculation date the facility agent is simply unable to calculate the interest payable. Estimating will not do: a 0.01% error on the rate amounts to +/– GBP50,000 on a GBP500m loan. A *Changes to the Calculation of Interest* clause is included to deal with just this problem.

In older CFAs, and as standard before the GFC, the clause was hubristically drafted—it assumed the only possible market disruption could arise from technical failure, and loosely defined market disruption as lack of a screen rate (i.e. lack of an official IBOR as communicated electronically to banks). In such a case, the market disruption clause stated, two or more reference banks had been identified to provide a substitute rate—their independent estimation of what the rate would be, based on their own borrowing in the money market. In effect, it recreated the calculation of LIBOR (involving 18 banks surveyed by the BBA regarding their borrowing costs) with a sample of two banks of similar standing.[37]

This form of market disruption clause was stress-tested during the GFC and subsequent scandal. During this period LIBOR not only rose dramatically, but Lenders became aware that LIBOR did not reflect the significant *actual* offering rate they were having to pay to obtain funds in the market. In short, the credit markets 'dried up'—banks were not prepared to lend money to other banks (1) because they feared they would not be repaid and (2) they wished to hoard capital on the balance sheet.

This meant that a screen rate *was* available but that no lender trusted it anymore. Nor did recourse to the reference banks help because quite possibly the reference banks would simply repeat the problem with the screen rate: they would quote a borrowing rate much lower than that at which they were actually borrowing. From the lender's perspective this is disastrous; for the floating rate CFA is supposed to insulate the lender against rising money market costs through the CFA's rate *floating* on top of the market rate. Now it was not floating, or rather it was floating on a LIBOR rate which was much lower than the lender's actual costs of borrowing. The lender was losing money. This was particularly so where the CFA included a floating rate RCF and term loans which the borrower was currently drawing down.

During this moment of stress, banks investigated the possibility of avoiding the obligation to lend by:

---

36 See further Thomas Miller and Aidan Lawes, 'Is It Time to Review Your "Standard" Increased Costs Clauses in Facility Documentation?' (2022) 5 JIBFL 347.

37 This was designed to avoid the lender simply specifying its own rate—an exercise of discretion which could be subject to an allegation of arbitrariness: *Paragon Finance plc v Nash* [2001] EWCA Civ 1466, [2002] 1 WLR 685.

(1) Triggering the market disruption clause. Much debate was had about how many lenders in a syndicate will need to have trouble funding for this clause to be triggered (30% was usual). Clearly, one bank collapse should not be a reason. If there is market disruption, a substitute for LIBOR is effectively cobbled together from pre-agreed reference banks.
(2) Looking to vary the contract to deal with the situation—where funding becomes impossible or prohibitively expensive, Lender may seek to argue frustration (dubious) or at least argue that a variation should be agreed.
(3) Calling a material adverse change (**MAC**). This is problematic—see our investigation into MACs in our CFA case study below.

Members of the LMA were very dissatisfied with the standard drafting, which seemed too loose to enforce and did not cover the risks that actually arose in the GFC. As a first step in response, the LMA standard form expanded the *Unavailability of Screen Rate* clause to pre-empt the need for such a variation by suggesting methods by which a reasonable reference rate can be calculated (for example by using shortened interest periods). In this way there is something of a firewall between systemic failure and the CFA. On the other hand, this clause does not protect Lender from price risk, which is the risk inherent to banking. This first move was then superseded by the introduction of SONIA, which did much to bypass the risk that reference banks might be less than transparent about cost of funds.

Yet it remains the case that disruption can occur, and the reference rates for the loan are not available on a given day. The LMA therefore introduced an addendum to the standard CFA which, while attractive to lenders, seems like a step backwards. The new clause provides that in the absence of a reference rate, a 'cost of funds fallback' applies.[38] This fallback initially calculates interest by reference to the actual cost of funds to the lenders party to the CFA, which cost is notified to the facility agent. This deals with the immediate problem of calculating a pressing interest payment; the clause then encourages the borrower and agent to negotiate a longer-term solution.

The principal difficulty with the cost of funds fallback is that it both repeats the error of the GFC—believing banks will always be transparent and honest when disclosing cost of funds—*and* confers on the lender a discretionary power to vary the interest rate of a loan in a non-transparent way.[39] To emphasize this latter point, the right to determine the interest rate payable was possessed by the respective parties as they negotiated the contract, and their agreement on the rate was embedded in its terms, so binding them to it. In the event this agreed rate became unascertainable, the contract conferred the borrower's residual right to agree to an alternative rate (to vary the contract) as a power on the lender. In exercising that conferred power, the lender is open to a claim that the exercise of the power was in bad faith and/or unreasonable pursuant to the *Braganza* doctrine.[40]

BRAGANZA v BP SHIPPING LTD [2015] UKSC 17, [2015] 1 WLR 1661 (SC)

The claimant's husband had been employed as chief engineer onboard a vessel operated by the defendant. It was a term of the contract that should the employee die while working, a death-in-service benefit would be payable to any surviving spouse. Excluded

38 Hanif Virji, 'Facing the End of LIBOR Addendum: A 'Cost of Funds' Fallback?' (2020) 2 JIBFL 84.

39 Something the pre-2009 drafting avoided by using two independent reference banks.

40 Charlotte Eborall and Sarah Parker, 'Bragging Rights: Termination Clauses and Implied Duties of Good Faith' (2022) 8 JIBFL 518; Hugh Evans and Shabaz Ahmed, '*UBS v Rose Capital Ventures*: Good Faith and Braganza' (2019) 34(5) JIBFL 336.

from this clause was death by suicide, and the contract provided it was for the employer to determine whether suicide had occurred. Sadly, the husband disappeared one night in the mid-Atlantic and was presumed drowned. The employer concluded the death was a result of suicide and declined to make payment to the claimant. The claimant sued, arguing that the employer's finding of suicide was self-serving, not being supported by any cogent evidence.

Held: The Supreme Court analogized from well-known administrative law approach to the review of decision-making developed by Lord Greene MR in *Associated Provincial Picture Houses Ltd v Wednesbury Corp* [1948] 1 KB 223 (CA).[41]

The Supreme Court held that where a contractual term gave one party the power to exercise a discretion or form an opinion as to relevant facts, it was not for the court to substitute its own decision, but where the decision would affect the rights and obligations of both parties this created a conflict of interest and the power could be abused.

The court would prevent this by implying a term in appropriate cases that the power should be exercised not only in good faith but also without being arbitrary, capricious, or irrational. In this regard, the Supreme Court referred to *Socimer International Bank v Standard Bank London Ltd* [2008] Bus LR 1304 (CA):

> a decision-maker's discretion will be limited, as a matter of necessary implication, by concepts of honesty, good faith, and genuineness, and the need for an absence of arbitrariness, capriciousness, perversity and irrationality. The concern is that the discretion should not be abused. [66]

In this case, this limitation would take the form of the *Wednesbury reasonableness* test, namely a decision would be impugned where (1) it was a decision that no reasonable decision-maker could have reached, or (2) even so, the decision-making process had failed to exclude extraneous considerations or to take account of all obviously relevant ones.

Baroness Hale said:

> Contractual terms in which one party to the contract is given the power to exercise a discretion, or to form an opinion as to relevant facts, are extremely common . . . the party who is charged with making decisions which affect the rights of both parties to the contract has a clear conflict of interest. [18]

Accordingly:

> unless the court can imply a term that the outcome be objectively reasonable—for example, a reasonable price or a reasonable term—the court will only imply a term that the decision-making process be lawful and rational in the public law sense, that the decision is made rationally (as well as in good faith) and consistently with its contractual purpose. [30]

In the instant case, a 4:2 majority of the Supreme Court held that the employer's decision was irrational. Suicide was such an 'inherently unlikely' event that in the absence of any 'cogent' evidence of suicide, no reasonable person could have reached a positive conclusion that suicide was the cause of death. The claimant was entitled to the death-in-service benefit.

41 But be careful: the *Braganza* test is not the *Wednesbury* test and the analogy should not be pushed too far.

While *Braganza* is the leading case on the exercise of powers under a contract, a slightly earlier case—*Paragon Finance*[42]—specifically considered the discretionary variation of an interest rate in the context of mortgage lending. In *Paragon Finance*, Dyson LJ said:

> It is one thing to imply a term that a lender will not exercise his discretion in a way that no reasonable lender, acting reasonably, would do. It is unlikely that a lender who was acting in that way would not also be acting either dishonestly, for an improper purpose, capriciously or arbitrarily. It is quite another matter to imply a term that the lender would not impose unreasonable rates. [41]
>
> It follows that if [the lender] encounters financial difficulties, it may feel obliged to raise the interest rates paid by its borrowers. In deciding whether to raise interest rates, it will have to make fine commercial judgments. But if it decides to take that course in order to overcome financial difficulties, it is not acting dishonestly, capriciously or in an arbitrary manner. It is not taking into account an irrelevant consideration. Nor is it acting in a way which is so unreasonable that it can be said of it that no reasonable lender would take that course if placed in that situation. [47]

These dicta received subsequent approval from the Court of Appeal.[43] They certainly provide some comfort to lenders, but given the historical evidence that banks have been motivated to be less than transparent about their cost of funds in a crisis, one cannot help but think a borrower faced with a skyrocketing floating rate derived, in the absence of the usual reference rate, simply from a unilateral communication from a lender, might well wish to question it.

2.5 Credit risk mitigation in CFAs

Up until now we have looked at how the CFA interfaced with the InterBank market/central bank. In this and the following lectures we will focus on the more obvious relationship between Lender and Borrower. Broadly speaking, the CFA attempts to mediate the following interests.

There is theoretical issue at play here too. In his *Finance Capital* (1910), Rudolf Hilferding advanced the thesis that German corporations had moved beyond the phase of being private fiefdoms of industrial magnates.[44] Yet unlike Berle and Means, he did not claim that control of the corporation had by default fallen into the hands of a new managerial class. Rather he claimed that corporations were subject to the discipline of the financiers who sat on German corporations' boards. While there is much in Hilferding's analysis that is contingent on corporations law and practice in Weimar Germany, the core argument that the providers of debt finance have significant control over corporates in comparison to providers of equity finance is not without merit. Hilferding's analysis was modernized by De Vroey in the 1970s but might benefit from further empirical research in light of our discussions today.[45] What we will see is that the CFA is capable of disciplining corporate behaviour through a number of mechanisms designed to maintain the creditworthiness of the Obligors within certain parameters over the term of the agreement.

42 [2005] EWCA Civ 760, [2005] 1 WLR 3412.

43 ibid. See also, *Abu Dhabi National Tanker Co v Product Star Shipping Ltd, The Product Star* (No.2) [1993] 1 Lloyd's Rep 397 (CA) [403]–[404].

44 For a recent edition: Rudolf Hilferding, *Finance Capital: A Study in the Latest Phase of Capitalist Development* (Routledge 2007).

45 Michel De Vroey, 'PART I: The Corporation and The Labor Process: The Separation of Ownership and Control in Large Corporations. Review of Radical Political Economics' (1975) 7 Review of Radical Political Economics 1.

Table 2.3 Key party interests when negotiating a CFA

Finance party side	Obligor side
That the debtor is in fact the person it claims to be	That the debtor is not forced into a representation it cannot make
That the debtor stays the same, but for planned growth	That the debtor is permitted to carry out its business without interference
That the creditor receives timely information from the debtor that it is staying the same (or that there is a problem)	That the debtor does not spend all its time managing loan covenants rather than the business
That if the debtor is at risk of default, the creditor knows well in advance	That the debtor is given time to 'turn things round'
That if default occurs, the creditor has immediate and effective access to any remaining capital in the business	That the debtor: (a) Has freedom to dispose of its assets in the conduct of its business; and (b) During insolvency it balances the interests of all its stakeholders, especially all its creditors

2.5.1 Overwriting contract's default rules

When you studied contract law, you often studied the default contractual rules—the rules that the court will apply if the parties are silent on the matter or have explicitly chosen the default rules. This is particularly the case for breach of contract, where you learnt about the rules for identifying conditions, warranties, and innominate terms, and the consequences of their breach in terms of damages and possibly entitling the innocent party to terminate the contract. You likely also learnt about misrepresentation—that a representee may void a contract if they entered into in reliance on a pre-contractual misrepresentation made by the other party. If you studied these basic rules as *the only rules*, then the borrower-facing risk mitigation clauses of a CFA will be utterly confusing. For here we find representations in the contract (not before it), covenants (aka undertakings) which look like conditions or perhaps not, and a whole regime for dealing with breach which is not termination but something called *acceleration*. It is as if the contract law you studied is irrelevant.

Yet one need not look far into the case law to find the basis for the CFA's approach to representations, breach of condition, and so forth. English contract law actively encourages contracting parties to design their own regime for handling misrepresentations and non-performance.

Given contract law's origins in medieval tort (assumpsit, trespass on the case), one might reasonably think that the focus of breach of contract is like that of breach of duty—one party has wrongfully failed to meet an obligation and the court should hold them to account for it, a fortiori when they volunteered to be bound by that obligation. But it is this very voluntariness which speaks to the opposite view: that the parties had in mind the consequences of breach when the made the contract and so assumed the same just in case they could not do what they had originally promised. For, if they did not accept these consequences, they should not contract in the first place knowing that the law would not impose the obligation against their will.

This view can be boiled down to the following analysis of a promise: I promise to do *x*, but if I do not do *x* then I will do *y*. E.g. I promise to deliver goods, but if I do not deliver goods then I promise to pay you a sum of money equal to any loss caused by non-delivery. In most cases the alternative *y* will be implicit, but should anyone ask two parties 'what happens if A does not do *x*?'

A and B will not say 'nothing, A can just walk away,' they will say 'well of course in that case we expect A to remedy the situation by doing some y.' This implied 'secondary obligation' view had an adherent in Lord Diplock.[46]

> Leaving aside those comparatively rare cases in which the court is able to enforce a primary obligation by decreeing specific performance of it, *breaches of primary obligations give rise to substituted or secondary obligations on the part of the party in default*, and, in some cases, may entitle the other party to be relieved from further performance of his own primary obligations. These secondary obligations of the contract breaker and any concomitant relief of the other party from his own primary obligations *also arise* by implication of law—generally common law, but sometimes statute, as in the case of codifying Statutes passed at the turn of the century, notably the Sale of Goods Act 1893. *The contract, however, is just as much the source of secondary obligations as it is of primary obligations; and like primary obligations that are implied by law, secondary obligations too can be modified by agreement between the parties*, although, for reasons to be mentioned later, they cannot, in my view, be totally excluded. In the instant case, the only secondary obligations and concomitant reliefs that are applicable arise by implication of the common law as modified by the express words of the contract. [Lord Diplock, *Photo Production Ltd v Securicor Transport Ltd* [1980] UKHL 2, [1980] AC 827]

One corollary of regarding consequences of breach as part of the contract, Diplock confirms, is that these consequences are within the power of the parties to agree. This is just what the CFA does: rather than rely on the default rules of the common law of contract, it sets out explicitly what the parties agree should happen where there has been a misrepresentation or non-performance. This permits the parties to control potential and actual default in an orderly fashion, potentially averting complete disaster, and intentionally allocating risk.[47]

Be careful, though: the default rules have not disappeared; the common law is always there, under the surface, ready to rise up through the slightest crack in the drafting. It is always possible for a party to demand that the contractual provisions be adhered to or, alternatively, that the default rules are applied instead. As an extreme example, liquidated damages clauses are an example of an expressly agreed alternative to the default rule (damages for loss), but the court may strike down what was expressly agreed if it goes too far i.e. the clause penalizes the defaulting party rather than remedies the loss to the innocent party.

2.5.2 Representation versus undertakings in the CFA

You may remember that English common law differentiates between representations and warranties, and between warranties and conditions (and innominate terms, but let's ignore these). Rather than rely on post hoc judicial interpretation, the CFA attempts expressly to identify which of its borrower-related terms are representations, warranties, and conditions.

First, the CFA distinguishes representations on the one hand and undertakings (aka undertakings or conditions) on the other. These play the following practical roles:

---

46 Lord Diplock infamously concurred with a HL opinion by stating words to the effect: 'Legal certainty demands that I concur with the majority, and I do so willingly, even though the majority are completely wrong.'

47 cf *Transfield Shipping Inc v Mercator Shipping Inc (The Achilleas)* [2008] UKHL 48, [2009] 1 AC 61; Oliver Wendell Holmes, 'The Path of the Law' (1897) 10 Harv L Rev 457.

(1) The representations clause:
  (a) Includes express representations by the borrower of the legal and commercial assumptions on which the deal is based.
  (b) Sets out the contractual basis of the loan.
  (c) Is investigatory—it forms part of the assessment of the creditworthiness of the borrower.
  (d) Requires that certain representations be repeated at certain times during the life of the loan e.g. utilization, rollover. This provides for continued investigation of the creditworthiness of the borrower. Repetition is usually tied to drawdown—every time a borrower draws down (borrows) any part of a facility, it will make representations on which the lender will rely before disbursing the funds.
  (e) Is, or should be, tailored for each borrower.

EXAMPLE: A REPRESENTATIONS CLAUSE

17. Each Borrower makes the representations and warranties set out in this Clause to each Finance Party on the Signing Date.

In the case of the Company, it is a public liability corporation, duly incorporated and validly existing under the law of its jurisdiction of incorporation.

There has been no material adverse change in its assets, business or financial condition (consolidated if applicable) since the date to which the Original Financial Statements were drawn up.

. . .

The Repeating Representations [as defined] are deemed to be made by each Borrower by reference to the facts and circumstances then existing on the date of each Utilisation Request and the first day of each Interest Period.

(2) The undertakings clauses
  (a) Specify performance obligations of the borrower.
  (b) Are particularly focused on obligations of the borrower to remain creditworthy, including by:
    (i) Maintaining its current line of business and assets, and not disposing of key assets.
    (ii) Not incurring more debt, and not granting security to other creditors.
    (iii) Maintaining its financial performance within certain parameters. On this see the final technical section of this chapter on financial covenants.
    (iv) Not acquiring new businesses (takeovers).
    (v) Complying with relevant law.
  (c) Are not absolute prohibitions. They usually contain exceptions:
    (i) for activity in the borrower's normal course of business (disposing of stock; trade credit).
    (ii) a de minimis 'basket' (the borrower is allowed freedom to dispose, incur indebtedness, etc, provided the value does not exceed e.g. GBP10,000).
    (iii) where the lender/facility agent grants permission.

As these clauses will interfere with the borrower's freedom to act, in practice they are some of the most heavily negotiated clauses in a CFA.

AN EXAMPLE CFA UNDERTAKING BY A REAL ESTATE BUSINESS

(a) The Borrower shall not be a creditor in respect of any Financial Indebtedness [defined to exclude this loan].

(b) Paragraph (a) above does not apply to:

(i) any credit extended by the Borrower to a tenant on normal commercial terms and in the ordinary course of its property investment business;
(ii) any advance payment made in relation to capital expenditure in the ordinary course of its property investment business.

The representations and undertakings broadly map onto the equivalent distinction between representations and terms in the common law of contract. If this were all, then apart from the novelty of including the representations in the contract, there would not be much more to add. As far as misrepresentation is concerned, the lender would hope to be able to point to the explicit recording of representations in the contract as proof that they were made, and the lender relied on them (grounding a claim for vitiation and damages under the Misrepresentation Act 1967). The undertakings would be analysed as innominate terms following *Hong Kong Fir*:[48] if breach of a term deprives the innocent party of substantially the whole benefit of the contract, innocent party is entitled to terminate the contract and sue for damages.

Yet this is *not* all. Rather, the CFA expressly provides for what happens when a misrepresentation has been made and/or an undertaking has been breached.

2.5.3 Default and acceleration

To repeat, the basic rule is that if a breach of a contractual term deprives the innocent party of substantially the whole benefit of the contract, then at common law the term is a condition, and its breach entitles the innocent party to terminate and sue for damages. Though traditionally every other term was regarded as a warranty, entitling the innocent party only to sue for damages, the *Hong Kong Fir* notion of the innominate term in reality fills this gap—it is quite possible for any term to be a condition in the right circumstances. Critically for our purposes, as we have noted, it is open to the parties to override these default rules by designating the effects of breach of any given term. This freedom is not absolute—secondary obligations are policed more heavily than primary ones. In *L Schuler AG v Wickman Machine Tool Sales Ltd*, infamously, the majority of the House of Lords held that a clause designated a condition was not, because it covered such a minor and irrelevant issue that to permit the other party to terminate for its breach would be absurd.[49]

The basic scheme of the CFA is to create a new clause—the **Events of Default** clause—which provides an overview of the effect of a misrepresentation or breach of any of the undertakings by the borrower. For each one it specifies where there is a default, whether it is possible for the borrower to remedy (cure) that default, and what rights the lender has on default. These rights boil down to what is called in the contract **acceleration**, which we will examine shortly.

The common Events of Default include:

(1) Non-payment. This would evidently be a condition at common law, but the CFA takes no risks and specifies that a failure to make payment when due which is not remedied will be an Event of Default.
(2) Insolvency (which usually amounts to non-payment of someone). Although slightly more oblique, there is a good argument that insolvency, which likely flows from an inability to pay, goes to the heart of a loan contract and so a requirement that one be solvent (drafting

48 *Hong Kong Fir Shipping Co Ltd. v Kawasaki Kisen Kaisha Ltd.* [1961] EWCA Civ 7, [1962] 2 QB 26; and see in a finance context *EMFC Loan Syndications LLP v The Resort Group plc* [2021] EWCA Civ 844, [2022] 1 WLR 717.

49 [1973] UKHL 2, [1974] AC 235. 'The fact that a particular construction leads to a very unreasonable result must be a relevant consideration. The more unreasonable the result the more unlikely it is that the parties can have intended it, and if they do intend it the more necessary it is that they shall make that intention abundantly clear.' Lord Wilberforce dissented.

as not being insolvent) would be a condition at common law. Again, explicit drafting must be preferable.

(3) Breach of financial covenants (examined in section 2.8).

(4) Breach of any other obligation of the CFA or related finance documents, including in particular the general undertakings, if not remedied within a specified time period.

(5) Misrepresentation. This can be very confusing. Rather than rely on the framework of vitiation afforded by the Misrepresentation Act 1967 and the common law, the CFA provides that the *fact* of a misrepresentation also amounts to an Event of Default. The reason is control of the consequences, which we discuss as part of acceleration.

(6) Cross-default, which you must always bear in mind in any dealings with a client. A cross-default would include a failure by the borrower to make payment under a contract or arrangement with a third party (such as payment of interest on bonds, or failure to pay rent). Lawyers outside of finance can be dangerously unaware that a non-payment under a transaction in their own field can trigger cross-default clauses at the heart of a corporate's borrowing.

(7) The **MAC Clause** (cl 23.15). The material adverse change clause turns on the definition of **Material Adverse Effect**. The sheer open-endedness of the definition makes it very attractive to Finance Parties clutching at straws but, because it benefits them, the MAC clause will be construed strictly against them. During the GFC it was mooted whether the MAC clause could be triggered in light of events, but market opinion came down on the negative side. A Material Adverse Effect has been interpreted (on the drafting of the particular contract) to require a post-contract event unknown before contracting which has a material and adverse effect on the Obligors' ability to perform the conditions of the loan agreement. The evidence establishing a MAC is also critical: market events or hearsay appear to be insufficient. A material adverse change in financial condition for example must be borne out by the financial information provided under the loan agreement. See *Grupo Hotelero Urvasco SA v Carey Value Added SL & Another* [2013] EWHC 1039, discussed in section 2.6.

Strictly speaking, the Events of Default clause distinguishes between **Defaults** and Events of Default, giving rise to a subtle area of negotiation. For example, the *other obligations* clause provides that a breach of any other term of the Finance Documents (a Default) will be an Event of Default if it is not remedied or remediable within a certain time period. During the period between Default and Event of Default we have a period (hidden away in the definitions clause of the CFA) when a Default is **continuing**. It will continue until remedied or waived. Depending on the drafting, the principal right of a lender when a Default is continuing is to enforce a drawstop: the lender's commitment to lend is suspended and its can simply refuse to disburse funds to the borrower. For corporate borrowers, who likely have an RCF to provide continuing liquidity, the time for drawing down funds may be uncomfortably close (a matter of weeks).

Some banks will seek to argue that a continuing Default is enough to trigger acceleration (see below), while others may regard one as continuing even if it has been waived—on the basis that Default is a breach of contract, and its remedy does not cause the fault to disappear; that is entirely in the gift of the innocent party (to waive). This latter argument was considered in *Grant v FR Acquisitions*,[50] where the court held that the test to be adopted is whether the identified event or state of affairs which constituted the event of default is continuing—the potential impact on a creditor's rights of the event of default should be disregarded. To put it another way, once continuing does not mean always continuing—the court will look to the mischief identified by the Event of Default and assess whether the event itself has ceased or not.

At the end of the Events of Default clause, one finds the contractual provision detailing the rights of the lenders when an Event of Default is declared: **acceleration**. Acceleration literally means

50 *Grant v FR Acquisitions Corporation (Europe) Ltd.* [2022] EWHC 2532 (Ch). This case recurs in our discussion of continuing defaults in derivatives contracts.

speeding up the term of any Loans made, indeed so much that they become entirely repayable immediately. More particularly, acceleration permits the lender (or agent at the instruction of the lender(s)) to:

(1) cancel the commitments i.e. the lenders are no longer obligated to lend any further funds to which they were committed under the CFA;
(2) declare all loans immediately repayable on demand;
(3) declare all sums owing under the Finance Documents immediately payable on demand (this would include interest and fees); and
(4) where the loans are secured, enforce any and all security (see Chapters 3 and 4).

An acceleration clause tends to be brutally short and effective; the more verbiage that creeps into such a powerful clause creating secondary rights and obligations, the greater the risk that it be recharacterized by the court in a way the lenders do not intend. After all, an upfront demand for e.g. GBP300m cash would render almost any corporate insolvent and so would be fatal. A court will think twice if seized by a desperate borrower pointing to an ill-drafted acceleration clause. A particularly interesting variation on this point occurred in the following case.

LOMBARD NORTH CENTRAL PLC v EUROPEAN SKYJETS LTD (IN LIQUIDATION) [2022] EWHC 728 (QB)

This was an aircraft finance case in which L had lent USD3,600,000 to Skyjets on a secured basis for the purposes of acquiring a Bombardier Learjet. L subsequently accelerated the loans for various reasons, enforced the security over the Learjet and realized its value of USD3.1m. L now claimed the balance from Skyjets.

One of the grounds for accelerating the loan had been Skyjets' failure to pay, when due, the sum of USD179.99 (one hundred seventy-nine dollars, ninety-nine cents)—a non-payment event of default. Skyjets argued that not only was it wholly unreasonable for L to accelerate the loan and demand immediate payment of USD3.6m for want of just USD179.99, but also the clause amounted to a penalty because it allowed L to recover the full amount loaned as a result of an event of little consequence.

Held: Foxton J was merciless ([148]):

> This argument is hopeless. Skyjets was obliged to repay the amount it had borrowed, on the terms of the Loan Agreement. Those terms provided for monthly instalments as the starting point, but entitled Lombard to require repayment of the full outstanding balance following events which, objectively, raised the risk of default. As Neill LJ observed in *The Angelic Star* [1988] 1 Lloyd's Rep 122 (CA), 126:
>
> 'I know of no rule that prevents a lender from stipulating that in the event of a failure to make an instalment payment on the due date the whole loan becomes due and repayable forthwith.'[51]

In a loan agreement, the whole purpose of which was to make a loan and see it repaid, the failure of the borrower to pay any sum when it fell due was fundamental to the whole enterprise.

51 See also *ZCCM Investments Holdings Plc v Konkola Copper Mines Plc* [2017] EWHC 3288 (Comm) [33]–[34].

Acceleration operates best as a nuclear threat in negotiation over default, and is not to be deployed thoughtlessly. Simply 'pressing the button' will destroy value: the corporate borrower will fall into liquidation, its customers and suppliers will desert it, and it will cease to be a going concern with the result that the lenders will recover much less on a distribution of the remaining assets. The lender is (or should be) looking for a long-term relationship in which the borrower generates profits to repay all the debt capital and pay all the interest expected under the arrangement. What is needed, therefore, is a lender which is prepared to negotiate a way through present difficulties with the borrower: a process called a **workout** or, if a more fundamental reconfiguration of the borrower business is required, a **restructuring**. Both of these can potentially occur without recourse to the various insolvency tools available, such as administration or a scheme of arrangement. They can occur without accelerating the loan.

It is a question of a spectrum of possible actions. If the default is minor, the lender may simply *expressly* **waive** the default either for the time being or permanently, by means of a letter identifying the breaches, waiving them, but otherwise reserving rights. Lenders will not want to rely on the default common law and equitable rules around waiver and promissory estoppel.[52] Waiver is only appropriate, however, if the default is itself of a temporary nature. One cannot waive a change of control (takeover), because tomorrow the borrower will still have been taken over. For situations where defaults are permanent, it is more correct to pursue a **variation of contract**. Such a variation would simply reconfigure the offending clause to expressly permit or carve out just the circumstance of concern.

At this point you may be reaching for *Foakes v Beer*[53] and similar variation cases,[54] noticing quite correctly that this is a case concerning varying terms relating to payment of a debt and so potentially falling foul of the rule that there can be no consideration for variation to a debt obligation, rendering any such variation unenforceable. There is possibly an argument here that in CFAs a debt is not payable until it falls to be payable, including by acceleration, and until then it is merely owing. On that basis, provided acceleration has not occurred, one might be able to argue that *Foakes v Beer* (which concerned a payable judgment debt) could be limited to debts now payable, and so be distinguished, and that we can rely instead on the flexibility of *Williams v Roffey Bros*,[55] which held that a variation of contractual terms in one party's favour could be enforceable if a practical benefit was afforded to the other. One could further point to the valid consideration identified in *Pinnel's Case* (which concerned a debt which was *not* payable when the debtor tendered part payment), such as the hawk or robe.[56] In the context of CFAs, the practical benefit to the lender wishing to vary is obvious, as we noted: the borrower is able to continue business, generating cash to make payments over the full term of the loan.

These musings are somewhat moot, however, because practising finance lawyers simply circumvent *Foakes v Beer*. Any variation of a CFA, normally documented in what is called an amendment and restatement agreement, is made by way of **deed**. A duly executed, witnessed and delivered deed is binding by its very form, having no need of consideration for its enforceability.

Working out a default is, in my experience, far more common than acceleration. Yet inevitably there will be borrowers who exhaust their lender's patience, or who fall so quickly that acceleration will be the better option to salvage value. In the next section we explore this scenario, examining one of the more questionable Events of Default on which lenders seek to rely: the Material Adverse Change clause. In the section after that, we consider the exercise of the power to accelerate in

52 *Central London Property Trust Ltd. v High Trees House Ltd.* [1947] KB 130.

53 [1884] UKHL 1.

54 Mann and Hoyle (n 30); *re Selectmove Ltd.* [1993] EWCA Civ 8, [1995] 1 WLR 474; and the near miss in *Rock Advertising Ltd. v MWB Business Exchange Centres Ltd.* [2018] UKSC 24, [2019] AC 119.

55 *Williams v Roffey Bros & Nicholls (Contractors) Ltd.* [1989] EWCA Civ 5, [1991] 1 QB 1.

56 *Pinnel's Case* [1602] 5 Co Rep 117a.

situations where there is more than one lender making the decision, and these lenders disagree on whether to accelerate.

2.6 Case study: MACs as events of default

This case study focuses on just one judgment: *Grupo Hotelero Urvasco S.A. v Carey Value Added S.L.* [2013] EWHC 1039 (Comm). The case is authority for how courts should interpret Material Adverse Change (**MAC**) clauses, but it also serves as a good illustration of how courts go about interpreting financial contracts more generally. You should have studied contractual interpretation when you studied contract law, but may have found the modern approach to contractual interpretation to be abstract and dry. In fact, interpretation is arguably the single most common task practising lawyers engage in, especially if you include drafting as an exercise in ensuring your contract will be interpreted as you intend. *Grupo Hotelero* is a complicated case but it puts flesh on the bones of those abstract rules of interpretation.

2.6.1 *Grupo Hotelero* facts and issues

2.6.1.1 Background

The Spanish company Grupo Urvasco S.A. (**GU**) was 100% parent of Grupo Hotelero Urvasco S.A. (**GHU**); GHU owned 100% of the shares of its own UK subsidiary Urvasco Ltd (**Urvasco**). Urvasco was a special purpose vehicle set up to hold land on the Strand, London (just by Aldwych and the High Court), which would be developed into a hotel. The purchase of the land and construction costs were financed under two loan contracts, one with BBVA (a bank) and one with the Carey group of companies (also from Spain). One can draw the relationships between the parties as follows:

The main things to grasp about the case are these:

(1) There are two loan contracts:
   (a) The 2004 BBVA Credit Facility Agreement between BBVA and Urvasco Ltd, under which Urvasco borrowed money from BBVA to build a hotel in the Strand, London. Urvasco's repayment obligation was guaranteed by GU i.e. GU promised BBVA that if Urvasco did not pay, GU would instead.
   (b) The 2007 Carey Loan Agreement between a Carey subsidiary, LVA, under which GHU borrowed money from LVA to try and save the Strand hotel project, which had gone badly wrong. GHU's repayment obligations were also guaranteed by GU.

(2) Remember that often we refer collectively to the borrower(s) and guarantor(s) under a loan agreement as Obligor(s).

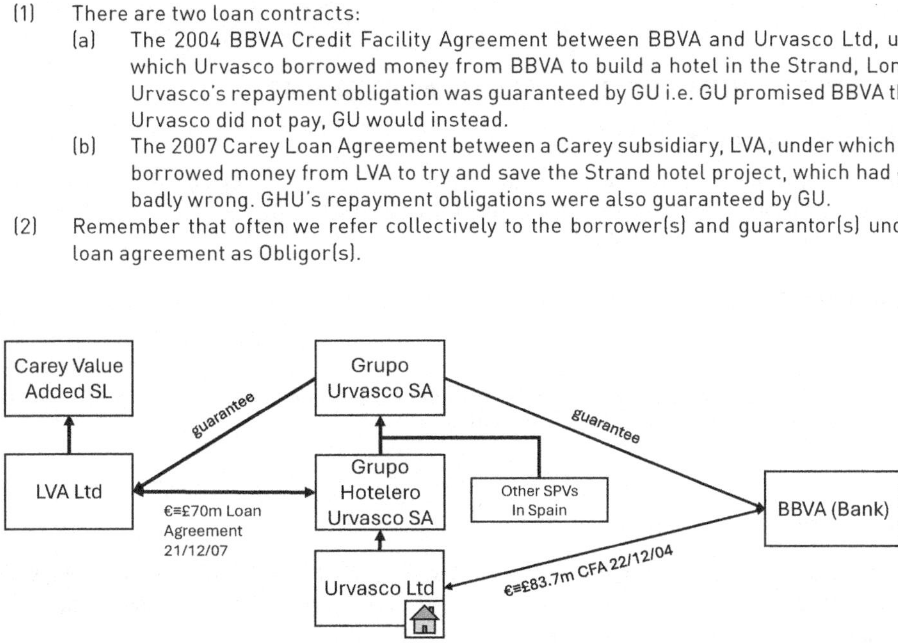

Figure 2.4 ***Grupo Hotelero*** **structure**

(3) Critically, because the Carey loan agreement was closely related to the BBVA CFA, several of the Carey loan agreement terms simply copied across or referred to terms of the BBVA CFA i.e. incorporation of terms by reference.

(4) Both contracts specified detailed contractual mechanics for dealing with when something went wrong. Later in this module, you will look at how the courts handle when something goes wrong as a matter of common law, but appreciate that modern contracts try to cope with problems themselves. Try not to confuse what the contract says should happen if one party behaves wrongfully (self-regulation) with the rules of common law for what happens in that case (regulation of self-regulation). Both the BBVA CFA and Carey loan agreement had terms of the following kind:
   (a) A promise by the obligors to make a representation on a specified date that there had been no MAC in the obligors' financial condition.
   (b) A term that if an obligor made such a representation and it was false, this would be a Default.
   (c) A term that if a Default occurred, then the lender would be able, among other things, to refuse to loan money to the borrowers.

CLAUSES FROM THE BBVA CFA

A repeating rep by GU:

Cl 16.10: 'In the case of [GU] only, there has been no material adverse change in its financial condition (consolidated if applicable) since the date the Original Financial Statements were drawn up.'

Repeated on different IPDs e.g. 1 July 2008.

Event of Default

Cl 21.4: A representation which was incorrect in any material respect when made or deemed to be repeated is a **default** (part of the events of default clause which deals with 'Misrepresentation').

CLAUSES FROM THE CAREY LOAN AGREEMENT

A repeating rep by GHU:

Cl 8(h): 'There has been no material adverse change in its financial condition (consolidated if applicable) since the date of this Loan Agreement [21/12/07].'

Repeated on various advance dates including 6 June 2008.

Event of Default

Cl 10(b)(iii): 'Any representation . . . proves to have been untrue when it was made in any material respect.'

Cl 10(b)(v): 'A BBVA Default occurs' = 'Any "Default" as defined under the BBVA CFA'—a cross-referral to the other contract's obligation of GU.

2.6.1.2 What went wrong?

Three key things led to trouble between the parties. First, in the first quarter of 2008, the Spanish property bubble burst. This largely affected the Urvasco group companies in Spain, but at the same time the Strand hotel project had being going badly and was expected to make a loss. No doubt Carey felt this was a Material Adverse Change that called into question the obligors' ability to repay the loans. Hence, second, in June 2008 Carey refused to lend any more money under the Loan Agreement. GHU claimed it lost profits as a result of Carey's wrongful refusal to lend, amounting to damage of GBP71m. Third, the hotel could not be completed on time because (GU claimed) of Carey's refuse to disburse funds to be sued to pay building contractors.

2.6.1.3 The key issues

Notice that Carey did not rely on the MAC clauses directly but on the fact that contractual representations the obligors had made denying a MAC had occurred were untrue. Carey claimed that it was entitled to refuse to loan money to GHU because there has been a Default, because either:

(1) GHU had represented there was no MAC on 6 June 2008, when in fact there was a MAC.
(2) Urvasco (or GHU) had represented that there was no MAC in respect of Urvasco on 6 June 2008, when there was a MAC.
(3) GU had represented to BBVA that there was no MAC on 5 June 2008, and it was a term of the Carey loan agreement that GU not be in default (e.g. by making a false representation) under the BBVA CFA, i.e. the one contract referred to the other.

GU, GHU and Urvasco denied each of these claims.

As noted in section 2.5, these contractual representations should not be confused with precontractual representations. The latter are not part of the contract and, if untrue, form the basis for a misrepresentation claim. The former are part of the contract: the obligor promises to make the representations and promises that, when it does, they are true. A breach of that promise has contractual consequences: (1) in contract law generally, damages for breach of warranty; but (2) in a standard CFA contractually defined consequences including a drawstop i.e. the lender is permitted to refuse to lend.

2.6.2 *Grupo Hotelero*: approach to interpretation

Blair J's discussion[57] of how he will go about interpreting the contracts takes place in 2013. *Investors Compensation Scheme*[58] (**ICS**) is now the authority for the approach, and *Chartbrook v Persimmon Homes Ltd*[59] and *Rainy Sky v Kookmin*[60] have been handed down. *Wood v Capita Services Ltd*[61] is still to come, however. Blair J does not mention ICS, though no doubt it is at the back of his mind. Rather, Blair J focuses on the dicta of Lord Clark in *Rainy Sky v Kookmin*:

> [The exercise of construction is a] unitary exercise in which the court must consider the language used and ascertain what a reasonable person, that is a person who has all the background knowledge which would reasonably have been available to the parties in the situation in which they were at the time of the contract, would have understood the parties to have meant. In doing so, the court must have regard to all the relevant surrounding circumstances. If there are two possible constructions, the court is entitled to prefer the construction which is consistent with business common sense and to reject the other. [21]

It is telling his citation only occurs a third of the way through Blair J's discussion. It emphasizes context, particularly market context, and that will guide Blair J's whole approach. One might have

57 [2013] EWHC 1039 (Comm) [334]–[362].
58 *Investors Compensation Scheme Ltd. v West Bromwich Building Society* [1998] 1 WLR 896 (HL).
59 [2009] UKHL 38, [2009] 1 AC 1011.
60 [2011] UKSC 50, [2011] 1 WLR 2900.
61 [2017] UKSC 24, [2017] AC 1173.

thought, following ICS, that one should be begin with textualism: read the words in the contractual clause in issue and apply their plain meaning. Blair J does not abandon textualism, but he does not begin with it; he opens his discussion with the market practice concerning MACs,[62] and this remains the guiding principle of his approach. This is not just a matter of applying 'business common sense' when deciding on conflicting readings. It is a stronger view that the reasonable person here who used the language is financially literate, so to speak, and so assumes the contractual terms in full knowledge of their meaning to the average City of London lawyer, accountant, or financier apprised of the nature of the deal in question.

The City of London context plays out in one particular interpretative puzzle with which Blair J dealt summarily. Carey had also argued that there was an implied term of good faith in the Carey Loan Agreement, with the effect that even if technically there was no default, the obligors had not shown good faith in failing to disclose their financial and construction troubles to Carey. Critically, Carey honestly felt this because they, like GU and GHU and even BBVA, were Spanish and as a matter of Spanish law and market practice, all parties proceed on the basis that good faith underpins contractual dealings.[63] Blair J refused to imply such a term.[64] His reasoning was quite correct, for as a matter of textualism there was not express term as to good faith in the contract, and he was therefore applying the clear words of the parties *provided that* one accepts absence is clarity. Nor was it necessary and reasonable to imply such a term into a contract governed by English law.[65]

Yet one cannot help but feel uncomfortable. Had an officious bystander[66] with relevant knowledge observed negotiations between Carey and GU, and pointed out that good faith applies, the parties would have responded 'of course' because they were negotiating in a Spanish business context. They may well have been surprised to find that by assuming good faith, an English court would regard the lack of an express term requiring good faith as an exclusion of good faith. One feels, as Taylor has argued,[67] that English law is imposing consequences on foreign litigants for which they had not bargained; rather consequences for which reasonable Englishmen would have bargained. In choosing English law, do foreign litigants hand over not just legal principles, but also linguistic meaning and social context to the English court? Should an Englishman's word be a foreigner's bond?

This concerned about adoption of the linguistic meanings of others is doubled in this case by a further fact common to financial contracts. When Carey's lawyers drafted the Carey Loan Agreement, it was important that it reflect the BBVA CFA accurately just because breaches under the latter were agreed to be breaches under the former, as we have seen. Yet to do this, Carey's lawyers copied across the language of the BBVA agreement—somewhat unsuccessfully, it turned out. The paradigm of contractual interpretation is two parties rationally negotiating the precise language that circumscribes their respective obligations, having the knowledge they have in that social context. If someone just copies the language from another negotiation, by definition they lack the particular knowledge of the negotiators and may well lack knowledge of the social context also. This problem is even more stark where a third party has assumed the rights and obligations of an original party, e.g. by novating into the contract. Saville LJ made just such an observation in *National Bank of Sharjah v Dellborg* (1997): how can third parties who assume the language of existing contracts understand the full meaning of the terms if they were not part of the negotiation of those terms?[68] The response to

62 *Grupo Hotelero* [334]–[339].

63 Art 1258 Spanish Civil Code.

64 *Grupo Hotelero* [342].

65 *Attorney General of Belize v Belize Telecom Ltd.* [2009] UKPC 10, [2009] 1 WLR 1988; cf *Marks and Spencer plc v BNP Paribas Securities Services Trust Company (Jersey) Ltd.* [2015] UKSC 72, [2016] AC 742.

66 To use one of the traditional tests which has not, it seems, fallen into desuetude: *Southern Foundries (1926) Ltd. v Shirlaw* [1940] AC 701 (HL).

67 Tim Taylor, 'The Englishman's Word as the Foreigner's Bond' (2002) 18 Arbitration International, 379, 400.

68 [1997] EWCA Civ 2070, [1997] 7 WLUK 892.

this, no doubt underpinning Blair J's analysis, is that the relatively standardized terms of LMA CFAs have a market meaning that has, in a sense, 'broken away' from the specific context of negotiations. When persons become party to a CFA they accede to a market meaning which is understandable and tradeable in that market. By agreeing to use English law, and to copy across words used in another English law agreement, Carey held itself out objectively to that market that it was assuming the legal-linguistic meanings of that market.[69]

With these observations, we understand why Blair J opened his interpretation by discussing that market context—the custom and meaning of MACs—and not the specific terms of the Carey Loan Agreement. This was a judgment very much facing every single loan agreement in the market which used the LMA MAC clause. The judgment did not contradict wider rules about contractual interpretation, but one can certainly detect a shift in the centre of meaning's gravity to market context.

2.6.3 *Grupo Hotelero*: decision

Having discussed his approach to interpretation, Blair J found that:

(1) Material Adverse Change to financial condition should be interpreted as:
  (a) referring to a change in the obligor's financial condition by reference to its accounts;
  (b) 'material' only if the change would impact on the ability of that obligor to perform an obligation under the Carey Loan Agreement (and any other effect was irrelevant);
  (c) referring to a change which was unforeseen by the lender, for if they had foreseen the problem the lender ought (i) either to have expressly provided for that specific problem in the contract; or (ii) priced the risk into cost of the funds; or (iii) both. The MAC clause was not to be used as insurance for a lender's poor credit assessments.

(2) While the collapse of the Spanish property bubble caused a MAC in the financial condition in GU—a Spanish construction company—GHU was not a construction company but rather ran hotels, and that business had been largely unaffected by the collapse. Thus, the change was immaterial and GHU's representation was truthful.

(3) Urvasco was not a party to the Carey Loan Agreement and so had simply not made a representation. Even if GHU had made a representation about the financial condition of Urvasco, Urvasco was simply a shell company and so any question about its financial condition was meaningless. Rather, as it received all its money from GHU and via the BBVA CFA, this question needed to be referred to the financial condition of GHU (see above) and the ongoing validity of the BBVA CFA.

(4) GU was affected by the Spanish property bubble collapse, and so there had been a MAC in its financial condition sometime before 6 June 2008, but certainly sometime *after* December 2007.

(5) GU had represented to BBVA that no MAC had occurred *on* 1 January 2008. This was truthful on that date, and so no default under the BBVA CFA was outstanding between 1 January and 1 July 2008.

(6) When GU represented the same thing to BBVA on 1 July 2008, the MAC had occurred and so there could have been a default under the BBVA CFA. But that was not in issue—we were only concerned with the Carey Loan Agreement.

(7) Consequently, when, on 6 June 2008, three weeks before the representation to BBVA, GU represented to Carey/LVA that no default was outstanding under the BBVA CFA because no false representations had been made thereunder, that was a truthful representation. The false representation had not happened yet.

(8) Accordingly, there was no default under the Carey loan agreement and Carey/LVA were not entitled to refuse to lend money to GHU.

69 See Adam Kramer, 'Common Sense Principles of Contractual Interpretation' (2002) 23 OJLS 173.

In fact, GU and GHU lost the case on other grounds: they had failed to pay the contractors building the hotel and this was a separate and specific default which did entitle Carey/LVA to withhold the loan.

Take some time to chew over the clauses, their interactions, and Blair J's findings. This is a complicated fact pattern but representative of financial legal practice, and far removed from the contract law world of men buying and selling oats for racehorses. By putting in the effort now you will gain a great deal of understanding of this field. Be prepared to draw diagrams, as I have done, to track what is going on in the different agreements between the different parties. And once you are comfortable with the case, step back and think about the issues of contractual interpretation policy that are raised. How would you respond to an exam question on contractual interpretation in light of *Grupo Hotelero?*

2.7 The power to accelerate in syndicated CFAs

In this section, we look at further features of the CFA which relate to creditor 'democracy.' It is not uncommon for more than one lender to commit to lend under a single CFA, and we will examine why and how this comes about in Chapter 6. For present purposes, we need simply assume that two or more lenders are parties to the CFA. The CFA provides for various situations in which lenders must make decisions, the most important of which concerns acceleration. The question then arises: what happens if one lender wishes to accelerate the loans, whereas the other disagrees?

As a first step, the CFA expressly defines a concept of creditor 'democracy' by defining how certain decisions, such as accelerating the loans, can be made by the majority of lenders. The following drafting provides an example:

EXAMPLE: MAJORITY LENDERS IN A CFA

Definition

Majority Lenders means a Lender or Lenders whose Commitments aggregate more than 66 2/3% of the Total Commitments (or, if the Total Commitments have been reduced to zero, aggregated more than 66 2/3% of the Total Commitments immediately prior to the reduction).

Acceleration

On and at any time after the occurrence of an Event of Default which is continuing the Agent may, and shall if so directed by the Majority Lenders, by notice to the Company:

(i) cancel the Available Commitment of each Lender whereupon each such Available Commitment shall immediately be cancelled and the Facility shall immediately cease to be available for further utilization;

(ii) declare that all or part of the Loans, together with accrued interest, and all other amounts accrued or outstanding under the Finance Documents be immediately due and payable, whereupon they shall become immediately due and payable; and/or

(iii) declare that all or part of the Loans be payable on demand, whereupon they shall immediately become payable on demand by the Agent on the instructions of the Majority Lenders.

This deals with how CFAs mediate between lender interests: it does so on a "1 currency unit of debt equals 1 vote" basis, much as in a creditors' meeting in an insolvency process. Yet things are not this simple. Analysed legally, these clauses confer a power on the majority lenders, and that power could be abused. For example, the Majority Lenders may well order acceleration not principally to recoup their debt but with a view to destroy the borrower's value and so cause economic harm to the minority lenders (the majority concluding that the harm to themselves is worth it). The contract, on its face, seems to permit such behaviour, but does the common law and equity? This observation leads us into some fascinating case law.

2.7.1 Basic concept: powers

A **right** might be regarded as a subsisting relationship one person A has with another B. It is therefore always double: if A has some right with respect to B, B is said to have some duty (in which I include obligation) to A. Critically, the right/duty in enforceable by way of a claim (*right* and *claim* are sometimes used interchangeably). A right may be regarded as inherent (the right to life) or acquired, for example as a result of forming a contract.

A **power** arises when A places her right in the hands of another, C, with a view that C will exercise that right on A's behalf. A power can look like a right, but it is this act of **donation** and exercise on behalf of another which distinguishes it. C may well be enforcing a right under a contract with B, but technically he is exercising a power on behalf of A to enforce A's right against B and B's obligation to A.

A classic example is agency. A (the principal) might give her right to contract to C (an agent), telling C to exercise the power of contracting to enter into a contract with B. If C does as instructed, C is not legally making a contract with A (even if de facto it looks that way); C is just standing in A's place, and when the contract is made it is a contract between A and B (C's power has been exercised and in this fulfilled). Notice that here, C has the power to bind A to B. A might have second thoughts about contracting with B, but if she does not instruct C to stop, B may rightfully claim C was authorized to bind A to B by way of a contract. Handing over a power is therefore no small thing. You might surmise that A would never hand over a power to someone else and allow them to wield that power to harm A.

Another, highly relevant contrast between rights and powers is afforded by looking at the CFA's acceleration clause from the borrower's perspective.

LOMBARD NORTH CENTRAL PLC v EUROPEAN SKYJETS LTD (IN LIQUIDATION) [2022] EWHC 728 (QB)

The facts were stated in section 2.5.3.

As a further line of defence, Skyjets argued that the lender's discretion to accelerate was subject to the implied duty of good faith and reasonableness deriving from the *Braganza* case (discussed in section 2.4.4). Accelerating the loan over just USD179.99 was an irrational exercise of that discretion.

Held: Skyjet's argument was flawed: the lender was exercising its contractual right, not a power conferred by another, and therefore was entitled to exercise it (or not) as it saw fit. David Foxton J said:

> When the occurrence of an Event of Default gives Lombard a right of termination, I do not accept that Lombard's decision whether or not to exercise that right is in the nature of a contractual discretion to which the *Braganza* duties apply. Rather Lombard's decision is what is sometimes described as an 'absolute contractual

right' for it to exercise for its own purposes, as it sees fit. The issue of whether rights to terminate and analogous rights could be subject to *Braganza*-duties was the subject of careful consideration by His Honour Judge Pelling QC in *TAQA Bratani Limited v Rockrose UKCS8 LLC* [2020] EWHC 58 (Comm), [44]–[53], who rejected the argument that rights of termination were to be analysed as contractual discretions. That reasoning is compelling, and I gratefully adopt it.

It is perhaps worth noting that Pelling J's judgment in *TAQA* adopted full square the counsel for the lender's argument. Counsel for the lender happened to be one David Foxton QC.

It is worth underlining, therefore, that we are not concerned with the discretionary exercise of a right to accelerate a loan as between lender and borrower. Rather, we are concerned with the discretionary exercise of the power to bind all lenders to a decision to accelerate as conferred by the minority lenders on the majority.

2.7.2 The problem stated

Imagine a contractual term in which several parties agreed that they will take decisions collectively. The term provides that in the case of certain decisions, it is enough that a 'majority' (as defined in the contract), consent to a particular course of action for that majority consent to bind all the parties. This means a minority could not consent to a course of action, but nevertheless they will be deemed to have consented. It is worth differentiating the two stages of this process:

(1) Deliberation: *every* party may vote in the decision-making process. Decisions are made by the 'majority.'
(2) Practical action: the *majority* may carry out the decision above, and in so doing have the power to bind all parties to that course of action.

We can analyse the above term using powers. In effect, every party has donated to the 'majority' of parties the power to carry out that course of action to which the majority, however constituted, consents.

In (corporate) finance law, one is likely to encounter this sort of voting arrangement in two situations: (1) in certain clauses of the statutory contract made between a company and its members inter se (known as the **articles of association**); and (2) in a CFA, in which one will almost always find a term providing for Majority Lender consent to certain courses of action such as accelerating the loans or waiving certain breaches by the borrower.

Our key case—*Redwood Master Fund v TD Bank*—demonstrates why this area is so contentious. The facts are simplified to emphasize the difficulty such cases present.

REDWOOD MASTER FUND v TD BANK EUROPE & ORS [2008] 1 BCLC 149

Under a syndicated loan agreement, United Pan-European Communications ('UPEC') had borrowed money from numerous lenders including TD Bank, ABN Amro, and Redwood

Master Fund ('Redwood'). Redwood was owed 2% of the total debt and so could be easily outvoted on any decision requiring 66 2/3% Majority Lender consent. The loan agreement provided that different currencies could be lent under different loan facilities of the agreement, each loan creating a separate debt. As it happened, Redwood had agreed to lend US dollars under 'Facility C,' whereas TD Bank and others had agreed to lend euros under 'Facilities A and B.' The relevance of this was that Redwood's debt was distinct from the debt of the majority of lenders.

UPEC entered into a period of financial difficulty, and it was agreed that the lenders would work with UPEC to work out the issues. After some negotiation it was agreed that various breaches of the loan agreement would be waived, certain amendments to the agreement's terms would be approved, and the debt owed by UPEC would be reduced by cancelling certain amounts owing (a 'haircut'). Critically, it was the Facility C debt owed to Redwood which would suffer the haircut.

The lenders voted on the proposal. Over 88% of the lenders voted in favour; Redwood voted against. Under the terms of the relevant contractual clauses, the proposal was approved and the Majority Lenders were authorized to carry out the amendments, waivers, and haircut. Redwood sued.

Redwood could be seen as advancing an intuitive argument behind the technical legal argument they made.

The *intuitive argument* was this: when a principal donates a power, the principal only does so in the belief that the donee of the power will exercise it on the principal's behalf and for the principal's benefit. No one expects an agent to bind his principal to a deal the principal does not want. But here Redwood had expressly voted against a course of action which the donees of the power to bind all lenders were now pursuing directly against Redwood's interests. In short, Redwood would never have instructed the Majority Lenders to expropriate Redwood.

The *technical argument* worked by analogy from the company cases where members of the company vote as a majority to bind a dissentient minority. We will look at the detail of the relevant case law shortly, but the essence of the argument was this: it is established law (they claimed) that a majority does not have absolute power to bind a minority, but rather must exercise that power bona fides for the lenders as a whole. As Redwood was not benefitting from the decision, rather only the majority at Redwood's expense, the majority were abusing their majority status to **oppress the minority**. In such a case the court should restrain the majority from carrying out their decision and order a revote.

In what follows we will need to make a detour through some company law cases, but to cut a long story short, the judge in *Redwood*, Rimer J, was able to both clarify the company law test for oppression of a minority into two tests, and then from the second of these tests develop a test suitable for application to finance contracts. If you have not studied company law, or do not wish to follow the preliminary reasoning in *Redwood*, you can skip ahead to section 2.7.4.

2.7.3 *Allen v Gold Reefs* (CA)

Happily for the minority members of a company, English law early on developed qualms about majorities abusing their voting power. The question is not so much as to the point of principal (stated in the next case), but on the basis and extent of that principal.

ALLEN v GOLD REEFS OF WEST AFRICA LTD [1900] 1 Ch 656 (CA)

In short: The majority members of a company voted to amend the statutory contract between them so that the company could prevent a shareholder who owed the company money from selling any of his shares (and not just the shares for which he had not paid).

Detailed facts: A limited company by one of its articles provided that it should have a lien—a kind of right to withhold property—'upon all shares (not being fully paid) held by such member' where that member owed debts or had liabilities to the company.

The company, by way of purchase-money for the property acquired by it, allotted fully paid shares to Z., a nominee of the vendor to the company. Z. also applied for and had allotted to him shares not paid up. He was the only holder of fully paid-up shares. At his death he was indebted to the company in arrears of calls on the unpaid shares, but his assets were insufficient to pay the arrears. Thereupon the company, by special resolution altered the above articles by deleting the words 'not being fully paid,' thus creating a lien on Z.'s fully paid shares.

Per Lindley MR:

> The power . . . conferred on companies to alter the regulations contained in their articles is limited only by the provisions contained in the statute and the conditions contained in the company's memorandum of association. Wide, however, as the language of [s 21 Companies Act 2006] is, the power conferred by it must, like all other powers, be exercised subject to those general principles of law and equity which are applicable to all powers conferred on majorities and enabling them to bind minorities. It must be exercised, not only in the manner required by law, but also bona fide for the benefit of the company as a whole, and it must not be exceeded. These conditions are always implied, and are seldom, if ever, expressed. But if they are complied with I can discover no ground for judicially putting any other restrictions on the power conferred by the section than those contained in it. How shares shall be transferred, and whether the company shall have any lien on them, are clearly matters of regulation properly prescribed by a company's articles of association. . . .
>
> But then comes the question whether this can be done so as to impose a lien or restriction in respect of a debt contracted before and existing at the time when the articles are altered. Again, speaking generally, I am of opinion that the articles can be so altered, and that, if they are altered bona fide for the benefit of the company, they will be valid and binding as altered on the existing holders of paid-up shares, whether such holders are indebted or not indebted to the company when the alteration is made. But, as will be seen presently, it does not by any means follow that the altered article may not be inapplicable to some particular fully paid-up shareholder. He may have special rights against the company, which do not invalidate the resolution to alter the articles, but which may exempt him from the operation of the articles as altered.

Held: the company did have the power to alter its articles in this way.

Notice first the stated basis on which Lindley MR intervened:

(1) Changing the constitution was a *power* of the majority to bind the minority.
(2) The exercise of a power engages principles of 'law and equity:'
   (a) as a matter of law, the power must be exercised as the law (here the statutory contract) requires.
   (b) as a matter of equity, the power must be exercised bona fide for the benefit of the [donors of the power] as a whole.

While this latter formulation will create significant debate, it seems that the central value claim is undisputed: unlike 'normal' property owners, shareholders do not have an absolutely unfettered right to vote as they wish when altering the constitution (because this interferes with the property of the minority).

So we have Lindley MR's test, but what does it mean?[70] In *Allen* it was held that the alteration, forcing shareholders to pay up what they owed the company, was evidently in the company's interest. But what does this term 'company as a whole' mean, because that seems to go beyond the SCP that is the company. And what would a breach of Lindley MR's test look like?

Rixon[71] has called 'the company as a whole' a Delphic term (i.e. mysterious and requiring irresolvable interpretation). A spectrum of academic thought developed as to its meaning. In a contractual context it means the aggregate of the donors of the power,[72] in which case it is the donors' collective interests which are relevant to the voting decision. But who are our reference donors?

- Subjectively all of them—but this amounts to requiring an actual unanimous vote; in which case, why the 75% threshold in the statute?
- Subjectively 75% plus of the voting members; in which case a minority could *never* question a procedurally correct vote, however abusive.
- Objectively what the court thinks is in the interests of the donors—but these are business interests, and the court knows nothing about those.
- Objectively all of the voting donors—i.e. what all reasonable members would regard as in the interests of the donors as a whole.
- Objectively a hypothetical donor—i.e. what one reasonable donor would have regarded as in the interests of the donors as a whole.
- Something else?

The cases provide variations on this them, setting the scene regarding the meaning of the *Allen v Gold Reefs* test right up to the moment when *Redwood* was heard (there have been cases since,[73] but as noted above the test for finance contracts has split off from the company cases).

---

70 FG Rixon, 'Competing Interests and Conflicting Principles: An Examination of the Power of Alteration of Articles of Association' (1986) 49 MLR 446, 448; LS Sealy, '"Bona Fides" and "Proper Purposes" in Corporate Decisions' (1989) 5 MLR 265, 269.

71 FG Rixon, 'Lifting the Veil between Holding and Subsidiary Companies' (1986) 102 LQR 415.

72 *Greenhalgh v Arderne Cinemas Ltd.* [1951] 1 Ch 286, 291.

73 *Citco Banking Corporation NV v Pusser's Ltd. and Another* [2007] UKPC 13, [2007] Bus LR 960; *Arbuthnott v Bonnyman and Others; Re Charterhouse Capital Ltd.* [2015] EWCA Civ 536, [2015] BCC 574. These cases are not, however, without interest if read in parallel with the finance law cases.

DAFEN TINPLATE COMPANY LTD v LLANELLY STEEL COMPANY (1907) LTD [1920] 2 Ch 124

The defendant company, not having power under its original articles of association to acquire compulsorily the shares of members, passed special resolutions altering its articles and introducing a power enabling the majority of the shareholders to determine that the shares of any member (other than a certain named company) should be offered for sale by the directors to such person or persons (whether a member or members or not) as they should think fit at the fair value to be fixed from time to time at stated intervals by the directors.

Per Peterson J:

> In my view it cannot be said that a power on the part of the majority to expropriate any shareholder they may think proper at their will and pleasure is for the benefit of the company as a whole.

The decision was much criticized: Peterson J proceeded on the basis that it was the court which was to determine what was for the benefit of the company as a whole. This was one of those situations in which a case on the same point was pleaded in parallel before a different judge—one who enunciated a different interpretation of the *Allen v Gold Reefs* test.

SIDEBOTTOM v KERSHAW, LEESE AND COMPANY, LIMITED [1920] 1 Ch 154

A private trading company, in which the majority of the shares were held by the directors, passed a special resolution to alter its articles by introducing a power for the directors to require any shareholder who competed with the company's business to transfer his shares, at their full value, to nominees of the directors. The plaintiffs, who carried on a competing business, held the minority of the shares, and had voted against the resolution. They brought an action for a declaration that it was invalid as against them.

Lord Sterndale MR said:

> [L]ooking at it broadly, I cannot have any doubt that in a small private company like this the exclusion of members who are carrying on competing businesses may very well be of great benefit to the company. That seems to me to be precisely a point which [A] ought to be decided by the voices of the business men who understand the business and understand the nature of competition, and whether such a position is or is not for the benefit of the company. [B] I think, looking at the alteration broadly, that it is for the benefit of the company that they should not be obliged to have amongst them as members persons who are competing with them in business, and who may get knowledge from their membership which would enable them to compete better.

The judgment was handed down in 1920 just before *Dafen Tinplate*, but states the test differently. Lord Sterndale seems to be adopting what today we might describe as 'the objective view of a reasonable business person having all the knowledge and facts about the company's affairs and business which the members did in fact have.' However, to muddy things, Lord Sterndale in fact imposed his own view in the judgment despite his theoretical recourse to the reasonable businessman. A generous reading is that 'his' view is his judgment as to the view of the reasonable business person above.

So, who is right: Peterson J or Lord Sterndale?

GREENHALGH v ARDERNE CINEMAS LTD AND OTHERS [1950] 2 All ER 1120 (CA) 1127[74]

The articles of association of A Ltd contained a clause prohibiting the sale of shares to persons other than members of the company. The majority of members wished to sell their shares to Mallard who was not a member of the company. To achieve this they held a general meeting and passed a special resolution amending the articles to permit sale to anyone designated by resolution. They then passed such a resolution designating Mallard as transferee and sold him the shares. G, a minority shareholder, sought a declaration that these resolutions were invalid as a fraud on the minority.

Evershed MR said:

> The phrase, 'the company as a whole,' does not (at any rate in such a case as the present) mean the company as a commercial entity as distinct from the corporators. It means the corporators as a general body. That is to say, you may take the case of an individual hypothetical member and ask whether what is proposed is, in the honest opinion of those who voted in its favour, for that person's benefit.

If *Sidebottom* takes the objective perspective of the members as to what would benefit the company as a whole, Evershed MR constructs what appears to be a combined subjective and objective test:

(1) did the members who voted for the alteration *subjectively* honestly think that . . .
(2) the alteration is for the benefit of a *hypothetical* (i.e. objective, 'third') member?

One can see that Evershed MR at least is trying to escape reasonableness tests because the *Allen* test was equitable, not common law—validly made resolutions should only invalidated if there is demonstrable *mala fides* on the part of the majority. There are at least two difficulties, however:

(1) By saying the 'company as a whole' means the 'corporators as a general body,' Evershed MR quickly slips into referencing the benefit to an *individual* member.
(2) How do we identify the hypothetical member? If a company has 100 members with one share each, there is at least a 75% chance that a member chosen randomly from that group subjectively regarded the alteration as beneficial. Why should our hypothetical member think any differently, and if they do, why should we regard them as representative?

---

74 Note that there are several *Greenhalgh* decisions on different elements of company law, and all are important. Use the right one!

2.7.4 Abuse of power by majority lenders in *Redwood*

Remember that Redwood's lawyers had been arguing that the Majority Lenders ought to have acted bona fide for the benefit of the lenders as a whole, as per *Allen v Gold Reefs*, but in forcing a haircut on Redwood they clearly were only benefitting the Majority Lenders' sectional interest. The judge, Rimer J, considered the cases we have just discussed and concluded that they contained an implicit but critical distinction between:

(1) Decisions which could benefit the company, then the test would be: bona fides for the benefit of the company as a whole.
(2) Decisions in which the company was disinterested—it only affected parties to the statutory contract inter se.

Evershed MR had appreciated the distinction in *Greenhalgh* but had felt so bound by *Allen v Gold Reefs* that he tried to fit decisions of type (2) above into the language of the test of type (1). Evidently, Rimer J observed, a test for member decisions which affect a company are wholly irrelevant to finance contract decision-making because there is no 'special' company standing over against its members under such a contract. Rather, we just have parties, all equal in status. Accordingly, if either of the tests applied at all, it was test (2) which concerns decisions that only affect voting members (being as they are all of equal status) and are of no concern to any company.

Yet Rimer J did not stop there. Appreciating that Evershed MR had been forced to do violence to the language of *Allen v Gold Reefs* with his hypothetical member formulation, he quite naturally asked counsel how the test should be phrased in this distinct context. Redwood's counsel responded: the test is 'bona fide for the benefit of the lenders as a whole.'

Rimer J's quite sensible response: it 'is meaningless to say "for the benefit of the members as a whole."'[75] The whole point, as a matter of construction, of a majority voting clause is to deal with just those situations where a minority would otherwise be able to block action. Such a clause broke deadlock. Majority control was predicated on there being a dissentient minority; had the parties foreseen consistent unanimity, they would not have agreed such a clause. While the clause in question did not specifically state that the result of a Majority Lender vote was that the minority would perhaps lose some benefit or otherwise be dragged along against its will, a straightforward application of *Shirlaw v Southern Foundries* to imply what was obvious to an officious bystander sufficed to fill the gap.

Yet Rimer J's thought process, no doubt greatly aided by TD Bank's counsel, one Tom Bingham QC, did not cease there. The basic principle on which *Allen v Gold Reefs*—that a power once conferred ought not to be abused—remained good law, and it evidently applied to the conferral of a power in this situation. The question was how? Rimer J's breakthrough was to observe that asking 'for whom?' a power be exercised was to ask the wrong question and so invite confusion. Rimer J stepped back, asking himself: what is the 'vice' that the basic principle regarding powers is attempting to combat? His answer: the vice was 'dishonest abuse of power' i.e. the concern was not about a 'who' but about a 'purpose.'

This reasoning led Rimer J to enunciate a disjunctive test for establishing abuse of power:

(1) was the power *not* used in good faith for purpose for which it was conferred (but rather for an ulterior motive); or
(2) was the power's use motivated by a malicious wish to damage the minority?

75 *Redwood Master Fund v TD Bank Europe Ltd. & Others* [2006] 1 BCLC 149, 180g, 182a.

The precise distinction between the two is less than clear, but by analogy from the agency and director authority cases, one might suggest the following. Test (1) concerns an ultra vires point. This aims at situations where a donee exercises a power in excess of the terms on which it has been conferred and/or for a purpose other than for which it has been conferred. There is a defence here where the donee did act ultra vires but honestly believed they were acting intra vires. By way of example, a finance contract majority voting clause often specifies that altering the total amount repayable requires unanimous consent (not in *Redwood*, however), so in such a case a Majority Lender attempt to do just that would fall foul of test (1).

Test (2) concerns situations where the donee acts intra vires the terms of conferral and/or purpose, but chooses a particular course of action primarily motivated by malice and with a view to harming the donor of the power. The classic example is fraud: the Majority Lenders may well have correctly voted to approve a decision which approved certain waivers of breach of contract with the borrower, but they did so because they were secretly bribed by the borrower and not because doing so was in any lender's interest.

Where does this leave Redwood's intuitive thought? Remember, Redwood basically felt that they would never have given someone the power to expropriate Redwood. Did Redwood have a point? Think back to the nature of a chose in action like a debt or other contractual right. As property, how is it delineated? The right is entirely circumscribed by the contract that creates it.

- If I own GBP100 of debt due on 1 March then:
  - I do not own GBP101 of debt or any other amount.
  - I am not entitled to repayment before 1 March.
- If someone denies me that extra GBP1, or earlier repayment, they have denied me nothing that was my right, for it was not.

Redwood was owed a debt, but that was circumscribed by the majority voting clause. That clause said, in certain circumstances the GBP100 could be reduced to GBP90: the circumstances were a majority vote. Redwood had not lost anything when the haircut was imposed. It had received no more than its contractually delineated right—a right limited by majority variation. Objectively, the contract defined the right as such; Redwood's subjective intent was irrelevant. This is a common error made by investors. They think they have put GBP100 into a company as capital, and somehow that GBP100 is 'in' the company and still 'theirs.' This is as false for creditors as it is for shareholders. Both *sell* their money to the company as capital, for the companies use. In consideration of that sale, they receive contractually delimited choses in action: debt obligations for creditors; shares for shareholders. These choses in action come subject to the majority voting provisions stated in the relevant contracts.

2.7.5 After *Redwood*

Although we will not look at them, Rimer J's analysis in *Redwood* greatly influenced subsequent company law cases also.[76] The thinking was adopted for ensuing contract cases also, though while *Redwood* provided needed clarity, cases continued to arise driven by the same intuitions that Redwood MF felt: that minorities were being forced into changes of circumstance for which they had 'never' contracted. The most important subsequent case is *Assenagon*, for here is a rare example of a court finding that a minority had been oppressed by the majority in an arm's-length commercial context.

---

76 See *Ciban Management Corporation v Citco (BVI) Ltd.* [2020] UKPC 21, [2020] 3 WLR 705; *re Charterhouse Capital Ltd, sub nom Arbuthnott v Bonnyman & Others* [2015] EWCA Civ 536, [2015] BCC 574.

ASSENAGON ASSET MANAGEMENT v IRISH BANK RESOLUTION CORP LTD [2012] EWHC 2090 (Ch)

A case in which the minority obtained relief from majority oppression. An Irish bank was insolvent, owing amounts to various creditors. The banking authorities sought to reduce this debt. Authorities offered to grant new 'exchange' debt to the majority lenders *if* the majority lenders voted to support a plan to redeem the minority lenders' debt for virtually nothing—to effectively cancel the minority lenders' debt.

Per Briggs J:

> It is entirely at variance with the purposes for which majorities are given a power to bind minorities . . . for the majority to lend its aid to the coercion of the minority by voting for a resolution which expropriates the minority's rights . . . for a nominal consideration. [84]–[85]

We have to be careful here.[77] The issue was not so much buying the vote but expropriation. One must make a distinction between a party agreeing to a majority lender power to redeem or cancel a debt, for example, and a majority lender power to vary the contract which is subsequently used to include a right to redeem/cancel debt. In the latter case, the varied agreement was not one the minority 'bargained for.' The thinking here is difficult. If one is concerned about having debt redeemed, one should bar this in the contract, as modern syndicate finance contracts almost invariably do as standard. If one agrees to majority lender variation without any limits, it is difficult to see why one did not bargain for *any* variation and consequent results whatsoever.

In moving towards a proper purpose test, *Redwood* also moved the relevant law into contention with another line of cases culminating in *Braganza*. In *British Telecommunications plc v Telefónica O2 UK Ltd*,[78] Lord Sumption said:

> in the absence of very clear language to the contrary, a contractual discretion must be exercised in good faith and not arbitrarily or capriciously. [37] [Lord Sumption]

Braganza v BP Shipping Ltd followed hot on its heels.[79] Yet in in contractual context, the party exercising discretion can act in self-interested manner. For this reason, *Braganza*, which distinguished but nevertheless drew an analogy with public law notions of *Wednesbury* reasonableness, has been criticized. Davies and Sales argue the *Braganza* 'analogy' with public law imports factors relying on different context and wider public values which are absent in contractual context.[80] In public law an officer acts in no way for her own interest but only the interest of the public; in private law, self-interest tends to be present in some degree. The parallel should therefore be with equity, where the key question is whether a discretionary power exercised 'for a proper purpose' or 'authorised by the power conferred.' Davies and Sales caution against introducing a 'good faith' criterion because of its vagueness and difficulty of reconciling with self-interested nature of contracting. Rather, they

---

77 See *Azevedo v IMCOPA—Importacao, Exportaacao e Industria de Oleos Ltda* [2013] EWCA Civ 364, [2015] QB 1.

78 [2014] UKSC 42, [2014] 4 All ER 907.

79 [2015] UKSC 17, [2015] 1 WLR 1661.

80 Paul Davies and Philip Sales, 'Controlling Contract Discretions: Wednesbury Reasonableness, Good Faith and Proper Purposes' (2024) 140 LQR 106.

strongly argue that the criterion for the exercise of a contractual discretionary power should be whether it was exercised for a proper purpose, as determined by the contract and its context (i.e., based on party intentions).

Notice how *Redwood* exemplifies the Davies and Sales approach by focusing on the purpose derived from a true construction of the contract. One can hope that *Braganza* will be 'clarified' in due course to bring it into line with the *Redwood* line. The question of good faith, however, may be a bar to reconciliation.

2.8 Financial covenants

This section is advanced and aimed at students with an understanding of corporate accounts. Although financial covenants are arguably the most critical borrower undertakings in a CFA (beyond payment), they do demand a great deal, and so this section is entirely optional.

One special group of conditions in the CFA are the financial covenants. These covenants are the most difficult for a lawyer to understand because they require familiarity with the accounting principles of corporate finance. Nevertheless, complying with these covenants are some of the most critical the borrower makes, and understanding them gives an important insight into finance capital, its discipline, and systemic risk.[81]

Simply put, a financial covenant is a promise by a borrower to maintain a certain **ratio** between two **defined numbers** derived from its **financial statements**.

Financial covenants are heavily tailored to the business structure of the borrower, and it will be the banks that determine what the financial covenants will require. The role of the lawyer is to try and turn those requirements into enforceable legal obligations. Nevertheless, there is a broad distinction between financial covenants depending on the following factual matrices:

(1) Monthly/annual/statutory accounts for investment grade financial covenants: the financial covenants aim to describe the current financial position of an established borrower and set parameters within which the borrower should operate over the term of the CFA.
(2) These are also relevant in investment grade real estate financing where the acquisition of developed commercial property is predicated on an established expectation that the property will generate predictable rental income.
(3) Financial modelling for leveraged and project finance: the financial covenants have nothing to describe because the business that will generate income and grow capital is either:
    (a) yet to be acquired (leveraged buyout);
    (b) not constructed yet (project finance);
    (c) currently in dire straits such that no party wishes to maintain the current economic position but rather has agreed how the borrower will aim to improve its financial position over time (insolvency workout).

These covenants therefore model the future.

Financial covenants operate as *early warning indicators* of the financial health of Borrower. This allows all parties to remedy the situation well before statutory mechanisms (principally insolvency rules) kick in, at which point the parties lose control of the process.

---

81 A useful illustration of failing to master financial covenants is provided by the Scottish professional negligence case of *Dunvale Investments Ltd. v Burness Paull & Williamsons LLP* [2015] CSOH 32, [2015] SCLR 567. Here the borrower's solicitors failed to point out that a Loan-to-Value covenant had been so drafted that if the borrower were to draw down a revolving credit facility without first providing security to the lender, the loan side of the ratio would so increase as to breach the covenant. The borrower drew down the funds, the lender declared breach, and the solicitor was found liable for negligence.

2.8.1 Financial statements

I assume familiarity with the basics of company accounts: the balance sheet and profit and loss account, how they are constructed, and what they can and cannot tell us. Should you require a refresher briefing, I have attached one as **Annex A**. Just be aware that this briefing covers a single corporate, but where companies are grouped (s 1161 CA 2006) they are also expected to produce **consolidated accounts** for the group.

Now the statutory accounts of a corporate are the balance sheet and P&L a/c which latter is also called the **income statement**. Banks, however, are unlikely to lend on the basis of what the law requires companies to disclose to the man on the Clapham omnibus. Banks will work closely with the CFO to fully understand Borrower's business (model). Appreciate, however, that the day-to-day inventories of a borrower are rough and liable to change as corrections are made. They do not form a satisfactory basis for a legal obligation, especially one as the financial covenant Event of Default. Thus these financial covenants tend to be based on financial statements which are as objective as possible; in the case of corporates, the (audited) balance sheet, income state, and the cash flow statement (hereinafter the **financial statements**).

To attain a level of objectivity, the finance statements are to be completed in accordance with international accounting standards, the international Generally Accepted Accounting Principles (**GAAP**). In the European Union corporates prepare financial statements in accordance with International Financial Reporting Standards (**IFRS**).

As mentioned, I expect you to know what a balance sheet and income statement are. A **cash flow statement** registers the net inflows and outflows of Cash and Cash Equivalents over a time period. Being cash focused, it is a hard figure; there is no estimating stock value, depreciation, or goodwill here. It is critical because cash flow goes to liquidity, which goes to ability to pay debts as they fall due. Cash flow statements are crucial in future-modelling CFAs because especially at the beginning of the term cash will be expended at a tremendous rate with little or no income until a capital base is created.

Each of the Financial Statements is the source for e.g. the following 'defined numbers':

(1) Balance sheet: tangible net worth; (net) borrowings.
(2) Income statement: EBIT(DA); finance costs.

Cash flow statement: funnily enough, (net) cash flow (if used), which feeds into potential deductions from (net) borrowings).

2.8.2 The 'defined numbers'

'Defined numbers' is not a term of art; I just use it to simplify and aggregate the inputs used in financial covenant ratios. Let us examine what some of these defined numbers are.

Consolidated [Tangible] Net Worth: This is *not* the same as net assets; rather, Net Worth looks at the capital structure of Borrower and relates this to which component is debt rather than equity finance. We look at the balance sheet and take capital plus reserves and deduct certain adjustments such as declared dividends, goodwill, variations in the value of own shares or of shares held in other Group companies.

As Net Worth depends on fair value of share capital, it can be volatile under IFRS, especially where Borrower starts altering its share capital by buybacks etc. This volatility is even worse in service businesses where valuations can differ wildly. Net Worth is thus recommended for use, if at all, with Groups focused on tangible assets or low-risk financial assets.

Consolidated Total [Net] Borrowings: This definition is tightly linked to the definition of Financial Indebtedness used in that undertaking. It is also based on the balance sheet but includes also contingent liabilities which would not necessarily appear there (but perhaps as notes to the accounts)—principally intra-Group guarantees and indemnities.

Some CFAs allow the netting off or deduction of Cash or Cash Equivalents. The point here is that if Group hits a liquidity crunch, it could mitigate this by quickly realizing highly liquid assets and using these to repay indebtedness. As this definition feeds into the gearing and leverage ratios, such liquidity is important. Examples of Cash Equivalents include commercial paper and gilts/ T-bills (see Chapter 8).

Consolidated EBITDA: Earnings Before Interest and Tax is just the US way of saying 'operating profit.' The basic idea is to strip back various charges on the business to determine its basic profitability. This is not quite fundamental profitability because it still includes overheads, but it does grasp the liquidity of the business over the period. By also excluding Depreciation and Amortization—which are non-cash charges designed to estimate the decline in value of tangibles and intangibles respectively—EBITDA gets very close to cash flow and so can be a basis for the cash flow statement. If one looks at an income statement, it is simply a case moving upwards from the bottom line, adding back in all the charges as you go.

Consolidated EBITDA aggregates the operating profits of Group members together (if so defined) with the share of profits/losses of associates (IAS 28 investor exerting influence over operating and financial policy)[82] and joint ventures (IFRS 11).[83]

Adjusted Consolidated EBITDA: the financial covenants may permit deviations from IFRS principles to better reflect the parties' agreed practice. The key reason for adjustment is an unusual item that is or will appear on the Group's accounts. Technically Depreciation and Amortization are such adjustments, but you can also see stipulations that permit Exclusion of gains/losses from:

(1) Acquisitions and disposals of significant items.
(2) Restructurings.
(3) Reversals of provisions (e.g. on bad debts which come good).

Occasionally adjustments will occur to allow the Group to operate under a variation of the IFRS schema. This happened in the UK during the transition period from national GAAP, for example.

Consolidated Finance Costs: All finance costs (whether in each case paid, payable or added to principal) incurred by the Group during a Measurement Period, calculated on a consolidated basis. Net finance costs is the foregoing less interest receivable in the same period.

2.8.3 The ratios

We have our building blocks, but how do they fit together? Commonly the financial covenants will deploy one or more of the following non-exhaustive list ratios:

Interest Cover: The Company must ensure that the ratio of Consolidated [EBIT/EBITDA] to Consolidated [Net] Finance Costs is not, at the end of each measurement Period, less than [x] to 1.

82 IFRS Foundation, 'Investments in Associates and Joint Ventures' (2024) IAS 28 <https://www.ifrs.org/content/dam/ifrs/publications/pdf-standards/english/2024/issued/part-a/ias-28-investments-in-associates-and-joint-ventures.pdf?bypass=on> accessed 16 September 2024.

83 See now IFRS Foundation, 'Joint Arrangements' (2017) IFRS 11 <https://www.ifrs.org/content/dam/ifrs/publications/pdf-standards/english/2021/issued/part-a/ifrs-11-joint-arrangements.pdf> accessed 16 September 2024; and IFRS Foundation, 'Disclosure of Interests in Other Entities' (2024) <https://www.ifrs.org/content/dam/ifrs/publications/pdf-standards/english/2022/issued/part-a/ifrs-12-disclosure-of-interests-in-other-entities.pdf?bypass=on> accessed 16 September 2024.

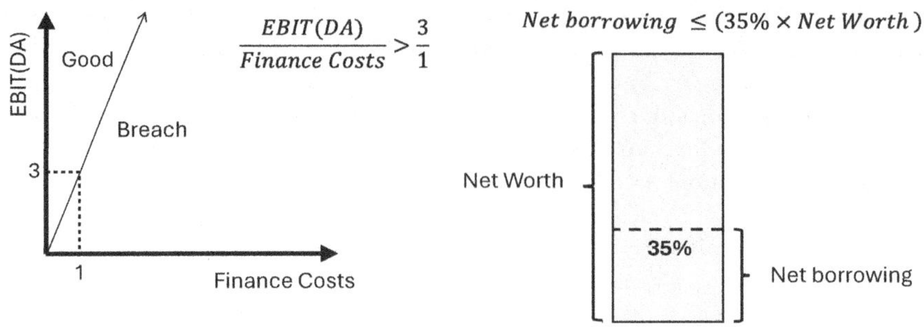

Figures 2.5 and 2.6 An interest cover ratio of 3:1, a gearing covenant of 35%

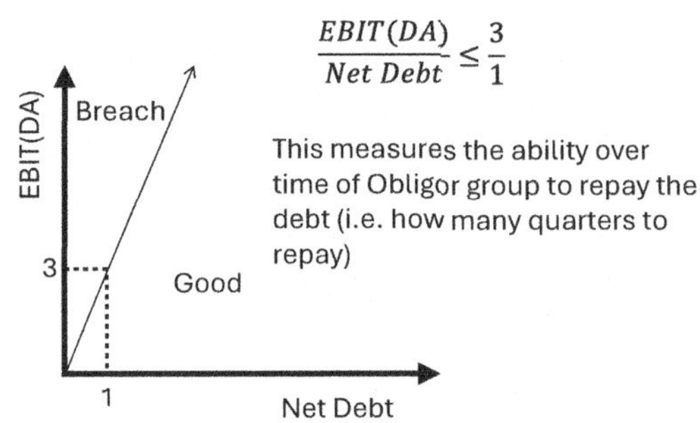

Figure 2.7 A leverage ratio of 3:1

Gearing: The Company must ensure that Consolidated Total [Net] Borrowings do not exceed [x]% of Consolidated [Tangible] Net Worth.

Evidently gearing will vary as Borrower draws down Loans. Gearing Ratios should take this into account and indeed other planned changes in capital structure e.g. share issues/buybacks/ cancellations.

Leverage: The Company must ensure that Consolidated Total [Net] Borrowings do not exceed [x] times Adjusted Consolidated EBITDA.

Please be aware that this definition of leverage is not the only definition in finance. For example, you might be more used to thinking of leverage as the ratio of debt to assets, not income.

2.8.4 The financial covenants in action

There are many instances where breaching financial covenants are the bases for an Event of Default and consequent restructuring or acceleration. Given the detail in which they are negotiated over and above almost any other term in a CFA, it is unsurprising that borrowers do not generally put the financial covenants in issue, as having questionable interpretation or otherwise. It does happen, however, as the following case illustrates.

STRATEGIC VALUE MASTER FUND LTD v IDEAL STANDARD INTERNATIONAL ACQUISITION SARL AND OTHERS [2011] EWHC 171 (Ch)

ISIA was part of the Ideal Standard group of companies. ISIA was borrower under a CFA, with Fund as one of the various lenders. The CFA contained an interest cover covenant in clause 22.2 to the effect that the ration of EBITDA to interests costs would be or exceed the ratio specified in that clause (actually it was a table of ratios varying over time.

The clause additionally permitted the ISIA to remedy any breach of the financial covenant as follows:

22.5 Equity Cure Right

> [I]f the requirements of any financial undertaking set out in clause 22.2 . . . are not met in respect of a Relevant Period, the cash proceeds ('Cure Amount') received by the Company pursuant to any New Equity ('Cure Subscription') or additional Subordinated Debt ('Cure Loan') invested in the Company for the purpose of curing such breach shall be included in a recalculation of such financial undertaking by making a pro forma adjustment to EBITDA (solely for the purpose of ascertaining compliance with the financial undertaking and not for any other purpose) such that (*x*) EBITDA for such Relevant Period is increased by an amount equal to the Cure Amount and (*y*) the Cure Amount does not count as cash to be deducted in calculating Total Net Debt.

When ISIA subsequently breached the covenant, it immediately tapped its other group companies for funds, receiving some EUR75m by way of intragroup loan. Some two-thirds of this is used to prepay the loan, reducing principal and therefore also interest payments thereon, and so bringing the interest cover ratio back into compliance with the clause.

The same day. The lenders instructed their agent to issue to ISIA a notice of acceleration of the loan, alleging inter alia that the cure was ineffective because it had been funded by a intra loan (increasing ISIA's leverage) and not in a valid way prescribed by cl 22.5, i.e. by injection of equity i.e. share capital.

Although the notice was later revoked, the Fund, as minority lender, sought to pursue its rights alone [let us assume this was permissible], further arguing that the Equity Cure Right as drafted made no sense if ISIA could *borrow* money to cure, because in borrowing it would simply incur further debt, worsening its financial position contrary to the intent of the financial covenant. The true interpretation of cl 22.5, it claimed, was that it allowed only for a fresh injection of *equity* capital (shares).

Held by Lewison J:

> On the true construction of the agreement, the cure was effective. A court should not adopt an interpretation of a contract that flouts commercial common sense, but where two rival interpretations both made commercial sense, one had to be careful. Lewison J cited the Court of Appeal in *Bank of Nova Scotia v Hellenic Mutual War Risks Association (Bermuda) Ltd* [1990] QB 818:
>
> It is nonetheless important, in attributing a purpose to a commercial transaction, to be sure that it is the purpose of both parties and not just one. If the purpose of the transaction is seen through the eyes of one party only an unbalanced view of the transaction may result. Many contracts represent a compromise between what one party wishes to obtain and the other is willing to give.

Had the commercial purpose of the interest cover ratio been to limit the net indebtedness of ISIA, then yes, it made perfect sense that capital injections by way of shares could be the only permissible mechanism of cure. New shares would add nothing to a company's indebtedness; a new loan be definition would.

This was not the purpose of the interest cover ratio, however. Rather, the interest cover ratio was there to ensure ISIA had sufficient cashflow to meet interest payments. It therefore mattered not where the capital came from that improved ISIA's interest cover ratio—the cure had been effective. The literal words of the clause allowed for a debt capital injection, and there was no compelling reason to read those words otherwise.

As noted above, of all the covenants in the CFA, the financial covenants are the most deeply negotiated and most closely watched by both borrower and finance parties. They set precise economic parameters within which the borrower must operate. Although complex, they are the disciplinary panopticon of the CFA from which all else the borrower and its group is observed. ISIA saved itself, but notice how quickly it jumped into action to borrow EUR75m from its group companies to avoid acceleration, just because of its interest cover covenant. Indeed, it was confirmed in that case that ISIA was not insolvent by any relevant measure and had at least in the short term staved off difficulties. ISIA would have been insolvent, though, had acceleration of the loans been carried through. A borrower facing financial covenant breach will normally do its utmost to return to compliance. Hilferding's observation that the centre of gravity of corporate governance lies not with shareholders but with senior creditors, one might say, finds its most striking instantiation in these contractual clauses.

Annex A—the balance sheet

Why do I need to understand the balance sheet?

Knowing how to read a basic balance sheet is a skill worth having, especially as you will be given one in the exam. *Note that balance sheets differ even in form, depending on the accountant.*

The structure of the classical balance sheet mirrors the misconception of the company as a creature of the shareholders to the exclusion of every other stakeholder. We will see that modern corporate finance, at least, makes little distinction between debt and equity.

Finally, the company accounts provide information to investors. By means of financial tests (ratios) the investors may determine the market price of shares (over/undervalued). The ratios are a key way in which managerial behaviour is disciplined by the market.

Capital employed/employment of capital

Suppose Zenon plc was incorporated to acquire and carry on the business of internet-based sales owned by Zenon Ltd. To do this it issued 200m GBP1 shares, secured their admission to a RIE, and allotted them to numerous investors, all on 1 April. In fact, the investors were so keen they bought shares at 3x the nominal value. With the proceeds of this issue, Zenon plc did indeed acquire Zenon Ltd's business assets and began trading on 1 May.

The above investment is called the **capital employed** by the company—the 'stock' given over to the company's power. It can also be called 'the capital attributable to the shareholders' or just 'capital [and reserves].' It sits at the bottom of the balance sheet and looks as follows. Note that all balance sheets are static—they are stated to show the balance **as at [date]**.

ZENON PLC
BALANCE SHEET (PART)
as at 1 April 2012

CAPITAL EMPLOYED	£m
Share capital	200
Share premium	400
Shareholder funds	600

Figure 2.8 Zenon plc balance sheet part 1

But this capital does not sit there; it is actually put to the use of the company. Above the Capital Employed section is a section telling us how that capital is employed (aka assets employed). Capital is in a sense everywhere in capitalism, but it is never somewhere as capital itself; it is always capital in the form of some asset. Capital is a bit like a substance—it is 'simply' the bearer of various modulations through time. In fact, on 1 April all of Zenon plc's capital had only one form: cash, being the proceeds of the share issue.

ZENON PLC
BALANCE SHEET (PART)
as at 1 April 2012

EMPLOYMENT OF CAPITAL	£m
Current Assets	
Cash	600
Net Current Assets	600
CAPITAL EMPLOYED	
Share capital	200
Share premium	400
Shareholder funds	600

Figure 2.9 Zenon plc balance sheet part 2

And that's a balance sheet—the capital employed at the bottom is faithfully reflected in the employment of capital above. Zenon plc was given GBP600m of capital represented by GBP600m of cash.[84]

By 1 May, Zenon plc has acquired its business assets. The balance sheet now looks more interesting, but it lists not each asset but each type of asset according to 'liquidity'—primarily identified by the current/fixed/long-term classification that roughly turns on availability/payability within 12 months or not.

ZENON PLC
BALANCE SHEET (PART)
as at 1 May 2012

EMPLOYMENT OF CAPITAL	£m
Fixed Assets	300
Current Assets	
Stock	300
Cash	100
Total Assets	700
Long-term liabilities	
Secured loan [debenture]	(100)

84 Cash implies Zenon plc is holding coins and notes. If we are precise, Zenon plc's cash will be at the bank. What Zenon plc owns is the debt obligation owed by the bank to Zenon plc.

EMPLOYMENT OF CAPITAL	£m
Net Current Assets (Liabilities)	600
CAPITAL EMPLOYED	
Share capital	200
Share premium	400
Shareholder funds	600

Figure 2.10 Zenon plc balance sheet part 3

Notice (1) liabilities are shown in brackets indicating a negative amount; (2) the fixed assets in all likelihood represents realty, while the secured loan, being long term, is likely to be secured on that realty; and (3) the reapplication of the capital has not changed the capital employed. We are keeping this simple i.e. assuming that all purchases were for the correct market value (no gains or losses were made).

Zenon plc now starts trading. This activity is shown in the profit and loss (**P&L**) statement, which unlike the static balance sheet, displays a duration of trading, usually **for the year to [date]**. Here is the Zenon plc P&L statement for the first year of trading:

PROFIT & LOSS A/C
for year ending 31 March 2013

	£m	£m
Turnover		3,000
less		
Cost of sales		(2,700)
Gross Profit		300
less		
Expenses (incl. directors' fees)	(100)	
Interest	(50)	
		(150)
Profit before tax		
		150
Appropriations		
less | Tax on profit		(40)
Profit after tax		110

Figure 2.11 Zenon plc P&L 2013

Turnover is the raw profitability of what it is Zenon PLC does. The cost of sales reflects all the expenditure Zenon plc must make to actually achieve turnover, from buying stock to sell, to paying wages, to running IT etc. The gross profit then reflects the 'internal' profitability of carrying on the underlying business, once we factor in these costs.[85] Another name for this is **EBIT** = earnings before tax and [loan] interest. If we also factor out amortization and depreciation, we have **EBITDA**.

So, we have a healthy, GBP110m profit. This now feeds back into the latest balance sheet:

85 I say 'internal' profitability because there may be costs which Zenon plc externalizes and never pays, such as the just value of labour, harms to involuntary creditors, and environmental degradation. These are called (negative) externalities.

ZENON PLC
BALANCE SHEET
as at 31 March 2013

EMPLOYMENT OF CAPITAL	£m
Fixed Assets	300
Current Assets	
Stock	310
Debtors	220
Cash	150
Total Assets	980
Current liabilities	
Creditors	(130)
Tax	(40)
Long-term liabilities	
Secured loan [debenture]	(100)
Net Current Assets (Liabilities)	710
CAPITAL EMPLOYED	
Share capital	200
Share premium	400
Profit and loss reserve	110
Shareholder funds	710

Figure 2.12 Zenon plc balance sheet 2013

Notice how the balance sheet shows the profit or loss as a somewhat mystical variation in the size of the capital employed. Specifically, the invested capital remains static; its growth or loss is treated as an additional factor. What you should realize is that it is the business shown above that has generated this value (the big question is, what is its source?). That growth is expressed in the various assets and liabilities. The balance sheet balances because we add the difference between the net assets and the share capital etc.—the profit—to the bottom of the sheet to *make* it balance.

We move the clock forward one year to see what happens if Zenon plc holds on to its profits (in the reserve) and then declares a dividend of 10p per share. I show an extract from the P&L statement and the Capital Employed section of the balance sheet.

PROFIT & LOSS A/C [part]
for year ending 31 March 2014

Profit after tax		£m 120
less	Dividend	(20)
	Profit retained (reserves)	100
add	Profit brought forward from previous years	110
		210

Figure 2.13 Zenon plc P&L 2014

ZENON PLC
BALANCE SHEET [extract]
as at 31 March 2014

Current liabilities	
Dividends declared	**(20)**
CAPITAL EMPLOYED	
Share capital	200
Share premium	400
Profit and loss reserve	210
Shareholder funds	810

Figure 2.14 Zenon plc balance sheet 2014

On more advanced balance sheets you will see a 'declared dividends' account in Capital Employed which will explicitly show the (20) as reducing shareholder funds from profits of 230.

Financial ratios—share markets disciplining management

The relevance of the above accounting information is that it is required to be given under Part 15 Companies Act 2006 (cf s 396 a/cs must comprise balance sheet and P&L a/c). It is one way that shareholders can assess the financial condition of the company. Certain tests are available to perform this financial analysis, but they must be considered in the round. For example:

- **Return on (invested) capital**: this basically asks how much money is generated by each GBP1 of capital invested in company operations. A classic form of the calculation is $(EBIT \cdot (1 - tax\ rate))/(Invested\ capital)$. This factors tax back in and factors out cash and cash equivalents. The factoring out of cash is important—if the company is holding on to cash, it is not investing it—it is not setting the capital in motion—and so is wasting capital that could be put to use elsewhere. If the company cannot use the capital, it should **return** it (but see the discussion of capital maintenance in Chapter 7).
- **Yield**: the agricultural reference is apt; yield means the growth the invested capital gives back in actual *dividends*—so it is cruder than ROIC. E.g. if a 5p dividend is declared, and the share price is GBP2, the yield is $\frac{5p}{200p} \times 100 = 2.5\%$.
- **P/e ratio**: the price-to-earnings ratio basically tells you how much current investors are prepared to pay to receive e.g. GBP1 of earnings. It is normally $(market\ value\ per\ share)/(earnings\ per\ share)$ and will be higher as where investors expect future earnings to increase. Notice the interaction between share price and ultimately dividends to transient investors.

Modigliani and Miller—from balance sheet to capital structure

The balance sheet's privileging of shareholder capital is anachronistic. Modern corporate finance theory follows the grandly titled Modigliani-Miller Theorem (**M&M**):

> The cost of capital to the business and the total value of the business are independent of the business' capital structure.[86]

The theorem basically states that *all else being equal*,[87] there is no economic reason why a company would issue shares rather than borrow—the cost of doing either is the same. From a M&M perspective, a company's balance sheet should look like this:

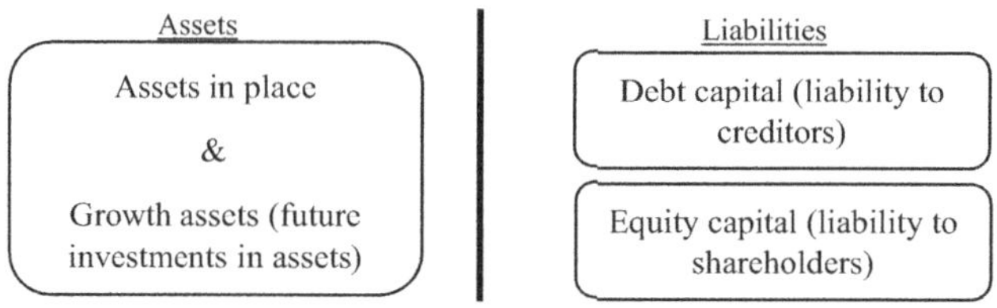

Figure 2.15 The M&M perspective on a business' capital structure

But in reality the cost is not the same, and the reason it is not the same is legal—e.g. the law actively decides that creditors should be paid off first in insolvency while, as recompense, shareholders control the company. A political decision has been made, and it affects **cost of funds**.

M&M allows directors to regard their **capital structure** as the entire right-hand side (RHS) of the balance sheet. Given this modern approach, should shareholders continue to be regarded as special, as pseudo-owners of the company?

In later chapters (Chapters 6 and 7) the capital structure will come back into focus. In Chapter 6 we will look at how, contractually, lenders can differentiate the capital structure further on the debt side using various subordination techniques. In Chapter 7, we examine the reasons for the basic structural distinction between debt and equity capital, and how this is used to great effect in leveraged buyouts. You can further deepen your knowledge, if you are studying corporate finance on the equity side, by investigating with your tutor the nature of different classes of shares (see section 629ff Companies Act 2006).

86 Franco Modigliani and Merton Miller, 'The Cost of Capital, Corporate Finance and the Theory of Investment' (1959) 49 Am Econ Rev 655.

87 There are actually some massive assumptions with M&M: no taxes; equal borrowing costs; efficient markets; perfect markets (i.e. no transaction costs).

Chapter 3

Security I

Basic principles and fixed security

Chapter contents

DOI: 10.4324/9781003457220-3

3.1 Game of chairs

A business is solvent if it can pay its debts as they fall due and, in many jurisdictions, the value of its assets is at least equal to the value of its liabilities. In such a situation, commercial actors—inherently optimistic by nature (how else would one start a business?)—are apt to disregard the counsels of lawyers who seem only ever to want to speak, at great expense, about what happens when it all goes wrong and the business collapses. But forewarning of doom is the lawyer's role, and one of the best reasons for appearing, Cassandra-like, in the marketplace, is that it is much, much easier to agree what will happen if things go wrong now, when the parties are positive and consensual, than later when they are fighting over the dying body of the business they funded.

In essence, the problem can be boiled down to a familiar children's game (I will be abusing this analogy later too): *musical chairs*. We can regard each child as an investor in a business, and their investment is represented by each participating child bringing one chair to the game, to be placed in a circle around which the children will dance and skip. Once the chair is placed in the circle, it ceases to be identified with the child that placed the chair; each child may use any chair, and we can regard the chairs as a fund available to all the investors. Nevertheless, each chair is considered an indivisible, discrete unit—no one may have an interest in e.g. half a chair, only a whole one.

Music is played and the children move in a circle, representing the passage of time and the business's turnover. During this phase a third-party referee will 'annihilate' one chair by removing it from the circle,[1] so that there is now one more investor in the business for that number of assets available to investors. In short, the chair business is balance sheet insolvent. In English law (but not, say, German law) this is not an issue until the music stops, for it is only when the music stops that the investors must recoup the value of their investment: one chair from the fund of chairs, which they claim by sitting on it. As there is one chair missing, one investor must go without. The investor who fails to recover a chair is thus eliminated, having lost their investment. The game then continues until one investor with one chair is left.

Anyone who has played this game as a child, or observed younger children playing it, will have remarked the brutality at the heart of it: the child who is timid, too polite, indecisive, or inattentive will be quickly culled. One may also see competitive and boisterous children dive for seats, hanging around a particular seat, barging each other aside and, in the worst cases, perching two-to-a-chair attempting to muscle their co-tenant off their prize. Tears are not unknown to the game.[2]

One can imagine a lawyer advising a child: the child's eyes glazing over as our lawyer explains the consequences of the rules and the risks run by participating. The child runs off before our lawyer has finished and starts to play, but is back five minutes later, face flushed with disappointment, uttering the immortal words: 'it's not fair!' Our lawyer, evidently unused to dealing with children, produces an attendance note of the advice previously given and imagines his professional indemnity insurance broker breathing a sigh of relief.

I labour this point because in finance, especially when inexperienced investors and business people are involved, the lawyer can be faced with creditors who only too late think 'it's not fair!' as their investment evaporates. So let us think what constructive advice we could have given to our investor *beforehand*. Imagine, for example, some modifications of the rules of *musical chairs* as follows, which proceed on the basis that players invest one chair each into the game:

---

1 The point is that the chair plays no further role and does not even 'belong' to the game's referee—*de jure* it has ceased to exit.

2 At least in the UK, where for schoolmasters the demarcation between children's games and brawling is often difficult to draw, and no doubt contributed to the codification of rugby.

(1) It is possible for a player, call them P, to carry one chair around with them. When the music stops they need only sit down; practically, no one else can access the chair in time.

(2) P is permitted by the rules to own a chair and so exclude the world from it at will. Ownership is demonstrated by a title deed to this effect, whose validity is confirmed by a referee for the game. Being P's property, it is not possible for anyone else to remove the chair and, when the music stops, P may simply produce the deeds, have any occupant evicted, and take their place.

(3) P is permitted to acquire a proprietary interest in a particular chair, signified by affixing a label to that chair marked 'P.' When the music stops, P is entitled to enforce this interest by evicting any occupant of the P chair and taking the place instead. However, if the chair was removed by the referee during the game, P's interest is likewise annihilated, and so they must compete for one chair as normal.

(4) It is possible for P to acquire a proprietary interest equal to one chair in the class defined as 'chairs in the circle from time to time,' evidenced by a deed. Any chair can be removed each round, but when the music stops P has a right to claim one of the remaining chairs as their own, evict any occupant, and take their place.

(5) It is possible for a second player, Q, to unilaterally promise to P that if P is ever left without a chair while Q has a chair, Q will surrender his chair to P, thereby assuring that at least in one round where both P and Q are participants, P will have a chair to sit on and Q will lose out.

These modified rules of *musical chairs* are unlikely to catch on among five-year-olds, but they do serve to provide examples of how a player could mitigate their risk of losing the game. Options 1–4 are rough equivalents of four kinds of **security** a creditor can obtain to protect their investment. Option 5 is roughly equivalent to obtaining a performance **guarantee**. We will examine all these legal forms of risk mitigation, and more, in this chapter. The effect of P adopting one of these options is to **prioritize** them ahead of the other players in the specified manner when it comes to determining who loses out in each round.

We have not quite finished with this tortuous analogy, though. After a singularly tiresome round of *musical chairs* in which our well-advised P determined to use option 2 to win the game, all the players and referee agree that granting title to a chair defeated the game and so banned this form of security. All the players now know they had better obtain legal advice too—a legal arms race has begun—and when a new round commences, we find that all players have been similarly advised: they all follow option 3 and affix their initial to one of their chairs. The effect of *everyone* following option 3 is this: they cancel each other out, for a random chair is removed extinguishing the interest of the player whose name is affixed to it, and the other players claim the remaining chairs accordingly. If everyone is prioritized in the same way, the effect is equivalent to no one being prioritized.

Or consider this: every player chooses option 4. Now we face a conceptual difficulty, for each player has an interest in exactly one of the chairs in the circle, but which, and who loses out? The rules of this game bar us from splitting chairs into parts, so we must determine some other way of prioritizing player interests. One way, which you may have plausibly inferred from your knowledge of property law, is differentiate the interests according to first in time. Using this method, we say that for any P, Q, if P formalized their deed evidencing option 4 earlier in time than Q formalized their deed evidencing option 4, then P ranks prior to Q. Applying this to every player to achieve a temporal ordering, it must be whoever formalized their deed last in time who ranks last, and so they must lose out first.

With this game we are starting to obtain a sense a ranking and priority of risk mitigation, and particularly security interests. This ranking is absolutely crucial to everything we learn about finance law and that is why I have laboured this naïve account. Hopefully we now have enough intuition to explore ranking and priority in a properly financial setting.

3.2 The insolvency waterfall

Francesca is a sole trader in wine, which she sources from the Saint-Mont area of the Gers department, France. She buys wine straight from the producers, often taking options on the grapes still on the vine on the hills around the village of Aignan, and ultimately imports crates of wine to London for sale to wine merchants. Buying the wine in advance, and the necessary payment of import duties and customs bonds, all require significant expenditure long before Francesca recoups that money in sales. Francesca therefore needs credit, which is provided by various financiers.

As a first step, consider that these various creditors have all lent money to Francesca and have not considered any additional risk mitigation techniques, such as taking security. The law states that if Francesca is unable to repay her creditors (and so is bankrupt), her remaining assets must be sold to realize their cash value, and this cash should be distributed to the creditors **pro rata**. Because cash is divisible (unlike chairs), it is possible to divide up the cash so that the creditors need not fight over who gets something; if there is not enough cash to distribute, they all receive less.

ESSENTIAL DEFINITION: PRO RATA

Where all debts rank equally between themselves, they shall be paid in full unless the assets are insufficient for meeting those debts, in which case they shall abate in equal proportions between themselves.[3]

Here, ranking equally just means no creditor being considered has an additional risk mitigation afforded by e.g. security or perhaps statute. **Abate** means 'be diminished' or 'reduce.'

The best way to grasp the notion of a pro rate distribution is to work through some examples. We will assume that Francesca's trustee in bankruptcy has 'got in' all her assets, which consists in wine, and has **liquidated** these, which means she has turned them into cash. 'Liquidation' here provides a very useful image—we can imagine the trustee in bankruptcy distributing the cash by pouring it into the waiting glass of each creditor.

EXAMPLES 1 AND 2

Let there be two creditors, C1 and C2. C1 is owed £75k; C2 is owed £25k.

1 On liquidation, it turns out Francesca's wine is worth £100k. As she owes £100k, her creditors can each be repaid in full.

2 On liquidation, the sale of Francesca's wine realizes £80k. This means creditors will lose, altogether, £20k i.e. 20% of the total debt, or 20p in the £. The losses are distributed in proportion to the amount lent:

   a C1 receives 80p back for every £1 lent i.e. 0.80 × £75k = £60k.

   b C2 receives 80p back for every £1 lent i.e. 0.80 × £25k = £20k.

In absolute terms, C1 loses more money (£15k) than C2 (£5k), but in absolute terms he did receive more of the distribution back. Critically, each of C1 and C2 have lost proportionately the same amount.

3 Based on Insolvency Act 1986, s 328 as this is a personal insolvency (bankruptcy). The basic principle applies to corporate insolvencies too, but is stated in Insolvency Rules 1986 SI 1986/1925 r 1.181(1).

We can visualize the foregoing example using wine glasses. Both C1's and C2's wine glasses are being filled at the same time, but C1's wine glass is bigger and so more wine is needed to fill it to the 80% full mark than is needed to fill C2's glass. Now let us make things more interesting . . .

Like our well-advised players of *musical chairs*, Francesca's creditors may not want to bear their losses according to the basic rules of the game; they may wish to negotiate some preferential treatment so that they can mitigate their risk of suffering loss. It may be fairly obvious to you why creditors would want to avoid losing any money at all, but this is only half the picture: if one creditor is to avoid a loss, some other creditor must bear that extra loss. This leads us to the question: why would any creditor volunteer to suffer greater losses?

Not all creditors are the same. They have what we call different risk profiles. Some creditors want to take on more risk (of losses), and they wish to do this because with more risk of loss comes (or should come) more reward. Here are some of the factors by which we can differentiate the risk profiles of creditors (and indeed investors more generally):

(1) While Francesca's business is healthy:
  (a) If interest is payable regularly to all creditors, who should receive a higher rate of interest?
  (b) If interest is payable e.g. at the end of the term of a loan, who should receive interest and repayment first?
  (c) If Francesca foresees financial difficulties, who should have the deciding say in whether and how Francesca's debt can be restructured?
(2) On Francesca's bankruptcy:
  (a) Who should bear the capital loss first (this may be a moot point if Francesca has no assets left)?
  (b) Who should have been permitted to take security?
  (c) Who should have the deciding say in whether and how Francesca's debt can be restructured?
  (d) Should a creditor be permitted to take on Francesca's business as a whole?

Let us consider two kinds of creditor. C1 is a very conservative provincial bank, and its primary concern is to protect its capital. C2 is a so-called business angel—a private equity investor who parachutes in to invest in small businesses with high-risk start-up capital. How might they respond to the risk profile questions above?

C2 is prepared to take a risk. Specifically, C2 is prepared to lose the money he lends. But he wants a greater reward for this risk. Therefore, C2 expects to receive more interest for the money C2 lends that C1 receives for C1's credit. C is happy with this, provided that C2 does indeed bear more risk; i.e. should Francesca's business collapse, C2 should be repaid capital first and only when repaid in full should any leftover cash be distributed to C1. To protect this position further, C2 would like to take security over Francesca's assets, not least in case the trustee in bankruptcy decides that C2 should receive more money back than C1 and C2 initially agreed. In this way C1 is in a relatively safe position compared to C2—it will not receive much interest every quarter while Francesca is doing well, but that is balanced against the greater chance that C1 will not lose the money it lent in the first place. As long as Francesca is doing well, C2 receives much more income by way of interest payments. But what if Francesca is starting to struggle to make repayments? In this situation C1 is less concerned, for if bankruptcy occurs, C1 knows that losses will be borne by C2 first. Indeed, C1 is actively counting on C2's investment as providing a 'cushion' which will absorb any economic shock long before C1's capital is diminished. Conversely, C2 is very concerned as soon as there is even a chance Francesca might default because C2 will lose out first. Therefore, the creditors might further agree that if Francesca is in difficulty, C2 can step in and help her, for example by lending her more money, by paying off some of the C1 debt, or even by stepping in to manage Francesca's business.

In this example we see how one creditor might volunteer to take on more risk of losses than another creditor, and how this plays out in practical legal mitigations such as the granting of security. The interplay of different risk profiles plays out all the time when it comes to structuring the debt and indeed equity finance of a business, and law plays a central role in the structuring, notably by permitting creditors to take security.

In the *musical chairs* analogy, we provided some naïve examples of the ways in which players could mitigate their risk of losing by taking 'security.' We will examine security in legal detail in due course, but let us remain at a relatively high level of abstraction so that we may focus on the effect of security in the context of our differing risk profiles. To do this we introduce further technical language. If creditors C1 and C2 have not taken security, we say each is an **unsecured** creditor. If they have both taken security, we say each is a **secured** creditor. If C1 and C2 are both unsecured creditors, we say that they both **rank equally**, which means that they should both receive a distribution on insolvency at the same time in equal rank with each other. This is known by the Latin name **pari passu**. If C1 and C2 are both secured, and have a security interest in the same property, they are likewise pari passu, but now as secured creditors. If C1 is secured, but C2 is unsecured, then we say C1 and C2 do *not* rank equally, are thus not pari passu, and that C1 ranks **prior** to C2.

ESSENTIAL DEFINITION: PARI PASSU

In equal step, that is, without preference.

This definition makes more sense if contrasted with the case where two creditors are not pari passu, for in such a case the creditor ranked prior is preferred over the other creditor, which roughly means that the prior-ranked creditor is repaid *in full before* the lower-ranked creditor.

It is common for lawyers to say that a given subset of creditors **rank pari passu and pro rata**, which just means that as between equally ranked creditors, the debts of those creditors are repaid in proportion to the amount owed to them, and that each rank is repaid in full before the next lower rank.

Once again, all this is made clearer by some examples. Do not worry just yet what security is; focus on the effect it has on Francesca's bankruptcy.

EXAMPLE 3

As before, let there be two creditors, C1 and C2. C1 is owed £75k; C2 is owed £25k. This time, C1 also takes security over certain crates of wine which Francesca has been holding in a cellar for several years, and which she does not intend to sell for some years to come. C2 is unsecured.

On Francesca's bankruptcy her assets are worth £80k, made up of £75k worth of the cellared wine granted as security to C1, and £5k of other assets.

C1 ranks prior to C2, and specifically is able to benefit fully from the value of the cellared wine granted as security. This wine is sold and C1 is paid in full. C2 must wait for the trustee in bankruptcy to distribute the remaining £5k. As C1 has been repaid in full, the £5k is distributed to C2, who thereby loses £20k of the money he lent to Francesca.

EXAMPLE 4

Let Francesca have three creditors. C1 has lent £40k, C2 has lent £40k, C3 has lent £20k. C1 and C2 agreed to take equal ranking security over the cellared wine crates. C3 is unsecured.

On bankruptcy, Francesca's assets are valued at £80k: £75k of cellared wine, £5k of other assets.

The cellared wine's value is realized. As C1 and C2 rank equally, they receive a pro rata distribution. As they lent equal amounts, the distribution is 50p for each £ owed, so each of C1 and C2 receive £37.5k.

C1 and C2 have not yet been repaid in full; they are still owed £2.5K each. C3 is yet to receive anything.

There being £5k of assets left in Francesca's bankruptcy estate, this is distributed to the remaining creditors of the next rank i.e. C1, C2, and C3 pro rata. As C3 is owed £20k, whereas C1 and C2 are owed only £2.5k each, C3 is entitled to 80p in the £ (or 80%) of the remaining estate. This comes to £4k. C1 and C2 receive 10p in the £ (or 10%) each, being £0.5 each.

Using the wine-pouring analogy, we can imagine the ranking of creditors as the stacking of wine glasses on top of each other, like a pyramid, and pouring wine into the top glass. Only this top glass fills at first, and only when this top glass is full does any excess wine flow over the sides and into the glasses of the next tier below. If there is not enough wine to go round, then at some point a tier of glasses will not be completely filled, and the tiers below that will remain empty. The tiers of the glass pyramid can be considered the ranks of the creditors, with higher tiers representing prior ranking creditors, and each tier receiving a distribution proportionate to the number and relative size inter se of glasses in that tier. One final example for now should illustrate this point.

EXAMPLE 5

As before, let there be two creditors, C1 and C2. C1 is now owed £50k; C2 is likewise owed £50k. C1 takes security over certain crates of wine which Francesca has been holding in a cellar for several years and which she does not intend to sell for some years to come. C2 is unsecured and so ranks lower.

On Francesca's bankruptcy her assets are worth £80k, made up of £75k worth of the cellared wine granted as security to C1, and £5k of other assets.

The security (the cellared wine) is sold, realizing £75k. C1 is only owed £50k, so he keeps only this amount and *must* return the surplus £25k to the trustee in bankruptcy. The trustee in bankruptcy moves to distribute the remaining value, observes that C1 has already being repaid in full, and so distributes the remaining £25k + £5k = £30k to C2. C2 therefore has lost £20k; C1 has lost nothing.

With these first few examples who have encountered a very simple version of what is known as the order of priority of debts on insolvency, and which finance lawyers sometimes call the **insolvency waterfall** (hence my example). In practice, there can be very many ranks to this waterfall, some imposed by statute—such as the preference afforded to trustee/liquidator expenses—and some effected more or less consensually, such as by way of granting and taking security. In the detail of the law of security that follows, do not lose sight of *why* creditors are taking security, and indeed why debtors are offering it to creditors with varying risk profiles. The law of security can at times be complex and even incoherent, but there is a strain running through the cases of commercial pragmatism: parties are creating security interests for the reasons discussed in this section, and the court often remembers that it is the effect of security, in terms of the insolvency waterfall, which is most important, and not the conceptual purity of the law.

3.3 The legal nature of security—general principles

We must always bear in mind the economic effects of taking security, for this is the purpose for which a creditor will require the debtor to grant security. These effects include:

(1) Providing an alternative source of value to satisfy a debt, should the debtor fail to make the promised repayment. This source is generally an asset, although loosely speaking it could extend to a wealthy person.
(2) Conferring control over the debtor by restricting their use or transfer of an asset, either now or should they default. Indeed, the risk of such control being exercised may be a useful bargaining chip.
(3) Allocating the value of the security to the secured creditor alone, and so removing this value from the capital available to any unsecured creditor. This has the ranking effect discussed in the previous section.
(4) Derivatively, by making the loan less risky because there is a 'backup' source of value to meet repayment:
    (a) allowing the lender to lower the cost of funds i.e. offer the debtor a lower interest rate; and,
    (b) making the loan more attractive to other investors (see syndication in Chapter 6).

The problem for the courts is that the routes to achieve these economic effects are many and varied, and as a result they do not fall neatly into a single doctrinal concept of security. A simple example would be the promise made by a wealthy shareholder that if a named company fails to repay that company's debt to bank, the shareholder will indemnify bank for any losses it suffers in consequence. In such a case, bank is economically more 'secure' than it would be had it only been able to sue the company for the debt—bank has now two chances to recoup its investment rather than one. Yet this indemnity is not 'security' in the strict (if 'archaic')[4] sense lawyers often have in mind, but in the more general sense that it is a legal arrangement that lowers the risk of ultimate non-repayment. At best it might be called a 'personal security' because it is a personal right of bank against the wealthy shareholder to demand indemnification and sue if that is not forthcoming.[5] Usually however, when lawyers speak of 'security,' especially when drafting security deeds in finance transactions, they mean **real security**.

---

4 in *re Rayner* [1904] 1 Ch 176 (CA), Farwell J interpreted a reference to 'security' in a will as a reference to pledges and other interests in property, even though the context made clear the word was being used in the then novel sense of 'investment.' The 'archaic' reading was overturned on appeal.

5 Indeed, statute has no qualms in extending security to such things as guarantees and even letters of comfort: Energy Act 2004, s 114.

> **ESSENTIAL DEFINITION: REAL SECURITY**
>
> Let debtor D be liable for a debt to creditor C, then D grants real security to C (or some third party) just when D makes available to C (or that third party) some identified or identifiable asset or fund such that C (or that third party) may appropriate that asset or fund for the purpose *only* of satisfying D's liability to C.

We will return to personal security and other 'quasi-security' later in this chapter, but for the time being we are going to focus on real security as the core of what is generally meant by security in finance law. In section 3.4 we will identify four types of real security, but there are features common to all or most of these which are worth dealing with together and in this section. These are the liabilities that are secured, attachment, perfection, enforcement and priorities, and the equity of redemption.

3.3.1 Secured liabilities

Security cannot exist on its own; it must be security *for* some liability (usually debt). If real security is granted, and the liability it secures ceases to be, then the basic position is that the real security ceases to be. It may be that the formerly secured party still in fact has possession, or legally has title to the asset, but they have neither by way of security and the former debtor will be entitled to return of possession and/or title.

Consider the following drafting from a security deed one might find used in a modern finance transaction:

[Definition] Secured Liabilities means all present and future obligations and liabilities (whether actual or contingent and whether owed jointly or severally or in any other capacity whatsoever) of the Debtor to the Finance Parties under each Finance Document to which the Debtor is a party.

Cl 2.1 Creation of Security

All the security created under this Deed:

(1) is created in favour of the Security Trustee;
(2) is created over present and future assets of the Debtor;
(3) is security for the payment of all the Secured Liabilities . . .

For this purpose, let us assume that the Finance Parties are certain banks that have made loans to the debtor and that they have asked one person—the Security Trustee, who is also a Finance Party—to hold the security and proceeds of its enforcement on trust for them. 'Finance Documents' would include the credit facilities agreement and this security document. Then we have a response to an important question: must security *only* be granted to the creditor of the secured liabilities?

A little thought suggests that the answer to the question must be yes, at least in a case such as this. We can proceed as follows: if security can always be granted to the creditor itself, then normal principles suggest that the creditor can direct a nominee or agent to hold that security on its behalf, for it remains the principal of that security. Similarly, a creditor can settle a trust on a trustee who holds the security interest on trust for a beneficiary, namely the creditor. Moreover, an agent, nominee, or trustee can hold for more than one creditor, and may even hold for a class of creditors from time to time. Thus agent, nominee or trustee need not be owed anything by the debtor (at least in English law)—at least in these cases security can be granted to a third party to whom the debtor is not liable. This is rather good news, because the use of Security Trustees and Security Agents is a standard feature of secured syndicated financing, as we will see in Chapter 6.

What, though, of other third parties? Could security be granted in favour of someone to whom no debt is owed, and who is neither a trustee, agent, nor nominee of any relevant creditor? The following case suggests that this too, is possible.

IN RE LEHMAN BROTHERS INTERNATIONAL (EUROPE) (IN ADMINISTRATION) [2012] EWHC 2997 (Ch)

Lehman Bros investment bank had organized its affairs in Europe through dozens of special purpose companies incorporated in jurisdictions such as England and Luxembourg. This added significantly to the complexity of its administration when in 2008 it collapsed into insolvency.

On interpretation of a master security document, the court held that a certain debtor 'A' had granted a type of security known as a charge to secure liabilities owed to Lehmans' entity C. However, the security had not been granted to C but to another of its special purpose companies: B. The question arose as to whether A could grant security to C for a liability to B, especially if B was not C's trustee.

Held per Briggs J:

> In my judgment, it is not inherent in the nature of a charge that the chargee must be, or be a trustee or fiduciary for, the creditor. All that is necessary is that the chargee has a specifically enforceable right to have the relevant property appropriated to the payment or discharge of the relevant debt or other obligation. It is that right of specific enforcement which transforms what might have otherwise been a purely personal right into a species of proprietary interest in the charged property . . . It is the right to specific performance that makes the critical difference.
>
> That being so, I can see no good reason why A should not confer a specifically enforceable right on B to have A's property appropriated towards the discharge of a debt which A (or someone else) owes C, without any requirement that B be C's trustee or fiduciary. B may have good business or personal reasons to wish to ensure that A pays his debt to C, and I cannot see why the law should prevent B taking an enforceable (and therefore proprietary) interest in A's property so as to give himself the power to achieve that objective, without making himself a trustee or fiduciary [agent] for C. In truth, it seems to me that the relationship between B and C is irrelevant to the enforceability of A's promise to B, if it derives from a specifically enforceable contract between them.

As Goode and Gullifer note, this judgment creates some conceptual difficulties.[6] As we have stated, security must be security for some liability—security and liability are surely inextricably entwined. The nature of a security trustee is that it holds a creditor's security for the benefit of the creditor, and that is important because should the trustee enforce the security, the proceeds are

6 Louise Gullifer (ed), *Goode and Gullifer on Legal Problems of Credit and Security* (7th edn, Sweet & Maxwell 2023) 1–16.

used to satisfy the outstanding debt to the creditor. Briggs J seems to be suggesting that this relationship is irrelevant. In Briggs J's favour, there is considerable common sense in permitting a creditor to direct a debtor to grant security to a third party. The general tenor of the judgment is if this is the way a creditor wishes to be satisfied, indeed wishes to mitigate its risk, so be it. But what happens if B enforces the security, for example realizing its cash value, but then itself becomes insolvent? In a trust or fiduciary situation, C, as beneficiary, would have a proprietary interest in the security and its proceeds. Without that relationship, would C only be left with personal claim against B, one perhaps worthless if B is insolvent?

Or what happens if B enforces the security and A repays C, or C releases A from liability? Briggs J appears to assume that the implicit terms of the relationship between A, B, and C is such that whatever A and B, or A and C, do, this will have an immediate effect on the rights of C or B, respectively. In particular, if B enforces the security and realizes sufficient value to repay the debt, A's debt to C is satisfied whether or not C receives the money. Likewise, if C releases A's debt, B's security is automatically released. This *should* happen, but by what mechanism, if not explicit agreement, is unclear. While *Lehman Bros* has been subsequently applied,[7] it would be most helpful if these difficult scenarios were placed before the court for specific adjudication.

3.3.2 Attachment

As we saw in section 3.2, taking security has the effect of prioritizing the secured creditor with respect to that asset. The secured creditor has prior right to the value realized from that asset; other creditors must wait to see if any surplus value remains once the secured creditor is satisfied. It follows that the court must be clear just which asset is subject to the security, and where to draw the line between what is subject to security and what is not. We therefore say that the security must *attach* to some identifiable asset. Conversely, if no attachment occurs, there can be no real security (yet).

There are several ingredients that make up the notion of attachment, some deriving from more general legal considerations of property and contract law:

(1) *Nemo dat quod non habet*: as a purported donor cannot transfer a property interest which he does not have, it follows that a debtor cannot attach an asset to security if he has no property interest in that asset. This does not exclude a debtor agreeing to attach an asset acquired in the future, but then the security is incomplete pending acquisition, and so attachment.

(2) *The parties must 'agree' to secure*: a creditor/debtor cannot unilaterally decide to take/give an asset as security. While most agreements will be valid contracts according to the requirements of contract law and any applicable statute,[8] in the case of a pledge (see section 3.4.1) it is enough that the debtor-owner intentionally give actual or constructive possession of the asset to the creditor by way of security, and the creditor willingly accept possession on that basis. Contrast this with the following scenarios:
   (a) Donor gives over possession in exchange for cash, but the donee of the asset believes she is buying the asset outright, not giving a secured loan.
   (b) Creditor demands security over debtor's car, but debtor forces creditor to take possession of a bike by way of security instead.
   (c) Debtor leaves an asset at the creditor's premises as security, but the creditor is not even aware that security has been offered.

7 *re Olympia Securities Commercial Plc (In Administration)* [2017] EWHC 2807 (Ch).

8 For example, the requirement that contracts transferring interests in land should be in writing: Law of Property (Miscellaneous Provisions) Act 1989.

(d) In each case, 'agreement' is understood in the more fundamental sense that we also find in the law of gifts: that both parties are as one[9] that security is being created and is attaching to *this* asset.

(3) *The asset must be identifiable*: this is most obviously satisfied in the case of a pledge, where the debtor manifestly hands over possession of a tangible asset, such as a diamond ring, to the creditor, by way of security. There can be little doubt that the ring is attached to the debt it secures. But as legal systems abstract from this most simple of cases, favouring commercial practicality over judicial certainty, the question of identifiability becomes difficult. Consider:

(a) Debtor hands over the keys to his car to creditor by way of security—while technically actual possession of the car has not been transferred, the keys enable all necessary control of the car, and their transfer to the creditor can only be *constructively* understood as transferring possession.

(b) Debtor executes and delivers of a deed of transfer of title to property to creditor by way of security—the deed is best understood as a further abstraction of the symbolism of handing over the keys to property. The constructive understanding refers to the asset described in the deed. Description, however, now raises the problem of the adequacy of words to identify their object.

(c) Debtor transfers title to 'my car' to creditor by way of security. It turns out, however, that debtor possesses two cars. It is not possible to identify which car is meant, and so neither car is attached. Debtor must perform an additional act of unqualified appropriation of one car to the security. Until such part, the transfer is a mere agreement to secure which is incomplete (and so ineffective against third parties).[10]

(d) Debtor transfers title to his '1/10th share in a bulk of fungible goods on the merchant vessel *The Gersoise*' to creditor by way of security. By extrapolation from the foregoing cars example, until such time as debtor definitively appropriates 1/10th as his own, separate bulk of goods, there is a mere agreement to secure.[11]

(e) Debtor transfers title to 'my car and any replacement car I may acquire' to creditor by way of security. Debtor subsequently replaces his old Ford Escort with an Audi Q4.

(f) Debtor transfers title to 'my assets from time to time' to creditor by way of security.

(g) These last two scenarios ((e) and (f)) require a little more thought, and we will review the relevant law in more detail in sections 3.4.4 and Chapter 4. Have a think about them and see if you can guess, by analogy from (a) through (d), how the law would deal with attachment in these cases.

(4) *Meeting any contractual conditions precedent* ('CPs'): it is a very common feature of financial legal practice that a party be obligated to meet CPs before the counterparty perform its obligation. Now, more often than not, it will be the bank who demands security be granted before the bank disburses any loan, but there are occasions when security will only be granted if some contingency occurs. It may be (as in case (3)(e) above) that the contingency is the debtor acquiring a new car. In high-level financial transactions, the parties may have agreed an unsecured loan that contains a provision that debtor must grant security should its financial condition breach a certain minimal threshold.

---

9 As you know, contracting parties must also be as one (*ad idem*) on formation, but additional conditions must be met: an intention to create legal (contractual) relations and critically, consideration.

10 *re London Wine Co (Shippers)* [1986] PCC 121, with thanks to Hugh Beale for his lectures on this subject.

11 See Roy Goode and Ewan McKendrick, *Goode and McKendrick on Commercial Law* (6th edn, LexisNexis Butterworths 2020) paras 8.02–8.22 and 8.92–8.98; Michael Bridge (ed), *Benjamin's Sale of Goods* (11th edn, Sweet & Maxwell 2021) para 5–068 onwards; Gullifer (n 6) 2–05; *re London Wine Co (Shippers)* (n 10); and Sale of Goods Act 1979 ss 20(a)(b).

EXAMPLE: CONTINGENT OBLIGATION TO GRANT SECURITY

In this clause of a credit facility agreement, the borrower will use the loan to purchase land it has identified in Germany. As the seller of the land has yet to agree to anything, the borrower can hardly grant security over the land now. Therefore, the creditor bank has required the borrower to undertake to grant German law security (to its agent) over the land in the future *if* the land is subsequently acquired by the borrower.

Specified Real Estate means the land at Miltenberg in the Free State of Bavaria in Germany marked 'A' and shaded yellow on the Agreed Plans.

Cl 22.19 Security

Upon acquisition of any of the Specified Real Estate (the **acquired real estate**) the Company shall ensure that the relevant German Obligor delivers within 10 Business Days a duly executed and notarized Land Charge over the acquired real estate to the Security Agent (together with such corporate authorities, legal opinions and other documents and evidence that the Security Agent may reasonably require).

3.3.3 Perfection

Attachment is a necessary condition for the creation of real security, but just because the debtor and creditor know which asset is subject to security does not make that security effective against third parties. This is extremely important because if debtor has made available a car to creditor, but has retained possession as is the case with certain kinds of security, what is to stop debtor selling the car to a third party dealing in good faith who knows nothing of the secured the debt? Does the third party take free of the security (normally, yes)? And what happens if our third party is also owed money by debtor, and takes security over the car oblivious to the existing security? Does the third-party security rank prior, posterior, or pari passu with the security granted to creditor (normally, prior)?

Perfection is the act of publicizing the grant of security so that third parties are **on notice** that the security exists and attaches to an asset. Being on notice, our third party cannot claim ignorance of creditor's existing security interest. In our example of debtor selling the car, the third party must take the car subject to creditor's security interest. In our example of a third party taking the car as security, the third party's security ranks posterior—in short, the existing creditor can use the value of the car to be repaid her debt in full, and any remaining value (if any) will go to repay what is owed to the third party.

So how does one perfect security? The simplest answer is that one should always check the technical, often statutory requirements for the particular asset being offered as security, and that this often amounts to recording the security interest on some public register. In the absence of explicit requirements, the safest option is to effect actual notice by informing third parties directly. Below are examples of some of the most commonly encountered perfection requirements in financial legal practice:

(1) *Taking possession of the asset*: in terms of perfection, there can be no more public manifestation that a physical asset is subject to a non-owner's interest than that non-owner rightfully holding onto the asset to the exclusion of its owner. It is difficult to sympathize with a third party who, where attempting to buy an asset or take it as security, fails to ask to see the physical asset the seller/debtor is offering. The inherently public nature of taking physical possession is at the heart of the security types know as **pledge** and **contractual lien**, and perfection by possession is inextricably bound up with their nature.

For non-possessory security some other perfecting mechanism is required, often dependant on either the nature of the security asset or the nature of the debtor granting security. This is often registration on a public register. Watch out, though: sometimes security might require perfection under more than one regime.

(2) *Registering a ship mortgage*: whatever other rules of security apply, should security for principal and interest be granted over a ship registered in the UK, that security should be registered under the Merchant Shipping Act 1995 with Form 4737.

What if the security is not registered? Then the security is ineffective against third parties, but this does not mean there is no security. There is effective security against the debtor. If a third party takes registered security over the ship, the first creditor's unregistered security will by pushed down the ranking (it will rank posterior to the perfected security).

(3) *Registering an aircraft mortgage*: like ship security, security over aircraft registered in the UK should be perfected by registration, this time in the Civil Aviation Authority's Register of Aircraft Mortgages.[12] Unlike ship mortgages, one can alternatively perfect security by registering it under the 'Cape Town' Convention on International Interests in Mobile Equipment.[13]

(4) *Registering a statutory charge of land*: perhaps more familiar to students who have already studied English law, the registration regime for land registered[14] in the UK is governed by the Land Registration Act 2002 (LRA 2002) and the Land Registration Rules 2003 SI 2003/1417. When it comes security, not all security interests are registrable—they must be registrable dispositions, which for our purposes means statutory mortgages of land, also known as charges of land (see section 3.4). Unlike ship and aircraft mortgages, this means there are some security interests which the creditor would very much like to make public, but which are not perfectible under the land registration system. Happily, it is possible to publicize these interests (e.g. equitable mortgages and charges (see section 3.4) by entering an agreed notice on the register.[15]

(5) *Registering a company charge*: thus far the lawyer has proceeded on the basis that the type of asset determines the mode of perfection. Sometimes, however, it is the nature of the security grantor which is relevant, and this is most commonly encountered when the grantor is a company registered under the Companies Acts[16] or for security granted before 1 October 2011 an 'overseas company' required to register as such in the UK.[17] Perfection is achieved by registration on the Register of Companies.

Failure to perfect security granted by a company has far worse effects that failure to meet the perfection requirements of specific kinds of assets. Whereas failing to register a ship mortgage still leaves in place a mortgage in equity, effective against the debtor and any third party with notice, failure to register security granted by a company means the security is void against other creditors, liquidators and administrators, even if they have actual notice. Things are little better for the debtor company, for another effect is that the debt immediately becomes payable, potentially rendering the debtor company insolvent.[18]

---

12 Governed by the Air Navigation Order 2016 SI 2016/765 and kept pursuant to the Mortgaging of Aircraft Order 1972 SI 1972/1268.

13 Implemented in the UK by the International Interests in Aircraft Equipment (Cape Town Convention) Regulations 2015 SI 2015/912, which it is believed survived Brexit: European Union (Withdrawal) Act 2018 s 2.

14 For unregistered land in the UK, granting a legal mortgage or charge of land triggers the requirement to register of the land itself (and consequently the security interest): Land Registration Act 2002 s 2.

15 Land Registration Act 2002 s 32.

16 Companies Act 2006 s 1046.

17 The case of overseas companies has been subject to legislative flip-flopping. Overseas Companies (Execution of Documents and Registration of Charges) Regulations 2009 SI 2009/1917, reg 9 (repealed by the Overseas Companies (Execution of Documents and Registration of Charges) (Amendment) Regulations 2011 SI 2011/2194 reg 2(3)), and the earlier case *Slavenburg's Bank NV v Intercontinental Natural Resources Ltd.* [1980] 1 All ER 955. See now ss 1–44 of the Economic Crime (Transparency and Enforcement) Act 2022 with respect to security over land.

18 Companies Act 2006 s 1046.

EXAMPLES: COMPANIES GRANTING SECURITY

Consider the following two common arrangements (do not worry about the kind of security interests involved just yet):

1. Quercus Ltd grants security by way of statutory charge over land to its creditor Bank. The statutory charge must be perfected 'twice': once by registration on the Land Register, and once by registration on the Register of Companies.
2. Silex Plc is the 100% shareholder of Quercus Ltd. It promises to pay Quercus Ltd's debt to Bank if Quercus cannot (this is called a guarantee). Silex Plc grants security for this promise by way of equitable mortgage of its shares in Quercus Ltd in favour of Bank. Equitable mortgages of shares need not be registered, so only the grant of security by Silex Plc *as company* need be registered against Silex Plc's entry on the Register of Companies. It is irrelevant that the shares are in a company that owns land.

The structure detailed in (2) is evidently more efficient for all parties because, if adopted on its own, it reduces the dealings with the public register, avoiding costs and delays.

(6) *Registering a mortgage of goods*: finally, but by no means exhaustively, we mention a particularly archaic but nevertheless common mode of perfecting security, this time non-possessory security over goods. Confusingly, this form of security (even if it really refers to a mortgage of goods) is called a **bill of sale**. The name derives from commercial practice in the Middle Ages, and refers to the way in which indeed the debtor sells the goods to the creditor (who takes legal title), but keeps possession of them for the debtor's use. This commercial practice was readily abused by debtors and the Victorians, being great fans of registers, enacted the Bills of Sale Act 1878 (BSA 1878) and the Bills of Sale (1878) Amendment Act 1882.

Perfection is achieved in a gloriously antiquated fashion, by submitting the relevant particulars to the registry located at the clerks' office of King's Bench, in the Royal Courts of Justice. The delivered particulars are stamped and key information is entered into a huge logbook that looks like it has been recovered from the shipping office of a seventeenth-century merchant. For this reason debts secured by bill of sale are called 'logbook loans.' People wishing to consult the register (usually me when I was a trainee) would have to do so by visiting the High Court and manually working through the texts in a draughty corner of the clerks' office waiting area.

Perfection occurs at the moment the delivered particulars are stamped by the clerk.[19] It can therefore occur that if two sets of particulars are delivered by competing creditors, one set posted after 4pm on Friday might reach the clerk's office the same day as particulars delivered by hand on Monday morning, and the clerk might stamp the hand-delivered particulars first, granting the security particularized priority in law, if not in fact. This is just one reason the Law Commission has described the Acts as 'outdated.'[20] The system also favours relative opacity—who really will pore through a physical logbook on the off chance of finding security in this day and age? The only reason I was ever sent to scrutinize the logbook was to investigate the convoluted transactions of high net worth individuals who were about to be subjected to a freezing injunction on account of alleged fraud. This is by no means the sole or even principal driver for use of bills of sale, but the system is manifestly open to abuse.

19 Bills of Sale Act 1878 s 10, confirmed *Nine Regions Ltd. (t/a Log Book Loans) v Office of Fair Trading* [2010] UKFTT 643 (GRC).

20 Law Commission, *Bills of Sale* (Law Com CP No. 225, 2015).

3.3.4 Enforcement and priorities

In the broadest terms, enforcement of security amounts to seizing the attached asset, if not already held, and selling it to realize its value, that value being applied to satisfy any outstanding secured liabilities, the remainder to be returned to the debtor. The practical advantages of seizure and repayment should not be underestimated; indeed, even the threat of seizure and realization may be enough to exert lawful negotiating pressure on a debtor long before actual default. It is not proposed to consider the technical detail of enforcement, such as the use of Law of Property Act 1925 receivers (who seize charged assets), court bailiffs, or insolvency administrators and liquidators. Of greater doctrinal interest is the relationship between secured creditors. We have seen, in our discussion of the **insolvency waterfall**, that security affords priority over unsecured creditors, which in practical terms means the secured creditor is paid first and in full before the unsecured creditors. How, though, does priority work as between secured creditors? Do they all rank pari passu and pro rata, and if not, how does the court determine which secured creditor's interest ranks prior?

The two basic rules, subject to a complex array of exceptions, are expressions of the same underlying logic:[21]

(1) As to **equitable** security interests (such as charges), the interest created first in time ranks prior to any created after (*qui prior est tempore potior est jure*).
(2) As to **legal** security interests (such as legal mortgages), no one may give a greater interest than he already has (the *nemo dat* rule, which you have seen before).

A little thought, as Goode and Gullifer explain, as to the *nemo dat* rule and one can see that if the debtor gives a legal security interest in an asset to a senior creditor first in time, whatever legal interest in that asset he thereafter gives to a junior creditor, that second interest must be reduced by the legal fact that the first interest has already been transferred away.[22] But then time is determinative of the greater and lesser interest, and so we recover the equitable rule.

The two rules should be kept separate for one good reason, however. There is a third rule, with which you will be familiar from your study of property law:

(3) A bona fide grantee of legal security interest for value without notice will **overreach** an equitable security interest even if the latter was granted earlier in time.

The following case, which is linked to the collapse of companies linked to disgraced tycoon Robert Maxwell, illustrates this point.

MACMILLAN INC v BISHOPSGATE INVESTMENT TRUST PLC (NO.3) [1995] 1 WLR 978 (ChD)[23]

Bishopsgate (BIT) held legal title in shares in a corporation Berlitz, Inc., as nominee for Macmillan (M). M therefore had an equitable interest in these shares. Subsequently, and

21 See the discussion of Lord Westbury LC in *Phillips v Phillips* (1861) 4 De Gex, Fisher & Jones 208, 45 ER 1164, 1166.

22 Gullifer (n 6) 5–04.

23 The case is heavily simplified and the legal aspects of priority were secondary: eight secured parties were involved, M and BIT were themselves part of Maxwell's empire, and the shares were subject to New York law so that significant conflict of laws issues were raised.

without M's knowledge, the share certificates and a signed stock transfer form were given to Crédit Suisse (CS) by way of security for a loan ultimately benefitting Robert Maxwell. CS needed only to date the form and submit it to Berlitz to obtain legal title, but did not do so. When Maxwell's business interests collapsed, M discovered what had happened and sought recovery of the shares. Initially, it obtained an interim injunction preventing CS from dating and submitting the stock transfer form to Berlitz. The injunction was later discharged, and CS was able to date and submit the form, obtaining legal title to the shares.

Held per Millett J: Before the collapse, CS possessed the necessary documentation to perfect a legal mortgage of the shares, but it had not done so. As equity treats as done what ought to have been done, CS had an equitable mortgage of the shares. Had CS been prevented from perfecting its security, its equitable interest would have competed with the equitable interest of M, and as M's equitable interest was prior in time, M would have been able to enforce its interest in the shares against CS.

However, the injunction had been lifted and CS had obtained legal title to the shares by way of security. Provided that at the relevant time CS had no notice of M's equitable interest, CS's legal title overreached M's equitable interest, leaving M with a mere personal claim against BIT for breach of fiduciary duty.

The relevant time for determining whether CS had notice was not when the transfer of legal title was effected, but when the equitable mortgage was created. On the facts, CS had no knowledge of M's interest when the equitable mortgage was created.

These basic rules seem clear enough, but the complexity begins to arise in virtue of the variety of rules specific to kinds of security, attached asset, and grantor. If we ask, which security interest is first in time, we must ask, which time is the relevant one? English law does not provide a universal answer.[24] It seems that if no further perfection step such as notice or registration is required, the security interest created prior in time prevails, but as we have seen, the notice and registration requirements are varied and overlapping. If a company grants a charge or mortgage, even one which normally need not be registered, the statutory requirement to register a charge granted by a company prevails. Statute provides for a holding period of 21 days in which to deliver details of the corporate security to the Registrar, with the effect that on registration the security subordinates other chargees who may have taken security in the meantime, even those without other notice of the first security interest.[25] Moreover, as between registration e.g. of an aircraft and of a company charge, the requirement for companies prevails in the sense that failure to register the company's grant renders the security ineffective against a liquidator, administrator or other chargees, irrespective of registration at the Civil Aviation Authority. The priority as between two or more secured creditors who all have failed to perfect their security is less than clear, and as we saw in *Macmillan*, the various rules as to notice applicable to property and its owner present further difficulties where notice is the priority point,[26] such as with a legal mortgage of a chose in action (see section 3.4.4). Add to this the possibility that creditors may agree to vary the usual priority rules, and English law on the timing of priorities is unsatisfactory.

24 For a detailed discussion of this convoluted area, cf Gullifer (n 6) 5–26 to 5–33.

25 Companies Act 2006 s 859(a).

26 By extension from *Dearle v Hall* (1828) 3 Russ 1.

3.3.5 Redemption

In some forms of security (as we shall shortly see), the debtor transfers legal title to the attached asset to the creditor; in others, he gives possession. This transfer of handing over gives an additional quality of security to the creditor, but the assumption is that once the debtor has repaid the secured liabilities, he should **redeem** title and/or possession back from the creditor, for surely the whole purpose of the security has come to an end. What, though, if the creditor refuses to retransfer title and/or return possession? What if debtor and creditor agree that the creditor can retain the asset?

It is the essence of a mortgage or pledge that in the eye of a court of equity it should be a mere security for money, and that no bargain can be validly made which will prevent the mortgagor or pledgor from redeeming on payment of what is due, including principal, interest, and costs. This is called the **equity of redemption** and has been expressed in the maxim *once a mortgage, always a mortgage*. It should be noted, however, that the equity extends to all forms of security, not just mortgages.

HOWARD v HARRIS (1683) 1 Vern 190; 22 ER 1074 (Ch)

Mr Howard borrowed £1,000 from Harris, secured by way of mortgage of his land, which meant that legal title was conveyed to Harris. As condition of the loan, it was agreed that if Mr Howard or his male heirs repay the principal and interest, they could redeem the land. Mr Howard, later realizing he would not have male heirs, willed his property to his wife. He subsequently died, and Mrs Howard sought to repay the debt to Harris and redeem the land. Harris refused to comply, claiming that on Mr Howard's death without male heirs, the mortgage had become irredeemable and the land his outright.

Held: Equity always questioned restrictions on the right to redeem, even voluntary, and could not countenance any restriction which converted a security into something it was not, such as a true sale. Mrs Howard was entitled to redeem the land.

The equity of redemption is extremely old, being traced back by Matthew of Paris at least to 1178 and the Lateran Council, which condemned usury and laid down that a creditor should, on repayment, restore a debtor's security.[27] The latter specification followed from the former general principle—the outright acquisition of the asset was regarded as the acquisition of loan interest in asset form, and thus one of the many ways merchants thought up to circumvent usury laws.[28] In favouring merchants, the common law was particularly harsh in this context. Where a loan agreement stipulated repayment of a precise sum on an exact day, and that failure to meet the exact requirements meant forfeiture of the security asset, the law would uphold the strict stipulation. Equity would have none of it; any attempt to prevent ('clog and fetter') a mortgagor's interest of redemption, by whatever indirect means, would be cut down.

Subsequently, the religious motivations for the equity of redemption fell into abeyance, but it continues to be a narrower principle of equity resting on the grounds that (1) logically, what is in substance a security is a security and not a true sale, whatever the 'form' it takes—a security grantor should be permitted to redeem; (2) equity will not uphold a bargain which is unconscionable e.g. because it is oppressive; and (3) equity will follow the common law where the law finds the security

27 Matthew of Paris, *Historia Major* (first published 1684, Rolls Series 2012) 114–16.

28 'A man shall not have interest for his money, and a collateral advantage besides for the loan of it.' *Jennings v Ward* (1705) 2 Vern 520, 23 ER 935.

agreement void or voidable. Within these limits, it is now possible to add collateral restrictions in secured financings.[29]

G&C KREGLINGER v NEW PATAGONIA MEAT AND COLD STORAGE CO LTD [1914] AC 25, [1911–13] All ER Rep 970 (HL)

In 1910, K agreed to lend to PNCS £10,000 at 6% interest, repayable September 1915, secured by floating charge (see section 3.5) on the assets of PNCS. PNCS was entitled to repay the loan at any earlier time and so redeem the charge at that point. It was further agreed that, until August 1915, K had a right of first refusal on all PNCS' sheepskins, the price to be the best price PNCS could obtain in London at any given time. If PNCS did sell the assets to a third party, K would receive 1% of the sale price.

In January 1913, PNCS repaid the loan and sought to argue that they were no longer bound by K's option to buy the sheepskins. In particular, PNCS argued that this right had been redeemed or, if it could not be, the option was a clog on the equity of redemption.

Held: the security agreement and the option for sale and purchase were wholly separate transactions. Considered in itself, there was no clog on redeeming the floating charge. The option agreement was a collateral contract, independent of the loan and security (even if business reasons had motivated taking the whole deal together) and was not brought to an end by the redemption of the charge.

Kreglinger is *the* modern authority, but the House of Lords understandably focused on collateral advantages and only gestured at the equity of redemption, not providing a precise statement of the limits of its application. Further judicial gloss was required, and the courts now look to the summary of the law set out by Morgan J in *Brighton & Hove City Council v Audus* [2009] EWHC 340 (Ch):

[46]. It is inherent in the concept of a mortgage or security interest that the borrower of money should be able to discharge the security interest, that is, to redeem the mortgage by paying the money and in that way performing the obligation performance of which is secured. At common law it was possible to include in a mortgage a contractual term which had the effect that the mortgagor would lose the right to redeem if he failed to repay the moneys due by a specified date. Equity regarded such a term as liable to work injustice and hardship and equity granted relief against the operation of such a contractual term by recognising an equitable right to redeem, notwithstanding non-compliance with the contractual term. . . . For present purposes, the modern law is stated in the speeches in the House of Lords in *G&C Kreglinger v New Patagonia Meat and Cold Storage Co Ltd* [1914] AC 25, [1911–13] All ER Rep 970. That decision restated some of the equitable rules and clarified the law in relation to suggested collateral advantages taken by the mortgagee from the mortgagor and relating to the circumstances in which the mortgagor could redeem the mortgage. This area of the law is often described by using the phrase 'clogs on the equity of redemption' but that phrase is not particularly helpful in identifying the detail of the relevant rules.

[47]. The relevant rules are threefold. The first is that a condition which is repugnant to the contractual right to redeem and the equitable right to redeem is void. The second rule is

29 *Biggs v Hoddinott* [1898] 2 Ch 307.

> that a condition which imposes a penalty in respect of the exercise of the equitable right to redeem, following a failure to exercise a contractual right to redeem, is void in equity. The third rule is that a provision which regulates or controls the right to redeem is invalid, if it is unconscionable.

The question of unconscionability—which you may remember as a vitiating factor in contract law—has been considered in several cases.[30] A fairly useful indication is provided by *Multiservice Bookbinding Ltd v Marden*, where it was held that a bargain could not be unfair and unconscionable unless one of the parties to it had imposed the objectionable terms in a morally reprehensible manner, that is to say, in a way which affects conscience. It was not enough to show that the term was 'unreasonable.'[31]

Study question: W lends GBP100k to S, repayable within five years, to finance S's theatre business. The loan is secured by mortgage over the theatre. In consideration, S will pay (1) 6% interest monthly, and (2) two-thirds of S's theatre ticket receipts for the next five years. S may prepay the loan at any time. A year later S prepays the GBP100k plus all interest due. W refuses to release the security, arguing that he has not received the two-thirds ticket sales for the remaining four years. Is the five years of ticket sales condition a clog on the equity of redemption, or a wholly independent arrangement?[32]

3.3.6 Distinguishing so-called personal security

In modern parlance, the word 'security' is reserved for the four kinds of consensual security to be detailed in the next section and for the floating charge. Roughly speaking, these all involve property rights and in the older cases where often referred to as 'real security.' The epithet was required because in the nineteenth century judges felt that certain other practices gave security in the vernacular sense of mitigating the risk of non-payment, but they did not strictly confer a property right. Rather, these other security practices created additional personal obligations (additional debts). The classic examples are the guarantee (including the bond) and indemnity. For example, with a guarantee, P may owe GBP1,000 to Q, and R may guarantee to Q that should P not pay, R will pay in his stead (and can be sued if R does not). To distinguish this 'security' from real security, the courts spoke of 'personal security,' for the claim against Q was a personal claim.[33]

We do not propose to delve deeply into the realm of guarantees and indemnities; many of the interesting cases arise in the context of international sales and construction, even though guarantees and indemnities are a standard feature of London-style financings. For our purposes, we will just indicate the nature of guarantees and indemnities, and later we will see how personal security helps risk mitigation in a practical context.

We should first note that, as with contracts for interests in land, guarantees must be made under hand. The magic words from Statute of Frauds 1677 section 4:

> No action shall be brought . . . to charge the defendant upon any special promise to answer for the debt, default or miscarriage of another person . . . unless the agreement upon which

---

30 *Cityland and Property (Holdings) Ltd. v Dabrah* [1968] Ch 166, [1967] 2 All ER 639; *Multiservice Bookbinding Ltd. v Marden* [1979] Ch 84, [1978] 2 All ER 489; *Knightsbridge Estates Trust Ltd. v Byrne* [1939] Ch 441, [1938] 4 All ER 618 (CA).

31 *Multiservice Bookbinding Ltd. v Marden* (n 30) 110.

32 Hint: read the discussion of *Santley v Wilde* [1899] 2 Ch 474 (CA), in *Bradley v Carritt* [1903] AC 253 (HL).

33 This older terminology comes up again when we discuss securities in Chapter 8.

> such action shall be brought, or some memorandum or note thereof, shall be in writing and signed by the party to be charged therewith or some other person thereunto by him lawfully authorised.

In practice the guarantee is normally included in the CFA, thus meeting the requirement. We have quoted the Statute of Frauds because it also provides the tradition definition of guarantee.

ESSENTIAL DEFINITION: GUARANTEE, INDEMNITY

A **guarantee** by G (the 'guarantor' or 'surety') is a special promise to a creditor C to answer for the debt, default or miscarriage of a C's debtor D's. The obligations could be contractual, debts or arising through tort or restitution.[34]

A **performance guarantee** makes clear G will ensure that D performs his obligations, or G will do it for D.

Where D fails to perform, normally C is expected to make demand that D perform, failing which C may demand that G perform in D's stead. However, a **first demand guarantee** permits C to go directly to G and demand performance without asking D first (provided it is time for performance under the underlying contract).

An **indemnity** is distinguished from a guarantee as follows: a guarantee is a secondary obligation which ensures performance of another's primary obligation, such as payment; an indemnity is itself a primary obligation to remedy some identified loss. An indemnified party is thus said to be 'held harmless' of any losses to the extent clearly provided for under the terms of the indemnity. It matters not that the losses arise from the breach of another's obligation e.g. under contract—the indemnity is an independent primary obligation.[35]

Guarantees and indemnities arise commonly in secured financings, especially financing of corporate groups. In such situations a bank may prefer to lend into an operating subsidiary, not least because the operating subsidiary owns the principal income-generating assets of the group. That loan will be secured using the mechanisms we examine in the following sections, but additionally the bank will seek 'personal security' from the parent company by means of a guarantee and indemnity. Why both a guarantee and indemnity? A practising lawyer will respond why have only one protection when you can have two. The granting of a parent company guarantee and indemnity is illustrated below, with the dotted circles highlighting secured assets. It is once again highly recommended that you draw diagrams when dealing with financing structures.

This deployment of the guarantee and indemnity will be examined again in Chapter 4 where we look at practical structuring concerns. For completeness, below is part of some example drafting from a CFA for a group of companies. As an exercise: (1) identify which elements create the guarantee and which the indemnity; (2) once you have read the chapter, come back and suggest an explanation for the function of the 'continuing guarantee' subclause.

34 *Moschi v Lep Air Services Ltd.* [1973] AC 331 (HL) [347]–[348] (Lord Diplock).

35 *Pitts v Jones* [2007] EWCA Civ 1301, [2008] QB 706.

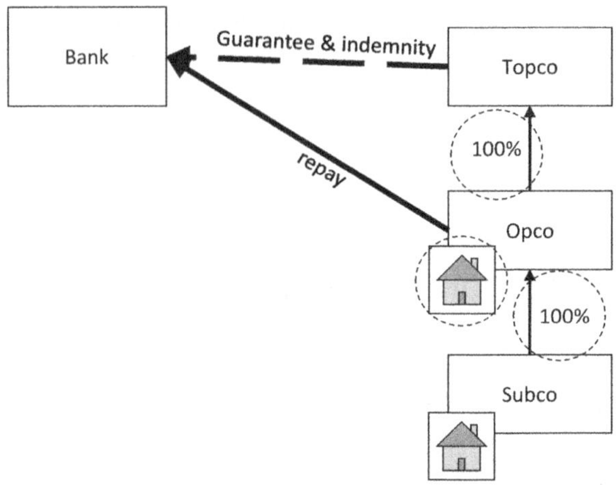

Figure 3.1 A simple guarantee and indemnity structure in a corporate group financing

EXAMPLE: PART OF A CFA'S GUARANTEE AND INDEMNITY CLAUSE

Cl 18.1 Guarantee and indemnity

Each Guarantor irrevocably and unconditionally jointly and severally:

(a) guarantees to each Finance Party[36] punctual performance by each Borrower of all that Borrower's obligations under the Finance Documents;[37]

(b) undertakes with each Finance Party that whenever a Borrower does not pay any amount when due under or in connection with any Finance Document, that Guarantor shall immediately on demand pay that amount as if it were the principal obligor; and

(c) agrees with each Finance Party that if any obligation guaranteed by it is or becomes unenforceable, invalid or illegal, it will, as an independent and primary obligation, indemnify that Finance Party immediately on demand against any cost, loss or liability it incurs as a result of a Borrower not paying any amount which would, but for such unenforceability, invalidity or illegality, have been payable by it under any Finance Document on the date when it would have been due. The amount payable by a Guarantor under this indemnity will not exceed the amount it would have had to pay under this Clause 18 if the amount claimed had been recoverable on the basis of a guarantee.

Cl 18.2 Continuing guarantee

This guarantee is a continuing guarantee and will extend to the ultimate balance of sums payable by any Obligor[38] under the Finance Documents, regardless of any intermediate payment or discharge in whole or in part.

---

36 i.e. principally the lenders and their agents.

37 i.e. principally the CFA and the security agreement (see the following).

38 i.e. sums owed by the borrowers *and* the guarantors and indemnifiers.

There are many areas of risk which may see a guarantee fail to be enforceable but which we simply do not have space to cover these here. One though should be flagged as it is a significant risk and one oft forgotten. Just as security can be released 'by accident,' so too a guarantee can be released by unwittingly tinkering with the underlying primary obligation. It is a well-established rule that any variation of the underlying obligations of the primary obligor which could prejudice the guarantor will, unless the guarantor consents, discharge the guarantee.[39] The key policy concern expressed in the cases is the natural one that if creditor debtor and primary obligor wish to change the nature of a guaranteed obligation, the guarantor should be consulted.[40] It is possible to so draft a CFA guarantee to include prior consent to a possible variation,[41] but the better practice is to do that which the law counsels: have the guarantor also execute any deed of variation of a CFA.

3.4 Real security interests

Having surveyed some of the general principles of security, it is now long past time to look at the kinds of real security interests recognized by English law. At this point it has become traditional to cite Millett LJ's (as he then was) formalistic statement in *re Coslett (Contractors) Ltd* [1998] Ch 495 (CA):

> There are only four kinds of consensual security known to English law: (i) pledge; (ii) contractual lien; (iii) equitable charge and (iv) mortgage. A pledge and a contractual lien both depend on the delivery of possession to the creditor. The difference between them is that in the case of a pledge the owner delivers possession to the creditor as security, whereas in the case of a lien the creditor retains possession of goods previously delivered to him for some other purpose. Neither a mortgage nor a charge depends on the delivery of possession. The difference between them is that a mortgage involves a transfer of legal or equitable ownership to the creditor, whereas an equitable charge does not. [508(F–G)]

These dicta are helpful, so let us examine each of the four interests in turn. A note of warning: do not be misled by nomenclature; focus on substance of each security interest as described. For example, and English pledge is not a civil law system pledge (*Pfand, nantissement*, or otherwise), and an English statutory mortgage of land is not even a mortgage by strict English standards.

3.4.1 Possessory security I: the pledge

Imagine Bob asks to borrow GBP50 from Shay, which he will repay 'when he can.' Shay is unconvinced that Bob will repay but says that if Bob will hand over his copy of Connelly's *Finance Law* until he repays, then he is willing to lend. Shay makes clear that if Bob does not repay within a year, Shay will take the book and sell it. If he receives more than GBP50 back from this sale, he will pay the surplus to Bob. If Bob repays in time, he will hand the book back.

This arrangement is colloquially called a **pawn** (whence *pawnbroker*)[42] and legally termed a **pledge**.

Before we turn to the legal mechanics, let us consider the practical benefits of this manner of taking security:

---

39 *Holme v Brunskill* (1878) 3 QBD 495, confirming *Croydon Gas Company v Dickenson* (1876) 2 CPD 46 at 51.

40 *Holme v Brunskill* per Cotton LJ at 505. See also *National Bank of Nigeria Ltd. v Alowesi* [1964] 1 WLR 1311.

41 *Hackney Empire Ltd. v Aviva Insurance UK Ltd. (formerly t/a Norwich Union Insurance Ltd)* [2012] EWCA Civ 1716, obiter that even if the variation had been prejudicial, it would have been permissible within the indulgence permitted by the guarantee clause.

42 Though in fact 'pawn' was used in the seventeenth-century cases: *Mores v Conham* (1609) 74 ER 946.

(1) Shay has the book under her physical control: she possesses it. If Bob fails to repay the debt, she need do nothing more than sell the book in her possession. There is no need to approach Bob, and certainly no need to enforce any right against him. Her right to sell the book and the factual reality of her physical power to do so coincide.

(2) Bob does not have the book under his physical control. Had Bob retained the book he might have been tempted to sell it, and while it is not impossible that Bob sell the book without delivering it to the third-party buyer, it will be harder for him to convince that third party to buy if he cannot produce the book for inspection.

(3) From a third party's perspective, if the third party has observed the act of pledging, or if not at least had the wit to ask Bob to permit them to inspect the book before buying, then they will be aware that there is something legally 'questionable' about property in the book. The publicity afforded by handing over possession to Shay acts as a 'red flag' to third buyers, thus further ring-fencing Shay's security and further motivating Bob to repay.

It is worthwhile labouring this naïve account of the pledge because it is foremost a socially developed practice, appearing to be the oldest form of security in several jurisdictions.[43] As such, when courts began to analyse the legal nature of the pledge in England, for example, it was not entirely clear where pledges fitted into the accepted categories of property. In short, is a pledge a property right in the hands of the pledgee?

MORES v CONHAM (1609) 74 ER 946 (KB)

Mores was owed £100 by one Lovet, who granted a pledge to Mores of goods. Later, Conham approached Mores offering to pay off Lovet's debt if Mores would in consideration deliver to Conham the goods pledged by Lovet. Mores accepted the contract, but later failed to deliver the goods. A question arose as to whether Mores had any property in the goods that he could transfer to Conham.

Held (Foster J dissenting): That a pledgee (Mores here) has a 'special property' in the pledged things which amounted to a power to hold, if appropriate maintain, and, on failure to repay, sell them to realize their value. This special property was stronger than a mere contractual right to detain the goods and so could be transferred to a third party. But no one can give more or other right than he himself has, and so a pledgee cannot transfer absolute title to third parties (until such time as the power of sales becomes exercisable).

As Mores was not yet permitted to sell the goods, no title transferred to Conham under their contract. Conham has a purely personal claim against Mores for breach of contract in failing to deliver the goods promised, a claim sounding in damages.[44]

It seems, therefore, that a pledge does transfer to the pledgee a special kind of property. This property right is extremely limited and seems to extend to a power to detain the property, to protect that detention against third parties, and sell it to realize its value for the purpose only of discharging the debt it secures. There may also be a right to maintain and use the property. For example, if the pledged property is a dairy cow, the majority in *Mores v Conham* considered it sensible that the pledgee be permitted to milk it (for the cow would be harmed if this was not done), but if the property

43 Alfred William Brian Simpson, *A History of the Land Law* (2nd edn, Clarendon Press 1986) 141.

44 I have modernized this: in the original the judges speak of an *assumpsit* which broadly was the forerunner of a contractual obligation 'assumed' by a party.

were clothing or some other thing that would be worn out by use, then there was no right to use it. On this, however, Forster J explicitly disagreed. On the other hand, a distinguishing limitation of the pledge is its possessory nature—if the pledgee willingly gives up possession, there can be no pledge.[45]

You may wish to think of the pledge this way: of the bundle of rights the pledgor has with respect to a thing, he has extracted the smallest rights possible from that bundle and granted these to the pledgee. The concern in *Mores v Conham* was that Mores was attempting to transfer to Conham more (or other) rights than he had received from Lovet, something impossible in property law. This rule, by the way, is often known by the Roman law maxim: *nemo plus juris ad alium transferre potest quam ipse haberet.*[46] This point is worth labouring because it is the transfer of often limited rights which is so central to a great deal of financial transactions, even if pledges themselves are uncommonly used in the kind of secured financing which features in this book.

Mores v Conham was approved in the leading case of *Donald v Suckling*, which contained a thorough review nor only of the common precedents, but also civil law doctrine and Roman law as well. This case tests our understanding of the principle in *Mores v Conham.*

DONALD v SUCKLING (1865–66) LR 1 QB 585

Donald had invested in the British Slate Company, and this investment was represented by a special kind of valuable debt instrument, called a debenture. Donald was indebted to Simpson, and so in August 1864 he agreed with Simpson that he would make due payment by February. To secure this debt, Donald pledged to Simpson his debentures, with an explicit power that if payment was not made on the due date, Simpson could sell the debentures to discharge the liability. Subsequently, but before February, Simpson became indebted to Suckling, and as security for this second debt, pledged the same debentures to Suckling. On hearing this, Donald sued Suckling, claiming that Simpson had nullified the pledge and that Suckling was wrongly detaining Donald's property.

Held (Shee J dissenting): Donald had not yet repaid his debt and so the pledge to Simpson remained in force. Simpson had transferred to Suckling no more right than he himself had, i.e. a power to detain the debentures and sell them to realize their value and discharge a debt if the secured liabilities were not discharged. The pledge and re-pledge were therefore both valid and Donald's claim failed.

Donald v Suckling confirmed *Mores v Conham*'s property law analysis of the pledge, but also provided greater clarity regarding the interaction between property law and contract. Cockburn CJ laid great store by terms of the contract for pledge, and, combined with Blackburn J's recourse to market practice regarding re-pledging, this strongly suggests that the rights of the pledgee can vary from pledge to pledge. If what is pledged is a unique work of art, it may well be a term of the contract of pledge that the pledgee may not re-pledge the property, but market practice concerning debentures, bills of exchange, and so forth strongly suggested that re-pledging was implicitly permitted unless expressly negatived.

45 See the Australian case of *TEA (1983) v Uniting Church (NSW) Trust Association* [1985] Victorian Rep 139.

46 As given in the case note: 'no one can transfer more or other right than he himself has.'

A further contractual aspect concerns a question which has no doubt occurred to you, and which motivated Donald: what happens if the pledgor does repay his debt on the due date, only to find the pledgee unable to return the pledged property because it is in the hands of a third party? It is always worth considering alternative hypothetical scenarios—here let us use Donald, Simpson and Suckling once more:

(1) Before the repayment date, Simpson purports to *sell* the pledged property to Suckling. Simpson is not absolute owner of the pledged property, so he is attempting to transfer something he does not have. Donald remains the true owner of the property and can seek its recovery from Suckling. But is the property still pledged? Attempting the outright sale of the pledged property is wholly inconsistent with the contract for pledge between Donald and Simpson. This contract of pledge can be treated as at an end and Donald can seek return of the property immediately. Donald's debt to Simpson is now unsecured. For his part, Suckling has a claim against Simpson for breach of contract of sale, for Simpson failed to transfer title.

(2) Donald repays on the repayment date but discovers Simpson has validly re-pledged the property to Suckling and is unable to return the property to Donald. As to property law, it seems Suckling has a valid if limited property right in the re-pledged property as extensive as that of Simpson i.e. Suckling can detain the property and sell it if Simpson fails to pay. Donald is barred from having the property returned because the right of detention rests with Suckling. As a matter of contract law, Simpson promised to return the pledged property on repayment, and has failed to do so. Donald is entitled to damages for breach of contract against Simpson.

(3) Donald repays on the repayment date but discovers that Simpson has invalidly re-pledged the property to Suckling in virtue of an express term of the contract of pledge prohibiting any re-pledge. Simpson is now unable to return the property. As to property law, Simpson's special property was more limited than a 'normal' pledge, and so he did not have a right of alienation of the pledged property. As such Suckling did not receive a special property and is simply holding it for Donald, who may claim its return from Suckling. As to contract law, Donald may sue Simpson for breach of the prohibition on re-pledging (receiving nominal damages if Donald actually recovers his property from Suckling), and Suckling may sue Simpson for failing to (re-)pledge the property as promised.

Apart from the market practice justification referenced by Blackburn J, the outcome in scenario (2)—the precipitous fear of which evidently excising Donald in the actual case—may be justified on the following ground. In giving up his special property, Donald voluntarily restricted for a certain time his absolute title, losing his right of possession (and use) and his right to realize the sale value of the asset. He may feel that Simpson's re-pledge is an interference with his property, but he voluntarily gave up just that subset of his rights with which Simpson subsequently dealt. Donald has lost nothing more than he already had as a result of pledging the assets. Moreover, had Donald wished to retain control over a possible re-pledge, he needed have done no more than explicitly prohibit the same in the contract of pledge.

3.4.2 Possessory security II: the contractual lien

The cases show that parties have often confused contractual liens with pledges. At their heart both are possessory: the party to be paid detains certain tangible property pending payment by the property owner. Yet there remains a critical distinction: a pledge vests a (special) property right in the pledgee; a lien does not. Rather, a lien creates a purely personal right as between what are called the bailor and bailee. The confusion arises because that right is nothing more than the right to retain possession of certain property of the bailor—something that looks to the layperson practically the same as a pawn.

The cases highlight a further distinction: with a pledge possession is given over from the beginning of the transaction with the principal purpose of securing some debt; with a lien, possession is given for some other reason to the bailee, and only subsequently, when a debt has arisen, does the bailee now retain its possession against the bailor pending satisfaction of the debt. This is just what happens in the most basic form of lien, the **possessory lien**.

EXAMPLE OF A POSSESSORY LIEN

L makes picture frames. W contracts with L that L will make picture frames for certain valuable artworks owned by W, and W promises to pay £1,000 on completion. For this purpose, W delivers up the paintings into L's possession at his workshop. L completes the frames and demands payment, but W wrongfully refuses to pay. L tells W that he will not deliver up the now framed paintings until payment is forthcoming. Legally, we say that L now has a possessory lien over the framed paintings.

This example stresses the manner in which a lien comes about only after a bailee has taken possession for some other purpose, but we should never lose sight of the other key feature of a lien: it does not amount to a property right in the things possessed, as the following case illustrates.

LEGG v EVANS AND WHEELTON (1840) 6 Meeson & Welsby 36, 151 ER 311

Legg was contracted by Williams to frame certain paintings. When Williams failed to pay and repay other debts to Legg, it was agreed that Legg could hold the framed paintings pending satisfaction of the debts. In a rather questionable development, Williams obtained a judgment in default against Legg and directed the Sheriff of Middlesex to seize the framed paintings, claiming that they were Legg's property. The framed pictures were seized and in fact sold. Legg complained that the Sheriff had no authority to seize the frames because a Sheriff could only seize goods that could be rightfully sold.

Held by Parke B:

> If we consider the nature of a lien, and the right which it confers, it will be evident that it cannot form the subject-matter of a sale. A lien is a personal right, which cannot be parted with, and continues only so long as the possessor holds the goods, It is clear, therefore, that the sheriff cannot sell and interest of this description, which is a mere personal interest in the goods. . . .
>
> Here, the interest cannot be transferred to any other individual: it continues only as long as the holder keeps possession of the subject-matter of the lien, either by himself or his servant. Then, as the sheriff cannot sell, neither, by the general rule of law, can he seize: and there must, therefore, be judgment for the plaintiff.

Legg was awarded damages.[47]

47 In the amount of the sale value of the framed paintings, being the damages payable for the tort of conversion (interference with his rights—the lien).

Notice that Parke B focused not on the frames but solely on the rights at play in the case: the proprietary right of Williams in the framed paintings (they were Williams' property) and the personal right of Legg against Williams to detain his property.[48]

To see this an analogy might be in order. Suppose Williams owned land and that at he contracted with Legg that Legg would be irrevocably permitted ('licensed') to come onto the land to paint pictures for a period of one month in consideration of Legg paying GBP5. After two weeks, Williams locks his gates and excludes Legg from the land. Legg sues. In such a situation the law does not regard Legg as having any property rights in the land; Williams is as absolute an owner of that land as English law can contemplate. Save in very unusual circumstances where the court exercises its residual prerogative, the law will not force Williams to reopen his gates and permit Legg access. Legg has no relationship to the land; all he has is a personal right against Williams to be granted access. What this means is that in suing Williams, all Legg is entitled to are damages for any losses caused by Williams breaching his obligation to Legg. Put starkly, Legg is not entitled to *the right in the land*; he is entitled to the value equivalent to not being allowed on the land *by Williams*.

This example of the difference between proprietary and personal rights is easier to grasp because the distinction between the two rights is brought out by Williams doing something—refusing a license to enter land—which we would regard as indicative of property ownership: excluding others from possession. When we map this distinction over to liens we have to trust our fundamental principles, for in the case of the lien it is Legg, as personal right holder, who is doing the exclusion—he is excluding Williams as property owner from possession. This seems counterintuitive, but a narrow focus on the detained property perhaps obscures the true picture. It seems Legg's detention consists in two components:

(1) On the one hand, Legg's detention of William's property amounts to no more than this: Williams could demand delivery up of his own property from Legg. Were Legg to refuse to deliver up the property, Williams could sue in the tort of conversion and seek an order for delivery up. However, where a lien subsists, Legg now has a defence against such a claim—he can refuse delivery up until payment.[49]

(2) On the other hand, Legg's refusal to deliver up would be meaningless if Williams could actually (lawfully) recover his own property with Legg's input. An additional feature of detention is important: that Legg uses his rights in property he does own to prevent that access. Strictly speaking, Legg is not directly preventing Williams' possession of the detained goods, but indirectly so by preventing access to them through Legg's property. To see this, imagine that Legg placed the paintings in an old-fashioned iron safe and locked the door with a key. If Williams were to demand his paintings, Legg could respond that he is welcome to them. Williams could try the safe door, discover it locked, and demand the key. At this point Legg could say, 'the paintings are yours, but you shall not have my key.' Extend the safe by analogy to Legg's workshop or a bailee's warehouse and one sees its generality. And from this, one sees why, when a bailee such as Legg loses possession, the lien is extinguished, for it is akin to emptying out the safe: Legg could keep the empty safe locked forever after, as is his right, but the act would be futile with respect to the formerly detained paintings.

48 Interestingly, in *Legg v Evans*, Parke B seems to have entertained the idea that the sheriff could have seized Legg's personal right, but quickly concluded that a lien is by its very nature incapable of seizure/sale because it can only subsist when the things subject to the lien are possessed by the bailee and is destroyed at the point of seizure/sale. Compare, as Parke B does at 42, a situation where Legg would have hired the frames from Williams. Then in this case Legg's right would be for the possession and use of the frames for a certain time, and the sheriff could have seized that right, for he could have sold the possession and use for the remaining time of the hire agreement (at which point the purchaser would be obligated to return the frames) without destroying the right.

49 *Richards v Symons* (1845) 8 QB 90, 115 ER 808.

The general thrust of *Legg v Evans*, then, is that we distinguish a lien from a pledge, because a pledge grants the pledgee a special property, whereas a lien confers only a personal right (or better, immunity) to refuse to deliver up property until payment. Yet it seems this distinction becomes very blurred in practice.

> ### *ROGERS v KENNAY* (1846) 9 QB 592, 115 ER 1401
>
> Rowe, a builder, obtained an advance of payment from Rogers, and as security for this he deposited various materials on Rogers' land, and it was agreed that if repayment failed to occur, Rogers could sell the materials to meet the outstanding debt. Kennay successfully sued Rogers for an unrelated debt, and sought enforcement, a sheriff seizing the materials on Rogers' land. Rogers sued Kennay for conversion of the materials, arguing that he had a special property in them.
>
> *Held* per Lord Denman CJ: '*Legg v Evans* . . . was a case much considered [in argument] and is directly on point.'
>
> Per Patteson J, Williams J concurring: '[In *Legg v Evans*] Parke B. said that "any person having a right to the possession of goods may bring trover in respect of the conversion of them, and allege them to be his property" and lien, as an immediate right of possession, was held to constitute such a property.'

Rogers appears to be authority for the proposition that a lien *is* a special property and not just a personal right, and thus much closer conceptually to a pledge than we might think. Yet this authority seems questionable. First, the quotation on which Patteson J relies is from an interjection Parke B makes during argument;[50] it does not form part of his judgment, which was quoted at length above. Moreover, Parke B was responding to an argument about procedure, being whether a bailee could bring a claim for conversion of detained goods. Combined with the final judgment of Parke B, which explicitly states a lien is a personal right, might it not be that Parke B is simply pointing out that for procedural purposes a bailee may 'allege' property in the goods. In other words, the allegation of property is a legal fiction for the purposes of maintaining a claim for conversion.

Second, the greater part counsels' argument in *Rogers v Kennay* concerned pledge and the special property this confers. Indeed, the plaintiff's case was that it had a property right and given the deployment of authority on pledges, seems to have anchored his claim in a pledge. It was the defendant who sought to argue that the matter concerned a mere lien.[51] Looking at the facts of the case, the materials were expressly handed over to secure a debt and for no other purpose: by our definition surely nothing other than a pledge. It seems, however, that the court did not feel it necessary to decide on whether there was a pledge or a lien; it sufficed to decide that even if Rogers had merely a lien, he had enough 'property' to maintain the action against Kennay for taking possession of the materials.

One corollary of Parke B's judgment is that the 'simple' lien in *Legg v Evans* carries with it no right to sell the goods, whereas a pledgee as a matter of law may always sell the pawn when the debt is due. In *Rogers v Kennay*, by contrast, such a right of sale on default of payment was created by

50 *Rogers v Kennay* (1846) 9 QB 592, 115 ER 1401 [41].
51 ibid 593.

express agreement. An agreement extending the rights and powers of a possessory lien converts it into a **contractual lien**.

DEFINITION: CONTRACTUAL LIEN

A possessory lien created by a contract, and so a truly consensual security.

As with a 'simple' possessory lien, possession must have been given over for some purpose other than securing a debt, with the contract providing that the lien only arise when a debt falls due.

Having introduced the possibility that a bailee may in certain circumstances sell the detained property and realize its value, it will have occurred to you that our basic notion of a lien has evolved in a direction which brings it closer still to the pledge. How much closer? Is a possessory security which permits the secured party to sell the detained property not equivalent to a pledge? Surely the right to alienate (i.e. transfer) is a key marker of a property right? The next case draws a fine distinction.

GREAT EASTERN RAILWAY CO v LORD'S TRUSTEE [1909] AC 109 (HL)

Lord was a coal merchant in Norwich and was supplied coal from London which was regularly transported by the Great Eastern Railway. It was a term of the contract of carriage that:

> (3) The company [Gt. E. Rly] . . . have a continual lien upon all . . . goods, minerals, articles and things hauled or conveyed on their lines, or which shall be at any time upon the railway or upon any ground allotted by or rented of the company for all tolls, rates, charges and moneys which shall be or become due or payable to the company . . . and the company to be at liberty from time to time and in such manner as they shall think fit, to sell and dispose of all or any of such . . . goods, minerals, articles and things in order to satisfy any such lien.

Subsequently Lord rented premises for coal storage in a railway freight yard, the premises being owned (as part of the yard) by the Great Eastern Railway. Lord fell into arrears to Great Eastern Railway, which took back its premises from Lord by changing the locks and preventing access to the coal stored therein. Lord's trustee in bankruptcy argued (A) if there had been a possessory lien, it had been extinguished when the company delivered the coal to Lord's store; (B) alternatively, that if this was a consensual security arrangement if was void because the legal formalities for a transfer of property to the company in the coal had not been satisfied; and (C) the power of sale in cl 3 was evidence that what had been granted to Great Eastern Railway by the agreement was a property right.

Held: (A) on the facts the Great Eastern Railway had not unconditionally delivered up the coal to Lord—the contract was clear that coal stored on land rented from the Great Eastern Company continued to be subject to the same possessory lien as subsisted while that coal was being transported.

(B) on a true construction of the contract no property had ever been intended to be transferred to the Great Eastern Railway. All the railway company had was a personal right against Lord and his successors to detain the coal, which remained entirely Lord's property, pending satisfaction of the debt.

(C) Again, on a true construction of the contract, Lord remained absolute owner of the coal. Clause 3 *authorized* the railway company, in certain circumstances, to act as Lord's agent and sell Lord's coal on Lord's behalf, the proceeds to be used, at Lord's direction in the contract, to meet any arrears.

The arrangement in *Great Eastern Rly v Lord's Trustee* was distinct from a pledge because no property was transferred, and remained a lien and not any other interest because the chain of bailee possession was not broken from the point of carriage, through the point of debts becoming due, to the point which Lord's Trustee sued for return of the coal. It is this latter distinction to which we now turn. Can a creditor purport, in a contract, to take a lien over goods which they do not possess before the debt becomes payable? And if not, have they created any security interest at all?

RE COSLETT (CONTRACTORS) LTD [1998] Ch 495 (CA)

Mid-Glamorgan County Council, as creditor, had contracted with Coslett Ltd for certain environmental coal-washing works. The contract between the parties provided, by clause 53.2, that all plant, goods and material were, when on site, deemed to be the property of the council. Clause 63.1 granted the council two rights: that if the contractor went into liquidation or abandoned the contract the council could enter the site and expel the contractor but without releasing it from any of its responsibilities under the contract, and that, in the event of the company being expelled

first, the council could retain possession of the plant and use it to complete the works without further payment to the company; and

second, the council could sell plant on completion of the works as well as plant not required to complete the works and to apply the proceeds of sale towards whatever sums might be or become due from the company under the contract.

Coslett Ltd subsequently became insolvent and the council expelled it from the site. Coslett Ltd's administrator demanded return of the plant and machinery which it regarded as Coslett Ltd's property.

Held: (A) on a true construction of the contract, cl 53.2 only 'deemed' the plant and machinery to be property of the council and did not actually transfer title. The fact that cl 53.2 applied indiscriminately to plant and machinery which belonged to sub-contractors also, i.e. title holders not party to the contract, strongly indicated that the clause did not intend formally to transfer title.

(B) the council's contractual right to retain possession in order to complete the works did not constitute an equitable charge (see below). One important reason given for this finding was that in the case of an equitable charge (as with a mortgage and a pledge, but unlike a contractual lien) property and/or possession is given for the purposes of a securing the debt. In this instance, however, it had been explicitly given for the purposes of completing the works, not for securing a debt should it become payable.

(C) So, did cl 63.1 constitute a contractual lien in that possession was granted for one reason, but later came to secure an unpaid debt? The judgment was no: for a possessory lien, as we have seen, bailee possession must continue from initial receipt through to the debt falling due and thereafter until repayment (or at least suit by the bailor). But in this case Coslett Ltd had full possession and use of the plant and machinery throughout the works right up until the point when they were expelled from the site for insolvency. There could be no lien in this case.

(D) However, cl 63.1 did create a new security interest at the time of expulsion because it granted a right of exclusive possession and sale of all plant and machinery on the site *at the moment of expulsion*. We will return to the nature of this new security interest when we examine floating charges (see section 3.2). For the time being, it suffices to note the CA's reasoning on one key point: that up until expulsion, Coslett Ltd could take plant and machinery onto and off the site at will further underscoring that the council lacked the requisite possession of these things to constitute a lien. It was only when expulsion occurred that the security attached to whatever plant and machinery happened to be on the site at that moment.

3.4.3 Study questions: possessory security

(1) R is in the habit of grazing his cow in S's field, paying a small fee in consideration to S. Subsequently, R becomes indebted to S and so they agree that the cow will remain with S 'wherever she may be' as 'security' for R's debt. One day R seizes the cow from S's field. S discovers the cow missing and after a short search finds the cow being led by R down a public road to R's farm. R refuses to return the cow and, when S sues for trespass against the goods, R argues that S has no right because he has no possession.
  (a) What kind of security, if any, is described in the facts?
  (b) Evaluate the merit of R's defence that S has lost any right to demand back the cow.

(2) T gives possession of goods to U as security for future debts. T runs up a large debt, and after some chasing by U, T writes a cheque to U in payment of the full sum. Satisfied, U returns the goods to T's possession. Subsequently, T's cheque is dishonoured, and U demands return of the goods.
  (a) What kind of security, if any, is described in the facts?
  (b) Is U entitled to return of the goods?

Hint: Have a look at the Australian cases of *Broad v Commissioner of Stamp Duties* [1980] 2 NSWLR 40; *TEA (1983) v Uniting Church (NSW) Trust Association* [1985] Victorian Rep 139, for inspiration. Would an English court decide in the same way?

3.4.4 Non-possessory security I: the mortgage

As we have noted, one way of dividing the kinds of security is into possessory and non-possessory security, and possessory security is taken by physical delivery of the chose in possession to the secured party. An alternative mode of granting security is not to hand over possession, but to transfer ownership, that is, legal or equitable title in the thing. The transfer is subject to two key provisos: first, that the new owner may have recourse to the thing, including by seizing possession of the thing on a default, in order to satisfy the secured liability, and second, the debtor is entitled to retransfer of ownership on satisfaction of the debt (a retransfer which in any event occurs in equity in virtue of redemption).

It is worth highlighting two confusions or misconceptions students often have about mortgages:

(1) It is perfectly possible for a chose in possession (a tangible thing) to be mortgaged. A mortgage is a transfer of title, and that could be title to a chose in possession, a chose in action, and anything else the law may care to recognize as property.[52] All that need happen is that title is transferred; possession remains with the mortgagor (debtor). It is only possessory security which is restricted as to things over which it can be granted—being inherently possessory it can only be granted over choses in possession.

(2) British vernacular confusingly uses the word 'mortgage' for a transaction which legally is not a mortgage. The difference is crucial: The British vernacular term 'mortgage' refers to the security British homeowners grant to lenders funding the purchase price of their residential property. This is not a mortgage at law. Rather, this security is a statutory creation of the Law of Property Act 1925[53] and is technically a statutory charge[54] (see the next section). Importantly, this statutory charge does not confer any ownership on the lender; ownership remains with the borrowers. A 'true' mortgage must involve a transfer of title.

Whereas the merit of possessory security is the practical power afforded by physical possession to the exclusion of others, the strength of the mortgage is the legal respect of mortgagee's title to the thing.

Yet this strength is also the legal mortgage's greatest weakness: it may be wholly inappropriate for a lender to become owner of the debtor's assets, and indeed it might open up the new owner to potential liability, or produce other unintended consequences. Scottish property and so security law is very different from English law, but the following modern Scottish case remains instructive because it concerned the equivalent Scottish form of security whereby absolute title is transferred, and the effect of that on a corporate group.

FARSTAD SUPPLY A/S v ENVIROCO LTD (THE FAR SERVICE) [2010] UKSC 18 (Scot), [2010] BUS LR 1087

The vessel's owner, Farstad, agreed with Asco UK Ltd ('Asco') to indemnify it and 'any of its affiliates' for any loss and damage caused to the vessel and any other property. 'Affiliate' was defined in that agreement to include any subsidiary company. At a later date Asco entered into a credit facility agreement with Royal Bank of Scotland ('RBS'), secured over various of its assets. One such asset was Asco's shareholding in Enviroco Ltd. Security over these shares was granted by assigning title to the shares to RBS[55] with a proviso of retransfer on repayment of the debt.[56] Subsequently a fire on the vessel caused damage to Enviroco Ltd's property and harmed its employees. Enviroco Ltd sought a declaration that Farstad was liable to indemnify Enviroco for the loss.

52 Before 1925 it was also possible, and conceptually correct, to transfer title to land by way of legal mortgage.

53 Law of Property Act 1925 s 85.

54 ibid s 85 refers to 'a charge by way of mortgage' which makes little sense given that there is no transfer of title. For a discussion of terminological confusion, cf Colin Bamford, *Principles of International Financial Law* (3rd edn, Oxford Academic 2019) 10.53.

55 Technically they were assigned to RBS' nominee, a security agent.

56 In Scotland, and indeed in many civilian jurisdictions such as Germany this is called a pledge of shares (in Germany a *Verpfändung*). It is not a pledge in the English sense; the closest approximation is a legal mortgage of shares.

Held: As a matter of interpretation of the indemnity and the then applicable UK company law,[57] for Enviroco to be an affiliate of Asco it needed to be a subsidiary, i.e. a company over 50% of the voting shares of which were held by Asco *and* of which Asco was a member. In assigning ownership to RBS, RBS had been registered as a member of Enviroco, replacing Asco. Therefore, at the relevant time Enviroco was not a subsidiary and so not an affiliate of Asco, and could not benefit from the indemnity.

Although this case must be read in the context of interpreting an indemnity against the person seeking to rely on it, and so narrowly, the core reasoning around the security is readily translatable to the English law context. *The Far Service* illustrates one danger in assigning title by way of security, but it also implies a further danger for the secured lender: that it becomes owner of the property, gaining the rights but also the responsibilities that follow with it. In the context of shares this means that the bank or its nominee becomes a member of the company the whares of which it taken legal assignment.

Consider the following scenario. Ali is a significant business investor, holding shareholdings in a number of start-up and mid-tier companies. All the shares of one of the latter companies, Zeno plc, have been admitted to the Official List of the London Stock Exchange. Ali is a 27% shareholder of Zeno plc, but he owes the company GBP9,000 for an unpaid portion of the shares he owns. Chris, who has no links to Ali, is a 5% shareholder of Zeno plc. In January, Ali enters into a loan agreement with Bank, secured by way of legal mortgage of Ali's shareholdings. The security is perfected that month. In February, Chris borrows money from Bank, secured by way of legal mortgage of his Zeno plc shareholding. As a result, Bank:

- is now the 32% member and shareholder of Zeno plc;
- will receive no doubt unwanted corporate information and notices from Zeno plc;
- transfer of ownership may trigger a forced sale or similar mechanism under non-model articles of a company (for example a joint venture company);[58]
- is under a regulatory obligation to disclose this significant shareholding, pursuant to the Listing Rules and the Companies Acts' Persons with Significant Control regime;
- has crossed the 30% threshold of the UK Takeover Code and must launch a formal takeover offer for all the shares of Zeno plc, or quickly withdraw in embarrassment;
- is liable for a call by Zeno plc to pay up the GBP9,000 outstanding on the shares formally owned by Ali;
- has crossed the 30% threshold under the pensions moral hazard regime and may be called to make a contribution to any pension scheme;
- if Zeno plc is or becomes insolvent, this could be:
  - regarded as a de facto or shadow director which ought to have exercised relevant skill and care with respect to the company's affairs and the interests of its other creditors;
  - and a connected person, allowing a liquidator to call into question the validity of the security granted.

The problem, then, with a legal mortgage of shares is that the security is just too secure—the legal and regulatory risks can often significantly outweigh the advantage.

57 Companies Act 1985 ss 22, 736.

58 *Wise v Lansdell* [1921] 1 Ch 420 (CA).

MOMENT OF REFLECTION: LEGAL MORTGAGES

Use your legal and commercial common sense to suggest risks and disadvantages of a bank taking legal security over the following things:

(A) The furniture of a trader who buys and sells furniture.
(B) Thirty tons of fertilizer, currently stored in a warehouse at an English port.
(C) An option to acquire cocoa at a set price, which expires in one month.

Can you think of a situation where a legal mortgage would be advisable?

If you have obtained the impression the legal mortgages are generally disfavoured in English financial practice, you are on the right track. As ever, however, equity intervenes to mitigate the worst excesses of common law formalism by offering us the **equitable mortgage**. The equitable mortgage is rooted in of the maxims of equitable which you have likely already encountered in your studies: equity regards as done that which ought to have been done.

> In equity it is not necessary, for the alienation of property, that there should be any formal deed of conveyance. A contract for valuable consideration, by which it is agreed to make a present transfer of property, passes at once the beneficial interest, provided the contract be one of which a court of equity will decree a specific performance. *Per* Westbury LC, *Holroyd v Marshall 41* [1861–73] All ER Rep 414 (HL) 417.

With an equitable mortgage this maxim is actively deployed to the parties' advantage as follows: they set out to grant a legal mortgage, but intentionally omit one action which the law requires in order for that legal mortgage validly to be granted. There can be no legal mortgage, but equity sees that a legal mortgage was in view and so finds the equitable mortgage in its stead. In *Swiss Bank Co v Lloyds Bank Ltd* [1982] AC 584 (HL), 594–595, Buckley LJ quoted Fisher and Lightwood's treatise on mortgages with approval:

> An equitable mortgage is created when the legal owner of the property constituting the security enters into some instrument or does some act which, though insufficient to confer a legal estate or title in the subject matter upon the mortgagee, nevertheless demonstrates a binding intention to create a security in favour of the mortgagee, or in other words evidences a contract to do so: see ELG Tyler (ed), *Fisher and Lightwood's Law of Mortgage* (9th edn, Butterworths 1977) 13.

As with a legal mortgage, an equitable mortgage does not create a new property right; rather, it transfers an existing right, here separating out the owner's equitable title to the property and transferring that to the mortgagee.

How is the equitable mortgage useful in practice? Let us take up again our focus on shares and see how an equitable mortgage is constituted and sidesteps many of the potential pitfalls. What is required is that the mortgagor set out to grant a legal mortgage, but in agree with the mortgagee, she omits one or more steps to complete title transfer. If we take an example of certificated shares, this can be achieved by:

(1) the mortgagor completing a signed but otherwise only partially completed (sometimes even blank) stock transfer form;

(2) the mortgagor depositing this stock transfer form and the relevant share certificates[59] with the mortgagee; and
(3) *ideally, but this is not absolutely necessary,* simultaneously committing to writing that the documents in (1) and (2) are deposited by way of mortgage, giving the mortgagor a power to complete the transfer and sell on default, and an obligation to return or reconvey the shares on repayment.

The legal effect is that the mortgagor remains legal title holder to the shares and therefore a member of the company that issued them, but strictly speaking the mortgagor should exercise its right, e.g. to vote, as directed by the mortgagee, who holds the beneficial interest. Often, however, banks will leave discretion to the mortgagor (not least due to the risk of being considered a de facto or shadow director if the voting rights are significant). Should the mortgagor default, then the mortgagee is entitled to complete and date the stock transfer form (and if necessary, pay duty), send it and the share certificates to the company, and thereby be registered as a member of the company and legal owner of the shares by way of transfer of the shareholding.[60]

The advantage of the equitable mortgage is the mortgagee does not yet take title and so defers all that follows from ownership. Yet title is only deferred—as soon as the default occurs, the mortgagee must decide whether she wishes to become owner, potentially triggering one or more of the events listed above in our discussion of legal mortgages of shares. It was mortgagee reticence which led to the legal mess in the following case.

WISE v LANSDELL [1921] 1 Ch 420 (CA)

Wise, his wife, and Lansdell and his wife were members of an eponymous company which today we would describe as a quasi-partnership company. Wise and his wife held a significant minority of the voting shares; the Lansdells the majority. It was a term of the company's articles that should a member become bankrupt, the company could force sale of the bankrupt's shares to the other members.

Wise granted an equitable mortgage of his and his wife's[61] shares to a creditor M to secure various liabilities. Subsequently Wise was declared bankrupt. Seeing the shares were worthless to Wise, his trustees in bankruptcy disclaimed any interest in them. There ensued a standoff: the company did nothing to force sale, but nor did M enforce the security, fearing that doing so would trigger the forced sale provisions of the articles.

A general meeting of the company was called. M, it seems, directed Wise to attend and to vote the shares in accordance with M's wishes. Mr Lansdell, as majority shareholder and chair, refused to recognize Wise's right to vote alleging he was a bankrupt and so non-member, and passed resolutions ignoring his protestations. Wise sued Mr Lansdell for abusing his majority power and denying his votes.

59 This move is practical and has limited legal effect. The certificates are not *per se* property in the shares; the only index of title is entry on the register of members held by the company. As such there is no possessory security at work in taking the certificates. Nevertheless, were the mortgagor to retain the certificates he may be able to convince a bona fide purchaser for value that no mortgage exists and could transfer title to him by way of legal mortgage (effectively mortgaging the shares twice). In such a case, the transferee would rank prior to the equitable mortgagee, and could have his debts satisfied first. Conversely, depriving the mortgagor of the certificates should put any third party on notice of some problem with the mortgagor's title. By analogy from the case of equitable mortgages of land: *Wilkes v Bodington* (1707) 2 Vern 599, 23 ER 991.

60 *Stubbs v Slater* [1910] 1 Ch 632 (CA).

61 Wise had caused his wife to make over to him a blank stock transfer form for his own use.

> The facts caused some difficulty because it was unclear what had happened to title in the shares once the trustees in bankruptcy had disclaimed Wise's interest. Understanding that affected how one understood M's equitable interest.
>
> *Held*: Primary responsibility for the confusion lay with the Lansdells, who really ought to have initiated the company's forced sale proceedings. Having failed to do so, Wise remained on the register as a member of the company and was entitled to vote. The resolutions were void.
>
> As to the question of the effect of the trustees' disclaimer, all they had disclaimed was Wise's residual 'beneficial' interest in the shares i.e. his interest in the return of M's equitable interest on repayment. As against the rest of the world, W remained legal owner of the shares and could vote the shares as directed. It would be absurd if trustees in bankruptcy could destroy, by disclaimer, the property rights of third parties such as those of equitable mortgage holders.

One way to understand *Wise v Lansdell* is to regard Wise as having lost any positive attribute of ownership once his trustees disclaimed the shares. This included rights to vote as he saw fit and to see any economic return. It is in this sense of *asset* that I read the term 'beneficial' used by the court. All that was left were the pure *burdens* of ownership, including *liability* for a call on winding up and here, given the equitable mortgage, a duty to use his legal status and voting power as M directed.

3.4.5 Non-possessory security II: the (fixed) charge

It is common when introducing the charge to note that in practice the charge, being a creature of equity, is often confused with the equitable mortgage, especially because the practical effect of both types of security is similar. At this point a sharp conceptual distinction is introduced: under an equitable mortgage there is a transfer of an existing property right—the equitable interest in the property—whereas an equitable charge creates an entire new property right, different from an ownership interest, which 'incumbers' the thing charged. Indeed, whereas a mortgage is effected by a transfer of title, and a pledge by delivery of a chose in possession, nothing changes hands with a charge. Rather, a charge is simply an agreement between a chargor and chargee that some thing owned by the chargor may on default of payment be appropriated by the chargee to meet the due debts of the chargor.[62]

The distinction is in principle correct and offers a solid point of departure for the student, but overstates the difference between the two types of security. If one considers again the equitable mortgage, it is not simply an incomplete transfer for title. If Jones contracts to sell his house to Powell but fails to execute the deed of transfer, Powell has an equitable interest in the house and can call for specific performance of the transfer, but this is a simple contract for sale of land and not a security transfer. What makes a transfer a mortgage is the purpose of the transfer, being to secure specified liabilities with a reconveyance on repayment (if it occurs). In other words, this purposive component amounts to a right of the mortgagee to appropriate the thing to satisfy an outstanding debt of the mortgagor. On this view, the mortgage and charge actually share a key attribute: an

---

62 'An equitable charge which is not an equitable mortgage is said to be created when property is expressly or constructively made liable, or specially appropriated, to the discharge of a debt or some other obligation, and confers on the chargee a right of realisation by judicial process, that is to say, by the appointment of a receiver or an order for sale': cf ELG Tyler (ed), *Fisher and Lightwood's Law of Mortgage* (9th edn, Butterworths 1977) 14.

agreed right to appropriate some thing to meet a liability. If the purpose of security is deemed of central importance for intentionally created security interests, we might, now armed with all that we have studied, venture the following classification:

- *Agreed*
  - *present right to appropiate thing*
    - *+transfer of*
      - *legal title = legal mortgage*
      - *equitable title = eq.mortgage*
    - *+possession = pledge*
    - *+nothing more = equitable charge*
  - *future right to detain thing*
    - *expressly in contract = contractual lien*
    - *impliedly by custom or law = (possessory) lien*

In light of this division, we may understand Atkin LJ's survey of English security:

> The first question that arises is whether or not this document [under consideration] does create a mortgage or charge, and to determine that it is necessary to form an idea of what is meant by a 'charge.' It is not necessary to give a formal definition of a charge, but I think there can be no doubt that where in a transaction for value both parties evince an intention that property, existing or future, shall be made available as security for the payment of a debt, and that the creditor shall have a present right to have it made available, there is a charge, even though the present legal right which is contemplated can only be enforced at some future date, and though the creditor gets no legal right of property, either absolute or special, or any legal right to possession, but only gets a right to have the security made available by an order of the Court. If those conditions exist I think there is a charge. If, on the other hand, the parties do not intend that there should be a present right to have the security made available, but only that there should be a right in the future by agreement, such as a licence, to seize the goods, there will be no charge. [in *National Provincial and Union Bank of England v Charnley* [1924] KB 431, 449]

Once one realizes that an equitable mortgage comprises a charge and an incomplete transfer of title, one can understand in part why the terminology of mortgage and charge are often used interchangeably, especially in the older cases. The student is forewarned. By way of example, in the following case Lord Westbury LC tells us that there can be no equitable mortgage of a thing one does not (yet) have, but nevertheless equity does appropriate that thing if it is after acquired. The question is: is he describing a mortgage or a charge?

HOLROYD v MARSHALL (1862) 10 HLC 191, [1861–73] All ER Rep 414 (HL)

Taylor, operator of a mill in Yorkshire, borrowed money from Holroyd secured by way of assignment of title of the machinery fixed in the mill. In additional, the mortgage purported to extend to any machinery Taylor might at some future time acquire and fix in the mill. Taylor failed to meet a third party's demand for payment, and Marshall, local sheriff, had been ordered to seize the machinery in satisfaction of the debt. Holroyd claimed that the machinery belonged to him in virtue of the security.

Held per Lord Westbury LC:

> It is alleged that [the contract cannot create a mortgage], because it relates to machinery not existing at the time, but to be acquired and fixed, and placed in the

> mill at a future time. It is quite true that a deed which professes to convey property which is not in existence at the time is a conveyance void at law, simply because there is nothing to convey. So in equity, a contract which engages to transfer property which is not in existence, cannot operate as an immediate alienation, merely because there is nothing to transfer. But if a vendor or mortgagor agree to sell or mortgage property, real or personal, of which he is not possessed at the time, and he receives the consideration for the contract, and afterwards become possessed of property answering the description in the contract, there is no doubt that a court of equity would compel him to perform the contract, and that the contract would in equity transfer the beneficial interest to the mortgagee or purchaser immediately on the property being acquired. This, of course, assumes that the supposed contract is one of that class of which a court of equity would decree the specific performance. If it be so, then immediately on the acquisition of the property described, the vendor or mortgagor would hold it in trust for the purchaser or mortgagee, according to the terms of the contract.

Lord Westbury has been criticized for the infelicity of his expression, particularly because it is unclear how wide the class of contracts where equity would decree specific performance is to be drawn.[63] Lord Chelmsford at least uses the language of mortgage *and* charge, but nor does he help matters by using both and so not specifying which is being considered in this case.[64] But we should not be too harsh—the neat categorization of security interests can obscure the equities that lie at the heart of appropriation of an asset by way security, and the merit of Lord Westbury's dicta is that they bring out this equitable heart, namely that in *Holroyd* the after-acquired machinery became an identified component of a variable fund (of machines) held by the chargor for the benefit of the chargee, and to which the chargee had recourse in priority to third-party creditors with merely personal claims against the chargor. In this, Lord Westbury's use of 'trustee' is revealing, if again perhaps too strong for modern tastes.

3.5 Conclusion

The decision in *Holroyd v Marshall* opens up an interesting possibility: if one can take an equitable charge over specific future property such as obvious major purchases of single units of plant and machinery, can one extend this thought further, taking a charge over any future-acquired asset? Do we even need to specify the asset, beyond it being acquired, possibly, by the charger at some point? And does this thought also work backwards, in that we simply allow the charger to dispose of assets for the time being, to be replaced by new ones? The motive for this thought is not the joy of conceptual games, but a very material one: companies buy and sell stock in trade every day, acquiring and disposing of what are in aggregate very valuable assets. Could a lender take security over these assets using a modified version of the rule in *Holroyd v Marshall*? In the next chapter, continuing our investigation of security, we find out the answer.

---

63 F Pollock, 'Re Wait' (1927) 43 LQR 293, 294. See also *Tailby v Official Receiver* (1888) 13 App Cas 523, [1886–90] All ER Rep 486.
64 (1862) 10 HLC 191, [1861–73] All ER Rep 414, 420.

Chapter 4

Security II

Floating security and secured finance

Chapter contents

DOI: 10.4324/9781003457220-4

4.1 Introduction

This chapter builds directly on the previous and its explanation flows directly from it. It is recommended that you study at the very least the account of the general principles of security, and the forms of non-possessory security, before continuing.

4.2 The floating charge

4.2.1 Introduction

The analysis of the court in *Holroyd v Marshall*—discussed at the end of the previous chapter—can be broken down into a set of concentric circles, each one pertaining to the extent of the security interests considered. It was not disputed that the mill operator's machinery at the time of granting security could be charged; this was a present fixed charge over each such item. The case itself is authority for the possibility of granting a fixed charge over identifiable future assets also, namely the machinery the mill operator would acquire at a later date. Yet Lord Westbury LC appears to have entertained a third, still wider possibility: the mill operator could have granted security over as yet unidentified future assets, assets which may have been acquired and then subsequently transferred on, only for their replacements to have fallen under the charge on acquisition, and so on until the charge was enforced or released. This is our first, crude notion of what is now known as the **floating charge**.

It is a matter of some judicial debate whether this was the court's intention, not least because any such opinion was probably obiter given the facts of the case, but it would be wrong to assume that the court was innovating—their Lordships approached the suggestion of this third option as if it were a matter of settled law not innovation, and so not meriting doctrinal discussion. This is important, because often when doctrinal writers introduce the floating charge, they trumpet the genius of English equity for having 'invented' such a useful security device, and thereby having stolen a march on more formalist legal systems. Consider though this report from Justinian's *Digest*:

> When a debtor [charged][1] a [market] stall to the creditor, the question was put whether this was invalid or whether by 'stall' the merchandise in the stall was to be taken as [charged]. And if he sold goods from time to time, bought others, brought them into the stall and then died, could the creditor in the [charge][2] action sue for all that was then on the premises, in view of the turnover of stock? Scaevola replied: What was in the stall at the debtor's death was subject to the security.[3]

Evidently the raison d'être for the floating charge was known to the Romans, and a very practical commercial reason it was: a trader, whose very business involves an ever-changing bulk of stock, wishes to grant security over that bulk of stock as it varies from time to time. The *Digest* suggests that the answer was the trader may do so, at least by reference to some locus of the stock such as a stall. The alternative would be that an agent of the creditor would have to stand by the market stall

1 The actual translation is 'impignorated' here used in a wider sense than 'mortgage,' to mean any non-possessory security, as is confirmed by the subsequent use of 'hypothec' to describe the same security in the case.

2 The actual translation is 'hypothec' here used interchangeably with 'impignorated.'

3 *Digest* 20.1.34.pr (Scaevola) (*Corpus Iuris Civilis*, T. Mommsen, P. Krüger, R. Schöll, W. Kroll eds. (var. ed. 1911, 1915, 1904)). See also *Digest* 20.1.15.1 (Gaius) and *Digest* 20.2.9 (Paul), ibid. For discussion, see HLE Verhagen, 'Ius Honorarium, Equity and Real Security: Parallel Lines of Legal Development' in Egbert Koops and Willem J Zwalve (eds), *Law and Equity: Approaches in Roman Law and Common Law* (Brill 2014) 129.

all day every day and maintain a running book of each item of stock as it is bought and sold by the trader, thereby fixing/releasing a charge at every moment.

The commercial driver for such a charge seems to be very old, but we must admit that the differences from the modern English law floating charge remain significant: formally, transactionally and conceptually. For a start, today an English unincorporated trader is unable to grant a floating charge;[4] that power is granted only to incorporated companies and subject to a perfection requirement of registration at Companies House. The reasons for these formal requirements are clear: third-party creditors must know, before they lend, what assets of the debtor are available to meet claims on insolvency. Often, with fixed security this information is identifiable, usually by reference to a register or some other form of notice (but not always). Yet if secured assets are changing daily, how can a third-party creditor keep track other than by having an agent stand at the factory gate with a clipboard? When the Law Commission was asked to consider extending floating charges to the assets of unincorporated traders,[5] it was just this issue which gave rise to pause—without an existing registration structure to fall back on, it would be necessary to legislate for one, and such additional formalities (and costs) would rather defeat the low regulation status of the unincorporated trader.

The transactional structure of the English floating charge likewise differs from the apparently implicit and haphazard form of the security in the *Digest* (and arguably *Holroyd v Marshall*). The modern deed of security used in finance transactions will grant fixed charges of present and future assets, and then use an additional floating charge to sweep up anything that escapes any of the fixed charges. This 'fixed and floating' charge is sometimes referred to as a 'universal charge' following US practice, though there is no legal import in this, the term being a portmanteau for the multiple charges and indeed mortgages the deed creates. More commonly, the document is called a **debenture**,[6] though strictly a debenture is a kind of debt instrument issued by a company[7] and often secured against the company's assets by way of floating charge, in which case it was called a 'mortgage debenture' [*sic*]. At some point in the later nineteenth century, the reference to security was dropped and the word *debenture* came to mean the security itself, i.e. a charge over all the company's assets from time to time.[8]

FLOATING CHARGE: THE BASIC IDEA

Building merchant company wishes to borrow for its general corporate purposes; Bank wishes to lend but on a secured basis. Taking fixed charges over company's stock-in-trade, cash and customer debts would be self-defeating—unless bank employed someone to stand at company's gates and create and release security over each screw and bolt, buying and selling would be impossible if the fixed charge requirements were to be met (and even then the whole process would slow business down considerably).

Company therefore offers a charge over its present and future assets from time to time, with license from the chargee bank to buy and dispose of any such assets as it sees fit in the course of business (without needing to ask bank each time).

4 The Bills of Sale Act 1878 and its Amendment Act of 1882: s 4 requires the trader's secured assets to be listed in a schedule; something inherently impossible with a floating charge; s 5 prohibits charges of future goods; and s 17 expressly exempts companies from these provisions.

5 Law Commission, *Company Security Interests* (Law Com No 296, 2005) paras 1.56ff.

6 From the Latin *debentur*, meaning to be owed.

7 s 738 Companies Act 2006: in the Companies Acts 'debenture' includes debenture stock, bonds and any other securities of a company, whether or not constituting a charge on the assets of the company.

8 See further, 'securities' (Chapter 8).

It is now understood this security constitutes a proprietary interest not in any particular assets, but in the company's assets *as a whole*, i.e. as a **fund** which is capable of mutating through time. The charge is a creature of equity, as is the fund, and bears some analogy with a trust fund in that the content of the fund may change over time; the beneficiary's interest is in the fund *qua* fund.

Either explicitly, or implied by law, the charge is potentially subject to **crystallization**. The term implied by law provides that if the company's management ceases to control the business—e.g. when a liquidator is appointed—the floating charge over the fund crystallizes, creating a *fixed charge* over every particular asset in that fund at that moment.

The moment of creation of the fixed charges determines their priority relative to any other fixed charge over these assets. For example, if a third party earlier created a fixed charge over an asset, the third party's interest ranks prior to bank's fixed charge. The effect is that the asset in question may be sold and its value realized to meet third party's claim first, any remainder to meet bank's claim. As between floating charges, the earlier in time is also prior.

Floating charges permit special enforcement rights which flow naturally from their whole-business nature. Pre-2002 'qualifying' floating charges allowed secured parties to appoint an administrative receiver who took over management of the business as if it were the creditors' own. Post-2002 floating charges continue to admit the appointment of an administrator out of court to guide the company through an insolvency process. These powers are additional to enforcing against individual charged assets, including appoint a receiver to seize and sell the assets.

Here is an example of wording you might find in a company's debenture or universal charge security document. Notice that it has a 'belt-and-braces' approach in which it seeks to create fixed charges over as much as possible, failing which there is a floating charge to sweep up everything else.

2 CREATION OF SECURITY

. . .

2.3 Investments

The Chargor charges by way of a first legal mortgage all shares in any member of the Group owned by it or held by any nominee on its behalf.

2.4 Plant and machinery

The Chargor charges by way of a first fixed charge all plant and machinery owned by the Chargor and its interest in any plant or machinery in its possession.

[*Further subclauses listing types of security and particular property subject to it.*]

2.10 Floating charge

(a) The Chargor charges by way of a first floating charge all its assets not at any time otherwise effectively mortgaged, charged or assigned by way of fixed mortgage, charge or assignment under this Clause.

(b) The floating charge created by this Subclause 2 will automatically convert into a fixed charge over all of the Chargor's assets if an administrator is appointed or the Security Agent receives notice of an intention to appoint an administrator.

Having identified everything that can be mortgaged or encumbered with a fixed charge, subclause 2.10 creates a floating charge over everything else. But notice precisely how the security works: subclause 2.10(b) states the conditions for crystallization of the charge into a set of fixed charges over specific assets—any property up to that point capable of falling under the floating charge's terms is now attached by a set of fixed charges. In this instance, the crystallization is expressly provided for in the security deed and is automatic on the appointment of an administrator to manage the insolvent company, or semi-automatic if the creditors pre-empt this by sending notice to the Facility Agent in advance.

EXAMPLE: FLOATING CHARGE PRIORITY

On 1 February, Hare Bank takes a floating charge over all the assets of X Ltd. to secure certain debts. Hare Bank registers the charge in the usual way directly thereafter. There is no negative pledge clause. On 1 March, Tortoise Bank secures a loan to X Ltd. by taking a fixed charge over the specified plant and machinery of X Ltd., which is duly perfected. On 2 March, X Ltd. defaults on its loan to Hare Bank, Hare Bank accelerates the loan, and the floating charge crystallizes. X Ltd.'s assets are now subject to a fixed charge in favour of Hare Bank, but the fixed charges over the plant and machinery were created *second in time* after the fixed charges in favour of Tortoise Bank, and so rank posterior. Thus, Tortoise Bank may enforce against the plant and machinery first to repay its loan to X Ltd., any surplus only being handed to Hare Bank to meet its claims, any remainder to X Ltd.

Such is the practice of the floating charge: it is an attempt to reconcile the interests of a lender in taking security with the interests of the corporate borrower (and any sensible lender) in being able to carry on its business without being subject to oppressive legal formalities around security creation and release.[9] There is though, a third interested party: the court as ever must determine whether the practice is enforceable, both between the parties and against third parties. This policy concern was neatly précised by Lord Millett:

> A second mischief arose from the very nature of the floating charge which allowed a company to continue to trade and incur credit despite the existence of the charge. This put the ordinary trade creditors of the company at risk, even though they would not normally know of the existence of the charge; for the holder of the charge could step in without warning at any time and obtain priority over them. Such trade creditors would include the suppliers of goods which the charge holder could appropriate to the security and realise for its own benefit leaving the suppliers unpaid. This was seen by many judges as an injustice and by Lord Macnaghten as a great scandal.[10]

A first step to evaluating this practice legally was to determine just what it was that nineteenth-century corporate lawyers were doing; just what this purported security was in law. It would be difficult to distribute justice as a matter of policy if the dividing lines of distribution—here between kinds of charge—were blurred.

9 And this practice was the express policy justification given in the early English cases: *in re Florence Land and Public Works Co ex p Moor* (1878) 10 ChD 530 (CA) 541 (Sir George Jessel MR); *Biggerstaff v Rowatt's Wharf Lt* [1896] 2 Ch 93 101, 103 (Lindley and Lopes LJJ).

10 *Agnew v CIR* [2001] UKPC 28 [10].

4.2.2 Judicial recognition

Given the House of Lords' apparent assumption that a charge over business assets *from time to time* was legally feasible, perhaps indicating knowledge of a Roman prehistory, we should perhaps not be surprised at the speed at which the floating charge concept was accepted and named as a distinct form of security by the English courts.[11] It began with lawyers drafting security documents which took security over an 'undertaking.'

IN RE PANAMA NEW ZEALAND AND AUSTRALIAN ROYAL MAIL CO (1869–70) LR 5 Ch App 318

A steamship company, having power to issue mortgages, bonds, or debentures, issued mortgage debentures, charging the 'undertaking, and all sums of money arising therefrom,' to meet the principal and interest payable under the debentures. Before the debentures became due the company was wound up, and the ships and other property of the company were sold to third parties.

Held: The debentures had created a charge over the 'undertaking' understood as the business assets of the company from time to time, including proceeds from their sale. The debenture holders were entitled to repayment from the proceeds of the sale of the ships and other property in priority to the unsecured creditors of the company.

A series of cases in the 1870s confirmed that a company could indeed charge its undertaking,[12] including future assets, so that by the turn of the century, Chancery judges regarded doing so as a common place and named it the 'floating charge.' The classic statement of just what a floating charge is, was given by none other than Lord Macnaghten in *Governments Stock and Other Securities Investment Co Ltd v Manila Rly Co Ltd* (1897):

> A floating security is an equitable charge on the assets for the time being of a going concern. It attaches to the subject charged in the varying condition in which it happens to be from time to time. It is the essence of such a charge that it remains dormant until the undertaking charged ceases to be a going concern, or until the person in whose favour the charge is created intervenes. His right to intervene may of course be suspended by agreement. But if there is no agreement for suspension, he may exercise his right whenever he pleases after default.[13]

These dicta are often cited approvingly along with Lord Macnaghten's further comments in *Illingworth v Houldsworth*,[14] and those of Romer LJ in the court below:

---

11 See however continued concern in the 1860s: *King v Marshall* (1864) 33 Beav 565, 569 (Romilly LJ). The case focused on whether uncalled capital of the company could be charged, however. Furthermore, in common with other sceptical cases of the time, a fatal defect of charges over an 'undertaking' was lack of wording indicating an intention to charge future property—something the lawyers in *re Panama* remedied. On these cases, see Simon Firth (ed), *Gough on Company Charges* (3rd edn, Butterworths Law 2025) 5.30.

12 *in re Florence Land* (n 9), *in re Hamilton's Windsor Iron Works; ex p Pitman & Edwards* (1879) 12 ChD 707; and *in re Colonial Trusts Corp; ex p Bradshaw* (1879) 15 ChD 465.

13 [1897] AC 81, 86.

14 [1904] AC 355.

> I should have thought there was not much difficulty in defining what a floating charge is in contrast to what is called a specific charge. A specific charge, I think, is one that without more fastens on ascertained and definite property or property capable of being ascertained and defined; a floating charge, on the other hand, is ambulatory and shifting in its nature, hovering over and so to speak floating with the property which it is intended to affect until some event occurs or some act is done which causes it to settle and fasten on the subject of the charge within its reach and grasp.[15]

In the Court of Appeal, where the case went under the name *re Yorkshire Woolcombers Association Ltd*,[16] Romer LJ had said:

> I certainly think that if a charge has the three characteristics that I am about to mention it is a floating charge. (1) If it is a charge on a class of assets of a company present and future; (2) if that class is one which, in the ordinary course of the business of the company, would be changing from time to time; and (3) if you find that by the charge it is contemplated that, until some future step is taken by or on behalf of those interested in the charge, the company may carry on its business in the ordinary way as far as concerns the particular class of assets I am dealing with.[17]

These remain the authoritative statements as to the general concept of the floating charge, though note Romer LJ's triple of characteristics is less solid than it first appears: characteristics (1) and (2) could equally apply to a fixed charge over present and future assets; only (3) is determinative, as we shall see.[18]

If the notion of a floating charge was accepted with speed, there were still significant questions about its precise nature relative to the classic fixed charge. Conceptual headaches included:

(1) In a sense the floating charge is not *toto caelo* different from a fixed charge; as *Holroyd v Marshall* suggested, it is a security interest that wants to be a fixed charge, just not yet. Where is the dividing line (if any) between a fixed charge over future-acquired assets, and a floating charge?
(2) We have a purported security interest, but an interest in what property? At least the future fixed charge could identify something that the chargor would acquire. With a floating charge the intention is to catch absolutely anything the company owns perhaps many years in the future, but also to exclude property the company alienates (so third parties take free). Can there be any property right here or is this just a fiction?

We look more closely at these questions in the next sections.

4.2.3 The key distinction from a fixed charge

In *Holroyd v Marshall*, Lord Macnaghten suggested that one could create a charge over future acquired property and build into the terms of that charge a license to deal with the property specific various conditions and mechanisms for permission. One could add that the list of property could be a list of all the assets a company could ever need to acquire, and conditions permitting disposal of the

---

15 ibid 358.
16 [1903] 2 ch 284.
17 ibid 295.
18 *re Spectrum Plus (In Liquidation)* [2005] UKHL 41 [111].

same. Such a charge would still be a *fixed* charge. What then distinguishes a floating charge from the fixed charge just described?

The question turns on the nature of appropriation—the notion that an asset must be sufficiently identifiable for a court to recognize that it is just *this* asset which is appropriated to the security. In short, the asset can be 'fixed' or 'pinned down.' Appropriation is not the same as enforcement. Appropriation just means that a given asset is now available *first* to meet the secured liabilities of the chargee on enforcement (if enforcement occurs), *second* any remainder to go to other creditors and then the company/members on winding up.

One asset class pushed the very limits of this need for fixity: the **receivable** (also known as a **book debt**).

ESSENTIAL DEFINITION: RECEIVABLE

A receivable is an obligation to pay (a debt) in the hands of the obligee. As property it is a chose in action.

E.g. Jones buys 1 tonne of concrete slabs from Tradeco Ltd., in consideration of £500 payable within 60 days of delivery. That contractual promise to pay, and subsequently due debt if unpaid, is now an asset of Tradeco Ltd., and will be recorded in its accounts (or 'books') as an asset under 'current debtors.' Hence receivables are also called '**book debts**.'

Trading business receivables are highly variable. Debts may be created, and debtors may pay some or all that is owed, from one day to another. The trading business may waive some debts for a valued customer, or charge interest on late debts. Each such debt is a chose in action and so each must be individually appropriated to the security. To grant a fixed charge over each would seemingly require a secured party to employ an accountant and lawyer permanently just to identify and create/release fixed charges over each debt (or part thereof) as they arise or cease to be. From the chargor's side, too, this would be unsupportable: receivables constitute the very liquidity of any trading business—the cash proceeds are needed to buy more stock, pay overheads and so on. The receivables themselves can be sold to specialist finance houses at a discount for money upfront (a transaction called **factoring**). Yet being the lifeblood of a trading business, receivables are often a significant part of the business's value. A major creditor of the company would ideally like to take security over the company's receivables. Which kind of security should this be given the tension between the formalities of fixing a charge and business practicalities?

This question raises the next driver of judicial difficulties. Given the everchanging quality of receivables, we might conclude that unless ridiculously formal steps are taken, a creditor will not be able to fix a charge on any given receivable. Let us assume, though we are still unsure as to why, that the court will allow the creditor to take a floating charge over receivables (our assumption would be correct). Very well, our creditor has their security. What is there to complain about?

The problem comes back to priority. A floating charge crystallizes very late in the day (say, appointment of an administrator), meaning that the newly constituted fixed charges over whichever receivables are now owned by the company rank posterior to any fixed charge over those receivables that may have been created even 24 hours earlier. The chances of this happening are not insignificant. When a company's management are desperate to save a moribund business, they will attempt to raise cash by any means possible. The result our creditor fears is that its floating charge turns out to be subordinated to other creditors, with two results: (1) the value of the realized security for our creditor is much less than expected; (2) attempts by our creditor to manage the business through insolvency are stymied by the loss of control over a key business asset: the receivables.

The priority problem became even more acute thanks to the intervention of insolvency legislation. Following the Preferential Payments in Bankruptcy Act 1897 (now reenacted as part of the Insolvency Act 1986, as amended),[19] a class of preferential creditors was created which ranked after fixed charges but ahead of floating charges. Preferential creditors included the liquidator (fees) and the tax authorities. This class was subsequently extended to employees and their pensions, and by reserving a 'prescribed part' to unsecured creditors.[20] All these claims reduce the fund left for distribution to floating charge holders.

Given these concerns around priority on insolvency, lenders to corporates have been sorely tempted to take security over receivables by way of fixed charge. The question was whether they succeeded, and that question turned on the dividing line between what makes a fixed charge fixed and not floating. It took some 130 years to settle the problem. Our first case has been subsequently overruled in *re Spectrum Plus* (see below), but this latter case makes much more sense if contextualized by what had gone before.

SIEBE GORMAN & CO LTD v BARCLAYS BANK LTD [1979] 2 Lloyd's Rep 142 (ChD)

RHM was a company which banked with Barclays and benefited from an overdraft facility. RHM's indebtedness to Barclays was secured by an all-monies debenture which inter alia created a 'first fixed charge' over the proceeds of its 'book debts.' One feature of this arrangement was that the book debts included the proceeds of certain instruments such as bills and letters of credit issued by banks abroad to facilitate international sales. Barclays would receive the instruments and 'clear' them i.e. present them at the issuing banks to obtain payment on RHM's behalf, the proceeds payable into RHM's current account. A second feature was that Barclays could assert a lien over the instruments for unpaid RHM debts, and, it claimed, it had a lien over the proceeds also.

Siebe supplied safety equipment to RHM. RHM ran into financial trouble and could not pay Siebe. Following negotiations, RHM assigned to Siebe the various instruments held by Barclays, sending a copy of the assignment to Barclays and instructing it to release the bills to Siebe.

Barclays refused to comply, claiming RHM was also in debt to Barclays, which had a first-ranking fixed charge over the proceeds from the book debts. Barclays cleared the bills it held and applied the money to reduce RHM's indebtedness to Barclays.

Held: Barclays had a valid fixed charge over the proceeds of the book debts.[21] Slade J felt the following factors were determinative:

(i) The express words of the debenture clearly intended the creation of a fixed charge.

19 s 175 and s 40 Insolvency Act 1986 (previously ss 2 and 3 of the Preferential Payments in Bankruptcy Act 1897). See also s 251 Enterprise Act 2002.

20 s 176A of the Insolvency Act 1986 and the Insolvency Act 1986 (Prescribed Part) Order 2003 (SI 2003/2097).

21 Strictly, the fixed charge only extended until Barclays became aware of the assignment to Siebe. Absent notice of the specific terms of the debenture, Siebe were entitled to assume RHM had an equity of redemption permitting them to recover the instruments and transfer them to Siebe (i.e. Siebe was a bona fide purchaser for value without notice (BFPFVWN)).

(ii) Barclays controlled the clearing process and therefore had the power to prevent the proceeds reaching RHM. This control conflicted with any sense of RHM being permitted to carry on its business with property as it saw fit.
(iii) Barclays had a lien over the proceeds, even, it seems, if RHM owed nothing to Barclays at a given moment.

Siebe Gorman was heavily criticized. For example, while it is by definition possible to take possessory security by way a lien over bearer instruments because they are capable of possession, it is an abuse of language to claim that lien extents into the intangible proceeds (a credit in an account).[22] As for the construction argument, we have seen that the express words will only get the parties so far, and that if the legal effects of an agreement contradict those words, the legal effects will prevail.

The main critique, however, was aimed at the argument from control: on the facts, Barclays did not have control of the proceeds, which entered an account from which RHM could freely withdraw money for its business purposes. Surely this freedom to dispose of the proceeds met the third condition for a floating charge identified by Romer LJ in *re Yorkshire Woolcombers*, namely a company's freedom to deal with specific assets (until crystallization)?

IN RE BRIGHTLIFE LTD [1987] Ch 200

By a debenture dated 11 April 1983 the company created a 'first specific [i.e. fixed] charge' over 'all book debts and other debts now or at any time during the continuance of this security due or owing to' the company. The debenture also created a 'first floating charge' over 'the undertaking and all other property, assets and rights whatsoever present and future.'

The debenture-holder crystallized the floating charge by serving notice, and at the same time sought assignment of the company's credit balances in accounts with various banks. The liquidator sought directions as to whether the credit balances could be subject to a fixed charge.

Held per Hoffman J (as he then was), applying *re Yorkshire Woolcombers* and distinguishing *Siebe Gorman*, that the company's ability to deal freely with the credit balances in its accounts was inconsistent with the nature of a fixed charge—the balances were subject only to a floating charge. Moreover, as a matter of construction the credit balances did not fall within the meaning of 'book debts' in the debenture.

Notice *re Brightlife*, being a first instance case, did not overrule *Siebe Gorman*. Enterprising lawyers therefore observed a gap: *re Brightlife* had ruled that one could not create a fixed charge over credit balances if the chargor account holder was free to deal with the balances, but *Siebe Gorman* had ruled that one could create a fixed charge over book debts from time to time. The credit balances are one sort of property (the chose in action which is a claim on the bank for payment); the book debts are another (the chose in action which is a claim e.g. on a purchaser under a sales contract). Lawyers

22 Per Lord Hope of Craighead in *re Spectrum Plus (In Liquidation)* (n 18) [59]–[60].

thus altered debentures to create a fixed charge over all book debts; a floating charge over all proceeds of book debts.

RE NEW BULLAS TRADING LTD [1994] BCC 36 (CA)

The company's debenture in favour of private equity house 3i created a fixed charge over all book debts and a floating charge over all proceeds of book debts. The debenture further created restrictions on dealing with the book debts. When the company became insolvent, 3i enforced against the receivables and directed all future proceeds of realizing the debts to be paid to 3i directly.

At first instance the court had ruled that the fixed charge over book debts was on its true construction a floating charge.

Held: The fixed charge was valid: it was possible to create a fixed charge over specific future acquired assets, including receivables, even if the proceeds of realizing the book debts could be freely disposed of.

New Bullas proved unpopular with the leading legal minds, not least because a receivable remains in practice a claim for payment, and pursuing accounts payable is part and parcel of a trading business.[23] Was it really the case that 3i were in control of the receivables as a debt collection agency, or in fact was the company still very much in charge of these book debts? If it was, surely that contradicted the nature of a fixed charge. Moreover, as 3i had practically demonstrated, a distinction between book debt and proceeds was surely 'theological,' for the first thing 3i had done was to enforce its fixed charge by converting the book debts into proceeds, claiming these enforcement proceeds were still covered by the fixed charge and did not fall under the floating charge.

A very similar fact pattern came via New Zealand to the Privy Council.

AGNEW v COMMISSIONERS OF INLAND REVENUE (in re BRUMARK INVESTMENTS LTD) [2001] UKPC 28

As with *New Bullas*, the debenture created a fixed charge over book debts, and a floating charge over the proceeds. Yet in fact the company continued to deal with the receivables as it saw fit, creating the debts through trading, pursuing them, and waiving payment as needed.

Held: The charge over the book debts was a floating charge. On the issue of whether one could distinguish book debts from the proceeds of their realization (and so create different security over each), Lord Millett, delivering the sole judgment, said:

> While a debt and its proceeds are two separate assets, however, the latter are merely the traceable proceeds of the former and represent its entire value. A debt

23 Roy Goode, 'Charges over Book Debts: A Missed Opportunity' (1994) 110 LQR 592; Sarah Worthington, 'Fixed Charges Over Book Debts and other Receivables' (1997) 113 LQR 562; see also LJ Millett in *Royal Trust Bank v National Westminster Bank Plc* [1996] 2 BCLC 682 (ChD).

is a receivable; it is merely a right to receive payment from the debtor. Such a right cannot be enjoyed in specie; its value can be exploited only by exercising the right or by assigning it for value to a third party. An assignment or charge of a receivable which does not carry with it the right to the receipt has no value. It is worthless as a security. Any attempt in the present context to separate the ownership of the debts from the ownership of their proceeds (even if conceptually possible) makes no commercial sense. [46]

From this it followed that analysis of whether a fixed charge could be created over book debts needed to be holistic: realization of book debts was a feature of them, and so one had to ask whether the company or debenture holder had control over realization also.

Expressly disapproving of *New Bullas*, Lord Millett and the Privy Council concluded that while in principle creating a fixed charge over book debts was possible, it was necessary for the chargee to have de jure and de facto control of the book debts, and that included their realization. This control centred on the ability of the chargee to prevent the company from dealing with (and so realizing) the book debts as it saw fit.

Complete control was unnecessary; the company could continue to realize the book debts provided that the proceeds could only be paid into a blocked account of the chargee i.e. the company could not expect to use those proceeds as part of its cashflow (without explicit release by the chargee).

The Privy Council indicated practical ways in which lawyers could achieve the desired result, notably appointing the company as agent debt collector on the chargee's behalf. The words 'on the chargee's behalf' are critical though. The proceeds must go to the charge who must have the right to prevent the company using those funds.

Siebe Gorman was now on very shaky ground, but as a matter of precedent it had yet to be formally overruled. This happened in *re Spectrum Plus*. The case can be a confusing for students of floating charges because a great deal of the judicial discussion is not about security at all but about the nature of precedent. In particular, and for good reason, the House of Lords was required to consider the effect of overruling *Siebe Gorman* on countless debentures that had been drafted on the basis of what *was* the law. One option mooted was to overrule *Siebe Gorman* prospectively only, but to otherwise enforce debentures drafted before the House of Lords' opinion was handed down. The House of Lords ultimately overruled *Siebe Gorman* retroactively also.

IN RE SPECTRUM PLUS (IN LIQUIDATION) [2005] UKHL 41

The facts follow a now familiar pattern: the company had an account with a bank. The bank extended an uncommitted overdraft facility to the company to help with its day-to-day liquidity requirements. All monies owing were secured by a debenture which *inter alia* purported to create a fixed charge over the company's book debts.

As part of the financing arrangements, the company would collect the book debts and pay them into the account held with the bank, these sums being applied to reduce the balance over any overdraft that had been drawn down.

When the company went into liquidation, the bank claimed it had a fixed charge over the book debts and demanded that the liquidator assign them to the bank directly. The liquidator sought directions from the court.

Held: On a true construction of the debenture, the charge over book debts was a floating charge.

Previous cases, such as *Siebe Gorman*, had become overly fixated with Lord Macnaghten's statement in *Holroyd v Marshall* that one could create a fixed charge over specific and ascertainable future property. This issue of appropriation was not determinative of whether the charge created was fixed or floating. Rather, the key distinction was the third limb of Romer LJ's test: whether the charged assets were only available to meet the debts owed to the chargee, or whether the company could still deal with those assets.

Lord Scott said:

> In my opinion, the essential characteristic of a floating charge, the characteristic that distinguishes it from a fixed charge, is that the asset subject to the charge is not finally appropriated as a security for the payment of the debt until the occurrence of some future event. In the meantime the chargor is left free to use the charged asset and to remove it from the security. [111]

By way of illustration, Lord Scott supposed:

> for example, a case where an express assignment of a specific debt by way of security were accompanied by a provision that reserved to the assignor the right, terminable by written notice from the assignee, to collect the debt and to use the proceeds for its (the assignor's) business purposes, i.e., a right, terminable on notice, for the assignor to withdraw the proceeds of the debt from the security. This security would, in my opinion, be a floating security notwithstanding the express assignment. The assigned debt would be specific and ascertained but its status as a security would not. Unless and until the right of the assignor to collect and deal with the proceeds were terminated, the security would retain its floating characteristic. [107]

His Lordship continued:

> Or suppose a case in which the charge were expressed to come into existence on the future occurrence of some event and then to be a fixed charge over whatever assets of a specified description the chargor might own at that time. The contractual rights thereby granted would, in my opinion, be properly categorized as a floating security. There can, in my opinion, be no difference in categorisation between the grant of a fixed charge expressed to come into existence on a future event in relation to a specified class of assets owned by the chargor at that time and the grant of a floating charge over the specified class of assets with crystallisation taking place on the occurrence of that event. [107]

This is perhaps a slightly trickier example to parse but Lord Scott just means that if you agree that a fixed charge arises only on the occurrence of some future event, then that event (even if acquisition of the asset) is no different from any other crystallization, and until crystallization any charge must be floating.

Lord Walker framed the distinction slightly differently, emphasizing control:

> Under a fixed charge the assets charged as security are permanently appropriated to the payment of the sum charged, in such a way as to give the chargee a proprietary interest in the assets. So long as the charge remains unredeemed, the assets can be released from the charge only with the active concurrence of the chargee. [One might question the commercial reasons as to why a chargee may agree or refuse to release the assets, but] under a fixed charge that will be a matter for the chargee to decide for itself.
>
> Under a floating charge, by contrast, the chargee does not have the same power to control the security for its own benefit. [138–139]

In view of all this, *Siebe Gorman* had been decided wrongly and would be overruled in the usual manner i.e. also retroactively.

It is perhaps easier to remember Lord Walker's distinction based on control of the security, but the words 'control' and 'security' are bearing a heavy load. As to 'control,' it seems more helpful to work with Lord Scott's temporal formulation: until such time as an asset is appropriated to meet payment of the secured liabilities owed to the chargee, it cannot be subject to a fixed charge. Appropriation means, and Lord Walker is equally expansive on this, such practicalities are put in place that the company cannot use the asset for its own purposes without express release of the asset by the chargee. The ways this arrangement can be achieved are various; the key economic point, as Lord Millett noted in *Agnew*, is that an asset subject to a fixed charge cannot form part of the freely circulating capital of the company.

The word 'security' occludes a problem. At the boundaries of the floating charge are future assets not yet acquired or generated by the company. Not just specified future assets but any asset to be acquired, whether thought of by the debenture drafter or not. How can Lord Walker speak of the company's 'control of the security' when by definition future assets cannot be under the company's control. The floating charge charges something, but that something is a set of assets wider than the assets now controlled by the company. So just what is the floating charge charging?

4.2.4 The equity in a 'fund'

Lord Walker's line of reasoning that control of an asset by chargee or company marks the distinction between fixed and floating charge leads him to a conceptual problem: just what is it that a floating charge charges if it is to cover even those assets not yet controlled by the company? His Lordship appears implicitly aware of Lord Millett's warning about asking the wrong question: questions about identifying specific assets are questions for fixed charges (*Holroyd v Marshall*); the true question for floating charges concerns control of the company's business as a whole.

IN RE SPECTRUM PLUS (IN LIQUIDATION) [2005] UKHL 41

Continuing directly from his comments above, Lord Walker added:

> The chargee has a proprietary interest, but its interest is **in a fund of circulating capital**, and unless and until the chargee intervenes (on crystallisation of the

> charge) it is for the trader, and not the bank, to decide how to run its business.[24] . . . So long as the company trades in the ordinary way (a requirement emphasized by Romer L J in the *Yorkshire Woolcombers case* [1903] Ch 284, 295, and by the Earl of Halsbury on appeal in the same case, [1904] AC 355, 357-8) the constituents of the charged fund are in a state of flux (or circulation). Trading stock is sold and becomes represented by book debts; these are collected and paid into the bank; the trader's overdraft facility enables it to draw cheques in favour of its suppliers to pay for new stock; and so the trading cycle continues. [139, my emphasis]

Much has been made of Lord Walker's fund analysis, its basis in equity and the obvious link to the concept of a trust fund. We can, however, go too far in thinking of the trust as the closest possible analogy. Certainly, it is right to speak of a fund if we mean as equity does, a pool of assets which may vary both as to capital and income, in which certain persons have equitable interests. Yet if a floating charge constituted some kind of trust in this sense, not only would the chargee have personal claims against the 'trustee' of the fund but there could be surely no conceptual objection on extending floating charges so that any natural person could grant them, given any natural person can hold on trust.

A far closer parallel is just what distinguishes the floating charge from the trust on that point of who may create it: the company as owner of a capital (fund) for its equity and debt capital providers. Company lawyers have long known how Baron Alderton solved the question what kind of property does a shareholder own: is it an equitable interest in the company assets or is the share a kind of property in its own right?

BLIGH v BRENT (1837) 2 Younge & Collyer 268, 160 ER 397

A testator willed his real property (land) to his son and his personal property to his daughter. Part of the estate were certain shares in a company that ran the Chelsea Waterworks. The son sought to argue, in line with a generally prevailing view, that the shares represented an equitable interest in the property of the company [*sic*]. As the company's property was the land of the waterworks, the shares were equitable interests in real property, and so properly belonged to him under the will.

Held by Alderton B that the shareholders had sold money capital to the company to put to its use to make profit, and in consideration the shareholders received personal claims on the company for a return of capital on the company's winding up. They had no property rights in the company's assets directly. Alderton B stated:

> Now, in the first place, we have a corporation to whose management the joint stock of money subscribed by its individual corporators is entrusted. They have power of vesting it at their pleasure in real estate or in personal estate, limited only as to amount, and of altering from time to time the species of property which they

24 Lord Walker referred to Sarah Worthington's, *Proprietary Interests in Commercial Transactions* (CUP 1996) 74–77; and on the CA's judgment in this case, her 'An Unsatisfactory Area of the Law-Fixed and Floating Charges Yet Again' (2004) 1 International Corporate Rescue 175.

> may choose to hold; and, in order to give them greater facilities and advantages, certain powers are entrusted to the undertakers by the legislature, and that even before they were constituted a body corporate, of laying down pipes, and thereby occupying land for the purposes of their undertaking. These powers render the use of joint stock by the body corporate more profitable, but they form no part of the joint stock itself; and one decided test of this is that they belong inalienably to the corporation, whereas all the joint stock is capable expressly of being sold, exchanged, varied, or disposed of at the pleasure of the corporate body. It is of the greatest importance to look carefully at the nature of the property originally entrusted, and that of the body to whose management it is entrusted: the powers that body has over it, and the purposes for which these powers are given. The property is money—the subscriptions of individual corporators. In order to make that profitable, it is entrusted to a corporation who have an unlimited power of converting part of it into land, part into goods; and of changing and disposing of each from time to time; and the purpose of all this is the obtaining a clear surplus profit from the use and disposal of this capital for the individual contributors.

It is this surplus profit alone which is divisible among the individual corporators. The land or the chattels are only the instruments (and those varying and temporary instruments), whereby the joint stock of money is made to produce profit. (294-295)

The distinction made is somewhat readily transferable to the case of debt capital. When a creditor lends to the company on a secured basis, the creditor has a claim in debt for repayment and interest, and ultimately a claim on the company's capital on a winding up (in priority to shareholders). One can view the debt capital invested as contributing to the capital employed or instrumentalized by the company. The money lent transforms in plant, land, machinery, stock-in-trade, receivables. What matters is not the form the capital takes but that capital is available to creditors in priority to shareholders on a winding up. Put a floating charge in place and ask to what the charge attaches, and the answer from the company law perspective is obvious: it attaches to the capital fund of the company, whatever constitutes it from time to time.

The argument here is that we must understand Lord Walker's 'fund' analysis as part of more general thinking about the company and its capital. It explains both why the courts of the 1870s were so accepting of the corporate debenture in the first place, and a line of thinking which informs the company to this day. To name just four examples, we have (1) the original sense of debenture as the instrument a company issues and which can be secured against its whole business; (2) the duties directors owe to creditors also under section 172 Companies Act 2006, duties which override those to shareholders on insolvency;[25] (3) the critical powers floating charge holders continue to have in appointing administrators, and generally by dint of their rights in all of the insolvency processes; and (4) the close link between the moment of crystallization of the charge and the moment when we consider the claims of the capital providers, i.e. on commencement of an insolvency process.

Using this company law line of thought, when we ask 'just what does a floating charge *charge*?,' we can now answer with Lord Walker that it is a charge on the fund of circulating capital of the company as such. And when we seek to distinguish the floating charge from the fixed charge, the

25 *BTI 2014 LLC v Sequana SA* [2022] UKSC 25, [2024] AC 211.

same company law analysis has no problem in pointing to the formal distinction between a creditor's residual interest in the capital of the company on a winding up, and the company's distinct property rights in its assets. It also may alienate these rights, for example by appropriating a given asset to a fixed charge and thereby handing over control of the asset to the chargee. The fact that fixed chargee and floating chargee are often the same person (with respect to different assets) does not change things; the analysis in each case is different (much as a person can be a shareholder, director and employee simultaneously within one 'hat' affecting rights and obligations while wearing another 'hat').[26]

4.3 The role of security in finance transactions

Let us now look at some of the problems of the law of security which typically arise in secured finance transactions.

The basic structure of secured finance is as follows:

(1) One or more lenders make loans to one or more corporate borrowers, usually documented in a single multiparty CFA. The standard interest payment and repayment terms apply.

(2) Where there are multiple lenders, this is called a **syndicated loan** (examined in detail in Chapter 6, but for our purposes you just need to know that there can be several lenders). To better coordinate the relationship between lenders and borrower, the lenders appoint an agent (sometimes called a **Facility Agent**). We examined this in Chapter 2's discussion of governance.

(3) The Finance Parties are more likely to seek security, and more of it, where the risk of non-payment is higher. Again, to better facilitate the management of multiple lenders' security interests, the lenders appoint a **Security Trustee** or **Security Agent** who holds and enforces the security on their behalf. The difference of name will be clarified shortly.

(4) The Security Trustee or Security Agent is likely to be a special purpose vehicle incorporated in an optimal jurisdiction having regard to (a) the situs (location) of the property to be secured; and (b) the extent to which that jurisdiction's legal system will respect the security interests created.

ESSENTIAL DEFINITION: SECURITY TRUSTEE/SECURITY AGENT

Given that a security interest is a property right, English law and similar legal systems permit a person to hold the security interests on trust for a beneficiary. Thus, a **security trustee** is a person who holds the interests securing a syndicated credit facilities financing on trust for the lenders.

England and Wales, Guernsey and the Cayman Islands are all common jurisdictions in which to locate security trustees.

In jurisdictions where the trust is not recognized (or runs the risk of recharacterization), lenders instead appoint an agent and nominee to manage the security interests in their name (agency being common to all private law systems). Naturally enough, such a person is called a **security agent**.

Luxembourg is often home to security agents for EU-based financings.

26 *Lee v Lee's Air Farming Ltd.* [1961] AC 12 (PC).

> Both trustee and agent are under duties inter alia to maintain the (validity of) the security and to enforce it as and when instructed by the lenders.
>
> As we shall see, a security trust offers certain advantages where legally feasible.

Appreciate that the law applicable to security, being a property right, is determined by the *lex situs*. Thus, in international financial transactions, while the CFA and other financial documents will be governed by English or New York law (or whatever is agreed), the security will be subject to security documents governed by law local to that property.

This fairly standard secured financing structure raises and responds to several technical legal problems of security law. We will examine the following selection:

(1) How might effective control be taken over receivables for the purpose of creating a fixed charge? This is especially pertinent in financings where the receivables form a significant portion of the loan to value, and/or provide substantially all the means of interest payment.

(2) If a lender's debt is repaid, or all the lenders are released in favour of new lenders, or if the borrower repays an entire revolving credit facility one month only to reborrow the next, does not the equity of redemption apply to release the security? Must the lenders seek fresh security every time?

(3) What problems does one face when one cannot appoint a security trustee because of local law considerations?

(4) In corporate groups, the parent company is often worth considerably less than operating subsidiaries because all the business assets are in the subsidiaries. What is the best strategy for taking security in the context of corporate groups?

In what follows, we examine these problems in turn to provide a sense of how the private law of security interacts with the practice of modern finance law.

4.3.1 Controlling receivables

When we discussed floating charges, we saw how the chargee's ability to control the receivables and their proceeds was a practical indicator of the appropriate of book debts to a fixed security. In *Agnew*, Lord Millett provided several illustrations of how this might be achieved. One of the most common, which we now examine, is control of specified accounts into which receivables proceeds are to be paid to the exclusion of the chargor until the proceeds are released by the chargee.

Our example comes from real estate finance, the providing of a loan to fund the acquisition of estates in land. In real estate finance the most valuable asset available for security is obvious: the land itself. Yet the land's value is without more a capital value. This is excellent should the lender require repayment of the loan, for provided it has taken a statutory charge over the land, it can now foreclose and sell the land to meet the principal debt. The problem is interest: we cannot sell bits of the land to make interest payments every quarter. We need a source of income, and as you may have guessed, the most direct source of such income is rent from letting the land to a third party.

It is this rent which is, as an obligation of third party to pay, a receivable. It is the second most valuable thing in most real estate financings and naturally the lender would like to take security over the receivables (and proceeds) too. As is shown in the following CFA drafting, this is achieved by creating a rent account which will receive rental payments and appropriate them first to pay liabilities to the finance parties, releasing only any excess once all monies then due and owing are paid. This payment 'waterfall' operates in parallel with the timings of the rental payment dates (and so the loan interest payment dates should also match the expected days on which money comes into the account). All this drafting assumes the creation of a separate all monies debenture which has taken security inter alia over the rent receivables and the proceeds of those receivables.

14 BANK ACCOUNTS

14.1 Designation of Accounts

(a) The Company must maintain the following bank accounts in the name of the Company with an Approved Bank:
  (i) a rent account designated the **Rent Account**;
  (ii) a current account designated the **General Account**;
  . . .

(b) The Company must not, without the prior consent of the Facility Agent, maintain any other bank account.

14.2 Rent Account

(a) The Facility Agent has sole signing rights in relation to the Rent Account and is only entitled to exercise this right in accordance with the terms of this Agreement (or as otherwise directed by the Majority Lenders).

(b) The Company must ensure that all Rental Income (other than amounts in respect of VAT which are payable by a tenant in connection with a Lease Document, which will be paid into the General Account) are paid into the Rent Account.

(c) If any payment of any amount referred to in paragraph (b) above is paid into an Account other than the Rent Account, that payment must be paid promptly into the Rent Account.

(d) On any day on which an amount is due to be paid by the Company (and has not otherwise been paid by or on behalf of the Company) under a Headlease, the Facility Agent may, and is irrevocably authorized by the Company to:
  (i) withdraw from the Rent Account an amount necessary to meet that due amount; and
  (ii) apply that amount in payment of that due amount.

(e) . . . on each Interest Payment Date, the Facility Agent must (and at any time after the security created by the Security Agreement is enforced in accordance with its terms the Security Agent may), and is irrevocably authorized by the Company to, withdraw from, and apply amounts standing to the credit of, the Rent Account, in the following order:
  (i) **first,** in or towards payment pro rata and pari passu of any unpaid costs, fees and expenses of the Facility Agent, the Security Agent, any Property Manager and of any other due put unpaid Facility Fee;
  (ii) **secondly,** payment pro rata to the Facility Agent for the relevant Finance Parties of any accrued interest, due but unpaid under the Finance Documents.
  (iii) **thirdly,** payment pro rata to the Facility Agent for the relevant Finance Parties of any amount of principal due but unpaid under the Finance Documents and any other amounts due but unpaid to the Finance Parties under the Finance Documents;
  (v) **fourthly,** payment of any surplus into the General Account.

(f) The Facility Agent must allow withdrawals at any time from the Rent Account to pay any amount due but unpaid under the Finance Documents.

14.3 General Account

(a) Except as provided in paragraph (c) below, the Company has signing rights in relation to the General Account.

(b) If no Event of Default is outstanding, the Company may withdraw any amount from the General Account and apply it at its discretion including, without limitation, making payments in relation to any Subordinated Loan.
(c) At any time when an Event of Default is outstanding, the Facility Agent may, and is irrevocably authorized by the Company to:
  (i) operate the General Account; and
  (ii) withdraw from, and apply amounts standing to the credit of, the General Account in or towards any purpose for which moneys in any Account may be applied.

Observe how this clause has been drafted with the dicta of Lords Scott and Walker ringing in the drafter's ears. The Facility Agent here, on behalf of the secured parties, has total control of the proceeds of the receivables (the rent) in an account with an approved bank (likely to be the Facility Agent or one of the lenders). This control is exercised for the sole purpose of appropriating those rents to payment of any sums due from time to time. The rent account 'waterfall' operates to appropriate to each such debt whatever account balances remain having satisfied debts further up the waterfall. Only when all such due debts are satisfied is any remaining balance paid into the General Account from which the borrower company is permitted to take withdrawals. That final stage of transferring the remaining balance to a new account is colourfully called a **(rent) sweep**. Given all this, the lenders might be confident that any fixed charge over the proceeds of these accounts will be upheld as a fixed charge and will therefore rank prior to any preferential creditors, floating charge holders and unsecured creditors.

For completeness, here is an example of the relevant drafting from the corresponding security agreement ('debenture'). The reference to the credit balance being restricted is technically not determinative for contractual interpretation purposes, but it is clearly the correct name for the clause given that it refers back to the Rent Account defined above.

SECURITY AGREEMENT: FIXED CHARGE OVER PROCEEDS

2.5 Restricted credit balances

The Chargor charges by way of a first fixed charge all of its rights in respect of any amount standing to the credit of the Rent Account and the debt represented by it.

Look at the general account in clause 14.3 of the CFA drafting—would it be possible to take a fixed charge over this account? Seemingly not, for here the borrower company is permitted to withdraw monies from it at will. It is only when a default is outstanding that the Facility Agent is authorized to prevent withdrawals. Thinking back again to our floating charge cases, we recognize what this is: because the balance of the General Account is only appropriated to the payment of debt on occurrence of some future condition, and otherwise remain part of the circulating capital of the borrower, there can only be a floating charge over the General Account balances, crystallizing on occurrence of the condition. Indeed, the drafting of the clause cannot be read any other way. Money swept from the rent account is clearly made available to the borrower company's use.

4.3.2 Equity of redemption: 'accidental' release

One feature of the equity of redemption presents a particular problem for modern finance transactions where more than one finance party is involved, either initially or by acceding to the finance documents at a later stage (see Chapter 6). As a corollary of the right of the mortgagor to redeem secured property on repayment of a debt, any discharge of the debt acts to release the security automatically (at least in equity).[27] This seems only fair, but in a modern financing we have a problem illustrated by the following scenario:

(1) Lender A has lent EUR50m to Enmerkar plc, secured by way of fixed and floating charge over the assets of Enmerkar plc. Lender A now wishes to leave the arrangement, selling the debt it is owed by Enmerkar plc to an incoming bank, Lender B.

(2) One way of legally achieving this is for Lender A to **novate** its contract with Enmerkar plc so that its contract is released and a new contract, on exactly the same terms, is created between Lender B and Enmerkar plc. Practically, no money need be repaid by the borrower; Lender B simply steps into Lender A's shoes and is now owed an equivalent EUR50m.

However, equity does not care about these practicalities: when the old Enmerkar plc–Lender A contract was released, the debt owed to Lender A ceased to be, and as a result of the equity of redemption the fixed and floating charge is automatically released. The result: when Lender B enters into its novated contracted with Enmerkar plc, its new EUR50m debt is unsecured. Enmerkar plc must grant new security for the new debt created by the new contract.

Observe the negotiating imbalance that results from this state of affairs—Enmerkar plc has what it needs (the EUR50m it has already borrowed and spent) and so lacks motivation to expedite granting new security. Depending on how the CFA is drafted, it may even argue that it has already provided the requisite performance in granting security once and is not obliged to do so again. Lender B is in a weak position because even if it can point to a contractual requirement to regrant security, until that fresh security is granted—and perfecting the security may take weeks, even months—it is an unsecured lender and runs several risks. These include (1) Enmerkar plc granting security to a third party, which will then rank prior in time to Lender B whenever Lender B is granted security; and (2) Enmerkar plc falling into insolvency, in which case Lender B will have to prove for its debts like any other unsecured creditor.

The following case involves a partnership, but it illustrates how a lender may, without appropriate legal advice, accidentally release its security.

GEORGE ROLFE AND EDWARD BAILEY, AND THE BANK OF AUSTRALASIA v FLOWER, SALTING AND COMPANY (1866) 16 ER 139 (PC)

Certain partners carried on business together and, borrowing money from Flower, Salting & Company (FS&Co), granted security to FS&Co. Later, the partners formed a new firm with two new partners who together assumed all the assets and liabilities of the old partnership. FS&Co accepted this new arrangement, receiving payment of interest from the new firm's partners and, when it became insolvent, proving for its debt.

R and B, who were also creditors of the new firm, did not want to share the insolvency distribution with FS&Co and so argued that (1) the new firm owed nothing to FS&Co, because FS&Co was owed money by the partners of the old business instead.

27 A security agreement may specify additional conditions be met, such as payment of release costs, but any clog or fetter on redemption is void.

(2) Bank of Australasia, also a creditor, for its part argued that even if FS&Co could prove in the insolvency, FS&Co had to deduct from the amount it proved for the value of the security granted to FS&Co by the old firm's partners i.e. FS&Co had asked for too much.

Held: (1) On the facts, all creditors knew full well that all assets and liabilities had been assumed by the new firm. In particular, FS&Co's continued dealings with the new firm as if its partners were all jointly liable amounted to sufficient assent to what was effectively a novation of the old firm's debts such that (a) the old partners' debts had been discharged; and (b) the new firm's partners were liable for new debts equal in amount to the old debt.

(2) The security secured the partners' old debt, not that of the new firm's partners, and by the equity of redemption had been released when the old debt was discharged.

(3) Given that the security had never secured the new debt, and had been released, its value should not have been used to reduce the amount for which FS&Co proved in the new firm's insolvency.

Rolfe is not really a recharacterization case because the parties were not attempting to do one thing legally only to end up achieving the other; this was the more common situation of parties doing something economically without having any regard to its legal affects. In the following case we do have recharacterization proper: a bank attempted to call a guarantee of a secured debt which had been novated.

COMMERCIAL BANK OF TASMANIA v JONES AND ANOTHER [1893] AC 313, [1891–94] All ER Rep Ext 1652 (PC)

Wakeham owed money to Bank, secured by way of legal mortgage of Wakeham's land in favour of Bank. Bonney guaranteed all liabilities owed by Wakeham to Bank from time to time. Subsequently, Wakeham agreed with the Bank and a further person—Marshall—that Marshall be liable for and secure Wakeham's debts. To achieve this Wakeham took back the land and sold it to Marshall. Marshall then declared himself liable to Bank for the sums owing, offering security by way of legal mortgage of his newly acquired land. Bonney died and Bank brought a claim for repayment against Bonney's estate.

Held per Lord Morris:

> In this case, the acceptance of Marshall as full debtor, in room and stead of Wakeham, which constituted a complete novation of the debt, necessarily operated as an absolute release of Wakeham, and it is, therefore, in vain to contend that such novation merely amounted to a covenant not to sue the debtor [Wakeham] for whom the respondent [Bonney] was surety. [316]

The key terms in the judgment are 'complete novation' and 'absolute release.' These suggest that something less that absolute and complete novation may not operate to discharge a debt and so release security. The next case concerns release of a surety—someone who guaranteed payment of the debt—but security was also in place the general principle extends to the equity of redemption.

BRADFORD OLD BANK LIMITED v SUTCLIFFE [1918] 2 KB 833 (CA)[28]

A company 'Samuel Sutcliffe & Son' borrowed money from Birmingham District & Counties Bank, secured on debentures and guarantee by Mr Frank Sutcliffe and his son Albert who were directors of the company.

Subsequently the bank amalgamated with United Counties Bank, selling all its receivables to that bank along with the benefit of all security and guarantees. Interest payments were now paid to the new bank, though the debentures remained in the name of the old bank.

When the company defaulted, United Counties Bank enforced the debentures and made demand under the guarantee against Albert. Albert contended that, following *Commercial Bank of Tasmania,* the loan had been novated with the effect that the sureties had been released (the status of the enforced debentures was not discussed as they did not concern Albert Sutcliffe as guarantor personally).

Held: What had happened here was to be distinguished from an absolute novation: this was a legal assignment of the benefit of certain contracts and of debts, the effect of which continued those contracts and in no way discharged them.

Scanlon LJ said:

> Novation means this: 'that there being a contract in existence, some new contract is substituted for it, either between the same parties (for that might be), or between different parties; the consideration mutually being the discharge of the old contract'; and, I may add, the undertaking of rights and duties by the new party: see per Lord Selborne in *Scarf v Jardine* (1882) 7 App Cas 345, 351. But where the suggested form of novation is that the obligation is transferred to a new creditor it is necessary to distinguish between a mere assignment and an assignment which amounts to a novation. Novation introduces a new contract and requires the assent of all parties; mere assignment transfers rights acquired under the old contract, and may be made without the assent of the debtor.
>
> [Scanlon LJ then distinguished *Bank of Tasmania*—there the debtor had changed; here the creditor had changed.]
>
> [A] statement that A., who is carrying on the business formerly carried on by B., will receive and pay all debts owing to or by the old firm does not necessarily, if acted upon, amount to a novation releasing B. and making A. liable. A. may be acting simply as agent or assignee of B. As assignee with notice, he can claim and receive B.'s moneys from B.'s debtors without having made a new contract with them by which B. is released and A. substituted as contracting party. [849–850]

The language in *Bradford Old Bank* is slightly muddy: there is not really any such thing as an assignment which amounts to a novation—an act is either a novation (entirely distinct obligations are created) or an assignment (the benefit of the *same* obligations are transferred to a new obligee). Some charity is in order, however, as this is a pre–Law of Property Act 1925 case and assignment of choses in action remained a difficult area.

---

28 This case is often cited for its two principal findings which we do not discuss: (1) the restrictions on a bank's ability to combine customer accounts; and (2) when the limitation period of a debt starts to run when the contract is silent as to when the debt becomes payable.

Financial practice has certainly taken this on board by developing a number of techniques to ensure the continuance of the underlying debt. A key one, which we examine in Chapter 6, is using assignment (plus assumption and release) as suggested by Scanlon LJ when transferring debts to incoming banks. This method only deals with transfers of debts; it does not help us situations where a debt is repaid (only to be reborrowed), as in *Rolfe*. This can happen more regularly than you might think:

(1) Lender A has agreed to provide a EUR50m revolving credit facility to Enmerkar plc secured in the usual way. On 1 March, Enmerkar plc uses the facility for the first time, borrowing EUR7m for three months for its general corporate purposes.
(2) On 1 June, Enmerkar plc 'rolls over' the EUR7m loan for another three months, paying interest for the first three months of borrowing.

Lender A just lost its security. What happened legally is that on 1 June, under the terms of the RCF, Enmerkar plc repaid all the money owing (principal and interest), then borrowed a completely new EUR7m. It matters not that no cash ever left Enmerkar plc's accounts; as soon as repayment of the first loan was completed on 1 June, the security was released by the equity of redemption. The new loan starting on 1 June is wholly unsecured.

This is a bit like the *Bank of Tasmania* problem. Though the debt has changed rather than the name of the debtor, strictly speaking there is a new debtor here also because the original debt has ceased to be, and we cannot have a debtor without a debt. By extension, any guarantees will be released also.

RCFs are not the only situation in which this problem can arise, for facility agreements provide for the possibility of loans over an agreed time period, even if the 'borrower' never actually utilizes the facilities by borrowing money. There may be multiple facilities, with the borrower using then repaying one, then utilizing another. We can multiply the examples to illustrate the risks. The question is: how can we deal with this problem and cover off novation issues occasioned by transfer too?

There are two principal methods:

(1) appropriate drafting of an explicit covenant to pay and definition of secured liabilities;[29] and
(2) use a security trustee.

Item (1) is essential; item (2) is nice to have if local law permits, otherwise a workaround is required.

The key is to ensure that when the borrower contracts, not only do they covenant to pay[30] what they owe[31] (important, but technically it will be implied by law), but that you explicitly draft this as

29 Jeremy Richmond QC, 'Covenant to Pay Clauses in Security Documents: Why Are They Needed?' [2020] JIBFL 245.

30 For a detailed discussion, see Richard Hardwick, 'The Component Parts of the Covenant to Pay' (2016) 5 JIBFL 288.

31 An explicit covenant to pay in a security agreement is recommended—something like 'The Chargor covenants with the Security Agent that it shall, on written demand by the Security Agent, pay and discharge the Secured Liabilities when due.' This helps determine a date on which certain rights become enforceable, including appoint of a receiver: *Cryne v Barclays Bank plc* [1987] BCLC 548. Some drafters make do with a halfway-house form of drafting which relies on payment being due because acceleration has occurred under the CFA. Parsons, however, thinks a debt payable under a contract and a demand to pay under a security agreement (which triggers enforcement rights) are doing two different things, and the best practice is to make a separate demand to pay under the security document as a prelude to enforcement to ensure such action cannot be questioned: Timothy N Parsons (ed), *Lingard on Security Documents* (7th edn, LexisNexis 2019) 7.4, and the original 'precedents' attached to old sch 5 Law of Property Act 1925. For a case where this distinction was in evidence—the mortgagor had expressly excluded personal liability to repay the debt; the mortgage was nevertheless enforceable against the land only—see *National Provincial Bank Ltd. v Liddiard* [1941] Ch 158 (ChD) 161 (J Farwell).

an 'all monies' or 'all liabilities' clause.[32] What this means is that you ensure the borrower is liable for anything that they owe now *and* anything they could owe under the CFA, *and* that this extends beyond principal and interest to any fees, indemnities, costs, judgment interest or anything else that could ever arise. The future-facing nature of this drafting is designed to ensure that even if at any point the borrower reduces its balance of debt to zero on a given day, it is still liable for debts that could arise in future and therefore the security continues to secure that liability too. By means of this continuing liability for future debts there is no point in time when nothing is or could be owing, and so the equity of redemption does not bite. The following drafting from a security agreement ('debenture') is designed to do just this:

AN ALL MONIES SECURED LIABILITIES CLAUSE

Secured Liabilities means all present and future obligations and liabilities (whether actual or contingent and whether owed jointly or severally or in any other capacity whatsoever) of the Chargor to any Finance Party under each Finance Document to which the Chargor is a party.

1. **Creation of Security**

1.1 **General**

1.1.1 All the security created under this Deed:

(1) is created in favour of the Security Trustee;

(2) is created over present and future assets of the Chargor;

(3) is security for the payment of all the Secured Liabilities; and

(4) is made with full title guarantee in accordance with the Law of Property (Miscellaneous Provisions) Act 1994, s 2.

That this securing of future, contingent liabilities works has been established in the cases.

RE RUDD (1986) 2 BCC 98955 (CA)

A mortgagee declined to vacate the mortgages because there were contingent liabilities still outstanding under counterindemnities given by the mortgagor against certain performance bonds issued by the mortgagee.

The mortgagor argued that allowing the secured party to retain the mortgages even as it had been repaid, simply because there was a mere possibility that some cost could arise in the future, amounted to a clog and fetter on the equity of redemption and should be struck down.

Held: Dillon LJ observed the mortgagee's position:

> would have the result that the mortgagor cannot redeem the mortgage while there are contingent liabilities to the bank, without making provision to the satisfaction of the bank for those liabilities.

32 Parties may not wish to use an all-monies clause, preferring a 'specific monies' definition of secured liabilities instead. This often occurs where a transaction involves multiple credit facilities agreements of different rank, such as senior and mezzanine loans. In such a case the senior lenders will wish to carefully circumscribe the obligations secured so that more junior creditors do not obtain security interests by accident.

and Nicholls LJ said:

> The consequence of this construction is that the mortgagor may find itself unable to redeem its property for an indefinite period, until it becomes known whether a contingent liability will become a present liability or not. So be it. I can see nothing surprising about such a conclusion.

Performance bonds are effectively guarantees of some third party's contractual performance and are not peripheral features of a financing but, where given, core obligations. As such it was a little strong for the mortgagor to seek to evade voluntary liability for something inherently contingent (third-party performance) just because the contingency had not yet arisen. In the next case the chargor sought to limit the scope of *re Rudd* to just this kind of core and explicit liability, arguing that future, contingent expenses and costs, being peripheral, were not covered by an all monies secured liabilities clauses.

RE INDUSTRIAL NORTH WEST LLP; KENDALL v MORLEY [2020] EWHC 3052 (Ch), [2020] All ER 93

INW sought to develop certain land, and financed this with a £61.5m credit facility provided by Fairfield secured on all INW's assets. The CFA and security agreement were in the standard form, the latter including 'Secured Liabilities' wording materially equivalent to the above.

Fairfield subsequently concluded that undertakings under the CFA had been breached and accelerated the loans, forcing INW into insolvency. Fairfield enforced against the security and were able to recoup sufficient money from selling the land to repay the entire £61.5m of principal and interest.

The administrators now sought directions that Fairfield, being repaid in full, were no longer a secured creditor. Fairfield argued that they continued to be secured because Morley, a partner of INW, had threatened to sue Fairfield personally for fundamental breach of the CFA by wrongfully accelerating the loans. These costs fell within the definition of future secured liabilities.[33] Note that this was only threat; Morley had not commenced any proceedings.

Held: The security agreement's 'secured liabilities' wording covered future liabilities, even ones considered contingent on future actions by third parties. Morley *might* sue, putting Fairfield to considerable expense in defending its rights under the CFA. Those liabilities were covered by the CFA and, even if the current debts had been reduced to zero, those contingent liabilities could arise and continued to be secured by the security.

---

33 On securing litigation costs and expenses, see *Gomba Holdings (UK) Ltd. v Minories Finance Ltd. (No.2)* [1993] Ch 171 (CA) 184H–185A: 'The principle that a mortgagee is entitled to add to the secured debt his costs, charges and expenses properly incurred is, therefore, firmly embedded in the law and is the principle underlying express contractual provisions such as those that must be construed in the present case.'

The 'all monies' drafting of the definition of Secured Liabilities in the covenant to pay is, as you can read from the suggested drafting above, allied to the use of a security trustee. Remember, we wish to ensure that a debt continues to exist in some form so that the security is not automatically released. If the all-monies drafting of Secured Liabilities deals with the liabilities themselves continuing to subsist, the use of a security trustee deals with the creditor ceasing to exist (for no creditor, no obligee) because of a novation or payment of one creditor but not another. Deploying trust law helps us sidestep these problems in two principal ways:

(1) As the drafting indicates, the chargor grants security to the security trustee, not to anyone else. The security trustee will not normally change, even as the creditors do, providing the desired continuity.[34] It is irrelevant that the security trustee is not itself a lender (and so not owed anything), for it is holding the security on trust for the creditors with respect to their liabilities—a legal arrangement of which the chargor has notice under the security agreement. This said, the security trustee will in fact be a creditor because its costs are indemnified by the chargor. Further, some 'covenant to pay' drafting might even create that covenant in the security trustees favour, for good measure.

(2) The security trustee deploys a further clever feature of trust law: the **class**. The security trustee does not hold the security on trust for a named set of creditors, perhaps replicating the problem of changing creditors, but on trust for a class of creditors. This class can be defined as each person from time to time who is a party to the credit facility agreement as a creditor. With class drafting, the identity of individual creditors is irrelevant, and we could have one creditor or 5,000, and any creditor could be replaced by another. There is even an argument we could have no creditors at any given point, given the future liabilities wording of the security agreement and a strictly logical interpretation of 'class.'[35]

The net result of the all-monies drafting of the definition of Secured Liabilities and the appointment of a security trustee is that the risk of the equity of redemption biting to automatically release any security is radically diminished. This permits syndication (lending by multiple creditors under a single CFA) and the secondary market in CFA debts, where financiers buy and sell debt obligations under CFAs. For more, see Chapter 6.

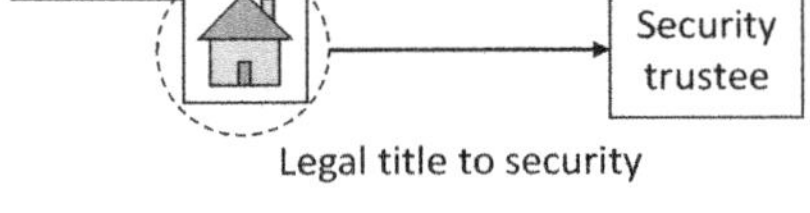

Figure 4.1 English law security trustee structure

34 For an example of a security trustee being removed because of a conflict of interest, see *London Capital & Finance Plc v Global Security Trustees Ltd.* [2019] EWHC 3339 (Ch).

35 It is logically possible to define a class which happens to be empty, e.g. the class of all five-sided squares. In this case it may just be that all lenders have been repaid, but the borrower has access to an as yet undrawn, uncommitted overdraft facility with one of the party banks.

4.3.3 Security trustees versus security agents

Appointing a security trustee helps mitigate the risks of accidental release of security, but what if the charged assets[36] and/or the security holder are located in a jurisdiction which cannot be relied on to recognize the trusts created? In such an instance, recharacterization could follow: the purported trustee is the holder of the security but only for itself; the security interests of the lenders *as proprietary rights* in the trust never subsisted.[37] At the least, this means the lenders only have personal claims against the purported trustee, and we can never rule out that even an SPV designed solely for this purpose could be pulled into insolvency proceedings. Worse, the local court may determine that no debt is owed to the purported trustee, and that as a result the security is released, or (as in Germany), the value of the security greatly exceeds the liabilities owed to the purported trustee, triggering overcollateralization principles which would see the security released at least in part.

In a cross-border transaction where the trust is at risk, appointing a security trustee could be regarded as reckless. We therefore require a solution with which civilian courts in particular are comfortable. That solution is to appoint a 'security agent' (although the name is not determinative of the legal effects of the role) to hold security by means of a **parallel debt** structure. Here is some example contractual drafting:

A PARALLEL DEBT CLAUSE

27.2 Security Agent as creditor (parallel debt)

The Borrower hereby irrevocably and unconditionally undertakes to pay to the Security Agent amounts equal to any amounts owing from time to time by the Borrower to any Lender under any Finance Document as and when those amounts are due.

(a) The Borrower and the Security Agent acknowledge that the obligations of the Borrower under this paragraph 27.2 are several and are separate and independent from, and shall not in any way affect, the corresponding obligations of the Borrower to any Lender under any Finance Document (its **Corresponding Debt**) provided that:
   (i) the amounts for which the Borrower is liable under paragraph (a) above (its **Parallel Debt**) shall be decreased to the extent that its Corresponding Debt has been irrevocably paid or (in the case of guarantee obligations) discharged; and
   (ii) the Corresponding Debt of the Borrower shall be decreased to the extent that its Parallel Debt has been irrevocably paid or (in the case of guarantee obligations) discharged; and
   (iii) the Parallel Debt of the Borrower shall not exceed its Corresponding Debt.

(b) For the purposes of this Clause 27.2, the Security Agent acts in its own name and not as a trustee, and its claims in respect of the Parallel Debt shall not be held on trust. The Security granted under the Security Documents to the Security Agent to secure the Parallel Debt is granted to the Security Agent in its capacity as creditor of the Parallel Debt and shall not be held on trust.

---

36 Appreciate that assets located in other jurisdictions should be secured using local methods as the *lex situs* is applicable. Nevertheless, an English debenture or New York universal charge attempts to secure anything owned by a company as a baseline.

37 For an example of such an argument, see *Akers v Samba Financial Group* [2014] EWCA Civ 1516, [2015] 2 WLR 1281 (law of Bahrain). On the some of the conflict of laws issues, including the Hague Convention of 1 July 1985 on the Law Applicable to Trusts and on their Recognition (in the UK, the Recognition of Trusts Act 1987), cf David Alexander and Stephen Robins, 'Samba and Its Implications for Insolvency Practitioners' (2015) 2 Corporate Rescue & Insolvency 55.

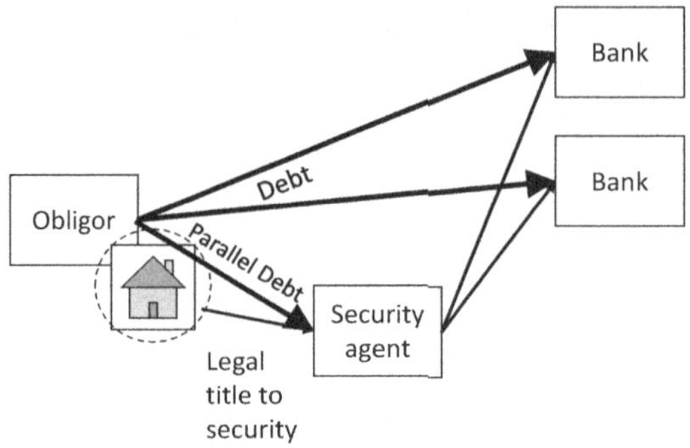

Figure 4.2 Security agent structure deploying parallel debt mechanism

> (c) All monies received by the Security Agent pursuant to this Clause 27.2, and all amounts received by the Security Agent from or by the enforcement of any Security granted to secure the Parallel Debt, shall be applied in accordance with this Agreement.

The drafting is slightly involved but the idea here is astonishingly simple: whatever the borrower owes to the lender(s)—call it *p*—the borrower has now promised to owe an amount *p′* to the security agent, where *p′* is always equal in amount to *p*. That parallel debt is secured in the Security agent's favour. The two parallel debts are wholly separate obligations and choses in action; the only link between them is that they are always the debts for equal amounts.

EXAMPLE: PARALLEL DEBT

Company owes £20m to Bank under CFA with parallel debt clause and Security Agent appointed. Company there also owes £20m to Security Agent. It does *not* owe £40m in total, but only £20m.

In June, Company repays £5m to Bank. Company now owes £15m to Bank *and in parallel* £15m to Security Agent.

In September, Company defaults and Security Agent enforces security against land which it realizes for £10m. Company now owes the only the remaining £5m to Bank *and in parallel* £5m to Security Agent. Security Agent applies the £10m it has received through enforcing the security: in accordance with the CFA it uses the £10m to pay down the debt to Bank (it turns the money over to Bank).

While a parallel debt structure cannot provide the comfort of granting lenders a proprietary interest in security held by a trustee, it at least mitigates the risk that the security be released for want of a debt owed to the security agent. Yet the creation of a parallel debt 'out of thin air' seems like another one of those sleights of hand by legal drafters. Surely a civilian court would see through the optical illusion of a debt which exists simply to recreate a trust structure using agency law and contract?

BELVÉDÈRE Case (*Cour de cassation, civile, Chambre commerciale*, 13 September 2011, no. 10-25.533), French *Cour de cassation*

Belvédère (B) was a French producer of alcoholic beverages with a corporate group structure based in France and Poland. The group had issued loan notes[38] via New York, and under the New York law contracts, a security agent had been appointed to take security over B's assets located in France and Poland. A parallel debt structure was in place: the USD375 of debts owed under the loan notes to noteholders were paralleled by an equivalent USD375 debt owed to a Security Agent.[39]

Insolvency proceedings were opened in Beaune, France. The Security Agent sought to enforce the security, but the French liquidators argued inter alia (1) that the parallel debt structure was contrary to public policy because it permitted double recoveries, and so void; and (2) the liquidators noted that some of the group companies were liable under the financing but had not granted security. Yet the charged assets secured the entire debt under the parallel debt clause. The liquidators claimed that at the very least, the security should only secure the debts specifically attributable to the group companies which had granted security (not the whole debt).

The court of first instance agreed, denying the Security Agent's rights to enforce.

Held: On the first point, the contracts clearly provided that the parallel debts would reduce in lockstep and there was no chance of a double recovery. On the second point, looking at the entire group financing as a whole, it was clear the entire group benefited from the financing arrangement and there was nothing to suggest any particular group company's indebtedness or grant of security should be avoided.[40]

It therefore seems that in France—a generally liquidator and debtor friendly jurisdiction—the parallel debt structure will be upheld. If one thinks about it, this is just an instance of what we have seen in the English courts, namely the parties have tried to achieve the economic effects of one *lawful* structure by means of a different *lawful* structure, and the court has affirmed that making such a choice is their right. Even before *Belvédère*, parallel debt was standard for London-style secured syndicated financings in continental Europe, and it was good to see the practice confirmed.

---

38 On loan notes as securities, cf Chapter 8. For current purposes you can treat the noteholders as lenders as it does not affect the question of parallel debt or security.

39 In fact, there were two security agents, one of which held the security on trust. It was a separate issue for the court whether to recognize the trust and, having determined the question should be referred to New York law, did recognize the trustee's legal title to the security for the purposes of proving in the liquidation. The case arose against a background of a legislative attempt to incorporate the security agent into French law (old art 2328–1 *Code civile*) which had proved unsuccessful. See further Reinhard Dammann, 'The Recognition of Trusts and Parallel Debt Structures by the French Supreme Court' (2011) 6 Corporate Rescue & Insolvency 181.

40 Two possible grounds which company lawyers will recognize are (1) lack of corporate benefit in a group company guaranteeing or securing the debts of another company (despite separate corporate personality, modern courts tend to see the economic rationale of intra-group financing structures, however); and (2) breach of capital maintenance rules where a subsidiary guarantees or secures the debts of its parents—the upstream guarantee problem. This is trickier, especially in jurisdictions like Germany, and specific advice is required to ensure both appropriate corporate approvals are obtained, and a contractual back-up is in place of the court voids the guarantee/security.

4.3.4 Taking security in (transnational) corporate groups

The principal risk of lending into a corporate group derives from the combination of the doctrine in *Salomon* (separate corporate personality), and the statutory grant of limited liability to companies which wish it (almost all of them). Although not strictly a finance law matter, the following case beautifully illustrates the problem.

COSTELLO v MACDONALD [2011] EWCA 130

Mr and Mrs Costello owned certain land. They incorporated a limited liability company for the sole purpose of developing that land. Critically, they retained ownership of the land; the company had no interest in it. They were the only shareholders of the company.

M, a building contractor, contracted with the company to develop the land, and carried out a significant amount of work. The company, however failed to pay. M now realized the company was impecunious so sought to bring a claim against Mr and Mrs Costello, arguing inter alia that (1) the company was just a sham for the real economic situation in which the Costellos used the land; and (2) though no contract existed between them, the Costellos would ultimately benefit from the works by M and so had received an unjustified gain at M's expense. M therefore demanded restitution on a quantum meruit basis.

Held: M had gone into the arrangement with its eyes open, contracting with the company, not the Costellos. Had it wished the Costellos to be liable, it should have made them a party to the contract and/or had them guarantee performance or provide security. The court would not save M from its own lack of caution. The way in which the Costellos had structured their affairs was perfectly lawful, being within the framework of the companies acts, and would be respected.

The lesson in *Costello v Macdonald* translates readily to the finance context. Take a simple two company group, for example: a parent ('Holdco') and operating subsidiary ('Opco'). In such a group the assets are most likely in Opco, namely land, plant and machinery, stock-in-trade and receivables; Holdco will be simply a holding company, set up to look for capital investment on securities exchanges. An example structure is illustrated in Figure 4.3.

If the Bank is ill-advised, it will repeat Macdonald's mistake—it will enter into a CFA with one of the group companies which has no (or few valuable) assets. Through intra-group loans and upstreaming of dividends, the borrower company can quickly disburse the loan to other group companies for their benefit, leaving the bank with a debt owed by a company which is all but worthless. The court will not be sympathetic save in the case of proven fraud;[41] banks and their lawyers especially should know better than to lend into a group this way.

Figure 4.3 illustrates just what the bank ought to be doing: (1) lend into the most valuable company, here Opco, creating a corresponding debt obligation the other way; (2) secure that debt obligation by means of registered debenture/universal charge over the entire assets of Opco for all liabilities of the transaction; (3) not forget about Holdco, but require that Holdco guarantee to Bank

41 e.g. *Trustor AB v Smallbone (No.2)* [2001] EWHC 703 (Ch), [2001] WLR 1177; but *VTB Capital PLC v Nutritek International Corp* [2011] EWHC 3107 (Ch); and Lord Sumption's and Lord Neuberger's discussions in *Prest v Petrodel Resources Ltd.* [2013] UKSC 34, [2013] 2 AC 415.

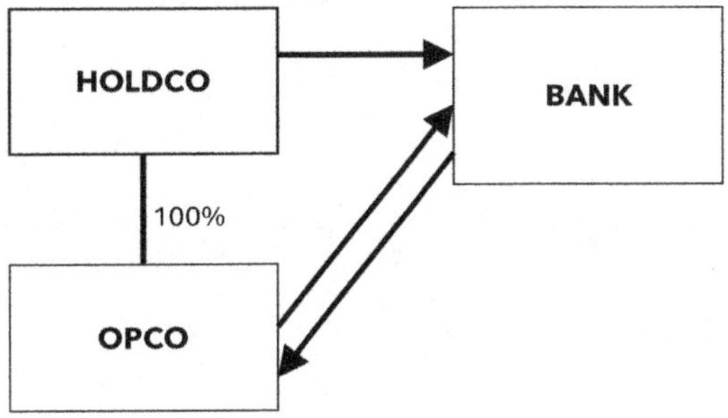

Figure 4.3 Lending into a corporate group

the debts of Opco, creating a further debt obligation; and (4) require Holdco to grant security over its shares in its subsidiary, Opco.

Step (4) is the neatest aspect of this whole arrangement—Bank has a debenture over Opco's assets, but enforcing all the fixed charges and the floating charge, e.g. by appointing a receiver can by quite cumbersome and time consuming. Foreclosing any statutory charge of land will take time, and selling the land even longer. Most critically, breaking up Opco's business through enforcement will destroy value. Opco as a going concern, with all its assets working in synergy, is worth considerably more than the mere sum total of its asset-parts. Provided Opco is not already in some insolvency process, it is therefore far more desirable for Bank to take control of Opco as a going concern. Under the pre-2002 UK insolvency regime this was effected by administrative receivership, but in fact step (4) provides a swifter mechanism which does not frighten other creditors quite so much and keeps Opco going. When the loan is accelerated, the Bank simply enforces the equitable mortgage of the shares of Opco. The effect is that the shares are now transferred to Bank, or its nominee, which becomes 100% shareholder of Opco. Bank can now effect a share sale to a third party of the whole business as a going concern. It is the shareholders of Holdco who are left with shares in a worthless shell company. Students who have studied mergers and acquisitions will recognize a parallel with the distinction between a share sale and an asset sale of a business.

Once the basic motivations of the above structure are understood, they can be replicated across corporate groups of greater size. As a matter of the law of security and guarantees, there is nothing in principle stopping every corporate group member both being a borrower and guaranteeing, and securing the repayments of every other group member, and indemnifying the lenders for any losses for non-performance. Company law, however, has something to say on the matter due to the doctrine of capital maintenance. As this takes us far from our discussion of security, we reserve discussion of this important topic to Chapter 7 and leveraged buyouts, where it is a critical feature.

Chapter 5

Commercial lending to sovereigns

Chapter contents

DOI: 10.4324/9781003457220-5

5.1 Introduction

In teaching finance law, it is often the case that students are also studying International Economic Law (**IEL**) and so are greatly interested in the financing of states, especially Low-Income Countries. At the postgraduate level one can also find a handful of students with practical experience of sovereign debt issuance and restructuring. The focus of IEL has traditionally been the public international law of sovereign debt and, accordingly, the powers and conditionalities of the Bretton Woods regime, including the International Monetary Fund (**IMF**) and World Bank, and the more informal Paris Club. To the extent that private 'commercial' lenders have been considered, they have played the role of holders of sovereign 'bonds' (more correctly 'securities' in Chapter 8's sense), most noticeably when these private lenders hold out against renegotiations of a poor country's debt burden led by the Paris Club and IMF.

Yet increasingly over the last couple of decades, more and more commercial lending to sovereigns has taken the form not of publicly issued bonds but of credit facilities documented by contract in the London Form discussed in Chapter 2.

> **DEFINITION: B2S**
>
> In this chapter, **B2S** means Bank-to-State and will be applied to any legal relationship between a bank or other private financial institution and a state, e.g. B2S contract means a contract between a private financial institution and a state.

Putting to one side momentarily the reasons for this shift, the increasing proportion of B2S debt has led to IEL practitioners and scholars calling increasingly for the expertise of private finance lawyers versed in the kinds of private legal techniques discussed in this textbook. Moreover, private finance lawyers have been able to bring new ideas from their subdiscipline to the IEL debates around sovereign debt.

In this chapter, I have selected a small number of topics and case studies in which private finance law has made and can make contributions to IEL.[1] It is hoped that such a chapter will be particularly motivating for IEL students, but it also provides a lesson for all regarding the interaction between finance law and the economic conditions upon which it operates. This is a huge area with great opportunities for country-specific research by students on the law and data relating to sovereign debt. This chapter provides examples of both, partly to indicate how a student might go about researching and writing various components of a dissertation on commercially sourced sovereign debt.

- First, we will look at an example of how you, the student, might go about gathering some quantitative empirical data on B2S lending which can be used to add evidence to qualitative trends we establish by other means, such as literature reviews (section 5.2).
- Second, we look at a case study which highlights one current problem area for B2S lending by means of CFAs, being lack of transparency (section 5.3). This culminates in possible proposals to improve transparency.

---

1 Sections 5.2 and 5.3 of this chapter draw on my research into the Tuna Bond Scandal, published as Stephen Connelly, 'The Tuna Bond Scandal: The Continued Lack of Transparency in Bank-to-State Credit Facilities Agreements' (2021) 24 Journal of International Economic Law 649, modified to suit teaching needs.

- Third, we turn (in section 5.4) to sovereign default and sovereign debt restructuring, and the continuing problem of a lack of an international Sovereign Debt Restructuring Mechanism. The focus here is on two research methodologies: (1) contextual research into the development of sovereign debt laws; and (2) transformative research in which academics analyse legislative designs and propose legislative drafting to governments.

These sections can be read in any order, though sections 5.2 and 5.3 cover closely linked material which is analysed quantitatively and then contextual-legally. The examples are provided to indicate the practice—the 'how'—of research in the hope of inspiring student dissertations.

5.2 Gathering empirical evidence of growth in bank-to-state loans

As noted in the introduction, this section aims at teaching you research by showing how research was undertaken. The fact that it provides financial information can be regarded as a bonus. It is aimed at students who would like to include quantitative financial data in their dissertation or thesis for example, though the methods here (once you get used to the financial databases) are simpler than they first appear. In what follows, I define categories (a typology) of things I wish to examine and then move on to gathering data about those things, presenting and analysing that data, and drawing conclusions. This is a very practical thing, and generally practical things are best learnt by practicing. This section may be best approached by those who are undertaking their own quantitative empirical research at the same time. By following my steps and observing my errors and perhaps successes, the student may through their own efforts learn 'how.' And like all practical things, trying and failing at creating research is important. Published research may look as if it has issued pristine from an oracle, but researchers do struggle, trip up, bodge, and bootstrap their way through until they have solved the problems they encounter, at which point the represent their research as if they had an infallible master plan all along. As long as everyone is honest through this process and open with the reader, all is well. So, student, do research. It is the best way to learn how.

5.2.1 The evidence

5.2.1.1 Typology

We are concerned with a very specific subset of what the IMF generally classifies as 'loans.'[2] Following legal practice, four categories can be distinguished:

> **DEFINITIONS IN THIS SECTION**
>
> **Multilateral Agency (MLA)** means international institutions with governmental membership which conduct all or a significant part of their activities in favour of development and aid recipient countries, and which include multilateral development banks.[3]
>
> **Private Finance Party (PFP)** means any person acting as lender, arranger, or agent which is neither a state nor MLA.
>
> **B2S CFA** means any CFA (see Chapter 2) whereby one or more PFPs agree to provide credit facilities to a state, or organ of a state, for consideration (usually fees and margin).

2 International Monetary Fund, *Balance of Payments Manual* (5th edn, IMF 2007) ch 5, 59.

3 The OECD DAC Statistics definition.

These definitions are terse and do require some familiarity with the jargon. The definition of B2S CFA is designed to capture bilateral and multilateral credit agreements under which banks normally agree to make credit available to a state. The state may then choose to draw down this credit, usually in a prescribed manner. In our case the majority of such facilities for which there is information are stated to be on a 'term' basis, that is, the borrower is expected to repay the loan according to a fixed amortization schedule. Such agreements have a relatively standard form, even if the governing law differs. This standard is the so-called London Form of credit facilities agreement as promulgated by the Loan Market Association.

The definition of B2S CFA is non-exclusive in that it captures any CFA to which a PFP is a party even if a non-PFP—a state or MLA—is also a party. The reason for this is that when states and MLAs do enter into agreements as part of a syndicate with PFPs, it is usual that CFAs still reflect the legal substance of the CFAs that interest us. It is also common, however, for PFPs and MLAs to provide funding under separate CFAs, their respective rights being dealt with by intercreditor agreement.

5.2.1.2 Method and empirical methodology

In this subsection I explain how I went about obtaining my data, or my **method**. The guiding principle here is replicability: can anyone else reading this obtain the same data assuming the database sources themselves have not altered. In a fairly simple piece of research, the method can be fully discussed at the start of an article or dissertation. In more involved empirical research, some or even all of this discussion will be relegated to appendices and even supporting websites, for space reasons.

DEFINITIONS

Method is the process adopted for the purposes of gathering data.

Methodology is the framework which sorts the data you have gathered into what is more or less valuable or significant according to that framework.

Example of two methodologies: A doctrinal lawyer and a sociologist both collect benefits forms issued by a social security office. To the doctrinal lawyer, the form is of little value; what is valuable are the statute and rules which authorize the secretary of state to provide for the issuance of these forms. The forms are only of any note if they are legally non-conforming. Conversely, for the sociologist the forms are everything, because society only interacts with the law through these very forms. As far as office workers and claimants are concerned, the forms are the only 'legally' meaningful encounter that occurs.

The data concerning B2S CFAs was collated on 11 October 2018 (the first reference date or '1RD'), and rerun on 10 November 2019 (the second reference date or '2RD,' and all data stated to be my own are drawn from this one dataset, crosschecking with available data from Jubilee Debt Campaign.[4] The data were sourced from a standard Bloomberg terminal and are not compared with data sourced from Bloomberg's chief competitor Thomson Reuters Datastream. The principal reason for this is that Datastream does not provide the granularity required to isolate B2S CFAs, being rather focused on fixed income debt (commonly known as bonds).

4 'Our Interactive View of Debt Across the Planet' (Debt Justice) <https://jubileedebt.org.uk/countries> accessed 13 July 2021.

As to Bloomberg, an LSRC loan search was applied to all active loans, ranging over deals and tranches. These were filtered using the BICS Classification for Sovereigns, within this selecting the subsets: governments, local government, regions, and government agencies. This excluded lending to central banks and other public financial institutions. The African data were filtered by country of risk 'all Africa,'[5] which limited the obligors, including guarantors, to that continent. They were further filtered (1) restricting to date of loan signing, from 1 September 2008 to 31 August 2018; (2) restricting to structure type: bilateral or (part-)syndicated; and (3) excluding public finance parties–only deals, which was done by manually filtering states and each relevant MLA.

The search garnered 234 results which provided the following information, where known: (1) parties; (2) dates of signing and maturity; (3) total commitments (amounts capable of being borrowed) and total outstanding; (4) guarantor; and (5) loan type.

The data were restricted in time and space for the following reasons:

(1) The Credit Crunch of 2008 is a marked macroeconomic event, particularly in the financial sphere. In the short to medium term, it offers, if not a 'year zero,' at least a point in time when finance retreated, and policymakers began their attempts to reconfigure financial regulation.
(2) The set of countries 'All Africa' is chosen as the initial impetus for this research came from a deal between European banks and an African state. The analysis could be readily extended to all emerging markets for which data are available.

It is important to be open about any restrictions ('boundaries') you place on your data gathering. Sometimes this is also called 'scoping.' Laws scope all the time: an English law will limit their research to the jurisdiction of England and Wales, for example; their findings on objective intention in contract law are hardly applicable to France. Scoping is thus not mere negative (I did not look at things) but an important positive feature of method (I know the things I did look at are not mixed up with irrelevant and misleading data). Being clear about your scope demonstrates you understand what you are looking at, aids replicability, and defines the validity and extent of the claims you derive from the data.

Likewise, one should be open and honest about the limitations of one's data. The data on B2S CFAs are subject to the following caveats:

(1) Unlike bonds, CFAs such as B2S CFAs are not subject to any generalized disclosure requirement. The data therefore represent what either states or PFPs have disclosed voluntarily. In the case of states, 'voluntarily' means either disclosure mandated by the state's own law, or disclosure otherwise by government action. PFPs are deemed to have disclosed to the financial press or data services voluntarily.
(2) The data are not raw but subject to classification, permitting my search. Errors in classification therefore cannot be discounted, particularly in cases where an MLA may have acted as arranger, but the lenders were PFPs. This should have not been excluded by the search, but the lenders may have been ignored by the classifier or not disclosed.
(3) The data indicated a handful of deals where PFP lenders were sub-participants. Legally speaking they are not parties to a B2S CFA, but to a back-to-back arrangement with a nominal lender under the B2S CFA and indirectly exercise many rights under the B2S CFA. It may be the case that synthetic structures such as this were included.
(4) Both active and matured deals were searched, though the results did not differ. This seems improbable, and perhaps matured deals were not picked up by the search.

---

5 As defined by Bloomberg's 'Countries & Regions' tool.

Having pulled the data together into a spreadsheet, I then started to interpret it. Being quantitative in nature, some statistical analysis seems reasonable. One should not get carried away with or intimidated by your ignorance of advanced techniques. A golden rule for statistics is the less statistical manipulation you engage in, the better, especially if you are primarily a lawyer. First order analysis—basically counting the number of things of a certain type—might look simplistic but it remains an extremely powerful technique. This is because (1) your reader understands counting, they can therefore follow your statistical argument, and so agree with it because they understand it; (2) given the transparency of the methodology, your legal readers can push back, which you should regard as healthy criticism; and (3) beyond your choice of just what it is you decide to count, the interpreted data are very close to the raw data and so less processed; the more you force the data through higher-order analyses, the more the sense that you are now telling others about the statistical techniques, not the data. So do not feel worried if your counting of the number of cases mentioning term x seems childish compared to a multivariate logistic regression analysis. As David Spiegelhalter writes: 'basic techniques take us a remarkably long way.'[6]

The data were then subjected to a largely first order statistical analysis, which revealed the following evidence of note. This evidence will be used to bolster the wider critical doctrinal methodology applied to the case for reform around B2S CFAs.

If we look at Figure 5.1, we see a growth trend from Q3 2008 to date, this being roughly approximated by the linear trendline shown.

We observe that these deals are somewhat cyclical, tending to occur in bunches biannually. The 12 largest deals, constituting commitments greater than or equal to USD20bn, severally involved Egypt, Mali, and Cameroon. The lenders were the following.

As we are primarily interested in the behaviour of the parties to B2S CFAs, it is most interesting to see who amongst those reporting these deals is most involved in the subsector. Seventy-one

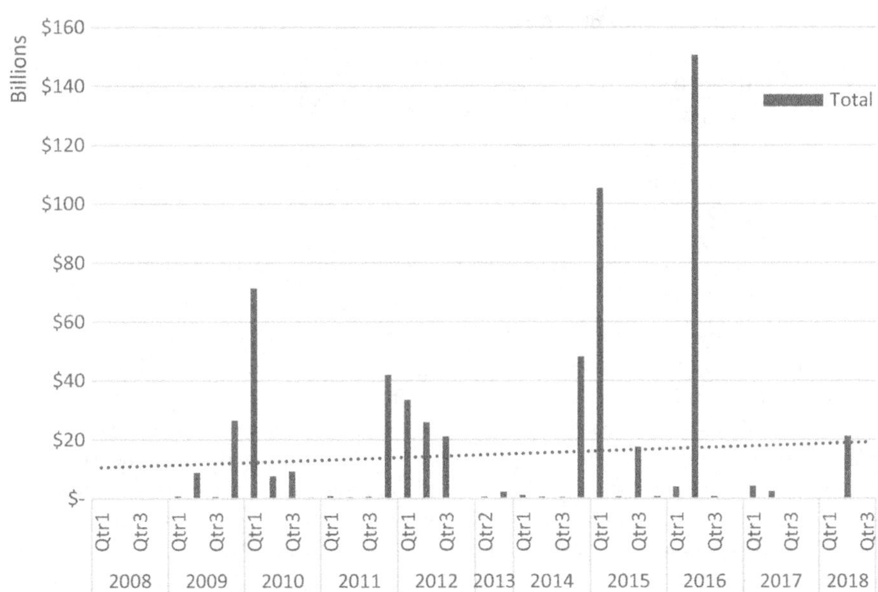

Figure 5.1 Total bank-to-state debt per year all Africa 2008–2018

6 David Spiegelhalter, *The Art of Statistics: Learning from Data* (Penguin 2019) 121.

Table 5.1 Twelve largest deals 2008–2018 grouped by state and lenders

Country of risk	Lenders
Mali	BNP Paribas, Banco de Unaio, Banque du Developpement de Mali, local banks
Egypt	Bank of Cairo, National Bank of Egypt, Islamic Development Bank, various Islamic finance funds, local development funds
Cameroon	Export-Import Bank of China, Federal Republic of Germany

Table 5.2 Leading B2S CFA lenders (lenders in three or more deals)

Bank	No. of deals
Undisclosed	14
EXIM Bank of India	14
Standard Chartered	10
Caixa Bank	7
National Bank of Egypt	6
Arab-Africa Int. Bank	6
Citigroup	6
Société Générale	6
Deutsche Bank	6
BNP Paribas	5
Bank of Cairo	5
Bank of China Ltd	5
Rand Merchant Bank	5
Export-Import Bank of China	4
Standard Bank of S. Africa	4
Banque Misr	3
BMCE Bank	3
Unicredit	3
African Export-Import Bank	3
Banco Bilbao	3
Banco Santander	3
Bankia	3

different banking groups were found to have signed B2S CFAs during the reference period. By this is meant that financial institutions may have signed agreements in various capacities and that it is not uncommon for different members of a banking corporate group to play these roles. For example, a secured loan will require a security agent, and where the security is subject to German law, for example, it is not uncommon for the security agent to be a separate legal person incorporated under German or Luxembourg law. Deutsche Bank's London Branch may act as lender and facility agent, while Deutsche Bank Luxembourg S.A. will act as security agent. These group entities have been counted as a single economic unit for the purposes of this analysis. Many such groups engaged in one or two deals during the reference period. Table 5.2 shows those 21 groups which signed three or more deals during the reference period.

As one can see, even where data have been collected, a number of deals took the option of not disclosing some or all of the lenders. In the instances considered there was no pattern to non-disclosure, as sometimes the disclosed arranger was an MLA, and sometimes some private banks were not disclosed.

Unsurprisingly, we find the UK's Standard Chartered as the leading 'pure' private bank in the sector. Standard Chartered has a long history of lending in territories of the former British Empire. In a similar vein, we find French banks lending in Francophone and North Africa, while Germany has developed links with Cameroon. MENA banks feature heavily, though their lending is concentrated in Egypt in the sample. Chinese and Indian finance also predominates, though interestingly Chinese banks are the primary vehicle for credit, whereas Indian finance comes largely from one source: the EXIM Bank of India.

A related factor for consideration is not the headquarters of a given bank, but the branch at which a B2S CFA was signed. This information was not provided in the majority of cases, but where it was, we found that many banks operated through their Johannesburg branch, or through London. The lack of data makes it difficult to draw conclusions on a preference for branch accounting purposes. One should note that where B2S CFAs are signed in these branch jurisdictions one would expect the choice of governing law to be English law. This is because an investment grade CFA is expected to be English law governed, whereas so-called South African Agreements are a deviation from the norm and are governed by local law.[7]

If we analyse the data by number of deals in a given year irrespective of value, a different picture emerges: the number of deals tends to fall over the decade even as total amounts increase. Figure 5.2 shows this.

What we see is an inverse trend: the number of discrete deals falls even as the value of these deals increases. Of particular note is the fall in deals and deal value in 2013. The reasons for this are not immediately obvious, but there are at least three macroeconomic factors which may have played a part. First, on the supply side spring 2012 broadly marks the end of the deepest point of

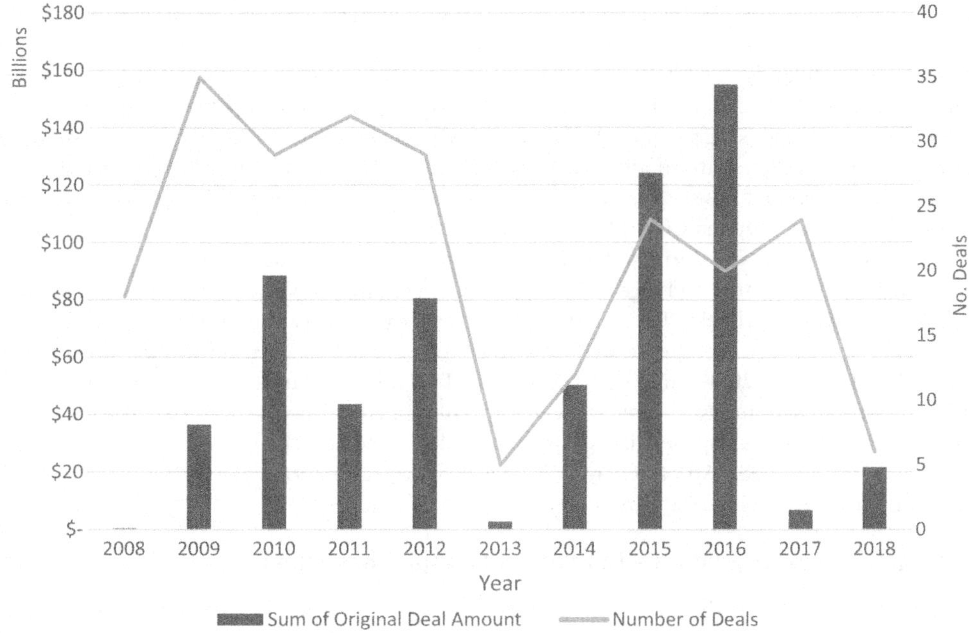

Figure 5.2 Number of bank-to-state CFA deals with African states by year 2008–2018

7 Slaughter and May LLP, 'LMA Loan Documentation in Africa' (July 2019) <https://prodstoragesam.blob.core.windows.net/highq/2496156/lma-loan-documentation-in-africa.pdf> accessed 6 November 2019.

the Eurozone crisis, when various measures had been put in place to shore up southern European banks and restructure Greek debt. Plausibly, this hangover from the 2008 crisis reduced the willingness of European banks to lend, especially in Emerging Markets. Second, 2013 marked a major tour of Africa by President of the United States Barack Obama, at which he announced a large aid programme to fund infrastructure. These funds may well have crowded out private debt that could have funded those projects. Third, 2013 also marks the end of a period of African debt relief under the Heavily Indebted Poor Countries scheme where mainly Paris Club creditors, but also some private creditors, provided a degree of debt relief. This scheme, which was largely focused on Africa, may have instigated a period of fiscal retrenchment under which financial indebtedness was constrained through to the end of 2013 before new rounds of borrowing, based on an improved debt-to-GDP ratio, began in 2014. Yet as we shall see when comparing B2S CFAs with all kinds of debt, all debt continued to increase in 2013. This is perhaps due to alternative forms of sovereign borrowing, such as B2S CFAs, bearing the brunt of reduced activity.

5.2.1.3 Lending concentration by state

Which states are contracting for Bank-to-State Debt? Using country of risk as the determinant, the data can be mapped in the following intensity chart (crosshatched states lack data). To do this I used the brilliant country charting tool provided in Excel. It allows you to present the data in a way meaningful to your audience and so to present a story about the data. A jurisdictional presentation is meaningful to lawyers, but note the perspective is the debtor country and that skews the presentation; I could have used a map linking the debt to the jurisdictions of the creditor instead.

One notices three zones of concentration: (1) Francophone Africa; (2) Tanzania and Uganda; and (3) variously South Africa and Egypt. South Africa and Egypt can be separately explained by the nature of their economies and the involvement of state and credit agencies in large projects in these states. High levels of Bank-to-State Debt should not be surprising for these states. The case of Francophone Africa is explained by the continued role of France in the affairs of these countries combined with France's *dirigiste* model of corporate governance. That is, French banks, like other major French corporates, are more likely to be involved in lending that would be undertaken by public bodies of other states such as the UK. However, while the data shows the significant presence of French banks in Mali and Côte d'Ivoire, Bank-to-State Debt is also provided to a large extent by MENA banks to Niger, and German state-backed finance houses to Cameroon.

What about Tanzania and Uganda? Surprisingly perhaps this concentration of Bank-to-State Debt is due to Japanese banks. TanzaniaInvest reports strong ties between these countries.[8] Exports from Japan to Tanzania has grown by 275% in ten years (2004 to 2014), amounting to approximately USD266.7m in 2014. Similarly, exports from Tanzania to Japan attained growth of 193% in the same period, amounting to approximately USD210m in 2014. The Ugandan investments appear to be linked to the use of Japanese banking corporations (as well as state bodies) to fund oil and gas projects there and in East Africa generally. This is driven by an internal assessment by Japan of its energy needs following the Fukushima disaster.[9]

5.2.1.4 Sources of lending—London and London branches

Finally, the data hint at the role of London as the locus for bank branches involved with B2S CFAs. To emphasize, our concern is with the current state of English law in its treatment of

8 'Tanzania Japan Relations' (*TanzaniaInvest*) <https://www.tanzaniainvest.com/japan> accessed 9 July 2021.

9 'Japan Looks to Grow Its Presence Across Africa' (*The World Folio*, 11 April 2017) <http://www.theworldfolio.com/news/japan-looks-to-grow-its-presence-across-africa/4264/> accessed 9 July 2021.

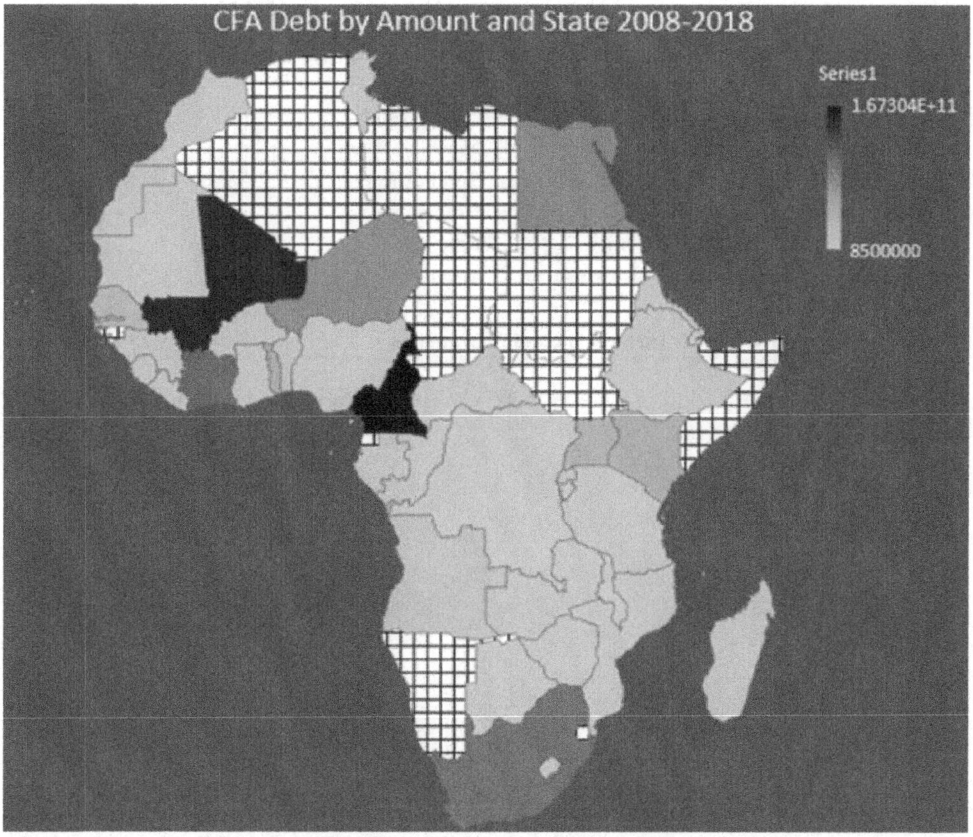

Figure 5.3 Bilateral and syndicated debt by amount and state 2008–2018

ultra vires state contracts, and questions of agency are governed by the law of the contract (English law), with London also likely to be the exclusive forum. Although data were sought on the governing law of B2S CFAs, insufficient data were forthcoming. I therefore assume a correlation between English law governed B2S CFAs and B2S CFAs to which UK banks or non-UK banks acting through London branches are a party. Indeed, as with the case of Johannesburg branches, one expects many more B2S CFAs to be governed by English law than just these London-originated deals.

Of the 235 deals analysed, 13 separate deals were found involving UK banks without a qualification as to a non-UK branch (Barclays, HSBC, and Standard Chartered) and 14 more which stated that the following banks (Table 5.3) operated from their London branches. The data on this issue suffers from three problems. First, the data were gathered pre-Brexit and so the EU law on company branches was in force. This allows a company incorporated in an EU Member State to establish a branch in any other Member State for accounting purposes.[10] The data do not capture whether a given non-UK bank is using a separate legal entity in the UK to lend, though FBN Bank UK Ltd may be such a case. Second, the data are highly reliant on the correct recording of branch information,

10 See further the Eleventh Company Law Directive 89/666/EEC, on disclosure requirements in respect of branches opened in a Member State by certain types of company governed by the law of another State.

Table 5.3 Lender London branches involved in B2S CFAs to Africa 2008–2018

Bank branch	Country of HQ	Instances
Citibank NA, London Branch	USA	2
Credit Suisse SA, London Branch	Switzerland	1
FBN Bank UK Ltd	Nigeria	3
FirstRand Bank Ltd, London Branch	South Africa	1
ING Bank, London Branch	Netherlands	1
Intesa Sanpaolo SpA, London Branch	Italy	4
Rand Merchant Bank, London Branch	South Africa	2
Total instances		**14**
Total Bank-to-State CFAs from bank's London branches		**USD 4,295,000,000**

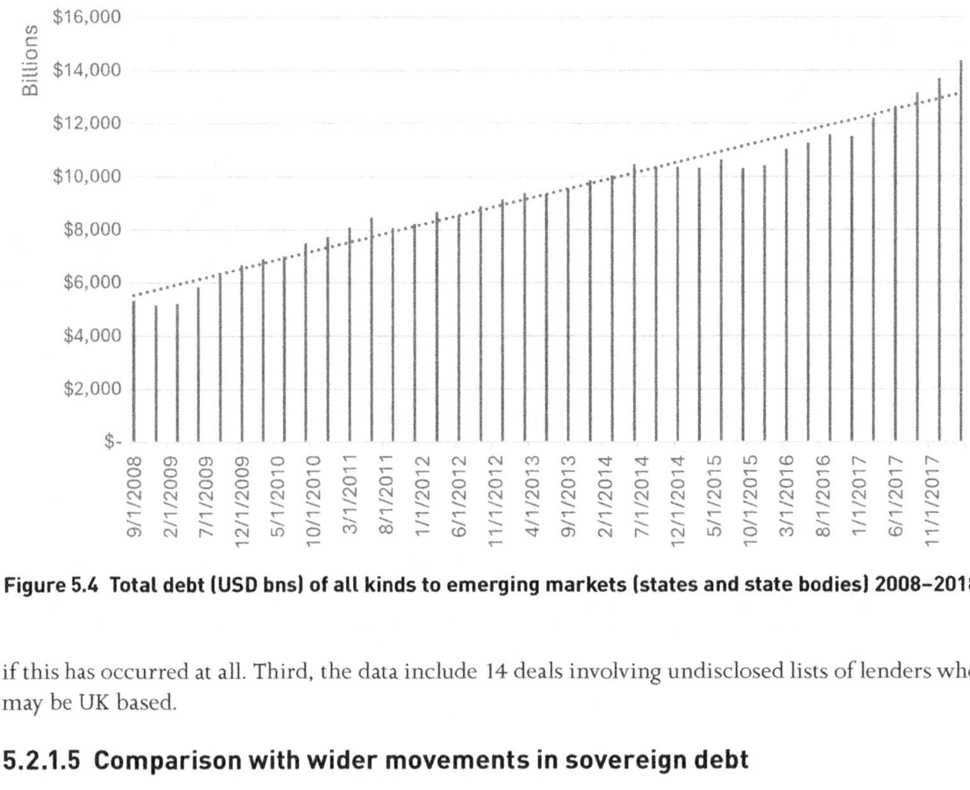

Figure 5.4 Total debt (USD bns) of all kinds to emerging markets (states and state bodies) 2008–2018

if this has occurred at all. Third, the data include 14 deals involving undisclosed lists of lenders who may be UK based.

5.2.1.5 Comparison with wider movements in sovereign debt

Returning to Figure 5.1, overall, the aggregate value of these deals expands over the decade to date. What does this expansion mean in the context of all African debt? Drawing on statistics from the Bank for International Settlements, Figure 5.4[11] charts the total debt lent to all Emerging Markets (Africa not being specifically differentiated in the BIS data) for the period.

11 Source data: Bank for International Settlements: BIS Statistics Explorer: Credit to the non-financial sector: F5.5 Total credit to the government sector (core debt)—at nominal value, USD billions (Updated: 19 September 2018 08:50).

The number of states, and level and instruments of indebtedness, are significantly greater in this instance, providing robustness to the positive growth indicated by the trendline. Given that the figure is cumulative, of most interest is the increasing trend for all debt which manifests growth (some USD2.2bn per year) of all debt over the period. The much looser fitting trend for B2S CFAs shows a smaller increase over the decade, being of a different scale (approximately USD214m per year). Thus, we only draw the simplest conclusion: that the growth in B2S CFAs into Africa increased at the same time that all debt increased into Emerging Markets, though the growth in B2S CFAs was intermittent, with bigger biannual leaps compensating for quieter intermediate periods. On this basis B2S CFAs do not seem to replace more traditional sovereign debt finance (bonds and MLA debt). Rather it appears that this form of financing—characteristic of corporates—is expanding to meet 'demand' for alternative forms of credit and potentially alternative 'corporate scale' credit purposes as markets are developed. In other words, there are only so many 'big ticket' infrastructure projects that can be built.

That is the general trend for all external debt, but can we find a more specific comparator? The International Debt Statistics of the World Bank provide such finely categorized data, though not fine enough to identify Bank-to-State Debt. Here we identified the debt disbursed and outstanding made available by external private creditors (principally financial institutions such as banks) to governments, aggregated on an annualized basis.[12] In other words we are observing at each data point the aggregate amounts of debt drawn down by sovereigns and the amounts to be repaid, noting that if an amount is outstanding for a period greater than 12 months then it will be counted twice, once on each reference date falling within that period. The states chosen were those of Sub-Saharan Africa. Data were available for 44 such states, the most notable omission being the Democratic Republic of Congo.

Figure 5.5 shows faster growth than that for the Bank-to-State Debt (see Figure 5.2). A similar visualization of the composition of these values by state over time is unhelpful, but the data does provide insights. South Africa is the leading debtor of the 44 states, being subject to private debt of almost six times that of the next most indebted Sub-Saharan state, with USD73bn in 2017 falling to USD68bn in 2018—some 49% of Sub-Saharan Africa's private creditor debt burden. Amongst the

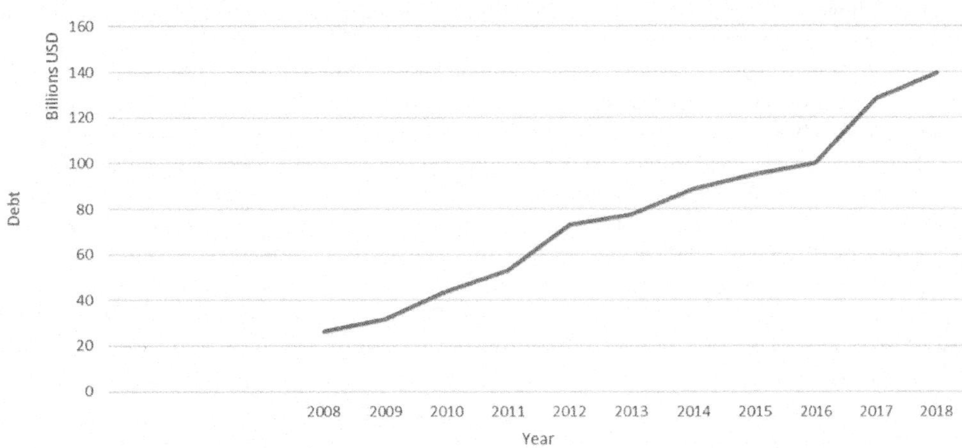

Figure 5.5 Total government debt disbursed and outstanding, owed to private creditors to Sub-Saharan Africa by state 2008–2019

12 Series code: DT.DOD.PRVT.GG.CD.

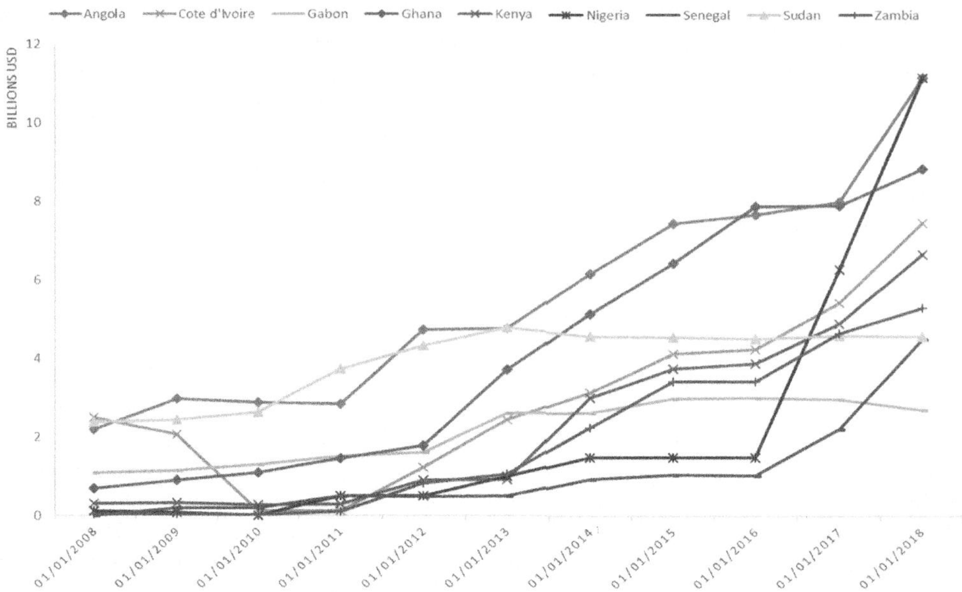

Figure 5.6 Total government debt disbursed and outstanding >USD2bn as at year-end 31 December 2018, owed to private creditors to Sub-Saharan Africa by state 2008–2019 (excluding South Africa)

remaining Sub-Saharan states with data for the time period, there are nine such states with disbursements and outstandings in excess of USD2bn as of 31 December 2018, accounting for roughly 42% of the total for Sub-Saharan Africa. These states manifest the greatest movements in indebtedness, as Figure 5.6 shows.

These absolute trends must also be relativized to the GDP of the individual states if we are to obtain a full picture. Figure 5.7 is a heat map of private creditor disbursements and outstandings in 2018 per state, as a percentage of GDP.[13]

While Cabo Verde is an outlier with private debt-to-GDP of 25%, six African states have the dubious honour of owing between 10% and 20% of their GDP to private creditors: in descending order, Zambia, (19.8%), South Africa, Côte d'Ivoire, Gabon, Ghana, Sudan, and Angola (10.6%).

Mozambique (the beginning of this research), though its borrowings from private creditors are in the hundreds of millions, not billions, has not bucked this trend. While its private debt-to-GDP ratio is some 5.0%,[14] the trend of increasing private debt in absolute terms has followed that of the major Sub-Saharan debtor states. In 2008 Government Debt (Disbursement and Outstanding) was USD7.2m, rising quickly to USD26m by end-2011 and exceeding USD412m by mid–2018. To put these pre-2019 figures in context, in 2020 Credit Suisse demanded that Mozambique repay USD622m in respect of the now restructured Finance Agreements[15]—an amount 150% bigger than the total disbursements and outstandings of 2019, and indeed 4.3% of Mozambique's 2018 GDP.

13 'World Economic Outlook' (*International Monetary Fund*, October 2019) <https://www.imf.org/en/Publications/WEO/Issues/2019/10/01/world-economic-outlook-october-2019> accessed 3 February 2025.

14 As of 2018: International Development Association and International Monetary Fund, 'Republic of Mozambique: Joint World Bank-IMF Debt Sustainability Analysis' (*World Bank*, April 2020) 3 <https://documents1.worldbank.org/curated/en/775751595863074749/pdf/Mozambique-Joint-World-Bank-IMF-Debt-Sustainability-Analysis.pdf> accessed 15 May 2018. The raw data show 2.87%, but Mozambique has subsequently rebased its GDP and so the DSA's figure from 2020 for 2018 is used.

15 'Credit Suisse Says Mozambique Liable for $622 Million Loan at Heart of Bribery Scandal' (*Reuters*, 22 January 2020) <https://www.reuters.com/article/us-mozambique-credit-suisse-idUKKBN1ZL1Q4> accessed 13 July 2021.

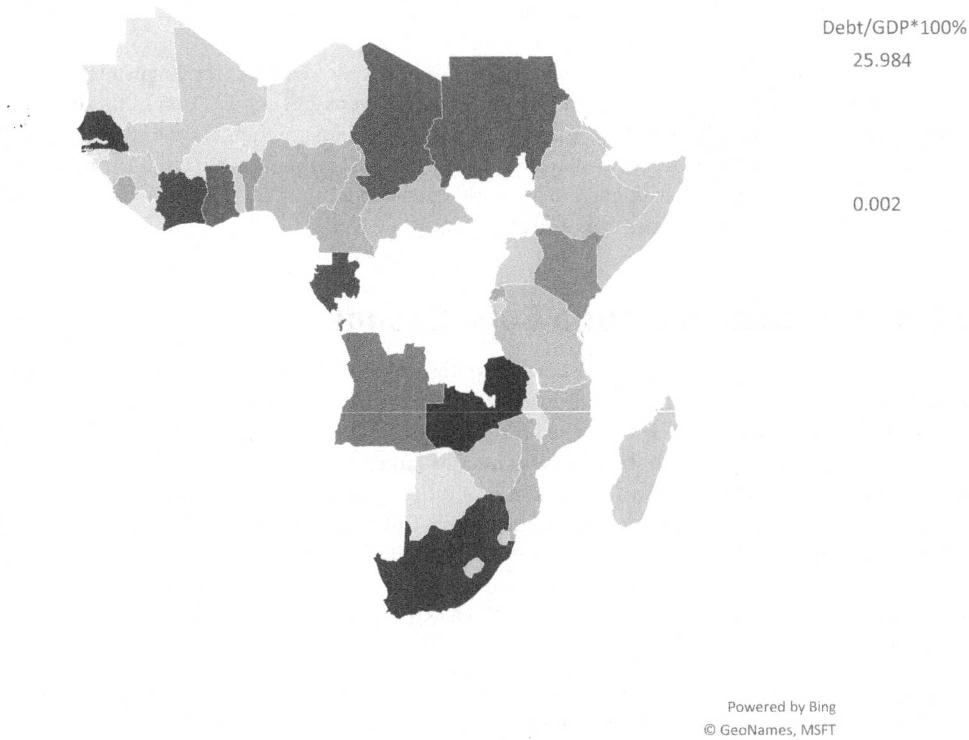

Figure 5.7 Private creditor disbursements and outstandings to Sub-Saharan African states in 2018, as a percentage of 2018 GDP

5.2.2 Drawing conclusions from the data

These data establish a general trend of increasing Sub-Saharan sovereign indebtedness to private creditors, providing context for the underlying growth in B2S CFAs established. While the identified B2S CFAs constitute only 2.8% of the total private creditor debt to governments, when we consider these amounts on a state-by-state basis we observe cases for concern, such as those of Mozambique, Angola, and Cabo Verde. The growth in B2S CFAs forms part of this generalized growth in private debt, but existing World Bank statistics do not have the granularity permitting us to identify the legal nature of the private creditor–originated indebtedness disbursed and outstanding. It has therefore proved necessary to glean such data as we can from other financial sources. These data are inherently incomplete because of the voluntary nature of reporting and the general confidentiality of B2S CFAs—a confidentiality which I claim aids fraudulent loan-making.

Why, as legal researchers, did we just trawl through all that data? One reason is that we wish to motivate specifically legal research, i.e. research about laws and their application. We may well have discovered a legal conundrum, but if it never arises in practice then we might struggle to convince readers as to why they should care to read about it. This need for motivation is particularly important where a legal question has fallen into obscurity—especially academically—but which has suddenly reemerged in practice in the face of financial developments. The data just examined are designed to show the increasing use of B2S CFAs raises real questions of transparency that do not arise with bonds because bonds are publicly issued and traded. In short: transparency is increasing in line with the number of confidential B2S loans governed by confidential CFAs. That observation motivates speaking about the legal risks of non-transparency (e.g. corruption and fraud), the law applicable in such cases, and, where the law is deficient, the need for legislation to reduce those risks.

Thus, our data is being deployed to motivate consideration of whether the English law of state liability for B2S CFAs should be reformed to increase transparency. Section 5.3 picks up this baton and takes it forward. It will undertake a case study of Mozambique which is used to demonstrate what can go wrong given the non-transparency of B2S CFAs. Together, the data and the case study claim that the chances of what happened in Mozambique happening again elsewhere could increase in line with the increasing number of non-transparent B2S CFAs.

5.3 Case study: the Tuna Bond Scandal

Given what we have learnt in section 5.2, we hypothesize that if the numbers of B2S CFAs from banks' London branches continues to increase, and increasingly burden states, then the opportunities for fraud—fraud relying on what I argue is the currently antiquated stance of English law—will only increase. The following case study of Mozambique (and as we shall see, Ukraine) demonstrates the stresses placed on the law of want and abuse of official authority and creditor knowledge, one would expect that we will also see an increasing number of cases before the High Court or arbitral tribunals in which the spotlight is thrown on City of London banking practices operating in the creditor-friendly shadow of English law. Therefore, this section asks whether English law unwittingly favours corrupt transactions involving B2S CFAs by placing the greater part of the risk of corruption on the side of states.

5.3.1 Credit Suisse and Mozambique

In 2013 and 2014 three Special Purpose Vehicles (**SPV**s) controlled by the Republic of Mozambique entered into contracts with three companies ultimately controlled by Mr Iskandar Safa (the **Privinvest Companies**) for the supply of fishing boats, security and facilities linked to the exploitation of the tuna fisheries of Mozambique's Exclusive Economic Zone in the Indian Ocean.[16] These purchases were financed by two CFAs in the London Form and a third private placement loan note style agreement also fairly standard in London financial practice (together the **Finance Agreements**). The leading lenders under the Finance Agreements were various entities of the Swiss bank, Credit Suisse, and the deals were arranged out of Credit Suisse's London branch: Credit Suisse Europe. The liabilities of the three SPVs under the Finance Agreements—including USD1.762bn of principal—were backed by sovereign guarantees under which the Republic was primary guarantor.

It subsequently became apparent that there was something amiss. Mozambique claimed to have no knowledge of these transactions, that it had never approved any aspect of them or received value. Mozambique alleges among other things that certain of its officials 'did not have authority to sign the sovereign guarantees, which were unconstitutional and illegal under Mozambican law' and that the signing of the guarantees was linked both to (1) 'large bribes [paid] to government officials' and (2) the supply agreements between the SPVs and the Privinvest Companies, all as part of an 'unlawful means conspiracy.'[17] These claims are denied. Mozambique—a Low-Income Country[18]—faces a bill for some USD2bn without, it claims, having ever been conferred a material benefit. Thus, during autumn 2019, while Credit Suisse had financed the asset purchases and had been less than

16 The facts are based on the summary by LJ Carr, in *Mozambique v Credit Suisse International* [2021] EWCA Civ 329.

17 ibid [22], [41].

18 Per the International Monetary Fund, 'List of LIC DSAs for PRGT-Eligible Countries' (IMF, 30 April 2024) <https://www.imf.org/external/pubs/ft/dsa/dsalist.pdf> accessed 16 September 2024.

diligent in investigating the authority of the signatories of the guarantees given by the Republic, it was initially believed that Credit Suisse was not (and specifically, certain of its employees were not) involved in the overarching conspiracy.

Since this research was initially prepared for publication, the Tuna Bond Scandal has moved on. It is worth highlighting two developments. First, in December 2018 the US Department of Justice commenced criminal proceedings against certain Credit Suisse Europe employees and, during the course of 2019, all but one admitted money laundering offences linked to the large 'commission' payments they processed (and skimmed) from Mr Safa's entities to various Mozambican officials.[19] While it is denied, Mozambique claims that these Credit Suisse employees also had knowledge of all material aspects of the conspiracy. Second, as part of several claims by Mozambique in the High Court of England and Wales which have subsequently been joined, Mozambique claims damages, for among other things unlawful means conspiracy, against Mr Safa, the Privinvest Companies, Credit Suisse, and others. On 11 March 2021 the English Court of Appeal determined that these claims were bound to considered by Swiss arbitral tribunal under an arbitration agreement between the Privinvest Companies and the SPVs.[20] It remains open whether Mozambique is bound by this arbitration agreement. In 2024, Credit Suisse settled the claims made by Mozambique, while judgment was given against the Privinvest Companies in July 2024.[21]

These events, particularly the admissions of guilt by the Credit Suisse employees, have shifted the initial legal analysis away from one focused on agency and abuse of power and onto unlawful means conspiracy, but all these questions remain in issue, and may once again become central with regards to claims against Credit Suisse if the bank and its now former employees make out their defence that they knew nothing of the wider conspiracy. Hence this research remains pertinent to the Tuna Bond Scandal, though, as stated earlier, the conclusions drawn are intended to be of general relevance.

The hypothesis is that the English law of powers and agency as it relates to sovereign states parties to CFAs between such states and private commercial parties (**B2S CFAs**), wrongly distributes the risk of an agent's abuse of power onto the state, and consequently the law as it stands will come under increasing pressure given the evidence of an increase in these types of contracts, unless there is legislative intervention to remedy current doctrine. The hypothesis suggests three research questions:

(1) To what extent do empirical data establish that sovereign states are making increasing use of relatively non-transparent private commercial party financing via B2S CFAs, rather than the more traditional public issuance of bonds and official debt? We have already done this work in section 5.2.

(2) Building on Theodor Meron's analysis of state responsibility, Lee Buchheit and others' account of contractual responsibility under New York law,[22] and Jeff King's related analysis of the enforceability of loan contracts having unlawful purposes,[23] what is the current English law of powers and agency as it relates to sovereign states entering into finance contracts, and on which party does the risk of agent abuse of power fall? (section 5.3.2)?

(3) Given the legal deficiencies and empirical evidence, what possible emendations to the English law of agency in these cases might counter the mischief of official agents and others conspiring to abuse their power when negotiating B2S CFAs? (section 5.3.4)?

19 Brendan Pierson, 'Ex-Credit Suisse Banker Pleads Guilty to U.S. Charge Over Mozambique Loan' (*Reuters*, 20 May 2019) <https://www.reuters.com/article/us-mozambique-credit-suisse-charges-idUSKCN1SQ2E1> accessed 13 July 2021.

20 International Monetary Fund (n 18).

21 *Republic of Mozambique v Credit Suisse International and Others* [2024] EWHC 1957 (Comm).

22 Lee C Buchheit, Mitu Gulati and Robert B Thompson, 'The Dilemma of Odious Debts' (2007) 56 Duke LJ 1201.

23 Jeff King, *The Doctrine of Odious Debt in International Law: A Restatement* (CUP 2016).

The analysis builds both on modern legal histories of the transactions and doctrine underpinning loans made to states, and, with its Mozambican-focus, country-specific analyses, which combine several legal subdisciplines: the private (international) law of loan agreements;[24] work on the G20 and Paris Club 2020 Debt-Service Suspension Initiative;[25] country-specific analyses of sovereign financing;[26] and work on the Highly-Indebted Poor Country debt forgiveness programme which foreshadows the move to Bank-to-State Debt.[27] The research adds to this literature by focusing on Mozambique, which to date has rather been the subject of studies on internal corruption.[28] One should also note an innovative study of creditor—China and its banks—rather than debtor state legal practices.[29]

Our focus is on a specific doctrinal issue relating to lending to sovereigns: where a credit facilities agreement is signed in abuse of authority by a corrupt official. This particular wrong would therefore fall foul of the 2012 restatement of UNCTAD *Principles on Responsible Sovereign Lending and Borrowing*, Principle 3 of which provides that:

> Lenders have a responsibility to determine, to the best of their ability, whether the financing has been appropriately authorized and whether the resulting credit agreements are valid and enforceable under relevant jurisdiction/s.[30]

Michael Waibel argues that the *Principles* 'reflect, to a considerable degree, how states and creditors of states act,'[31] and while Waibel's focus is primarily on the restructuring aspects of these Principles, there is a need for empirical analysis of actual loan agreements to assess whether compliance with Principle 3 is indeed the norm. Anna Gelpern is more circumspect,[32] writing '[a]gency problems, time inconsistency, information asymmetries, and moral hazard are perennial risks in sovereign lending and borrowing. Public officials borrow in the name of the people, but not in their interest.'[33] She argues that there is a need for 'substantive and technical elaboration over time,' and that the Principles could support best practices, due diligence and domestic legislative efforts.[34] One

---

24 Lee C Buchheit and Mitu Gulati, 'Responsible Sovereign Lending and Borrowing' (2010) 73 Law & Contemporary Problems 62.

25 See Schwan Badirou Gafari and Arthur Bauer, 'l'Action du Club de Paris et du G20 en matière de traitement de dette à l'heure de la Covid-19' (2021) 141 Revue d'Économie Financière 255; Juuso Kaaresvirta and Helinä Laakkonen, 'China as an International Creditor' (2021) 5 BOFIT Policy Brief 3.

26 Thomas Laryea, '*Donegal v Zambia* and the Persistent Debt Problems of Low-Income Countries' (2010) 73 Law & Contemporary Problems 193. This was collected together in the journal with articles by: Manuel Monteaguado (Peru) 201, Jeanne C Oliver (Argentina) 241, Arturo C Porzecanski (Ecuador) 251, and Mark H Stumpf (Bosnia) 301.

27 Celine Tan, 'Reframing the Debate: The Debt Relief Initiative and New Normative Values in the Governance of Third World Debt' (2014) 10 International Journal of Law in Context 249; Leonie F Guder, *The Administration of Debt Relief by the International Financial Institutions: A Legal Reconstruction of the HIPC Initiative* (Springer 2009); Mark A Walker and Barthélemy Faye, 'Sovereign Debt Renegotiation: Restructuring the Commercial Debt of HIPC Debtor Countries' (2010) 73 Law & Contemporary Problems 317.

28 David Stasavage, 'Causes and Consequences of Corruption: Mozambique in Transition' (1999) 37 Journal of Commonwealth & Comparative Politics 65. For a recent economic survey of corruption across Mozambican society see Inge Tvedten and Rachi Picardo, '"Goats Eat Where They are Tied Up": Illicit and Habitual Corruption in Mozambique' (2018) 45 Review of African Political Economy 541.

29 Anna Gelpern and others, 'How China Lends: A Rare Look into 100 Debt Contracts with Foreign Governments' (2021) Center for Global Development Working Paper No. 573 <https://www.cgdev.org/publication/how-china-lends-rare-look-into-100-debt-contracts-foreign-governments> accessed 16 September 2024.

30 United Nations Conference on Trade and Development, 'Principles on Promoting Responsible Sovereign Lending and Borrowing' (2012) <https://unctad.org/system/files/official-document/gdsddf2012misc1_en.pdf> accessed 1 July 2021.

31 Michael Waibel, 'Out of Thin Air? Tracing the Origins of the UNCTAD Principles of Customary International Law' in Carlos Espósito and others (eds), *Sovereign Financing and International Law: The UNCTAD Principles on Responsible Sovereign Lending and Borrowing* (OUP 2013) 88, 111.

32 Anna Gelpern, 'Hard, Soft, and Embedded: Implementing Principles and Promoting Responsible Sovereign Lending and Borrowing' in Esposito (ed), *Sovereign Financing* 347–82.

33 ibid 347–48.

34 ibid 381.

attempt at this augmentation has been the Institute of International Finance's 2017 *Voluntary Principles for Debt Transparency*,[35] but while expanding on the notion of full disclosure they too are voluntary. In analysing one such substantive and technical aspect, and in proposing binding legislative reform, this research also builds on Gelpern's call to action in concrete ways.

5.3.2 The current state of the law

As LJ Garay Salamanca has shown, B2S CFAs are hardly new, having developed in the Eurodollar market in the late 1960s, before taking off in the late 1970s, particularly as more actors entered the market.[36] Thus:

> Gradually, the criteria for credit extension as well as the borrowers' objectives deemed eligible for financing became more flexible, and more financing was granted to the public sector. . . . In the Latin American case, the public sector share in the stock of medium- and long-term external commercial bank debt increased from 53 percent to 58 percent between 1975 and 1981, while the share of commercial bank debt increased from 49 percent to 65 percent of the total stock of medium- and long-term external government debt. Meanwhile, the share of short-term debt in the total commercial debt balance increased from 21 percent to 28 percent during this period.[37]

The consequences of defaulting on these loans are well-known. States languish in a pre-insolvency law realm in which sovereign pseudo-bankruptcies descend into a creditor free-for-all. Nor need we rehearse the many instances of (un)successful workout, the calls for some kind of international insolvency regime perhaps modelled on the US Bankruptcy Code Chapter 9,[38] or the ad hoc efforts of stakeholders to ameliorate this situation, for example through recommendations on the adoption of Collective Action Clauses,[39] or the HIPC programme.[40] Our concern, however, is not the endgame of indebtedness but rather the moment of creation of the indebtedness, a moment in which debts may be incurred in a questionable manner.

Our particular concern is just those situations where one or more banks lends to a state on the basis of a credit facilities agreement governed, for the sake of argument, by English law (though the discussion is generalizable to other common law systems which follow English agency law, such as Singapore and Malaysia). As noted above, UNCTAD Principle 3 promotes the idea creditors have responsibility to determine whether a creditor has been authorized, but this responsibility is not reflected in English law. First, the state must act through its officials and, as in the case of the Mozambique loans scandal, those officials may be acting for some alleged ulterior motive in binding the state to a credit facilities agreement. As a matter of applicable law, will the state be bound to such a contract? Excluded from this analysis are cases identified by Jeff King where the contract is contrary to public policy or otherwise for an unlawful purpose—there may

35 Institute of International Finance, 'Voluntary Principles for Debt Transparency' <https://www.iif.com/Portals/0/Files/Principles%20for%20Debt%20Transparency.pdf> accessed 12 July 2021.

36 Luis Jorge Garay Salamanca, 'The 1980s Crisis in Syndicated Bank Lending to Sovereigns and the Sequence of Mechanisms to Fix It' in Barry Herman and others (eds), *Overcoming Developing Country Debt Crises* (OUP 2010) 111.

37 ibid 113.

38 Anne Krueger, *International Financial Architecture for 2002: A New Approach to Sovereign Debt Restructuring* (International Monetary Fund 2002) <https://www.imf.org/external/pubs/ft/exrp/sdrm/eng/sdrm.pdf> accessed 20 April 2024. Barry Eichengreen, *Towards a New International Financial Architecture* (Peterson Institute for International Economics 1999); Kunibert Raffer, 'Applying Chapter 9 Insolvency to International Debts: An Economically Efficient Solution with Human Face' (1990) 18 World Development 301.

39 Nancy P Jacklin, 'Addressing Collective-Action Problems in Securitized Credit' (2010) 74 Law & Contemporary Problems 175.

40 Guder (n 27).

well be fraud in cases such as the Tuna Bond Scandal but the fraud in such cases uses the lawfulness of a contract as a façade.[41]

The basic principle, from which our analysis follows, is that as a matter of English law a foreign state which enters into a private English law agreement with a private entity is regarded as acting analogously to a corporation.[42] Indeed, 'the case of a foreign government is the same as that of a corporation, and the ordinary practice applicable to a corporation must be adapted, as well as it would admit.'[43] In what remains the leading international law analysis of state's liability for contracts and their right of repudiation, Theodor Meron finds that in the municipal laws that he has examined, states are either explicitly regarded as corporations, or implicitly so in that the analysis of authority that follows assumes an equivalency.[44] English law appears to adopt the implicit approach, which the Court of Appeal quoted in *Law Debenture Trust Corporation v Ukraine* (2018):

> In conclusion, it appears that although analogies with corporations might usefully be drawn in particular respects, a foreign State in English law is not a foreign corporation, or an English corporation, either sole or aggregate, or a 'quasi-corporation,' or even an English legal person of whatever kind.[45]

The Court of Appeal qualified this formulation: Ukraine was present for the purposes of private rights in England because of recognition by the Crown, acting through HM Government.[46] The recognition conferred legal personality (though not a personhood constituted *ex nihilo* by English law or foreign law), and the cases were clear that this personality was its own and not the same as that of individual state officials. Further, some analogy could be drawn with international organizations which are explicitly regarded as corporations.[47] In any event, it was enough to observe that having legal personality, a foreign state had the power to make contracts and to authorize agents to make them on its behalf.

The finding that a state has a capacity analogous to a corporation leads us to the follow analytical questions: (1) Can a state only act in furtherance of its objects? (2) May a state only act by deploying its powers? (3) How does a state, being a legal person, act through its duly authorized agents (directly or indirectly, natural persons)? Questions 1 and 2 are usually regarded as part of the ultra vires rule and should be considered first in any legal analysis. Question 3 initiates a secondary consideration of the rules of agency which tie directly back to UNCTAD Principle 3.

5.3.2.1 Ultra vires

On the above assumptions, the Court of Appeal in *LDTC v Ukraine*,[48] regarded the application of the doctrine of ultra vires as fairly straightforward:

> English law imposes no restrictions on the capacity of those who have legal personality under English law, so as to render any act by them *ultra vires* and void . . . . There is no

41 King (n 23) 146–53.

42 *Prioleau v United States and Johnson* (1866) LR 2 Eq 659 (Ch).

43 *Peru v Wegelin* (1875) LR 20 Eq 140 (CA) 141–2 (VC Hall).

44 Theodor Meron, 'Repudiation of *Ultra Vires* State Contracts and the International Responsibility of States' (1957) 6 International & Comparative Law Quarterly 273, 289.

45 [2018] EWCA Civ 2026 [63], quoting Geoffrey Marston, 'The Personality of the Foreign State in English Law' (1997) 56 CLJ 374.

46 ibid [55]–[75].

47 s 1(2)(a) International Organisations Act 1968.

48 [2018] EWCA Civ 2026 (n 45). The Supreme Court heard Ukraine's appeal (unsuccessful on the ultra vires point) in [2023] UKSC 11.

> prerogative or statutory authority for limiting the capacity and powers enjoyed by a foreign state, which has legal personality in English law by virtue of its recognition as such by HMG. It follows from the absence of any limits at common law that as a matter of English law the foreign state enjoys unlimited capacity. Where it enters into a contract governed by English law, a foreign state will not therefore lack capacity to make and perform the contract, irrespective of the provisions of its own domestic constitution and laws.[49]

Thus, 'recognized foreign states have unlimited capacity (objects and powers) to contract and dispose of their assets notwithstanding any restrictions there might be in their constitutions.'[50] That a local law or constitution purport to limit a state's capacity and so render an ultra vires contract void (as in *LDTC v Ukraine*) was beside the point. English common law followed public international law in regarding a state as labouring under no such restriction and so the contract was valid.

5.3.2.2 Authority

We therefore turn to the third question: whether the purported agent of the state has due authority to bind the state to the credit facilities agreement in question. As far as English courts are concerned this is a matter of the English law of agency as it pertains to contracts.[51]

The first principle is that it is the state that has the power to do some act, and that an agent can only do that act if that power is donated to it.[52] The second principle is that where an agent is the donee of a power, they must use that power to pursue the objects of the donor and not for an improper purpose. Upon these two pillars is erected the following structure: an agent may have actual express, actual implied, or ostensible authority to bind the state. In short, actual authority is where the agent has expressly been donated a power to some specific act, or more commonly has been appointed to some office or other role which implies that they have authority to carry out a range of acts.[53] Thus as the law stands (and local legal opinions will confirm), a finance minister implicitly has authority to sign off on a bond issuance just by virtue of being finance minister, but this is less likely to be the case for a junior undersecretary for sports affairs.[54] Up to 2006, ostensible authority arose fairly often in the domestic courts because they dealt with cases where a third party was led to believe that a person was an agent of a corporation. Lord Diplock settled the rules for determining whether the corporation were bound, namely that: (1) there be a representation to a third party by a principal that the agent has authority; (2) the principal itself have the power to make such representation; (3) the third party be induced to contract; and (4) the corporation's constitution permits the contract. It is enough that those with actual authority acquiesce where the agent purports to act.[55]

Nevertheless, arguments as to want of authority have proved to be a battleground in cases involving states.[56] We need look no further than *LDTC v Ukraine*, where Ukraine's argument was that the Finance Minister who executed a trust deed constituting notes to be issued to the Russian Federation lacked authority due to internal borrowing limits.[57] The Court of Appeal held in 2018 that either the Finance Minister had usual (sc. actual implied) authority or failing

---

49 ibid [71].

50 The editors of PG Watts and FMB Reynolds, *Bowstead & Reynolds on Agency* (22nd edn, Sweet & Maxwell 2021) 2-011, citing [2018] EWCA Civ 2026 (n 45).

51 And Buchheit and Gulati confirm a similar approach in New York. Buchheit, Gulati and Thompson (n 22) 1238ff.

52 *AG for Ceylon v Silva* [1953] AC 461 (PC) 479; Watts and Reynolds (n 50) 8–042.

53 See *Hely-Hutchinson v Brayhead* [1968] 1 QB 549 obiter.

54 *Marubeni Hong Kong & South China Ltd. v Government of Mongolia* [2004] EWHC 472 (Comm), [2004] 2 Lloyd's Rep 198; *Donegal International Ltd. v Republic of Zambia* [2007] EWHC 197 (Comm).

55 See *Freeman & Lockyer v Buckhurst Park Properties (Mangal) Ltd.* [1964] 2 QB 480 (CA).

56 *Marubeni Hong Kong & South China Ltd.* (n 54). cf *JE Verreault et Fils Ltée v AG for Quebec* [1977] 1 SCR 41.

57 [2018] EWCA Civ 2026 (n 45).

that that he had ostensible authority *unless* LDTC knew or ought to have known that the Finance Minister was exceeding these internal borrowing limits. The CA determined that LDTC did not and could not be expected to have such knowledge (even Ukraine was initially unaware of the limit breach).[58]

If the Supreme Court confirms the existing view that state finance officials possess actual implied authority to bind the state to credit facilities agreements (unless the third party has notice of an actual internal restriction on that authority), then—in cases such as the Tuna Bond Scandal where deceit is in issue—much of the weight of argument will fall not on whether an agent had authority to exercise a state power, but on whether they exercised it for an improper purpose. This appears to be a straightforward question, but because the improper purpose may be bound up with some fraud, the case law is difficult. This is because a third party dealing with a 'corporation' can be expected to know the powers of that corporation given the public nature of its constitution. But it can hardly be required to investigate whether the internal procedures of the corporation have been followed such that an agent, actually having the power to do some act, is acting for its principal's benefit and not for an improper purpose. Rather, the third party is entitled to assume, absent notice, that the internal management of the company is sound: the so-called rule in *Turquand*[59] extended to states in *Donegal International Ltd v Zambia*.[60]

Following the courts' analogy, the leading English corporations law case is *Rolled Steel Products Ltd v British Steel*, where RSP's director (a Mr Shenkman) signed a guarantee in favour of SSS Ltd, in which he was personally interested.[61] RSP had the general power to guarantee, but this guarantee in no way benefited RSP, rather it benefited Mr Shenkman personally via SSS Ltd. All parties knew of this abuse. It was held that (1) the act was intra vires; (2) the power was not used to further the company's objects; (3) SSS Ltd, being the 'creature' of Mr Shenkman, had actual knowledge of the fraud; and (4) having such knowledge, SSS Ltd could not rely on the rule in *Turquand*. The *Rolled Steel* approach can also be used to explain the decision in *Hopkins v TL Dallas Group Ltd*, in which a deputy managing director fraudulently signed highly disadvantageous letters in his favour and to the knowledge of the counterparty.[62]

An initial reaction to the Mozambique scandal followed *Rolled Steel*, or at the very least analogized from the basic contract law principles that a fraud between agent and third party does not bind a principal.[63] The problem with this 'gut reaction' was that it ignored a rather central distinction between *Rolled Steel* and the Mozambique scenario, at least as initially reported. Remember, at the time it was not known that Credit Suisse employees had been involved in bribery, and these same employees continue to deny that they knew of any conspiracy directed at the Republic. In *Rolled Steel* the third-party beneficiary, SSS Ltd, was a co-conspirator with the agent director. That is why the third party could not rely on *Turquand*: it knew or was deemed to know that the agent director was abusing his power. In the Mozambique scandal, on the facts as we understood them in late 2018, the banks did not know that the state officials were abusing their power. As such, *Rolled Steel* says that the banks could by analogy rely on the *Turquand Rule*, and that they could assume that the agent, having actual implied authority, had been internally authorized to sign the Finance Agreements. The agreements were binding on Mozambique, and if the officials had breached fiduciary duties to *their* principal, Mozambique's claim was against these officials and not the banks.

---

58 ibid [125].

59 *Royal British Bank v Turquand* (1856) 6 6 El & Bl 327, 119 ER 886.

60 *Marubeni Hong Kong & South China Ltd.* (n 54), cited in [2018] EWCA Civ 2026 (n 45) [110].

61 *Rolled Steel Products Ltd. v British Steel Corp* [1986] Ch 246 (CA).

62 *Hopkins v TL Dallas Group Ltd.* [2004] EWHC 1379 (Ch).

63 Matthew Hill, 'Mozambique Bribe Claims Could Void Debts, Law Professor [Mitu Gulati] Says' (*Bloomberg*, 7 January 2019) accessed 20 April 2024.

5.3.3 Consequences and policy implications

Let us now summarize our results. Ultra vires is inapplicable to a foreign state. It has unlimited capacity to enter into a contract such as a B2S CFA under English law. Where the validity of the contract is called into question due to want of authority of an actual or purported agent of the state, then on a finding of lack of authority the contract is voidable—the state may elect to affirm the contract or treat it as void. If an agent has authority but the third party knows that the agent is abusing that authority for an improper purpose, the contract will be voidable. If the third party has no notice of the abuse, they are entitled to assume the agent's actions are approved by the state and the contract is enforceable.

The voiding of a disbursed B2S CFA can be disastrous for a bank: evidently the property (money) has gone somewhere and the bank may be out of pocket several million USD. If a contract procured by fraud against the principal is upheld and is enforceable, it is the state that bears this loss. It is of less concern to the bank who must repay the loan, for the bank has performed its side of the bargain and is entitled to delivery of the specified sums in repayment by the named obligor.

The consequences of the current state of the law for a country such as Mozambique appear to be this. Mozambique has unlimited objects and capacity to enter into loan contracts. Depending on their status, an official of Mozambique has implied actual authority to bind Mozambique to B2S CFAs and may have ostensible authority in certain circumstances. In the absence of actual notice that an official is abusing their power to bind Mozambique to a CFA, a foreign party is entitled (*pace* the UNCTAD Principles) to assume that the official is authorized to bind Mozambique. The B2S CFA is therefore valid, and Mozambique has only an 'internal' claim against its official.

Buchheit and others neatly set out the policy question that is put in issue in the context of New York law:

> the sovereign debt context raises a typical concern of agency law—that of faithless agents who purport to bind principals to an obligation to third parties when the fruits received in return for the obligation only accrue to the agents. Who, as between the principal (country and citizens) and the third party (the lender) should bear this risk of the faithless agent?[64]

As we have seen, UNCTAD Principle 3 places responsibility on creditors to verify authority, but we have established that English law disagrees with that view. Likewise, Buchheit and others affirm that as in England, the risk under New York Law 'usually lies at the feet of the principal' for reasons that reflect 'both business expediency and some element of efficient risk bearing' factors which we have seen also informed the English law approach to corporations and agency since *Turquand*,[65] and indeed the international arbitral awards identified by Meron.[66] Yet whereas it seems that English law will only overturn the presumption that a third party may assume internal management is sound if the third party has actual knowledge of some fraud, Buchheit and others inform us that the New York cases are more forgiving.[67] So, for example, if objectively a guaranty is of no corporate benefit to the guarantor corporation, then a third party is put on notice and should carry out further due diligence to establish why such an otherwise inherently ultra vires act is being undertaken.[68] Likewise, a third-party beneficiary of a guarantee cannot rely on a representation by a vice president and treasurer of a corporate guarantor as to their authority to bind that corporation in the face of visibly suspicious circumstances or behaviour.[69]

---

64 Buchheit, Gulati and Thompson (n 22) 1240.

65 ibid.

66 Meron (n 44).

67 International Monetary Fund (n 2) 1240.

68 *Strip Clean Floor Refinishing v NY Dist. Council No. 9*, 333 F. Supp. 385, 396 (E.D.N.Y. 1971).

69 *Gen. Overseas Films, Ltd. v Robin Int'l, Inc.*, 542 F. Supp. 684, 690 (S.D.N.Y. 1982).

The line English law has drawn is hardly immutable. Rather, it rests on a weighing of where the burden of due diligence and so risk should fall. Even if the view in *Turquand* is correct, it surely engages a balancing of interests materially distinct from our scenario in which state and private party are engaged. Indeed, this is the lesson of Meron's review of the cases; up to his time the trend was towards protecting foreign private parties from the sovereign power of state parties by placing the risk of official faithlessness on the state. The policy here is plain enough. The state should get its house in order, being deemed to be either corrupt or mismanaged such that corruption is prevalent. The whole discourse of 'corruption' is highly problematic and this work does not seek to engage with it. At the other end of the spectrum, we have the 'underlying' English law rule which *Turquand* sought to mitigate, that a corporation registered under the Companies Acts was required by statute to publish its constitution and other information and that to give effect to regulation through publication a third party was deemed to have notice of constitutional limitations on authority irrespective of whether it was ignorant of them. In our case of state and foreign third party, it seems that English law has tended with the international cases to move towards protecting the third party. Only if there is actual notice of fraud will the third party bear the risk.

English law's implicit policy assumptions seem to be that (1) foreign private parties are not in a position to monitor the internal bureaucracies of states (cost/benefit calculation); (2) the power imbalance of the relationship means that foreign private parties feel unable to carry out due diligence (a pseudo-duress argument); and (3) the law ought to encourage states to improve their internal management to a standard the English court expects (the moralizing argument). The Court of Appeal in *LDTC v Ukraine* tacked towards a doctrinal discussion, and there are only hints that the cost/benefit calculation may be playing a part. It was tellingly silent on the UNCTAD Principles. The policy question must be asked however, and one can argue that the above bases are at least subject to some qualification, as the Mozambique scandal shows. First, as to cost/benefit, Mozambique is one of the poorest states whereas Credit Suisse is a Global Systemically Important Bank whose business is assessing the creditworthiness of borrowers.[70] Mozambique's GDP was USD14.396bn in 2018; Credit Suisse had annual revenues of USD23.66bn and profits of USD4.94bn in 2019.[71] The bank is more skilled and economically more capable in carrying out due diligence in the area. Nor would requiring due diligence impose an additional burden, for a cursory review of any investment grade loan agreement shows the lengths banks go to, through conditions precedent and representations, to establish the capacity of obligors and their agents. To hold banks to a lower standard of diligence is to hold them to a standard they themselves do not accept. While Credit Suisse's relative economic size and skill support placing it under the greater risk burden, the UNCTAD Principles underscore that all creditors should be engaging in responsible lending, and in particular should be checking that appropriate authorization is obtained.

For its part, an argument from some form of duress remains highly specific to the facts, but the general trend of English courts has been to look to actual wrongdoing (such as a deceit or threat of breach of contract) as a basis for so drastic a finding. The advantage in this context of seeking an identifiable wrong is that this must be preferable to the vague prejudices about southern states which haunt the older international arbitral awards. If a state has prevented due diligence in some way, let this be pleaded out.

Finally, the moralizing argument is outmoded and arguably ineffectual. States such as Mozambique lack the resources to enforce strict internal oversight processes. As David Stasavage has shown, where Mozambique has been able to reduce corruption it has been because of increasing the

70 '2020 List of Global Systemically Important Banks (G-SIBs)' (*Financial Stability Board*, 11 November 2020) <https://www.fsb.org/2020/11/2020-list-of-global-systemically-important-banks-g-sibs/> accessed 12 July 2021.

71 Full Year and Q4 Results, 13 February 2020.

wages of functionaries and reducing the gap between the black market and official exchange rates for the metical.[72] Yet, Stasavage continues, this has not been enough: Mozambique cannot afford to employ sufficient officials, which results in individual officials having wide-ranging economic power and discretion. Furthermore, as Tvedten and Picardo confirm, while initial anti-corruption efforts made headway in the 1980s, the transition to a market economy led to increasingly complicated forms of corruption which the state was simply ill-equipped to investigate despite its best efforts.[73] Finally, there has been a critical shortage of people skilled to take on official roles, either as civil servants or as prosecutors. The most capable are offered much better wages in the private sector or outside Mozambique.[74] In short, judicial attempts to chastise states such as Mozambique into stamping out corruption are misguided and patronizing. English law should work to facilitate the diligent work of the vast majority of skilled and committed Mozambican officials working to combat corruption.

Such is the state of the law at present: banks know that the English court places the risk of a corrupt state agent upon the state-principal, and that irrespective of the ultimate destination of disbursed funds, the bank's balance sheet will continue to note the liability of a sovereign state as an asset. This subsection has posited policy arguments as to why such a legal settlement is unacceptable, motivated by the empirical evidence showing why this apparently niche issue may well become increasingly important, and a source of further injustice orchestrated from London's financial and legal centres of gravity. What though, is to be done?

5.3.4 Developing reform proposals

5.3.4.1 Introduction

As Sonja Gibbs has noted, there are 'significant disclosure gaps in both private sector and official bilateral lending to EM sovereigns' and 'a lack of transparency [which] contributes to a range of problems.'[75] Such concerns motivated the UNCTAD Principles and drove the IIF's 2017 *Voluntary Principles for Debt Transparency*. Both sets of principles are voluntary. My interest here is to discuss certain binding legislative options which may concretize these proposals by mandating some form of transparency or achieve that aim by other means.

Our focus is on B2S CFAs governed by English law and having English courts as their forum, which are made without the knowledge or due authorization of that state's proper organs, the funds of which may be disbursed for actual purposes which do not benefit that state. This part evaluates legislative, regulatory, and voluntary options whereby the practice of concluding corrupt B2S CFAs could in some way be curtailed, including by means of restricting their enforceability in England and Wales.

The options are ordered so that changes which may be easier to implement come first. It should in my view be easier to change regulatory guidance than enact Parliamentary legislation, especially at this time.

5.3.4.2 Discussion of options

In of the following proposals the term **Institutions** is used. Following UK and EU practice, Institution means a credit institution or investment firm as defined in Art 4(1) Capital Requirements Regulation, itself 'Retained EU law' after Brexit. This includes investment firms because my own

72 Stasavage (n 28).
73 Tvedten and Picardo (n 28) confirming Stasavage (n 28) 79–85.
74 Stasavage (n 28) 85–86.
75 Sonja Gibbs, 'Debt Transparency to the Rescue? Possibilities and Limitations?' (Lecture at UNCTAD's 12th Debt Management Conference, Geneva, 17 November 2019).

research indicates notable growth since 2008 in the role of non-banks and shadow banks in providing lending globally.[76]

5.3.4.2.1 Voluntary or mandatory register of Bank-State CFAs

Certain Institutions have proposed creating a register of loans to states which could be inspected by the public. Entering a transaction onto such a register would be a good 'safe harbour' for Institutions seeking to escape the deeming provisions discussed in section 5.3.4.2.3 below. This registration process can be voluntary or mandatory. It would be hoped that transparency would be enough to prevent corrupt B2S CFAs, but there will be a question of what happens if an Institution fails to register a B2S CFA. Several other questions arise with respect to such a register, including:

(1) What is the time frame for registration? Comparable registers tend to admit of registration within a short time after a transaction is agreed. Would post hoc registration be acceptable, when it is too late? Proposal 3 attempts to solve this.
(2) How public is public? Even if the register may be accessed by anyone, how much information should be provided? One could follow US SEC practice and require a filing of the text of all relevant finance documents.
(3) Who should maintain the register? The UK FCA, which already maintains a register of regulated persons, would seem the most appropriate choice. One would expect the cost of register maintenance to be borne by registering Institutions who would pay a fee per registration reflective of the total commitments of a given B2S CFA.

The principal benefit of this proposal would be that, if voluntary, it can easily be established without legislative intervention.

5.3.4.2.2 Reporting requirement

In keeping with recent trends to regulate corporate behaviour (for example, the Modern Slavery Act 2015 (the **MSA 2015**)), an Institution would be required to engage in internal due diligence regarding B2S CFAs and to report these processes in its annual report, making a statement in its annual report that no B2S CFA have been made in breach of the UNCTAD Principles (or if so, explaining how).[77]

This kind of reporting requirement tends to be enforced by means of summary criminal sanction (a fine or in the most serious cases imprisonment) for Institution officers. This method of regulation does not attack the B2S CFAs themselves, and states will still be liable under the relevant agreements.

The principal inspiration is the MSA 2015 but with one substantial change: the MSA 2015 is founded on specified criminal offences linked to slavery, whereas no such basis exists for CFAs. Therefore, I propose integrating the approach of the Money Laundering Regulations 2017[78] (**MLR 2017**), which focus on improving institutional behaviour with respect to preventing and monitoring what Institutions suspect to be unauthorized B2S CFAs (cases where authority cannot be completely verified). This suspicion is defined analogously with MLR 2017 and avoids requiring non-legally qualified actors to make an essentially legal judgment as to whether corruption linked

---

76 Stephen Connelly, 'When Overseeing Becomes Overlooking: The Post-GFC Reconfigurations of International Finance' (2016) 16 Journal of Corporate Law Studies 403.

77 I would like to thank Dr Marie Pillon, for her assistance in understanding the MSA 2015.

78 Money Laundering Terrorist Financing and Transfer of Funds (Information on the Payer) Regulations 2017, SI 2017/692, replacing the Money Laundering Regulations 2007/2157.

to a B2S CFA is taking place, shifting the focus onto a more subjective risk assessment of the satisfaction of conditions precedent—such as written proofs of authorization and ratification by state legislatures—already part of good banking practice.

Analogous norms, such as the MSA 2015 or MLR 2017, all have a basis in a general legislative provision and so one would expect this proposal likewise to derive from legislative change.

5.3.4.2.3 Legislative reform on voidability of CFAs

This option makes a small but effective statutory or legislative change to the existing common law to create a rebuttable presumption that Institutions have notice of any lack of authority of a state's agent who attempts to bind the state to a B2S CFA. In other words, it is motivated by and builds on the legal analysis undertaken in section 5.3.2 above.

As we saw, the common law of state's agent authority is out of sync with UNCTAD Principle 3 in that a bank need not enquire terribly deeply as to the lack of authority of an agent, and a state may be bound even where an agent lacked actual authority or abused it.

This prevailing presumption is inappropriate in the context of B2S CFAs. Rather, the presumption, to be set out in statute, should be that Institutions are deemed to have notice of any want of authority of an agent unless the Institution has met certain 'safe harbour' conditions of due diligence. The best such safe harbour would be to register the B2S CFA on closing (option A), giving the world notice of the transaction before drawdown.

The effect of a finding of (deemed) notice of non-authorization is that the state may not be bound by the B2S CFA. The B2S CFA is declared voidable, which means that the state may unilaterally opt to treat the B2S CFA as void. If the state does decide to treat the B2S CFA as void, then it is as if the B2S CFA had never existed; the state is under no further obligations because the obligations never arose. If an Institution has disbursed funds, the funds have been transferred unilaterally and in error, and the onus is on the Institution to recover them from whichever actual recipient of the funds, by means of certain technical procedures available for this purpose.

Unlike the reporting requirement approach above, the voidability approach catches all English law–governed B2S CFAs, and it is for the Institution to ensure that appropriate due diligence is undertaken to overturn the presumption of lack of authority. This ought to be no difficulty for Institutions, given that CFAs normally require proofs both as part of their representations and conditions precedent, and this is in line with UNCTAD Principle 3. Yet such a fundamental change to private law would require primary legislation.

5.3.4.3 Conclusions on reform

A combination of the registration and voiding options would provide the neatest 'surgical' reform with teeth sufficient to emend bank (and rogue officials') behaviour. The registration or voidability option has the benefit of travelling a legal furrow well-known to English banks: a failure to register a floating charge already leads to the unenforceability of that security against third-party creditors. Furthermore, inverting the onus on due diligence to banks from states allocates burden and risk to the party most able to bear it in line with UNCTAD Principle 3. A registration requirement alone would still benefit from public oversight by civil society, and one would expect such transparency to be as effective as that provided for under the MSA 2015. Yet no one can wait months for an annual report to disclose a problematic loan; states and civil society need to be able to respond in the crucial period between signing of the contract and drawdown. Furthermore, there are surely benefits in an ex ante voidability option mirroring the existing floating charge regime which places the burden on banks to undertake the due diligence we should surely expect of them and their professional advisors.

5.3.5 General conclusion

In late June 2019, following representations by Jubilee Debt Campaign, the UK Labour Party adopted a proposal regarding the registration versus voidability law for CFAs. This proposal subsequently formed part of the Labour Party Manifesto in the December 2019 UK General Election. In January 2020 Credit Suisse issued a counterclaim against Mozambique for recovery of the USD622m it claims is owing, Mozambique having attempted to obtain a legal declaration that the CFA in issue be cancelled (along with its guarantee).[79] Once again English law will be the crucible for adjudicating claims between international capital and states, and once again a light will be shone on certain banking practices occurring in the City of London and involving branches of banks from around the world, practices benefitting from the current approach of English law.

The empirical data sketch a context of increasing borrowing by Sub-Saharan states from private creditors, and borrowings which in some cases exceed 10% and even 24% of GDP. Further, the amounts owing under B2S CFAs have increased against this wider backdrop. This suggests that if English law continues to place the risk of an agent's abuse of power on Low-Income Country principals, rather than on the skilled banks and their advisors, we are likely to see an increasing number of cases in which English law and the City of London are brought into disrepute.

5.4 Bank-to-state lending and sovereign default

The issues raised by contracting between banks and states are one matter; what happens should a state-borrower default is another. It is sovereign default which has generated the most headlines and for good reason. When a private corporation, such as a UK company, is unable to pay its debts as it falls due, the creditors do not face a battle of all against all to recover whatever money they can from the failing company. Rather, legislation provides for a backstop procedure which weighs the relative claims of all creditors of the company and seeks first to try to restructure the debt (often by varying repayment terms) so the company might survive, and second, failing that, to wind the company up in an orderly fashion by repaying creditors as much as possible according to legislatively established principles. It is generally accepted that a creditor free-for-all would result in destroying more value than an orderly restructuring or winding up, not just be driving the company itself more quickly into failure as creditors seek to protect their position at the first hint of trouble, but also by minimizing financial contagion by averting a mass creditor panic as they scramble to recover what they can.

When it comes to sovereign debtors, however, no such legislative or treaty-based backstop is in place, despite people advocating for one since the time of Adam Smith.[80] As a result, when a sovereign defaults, it can feel like a creditor free-for-all, and it is this that has generated the headlines. Schumacher and others summarize the early 2000s boom in creditor unilateralism which saw individual creditors attempting to bypass restructuring negotiations with majority creditors and seize state assets directly:

> Examples of attempted seizures include presidential airplanes, central bank assets and social security funds held in the US, a famous vessel of the Argentine Navy (the ARA

---

79 Brendan Pierson, 'Ex-Credit Suisse Banker Pleads Guilty to U.S. Charge Over Mozambique Loan' (*Reuters*, 20 May 2019) <https://www.reuters.com/article/us-mozambique-credit-suisse-charges-idUSKCN1SQ2E1> accessed 13 July 2021.

80 Charles Seavey, 'The Anomalous Lack of an International Bankruptcy Court' (2006) 244 Berkeley J Intl L 499 (citing Adam Smith, *The Wealth of Nations* (first published 1776, Methuen and Co. 2000) 468: 'When it becomes necessary for a state to declare itself bankrupt, in the same manner as when it becomes necessary for an individual to do so, a fair, open, and avowed bankruptcy is always the measure which is both the least dishonourable to the debtor, and least hurtful to the creditor.').

> Libertad), Argentina's stake in the satellite launch firm SpaceX, and even Argentine dinosaur fossils on exhibition in Europe. Most of these attempts have been legally unsuccessful, in the sense that they were ultimately rejected by US and European courts. Nevertheless, the attempts increased the 'nuisance value' of the ongoing lawsuits, sometimes causing externalities that far exceeded the value of the litigated claims. In the Republic of Congo, for example, a small group of creditors holding less than $500m of debt succeeded in blocking the country's entire oil exports for years, thereby disrupting a multi-billion industry.[81]

The increasing litigiousness of private creditors coincided a developing country sovereign debt crisis; one which became so acute that the multilateral agencies and key creditor states concluded a debt relief programme: the Highly Indebted Poor Countries (**HIPC**) programme. Under HIPC, about 30 sovereigns saw their debt owed to public creditors reduced by up to a third, staving off the worst consequences of default. Yet HIPC also created policy problems:

- HIPC reduced debt owed to public creditors (such as the UK or IMF) but did not reduce the debt owed to private creditors. In effect, public creditors were being subordinated to private creditors, such that public creditors accepted the actualized risk of insolvency—non-payment—first, before private creditors. Put simply, public creditors subsidized private creditors.
- HIPC did not stop private creditor litigation. Indeed, private litigators would sue just to enforce the indirect subsidy they had received from public creditors. One had the situation where a private creditor would use the English courts to enforce a debt which the United Kingdom, as creditor, had compromised (i.e. agreed to reduce). A public was not just subsidizing private creditors, it was actively helping private creditors to enforce.
- Faced with continued, full claims by private creditors, HIPC debtors were required to devote funds, theoretically intended for public expenditure such as healthcare, paying private debt and fighting off litigation. This reduced the efficacy of HIPC.
- The debt relief created a space for new creditors to enter the sovereign debt market, encouraged in part by the public creditor cross-subsidy.

We will examine some of the legislative responses to these events shortly.

While HIPC provided relief, Low-Income Country sovereign debt ballooned again in the 2010s, fuelled by the growth of private lending to states and by the increasing role of China as a bilateral lender. The diversity of creditors in number and profile has thus dramatically increased. Repayments under bond and credit facilities agreements entered into in the mid-2010s would start to fall due in 2020 onwards: a so-called debt cliff-edge. This already precarious debt situation became critical with the onset of the COVID-19 pandemic, which saw major economies' GDP collapse and so their consequent demand for the resources, such as oil, extracted from the Global South. Since 2019, the nexus of crises has threatened a wave of sovereign defaults, with countries such as Zambia and Ghana becoming unable to meet payment schedules. Sovereign debtors now face negotiating not with a small number of experienced MLAs and public creditors, but a highly diverse range of

81 Julian Schumacher, Christoph Trebesch and Henrik Enderlein, 'Sovereign Defaults in Court' (2018) European Central Bank Working Paper Series No. 2135, 12–13 <https://www.ecb.europa.eu/pub/pdf/scpwps/ecb.wp2135.en.pdf> accessed 15 March 2024. Jonathan I Blackman and Rahul Mukhi, 'The Evolution of Modern Sovereign Debt Litigation: Vultures, Alter Egos, and other Legal Fauna' (2010) 73 Law and Contemporary Problems 47; George Foster, 'Collecting From Sovereigns: The Current Legal Framework for Enforcing Arbitral Awards and Court Judgments Against States and Their Instrumentalities, and Some Proposals for Its Reform' (2008) 25 Arizona Journal of International & Comparative Law 666.

public and private creditors between whom coordination of any kind of restructuring agreement is increasingly difficult.

Despite this, there remains no international consensus to create an international sovereign debt restructuring mechanism (**SDRM**). Such a mechanism was proposed by the Managing Director of the IMF in 2001 but was subsequently shelved for want of support. The legal vacuum was partially filled by market initiatives which focused on building creditor workout mechanisms into debt contracts themselves, but among several deficiencies with this approach, the greatest is that the mechanism must be negotiated *before* default occurs and ideally when a given contract is formed—contractualist solutions offer little hope to debtors bound by older contracts that lack these mechanisms, the repayment schedules of which can potentially run for decades.

The sovereign debt crisis, the failure of the SDRM initiative and the limitations of contractualist approaches have given impetus to calls for solutions at the national level. A particular characteristic of sovereign debt makes focusing on national legislatures a viable option for civil society: over 90% of relevant sovereign debt is subject to English or New York law, and so NGOs can heavily focus their efforts on the UK Parliament and New York State Senate. It is on these efforts, and their potential effects on private financial law, that the remainder of this chapter will focus.

For this purpose, we can broadly divide these legislative approaches into four categories, to be examined below:

(1) Legislation in support of contractualist measures.
(2) Anti-vulture fund legislation.
(3) Anti-holdout legislation.
(4) Legislation in support of a local law debt restructuring mechanism (which for historical reasons are discussed alongside the New York anti-holdout bill).

Over the last two to three decades these different approaches have gone in and out of fashion, having more or less success depending on political contingencies. The precise story is best told as we explain these four categories in turn.[82]

5.4.1 Legislation in support of contractualist measures

Given the absence of a legislatively mandated insolvency mechanism, the baseline for insolvency restructurings is private and contractual: the state simply lets debtor and creditors 'get on with it,' respecting laissez-faire and freedom of contract. On the spectrum of public intervention in contractual ordering, the next most minimal proposal (beyond issuing guidance and promoting self-regulation) one finds in the field of sovereign debt, and by far the most popular with governments during the 2000s, is implying an insolvency decision-making process into debt contracts themselves. Such a move is no doubt important. Under a standard debt contract, the rights of the creditor are absolute: if they are owed GBP100, they are owed GBP100 until payment in full, and neither the debtor nor any other creditor can interfere with that.[83] This meant that any creditor could hold out against otherwise agreed variations of contract, benefitting from others taking a haircut and even suing other parties if they felt their rights were infringed. Such 'holdouts' prove a significant negative block (or 'anti-commons') to good faith restructuring of sovereign debt.

---

82 The author has been heavily involved in the development of sovereign debt legislation for a number of years and this section draws from experience, but in terms of structuring I am also grateful to the following paper: erlassjahr.de, 'The Potential of National Laws for the Fair Resolution of Global Debt Crises' (2023) Focus Paper No. 9 <https://erlassjahr.de/wordpress/wp-content/uploads/2024/01/Focus_Paper_9_2edition–230130.pdf> accessed 5 December 2023.

83 See for example in England *Foakes v Beer* [1884] UKHL 1.

Matters came to a head when EU Member States were forced to renegotiate Greek sovereign debt and faced dissentient bondholders. Faced with deadlock, the EU agreed that it would require inclusion of decision-making clauses in all new bonds which permitted majority creditors to approve a course of action (such as a variation of terms) and bind all creditors to that decision. In this context, these terms are called Collective Action Clauses and are standard form of the term was mandated under Article 12 of the Treaty Establishing the European Stability Mechanism. The existing euro area model collective action clause ('CAC') became mandatory in all new euro area government securities with a maturity over one year issued on or after 1 January 2013.

The 2012 version of the Euro Area CAC introduced aggregated voting under which different series of bonds could be aggregated together for voting purposes (referred to in the CAC as a 'cross-series modification'). This version of aggregated voting is achieved through a 'double limb' voting arrangement which requires both a positive vote (above an individual series threshold) at the level of each affected individual bond issuance together with an overall aggregated positive vote (above an aggregate threshold) by reference to all affected series of bonds taken as a whole. In 2021 the EU updated this form in line with the CAC terms suggested by the International Capital Market Association (replicated below) to create a single-limbed model. Under this version all debt is simply aggregated as one and a majority of debtholders may approve a course of collective action.

> Modifications proposed by the Issuer to the terms and conditions of the Bonds of a single series, or to the Governing Instrument insofar as it affects the Bonds of a single series, that are not Reserve Matter Modifications . . ., may be approved by Bondholders (by vote at a Bondholders' meeting or by a written action), and future compliance therewith may be waived, with the written consent of the Issuer and the affirmative vote (if approved at a Bondholders' meeting) or consent (if approved by a written action) of holders of more than 50% of the aggregate principal amount of the outstanding Bonds of that series.[84]

The principal deficiency of these CACs is well-known: they are only forward looking, applying only to debt contracts in which they are terms. Sovereign debt as a whole includes debt which can have a term of 100 years (and there is even such a thing as 'perpetual debt'). If one is seeking to restructure the debt of a nation holistically, all pre-CAC debt simply escapes the effect of the CACs in relevant contracts. For CACs to become effective, states will have to wait decades for old-style debt contracts to terminate through performance. Moreover, CACs leave decision-making power to creditors whose interests are focused on profit maximization. Compare this to multilateral and bilateral public creditors who (ought to) take into account if not privilege the human rights of the citizens of indebted nations. For these reasons, CACs ought only to form part of a suite of measures designed to restructure sovereign debt.

5.4.2 Anti-vulture fund legislation

Trafficking in debt litigation has long been seen as problematic (see Chapter 6): to buy a debt owed to some other creditor and enforce it in the courts is one thing; to buy and enforce it for an ulterior purpose, such as to exert pressure to achieve concessions on an unrelated matter is quite another. Consider, for example, an investment vehicle—a fund—which attracts capital to be used to buy

84 International Capital Market Association, *Standard Aggregated Collective Action Clauses ('CACs') For the Terms and Conditions of Sovereign Notes* (August 2014) <https://www.icmagroup.org/assets/documents/Resources/ICMA-standard-CACs-August-2014.pdf> accessed 19 February 2025.

non-performing sovereign debt (i.e. debt in default). This can be profitable where the original creditor sells the debt at a steep discount due to the default (e.g. 20% of nominal value), and the fund is able to recover more than it paid (e.g. 30%). One might agree that enforcing payment of the debt is integral to the property in that debt, and that there is nothing questionable in such a business model, even if enforcement means seizing state-owned merchant vessels and shares.

Now consider a scenario in which the sovereign debtor is engaged in debt restructuring negotiations. The majority of its creditors agree that a significant debt haircut should be accepted in exchange for some repayment now and/or new debt, but the fund disagrees. Indeed, it disagrees because it has calculated that if the other creditors bear the losses occasioned by the haircut, the fund will increase its chances of recovering more. This would normally not be possible under a national law insolvency process because state legislation almost invariably permits the majority creditors to force ('cram down') the minority to accept a restructuring deal. Without an SDRM, our fund is free to regard itself as unbound by any restructuring agreement others have made. The fund therefore proceeds not only to enforce for the full amount, but actively targeting monies set aside either to pay the majority creditors or to meet public expenditures. The tactical thought behind such enforcement is this: even if these monies cannot be recovered for the fund, they can at least be tied up in litigation, thereby thwarting the agreement made between the sovereign debtor and majority creditors. It is therefore a sort of cutthroat defence, with the fund threatening to destroy the majority deal unless the fund obtains repayment of its debt.

The high-profile enforcement actions of funds should be seen in this light. The point of seizing dinosaur bonds and naval vessels was as more about causing very public trouble for the sovereign debtor, and its restructuring deal, than actually recouping losses, with a view to forcing concessions. Such behaviour led to the funds receiving the sobriquet **vulture funds**.

The case of *NML Capital v Argentina* provides an illustrative example of this tactical litigation.[85] Argentina had issued dollar-denominated bonds. As is common in this sort of transaction, the bonds were held by and payments of interest made through a bond trustee, here Bank of New York Mellon (**BNYM**), based in New York. Argentina reached a restructuring agreement with its majority creditors, but not NML, that they would take a haircut in exchange for immediate payments of money and new debt, to be distributed by BNYM. It was a term of the bond contract with each debtor that the creditor would never treat one debtor more favourably than any other creditor, e.g. by repaying one earlier or more than the other (a *pari passu* clause common in bonds). The majority creditors had agreed to waive this requirement as part of the restructuring; NML had not and, correctly as a matter of contract law, sought to enforce the terms of its agreement with Argentina and every other creditor. Argentina had put BNYM in funds so that the bond trustee could distribute the same to the majority creditors, and it was then that NML struck. It sought an injunction restraining BNYM from releasing any funds to the majority creditors on the basis that to do so would be to pay some creditors before others in breach of the pari passu clause. NML further 'offered' to withdraw the injunction if Argentina would pay NML in full. The funds were tied up in New York for a decade, the injunction finally being lifted in 2016 when Argentina reached new settlement with bondholders. Other funds imitated the litigation, for example in London.[86]

There is a deep policy question about the vulture funds' behaviour here. On the one hand the funds are simply exerting their property rights and precisely and voluntarily delineated in the contract with the debtor (and other creditors). On the other, those property rights appear to have been exercised abusively. The majority of creditors thought it best to restructure the debt to secure

85 *NML Capital Ltd. v Republic of Argentina*, 680 F.3d 254 (2d Cir. 2012).

86 *Knighthead Master Fund LP & Others v The Bank of New York Mellon & Anor* [2015] EWHC 270 (Ch).

payment; a small minority not only disagreed with the restructuring (as is their right) but actively used the good faith restructuring agreement of the majority to force concessions from the debtor. Is that still within the limits of the free exercise of such rights, or have we crossed a boundary into unduly harming others? And what of the policy considerations: surely a majority restructuring agreement reflects the utilitarian outcome as it benefits the most people, not just one.

Whatever one thinks about the policy here, the legislatures of Belgium and France strongly felt that the vulture funds had gone too far and proceeded to pass anti-vulture fund legislation. Belgium's law 'on combatting the activities of vulture funds' can be seen as a direct response to *NML v Argentina*.[87] Argentina had also used a clearing house (see Chapter 10) based in Belgium—*Euroclear*—to process payments to bondholders. Aware of this, NML had also served an injunction on Euroclear restraining payments there. This assault on Belgium's critical financial infrastructure, Euroclear being a major success story for Belgium's financial sector, could not stand. In the face of objections from financial lobby groups, the Belgian law was passed in July 2015.[88] NML immediately sought to review of the law in the Belgian Constitutional Court, but in 2018 the Court dismissed the suit and upheld the law in full.[89]

At its heart the Belgian law limits the enforceability of claims and the enforcement of foreign judgments relating to any sovereign's debt A key limitation, for example, drew up a shield about Euroclear payments, ensuring they could be made unhindered. Other restrictions included limiting the amount of any sum recoverable by a creditor which had taken 'unlawful advantage' to an amount equal to the sum that creditor paid for the debt in the secondary market. Thus, if a vulture fund had paid 40 cents for USD1 of debt acquired from another creditor, it could only ever recover up to 40 cents in the Belgian courts. For this purpose, 'unlawful advantage' was tested by reference to several criteria, including:

- The is a clear discrepancy between the discounted amount the creditor had paid for the debt of *any* state it had acquired in the secondary market and the amount it was now seeking to claim and/or enforce (e.g. the full amount owed).
- And one or more of inter alia:
  - the creditor had acquired the debt when the sovereign was already in default;
  - the creditor had refused to participate in restructuring negotiations;
  - the creditor is exploiting the weak position of the sovereign to exact an unfair advantage; or
  - full repayment of the debt would have a demonstrably adverse effect on the sovereign's finances and on the socio-economic wellbeing of that state's people.

Notice how the Belgian law does not seek to define 'vulture fund' but rather identifies a particular practice—third parties acquiring debts at a discount then enforcing for the full amount, using others' restructuring as leverage—as against public policy. If there is a downside, it is just this targeting, for the law provides no general mechanism for supporting sovereign debt restructurings, and indeed it will be hard to demonstrate a 'clear discrepancy' in debt values where any restructuring

87 'Projet de loi relative à la lutte contre les activités des fonds vautours' (2014/2015) DOC 54 1057/005 <https://www.dekamer.be/FLWB/PDF/54/1057/54K1057005.pdf> accessed 1 April 2024.

88 See further: LA Sourbron and L Vereeck, 'To Pay or Not to Pay? Evaluating the Belgian Law Against Vulture Funds' (2017) 8(1) Journal of Globalization and Development <https://doi.org/10.1515/jgd-2017-0010> accessed 16 September 2024.

89 Astrid Iversen, 'Vulture Fund Legislation' (2019) 38(5) Banking & Financial Services Policy Report, University of Oslo Faculty of Law Research Paper No. 2019-57 <https://ssrn.com/abstract=3456479> accessed 16 September 2024.

itself provides for a deep haircut. The general problem of high indebtedness of sovereigns is not tackled; only one particularly egregious subset of creditor practices.

Not long after passing its anti-vulture fund law, the Belgian legislature clarified in amending legislation that sovereign assets used for diplomatic purposes were immune from enforcement in any event.[90] Yet it stepped back from protecting assets made available for the payment of creditors, so it remained possible for a creditor not participating in any restructuring, but also not meeting the vulture fund criteria, to enforce against monies set aside for restructuring payments. Aware of this problem,[91] also hosting NML litigation,[92] and keen to support good faith restructuring of sovereign debt, France passed its *Sapin II* law in December 2016.[93] *Sapin II* targeted any post-2016 purchases of sovereign debt of 'developing countries' in the secondary market *after* the developing country had defaulted. The law granted a moratorium on suit and enforcement of such claims for four years pending conclusion of restructuring negotiations, extendable by the judge to six years. Article 60 of the law specifically ring-fences public assets, even commercial assets set aside for payment of creditors participating in a restructuring.

All this would have perhaps been empty—a vulture fund need only wait four to six years to recover—had the law not also actively aided restructuring by setting any restructuring agreement as the standard against which non-participating creditors' recoveries were to be measured. Where creditors holding 66% of the amount of outstanding debt agree to a haircut, say reducing the debt to 70% of the original amount owing, then non-participating creditors' recoveries in France would be so limited: the court would only allow them to recover, e.g. 70% of their claim. This addition converted a mere anti-vulture fund law into something positively encouraging good faith restructuring by imposing comparable treatment on all, participant or not.[94]

5.4.3 Anti-holdout and restructuring legislation

Anti-vulture fund legislation operates negatively by targeting blameworthy creditor behaviour. Anti-holdout legislation (a term coined by debt NGO erlassjahr.de)[95] encourages good creditor behaviour by protecting creditors who participate in debt restructuring from those who hold out for full repayment. Part of the vulture fund business model is holding out, i.e. refusing to agree to any restructuring in the hope of obtaining full repayment (a kind of anti-commons tactic). It is thus not surprising that *Sapin II* extended beyond Belgium's anti-vulture provisions to include positive mechanisms of court support for restructurings. Yet not only vulture funds hold out. Otherwise, well-behaved creditors may also not agree to a restructuring deal because, on balance, there is no normative impetus for them to participate in restructuring rather than not. The scope of anti-holdout legislation is therefore wider. It has in view all creditors by lending legal protection to the restructuring

---

90 See now Article 1412-5 of the Loi insérant dans le Code judiciaire un article 1412 quinquies régissant la saisie de biens appartenant à un État tiers ou à une organisation internationale, Doc 54 1241/001, 2 July 2015.

91 *Romak v Uzbekistan* (Court of Cassation, civ 1, 5 March 2014, No. 12-22.406); and more recently. *Commisimpex v Congo* (Court of Cassation, civ 1, 10 January 2018, No. 16-22.494; Court of Cassation, civ 1, 24 January 2018, No. 16-16.511; and Court of Cassation, civ 1, 3 February 2021, No. 19-10.669). On this, E Glucksmann, '*Commisimpex v Republic of Congo*' (2017) 111 AJIL 453.

92 *NML Capital v Argentina* (Court of Cassation, civ 1, 28 September 2011, No. 09-72.057 and Court of Cassation, civ 1, 28 March 2013, No. 10-25.938).

93 Loi No. 2016-1691 du 9 décembre 2016 relative à la transparence, à la lutte contre la corruption et à la modernisation de la vie économique. See now articles L 111-1-1 to L 111-1-3 of the French *Code of Civil Enforcement Proceedings*.

94 For cases considering *Loi Sapin II* see Court of Appeal of Versailles, 6 June 2019, No. 18/00534; Court of Appeal of Paris, 5 September 2019, No. 18/17592; Court of Appeal of Paris, 9 January 2020, No. 19/11412 quashed by Court of Cassation, civ 1, 7 July 2021, No 20-15.994; and Court of Appeal of Paris, 11 February 2021, No. 20/08151.

95 Erlassjahr.de, 'The Potential of National Legislation for the Fair Resolution of Global Debt Crises: An Overview and Assessment of Existing Laws and Legislative Proposals' (July 2023) Focus Paper No. 9 <https://erlassjahr.de/wordpress/wp-content/uploads/2024/01/Focus_Paper_9_2edition–230130.pdf> accessed 16 September 2024.

agreements of majority creditors against holdouts seeking full repayment, thereby actively encouraging creditors to participate. The legislation does this primarily by restricting holdout recoveries to no more than the holdout would have received had they simply participated in the restructuring.

Anti-holdout legislation does not provide for an insolvency mechanism, even in the most minimal sense of sanctioning 'qualifying agreements' as Creditors Voluntary Arrangements or Schemes of Arrangement. All anti-holdout legislation does is direct the court to refuse to lend aid to holdout creditors, thereby granting a legal benefit to participating creditors by supporting whatever restructuring to which they have agreed against holdout litigation. A useful analogy may be drawn with the illegality (public policy) defence in private law. Two highwaymen may agree to share the spoils of their robbery from a third party, but later one highwayman refuses to turnover half of the ill-gotten loot to the other. The other highwayman sues for breach of contract. In such a situation, the court will simply refuse to enforce the contract. The reason for this is not because the highwaymen have committed a crime (one bound up with the contract), nor because of some desire to protect third-party victims. The judicial policy, rather, is that it would be repugnant to the court to lend its aid to criminals by declaring such contractual rights as valid and enforceable. If highwaymen wish to agree, that is up to them; they just cannot expect a court to sully its hands with the affair. Something vaguely similar occurs with anti-holdout legislation: it tells the court that while holdout creditors have valid agreements, should they ask the court to assist them in declaring their rights valid and/or ordering enforcement, the court is entitled to withhold support. The difference from illegality is the policy here is not concern about bringing the court into disrepute, but about favouring creditors who engage in restructuring.

Given that anti-holdout legislation covers all creditors, should such legislation support *any* restructuring of sovereign debt by limiting otherwise valid contractual rights of non-participating creditors? Legislatures have been very reluctant to go that far, preferring to support identified, time-limited restructurings involving multilateral agencies and a low-income subset of sovereign debtors, though pressure from civil society for anti-holdout legislation of general, forward-facing scope is increasing.

A further key problem for any legislation restricting recoveries to no more than the amounts participating creditors received under the restructuring, is to define what 'no more than' means. The key phrase here, derived from Paris Club practice, is **Comparability of Treatment**. Comparable treatment is fairly easy to identify where all participating creditors take a 33.3% haircut to debt capital—just ensure that holdouts recover no more than 66.6% of their own debt. What do we do when the restructuring deal is complex, with multiple classes of creditor, exchange debt, amendments to amortization and service schedules, varying coupon rates and so on. How would a court map all these variations onto plain-vanilla bonds held by a holdout? Moreover, it is one thing to limit enforcement up to 66.6% (or whatever) and quite another to start varying a holdout's contract to incorporate terms to which they *ex hypothesi* have not agreement.

Since the Global Financial Crisis, anti-holdout legislation has been an area of significant reform activity, if limited legislative success, as we shall now see. The current high-water mark remains the UK's debt relief legislation of 2010, though this may be about to change.

5.4.3.1 The Debt Relief (Developing Countries) Act 2010

Emerging attempts to curb vulture funds in New York, Belgium saw a parallel in the UK, where members of the legislature introduced a Developing Country Debt (Restriction of Recovery) Bill under the ten-minute rule in the 2008–09 Parliamentary session.[96] This Bill was extremely

96 A rule which allows MPs who are not part of the executive to propose legislation on which the House of Commons can vote to take forward. The majority of such proposals tend to fail, if they are heard at all, and rely heavily on attracting support from the executive.

wide-ranging: it applied to the debt of any country which had been acquired at a deep discount, limiting private creditor recoveries to an amount equal to the discounted sum paid. It also required creditors seeking recovery to make extensive disclosures to aid transparency and granted sovereign debtors rights to stay claims and enforcement contravening the proposed measures.

Sympathetic to the need for some action on sovereign debt but concerned as to generality of the 2009 Bill, the UK Labour Government took evidence on measures to support the IMF's HIPC programme and made time in its final session before the 2010 General Election to pass the Debt Relief (Developing Countries) Act 2010 (the **2010 Act**).

The 2010 Act aimed to protect the 40 state participants under the HIPC Initiative from enforcement action by private creditors who held out against otherwise agreed debt reductions. This restriction also afforded simplicity because the fairly precise restructuring terms of the HIPC Initiative were known. Rather than capture, in vague terms, every possible restructuring imaginable, the 2010 Act could identify and enforce the specific debt reduction of one-third under the HIPC Initiative against *any* creditor of the long-term debt of a participating state. By way of example, imagine a private creditor being owed GBP100 by a HIPC participant, and this private creditor refusing to accept the debt haircut of one-third under the Initiative. This creditor now seeks to enforce that claim in the English court. The 2010 Act provides that the creditor may only recover GBP66.66 i.e. no more than the holdout creditor could have recovered had they actually participated in the Initiative. The following case shows the 2010 Act in action.

HAMSAH INVESTMENTS LIMITED & WALL CAPITAL LIMITED v THE REPUBLIC OF LIBERIA (2010) unreported

Liberia had incurred debt with a US bank in the late 1970s. Following default, the debt had been sold and resold several times before ending up in the hands of the claimants, who were described as 'vulture funds.'

In 2009 (i.e. before the 2010 Act), the claimants obtained judgment in the High Court in the sum of USD20m. Had the claimants participated in the HIPC Initiative, the recoverable sum would have been reduced. The 2010 Act came into force as the claimants sought to enforce the judgment in England. Faced with a legally mandated reduction in recoveries, the claimant creditors were forced to the negotiating table with Liberia, and the parties were able to reach an out-of-court settlement of USD1.3m.[97]

The 2010 Act could claim several successes. First, the fact that it was enacted at all in a jurisdiction whose law governs 90% of sovereign debt contracts demonstrated there were limits to England's famously creditor-friendly legal system. Second, the 2010 Act worked, primarily as a deterrent to claims. The *Liberia* case provided an object lesson. Third, as anti-holdout legislation, the 2010 Act shifted the focus away from the misbehaviour of a subset of creditors—vulture funds—and onto the plight of the victims: HIPCs. This circumvented the need for clumsy, moralizing definitions of wrongdoing and aligned with the prevailing policy of

97 'Liberia Agrees Deal with "Vulture Funds"' (*BBC News*, 23 November 2010) <www.bbc.co.uk/news/world-africa-11819276> accessed 10 May 2024.

corporate insolvency law, rescuing debtors so that value can be maximized for all. Fourth, despite objections from the City that the 2010 Act would see investor flight to jurisdictions which would respect their claims in full, the UK Parliament concluded there has been no evidence of creditors abandoning English law.

> No evidence has been presented to the Government suggesting that the legislation has negatively impacted the UK as a centre for financial services or has resulted in changes in the choice of law or jurisdiction for financial contracts.[98]

The greatest limitation of the 2010 Act was its scope: it only applied to HIPC countries participating in the Initiative, and only then for a limited time (though this limit was subsequently removed when it became clear there were no adverse effects for City business). As a political stepping stone, the 2010 Act established that anti-holdout legislation was possible, but was not able to establish a mechanism of general application to all countries and future claims. With time there would be need for a new round of legislation to deal with new crises.

5.4.3.2 A UK DSSI-support bill (2020)?

The 2010 Act focused on denying holdouts judicial support to recover debt in excess of those received by participating creditors i.e. it supported an internationally agreed reduction in the principal owed by HIPCs. Over-indebtedness, however, is only one solvency problem that states (like private persons) may face; the other concerns liquidity: the ability to pay sums as they fall due. Repayments of principal, especially bond debt, may only be due after several years, but payments of interest/coupon can be annual, biannual, or even quarterly. Due to their regularity, meeting interest payments—debt service—can often threaten to push a debtor over the edge either as an early warning of a deeper solvency crisis which will see the state defaulting on principal payments, or simply because in a given time frame the state simply lacks cash to make that interest payment: a liquidity crunch.

A liquidity crunch occurred when the COVID-19 pandemic hit, and states' GDPs fell to unheard-of peacetime levels. Foreseeing multiple, Low-Income Country defaults due to a failure to service debt, the G20 and IMF proposed a Debt-Service Suspension Initiative (**DSSI**). As the name suggests, the initiative proposed the suspension (but not cancellation) of the contractual obligation to service debt i.e. pay interest and other sums falling due. Debt-service suspensions of this kind are a common feature of corporate workouts. The DSSI committed G20 and Paris Club official creditors to a time-bound suspension of debt service for eligible countries that request such forbearance. The Institute of International Finance developed terms of reference for voluntary private sector participation to support the DSSI; support which was largely unforthcoming. As of 2023, 48 out of 73 eligible countries benefited from the DSSI.

The DSSI did suffer from two notable defects. First, it is often a term of financial contracts that where the debtor participates in a 'creditors' process'—often defined widely to include any renegotiation of debt payment terms—this participation constitutes a default. Several low-income countries held themselves back from applying to the DSSI in fear that they would trigger defaults, or at least negatively affect credit ratings.[99] Second, as with previous initiatives, the DSSI was led

98 House of Commons, Second Delegated Legislation Committee, Monday 16 May 2011, Mr. George Howarth in the Chair, Draft Debt Relief (Developing Countries) Act 2010 (Permanent Effect) Order 2011, Session 2010–2011, col 4.

99 Danny Cassimon, Dennis Essers and Andrea F Presbitero, 'Debtor (Non-)Participation in Sovereign Debt Relief: A Real Option Approach' (2023) IMF Working Papers No. 187/A001 <https://www.imf.org/en/Publications/WP/Issues/2023/09/08/Debtor-Non-Participation-in-Sovereign-Debt-Relief-A-Real-Option-Approach-535875> accessed 14 May 2024.

by official creditors as private creditors wanted little to do with it. The result was that money freed up by suspending debt service on debts owed to official creditors was simply diverted to servicing the debt of private creditors. As a result, the DSSI amounted to a risk subsidy to private creditors at the expense both of public creditors (and their taxpayers) and the citizens of law income countries who would otherwise have benefitted from healthcare support during the pandemic.

Although the DSSI focused on interest payments rather than capital repayments, it was evident that private creditors were once again free riding on the concessions on public creditors. Working with Celine Tan and Karina Patricio Ferreira Lima, and NGOs Oxfam and Debt Justice, the author moved to replicate the 2010 Act by proposing a UK bill which would support the DSSI against private creditors holding out against this new initiative.[100] Notice the key technical difference: the DSSI did not cut principal owed; indeed, it did not cut the interest debtors owed. Rather, it simply suspended interim payments during the pandemic to support sovereign liquidity. Any bill needed to focus on producing the same effect for private creditors, i.e. private creditors should not be able to claim and enforce against interest payments during the applicable DSSI suspension period.

The aim of the proposed bill was to complement the DSSI by granting a statutory standstill on recovery of qualifying debt owed to private creditors by DSSI-eligible countries that are governed by English law. In short, where a country benefitted from a DSSI suspension, holdout private creditors could seek the aid of UK courts in enforcing payments. They would either have to agree a voluntary payment or simply wait until the DSSI suspension was lifted. The proposal covered 90% of bonds contracted by these countries. It granted a DSSI-participating countries a stay of legal or arbitral proceedings where those proceedings concerned a qualifying debt owed by that country. The proposed legislation did not directly intervene in a contract to suspend debt payments, and as such it would still have been open to creditors to declare a default under the relevant contract. Instead, the legislation mirrored existing insolvency legislation in suspending the link between contractual default and the execution and enforcement of contractual rights, including with the aid of the English courts.

Civil society aimed for the proposed bill to be integrated into the Corporate Insolvency and Governance Act 2020, failing which, the Finance Act of the same year. However, despite liaising closely with HM Treasury and MPs, the Government concluded that the exigencies of the pandemic were such that adding in the debt suspension proposal would only distract from other urgent domestic measures. The proposal was thus shelved in September 2020, with no Parliamentary time available to propose a standalone bill.

5.4.3.3 New York legislative initiatives from 2021 on

The DSSI gave fresh impetus to legislative reforms in the State Assembly and Senate of New York. Whereas moves in the UK had faced the difficulties of carving out Parliamentary time in the context of emergency COVID-19 legislation, the New York proposals ran into a very different problem, namely competing reform proposals, with three vying for Senate attention:

(1) The July 2022 New York Taxpayer and International Debt Crises Protection Bill[101] proposed by Patricia Fahy AM (the **Fahy Bill**)—an anti-holdout bill in the style of the UK 2010 Act but

100 Stephen Connelly and others, 'COVID-19: Suspending Debt Service for Indebted Countries' (2020) GLOBE Centre Warwick Law School Briefing Note <https://warwick.ac.uk/fac/soc/law/research/centres/globe/policybriefs/pn2_connelly-tan-patricio-tassis_june_2020_002.pdf> accessed 16 September 2024.

101 Bill A2970.

with application to a wider range of future possible initiatives. The Fahy Bill was proposed on the New York Assembly, with a parallel bill but forward by Senator Brad Hoylman-Sigal in the Senate.[102]

(2) A New York **Model Law** to restructure unsustainable sovereign debt, first introduced in May 2021 and reintroduced in the 2022–23 Senate session—a bill which provided in broad terms for an insolvency restructuring mechanism within New York law itself, and not merely support to international initiatives.

(3) A bill, supported by Lee Buchheit, resurrecting New York's champerty law and affirming its application to vulture funds—effectively reversing the *Elliot* decision.

The Fahy Bill possessed several advantages over the UK 2010 Act.[103] It was forward-looking, attempting to cover possible future international initiatives on sovereign debt restructuring. In doing so the Bill could not predict the precise nature of any such restructuring (e.g. would there be a common reduction factor, debt service suspension, variation of term etc?). It therefore needed to be creatively vague and so spoke of a concept, emerging in Paris Club practice, of Comparability of Treatment. This meant that a claimant debtor in a New York court would only recover sums to the extent doing so resulted in no better treatment than a creditor which had participated in a given initiative. The Fahy Bill also resurrected a demand for transparency seen in the UK private member's bill of 2009, requiring that any debtor disclose relevant documentation as a condition of pursuing proceedings. That the scope came at the price of perhaps too great a degree of vagueness. Detractors pointed out that a New York Court may struggle to apply such a vague principle without more guidance.[104] There was also a sense that, tying the law only to initiatives in which the US participated overemphasized the advantages the law conferred on just this one creditor (we have seen private creditors opposing the UK 2010 Act likewise felt it was a subsidy to public creditors).

Political factors saw the emergence, as we have said, of the Model Law bill sponsored by State Senators Rivera and Davila. This was more ambitious: rather than simply providing procedural support for negotiated agreements at the transnational level, the Model Law bill proposed a New York law restructuring process applicable to private and public bilateral and multilateral claims governed by New York law. Any country would be entitled to apply to enter a court-backed restructuring of its New York debt, and overseen by an independent party, any restructuring plan could be imposed on all creditors, minority holdouts included. In this way, even New York created by contracts in which CACs were not included, would now be subject to collective action. The effect of a court sanctioned plan would be not simply to prevent enforcement of claims, but to substantively alter the claims themselves, e.g. reducing debt burden.

Given its scope, the Model Law bill was surprisingly light on legislative specifics. This is not per se problematic. After all, Schemes of Arrangement under UK company law, which also provide for court-sanctioned restructuring and cram down, are created under statutory provisions which leave much to the courts and legal practice.[105] Here, however, we were dealing with highly political restructurings being conducted in a novel forum, the New York Court, only applicable to New York law-governed debt, and against a potential backdrop of other restructuring initiatives such as multilateral initiatives. The Model Law as drafted was silent on most of these critical variables. What if, for example, the G20 and Paris Club were conducting their own restructuring and agreed different

102 Bill S4747.

103 Joseph Stiglitz, Martin Guzman and José Antonio Ocampo, 'Support Memorandum to the New York Taxpayer and International Crisis Protection Act (Hoylman-Signal/Fahy Bill)' (*Policy Dialogue*, 2023) <https://policydialogue.org/files/publications/papers/SUPPORT-MEMORANDUM-Guzman-OcampoStiglitz.pdf> accessed 27 May 2024.

104 Seavey (n 80).

105 Part 26A Companies Act 2006. This point has been forcefully made by Karina Patricio Ferreira Lima.

terms? The Model Law proceeded on the basis that multilateral negotiations had to have been agreed by any debtor seeking protection under the Model Law, but this surely undermined what the Model Law was trying to do—if debtors were required to negotiate multilaterally, why then renegotiate in New York? The generality of the Model Law meant many loopholes and aporias could be and were spotted by critics. Nevertheless, it did offer the prize of a sovereign debt restructuring mechanism and so a leap forward.

The third proposal was the very opposite of the Model Law in its surgical precision. As noted above, Lee Buchheit's highly achievable proposal involved reversing *Elliot* by affirming the application of New York's champerty law to sovereign debt acquired by vulture funds. Legally, the measure was unimpeachable, provided one accepts champerty has a role to play still in modern finance law. The problem it faced was political: the measure was conservative relative to the Fahy Bill and Model Law, and some felt it was dealing with a now relatively minor problem of vulture funds, when the bigger issue was the magnitude of all sovereign debt, acquired at cost or otherwise. That problem at least required anti-holdout legislation.

Both the Model Law bill and the Fahy Bill managed to secure legislative time at the New York Senate during the 2022–23 session. Initially things went well, much to the surprise of the banking lobby: the Senate permitted the Fahy Bill to proceed to a review by the NY Senate Judicial Committee, a review which concluded the Bill was acceptable. Things looked promising when the proposals returned to the Senate Chamber, it was just a question of finding Senate time to debate and vote on one of the Bills. Here though, progressives engaged in self-sabotage. Your author understands from those close to events that, faced with limited time, the Chair of the Senate could only put forward one bill for debate at the end of the session, leading to arguments over which bill should be prioritized. The bills' supporters ultimately ended up cancelling each other out, with neither bill reaching the Senate floor and so falling by the wayside.

Following much backroom negotiation between the two sets of supporters of the Fahy Bill and Model Law Bill, a second attempt on the Senate was made in 2024. Agreement had been reached to splice together the best parts of both bills into a single all-encompassing bill, though in reality the generality of the Model Law meant the new Bill S5542A (the **Amended Model Law Bill**).[106] While the Amended Model Law Bill permitted debtor states to elect which measures it would seek to rely on—anti-holdout measures or a full restructuring—by effect of this political 'fudge,' according to Reichert-Facilides and others, was to introduce all the problems of the individual bills into the one document for no legal benefit.[107] These include the vagueness of key provisions and a blindness to the interaction between New York decisions and debt being dealt with in London, or under a Paris Club arrangement. As at the time of this edition, we await a vote on the Amended Model Law Bill in the face of organized resistance from New York's financial lobby.

5.4.3.4 Proposals for further UK anti-holdout legislation 2023+

The fresh momentum in New York motivated civil society in Belgium, Germany, and the United Kingdom to put fresh legislative proposals to legislators. A key thought was that a push in tandem on several fronts would assuage legislators' concerns that being a first mover on sovereign debt legislation would lead to an exodus of financial deals (a concern not borne out by the experience of the 2010 Act (see above). We focus on the new UK proposals (the **Connelly Proposal**) drafted

106 As amended 1 February 2024: An act to amend the debtor and creditor law, in relation to restructuring unsustainable sovereign and subnational debt, sponsor Sen. Rivera.

107 Simon Hinrichsen and others, 'Designing Sovereign Debt Legislation: Learning from the Comparative Experience' (2024) <https://ssrn.com/abstract=4802614> accessed 27 May 2024.

by me with the aid of Celine Tan and Karina Patricio Ferreira Lima. The Connelly Proposal reflects the recent trend of drawing together the lessons of previous legislation, both enacted and proposed. Adopting Hinrichsen and others' typology of design choices for sovereign debt legislation, the Connelly Proposal can be classified as follows:

(1) *Anti-vulture vs comprehensive*: the Connelly Proposal replicates much of the 2010 Act in applying to all debt rather than targeting 'wrongdoing' creditors. This choice is driven both by Parliament's acceptance of the 2010 Act in principle, and because recent thinking has aligned with wider insolvency policy in eschewing blame for indebtedness in favour of solving unsustainable debt whatever the source.

(2) *Majority vote vs international initiatives*: like the 2010 Act and Fahy Bill, the Connelly Proposal supports international initiatives; it does not provide for a local mechanism whereby majority creditors can force a restructuring decision on a minority (as in the Model Law Bill). Like the Fahy Bill, the Connelly Proposal is forward-looking: it grants the Secretary of State a power of designation of any international initiative as falling within the proposed act, allowing that initiative (e.g. a specific Paris Club restructuring of one nation's debt) to benefit from anti-holdout support under the proposed act.

(3) *Comparable treatment vs flat reduction*: the 2010 Act supported the flat 66 2/3% reduction of debt under the HIPC Initiative. Yet often restructurings use alternative techniques, such as extending payment deadlines, varying interest rates and so on. The 2010 Act's choice was determined by the HIPC Initiative itself. The question future-facing legislation faces is how to predict what restructuring mechanisms will be put in place. Complete openness to any mechanism risks utter vagueness, leaving courts applying such an act unclear on what basis it should proceed, likely with creditors arguing over the fairness of any given choice. One could adopt the Paris Club's notion of 'Comparability of Treatment' but this notion names an indicative practice of the Paris Club which could well change, and which is limited to a subset of all possible restructurings and initiatives. At the other extreme, trying to specify a Procrustean solution in advance would almost certainly produce unfairness, if it works at all. The Connelly Proposal advanced a mediate solution: it appreciated that various, sometimes conflicting restructuring tools would be in play in any given case and proposed to price these as a single monetary value rather than have the UK courts replicate complex restructuring provisions. The Connelly Proposal carried over the percentage reduction factor of the 2010 Act, but now, following Reichert-Facilides, used the current market value of the debt over the nominal (original) value of the debt as the fraction to determine the reduction. The thinking here is that by so doing, the current market value prices in any reduction in value of the debt as a result of actual and anticipated restructuring terms.

(4) *Enforcement vs contract variation*: The New York Model Law Bill (both original and amended) deviates from previous practice by actively changing the contractual rights and obligations of parties to sovereign debt contracts. The Connelly Proposal prefers to restrict enforceability of those claims in local courts as this is consistent with its aim of supporting international initiatives.

(5) *Attachment limitation vs defence*: Sapin II provided for a very specific restriction on enforcement against certain state assets; it did not prevent creditors bringing claims in France (and then enforcing them elsewhere). The Connelly Proposal follows the 2010 Act in having a wider effect, not just restricting types of enforcement but providing a defence to a claim as such, namely that the claim can be subjected to a reduction factor based on a relevant international initiative, thereby also limiting the extent of enforcement. The general thought is that the 2010 Act is to be preferred, not least because all litigators know that claims themselves offer tactical advantages and place pressure on debtors, such that after a fashion, claims can bring about compliance and so act as a mode of 'soft' enforcement.

(6) *Standstill*: The DSSI Bill aimed at providing for a moratorium not just on debt service but on claims for and enforcement of that debt service. Moratoriums are a key feature of modern insolvency legislation for individuals and companies; they provide breathing space to renegotiate and prevent a creditor stampede which, as the *NML* litigation demonstrated, is

so destructive of value. In view of this, the Connelly Proposal incorporates such a standstill mechanism to protect state debtors in the period leading up to formal entry into an international initiative.

(7) *Clawback:* clawback provisions in insolvency encompass a variety of powerful judicial mechanisms to seize back assets that ought not to have been received by a creditor. In the context of sovereign debt, one can imagine a mechanism which claws backs monies received by a creditor in excess of a common reduction factor applied to all creditors by an initiative. The Connelly Proposal adopts a transactional version of such a clawback, called a *turnover*. This provides that should a creditor receive monies in excess of a reduction factor under the Connelly Proposal, they hold the excess on trust for the debtor or, if the trust fails, owe an amount equal to the amount of the excess they received to the debtor, and in either case must turn those monies or that amount to the debtor forthwith. Given that funds tend to be held in international settlement systems, this mechanism can be a highly effective bootstrapping for the proposal.

The Connelly Proposal attempts to draw together the best elements of previous proposals and legislation while also ironing out some of the concerns around scope and vagueness. The chief difficulty with the Connelly Proposal is that it is drafted in a manner highly specific to the UK context. While some of this is unavoidable—it must work within the UK legal frameworks—the principal contingency is that it mirrors the 2010 Act for reasons of political expediency at the expense of some clarity. The thinking here is that Parliament is familiar with the 2010 Act and so a 'mark 2' will be more palatable and communicable than a conceptually novel proposal. Yet at the same time this restricts the proposal's utility to other jurisdictions seeking a model. As at the time of writing the incoming Labour government has indicated interest in the proposal, or at least legislation in the area, and it has a range of backbench support. It is in the nature of transformative legal research to be beholden to political winds.

5.4.4 Restructuring legislation

These are laws that affect (private) creditors regardless of whether they are vulture funds and, like anti-holdout legislation, aim to secure multilaterally agreed-upon debt restructuring. In addition, they explicitly require the consent of a qualified majority of creditors as a condition of successful restructuring. This consent can produce several effects, from triggering anti-holdout legislation to varying existing contractual rights. Following erlassjahr.de's classification, we refer to these legislative proposals, which are a specific subcategory of anti-holdout laws, as laws for safeguarding majority decision voting.

Daniel Reichert-Facilides has proposed a law for safeguarding majority decision voting which stands at the more conservative end of the scale (for sensible reasons).[108] This proposal is in effect an anti-holdout legislation providing enforcement support for debtors who have agreed a restructuring internationally. Which restructurings should be protected? The Connelly Proposal solves this question by giving power to a government minister to designate qualifying initiatives; Reichert-Facilides offers a less-politicized solution (and so one legally predictable) by defining qualifying restructurings of long-term commercial debt by reference to qualified majority support. In short, if a qualified majority of creditors support a given restructuring, then the debtor may now avail itself of the remaining anti-holdout provisions of the Reichert-Facilides proposal to cram down holdouts. The problem-solving nature of drafting really comes out in this solution, for while it provides a measure of certainty it also raises further questions demanding

---

108 Daniel Reichert-Facilides, *Draft Proposal for a Foreign Sovereign Debt Restructuring Law* (Institute for Law and Finance 2022) <https://papers.ssrn.com/sol3/papers.cfm?abstract_id=4164656> accessed 15 March 2024.

solution. First, should multilateral debt be caught up in the legislation? Should multilateral debt be covered if the legislating state is also a creditor bit does not participate in a restructuring of the debt? Would the legislation create unwanted difficulties for negotiating multilateral debt? To avoid broaching these problems of the interaction between national and international insolvency mechanisms, the Reichert-Facilides proposal excludes multilateral debt from its purview. Doing so, however, entrenches the informal seniority of multilateral debt and the feeling amongst commercial lenders that they must fight for what they can get in an unfair international system i.e. an encouragement to vulture practices. Second, encompassing *any* agreed private creditor restructuring is perhaps just too open, including open to abuse if debtor and majority creditors agree to abuse minority creditors. The Reichert-Facilides solution is to place an additional condition requiring debtor states to generate a primary surplus while restructuring is underway, with a view, presumably, to encouraging positive fiscal behaviour by the debtor as part of a good faith restructuring. This seems like legislative overreach: for one, legislature seeking to impose fiscal restraints (like a fiscal brake of stability pact) on another generates significant political and diplomatic tension.

At the other end of the spectrum, the New York Model Law bill, and its amended successor, do not just uphold the qualified majority voting of a trans- or international restructuring, but provide for that restructuring to take place in New York under a court-sanctioned regime. In similar vein, Karina Patricio Ferreira Lima has proposed extending UK Companies Act Schemes of Arrangements to sovereign debtors.[109] Under these schemes, the restructuring is entirely organized on such terms as debtor and creditors think fit, but the court has the power to sanction any qualified majority creditor agreement and so force that agreement on dissentient creditors. Both options offer powerful restructuring mechanisms which fill the lacuna where an international Sovereign Debt Restructuring Mechanism should be. The difficulty they face is their interaction with international initiatives and with what happens to debt governed by, say, English law. As to international initiatives, while the Model Law bill required that an active IMF programme must have been completed to qualify, the IMF has had concerns that restructurings in New York might conflict with international restructuring efforts, permitting creditors to play off the two centres against each other, e.g. by threatening to run to New York if concessions are not granted internationally. The requirement of a completed programme also greatly restricted the scope of the law. The problems are perhaps even greater when it comes to debt governed by laws other than New York law. The New York Model Law bill assumes that other jurisdictions will pass equivalent laws (hence the nomenclature of 'model law'), thereby allowing all debt to be restructured. This is frankly unrealistic, given both the legislative difficulties such laws face and the peculiarities of different legal systems. It would be far better for the Model Law to support whichever laws are enacted globally, be they anti-vulture fund, anti-holdout, or some other mechanism, by restricting enforcement of debts covered by such foreign laws in New York. Given that the Amended Model Law Bill has taken in the Fahy Bill's anti-holdout mechanism, there is no principled objection to extending the Fahy Bill's enforcement restrictions on a comity basis from debt covered by multilateral initiatives to debt governed by e.g. English law and subject to specific UK legislation, anti-holdout, restructuring or otherwise.

5.4.5 Conclusion

As Hinrichsen and others note, the variety of legislative proposals in circulation in the last few years suggest no path-dependent convergence on a consensus view on what national legislation should

109 Stephen Connelly, Karina Patricio Ferreira Lima and Celine Tan, 'Proposal for Debt Suspension Legislation' (3 June 2020) 2022 The IEL Collective, Law & Finance Working Group.

look like.[110] This is exemplified by the Amended Model Law Bill which merely splices together two different bills and leaves it to the debtor state to decide in each case whether it prefers national or international restructuring. The Connelly Proposal is a first attempt to distil best practice into a single bill, but UK legislative history means it cannot present itself as a conceptually self-contained model law. Appreciation of the winding road of legislation is very important for contextual legal scholarship, and much remains to be written by students of sovereign debt on the matter.

110 ibid 31.

Chapter 6

Syndication

Chapter contents

DOI: 10.4324/9781003457220-6

6.1 Introduction

When Borrower draws down a Loan under a CFA, this creates corresponding contractual obligations to pay interest and repay capital. Each obligation is an asset (a chose in action) in the hands of the Lender, and, as an asset, he can sell it to third parties.

Syndication is a special case in which the sale of debt obligations is pre-planned, and indeed syndication may occur before any Loans have been drawn down—the syndicate banks may agree already to commit themselves to lend. Syndication developed as the borrowing needs of corporates expanded and it was no longer possible or prudent for one bank to be the sole Lender.

Syndication evolved into structured finance, in which creditors contractually differentiate their risk of losses on debtor default. States already provide for creditor hierarchies which are determined as a matter of public policy, but structured finance seems to subvert such policy decisions and indeed in some debtor-friendly jurisdictions some structured finance methods may be struck down.

DEBT OBLIGATIONS AND DEBT INSTRUMENTS

The following point merits emphasis: this chapter is all about the buying and selling of debt obligations constituted by *contracts* (and so governed by the English common law).

Enforceable debts can also be created by drawing up instruments such as IOUs. These are *not* contracts but debt instruments (known now as securities), which derive their enforceability and other attributes from the *law merchant* largely codified in the Bills of Exchange Act 1882. We look at securities in Chapter 8.

Do not worry about debt instruments now, but do make a note that presently we are *only* concerned with buying and selling contractual debt *obligations*.

6.2 The legal notion of debt: the law

In this section we give an overview of the legal analysis of debt. If you are happy to accept these things on faith, feel free to ignore the next section in which we examine some historical reasons why the law categorizes debt in the way that it does. In any event, it helps to deal with the terminology in one place as briefly as possible.

Let us first observe that law might be characterized as a number of languages lawyers use to speak about social states of affairs. By states of affairs, I mean facts which come to be or pass away by means of social utterances. A classic example, due to JL Austen, is the performative utterance 'I pronounce you man and wife.'[1] Nothing physically changes in the natural world when a registrar or priest utters these words, but we generally understand these words to have some effect: they bring about state of affairs called marriage, with all the attendant legal consequences of this status. Utterances such as 'I promise that x' and 'I owe you' are similar—in certain circumstances they produce new states of affairs with legal consequences. Generally, I will say that these kinds of states of affairs *subsist* to mark them out from natural facts, such as the natural fact that you, a living being, *exist*.

Now I said above that law is a number of languages. What I mean by this is that law is not a homogenous, unitary language which ascribes one and only one legal term or set of consistent, interrelated terms to a given state of affairs. In fact, and you know this though you

1 JL Austin, *How to Do Things With Words* (Clarendon Press 1962).

may not have consciously considered it, law offers different sets of terminology, sometimes inconsistent, to describe the same state of affairs. For example, if Boris punches Matt in the face, criminal law will interpret this state of affairs as battery and perhaps actual bodily harm, whereas the law of torts will interpret the same event as a trespass against the person of Matt. You will appreciate that if you answered your tort exam with references to offences against the person, you would not do very well. Accordingly, you learn, often unconsciously, not to mix the legal languages.

In the context of finance law, we have already seen that two legal languages are sometimes confused: the languages of obligations (mainly contract), and of property. When we considered contractual liens we saw several cases where the personal rights of a lienee to detain goods were often confused with the property rights of a pledgee in pledged goods. Our ability to hold the languages of obligation and property apart will once again be tested as we consider debt, and particularly the transfer of debt.

First, the *law of obligations*. If *a* is obligated to *b*, then *a* is bound to do something to *b*'s benefit. We say *b* has the benefit and *a* has the burden (is the **obligor**) of e.g. a contract. I note this relationship with an arrow: $a \rightarrow b$. This arrow just indicates that *a* is obligated to *b*.

With a contract there must be consideration i.e. *b* is also obligated to *a* thus: $a \leftarrow b$. Now we want to show both obligations, so in this case I write: $a \leftrightarrows b$.

Now the obligation $a \rightarrow b$ may consist in this: that *a* must repay to *b* some certain sum of money at a specified time. If *a* does not, he is in breach of contract. What is *b*'s remedy? If you have studied contract law your likely response will be: *b* will sue for breach of contract and request damages in the amount he expected to receive. This is not technically correct, however, for the law makes a distinction between a claim for a debt, and a claim for damages for breach of an obligation. There is no single statement as to what 'debt' means, for the cases turn on the interpretation of specific statutes and contracts, but a claim for a debt is most often defined by contrasting it with a claim in (contractual) damages:

(1) A debt claim is for a specific, agreed sum due pursuant to a *primary* obligation of the contract: *Phillips & Co (a firm) v Bath Housing Co-operative Ltd*.[2]
(2) A claim for damages is a claim arising out of losses caused by a breach of the terms of the contract: *President of India v Lips Maritime Corpn (The Lips)*.[3]

The distinction is not always clear in practice, and certain authorities do present anomalous outcomes in technical areas such as the statute of limitations and bankruptcy.[4] For example, some contracts contain a term that if one party delays performance, then 'liquidated damages' of a specified amount are payable to the other party. The innocent party may well feel that if GBP5,000 is payable under this liquidated damages clause, it is a debt owing to them. Yet they would be wrong, for all the clause does is convert a damages claim from a claim for as yet unquantified damages into a claim for mutually agreed quantified damages, but it is still a claim for damages (the secondary obligation), and not a claim in debt (i.e. a primary obligation to pay).[5] For the purposes of finance law, it suffices to grasp that the law of obligations sees a difference between a primary obligation to pay and a secondary obligation to pay such damages as may be assessed. Using our languages of

2 *Phillips & Co (a firm) v Bath Housing Co-operative Ltd.* [2012] EWCA Civ 1591, [2013] 2 All ER 475 [30].
3 *President of India v Lips Maritime Corp (The Lips)* [1987] 1 Lloyd's Rep 131 (CA) 422.
4 It is perhaps most commonly encountered in the courts in the context of Civil Procedure Rule 24 concerning summary judgment. Here the claimant in a debt claim has the distinct procedural advantage that a debt owing is usually 'obvious' to the court once a contractual obligation is put in evidence and an allegation of non-payment is made. The defendant will attempt, where possible, to argue that no debt is owing or, if anything is owing, it is in the form of damages which require a detailed assessment of the facts in a full trial (thereby delaying judgment day).
5 *President of India v Lips Maritime Corp (The Lips)* (n 3) 422.

arrows above, if we imagine a situation in which *a* owes money to *b* but also has caused *b* damage by failing to pay on time (because *b* lacked the money to pay a third party), it is as if there are two, distinct and severable arrows between *a* and *b*: $a \rightrightarrows b$, representing the debt claim and the damages claim, respectively. This distinction becomes also becomes important when we look again at a financial relationship using the language of property law.

Let us focus solely on the debt claim $a \rightarrow b$ for the time being. As we just seen, the law of obligations interprets this state of affairs as a relationship between *a* and *b*. How does property law interpret this state of affairs? In a manner of speaking, something quite mystical happens: property takes the arrow that in obligations law signifies a *relationship between people* and regards the arrow as a *thing* in its own right. It is as if someone has come along and picked up the arrow, declaring that it is now theirs.

The situation is slightly more nuanced—at least initially the arrow is not wholly divorced from the relationship. Ask yourself this: if *b* can be said to own any property i.e. any thing, what property does *b* own? Well *b* owns the benefit of *a*'s obligation to pay her a sum of money. To put it another way, this component of the contract:

$a \rightarrow$ is *b*'s *property*: $a \rightarrow$ is a thing owned by *b*. As you can see, one aspect of the relationship between *a* and *b* remains relevant: the arrow now apparently represents *a*'s obligation to pay, but it is no longer necessarily an obligation to pay *b*, but an obligation to pay someone. Who? The owner of arrow from *a*. In view of this, there needs to be a shift of perspective. As a matter of obligations, the arrow is *a*'s obligation to pay, but from a property perspective we are concerned with who owns the property, and so it is more correct to say that the arrow now represents the owner *x*'s **claim** in debt on *a*.

This claim gives us a hint as to the kind of property with which we are dealing. This property evidently is not land (immoveable) so it must be personal property (moveable). It is what we call a *chose* (law French for 'thing'). There are two types of chose, the chose in possession and the chose in action. Cast your mind back to the pledge and lien (Chapter 3) and hopefully you can see that a debt claim cannot be a chose in possession, for how would you be able to tell that *a* has a debt claim against *b*. Things in possession are *de facto* possessable because we can sense them with eye, touch, and so forth—hence we call then **tangible**. This physicality allows third parties to see who possesses the thing and so who may legally be interested in the thing. But a debt cannot be an object of our external senses; it is **intangible**. It is not a matter of a creditor holding up a unique object in his possession, for if *a* simply tells you he has a debt claim, what is stopping *c*, *d*, and *e* all telling you they are the rightful owners of the very same debt claim? How would you determine who is right? By deduction we must be dealing with a chose in action, but we can also provide a positive explanation as to why. It comes back to the question just asked: how does one establish who has the right to the debt claim against *a* if it is impossible physically to possess this claim? The answer is that we ask the court to adjudicate. That is what 'judge' literally means—it comes from the Latin *iudex* (*ius* + *dicere*) which means 'to say or declare the right.' So, in order to establish who is the rightful owner, one needs to bring a claim or action in a court. That is why we call these kinds of intangible things **choses in action**—they are things the ownership of which is only provable in a court action.

ESSENTIAL DEFINITION: CHOSE IN ACTION

'all personal rights of property which can only be claimed or enforced by action, and not by taking physical possession.'

This definition is offered by *Snell's Equity*[6] (and quoted by Bamford). The term 'personal' here could confuse; in this definition it refers to property which is not real i.e. is not land.

There are many kinds of chose in action, including:

- Claims in debt;
- Contractual rights;
- Claims in damages;
- Intellectual property;
- Company shares; and[7]
- Equitable choses in action, such as beneficial interests in a trust.

A detailed list would indicate that various rights have been recognized and subsequently grouped under the heading 'chose in action'; that English law did not start with a conceptual definition and derive the various kinds of chose in action from it. Rather, it established who had an enforceable claim in a given case, and through generalization this claim became one kind of chose in action.

For the purposes of this book we do not need to examine most of the choses in action—we will focus almost exclusively on debt claims, contractual rights, and claims for breach of contract.

Think back to the distinction we made between debts and damages for breach of contract. Now you have a better idea as to why the language here was slightly more convoluted. For we made a distinction between a claim in (or to) a debt, and a claim in damages for breach of contract. What is being grasped by this chose in action is not simply the debt considered as a sum of money, but the claim on *a* for delivery up of that sum of money, the 'claim' being the 'action' in the term 'chose in action.' Both elements must be present, for the essence of a chose in action is that it is (1) property that (2) is only realisable through an action. Put another way, without the action the chose is de facto ineffectual, and without the chose the action is bare litigation having no valid purpose.

As soon as the debt relationship is reinterpreted as a thing, as the property $a \rightarrow$, the other attributes of property seem to follow. One such attribute, which will be central to the rest of the chapter, is alienability—being *b*'s property, *b* is entitled to transfer $a \rightarrow$ to some *c*. It is as if *b* has picked up that arrow projecting from *a* to *b* and turned it to face *c* like a weathervane. It is again obvious if we draw what has happened:

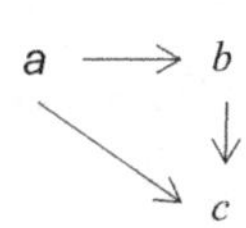

Even with this simple example we suddenly have a proliferation of property resulting from the various obligations. *b* owns a chose in action, the claim in debt on *a*. *b* now promises to *c* to transfer this claim on *a* to *c*. *c* now has a claim on *b*: a chose in action representing his personal right to force *b* to transfer *b*'s claim in debt on *a*. This is a wholly distinct chose in action, which

6 John McGhee KC (ed), *Snell's Equity* (3rd edn, Sweet & Maxwell 2015) 3-001.

7 See now s 541 Companies Act 2006, where the language of 'personalty' is used. The reason the Companies Acts felt it necessary to state this have their origins in *Bligh v Brent* (1837) 2 Y & C Exch 268, 160 ER 397. For an explicit link to the chose in action, see *Colonial Bank v Whinney* (1886) 11 App Cas 426.

I denote $b \rightarrow$, from that chose in action $a \rightarrow$ which *b* owns. The effect of *b* transferring $a \rightarrow$ to *c*, is that now *c* has a claim in debt on *c*.

You may remember from your contract law course that this kind of diagram is an example of something impermissible: a third party *c* cannot normally obtain the benefit of a contract between *a* and *b*. And that is correct, but only within the law of contractual obligations. I stress again that now we are using a property law analysis. As a matter of property law, by composition with $b \rightarrow c$ the chose in action $a \rightarrow b$ has become $a \rightarrow c$. This contradicts the rule of contract law, but nothing requires contract law and property law to be mutually coherent, though many have tried to maintain consistency. Professor Goode has written:

> The essential point is that a debt is a species of property only in the relations between the creditor and a third party who takes the assignment of the debt. As between the debtor and the creditor a debt is purely an obligation. The creditor does not own the debt, he is owed it.[8]

This seems to be an attempt to attain coherence by sequencing obligation and property in time. But surely the third party steps into the shoes of the original creditor, unless we are to hold that the third party is not owed money, a result which surely renders owning the chose in action pointless. And if there is a point at which obligation transforms into chose in action, even if only to transform back into obligation, at what points in time are these transformations occurring? Would it not be better to adopt a parallelism between the obligational and proprietary interpretations of this state of affairs, one interpretation being applied as the legal question being asked demands?

We might add that $b \rightarrow$, being a chose in action, is itself assignable by *c* to some *d*, and so on ad infinitum.

But, and this is a big BUT, we must not ever forget about the respective burdens. While *b*'s property was $a \rightarrow$, *b* is certainly not the owner of $\leftarrow b$, for that chose in action belongs to *a*. **An obligor cannot own her obligation to another** or more correctly, an obligor cannot own a claim against herself. This may seem a fairly self-evident point, but it has proved to be a matter of some legal contention. In the following case, the question arose whether a debtor could take security over a debt they owed to their creditor. As security is a proprietary right, the court's approach first required asking: can a debtor have any proprietary right over a debt it owes to another?

RE CHARGE CARD SERVICES LTD (No.2) [1987] 1 Ch 150.[9]

Charge Card (the 'Company') issued payment cards to the employees of other businesses. The employees would use the cards to buy petrol, and the Company would make these payments and seek repayment of the amounts disbursed from the employer businesses. As result, the Company owned a running balance of several debts owed by multiple businesses at any one time. To improve liquidity, the Company sold these choses in action (claims in debt on the employer businesses) to a factoring company called Commercial Credit, and in consideration received cash up front from Commercial

8 Louise Gullifer (ed), *Goode and Gullifer on Legal Problems of Credit and Security* (2nd edn, Sweet & Maxwell 1998) 125.

9 This case is discussed in great detail in Colin Bamford, *Principles of International Financial Law* (3rd edn, Oxford Academic 2019) 4.58–84.

Credit, less a discount for providing the cash earlier than the debts would be repaid by the employer businesses. One part of this factoring arrangement was an agreement that the Company would guarantee and indemnify Commercial Credit for any losses on bad debts (i.e. debts not paid by employer businesses within 120 days) and that to support this guarantee and indemnity, Commercial Credit could retain 15% of all monies Commercial Credit owed to the Company from time to time under the wider factoring arrangement.

The Company collapsed into insolvency, and its liquidator argued inter alia that Commercial Credit's right to retain the 15% of monies payable to the Company was void because it amounted to a charge on book debts (security) which had not been registered as required by the Companies Acts.[10]

Held: per Millett J (as he then was): if the retention clause created a charge, then it was 'clearly' a charge over book debts[11] and so void for want of registration. Yet the matter merited closer analysis:

> But is it a charge at all? The sum due from Commercial Credit to the company under the agreement is, of course, a book debt of the company which the company can charge to a third party. In my judgment, however, it cannot be charged in favour of Commercial Credit itself, for the simple reason that a charge in favour of a debtor of his own indebtedness to the chargor is conceptually impossible (175C-D). . . .
>
> The debtor cannot, and does not need to, resort to the creditor's claim against him in order to obtain the benefit of the security; his own liability to the creditor is automatically discharged or reduced.

It helps to unpack this by proceeding in stages. Ignore the question of security for one moment. The Company owns a chose in action: the employer debt $e \rightarrow Co$ arising because employer businesses have promised to reimburse debts arising under their employees' charge cards. The Company sold these choses in action $e \rightarrow$ to Commercial Credit. In consideration Commercial Credit now owed discounted sums of money to the Company i.e. the Company now owns a new chose in action, the debt owed by Commercial Credit: $CC \rightarrow Co$. Now imagine the Company assigned this chose in action $CC \rightarrow$ back to Commercial Credit. Then Commercial Credit would own a chose in action which is a debt to itself $CC \rightarrow CC = CC^{\circlearrowright}$. But that is absurd—a person cannot owe themselves a debt. Therefore, the assignment must extinguish the debt and destroy the chose in action.

There was not an absolute legal assignment of ownership in this case, however. Instead, the court held there was an attempt to grant security by way of charge. But the effect was similar: Commercial Credit purported to take security over a chose in action $CC \rightarrow Co$ which was its obligation to pay the Company. Yet were the security to be enforced, the chose in action would disappear because enforcement would immediately result in Commercial Credit owing a debt to itself $CC^{\circlearrowright}$—again an absurdity. As a result of this absurdity, Millett J held that there simply could be no security at all.

10 s 95 Companies Act 1948 at the time. See now s 859A Companies Act 2006.

11 For a discussion of equitable charges of book debts, see Chapter 4.

This view, that one cannot owe oneself a debt, seems obvious.[12] Yet it proved controversial: it was strongly criticized by Philip Wood[13] and Fidelis Oditah.[14] Though Lord Millett had his supporters, such as Professor Everett,[15] the debate came to a head in a House of Lords judgment relating to the collapse of the Bank of Credit and Commerce International.

IN RE BCCI S.A. (No.8) [1996] Ch 245 (CA); [1998] AC 214 (HL)

Jessa was the ultimate beneficial owner of the shares of a Panamanian company, Rayners, Inc. The company owed money to Bank of Credit & Commerce International, SA (BCCI). Jessa held deposit accounts with BCCI and agreed to provide comfort to BCCI for the company's debts by granting security over his account with BCCI to BCCI to meet the company's liabilities. In effect Jessa would allow BCCI to have recourse to his deposits if the company defaulted.

When BCCI collapsed, Jessa faced having the liquidators immediately claim repayment in full from the company, whereas Jessa would have to wait a long time to recover a much reduced amount of his deposit via the insolvency process. Jessa's aim therefore was to argue that the company's liability should be immediately set off against the debt BCCI owed to Jessa. This would mean Jessa would receive nothing back, but the advantage would be that the whole value of the deposit would reduce the company's liability to BCCI. To achieve this aim, Jessa sought to argue, following *re Charge Card*, that the purported 'security'—purporting to constitute a proprietary right granted to BCCI over a debt BCCI owed to another—was 'conceptually impossible' and that all the agreement did was create a personal liability from Jessa to BCCI. As this was linked to the liability of the company to BCCI, Insolvency Rule 4.90 permitted Jessa immediately to set off the opposed liabilities as desired (this rule provides for mandatory set-off on insolvency and is discussed in more detail later in this chapter).

BCCI's liquidator's aim was to claim the full amount owing from the solvent company now, and force Jessa to prove for his deposit, which would be paid out later and subject to a reduction due to the insolvency. They countered that the security was valid, with the result that there was a proprietary interest incapable of being set off against the deposit liability under r.4.90.

12 Nor was the decision original: cf *Halesowen Presswork & Assemblies Ltd. v National Westminster Bank Ltd.* [1971] 1 QB 1 (CA) 46 (LJ Buckley): 'No man can have a lien on his own property and consequently no lien can have arisen affecting that money or that credit. . . . I cannot myself understand how it could be said with any kind of accuracy that the bank had a lien upon its own indebtedness to the company.' That passage was subsequently approved by the House of Lords [1972] AC 785, 802 (Viscount Dilhorne), 810 (Lord Cross of Chelsea). *Per* Lord Cross: 'I agree with Lord Denning MR and Buckley LJ that a debtor cannot sensibly be said to have a lien on his own indebtedness to the debtor.' See also the Australian case of *Broad v Commissioner of Stamp Duties* [1980] 2 NSWLR 40 in which Lees J held that 'there can be no mortgage or charge in favour of oneself of one's own indebtedness to another.'

13 See Philip Wood, 'Three Problems of Set-Off: Contingencies, Build-Ups and Charge-Backs' (1987) 8(6) The Company Lawyer 262–269 at 265; Philip Wood, 'Comment' (1998) 17 Intnl FLR 10; Philip Wood, *English and International Set-Off* (Sweet & Maxwell 1989) 5-134-5-181.

14 See Fidelis Oditah, 'Financing Trade Credit: *Welsh Development Agency v Exfinco*' [1992] JBL 541. Rory Derham took a middle view in *The Law of Set-Off* (Clarendon 1987) 301–5.

15 Professor Everett, 'Security over Bank Deposits' (1988) 16 Australian Business Law Review 351. Support was also found in the courts, in cases such as *Morris and Others v Agrichemicals Ltd. and Others* [1996] Ch 245.

Held on appeal: The Court of Appeal approached the matter, as Millett J had done, from first principles and came to the intermediate conclusion that as far as one may speak of debts, a debtor cannot be the owner of a debt claim against itself:

> (262) Other criticisms of the reasoning in *in re Charge Card Services Ltd.* seem to us to carry little weight. It is said that Millett J attached too much importance to the fact that the debtor cannot sue himself; an unenforceable debt is still a debt even if it is unenforceable by action, for example if it has become statute-barred. That is true, but there is something distinctly odd about a chose in action which could never have been the subject even of an unsuccessful action. The concept of a debt which one owes to oneself must, we think, inhabit the same territory as a covenant with oneself and the grant of a lease to oneself.

For this reason, there could be no proprietary interest, and so no security, in such a purported 'self-owned' debt. Rather, the CA held that the agreement created a 'flawed asset,' that is, it regarded the deposit owed to Jessa as contingent on the company repaying the bank. On its terms, as long as the company had not repaid in full, the bank owed nothing to Jessa. So, while there were only personal rights as between the parties, Jessa's right did not exist at the time of insolvency and so he could not set it off against the company's liabilities at that time; he would have to wait.

Held by the House of Lords: The House of Lords did not disagree with the CA's view; rather it proceeded from a different starting point (the nature of an equitable charge) and reached a decision without needing to opine on whether debts could be owed to oneself. That decision was taken as overturning Millett J's narrow finding that it be conceptually impossible that a debtor take a charge over a debt he owed to another, but a close analysis of the House of Lords' reasoning (delivered by Lord Hoffman) indicates that *re Charge Card* and *BCCI (No.8)* are in fact very close, only dividing on the result.

Lord Hoffman's argument seems to be this: (1) An equitable charge is a species of charge, which is a proprietary interest granted by way of security. A proprietary interest provided by way of security entitles the holder to resort to the property only for the purpose of satisfying some liability due to him (whether from the person providing the security or a third party) and, whatever the form of the transaction, the owner of the property retains an equity of redemption to have the property restored to him when the liability has been discharged. (2) It is accepted that a depositor could charge its claim against a bank to a third party. (3) What objection is there that the third party could be the same bank? (4) Assume that the charge is valid; then if the bank were to enforce the security it would own its right to sue itself (in order to realize that claim and meet the depositor's liability). (5) But, as Millett J noted, as soon as this occurred the debt the bank owed to itself would be extinguished or cancel itself out. (6) *Pace* Millett J, is this not exactly what the bank intended in taking the charge? Namely, the bank intended to satisfy the depositor's liability to the bank by cancelling it out through seizing its liability to the depositor. (7) This confers the benefit that enforcement is somewhat automatic, and does not require the court's involvement. (8) Therefore there was no conceptual bar to the bank taking such a security—its self-annihilating nature *on enforcement* was what was intended, and there was consequently no reason why the courts should deny the practice.

Accordingly, the security was valid, it constituted a proprietary not a personal right, and Jessa would have to prove for his deposit in the insolvency.

As should be clear from my reconstruction of the argument in BCCI (No.8), Lord Hoffman felt that Millett J's conceptual objection in fact disclosed the conceptual intention behind taking security over a debt one owes to another (to secure liabilities of a third party). The basic propositions stand—that one cannot owe a debt to oneself, and that as a result taking an equitable charge over that debt, the debt must extinguish itself on enforcement. The House of Lords' objection is rather to Millett J's blanket and formalist denial that the charge can be taken in the first place; it could be taken precisely because it was designed to self-annihilate on enforcement.

Let us step back from security now and focus once again on debt more generally. One corollary of the view that one cannot assign one's own debt, is that if an obligor cannot own her obligations to others, necessarily she cannot assign that obligation to others. **An obligor cannot assign her obligation** for she cannot give what she does not have.

This means that when b assigned $a \rightarrow$ to c, the chose in action $\leftarrow b$ (being a's property) stayed where it was. The benefit became separated from the burden, resulting in this state of affairs:

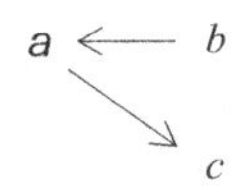

Accordingly, *c* has the benefit of the original contract, while *b* has the burden. Economically as much as legally this is likely to be undesirable for *b*.

The separation of benefit and burden is not problematic however if b's obligation to a has in fact been performed. In that case, the obligation is satisfied and so extinguished. E.g. if b has lent the GBP100 to a, then the arrow $\leftarrow b$ disappears: we go from $a \leftrightarrows b$ to $a \rightarrow b$. Then b only has the benefit and can assign this as she sees fit.

What if b has not performed her obligation, though? Then she cannot assign it away, even if a consented—an obligor cannot assign her obligation. The solutions to this are slightly cumbersome, and we will examine them when we look at syndication later in this chapter.

This section has tried to set out a simple diagrammatic way of representing debt obligations arising from contracts. By representing these obligations as arrows, we can then treat the obligations as 'things' which can be transferred at law to third parties by the beneficiary of the obligation. It is a very useful way of keeping track of things, especially in complex financial transactions and in attempting to understand the cases.

6.3 The legal notion of debt: the history

By the end of this chapter, you will understand that financial institutions buy and sell debt obligations created by loan contracts (CFAs), and that the law facilitates this. Yet the law did not always tolerate this practice, and it pays to question our fundamental legal notions if only to explain some of the peculiarities of the modern law.

Given what we learnt in Chapter 1 about the socio- and ethnological understanding of debt as a relationship of belief (creditworthiness) between two persons—creditor and debtor—should we not find the notion of selling debt to be problematic? If the social function of debt is to bind us together, and the act of settling a debt is regarded as an insulting casting off of that relationship, then it does seem strange that a creditor should be permitted to break up their relationship with the debtor and simply hand over that obligation to a third party whom the debtor may never have met. Imagine a parent, to whom the child owes so much—more than can be expressed in monetary terms—simply selling a particular child's obligation 'to honour one's parents' to a third party. If that makes you think twice about selling relationships, then you have an intuition as to the common law's attitude to attempts to sell relationships of indebtedness.

So why did the common law's attitude change? Socioeconomic factors, such as the development of mercantile commerce, played a significant part, but as lawyers we can also point to the expression of the change in the very conceptual apparatus of the law itself. If you look at the previous paragraph closely, you can see that there are two ways of speaking about debt competing with each other: the 'moral' way, which focuses on a *personal relationship* between two determinate individuals, and a more transactional way, which focuses on debt as a *thing* which can be sold like a commodity. We might baulk at selling a person or a personal relationship but have no qualms about selling a thing because naively we may regard a thing as neither a person nor a personal relationship. Yet in the law of debt, personal relationship and thing become confused; over time the personal relationship comes to be reconceptualized as a thing. Theorists call this process **reification**.[16]

REIFICATION IN LAW

Reification is a concept from critical theory, based on Marx's notion of commodity fetishism. Per Georg Lukács:

> 'the personality can do no more than look on helplessly while its own existence is reduced to an isolated particle and fed into an alien system.'[17]

On this view, the history of the transferability of common law obligations is one of the legal system finally acceding to the demands of financial practice—the entirely personal relationship of one individual with another is 'liberated' to freely circulate now as a commodity within the financial system, whether the obligor wishes it or not. And being free to circulate in a market, the debt now attains a new value which is not the amount the obligor nominally owes, but rather the value of that debt relative to every other debt in the market. In short, the debt attains an exchange value over against its nominal value as between the original parties.

In what follows, we look at the old view of the common law which respected the personal relationship account of debt, and the policy reasons for this, before examining how this notion was superseded by a 'thing' account of debt which permitted its transfer.

6.3.1 The old common law attitude to selling debt obligations

As Holdsworth has shown, the common law had two principal objections to the selling of debt obligations: one axiomatic, the other a matter of public policy.[18]

The axiomatic objection rested on our observation above, namely that a personal obligation is just that, the relationship between two identified individuals. On this view it is not the object of the relationship ('a debt of GBP5') which matters, but the legal subjects in 'I owe *you* GBP5.'

The common law provided (and still provides) the following analysis of this state of affairs. Using the discursive framework we call the law of obligations, we say that I have *promised* to you to deliver up the sum of GBP5 (on demand by you). I am a promisor (or obligor) and you are a promisee (or obligee), but only with respect to my promise to you. To the extent that this promised is legally recognized as enforceable, you are said to have the right to enforce my promise

16 There a number of variations on this basic idea expressed in the key literature. It is tailored here to the context of debt. For more, see Hanna Pitkin, 'Rethinking Reification' (1987) 16 Theory & Society 263, 293.

17 Georg Lukács, *History and Class Consciousness* (first published 1923, Rodney Livingstone tr, MIT Press 1972) 90.

18 WS Holdsworth, 'The History of the Treatment of 'Choses' in Action by the Common Law' (1920) 33 Harv L Rev 997.

to you, and, because this right pertains to my promise, we say that it is a *personal* right, or in the Latin, a right *in personam*.

The language of rights *in personam* is used to distinguish these rights from those rights that pertain to things, which are called rights *in rem*. We have already seen this distinction at work in Chapter 3, in the distinction between the rights of a pledgee and a lienee/bailee. If a pledgee loses possession of the pledged goods, her pledge stills subsists and she demands return of the goods from third parties, because his right is in the goods (*in rem*) versus the rest of the world. If a lienee loses possession of the bailed goods, the lien is usually extinguished, because the lien consisted only in a personal right or immunity against the lienor.

As stated, the common law still uses this framework of obligations when appropriate to do so (for example in contractual claims). Critically, what was different in the Middle Ages[19] was that the courts of common law drew the following axiomatic conclusion from the personal nature of obligations: to transfer a personal right was incoherent, for a personal right was entirely defined by being the relationship between me and you, and was extinguished when either me or you, or both, were subtracted from the relationship. Holdsworth writes:

> but it is clear that a personal action brought either on a contract or a tort is an essentially personal thing. The two parties have agreed, or the plaintiff has been wronged by the defendant. In both cases the cause of action arises from matters affecting these two persons and these only. On that account the common lawyers saw as clearly as the Roman lawyers that such rights of action were personal matters between these two persons. Therefore the assignment of such a right of action by the act of the two parties was unthinkable.[20]

The second justification for prohibiting the assignment of debts the ancient doctrine of **maintenance**. To understand the nature of maintenance, it helps to observe that the doctrine arises as a matter of public policy and is a basis on which a court may refuse to entertain a suit or enforce a legal act otherwise formally permissible. If you have studied illegality as a vitiating factor in contract law, you will appreciate there is often a judicial struggle[21] to rigorously define just what is or is not objectional about a particular contract, based on a somewhat vaguer sense that something about a transaction is not 'right.' Thus, it helps also to approach maintenance, and its offshoot, champerty, by providing some context—some of the historical motivations for the doctrine's development.

As just noted, for a long time the Roman lawyers regarded the great majority of obligations as wholly personal matters incapable of being transferred, but it is true that by the time of the Byzantine Empire some choses in action could be assigned. This led to a new and extremely objectional practice: powerful men, often landowners, would purchase the rights of claim of those unable to afford a court action, and would use these claims to pursue their own personal vendettas. In this, one already sees a principled objection: for it is one thing for Isaac to borrow from Theodore, his social peer and a forgiving man who will no doubt agree some variation of repayment terms if times are hard, and quite another to borrow from Valens, a powerful man and magistrate who has had his eyes on Isaac's farm for some time. In short, Isaac's burden to Theodore is as personal as Theodore's claim on Isaac. And it seems such abuses became widespread, leading to the Code of Justinian introducing a ban on assigning claims to those more

19 Another significant difference is that medieval courts did not speak of contract, and only very late of assumpsit (the forerunner of contract), but this is not material to the point being made about personal claims.

20 Holdsworth (n 18) 1003.

21 *Patel v Mirza* [2016] UKSC 42, [2017] AC 467.

powerful than the assignor, and limiting recoveries on assigned claims to no more than the amount paid in consideration of assignment.[22] By the Middle Ages, lords of the manor were buying up land and titles to pursue claims against neighbours, and suborning and bullying their peasants to stand as witnesses in wager of law[23] claims against whichever target they chose. The result was 'much unquietness, oppression, vexation, troubles, wrongs, and disinheritance' and an acknowledge threat to the civil peace.[24] In response, Henry VIII introduced his Maintenance and Embracery Act 1540 to bolster the law.[25]

This brief historical sketch gives one a sense of the public policy concerns that gave rise to the prohibition of maintenance, but in legal terms applicable to debts, just what is it? The essential idea, if we restrict ourselves to choses in action, is this: that the assignee of the chose in action has no material interest in the chose itself, but purely in the action, for she seeks to pursue that action for some unjust, ulterior motive often linked to placing economic and legal pressure on the defendant. One objection may have occurred to you, being that if someone takes a chose in action, surely they have acquired property and so do have some proprietary interest in the chose as well as an interest in the action. It seems difficult to imagine divorcing chose from action. This is, however, quite possible, and we call this situation a **bare right of action**.

ESSENTIAL DEFINITION: BARE RIGHT OF ACTION

A right to make a claim which is assigned to a person who has no legitimate interest in the outcome of the claim. Any attempt to assign such a right is contrary to public policy and void.[26]

Examples:

- *Defamation*: a newspaper defames Hayley. Hayley assigns her claim to Gilbert. Gilbert has suffered no reputational damage, so he has no legitimate interest in the outcome of the claim.
- *Insolvency law*: PSR Co Ltd fails to pay its debts as they fall due, and Powys presents a winding up petition to court. Vickers agrees to pay Powys' debt and all costs to date in exchange for an assignment of the right to continue the petition. Vickers happens to be a shareholder of the company, and on acquir-

22 Code of Justinian, IV 35, 22. The Emperor Anastasius to Eustachius, Praetorian Prefect: 'By two different reports which have been made to Us, We have ascertained that certain individuals, being desirous of obtaining the property and fortunes of others, have exerted themselves to have rights of action assigned to them by third parties, and in this way litigants are subjected to many annoyances; and as it is certain that, so far as undoubted obligations are concerned, men are more desirous of claiming their own rights than of transferring them to others, We order by this law that hereafter attempts of this kind shall be prohibited. There is no doubt that those should be considered the purchasers of the rights of action of others who desire assignments of this kind to be made to them, so that if anyone, after having paid money, should obtain such an assignment, he shall only be permitted to bring the actions which he has purchased to the extent of the amount of money which he has paid, even though the term "sale" has been inserted in the instrument evidencing the assignment.'

23 A 'wager of law' required a plaintiff to prove his case by bringing supporting witnesses to court. A powerful lord could easily summon enough conspiratorially minded peers and browbeaten serfs for his purpose, making a mockery of the whole process and driving the court to embrace documentary evidence, such as deeds under seal.

24 Statute of 32 Hen VIII C 9, Preamble.

25 ibid s 3 prohibits champerty, maintenance, and related practices such as buying witnesses. The greater part of the act restricted buying land and titles to maintain suit.

26 The reasons are discussed in the next section.

ing the right attempts to have the petition stood over (paused). Powys' assignment is void.[27]

Notice that the question is not whether conceptually any given right of action is a chose in action (for it is), but whether the assignment of the given chose in action is void as contrary to public policy.[28]

The common law's thinking appears to have been this. Debt is a chose in action, but the chose in question is strictly personal to a given creditor with respect to a given debtor. Only *this* creditor could be interested in the debt in a manner analogous to the way a libelled person can only be interested in their own reputation. On this view, no third party could be legally interested in a debt, and by extension they could not become interested in a debt i.e. they could not take assignment of another's debt. When *this* creditor purported to assign the debt to a third party, they separated *this* creditor's personal interest in the chose (which could not be transferred) from the action to enforce the rights in the chose. The result: our third party had taken assignment of a bare right of action. Being contrary to public policy, the court would refuse to enforce any such assignment. Indeed, in many cases the court might go further, regarding attempts to traffic in bare rights of litigation as highly abusive.

If we understand **maintenance** more generally as the prohibition on improperly supporting the pursuit of litigation in which one has no interest,[29] then in the context of choses in action it seems there is no material difference between a disinterested person improperly funding the litigation of the owner of a chose in action, and that same disinterested person extracting and taking assignment of that bare right of action constituting part of the chose in action and improperly pursuing the litigation himself. *A fortiori* where the maintenance is aggravated by an agreement whereby the assignee takes the chose in action now but need only pay for the assignment later from the proceeds of what they speculate will be successful litigation[30]—this aggravated maintenance being called **champerty**.[31] To strike down the latter to is to strike against the mischief at which the doctrine of maintenance aims. A corollary of this is that any contract or assignment purporting to transfer such a bare right of action is void, producing the rather neat effect that the purported assignee's claim must fail, for she has no claim to pursue.

These two justifications—the personal and thus apparently inalienable nature of debt obligations and the prohibition of maintenance—combined to void the assignment of debts well into the nineteenth century. As one might expect, merchants and bankers already at the end of the Middle

27 *in re Paris Skating Rink Co (No.1)* (1877) 5 ChD 959 (CA).

28 This two-stage analysis is made explicit in the personal injury case *Simpson v Norfolk & Norwich University Hospital NHS Trust* [2011] EWCA Civ 1149, [2012] QB 640.

29 *Martell and Others v Consett Iron Co Ltd.* [1955] Ch 363 (CA) where an unincorporated association had no strictly legal interest in protecting a river from pollution, but their collective concern (one might venture 'purpose') in supporting a claim to protect that river rendered the maintenance proper; *British Cash and Parcel Conveyors Ltd. v Lamson Store Service Co Ltd.* [1908] 1 KB 1006 (CA); and see *Plating Co v Farquharson* (1881) 17 ChD 49 (CA); *London and Regional (St George's Court) Ltd. v Ministry of Defence* [2008] EWHC 526 (TCC), (2009) 121 ConLR 26; cf *Trendtex Trading Corpn v Crédit Suisse* [1982] AC 679 (HL); *Giles v Thompson* [1993] 3 All ER 321 (CA) 333 (LJ Steyn); affirmed [1994] 1 AC 142 (HL).

30 *in re Trepica Mines Ltd. (No.2)* [1963] Ch 199 (CA); *Laurent v Sale & Co.* [1963] 1 WLR 829, which both concerned sales of claims in debt. See now *Trendtex Trading Corpn v Crédit Suisse* [1982] AC 679 (HL) discussed below.

31 Via law French (*champs parti*) from Latin *campi partitio* = division of the field (e.g. spoils of battle).

Ages began developing ways of sidestepping the harsh application of the common law.[32] One of the earliest and most widespread was for the creditor to appoint the person wishing to purchase the debt as the creditor's attorney with full authority to claim repayment on behalf of the creditor. It just so happened to be the case that the fee payable to the attorney was equal in amount to the value of the debt claimed.

GERARD v LEWIS (1866–67) LR 2 CP 305

Lewis and one other were owed debts by several people, including £250 by one Hullman. They 'assigned' these debts to Gerard, but aware this was not legally enforceable, they appointed Gerard their attorney to recover the debts on their behalf, though in fee Gerard would keep the recoveries. Gerard now sued Hullman for more than £250 and was able to obtain an order that Hullman be detained in a debtor's prison. Apparently shocked, Lewis obtained the release of Hullman, arguing that Gerard had exceeded his attorney's authority by suing Hullman for more than £250. Gerard sued, claiming Lewis had breached an implied promise not to block the debt claims.

Held: The amount claimed would be corrected to £250, but claiming the incorrect amount did not wholly discharge Hullman from liability, nor did it justify Lewis' actions. Willes J said:

> The defendant [Lewis] appears to have joined his partner in assigning certain debts to the plaintiff [Gerard], giving the plaintiff the ordinary power of attorney to sue in the name of the firm. The rule against assigning a chose in action stood in the way of an actual transfer of the debt, so as to enable the plaintiff to sue in his own name; and, therefore, it became necessary to give the power of attorney. But the intention of the parties in giving that power was to give the assignee the conduct and control of the litigation necessary for enforcing payment of the debts assigned. The defendant, therefore, who interfered to thwart or impede the remedy of the assignee under this deed, unquestionably broke the covenant implied from the words 'with full power and authority in the name or names of Bromham and Lewis, or either of them, their or either of their executors, &c, to ask, demand, sue for, recover, &c, the said debts, or any of them.' [309]

It should be stressed that this case discusses an obsolete method of transferring debt.

32 For pedagogic reasons I have sidestepped discussing bills of exchange and particularly promissory notes in this chapter. Their transferability (normally termed 'negotiability') has traditionally been considered an anomalous outgrowth of medieval transnational banking (e.g. J Milnes Holden, *The History of Negotiable Instruments in English Law* (Athlone Press 1955), and is only now sanctioned in virtue of statute: now the Bills of Exchange Act 1882, with promissory notes having received statutory support already in the Act of 1704 (3&4 Anne c 8). Indeed, JS Rogers makes a powerful case that the pre-1704 law saw no such anomaly, for it regarded all exchange transactions as reducible to agency/attorney relationships—bills and notes were originally only ever handed to presented by agents, with cases continuing to be brought in the name of the original debtor and creditor. JS Rogers, *The Early History of the Law of Bills and Notes: A Study of the Origins of Anglo-American Commercial Law* (CUP 1995) ch 3.

One further method of avoiding the strictures of the common law, and perhaps decisive in ultimately procuring the legal acceptance of the market for debt, was to avail oneself of the courts of equity. It is true the fear of maintenance excised equity as much as it did the common law, but the difference was that equity was unconcerned with formal requirements as to the personal nature of an obligation. Beginning, as one might expect, with an acceptance that beneficiaries under trust and legatees had an equitable interest in any choses in action held on trust for, or willed to them, respectively, equity managed to distinguish the debt a person owed from the trust fund or estate which comprised the debt as an asset. As a result, the equitable interest of assignees was not an interest in the particular debt but an interest in the fund, which fund could comprise various kinds of property from time to time. To transfer a debt, then, the assignor retained legal title to the debt and effected an equitable assignment of the interest in the debt fund to an assignor, who in commercial practice would purchase this 'equity' in consideration of a price. To enforce the debt, the equitable assignee had recourse to the Chancery Court and its great range of enforcement remedies. The following case provides an account of this context and logic. It is perhaps worth noting that the Lord Chancellor here, Lord Hardwicke, owed his position to the then Prime Minister, Robert Walpole. The Horace Walpole in the case is Robert's son, for whom Robert had secured first a position at the head of the Customs & Excise, then as Usher of the Exchequer (the British tax authority).

ROW v DAWSON (1749) 27 ER 1064 (Ch)[33]

Tonson and Cowdery had lent money to Gibson. Gibson was himself owed money by Horace Walpole in his official capacity as head of the Exchequer (i.e. the tax authority of state). In lieu of payment, Gibson made out a draft[34] in favour of Tonson and Cowdery as follows: 'Out of the money due to me from Horace Walpole out of the Exchequer, and what will be due at Michaelmas pay to Tonson £400, and to Cowdery £200 value received.' The draft was then sent to Swinson, Walpole's deputy at the Exchequer.

Gibson became bankrupt. Tonson and Cowdery argued that the debt in Gibson's estate belonged in equity to them, whereas the trustees in bankruptcy alleged the assignment of the debt was void 'in law and equity.'

Held per the Lord Chancellor:

> This demand, and the instrument under which the defendants claim, is not a bill of exchange, but a draft; not to pay generally, but out of his particular fund, which creates no personal demand: therefore not a draft on personal credit to go in the common course of negotiation, which is necessary to bills of exchange, by draft on the general credit of the person drawing, the drawee, and the endorser, without reference to any particular fund.
>
> It is an agreement for valuable consideration before hand to lend money on the faith of being satisfied out of this fund; which makes it a very strong case. If this is not a bill of exchange, nor a proceeding on the personal credit of Swinburn

33 If you are puzzled by the case name, Cowdery had died and so it was his executors who brought suit. The defendants were what we would now call Gibson's trustees in bankruptcy.

34 In this context, a draft is an instruction by the beneficiary of a fund to the holder of that fund to pay out a specified sum to a named person; see also 'cheque' and now *Coghlan v Bailey* [2017] EWHC 570 (QB).

> or Gibson, it is a credit on this fund, and must amount to an assignment of so much of the debt: and though the law does not admit an assignment of a chose in action, this court does.

The Lord Chancellor went on to note that the equitable interest thus created bound Swinson because the draft had been communicated to him i.e. he had actual notice of the order to pay out monies at Michaelmas. Had he instead paid out to Gibson (assuming he was not bankrupt) he would have been liable in equity to Tonson and Cowdery.[35]

With the Judicature Act 1873, which merged the streams of law and equity, it became possible for these equitable interests to be enforced in any court, not just in Chancery. Section 25(6) of the Act even enacted a first legislative attempt to provide for an effective form of legal assignment, which would be repealed and replaced in 1925.[36] Being outflanked on the one side by equity and the other by appointing legal attorneys for debt, the old law looked increasingly outmoded and, with its confusions as to what was caught by terms like 'chose in action' and 'maintenance,' overcomplicated. Such was the state of the law of debt when Holdsworth wrote in 1910:

> Some of these difficulties might be perhaps mitigated by a codifying Act, for which there is plenty of material. But it is probable that a branch of the law which comes at the meeting place of the law of property and the law of obligation can never be anything but difficult to formulate and apply.[37]

Holdsworth would only wait 15 years for something approximating a codifying act.

6.3.2 Debts under the new law: debt as legally transferable

The restructuring of English property law of the 1920s permitted Parliament to clarify some of the more controversial aspects of choses in action, and legislatively to recognize the financial reality that people bought and sold debt. Legal transfer of a chose in action, and consequently debt, is now achieved by a **legal assignment** under s 136 Law of Property Act 1925 (LPA 1925).

ESSENTIAL: s 136 Law of Property Act 1925

136 Legal assignments of things in action

(1) Any absolute assignment by writing under the hand of the assignor (not purporting to be by way of charge[38] only) of any debt or other legal thing in action, of which express

35 Returning to the 'anomalous' case of bills of exchange, JS Rogers (*Early History of the Law of Bills*, 170ff) argues that even when indorsement—signing over a bill or note drawn by a debtor to the benefit of third party by marking the document itself—became common, the bills or notes were only tokens of an interest in an underlying fund of the debtor. This made sense where the various creditors had goods sales and purchase accounts with the same debtor, and it was a matter of the debtor recording credits and debits when the bill or note was presented.

36 For a discussion, see JC Hall, 'Gift of Part of a Debt' (1959) 17 CLJ 99.

37 Pitkin (n 16) 1030.

38 Therefore, this does not exclude legal mortgages by way of assignment, which are not charges.

> notice in writing has been given to the debtor, trustee or other person from whom the assignor would have been entitled to claim such debt or thing in action, is effectual in law (subject to equities having priority over the right of the assignee) to pass and transfer from the date of such notice—
>
> (a) the legal right to such debt or thing in action;
> (b) all legal and other remedies for the same; and
> (c) the power to give a good discharge for the same without the concurrence of the assignor:
>
> Provided that, if the debtor, trustee or other person liable in respect of such debt or thing in action has notice—
>
> (a) that the assignment is disputed by the assignor or any person claiming under him; or
> (b) of any other opposing or conflicting claims to such debt or thing in action;
>
> he may, if he thinks fit, either call upon the persons making claim thereto to interplead concerning the same, or pay the debt or other thing in action into court under the provisions of the Trustee Act 1925.

The formalities of written document and notice are there, because how else would the world (and specifically an obligor) know that the intangible had changed owners?

Technically, the new statutory regime does not change the common law but rather overrides it. Much as the Companies Acts forced the common law to recognize the company's separate corporate personality,[39] and indeed to defend the settled will of Parliament even in the face of manifest injustice,[40] so too s 136 LPA 1925 provided an explicit, statutory validation of transfer on which traffickers in debt could rely before the courts. The s 136 assignment, being an absolute legal assignment, granted a much firmer basis also for debt transfers. The net result was that while equitable transfers of debt interests remained of a feature of the financial landscape,[41] legal assignment of a debt under s 136 LPA 1925 is now the principal and safest mechanism of selling and buying debt.

While statute had finally put paid to any residual formalist objections the common law had to the legal assignment of personal obligations, it made no adjustment to the other factor which caused the common law (and equity) to be uncomfortable with debt sales: maintenance and champerty. Yet here too, the courts began to chip away at the rigours of the old law, first in England and then in New York, which latter had inherited and indeed codified the law against maintenance.[42]

TRENDTEX TRADING CORP v CREDIT SUISSE [1982] AC 679 (HL)

Trendtex contracted with Central Bank of Nigeria (CBN) that CBN would provide a letter of credit facility to be drawn down when a supply of cement was supplied to Lagos. CBN did

39 *Salomon v A Salomon & Co. Ltd.* [1893] UKHL 1, [1897] AC 22.

40 *Adams v Cape Industries plc* [1990] Ch 433 (CA).

41 See Chapter 8.

42 A right to receive specified statutory compensation for damage to land was considered a payment due, and assignable to a new owner of land already in *Dawson v Great Northern & City Rail Co* [1904–07] All ER Rep 913, but the new owner could not claim for more damages where he subsequently increased the value of land.

not honour the letter of credit, and Trendtex lost USD14m. Trendtex sued but lacked the funds to pursue the complicated international litigation. Credit Suisse (CS) had lent money to Trendtex and honestly feared Trendtex would collapse if it could not recoup its losses. Therefore, Trendtex agreed to assign its right of action against CBN to CS in exchange for USD800k. As part of this agreement, cl.1 acknowledged that Credit Suisse could assign the right of action to a third party. This CS did, selling the right for USD1.1m, payable if the claim proved successful. The third party subsequently settled the action with CBN for USD8m. Trendtex, seeing the third party recover 10 times as much as Trendtex had received, now sought a declaration that the agreement was champertous and void.

Held: Each assignment envisaged under the agreement was considered in turn:

(A) *Trendtex to CS*: CS had a clear interest in the claim against CBN because of its economic interest in the survival of Trendtex. The economic effect of taking assignment of the claim was to support Trendtex's liquidity needs and recoup potential losses on its loan to Trendtex directly. This assignment was not contrary to public policy.

(B) *CS to the third party*: 704 (Lord Roskill):

> [T]he purpose [of the agreement] was to enable the claim against CBN. to be sold on to the anonymous third party for that anonymous third party to obtain what profit he could from it, apart from paying to Credit Suisse the purchase price of US$1,100,000. In other words, the 'spoils,' whatever they might be, to be got from CBN. were in effect being divided, the first US$1,100,000 going to Credit Suisse and the balance, whatever it might ultimately prove to be, to the anonymous third party. Such an agreement, in my opinion, offends for it was a step towards the sale of a bare cause of action to a third party who had no genuine commercial interest in the claim in return for a division of the spoils, Credit Suisse taking the fixed amount which I have already mentioned.

Trendtex needs to be read carefully in light of the history of maintenance. Remember that inroads were made into the hard application of the maintenance prohibition by referring to the legitimate interests of a transferee of a chose in action in pursuing the action. *Trendtex* is no more than an extension of that line of cases, for the House of Lords did not opine that all assignments of debt for value were valid, but only those assignments to a party with a legitimate interest—here CS's linked investment in Trendtex's business. It therefore remained open for a debtor to argue that an assignment of a chose in action to a third party who lacked this additional 'legitimate interest' was, even if not champertous, void in common law and equity for amounting to maintenance. This more general argument was made by Bank of Zambia in another sovereign debt case.

CAMDEX INTERNATIONAL LTD v BANK OF ZAMBIA (No.1) [1996] 3 All ER 431 (CA)

A Kuwaiti bank, CBK, made a large time deposit into an account at Bank of Zambia (BZ) in consideration of interest payable. BZ defaulted on making interest payments, and after several variations of the debt, CBK made a s136 LPA 1925 assignment of the debt, interest and any claims to Camdex. Camdex sued, and in the Court of Appeal BZ argued that the assignment was void for maintenance and champerty.

Held per Hobhouse LJ:

> Thus, none of [the maintenance] authorities alters the effect of the statute . . . . An assignment of a debt is not invalid even if the necessity for litigation to recover it is contemplated. Provided that there is a bona fide debt, it does not become unassignable merely because the debtor chooses to dispute it. Suing on an assigned debt is not contrary to public policy even if the assignor retains an interest. What is contrary to public policy and ineffective is an agreement which has maintenance or champerty as its object; such a consequence will not be avoided by dressing up a transaction which has that character and intent as an assignment of a debt. But, because the assignment of a debt itself includes no element of maintenance and is sanctioned by statute, any objectionable element alleged to invalidate the assignment has to be proved independently and distinctly, in the same way as any other alleged illegality has to be proved in relation to a contract which is on its face valid. [445]

Hobhouse LJ had spent a considerable amount of time reviewing the cases before coming to this conclusion, but he is surely right that those post-1925 cases all proceeded on the assumption, largely implicit, that s 136 LPA 1925 validated assignments which might otherwise have been void for maintenance. Before 1925, at common law it simply was not possible legally to assign a chose in action, that is the *thing*, and various attempts to circumvent this rule could be recharacterized as assignments of the bare right of action (although we have seen that uses of equity and agency came very close to doing just this). Section 136 LPA 1925 now made it legal to assign the chose and its action, and it was no longer the business of the courts, in the name of 'public policy,' to overturn Parliament's determination that the assignments provided for by s.136 were in the public interest. What remained to the courts was to police those purported assignments which were not authorized by s 136, namely those assignments which in substance aimed at transferring a bare right of action (rather than the whole chose in action). These would be rare occurrences, determined on the facts in each case, and often marked out by a champertous component of profiteering from litigation as in *Trendtex*.

Two years later, in New York, Peru advanced a maintenance and champerty defence to a sovereign debt claim. Peru hoped that it would have better luck than Bank of Zambia in England, not least because New York had strengthened its laws against champerty by positive State Senate enactments.

ELLIOTT ASSOCIATES v BANCO DE LA NACION AND REPUBLIC OF PERU, 194 FRD 116 (SD NY 2000)

Elliott, described as a speculative 'vulture' fund, had acquired ca. US$20m of Peruvian sovereign debt at a discounted price of ca. US$11m. Peru failed to respond to Elliott's demands for payment, and Elliott brought suit in the Southern District of New York (the usual jurisdiction of financial claims). In particular, Elliott sought to enforce against certain Treasury Bonds held by Peru in a New York deposit. In its defence, Peru argued that the assignments under which Elliott had acquired the sovereign debt violated s.489 of the Champerty Law and were void.

Held: The court echoed the reasoning in *Camdex*: 'Section 489 . . . is not violated when, as here, the accused party's "primary goal" is found to be satisfaction of a valid debt and its intent is only to sue absent full performance.'

With these two cases in the leading financial jurisdictions, maintenance and champerty—the final policy risks to legal assignments of choses in action—were positively restricted to a very limited set of circumstances. Moreover, the courts explicitly recognized the validity of the financial market for buying and selling debt. Good news indeed for the burgeoning sector of debt syndication.

6.4 Selling debt

6.4.1 Why?

In Chapter 2, we examined a simple CFA in which a bank set up a facility for a corporate borrower. The bank committed to lend a certain amount of funds when requested. The corporate borrower could submit a utilization request and, provided certain conditions precedent were met, the bank would lend—a so-called drawdown. From this moment on, under the CFA, our borrower is under an obligation to repay the debt and pay interest according to the timetable scheduled in the agreement. It is this debt obligation which can now be sold by the bank to other banks, in a process called **syndication**.

Why would the bank sell the debt obligation? The reasons are many, but it is worth covering a few of the more common motives. A significant driver is diversification of portfolio risk. A bank which lends EUR500m to one borrower is at risk of losing the lot should the borrower collapse. Selling some of the debt would mitigate that risk by (1) sharing the losses with whomever buys a portion of the debt; and (2) providing cash now which can be reinvested as debt capital in a different business which may survive. Sometimes the debt lent is simply too big for one bank even to originate (i.e. contract for). Diversification of risk can then be achieved either by joining other banks as lenders to the original CFA or, and this is just as common, agreeing the CFA and then novating portions of the commitments to lend *before* drawdown occurs. This is particularly popular where a loan is **investment grade**, that is, the debt is owed by a borrower with a good credit rating. Note that the loan will not itself be rated by a Credit Rating Agency (though the lenders will have undertaken their own analysis). Rather, the loan will not be the only debt capital invested in the company. An investment grade borrower is highly likely also to have sought finance on the securities markets, and it is these securities which will have been rated by a credit rating agency. An investment grade loan 'piggybacks' on that analysis when it comes to selling portions of the debt to other banks.

As noted, selling portions of debt obligations converts the debt into cash which can be invested as debt elsewhere. This is the basis for the originate-to-distribute model in syndication.[43] On this model, the lead bank—called the **arranger**—negotiates the CFA with the borrower for a not inconsiderable fee. The arranger then syndicates the loan, freeing up liquidity that was otherwise locked in to the CFA obligations. It is quite possible, though less common, that the arranger entirely exit the CFA, but it will certainly reduce its exposure. With the liquidity released, the banks' capital reserves

43 It is more (in)famous as a securitization practice, but syndication is the older transaction.

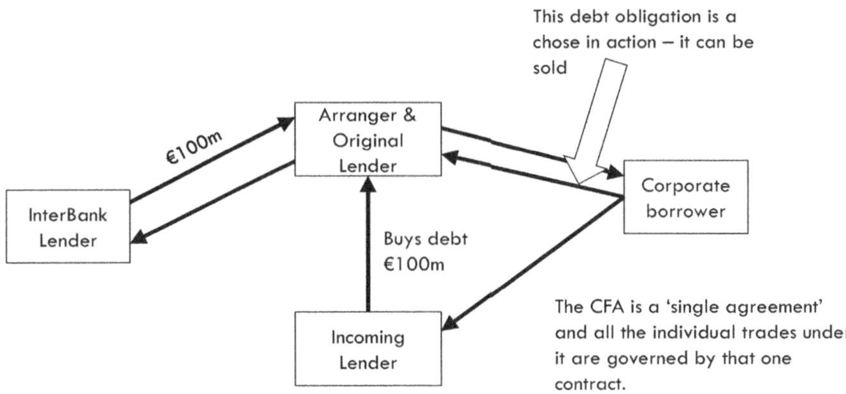

Figure 6.1 Arranging a syndication

are free to support a new CFA which the bank arranges once more for a fee before syndicating. The shorter the time between origination and distribution, the shorter the cycle to receiving new fees for new CFAs, in a very procyclical process (as the credit market booms, more deals are done, releasing capital more quickly in such of further deals, driving down the cost of credit and inflating the bubble further). As bankers' bonuses are closely tied to these fees, the agents themselves are highly motivated to continue and accelerate this originate to distribute cycle.

One further catalyst is regulation, or the lack of it. As you may now, when a corporate, aided by an investment bank, publicly issues securities (shares, bonds, etc), that issuance is heavily regulated and rightly so. By comparison, the syndication of CFA debt is virtually unregulated beyond the general oversight of banking capital requirements. Legislation such as the Financial Services and Markets Act 2000 simply is not relevant here. The syndication market for debt is regarded as a closed shop between banks and private equity outfits, to be handled by the private law in bilateral arrangements between the most sophisticated investors. If nothing else, this makes syndication quick. To sell debt you need only call up a syndication desk at another bank and have your lawyer fill in a two-page form attached to the CFA in question. For a discussion of whether this lack of oversight is desirable, especially as private equity has flooded into the syndication market after 2008, see my 2016 article on the topic.[44]

6.4.2 How?

At the legal heart of syndication is the transfer for consideration of a borrower's debt obligation. We have studied the first and second 'parts' of the CFA which deal with InterBank and borrower-facing issues, respectively. We now turn to the third part, which deals with syndication. Section 9 of the CFA usually begins provides how debt transfer is to occur. It will commonly state an Existing Lender may:

(1) assign any of its rights; or
(2) transfer by novation any of its rights or obligations to another financial institution,[45] trust, fund, or similar entity.

Let us examine the mechanics of these methods.

44 Stephen Connelly, 'When Seeing Becomes Overlooking' (2016) 16 Journal of Corporate Law Studies 1.

45 For a discussion of the meaning of 'financial institution' in this context, see *Argo Fund Ltd. v Essar Steel Ltd.* [2005] EWHC (Comm) 600.

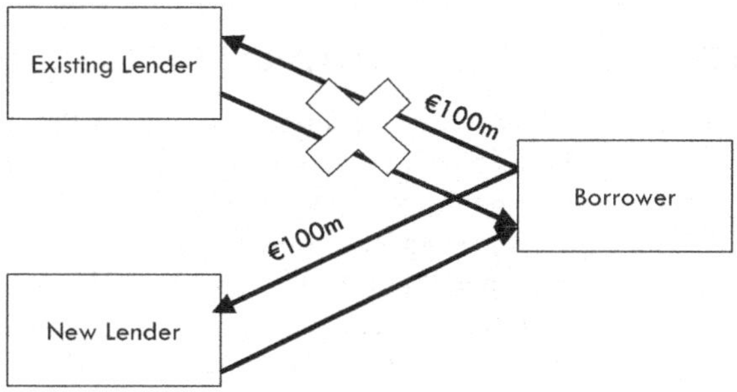

Figure 6.2 Transfer by novation cancels the old contract and replaces it with a new contract on equivalent terms

6.4.2.1 Novation

Novation is the most common method deployed in the London market. As the name suggests, the effect is to cancel the old debt contract, discharging the respective rights and obligations of the existing lender and the obligors (e.g. the borrower), and create a new contract between the existing obligors the new lender on exactly the same terms, both as to rights (e.g. to be repaid) and obligations (e.g. to fund).[46] Where there are several lenders, and some wish to remain involved, when simply includes these remaining lenders as parties to the new contract also.[47]

Novation of syndicated CFAs raises an interesting question. Let there be a CFA where two banks P and Q are each are lending GBP50m to borrower (GBP100m in total). P now proposes to transfer its debt to R by novation, and enters into a binding contract with R. This will create a new contract to which R, Q, and borrower are all party, but at which point in this contracting process was an offer made to Q and borrower, and when did they accept it? What consideration is being given? In short, is the new arrangement even a contract?

The CFA solves this problem by drafting in the explicit **advanced consent** of all parties to novation of the contract by any lender. Yet what is happening legally here? Our problem is that if we characterize the selling and buying lenders as making an offer of the new contract to which the buying lender will be a party, then that offer must be accepted. Is it possible for a party to accept an offer from *any* person who might turn up as a new lender offering a contract in predetermined form? A little thought back to your contract law days and you will recall that we have the ingredients of a unilateral contract—a contract where one party objectively makes an open offer on definite terms to a class of persons meeting certain conditions.[48] Should any person, such as a Mrs Carlill, meet the conditions, then the offeror Carbolic Smokeball Company is bound. On this view, the remaining parties are not accepting an offer from the new lender; they have made an open offer to any new lender which the new lender accepts by completing the requisite novation form and procedure in the CFA.

That is one possible legal analysis, but have the courts agreed?

---

46 See *GSO Credit-A Partners LP v Barclays Bank plc* [2016] EWHC 146 (Comm), where the new lender denied it was obligated to fund a guarantee facility when it took transfer of some of the debt.

47 Though there is some debate as to whether the novation is *partial* as between borrower and new lender, with the remaining parties simply carrying on with the old contract. cf *Graiseley Properties Ltd. v Barclays Bank plc* [2013] EWCA Civ 67 (Comm) [33], [37]; *Deutsche Bank AG v Unitech Global Ltd.* [2013] EWHC 471 (Comm) [50].

48 *Carlill v Carbolic Smokeball* [1892] EWCA Civ 1.

ARGO FUND LTD v ESSAR STEEL LTD [2005] EWHC 600 (Comm)

Essar had borrowed some USD40m some years earlier under a CFA which was subsequently syndicated. One of the incoming lenders was Argo, an investment fund, which acquired USD29m of the debt owed by Essar by way of what cl 27 of the CFA termed a 'novation.' Essar defaulted and Argo sued for payment.

In its defence, Essar complained that it had only ever envisaged contracting with a bank, and had never agreed to Argo, as a fund, becoming a party to the loan agreement. During counsels' argument, the court realized that there were treading new legal ground as no case had analysed such a situation before. It was necessary therefore to return to fundamentals.

Held: Novation was a valid means of transferring the debt. Aikens J said:

> if Essar takes no positive part in the mechanics of the transfer, how does the novation come about, as a matter of legal analysis of 'offer,' 'acceptance' and 'consideration'? In particular, how does Essar agree to the termination of the contract with the original participant and agree to the new contract with the transferee? Once again, counsel agreed that both contracts were unilateral contracts. (cf: *Carlill v Carbolic Smoke Ball Co* [1892] 2 QB 484, 56 JP 665; *New Zealand Shipping Co Ltd v AM Satterthwaite & Co Ltd: The Eurymedon* [1975] AC 154; [1974] 1 All ER 1015) In each case there is a 'standing offer' by Essar, which is contained in Clause 27 of the Agreement. The offer to terminate the old contract is made to each original participant. The offer to conclude a new contract is made to all those who are eligible, i.e. are within the definition of 'bank or other financial institution.' In the case of the old contract, the offer of Essar is accepted by the original participant by the delivery of the Transfer Certificate. In that case there is mutual consideration, because each side agrees to give up all its rights and obligations as against the other. [51]
>
> In the case of the new contract, Essar's standing offer to all those eligible has to be accepted by a Transferee. The act of acceptance by the Transferee is not spelt out in Clause 27. It must be the fact that the Transferee agrees to the transfer with the Transferor on the terms of the Agreement. [52]

The court further held that Argo, as a fund, fell within the class of banks or financial institutions referred to by cl 27 of the CFA.

Aikens J's reasoning on this point was affirmed on appeal,[49] and again by the Court of Appeal in a different case five years later.

49 *Argo Fund Ltd. v Essar Steel Ltd.* [2006] EWCA Civ 241, [2006] 1 CLC 546.

HABIBSONS BANK v STANDARD CHARTERED BANK (HONG KONG) LTD [2010] EWCA Civ 1335

StanChart was one of the lenders in a USD118m syndicated CFA. It agreed with H Bank to transfer to H Bank by way of novation USD2m of that debt. As the transfer was being processed, the borrower announced it was insolvent, spurring H Bank to back out of the transfer. StanChart regarded the transfer as agreed, however, and debited USD2m from H Bank's account with StanChart as payment. H Bank sued for its recovery, arguing inter alia that the novation was partial and ineffective for want of consent from the borrower.

Here the transfer clause was broadly in the LMA form for novations.

Held: The CA, led by Longmore LJ, agreed with Aikens J's unilateral contract analysis. It followed from that analysis that the other syndicate banks, too, had given **advanced consent** to the novation provided it was on the terms of the CFA and carried out in the form expressly provided therein.

All seems well with debt transfer by novation. Kwan Ho Lau has noted that advanced consent does generate some difficult legal puzzles.[50] Consider, to build on his example, a CFA in which two banks P and Q commit to lend GBP50m each to borrower B. Borrower B plans to use the full amount to acquire all the shares of a target listed company when the price dips below a certain level, as B hopes. Just before acquisition, however, Q realizes it will be unable to fund its commitment and so, facing technical insolvency, it novates the CFA to R, an entity rich in speculative intent but poor in actual cash. R fails to fund and B makes a loss in failing to acquire the target. Of course, B can sue R for breach of contract, but R is worthless. What B wants to do is sue Q for bringing about these circumstances. What claim does B have, if any? Kwan Ho Lau writes:

> In recent memory there has been one occasion in the English courts where protection was expressly mooted for the hapless obligee. That arrived in the form of an obiter dictum in *Argo Fund* [in the Court of Appeal], where Rix LJ remarked that an obligor who deliberately 'shuffle[d] off' its contractual obligations to a third party that was not capable of fulfilling them might breach an implied term to the effect of a warranty that the third party was capable of performing them.[51]

The concern is real, but it is difficult in a finance context to see these obiter dicta being taken further. The main thrust of *Argo Fund* and *Habibsons Bank* is that the person granting advanced consent should seek all the protection they require in the drafting of transfer provisions of the original contract. If, like Essar, they wish to limit transferees to a certain kind of bank, they should say so explicitly, for they have the advisers to guide them as to the risks.

In practice, the question of unexpected novatees took a different turn in the late 2000s, briefly in the borrower's favour. Borrowers began to realize they could deploy friendly third parties to acquire token portions of their own debt. Now they had a presence 'in the room' of the syndicate banks which proved invaluable in the context of restructuring and insolvency negotiations. Banks

50 Kwan Ho Lau, 'Novation and Advance Consent' (2022) 81 CLJ 581.

51 ibid 601. The reference is to *Argo Fund v Essar Steel* (n 45) [70].

wondered how borrowers knew so much about what had been negotiated in secret on the lender side. Eventually the lenders became wise to this trick and began amending the transfer clause to expressly exclude transfers to borrower-linked entities.

A further problem created by novation is its effect on security. The advantage of novation is that all aspects of the CFA are transferred, including the Commitments of the Obligors to lend, and the obligations of the administrative parties. The major disadvantage is that novation cancels existing debts and, because of the equity of redemption (see Chapter 3), this leads to an equitable release of any security.

Given such a substantial risk you may wonder why novation is considered at all. The reasons are that:

- Syndicated loan agreements in England and Wales will provide for a security trustee to hold the security on trust for a class of Lenders easily identifiable through the CFA (the original lenders and any new lender). The CFA will state that an equivalent debt is owed to the Security Trustee for the lenders' benefit. Changes in the beneficiaries will not alter the class of beneficiaries and the trust will endure (subject to the usual 80-year perpetuity period).
- English law (among others) permits security to be granted for future debts, and so even if the debt owed to the new lender is regarded as new, it is still a Secured Liability within the meaning of the security agreement.

These reasons are very jurisdiction specific, being closely linked to the trust mechanism. They are discussed in detail in Chapter 4.

6.4.2.2 Legal assignment

Legal assignment is the preferred method of transfer for any CFA with linkages to jurisdictions in which the method of novation, the hardening periods of security, or the viability of trusts could be questioned. Continental European CFAs, even if English law governed, should adopt this method. I tend to call this method assignment, assumption, release as this helps us to remember the transfer involves three distinct legal acts to achieve transfer, as follows:

(1) **Assignment** of the benefit of the obligations owed by the borrower from the existing lender to the new lender. This preserves the debt, and indeed all obligations owed to the existing lender under the current CFA.

(2) **Assumption** by the new lender of obligations equivalent to those owed by the existing lender (e.g. to fund on drawdown).

(3) **Release** of the existing lender from those obligations. This is not a gratuitous act by the obligors, for not only do the CFA's terms make a good case for the whole CFA being

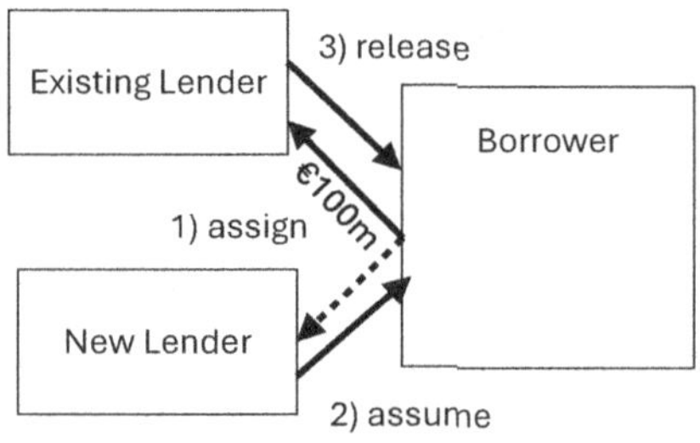

Figure 6.3 Assignment, assumption, release—note how the existing debt of GBP100m remains in existence and is assigned under s136 LPA 1925 to the new lender

contracted on the basis of the borrower agreeing to such a release on transfer, but the new Lender does assume real, continuing obligations, not just to fund, but to abide by syndicate democracy in such matters as enforcement.

As per s 136 LPA 1925, the assignment mentioned requires notice to the Obligors, while the release is conditional on consent of the Obligors. While the latter is pre-agreed, it must still be agreed, and powerful Obligors may limit the classes of potential transferees to so-called whitelists.

As we trailed above, the principal driver for this method of transfer is the maintenance security. Appreciate that the Security Agent is an agent and so holds as agent of the principals (the Lenders). Legal assignment should operate in tandem with the parallel debt clause discussed in Chapter 4. The parallel debt clause constitutes an equivalent debt in favour of a security agent of the lenders, secured by assets identified for this purpose. While assignment seeks to preserve the existing debt, the parallel debt clause adds further protection by creating a debt equal to the sums owing at any time to the varying class of lenders under the CFA.

6.4.2.3 'Silent' (equitable) assignment

A legal assignment concerns a transfer effected at law, but in Anglo-Saxon jurisdictions it may also be able to achieve a practically unsatisfactory transfer in equity. This style is used in certain US states, and there is called silent assignment or US-style assignment. As one might expect, a silent assignment is constituted by a transfer of the existing lender's rights to the new lender without the all-important formal notification to the obligors. Indeed, the obligors may in fact know nothing of the assignment. The question for the English lawyer, sceptical of this practice, is what happens when the obligors enforce their rights against the existing lender? The existing lender remains such at law. Is the existing lender still bound? If so, should new lender make existing lender good, or step into its shoes? What about other equitable rights, such as set-off? There appears to be no case on the matter, but a trusts-based analysis seems to be the most promising. The existing lender remains legally entitled to the benefit of the contract and legally burdened by its obligations, all on behalf of its equitable assignee, to which it must pass that benefit and from which, in equity, it may claim to be made whole again where it has paid out to the borrower. This remains an open question.

6.4.2.4 Synthetic transfers

These two modes of debt transfer identified in the LMA form—novation and assignment, assumption, and release—are standard, but there are at least three other ways (not provided for in the London Form of CFA) where the economic equivalent of debt transfer can occur.

Sub-participation: this a contractual agreement between the existing lender and a third party (the sub-participant) under which the sub-participant makes a payment to the existing lender to acquire the right to receive sums equivalent to those received by the existing lender under the CFA. It can come in two forms:

(1) *Funded*: the sub-participant pays the Existing Lender a capital amount equal to the amount the Existing Lender has lent (or is committed to lend) under the CFA. In consideration Existing Lender pays the sub-participant amounts equal to the income received (the interest) and, on repayment, amounts equal to the capital repaid.

(2) *Guaranteed (or risk)*: the sub-participant agrees to make payments to the Existing Lender on default by an Obligor. For example, if Obligor fails to pay EUR10m, sub-participant pays EUR10m to Existing Lender. This amounts to a kind of credit insurance; the Existing Lender pays a 'premium' to the sub-participant the value of which is linked to the Obligors' payment schedule under the CFA.

It is not uncommon for sub-participation agreements to grant the sub-participant rights to direct the Existing Lender e.g. to vote for or against waivers and amendments of the CFA.

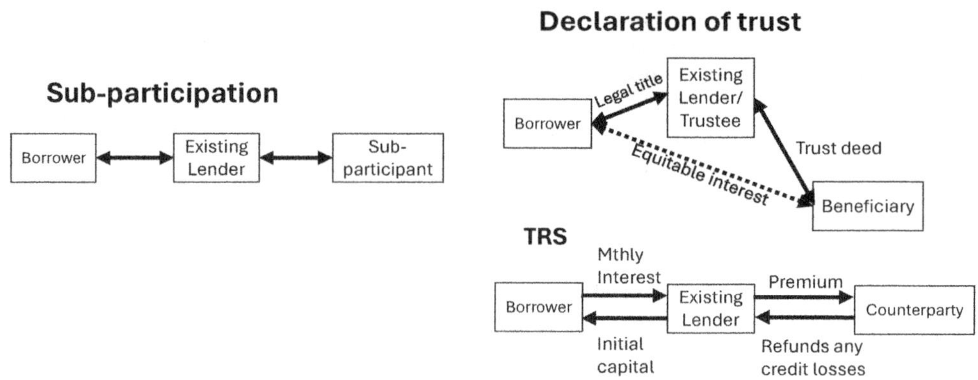

Figure 6.4 Three synthetic modes of transfer

Sub-participation is a doubled risk for the sub-participant. If the Obligors default it loses out, but even if the Obligors perform, payments made to the Existing Lender may be lost if the Existing Lender defaults, e.g. if it becomes insolvent.

Declaration of trust: here the Existing Lender declares a trust of the benefit of the Obligor obligations in favour of a third party (see *Don King Productions v Warren*).[52] The third party in effect buys this benefit, the economic effect being that the Existing Lender receives capital equal to that lent to the Obligors. In consideration the Existing Lender agrees to pass on any payments received from the Obligors 'as if' the third party were a New Lender. The Existing Lender need not 'sell' all its rights in this way.

Total return swap (TRS): the Existing Lender remains at all times Lender, but seeks to protect against the risk of Obligor default. Existing Lender pays a fixed rate over the term of the TRS to a counterparty in return for the right to put the risk of the loans on the counterparty on settlement. The TRS is thus a form of credit default swap. The swap may be physically settled or cash settled:

(1) In *physical settlement* the counterparty will pay to the Existing Lender the full amount of the loan made, and in return the Existing Lender will transfer the loan to the counterparty as New Lender.
(2) In *cash settlement* the counterparty will pay Existing Lender the difference between the amount of the loans actually made to the Borrowers and the market value of the loans. In other words, of the loans are distressed, the counterparty is compensating the Existing Lender for the loss it would make in selling the debt into the distressed debt market. The counterparty does not take the debt; it just pays the difference in value.

Key concerns for all these 'synthetic' modes of transfer include tax and regulatory treatment. Regarding the latter, capital adequacy rules will interrogate whether risk has properly transferred to a third party before lender can remove the risk from its balance sheet.

52 [2000] Ch 291 (CA). Cf. *Linden Gardens v Lenesta Sludge* [1994] 1 AC 85 (HL) for an attempt contractually to benefit a non-party.

6.4.3 Towards structured finance

The foregoing discussion of syndication assumed that the debt was homogenous and that each lender holding debt ranks pari passu with the other lenders e.g. if there are ten lenders each holding USD5m of a USD50m debt owed by borrower, and on enforcement only USD25m is recovered by the security agent, then each lender will receive, for each USD1 invested, 50 cents of capital returned. In other words, each Lender takes equal risk of Borrower default. Yet it does not have to be this way: the lenders could agree that some lenders will not be repaid until such time as the other lenders are repaid in full. It is certainly possible to draft a contract which would have this effect of diverting all repayments to some of the lenders first. We call this splitting up and ranking of debts so that some are paid in priority to others **structured finance**, to which we now turn.

6.5 Structured finance

We have seen that once Parliament had decided it was possible to buy and sell personal obligations as legal assignments of choses in action, there remained only one concern: maintenance. While it was now possible to contract to buy and sell (debt) obligations in law, these contracts and the legal assignments they provided for could still be void or at least unenforceable for public policy reasons. The current state of play in England is that unless there is a bad faith ulterior/illegitimate motive for acquiring a bad debt, then such a contract and its assignment will be valid and enforceable.

We now turn to another area in which contracts and public policy are likely to conflict: structured finance and its relationship with insolvency law. We are not going to delve into the finer details of insolvency law; we are just going to grasp enough to be able to consider the key contractual challenge: Parliament has seen fit to determine public policy on the fair distribution of assets in the case of an insolvency, so *to what extent can and should private parties be able to contract out of insolvency rules?* In particular, if structured finance involves contracts which appear to interfere with the normal distribution of assets on insolvency, should those contracts by void and unenforceable as a matter of public policy.

This is an area where examples help a lot. First, some English law terminology:

(1) If a person is unable to pay their debts as they fall due, they are said to be **illiquid** or **insolvent**.
(2) If they value of a person's debts exceeds the value of their assets, they are said to be **balance sheet insolvent**.
(3) If a natural person is found to be insolvent, they can be declared **bankrupt** and their insolvent estate (assets and liabilities) will be transferred to a **trustee in bankruptcy** for management.
(4) If a corporate person is found unable to pay their debts as they fall due, it can be declared formally insolvent and roughly speaking control of the corporate is handed to an administrator or **liquidator**.
(5) The role of the trustee in bankruptcy/liquidator is to get in all the remaining assets of the insolvent, turn these into cash, and then use this to pay off all the liabilities of the insolvent in accordance with insolvency law.

If there are enough assets to meet liabilities, then no one need worry. But if the person is insolvent, then things get interesting (for lawyers): there is not enough money to go round. We arrive at the key policy question: if someone is to receive less than they are owed, who should that be? Who should bear the risk and the loss? Parliament has provided the answer in its insolvency legislation. Here is a very general example which would also cover debts incurred under a single syndicated CFA.

EXAMPLE

Borrower B owes £1.2m to C Bank and £800k to D Bank under a syndicated CFA. If B has £2m then he can simply repay C and D in full, and everyone is happy. But what if B is insolvent and only has £1m? B cannot pay what is owed. Should C receive £1m and D do without, or should B give 50p to each of C and D?

Parliament has taken the view, which might accord with your intuitions that, all else being equal, every creditor should bear the losses on insolvency equally according to the debt they are owed. In this example it means:

(A) As B can only repay 50% of the amount it owes to all the creditors, *each* creditor should only receive 50% of what is owed to each of them.
(B) Accordingly, C should receive £600k (i.e. half of the £1.2m owed to it) and D should receive £400k (i.e. half of the £800k owed to it).

The rule that distributes the losses equally in this way amongst equal creditors is called the **pari passu rule**. It means 'in equal step,' implying that every creditor of equal rank bears the loss equally. It is often expressed more fully by the phrase **pari passu and pro rata** to emphasize that while all equally ranked creditors bear the loss equally, they do not bear equal amounts of loss. As in the example above, the loss bearing is proportionate to the amount owed: the absolute value C received (GBP600) was greater than that received by D (GBP400k) because C was owed more. Sometimes it is easier to think in terms of the debt itself as being owed—for every GBP1 owed, 50p was returned—and then work out how many GBP1s were actually held by the different creditors.

And with that groundwork we can begin to more precisely state our concern: given that the above pari passu rule is sanctioned by Parliament[53] and so a matter of public policy, is it possible for B, C and D, or any combination of them, to make a contract in which they promise to circumvent it? For example:

(1) Could B and C contract that B's GBP1m will become the property of C just when B is declared insolvent? The pari passu rule would then be applied, but B's estate has less to be share equally between creditors. Indeed, B and C's contract would deprive D of any recoveries as B would be left penniless.
(2) Could B, C, and D agree that once the liquidator has distributed the GBP1m as discussed above, they will then redistribute the GBP1m a different way as they see fit, in effect overruling Parliament's intention?
(3) Could B, C, and D agree that the sums loaned by C and D create debts but they will not be payable save on the occurrence of a specified event: namely, B's insolvency, when *only* the debt to C becomes payable in full.
(4) Could D and C agree that C will hand over any money he receives from the liquidator to D?
(5) Could B and C agree that C simply will not ask for repayment (prove for the debt) on B's insolvency, so that D receives the whole GBP800k by default?

We could keep going thinking up ways of interfering with the pari passu rule, but it is the principled question that is important—should freedom of contract trump public policy? Should contracting parties be able to contract out of insolvency policy?

53 While the pari passu rule is provided for in the Insolvency Acts, it is also part of the common law and subsists as a principle even if the statute does not apply.

ESSENTIAL DEFINITION: CONTRACTING OUT OF INSOLVENCY RULES

The basic rule is as follows: *parties cannot contract out of the insolvency legislation.*[54]

This basic rule is too broad to be applied predictably, so it manifests in two distinct rules which may sometimes overlap.

Rule 1: the anti-deprivation rule

'[A] simple stipulation that, upon a man's becoming bankrupt, that which was his property up to the date of the bankruptcy should go over to some one else and be taken away from his creditors, is void as being a violation of the policy of the bankrupt law.' *Ex p Jay* (1880) 14 ChD 19 (CA) 25 (James LJ).

Notice that in this instance the purpose of the (contractual) stipulation is relevant.

Rule 2: the pari passu rule

You saw this rule in action above, but now it is being understood in a prohibitive sense:

> [W]here the effect of a contract is that an asset which is actually owned by a company at the commencement of its liquidation would be dealt with in a way other than in accordance with [the pari passu rule] . . . then to that extent the contract as a matter of public policy is avoided. *Carreras Rothmans Ltd v Freeman Mathews Treasure Ltd (In Liquidation)* [1985] Ch 207, 226 (Peter Gibson J).

Notice that in this case the purpose of the contract need not be to interfere with the pari passu distribution; it suffices that the contract have that effect irrespective of the parties' intentions.

Both rules are subject to several qualifications limiting their potential ambit, but these are best stated when considering the cases.

As traditionally stated, these rules would seem to scythe through all kinds of modern financial arrangements in which the parties have contracted to mitigate their credit risk in various ways. Yet the rules do not, and they do not, it is submitted, because the traditional statements omit at least one crucial additional element: the (contractual) stipulation in question was not entered into for a legitimate commercial reason but for some ulterior purpose that offends the insolvency rules.

The distinction between the two rules is hardly clear cut, and several of the key cases approached the contract in issue using one rule, whereas later cases opine that the other rule should have been used instead.[55] As a starting point, we can use our running example to indicate the mischief(s) these rules are aiming at, and then consider some of the key cases.

Scenario (1), where Bob and Colin contracted that Bob's GBP1 would become Colin's property on the event of Bob's bankruptcy. The effect of this contract is that purports to remove from Bob's

---

54 Affirmed by Lord Collins in *Belmont Park Investments Pty Ltd. and Others v BNY Corporate Trustee Services Ltd. and Another* [2011] UKSC 38, [2011] 1 AC 383, 397A.

55 See *British Eagle International Airlines Ltd. v Compagnie Nationale Air France* [1975] 1 WLR 758 (HL), and the discussion thereof in *Belmont Park* (n 54) 398–99.

estate an asset which properly should have vested in the trustee in bankruptcy for the benefit of *all* the creditors (including Colin). The sole or at least principal purpose of the contract is to deprive the other creditors and so it is void—the transfer of the money never occurred.

Scenario (3), where all three people contracted to pretend the money transfers were notional accounting entries, not loans, but that on bankruptcy Bob would invent a single loan payable to just Debbie. This artificial construction does appear to offend against the pari passu rule (and arguably, in creating a new claim on the estate, the anti-deprivation rule too). The trustee in bankruptcy will want to pay Debbie just 40p, not GBP1, and let Colin prove for his claim.

These matters are best dealt with by considering the cases.

6.5.1 The first public policy principle: *anti-deprivation rule*

Any attempt to contract out of the mandatory provisions of insolvency law, and particularly an attempt to rank creditors differently with the effect that some are deprived of what they would have received had the prescribed procedure been followed, would be void.

RE JEAVONS, EX P MACKAY (1872–73) LR 8 Ch App 643

Jeavons sold the use of a ship-cladding patent to B and also lent to B £12,500. Matters were so arranged that all royalties for the patent's use by third-party ship-buyers were paid directly to Jeavons, who in effect acted as collection agent for B. It was agreed that (1) Jeavons would retain[56] 50% of any royalties and apply this to repayment of the £12,500 debt, and Jeavons would hand over the remaining 50% to B; but (2) should B be declared bankrupt, Jeavons would immediately take ownership of the 50% he had previously been required to hand over.

Held: Stipulation (1) was a valid commercial stipulation, but stipulation (2) was clearly designed to be a direct fraud on the bankruptcy laws. A person could not make it a part of his contract that, in the event of bankruptcy, he gain some additional advantage which prevents the property being distributed under the bankruptcy laws.

Ex parte Mackay underscores the principal mischief aimed at contractual provisions which remove an asset from the bankruptcy estate for the purposes of gaining an advantage over the other creditors, which latter must share a reduced estate. A simple example suffices:

> Bob owes GBP1,000: GBP500 to Colin and GBP500 to Debbie. Bob and Colin agree that Bob will store his van in Colin's garage and, if Bob is declared bankrupt, Colin will take ownership of the van. The van is old, but worth GBP500. Later Bob is bankrupted, and is found to have only one asset: the van. Except he does not own the van because of the purported transfer to Colin. The effect is that Colin has been repaid in full, for he has received a GBP500 asset which can be realized to meet Bob's debt, but Debbie is faced with a bankrupt's estate worth GBP0. Colin's contractual stipulation has clearly deprived Bob's estate and thwarted the proper operation of bankruptcy law: both Colin and Debbie ought to have received GBP250 each. The contractual stipulation is thus void and the van will be considered part of Colin's estate.

56 By way of contractual lien over the account monies.

Creditors take debtors goods in payment or at least security for payment all the time, but the anti-deprivation rule does not void all such transactions. The following two cases are illustrative of the line between valid and invalid contractual stipulations.

IN RE HARRISON, EX P JAY (1880) 14 Ch D 19 (CA)

A builder contracted with the landowner to build on his land, on completion of which the builder would take a lease of it. It was agreed that during development, should the builder be declared bankrupt, the building materials on the land would be transferred to the ownership of the landowner, no doubt so that he could complete the works himself. The builder was declared bankrupt and the trustee in bankruptcy sought to recover the materials.

Held: The stipulation offended against the anti-deprivation rule.

IN RE GARRUD, EX P NEWITT (1881) 16 Ch D 522 (CA)

A builder contracted with a shipbuilder to enter onto the latter's land and build a ship. It was further agreed that should the builder breach the contract, for example by failing to complete on time, the builder would pay liquidated damages by forfeiting any and all building materials on site. The builder breached the contract and, no doubt for linked reasons, was declared bankrupt. It was not clear which occurred first. The shipbuilder then declared the building materials forfeit under the contract. The trustee in bankruptcy sought to recover the materials.

Held: The contractual stipulation was valid: the cause of the transfer of property was the builder's breach and consequent liquidated damages clause; the stipulation's purpose was not to evade the bankruptcy laws.

There is, to be fair, judicial scepticism about the decision in *in re Newitt*. In *Belmont* in the Court of appeal, Neuberger MR and Patten LJJ (as they then were) thought that the stipulation did offend the rule and, had it been decided after *British Eagle*, would have fallen foul of that case also. Lord Collins declined to form an official view in the Supreme Court, however, though he too thought that the case problematic, especially as forfeiture occurred after bankruptcy.[57]

Consider the following set of clauses as a whole. Do you think they offend the anti-deprivation rule?

Cl.1 The following are Events of Default in this Agreement:
  1.1. Bob is declared bankrupt or is otherwise subject to any bankruptcy process . . .
Cl.2 The occurrence of any Event of Default will constitute a repudiatory breach of this Agreement.
Cl.3 On the occurrence of any repudiatory breach of this Agreement, full legal title in all building materials owned by Bob and located on the land of Colin at 13 Acacia Avenue shall transfer immediately and irrevocably to Colin.

57 *Belmont Park* (n 54) [82].

We have noted a key feature of the anti-deprivation rule: intention. The principal aim of the contractual provision must be to evade the operation of insolvency law. Yet if that is so, any clever drafter will certainly avoid being explicit; they will aim to produce the desired deprivation under the guise of an innocent transaction. Now the courts will look to substance, not form, to establish whether the rule is contravened, but if that is so, this leaves space for a liquidator to question seemingly innocent financial transactions. In 2011 it proved necessary for the Supreme Court to provide some comfort.

BELMONT PARK INVESTMENTS PTY LTD AND OTHERS v BNY CORPORATE TRUSTEE SERVICES LTD AND ANOTHER [2011] UKSC 38

Various investors provided money to a Special Purpose Vehicle to acquire government bonds (the collateral). The collateral was to generate income, which would be used by the SPV to make predetermined payments to the investors. However, this income was variable and so there was a risk the SPV would not be able to pay the investors. Therefore, a Lehmans entity agreed with the SPV that if the amount of income from the collateral fell below the amount payable by the SPV to the investors, the Lehmans entity would pay the shortfall. But, if the collateral income exceeded the amount due to the investors, the Lehmans entity would receive the excess.

It was further agreed that the collateral would be available as security for any sums due from the SPV to the Lehmans entity and/or the investors. The key provision in issue stated that the collateral was to be used to meet any debts owed to the Lehmans entity first, and only any remainder would go to the investors' claims. It also stated, however, that if Lehmans became insolvent, the priority would be immediately reversed: the collateral would be used to pay the investors' debts, and any remainder would go to the Lehmans entity.

Lehmans' liquidator sought a declaration that the provision which 'flipped' the collateral in favour of the investors was void as it offended against the anti-deprivation rule—it deprived Lehman's creditors of the value of the collateral just when Lehmans became insolvent.

Held: 106-108 (Lord Collins):

> If the anti-deprivation principle is essentially directed to intentional or inevitable evasion of the principle that the debtor's property is part of the insolvent estate, and is applied in a commercially sensitive manner, taking into account the policy of party autonomy and the upholding of proper commercial bargains, these conclusions on the present appeal follow. . . .
>
> The answer [to the question raised in the appeal] is to be found in the fact that this was a complex commercial transaction entered into in good faith. Although, as a matter of law, the [collateral] was provided by the issuer out of funds raised from the noteholders, the substance of the matter is that the [collateral] was provided by the noteholders and subject to a potential change in priorities.'

Accordingly, the priority 'flipping' provision did not offend the anti-deprivation rule. It had been agreed in good faith with a view to restoring property to the persons who had funded the acquisition of that property in the first place.

Notice once again that good faith and a general sense of legitimacy have been factored in to rescue a financial transaction from a principle of public policy.

6.5.2 The second public policy issue: pari passu

> Where the effect of a contract is that an asset which is actually owned by a company at the commencement of its liquidation would be dealt with in a way other than in accordance with [the pari passu rule], then to that extent the contract as a matter of public policy is avoided.

The key case exemplifying the rule is *British Eagle*, but to understand it we need to understand some further technical matters. The case involved a multilateral netting arrangement created by contract and the subsequent claim, by the liquidator of one of the now insolvent participating companies, that this contractual arrangement offended either the anti-deprivation rule or the pari passu rule, or both. Modern cases regard *British Eagle* as offending the latter even if their Lordships at the time regarded it as case of deprivation. We proceed on the modern interpretation that *British Eagle* concerns contractual interference with the pari passu rule.

It can arise under some business transactions that two or more parties end up promising to pay each other sums of money at various times. For example, if the parties sell each other commodities, or sell goods and services as agents for each other. Let us imagine we have two airlines which sell their own air travel tickets but also sell each other's tickets as agents and then pass through these fees less commission. For ease, each party will sell tickets for a month and make an accounting note of the fees to be handed over to the other party, and then will at the end of the month pay over an amount equal to that sum to the other party, and vice versa. Then one party, 'BE' may for the sake of argument end up at the end of a month owing GBP1,000 to the other party 'AF,' and at the same time AF may end up owing GBP900 to BE. Now in this situation BE could send GBP1,000 to AF, and simultaneously AF could send GBP900 to BE. Yet this is grossly inefficient (especially if we are talking millions, not hundreds). BE must find GBP1,000 in cash and wait while GBP900 hopefully arrives. If BE sends cash, it risks AF not doing the same, for example if AF becomes insolvent or the money is diverted en route. In any event, GBP1,000 is a lot of money that could have been used elsewhere.

One solution is for AF and BE to agree as follows: at the end of the month each notifies the other of the amount each owes to the other, then then subtract or 'net off' one amount from the other and who ever owes the difference or net amount must only pay that net amount to the other. In our example, GBP1,000 owed by BE less GBP900 owed by AF netted off gives GBP900 pounds owed by BE to AF. This contractual **netting** means BE only needs to find GBP900 cash, reducing its liquidity demand by 90%, and also immediately reduces the risk of AF's insolvency because by netting the value of what AF owes is used to reduce BE's liability to AF.

Look more closely, however. We have a contract which stipulates that one party's asset—the liability of the other party—will somehow be wiped out by being netted against its liability. Imagine you are BE's liquidator: BE has an asset, being owed GBP900 by AF. AF will no doubt claim that asset no longer exists because of the netting provision, but you are sceptical. You would much prefer to get in the GBP900 right now and distribute it pari passu to all the creditors. AF can worry about its GBP1,000 separately by proving for that debt in the insolvency i.e. AF can get in line with all the other creditors and bear its loses pari passu with those others. On this view, the contractual netting provision looks like it does offend the pari passu rule. The liquidator's behaviour here—choosing which assets and liabilities to demand now and which to disclaim or at least deal with later—is called **cherry-picking**.

Now, in fact the current example is exempted from the usual prohibitive rules by another provision of insolvency law: **insolvency set-off**. Insolvency set-off respects the commercial reality and indeed economic efficiency that if two parties have mutual debts it is much better for everyone that they can cancel out their debts, freeing up cash on the part of the solvent party which can (1) prevent illiquidity and so reduce the risk of contagion of insolvency; and (2) free up that money to flow around the economy. Accordingly, r 4.90 Insolvency Rules allows two parties to set off their liquidated debts on one party's insolvency provided the debts have mutuality, broadly understood as arising from some connected commercial relationship (as in our example). Rule 4.90 is set out below as it is fairly self-explanatory.

INSOLVENCY RULES 1986

Mutual credit and set-off

Rule 4.90.—(1) This Rule applies where, before the company goes into liquidation there have been mutual credits, mutual debts or other mutual dealings between the company and any creditor of the company proving or claiming to prove for a debt in the liquidation.

(2) An account shall be taken of what is due from each party to the other in respect of the mutual dealings, and the sums due from one party shall be set off against the sums due from the other.

(3) Sums due from the company to another party shall not be included in the account taken under paragraph (2) if that other party had notice at the time they became due that a meeting of creditors had been summoned under section 98 or (as the case may be) a petition for the winding up of the company was pending.

(4) Only the balance (if any) of the account is provable in the liquidation. Alternatively (as the case may be) the amount shall be paid to the liquidator as part of the assets.

This rule is mandatory (i.e. once the set off is implemented, it cannot be unravelled), but it is also limited in application. As soon as more than two parties engage in this kind of netting relationship the mutuality requirement ceases to be satisfied—insolvency set off works between mutual debts of two parties; as soon as third party is involved the net amount represents the non-mutual debts of three parties. Specifically, if the net amount is calculated by netting off debts owed by BE to AF and by a third party SB to AF, then the final net amount involves not mutual debts but two debts between different parties. Insolvency set-off does not apply.

Let us augment our scenario. BE, AF, SB enter into a contractual arrangement under which IATA, their industry body, will operate a **multilateral netting** system. As before we have a number of airlines, and they sell each other's tickets and now also rent out their stands at airports to each other. At the end of the month, they send an account to IATA detailing how many tickets they sold and how many times they rented out their stands to each of the two other parties. IATA then collates these accounts and nets them off. So, let the following hold at the end of a given month: BE owes GBP500 to AF and GBP600 to SB; AF owes GBP600 to BE and GBP600 GBP400 to SB; SB owes to BE and GBP400 to AF. First, let us net off the bilateral amounts: we have AF owing BE GBP100 and owing GBP200 to SB, while SB owes nothing. BE owes GBP200 to SB. Pay particular attention to the GBP100 owed by AF to BE—this chose in action on BE's balance sheet which could be called in by a liquidator and distributed to all creditors. Now the clearing house mechanism netted off these balances: BE 'owes' GBP200 into the 'clearing house' but is due to be paid GBP100 out of it, so net it was contractually required to pay GBP100 into the clearing house pot. AF 'owed' GBP200 + GBP100 into the clearing house, so it was contractually required to pay in GBP300. The net amount paid in (GBP100 from BE and GBP300 from AF) was equal to the total GBP200 + GBP200 = GBP400 payable to SB. BE and AF would pay in their respective amounts to IATA, who would pass on the GBP400 to SB in settlement.

The principal concern for BE's liquidator was that the contractual arrangement caused the GBP100 owed by AF to BE to 'disappear.' The GBP100 was netted off in the clearing house to reduce the amount BE owed to SB. What then is the issue? The liquidator wanted to receive the GBP100 asset now to distribute to creditors, and it would let SB prove for the GBP200 debt later, if anything was left. Add some zeroes to those figures and you can imagine the serious effects the liquidator's demands could have on the other airlines' liquidity.

You can understand why initially *British Eagle* was understood as an anti-deprivation case—the contractual arrangement made that GBP100 BE asset 'vanish.' However, on a better view the GBP100 has not vanished but been used to reduce BE's liability to SB. This placed AF and SB in a much better position than other creditors: they were able to use the full value, without pari passu reduction, of the sums BE owed. AF could use the full value of the sums BE owed into the clearing house to wipe out its debt to BE (BE's asset). SB would receive the full amount owed to it by BE (GBP200) without any reduction pari passu the other creditors.

Had the credit and debt been mutual, i.e. both arising from related transactions between AF and BE, setting them off against each other to reduce a liability would have been permitted by statute. But setting off an AF credit to BE against a BE debt to SB lacked the requisite mutuality, and so the statutory exception did not apply.

BRITISH EAGLE INTERNATIONAL AIR LINES LTD v COMPAGNIE NATIONALE AIR FRANCE [1975] 2 All ER 390, [1975] 1 WLR 758 (HL)

IATA ran an arrangement, called 'the clearing house' where air companies could manage the sums they owed each other for taking passengers, using planes and infrastructure. As a company incurred a debt the corresponding air company would notify the clearing house. All these mini-debts were then added up and at the end of each month the debtor air company would pay a net sum in settlement. BE and AF were two of the 'clearing house' members and when BE was declared insolvent, AF happened to owe a small net sum to BE. The effect of the arrangement however was that 'net' BE owed a single sum into the Clearing House. The liquidator claimed the contractual arrangement deprived BE of the asset (AF's debt owed) and/or offended the pari passu rule.

Held: AF was liable for the gross amount owing. It would have to prove the amount owed to it by BE in the subsequent liquidation.

Per Lord Cross in the 3–2 majority opinion:

> what the respondents are saying here is that the parties to the 'clearing house' arrangements by agreeing that simple contract debts are to be satisfied in a particular way have succeeded in 'contracting out' of the provisions contained in [statute] for the payment of unsecured debts 'pari passu.' In such a context it is to my mind irrelevant that the parties to the 'clearing house' arrangements had good business reasons for entering into them and did not direct their minds to the question how the arrangements might be affected by the insolvency of one or more of the parties. Such a 'contracting out' must, to my mind, be contrary to public policy. The question is, in essence, whether what was called in argument the 'mini liquidation' flowing from the clearing house arrangements is to yield to or to prevail over the general liquidation. I cannot doubt, that on principle the rules of the general liquidation should prevail. [411]

Lord Morris, in his intuitively compelling dissenting judgment (with which Lord Simon agreed), said it was not possible to infer that the multilateral arrangement was designed to subvert insolvency law, and that it was a good faith contract. The difficulty here is that this argument is premised on the this being a case of deprivation, where intent is required. Once *British Eagle* is understood as concerning the pari passu principle, to which intent is irrelevant, Lord Morris' judgment simply does not bite. An attempt to overturn *British Eagle* from within by using the dissentient opinion will struggle.

You may well have been sympathetic with the trustee in bankruptcy in *ex parte Mackay* because the contractual provision was obviously attempting to circumvent the will of Parliament and deserved to be struck down. Yet here there was no suggestion these major airlines set out to evade insolvency law; the financial justifications for the netting arrangement they had created were manifest. Yet nevertheless the House of Lords—by 3–2, we must underline—preferred formalism i.e. they preferred to apply the law strictly, rather than to give effect to the 'innocent' reality of the agreement before the court. In the next two sections on structured finance, we find the courts maintaining the fundamental principle enunciated in *British Eagle* but managing to accommodate financial practice via a series of exceptions and policy justifications.

CONSIDER THE FOLLOWING SET OF CLAUSES AS A WHOLE. DO YOU THINK THEY OFFEND THE *PARI PASSU* RULE?

The same clauses as existed in *British Eagle* save for the addition of the following clause.

> 9(a) With respect to transactions between members of the Clearing House which are subject to clearance through the Clearing House . . . no liability for payment and no right of action to recover payment shall accrue between members of the Clearing House. In lieu thereof members shall have liabilities to the Clearing House for balances due by them resulting from a clearance or rights of action against the Clearing House for balances in their favour resulting from a clearance and collected by the Clearing House from debtor members in such clearance.

6.6 Pari passu in the context of structured finance

We have established that a creditor and debtor may contract to lend and borrow a sum of money (forming a Credit Facility Agreement). On borrowing the money, the debtor owes a debt obligation to the creditor (a promise to repay), and since 1925 this debt obligation is legally a kind property—a chose in action—which the creditor owns and can assign to third parties. We can now complicate the picture by considering contracts under which multiple creditors commit to lend a percentage of a total amount to the borrower, or one lender lends and then sells aliquot parts of the debt to third parties (who accede to the contract simultaneously) with the same result: the borrower owes multiple lenders a percentage of the whole debt. The process of originating such a contract either (1) initially with multiple lenders or (2) in such a way that the contract can accommodate assignment of parts of the debt to different lenders is called syndication. It is quite possible for there to be multiple borrowers, almost always from the same group of companies, but that will not concern us here.

Under a standard credit facility agreement, the borrower will owe the lenders pari passu and pro rata. That means each lender will receive funds back on liquidation at the same time as the others, not one after the other, in proportion to the debt they hold. If there are three lenders owed GBP100m each, they will each receive 33.3p in the GBP1 on a solvent liquidation of the borrower.

The lenders may wish to modify this distribution, however. If we have two banks, Senior and Junior, they may contract that if borrower insolvency occurs, Junior will only be paid *after* Senior is paid in full. Why would Junior agree to this? One reason is risk diversification once again. Imagine our GBP300m loan receives 10% interest per annum. A conservative lender may focus on the return of its capital investment and be prepared to forgo interest to ensure repayment; a risk-taking lender may be prepared to risk its capital for an upside, such as a greater interest payment. Thus, if Junior prefers risk, it might agree to act as a debt cushion for Senior by absorbing losses while Senior is paid in full, but only in consideration of receiving a greater part of the total interest the borrower pays while it is solvent. For example, if the borrower pays 10% interest to the facility agent, the agent will be instructed by the lenders to send not 3.33% to the Junior lender but 6%, and to send the remaining 4% to Senior. In this way Junior's risk-taking is rewarded in high income just as long as the borrower survives. An agreement between lenders which modifies the pari passu rule is often called an intercreditor agreement (though 'subordination agreement' is sometimes used as a generic term).

Structured finance is the legal technique of differentiating an existing homogenous debt into different parts—or tranches—possessing different risk profiles. We will see, when we discuss leveraged buyouts, how this ranking of risk can be achieved by using the structural subordination afforded by companies. Another, legally weaker but more flexible method is contractual subordination. This is achieved by what is known as a subordination agreement in many transactions when all the parties are aware of its existence and are merely seeking to order the claims bilaterally between two parties, or two types of party. Thus, shareholders or mezz debt might be subject to a **subordination agreement**—a contract where the parties agree that at least one party will not be repaid by an identified debtor until other persons are repaid in full. When, however, the subordination is planned for the purposes of syndication, or indeed securitization, we tend to use more complicated subordination contracts called **intercreditor agreements** (**ICAs**). We tend to call the parties who will be repaid first on a default **Senior**, and those who will be paid last **Junior**. **Mezz(anine)** and in the US **Second Lien** are terms for middling debtors. When several tranches of debt are created, we use **letters**: A for most senior, B next senior, and all the way down to Z and even ZZ, which tends

In this scenario, Borrower owes €50 to each bank (total €100), but only has assets of €80

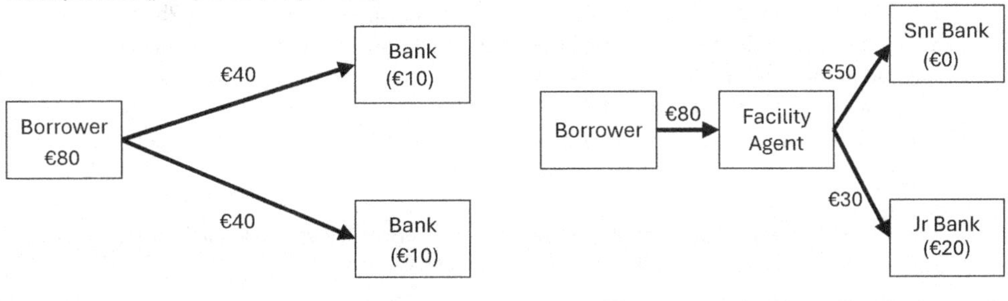

Figure 6.5 An intercreditor agreement, managed by the facility agent, prioritizes distribution to the senior creditor

not just to be junior but actually junk. Frankly, you may use any term you like for it is all a matter of contractual drafting.

Subordination only makes sense when there is not enough money to go round. If the borrower can repay 100% of what is owed, it does not matter who is entitled to be paid 'first'—everyone will be repaid. It is when less than 100% is recovered from a defaulting borrower that subordination is important. When subordination is in effect, certain parties will be paid in full before other parties, who as a result will bear disproportionately greater loss (and so risk). In Figure 6.5 we see that borrower owes EUR100 to two banks under a CFA, EUR40 each. However, borrower is insolvent, having only EUR80 in assets. On distribution the banks will only receive EUR40 each, both bearing an equal loss of EUR10. The right-hand diagram shows the effect of an ICA which is being administered by a facility agent for the banks. Here the borrower is still insolvent, with only EUR80 to be distributed, but this is going to be redistributed by the facility agent in accordance with the ICA. The ICA provides that one bank is senior, the other junior, such that all distributions will go first to repay the senior lender in full and only when senior lend is fully repaid will any surplus go to repay the junior lender. The effect in the example is that the senior lender is repaid the full EUR50, leaving just EUR30 to go towards repaying the junior lender.

ICAs demand a certain degree of abstract understanding. Unlike structural subordination (detailed in Chapter 7), an ICA does not change underlying legal rights on enforcement and insolvency; it creates a parallel world in which whatever does happen to the underlying debt 'in the real world' is altered in the parallel world that exists only between the ICA signatories.

Let us consider a more advanced example.

EFFECT OF AN INTERCREDITOR AGREEMENT

J is a corporate owing GBP300m (the Debt) under a fully drawn English law term CFA. The Debt is owed to the banks A, B, C, and D, each holding GBP75m of the Debt. Unbeknownst to J, banks A, B, C, and D have signed an ICA, to which F is party as Facility Agent under both the CFA and ICA. The ICA tranches the Debt as follows: the first GBP100m is named Senior Debt and ranks senior, then the next GBP50m is 'B Debt,' the next GBP75m is 'C Debt' and the final GBP75 is called 'Junior Debt.'

The Debt is owned as follows:

A Bank: GBP50m of Senior Debt and GBP25 of Junior Debt.
B Bank: GBP25m of Senior Debt and GBP50m of B Debt.
C Bank: GBP75m of C Debt.
D Bank: GBP25m of Senior Debt and GBP50m of Junior Debt.

J defaults, the loan is accelerated and enforced. The Agents recover GBP250m and the remaining debt is written off, J being liquidated. As far as J's liquidator is concerned, that is the end of the matter—the creditors have been satisfied as far as possible.

However, for the Facility Agent it is necessary to consider the contractual effect of the ICA. F does not distribute the recovered amount pari passu, but follows the debt ranking in the ICA, which gives the following result:

1 GBP250 goes first to the Senior Lenders: A receives back the full GBP100m; B receives the full GBP25m; D receives the full GBP25m.

2 GBP250m - GBP100m = GBP150m goes next to the B Creditors. B receives back the full GBP50m of B Debt.
3 GBP150m - GBP50m = GBP100m goes next to the C Creditors. C receives back the full GBP75m of C Debt.

The remaining GBP25m goes finally to the D Creditors. However, the D Debt is said to be GBP75m; the GBP25m will not meet this in full. A is owed GBP25m of Junior Debt and D is owed GBP50m of Junior Debt. As Junior Creditors A and D rank equally and the GBP25m recovered will be distributed to them pari passu. As A holds one-third of the Junior Debt while D holds two-thirds, one-third of the GBP25m will go to A and two-thirds to D. In other words, A receives 33.3p for every pound of Junior Debt it holds = c.GBP8.333m. D receives GBP16.667m.

The are many ways to achieve this outcome contractually, and indeed the borrower and other parties can also become involved. For example, the borrower may have a parent company which is not a party to the A, B, C credit facilities agreement, but which has separately lent money to the borrower as an intra-group loan. Being a creditor of the borrower, the parent would then compete with A, B, C in any borrower insolvency. If parent lent GBP100m, the insolvency dividend would have to be split equally four ways. To avoid this, A, B, C might require (as a condition precedent of lending to borrower) that the parent enter into a separate contract under which the parent agrees that A, B, C will be paid first and in full before the parent receives anything.

The question is whether these contractual arrangements are void for public policy reasons, specifically because they offend the pari passu rule. Given the policies which drove *British Eagle*, one might at least be suspicious of them, and indeed liquidators have so been. Yet what we will see is the court moving to a permissive stance: the pari passu principle become merely a default rule in situations where one party contractually volunteers to forgo its rights on insolvency. Whether it has volunteered, and to what extent, has become a matter of contractual interpretation.[58]

6.7 Contract versus pari passu?

What follows are just three of the ways lawyers have contractually 'modified' the workings of the pari passu rule. In each case the borrower's liquidator sought a declaration that the modification offended the rule. Note that subordination agreements may well include all three mechanisms just in case one or more fails in the courts.

To cut a long story short though, the courts have shifted from the censoriousness of *British Eagle* to permissiveness. The current thinking is that the pari passu is now merely a default rule out of which creditors may contract if they fall into one of two classes. Given a set of creditors X of a debtor, either:

(1) a given creditor A contracts to deprioritize itself, thereby causing all other creditors X—A to rank senior to it; or

58 *in re Golden Key Ltd.* [2009] EWCA Civ 636 [5]–[6].

(2) a given creditor A contracts with a subset of creditors B such that A ranks senior to just that subset B of creditors, but pari passu with all other creditors X—(B and A).[59]

The central lack of objectionableness in all this turns on consent. On the one hand, every creditor in a worse position than under pari passu consented to be in that position; on the other, every creditor not asked to give its consent on the matter is no worse off, and sometimes even better off, than under pari passu. Hence these recent dicta of Lewison LJ:

> Since there is nothing objectionable about a creditor agreeing to occupy a place in the queue which is further back than the place that he would otherwise have occupied, there is equally nothing objectionable in one creditor who might otherwise have shared pari passu with another agreeing that he will occupy a place even further back than that other. Nor, in my judgment, is there anything objectionable in a creditor who is entitled to a provable debt agreeing not to prove until some particular event has occurred. In other words creditors who would otherwise have occupied the same place in the waterfall may agree to subordinate their claims to other such claims. The question is whether the various instruments evince an intention that distribution should be on some basis other than pari passu.[60]

In in *re Golden Key Ltd* [2009] EWCA Civ 636 (CA) Arden LJ emphasized the default rule approach:

> Pari passu provisions are commonly found in debentures. A provision for pari passu repayment can, however, be implied if it is clear that the debenture holders are to stand on an equal footing (see for example *Murray v Scott* (1884) 9 App Cas 519). Accordingly, where a document on its true interpretation provides for the distribution of assets to a group of persons as between whom no distinction is to be drawn, the court will imply a requirement to make distributions proportionately even though the words 'equally' or 'pari passu' are not used. Such an implication is not, however, possible where the document evinces an intention that the distribution should be on some other basis. 6. Given its importance, the concept of pari passu distribution can be taken to be part of the background to the issue of the [commercial paper] that would have been known to the parties . . . The concept of pari passu distribution may also be a factor which makes one interpretation more plausible than another. [5]

There are a number of theoretical assumptions at the heart of this shift from prohibition to permission. Before we consider those assumptions, let us flesh out the story of this shift by examining the kinds of subordination and how they came to be recognized from the 1990s onwards.

The current thinking is that there are three species of contractual subordination. These are:

(1) contractual subordination;
(2) contingent subordination; and
(3) turnover trust.[61]

We examine each in turn.

---

59 *re Lehman Brothers International (Europe) (In Administration) (The Lehman Waterfall Case)* [2017] UKSC 38 [66].

60 in *re LB Holdings Intermediate 2 Ltd.* [2021] EWCA Civ 1523 [19] (LJ Lewison).

61 Bruce Johnston, 'Debt Subordination—Is All Okay Following the Lehman Waterfall Case?' (2017) 32 JIBLR 507. See confirmation in *LB Holdings Intermediate 2 Ltd.* (n 60) [21].

6.7.1 Method 1: contractual subordination

Where solvent parties agree, before a liquidation, to forgo their own rights to distribution, this does not contravene the either the anti-deprivation rule or the pari passu rule. The following case was considered, following *British Eagle*, as potentially falling foul of the anti-deprivation rule but, following *Belmont* we would consider this as a case concerning the pari passu rule.

DEFINITION: CONTRACTUAL SUBORDINATION

> [S]imple contractual subordination can *only* serve to demote the creditor's interests in relation to other creditors. But, whereas this is achieved through the articulation of a contingency in the case of contingent debt subordination, simple contractual subordination simply enables the creditor to select at what point in the waterfall his or her interests will be considered, provided: (1) That point is lower than the priority accorded to the creditor by the legal waterfall; and (2) All the creditor is doing is selecting a point in the legal waterfall, without re-writing that order. In other words, all a creditor is doing is waiving his or her right to be paid at a certain priority and electing to sit at a priority lower than would be the case according to the rules of legal subordination. [*in re LB Holdings Intermediate 2 Ltd* [2020] EWHC 1681 (Ch) [115] (Marcus Smith J)]

In earlier cases, the justificatory emphasis for distinguishing contractual subordination from the rule in *British Eagle* was not so much on consent as on market convention: these sorts of clauses were so widely used, and so useful for attracting investment, that it would be wrong for the court to strike them down. Vinelott J stated as much in 1993:

> In my judgment I am not compelled by the decisions of the House of Lords in . . . *British Eagle* . . . to conclude that a contract between a company and a creditor, providing for the debt due to the creditor to be subordinated in the insolvent winding up of the company to other unsecured debt, is rendered void by the insolvency legislation. A contrary decision would have wide-reaching repercussions. It is not infrequently the case that a company can only continue to trade and incur credit with the financial support of a parent or associated company, or a bank which is willing to subordinate its debt to the debts owed to the other unsecured creditor. Subordinated debt is in many contexts treated for accountancy purposes as if it were part of the company's capital.[62]

We see an example of just such a commercially beneficial arrangement in *in re SSSL Realisations*:

IN RE SSSL REALISATIONS (2002) LTD [2006] EWCA Civ 7

[You already encountered these facts when we discussed guarantee facilities in Chapter 2.]

Save Group plc (SG) was the parent company of SSSL and other operating subsidiaries that each ran a petrol station. As raiser of capital for the entire group, SG had lent

62 *in re Maxwell Communications plc (No.3)* [1993] 1 WLR 1402, 1416 (ChD).

capital to its subsidiaries. As such one of its major assets was the debt owed by *inter alios* SSSL to SG.

This loan was subject to a subordination agreement under which SG and SSSL agreed that any debt owed by SSSL to SG would be subordinated to any debt owed by SSSL to a petrol duty bond provider, AIG. The whole group entered liquidation. The liquidator of SG contended that the subordination defeated the mandatory anti-deprivation rule.

Held: the difference from *British Eagle* was that here the only creditor deprived had volunteered, before the liquidation, to forgo its rights to a distribution before AIG were paid in full. The anti-deprivation and pari passu rules were designed to protect unwitting third-party creditors. Where a creditor volunteered to forgo its rights to equal treatment, this left more value for third-party creditors and so did not contravene public policy.

6.7.2 Method 2a: contingent debt subordination

We already encountered the central thought behind this workaround when we looked at clearing houses—in the *Ansett* Case. The essential idea is that the junior 'debt' is not legally enforceable but a notional amount or accounting fiction which, on full repayment of the senior debt, is used as a reference value for the creation of a new debt payable to the junior lender. In short, if the senior lender is paid in full, a junior debt springs into existence. The following judicial definition has been approved by the Court of Appeal.

DEFINITION: CONTINGENT DEBT SUBORDINATION

Contingent debt subordination involves the creation of a debt that is payable only in the event of a given contingency being satisfied. By modifying the nature of the obligation owed by the debtor to the creditor, the operation of the rules of legal subordination changes. It is not that the rules themselves are changed, but they apply differently *because* of the contingent nature of the debt. [*in re LB Holdings Intermediate 2 Ltd* [2020] EWHC 1681 (Ch) [111] (Marcus Smith J) (emphasis in original)]

The cases on this are complicated, and so I have provided a naïve version of *Gemini* and then a more detailed iteration of the facts.

GEMINI (ECLIPSE 2006-3) PLC AND ANOR v DANSKE BANK A/S [2012] EWHC 3103 (COMM)

NAÏVE VERSION

Danske Bank agreed with the debtor Gemini and its various other creditors that amounts owed to it by Gemini would:

> only be due and payable if and to the extent that [Gemini] has funds available to be applied . . . towards payment of [Danske Bank] and all other amounts due to it in accordance with the terms of this Agreement after all amounts required to be paid in priority thereto . . . have been discharged or paid in full.

Further subordination was in place: all the other creditors were divided into A, B, C, D and E creditors, A being the most senior. Danske Bank ranked below all of these.

Danske Bank incurred regulatory costs which were to be refunded under the Agreement as subordinated debt. When Gemini became insolvent, it was unable even to pay the D and E creditors, let alone Danske Bank. Danske Bank promptly sued for payment.

Held: On interpretation of the contracts, clauses which had the combined effect that debts to a creditor were not due and payable unless and until another creditor was paid in full had the effect in the instant case that the thus subordinated creditor had no right to payment of sums it alleged were owed.

The following is a fuller version of the case (optional) if you are interested in securitization structures. You may wish to read the securitization section in Chapter 8 first and return to this.

GEMINI (ECLIPSE 2006-3) PLC AND ANOR v DANSKE BANK A/S [2012] EWHC 3103 (COMM)

ADVANCED VERSION

The case involved a securitization and the various contracts related to that transaction. Essentially an SPV (Gemini, the **Issuer**) issued notes to various classes of investors. The notes were tranched into an order of payment (a payment waterfall) pursuant to a cash management agreement (**CMA**) operated by a cash manager. In order to ensure the Issuer had sufficient liquidity to meet payments to noteholders, the SPV entered into a secured swingline facility (here called a Liquidity Facility) offered by Danske (the **LFP**).

The CMA payment waterfall provided inter alia that certain Liquidity Subordinated Amounts would be subordinated to payments to Class C, D and E noteholders. The Liquidity Facility itself confirmed the subordination:

> the Liquidity Subordinated Amounts . . . will only be due and payable if and to the extent that the Issuer has funds available to be applied in accordance with the CMA and the Issuer Deed of Charge in or towards payment of the Liquidity Subordinated Amounts and all other amounts due to it in accordance with the terms of this Agreement after all amounts required to be paid in priority thereto under the Cash Management Agreement and the Issuer Deed of Charge have been discharged or paid in full.

During the Credit Crunch Issuer became concerned that the LFP would not be able to provide credit and so drew down the entire facility. Interest accrued accordingly. This huge credit placed stress on LFP's capital reserves and following negotiation with its central bank, a special notice was issued allowing the LFP to treat the Liquidity Facility debt in a special manner for capital adequacy purposes. This still meant that the LFP suffered increased regulatory costs in complying with Basel II (at the time). Under the Liquidity Facility these costs were passed to Issuer as Increased Costs.

Under the Liquidity Facility and related documents, the Increased Costs were Liquidity Subordinated Amounts.

In July 2012 the cash manager and Issuer determined that the Issuer had insufficient funds to meet the demands of all creditors. Applying the waterfall the C noteholders were part paid, but the D and E noteholders were unpaid. Likewise significant Increased Costs were not paid. The LFP sued, claiming that on the terms of the various agreements the Increased Costs were a debt that was due and payable.

Held: Following the principles of construction in *Investors Compensation Scheme* (1998) and *Rainy Sky* (2011) the coherent, commercial sense of the documents was that where a prior ranking creditor had not been paid in full, no 'funds were available' for the calculation of sums payable to junior creditors and therefore no sums were due and owing to those junior creditors. Accordingly, the LFP had no debt claim against the Issuer.

Gemini raised a problem which would crop up again with derivatives—clearly Danske Bank could identify amounts that it thought it was owed, and the contracts provided for a definite amount to be identified for this purpose, but that 'economic' amount was not the same as a legal debt that is 'due and payable.'

6.7.3 Method 2b: promise to forebear

This mechanism is not a standalone subordination method identified by the courts but usually accompanies the other forms of contractual subordination.

Here the junior debtor obligates itself at a procedural level; the senior creditor may well admit that the debt exists and is payable to the junior lender, but requires the junior lender simply promises not to claim, enforce, or prove for the debt until the senior lender pays in full. In short, the junior lender is rendered passive. To enforce this promise to forebear, the senior lender's first step would be to bring a restraining injunction by way of application, using the contract containing the promise as evidence. The weakness of this method is that it does not stop the borrower or liquidator voluntarily sending money to the junior lender, and so the promise to forebear is unlikely to be used in isolation; it will 'bootstrap' one or more of the other methods discussed.

GEMINI (ECLIPSE 2006-3) PLC AND ANOR v DANSKE BANK A/S [2012] EWHC 3103 (Comm)

As part of the transaction discussed above, Danske Bank also promised that:

> it will not demand or receive payment of any distribution in respect of, or on account of, any amounts payable by the Issuer or the Trustee (as applicable) to [Danske Bank] under the Transaction Documents, in cash or in kind, . . . unless all amounts then due and payable by the Issuer to all other Issuer Secured Creditors ranking higher in the order of priority . . . have been paid in full.

Held: Enforceable.

6.7.4 Method 3: turnover trust

For completeness, but really a matter of trusts law, which you have not studied, we have the turnover trust. The idea here is to identify the money junior lender legally receives from the liquidator and grant an equitable (beneficial) interest in the same to the senior creditor. The result is that the senior lender has something stronger than a mere *in personam* claim against the junior lender, but has a property right in the money itself as against the whole world. The ICA will be executed and delivered as a deed for the purposes of settling the trust, and as part of its terms the junior lender will be obligated to turn over any moneys it receives with respect to the debt to the senior lender.

In the following case, a turnover trust was taken not to convene the anti-deprivation rule, although this point was not directly at point in this case, which concerned whether certain junior creditors had voting rights.

BRITISH COMMONWEALTH HOLDINGS PLC (NO.3) [1992] 1 WLR 672

BCH was a financial services company in severe difficulty. A meeting of capital holders was called with a view to approving a Companies Act Scheme of Arrangement (**SoA**). Amongst bondholders there were two classes constituted by a subordination agreement: senior and junior bondholders. The junior bondholders objected to the SoA and had sufficient voting rights to block a creditors' resolution approving it.

The administrators of BCH argued that the junior bondholders had agreed to subordination and in particular to a turnover trust. Under this particular trust various sums were held on trust for all noteholders by a bond trustee subject to the subordination. Following calculation of the assets of BCH as against the liabilities to the bondholders, it was clear that there was not enough to repay the senior bondholders in full and that the junior bondholders would receive nothing. Thus any sums held on trust for the junior, were now turned over on trust for the senior. Furthermore, the junior bondholders having no claim on these sums, had no rights as creditors of BCH and so no power to vote in any creditors' meeting.

Held: the turnover trust was on its face valid, there were indeed insufficient funds to meet senior creditor claims, and accordingly the junior creditors' claims were worthless and they had no rights to oppose the SoA.

6.7.5 Optional: supporting subordination

The following may be considered as further reading and not 'assessable.' The following are further contractual fixes which support subordination:

- Payment blocks and repayment schedules. If the senior creditors control the flow of money and where it is held (a controlled bank account), then they can de facto stop it from reaching Junior Lenders until they are paid.
- Allowing the Senior to prove for Junior Debt on insolvency. We saw a version of this in section 6.3, where creditors appointed agents and paid them for the service in an amount equal to the debt recovered. Here the Senior Lender applies recoveries to its own debt then passes the surplus to the Facility Agent for distribution to the Junior Lender.
- Standstill on Junior enforcement. The Junior lender agrees a procedural standstill which the Senior Lenders can put in evidence to support an injunction to restrain any insolvency action by a Junior Lender.
- Loss sharing. A recovering creditor promises to account to the Facility Agent for all proceeds, allowing the Facility Agent to redistribute those recoveries in accordance with the ICA.
- Tacking. This is a very technical legal right, recognized but questioned in English law. Tacking is the right of a Senior Debtor who 'adds' some debt, for example by making an advance during a Borrower restructuring, to have that debt considered Senior, even though it is given later in time than the Junior Debt. In effect it pushes the Junior piece further underwater, but thus far it seems to be upheld.

The ICA may also contain various technical devices which allow junior creditors to protect their risk. The junior creditors may feel for example that if acceleration occurs the resulting fire sale will wipe out their Debt and so regard a further capital injection as protecting their investment. This is particularly so if the Junior Debtors are closely involved with the Obligors e.g. they are project sponsors, or also equity.

- Cure right: the Junior Creditors may elect to 'fix' an Obligor Default, principally by making a cure payment to meet any shortfall. Normally this payment will rank junior or even lower than that.
- Call option: this is an option of the Junior Creditors to purchase (all of the) Senior Debt. So doing will de facto 'collapse' the subordination, but just as importantly it gives the Junior Creditors greater control of any default scenario e.g. to agree a restructuring/hold off acceleration.
- A reconfiguration of syndicate democracy. Despite the one unit of debt = one vote rule of the CFA, the ICA very often grants a particular tranche control. As the Junior Creditors will be most motivated to save a deal, while Senior Creditors can assume repayment come what may, the Junior Creditors will be given power to approve certain amendments and waivers i.e. restructure the terms of the CFA. However, once enforcement begins power will shift into the hands of the Senior Creditors, the Junior Creditors being assumed to be wiped out.

6.8 Is finance making a mockery of public policy?

The cases have not engaged in a detailed policy analysis of why debt subordination should be allowed in the face of the pari passu rule. Every court has affirmed *British Eagle*, but this has in a sense made things worse: faced with a House of Lords precedent, greater judicial effort is directed into distinguishing present facts from *British Eagle* than asking the question: in principle, is any arrangement other than pari passu distribution justified?

This said, we have seen at least two justifications subtending the cases:

(1) *The market justification:* these kinds of subordination are 'commonly found' (*Golden Key*) and serve legitimate commercial functions such that any decision to strike them down would have 'wide-reaching repercussions' (*in re Maxwell Comms* (1416F)).
(2) *The consent justification:* in the kinds of subordination only the parties who volunteer to be worse off are left worse off; no one is involuntarily deprived of the benefit of treatment pari passu (e.g. *Waterfall I*).

Both of these justifications would readily appeal to contract theorists. The first could be justified on the Humean grounds that the practice of debt subordination is conventionally regarded as socially beneficial (in the market) and so should be enforced not struck down. The second rests on the Hobbesian notion of personal liberty and the normative force of freely transferring one's power and right (to a pari passu distribution) to another in consideration of some benefit.

Our problem is that these justifications do not obviously speak from insolvency theory, only from contract theory. Is insolvency theory different? Would it agree with contract theory on these points, or propose different justifications with different results for contracting out? One might expect some difference, for insolvency theory should consider all creditors, not just parties to a given contract.

First, we need a conceptual framework to think about insolvency.[63] We can divide time up into the periods before insolvency and after insolvency as follows. This provides us with a timeline which has an **I**nitial state (a solvent borrower), one or more decision making **P**rocesses, and the **O**utcome of those processes. A Process may occur before (**ex ante**) it is discovered that there are not enough resources to go round (i.e. insolvency); or it may occur after (**ex post**) the discovery. This can be represented as follows:

$$\textit{Initial state} \gg \textit{Process}_{ex\ ante} \gg \textit{insolvency} \gg \textit{Process}_{ex\ post} \gg \textit{Outcome}$$

Insolvency theories may be usefully compared by mapping them onto this decision timeline, because they all advocate for the normative force of decisions about how to distribute assets by reference to the decision-making processes and when they occur.

One of the most influential insolvency theories is the creditors' bargain theory developed by Jackson and Baird.[64] In short, this theory asks us to consider a *hypothetical* contract the creditors would have made *before* insolvency occurred, in which contract they agree how to distribute the limited resources of the insolvent.[65] The general thought here is that once insolvency has occurred and in the absence of mandatory laws controlling creditor behaviour, the creditors will face a dilemma: on the one hand they could now, *ex post*, agree a consensual way of dividing up the insolvent's remaining assets, but on the other hand, it only takes one creditor to strike first and seize what it can for consensus to be impossible and every other creditor to lose out as a result. Far better, therefore, for the creditors to agree *before* insolvency, when they are not panicking and do not know if they could strike first, some consensual distribution of the assets should the borrower become insolvent.

63 This model builds on John R Danley, 'An Examination of the Fundamental Assumption of Hypothetical Process Arguments' (1978) 34 Philosophical Studies 187.

64 TH Jackson, 'Bankruptcy, Non-Bankruptcy Entitlements, and the Creditors' Bargain' (1982) 91 Yale LJ 862–63; DG Baird and TH Jackson, 'Corporate Reorganizations and the Treatment of Diverse Ownership Interests: A Comment on Adequate Protection of Secured Creditors in Bankruptcy' (1984) 72 UCLR 51; TH Jackson, *The Logic and Limits of Bankruptcy Law* (Harvard UP 1986).

65 For a modern critique, see Riz Mokal, 'The Creditors' Bargain and the Collectivity of the Liquidation Regime' in *Corporate Insolvency Law: Theory and Application* (Oxford 2005) ch 2; Ronald Davis and others, 'Principles and Theoretical Foundations of an Effective Financial Institution Resolution Regime' in *Financial Institutions in Distress* (OUP 2023) ch 7.

The creditors may not actually have agreed such a contract, but the creditors' bargain theory has a response to this: when a judge or legislator is considering how to distribute assets on insolvency, it should suppose the creditors did agree, ascertain what they would have agreed as a hypothesis based on efficient maximization of wealth, and distribute the assets accordingly. Doing so would maximize returns and garner *ex post* consent because it, at least, precludes individualistic behaviours which destroy value—it solves the 'common pool problem' of destruction of the common wealth by one person's selfish behaviour. Jackson writes:

> bankruptcy law at its core should be designed to keep individual actions against assets, taken to preserve the position of one investor or another, from interfering with the use of those assets favored by the investors as a group. . . . Bankruptcy law should change a substantive nonbankruptcy rule only when doing so preserves the value of assets for the group of investors holding rights in them. For this reason, bankruptcy law necessarily overrides the remedies of individual investors outside of bankruptcy, for those 'grab' rules undermine the very advantages sought in a collective proceeding. Changes in substantive rules unrelated to preserving assets for the collective good of the investor group, however, run counter to the goals of bankruptcy.[66]

Applying creditors' bargain theory to the case law around anti-deprivation and pari passu demonstrates some of its weakness. From what does the creditors' bargain theory derive its normative force? Why *ought* we to impose it on others, creditors, who might regard the individualistic 'grabs' for assets as perfectly justified in a free market system, perhaps on libertarian grounds?[67] Creditors' bargain theory attempts a sleight of hand common to all hypothetical contract theories: it derives its normativity from voluntariness—the consent inherent in lawful contracting—but is missing the key component, namely actual consent. As students of contract, you have encountered this situation many times in formation problems. We are trying to establish whether the parties consented to enter into legally binding relations, and we are careful not to bind people to agreements to which we are certain, objectively, that they did consent. Yet creditors' bargain theory is anything but careful, for it admits there is no actual contract and yet still asks us to pretend there is one, that all creditors consented to it, and to impose its terms upon them. If this were the general position of contract law, we would be in a very different world.

Consequent on pretending there is a contract follows trying to determine the terms of the contract. Again contract students will remember the discomfort of the judiciary in the face even of implying terms to make contracts work. Jackson et al. have no problems deciding which terms this creditors' bargain should have—the bargain should efficiently maximize the wealth of all creditors (perhaps by a pari passu distribution). Why, though, is *that* the bargain our creditors would have made? Why not another?

This is where we come to our cases: for in each of them, in fact, the key creditors *actually* made an *ex ante* bargain: some variation on a subordination agreement. The normative advantage of these actual contracts is that the creditors *actually* consented to them; actually did sit down and think about possible insolvency and came to just this bargain as to how to deal with the common pool problem in these circumstances. Through time and market practice, standard forms of subordination and particularly intercreditor agreement have developed to which creditors will agree (with appropriate) amendments. So we return to the original normative justifications for such contracts: the Hobbesian voluntariness argument and the Humean conventional social utility argument. Why should a judge

---

66 Jackson (n 64) 100–1.

67 E.g. due to a minarchist view that we should have basic rules around acquisition and protection of property, but no further state interference with what we do with our property: Robert Nozick, *Anarchy, State, Utopia* (Basic Books 1974).

or legislator, from an ex post position, cast aside an actual creditors' bargain and impose a purely hypothetical one?

The recent case law on structured finance does not explicitly consider these aspects of insolvency theory, but it turns out that it has the tools to respond to insolvency theory's most influential position on the distribution of assets. The case law can oppose the actual ex ante contractual process of a subordination agreement to the merely hypothetical ex ante contractual process of Jackson and Baird's creditors' bargain.

These two contractual theories by no means exhaust insolvency theoretic accounts of how one should distribute an insolvent's assets. A utilitarian, for example, might seek to develop a rule which if followed maximizes utility of all, and which is to be enforced ex post if it is not.[68] Such a rule could be none other than the pari passu rule, and, if a given subordination arrangement conflicts with it, a utilitarian would wish to see the pari passu rule enforced. A (later) Rawlsian process theorist may be concerned by pre-insolvency bargaining,[69] especially because it tends to exclude creditors who were in a weak initial position and who may never have been asked to contract (think unsecured creditors such as employees of the environment). Such a theorist may wish to introduce an ex post decision-making process which is fair just in virtue of its engagement of *all* creditors in some kind of creditor democracy—just the kind of process insolvency law does provide in the form of creditors' meetings in a creditors' voluntary administration or scheme of arrangement. In this instance the normative force comes from consensual voting and our intuitions around a democratic mandate. A Rawlsian may well be concerned that judges would prefer to enforce the private subordination contract of a subset of creditors over the will of all creditors expressed by vote in general meeting.

These wider insolvency policy considerations take us far beyond the private finance law concerns around contractual validity addressed in the cases. The judicial presumption is clearly in favour of freedom of contract and so the enforceability of structured finance techniques such as contractual subordination *unless* they intend to deprive other creditors of assets or work to place a contracting party ahead of other non-contracting creditors of otherwise equal rank in an insolvency distribution. You may wish to ask yourself, nevertheless, whether the balance between freedom of contract and public policy has been correctly struck.

---

68 See for example Nicolaes Tollenaar, 'Insolvency Law: Objective and Justification' in *Pre-Insolvency Proceedings: A Normative Foundation and Framework* (OUP 2019) 2.6.5.

69 Rawls' earlier position was much closer to a hypothetical contract theory, but seeing its flaws he moved to a pure process theory of what might now be regarded as stakeholder decision making. See John Rawls, *A Theory of Justice* (Harvard UP 1971); John Rawls, 'Justice as Fairness: Political Not Metaphysical' (1985) 14 Philosophy and Public Affairs 515.

Chapter 7

Leveraged buyouts

Chapter contents

DOI: 10.4324/9781003457220-7

7.1 Introduction

If you have studied contract law and company law, and have followed this book thus far, this chapter will present no legal principles which you have not encountered before. This is very much a chapter about application of a great number of those principles in a single transaction: the leveraged buyout (**LBO**). The LBO offers a great opportunity to see otherwise abstract principles in action, deployed by lawyers to produce remarkable results. Given everything going on in an LBO, it has been necessary to be selective. Our primary focus will be the use of (structural) subordination, the capital maintenance rules, and pre-emption rights. This chapter assumes you have studied some UK company law, though appreciates many company law courses avoid capital maintenance like the plague because it is hard to motivate in the lecture hall unless one is confident around advanced corporate finance; and the LBO is very advanced corporate finance.

The LBO is a transaction combining various legal techniques, and so we cannot look to the law to provide a founding definition. We need to describe in broad terms what an LBO does.

ESSENTIAL DEFINITION: LEVERAGED BUYOUT (LBO)

A **buyout** (or 'acquisition') is the acquisition of the entire issued share capital of a company (the **target**) by one or more persons who are either not members of the company or are only minority shareholders. If these persons happen to be the directors of the company, this is called a **management buyout** (**MBO**).

In any significant buyout, the consideration paid by the buyers of the shares will be financed:

(1) always by some equity[1] (and debt) investment from:
  (a) private equity; and
  (b) management, where this is an MBO;
(2) sometimes by debt investment from investment banks.

Where there is significant relative debt investment—we are talking a debt-to-equity ratio of 2x or even 3x—the buyout is called a **leveraged buyout**. In terms of the capital structure of the target, this would look something like 20–25% equity capital, 75–80% debt capital.[2]

Where the target's shares are listed on a public securities exchange, the transaction is sometimes called **bid finance** (though from a debt finance perspective 'LBO' is still used interchangeably with 'bid finance').

The ostensible goal of most buyouts is to improve the value of the target over five to seven years and then sell the business for a profit.

1 i.e. share investment.

2 Another indicator is the bid price paid to target EBITDA ratio, which in 2007–2008 was as high as 9.7x. What this means is it would take the company almost ten years at current earnings to generate the amount paid for its shares. The buyers are hoping it will as this money will ultimately be distributed to them. For an example of the pricing before the GFC, see *Cobden Investments Ltd. v The RWM Purchaser Ltd, Southern Counties Fresh Foods Ltd, Romford Wholesale Meats Ltd.* [2010] EWHC 3334 (Ch).

Going forward, we will take Leveraged Buyout to mean the leveraged acquisition of the entire issued share capital of a target company public listed on a (UK) regulated share exchange. The LBO therefore combines a number of legal practice areas:

- Mergers and acquisitions (M&A)
- The regulation of public securities exchanges
- Finance law.

In addition, there will be input from the tax lawyers, derivatives lawyers, and depending on the target business the employment team. LBOs have numerous moving parts and combine the most difficult, high-stress aspects of practice areas which are already known for their demanding nature and high-quality legal work.

There is one further feature of LBOs which is not obvious from the nomenclature. One's natural assumption is that it is the buyers who will be borrowing money to fund the purchase, even if through one or more SPVs. This would be correct *before* the acquisition. *After* the acquisition it is a different matter—the buyers have taken the view that the target will generate enough earnings to justify their investment, but rather than wait for dividends that would pay the buyers' debt, the buyers foist that debt onto the target. This creates one of the most controversial aspects of the LBO: the target company ends up footing the bill for the buyers' privilege of acquiring its shares.

If, after reading that, you feel something is amiss, you can congratulate yourself on having developed something essential to every lawyer: a nose which can smell if something is potentially 'off.' This does not mean something wrongful has occurred; it does mean you should investigate the matter legally to make sure nothing wrongful has occurred. A good chunk of this chapter will be focused on exploring the question of whether making the target foot the bill of its own acquisition is lawful (and if it is, justified in policy terms).

This chapter proceeds as follows. (1) In the next section we situate LBOs in the context of specialist finance generally. The idea is to set you thinking about how the standard financing to a corporate needs to be modified to take into account the economic risks posed by other kinds of financing. This helps us see why LBOs are particularly risky. (2) We the introduce our case study to motivate understanding: the leveraged buyout of Manchester United plc—yes, the football club. (3) In section 7.4, we examine the doctrine of capital maintenance which will have considerable bearing on LBOs, and (4) in section 7.5 we demonstrate how lenders used the doctrine to their advantage to subordinate junior debts in the Manchester United plc takeover. (5) In section 7.6, we examine the exceptions to the doctrine of capital maintenance and how these were used by Manchester United plc's defending management and hostile buyers in the battle for control.

It will prove necessary to pass over many other legal aspects of LBOs, or deal with them only in a cursory manner (particularly M&A and the regulation of public takeovers, for which specialist works can be consulted). Our main aim is to bridge the gap between foundational legal subjects and finance law in what may be corporate finance law's most exciting and demanding context. It is hoped the chapter will be particularly rewarding for students of company law and any corporate finance or M&A module.

7.2 LBOs as a form of specialist finance

Up to now, we have been largely focused on one particular kind of financing: the (secured) investment grade CFA entered into with a mid- to large-sized trading corporate. We have assumed typical corporate borrower: it is an established group which owns production facilities (a capital base), and which has relatively predictable income flows from the sale of its goods and creation of receivables. Importantly its value consists in the structuring of the various capitals that form its business into a production process. Yet can we use the same standard form of London-style credit facilities agreement when we are not lending to such a borrower? What if the borrower does not trade but simply exists to own capital assets? What if the borrower is an SPV that owns just one asset and leases it to another? What if the SPV exists solely to develop a project that is yet to exist? What if that project is the acquisition of a business that we know nothing about and which might never even happen?

The essential mechanics of the London form of credit agreement bear a lot of variation whilst remaining 'standard.' In what follows we survey some common specializations of the CFA. The idea is that by emphasizing how the CFA changes to accommodate these specifics you will further appreciate how risks vary, and the law is used to mitigate them. Here we are less interested in 'exogenous' risks—land could be eroded, a ship sunk, an LBO financer becoming insolvent—than the risks inherent in the deal itself. The core risk arises from the lender's ability to recoup the value into which it is lending. At one extreme, we might have a secured loan for 80% of the purchase price of gold bullion stored by the Bank of England. Here if the borrower fails to repay, the gold is likely to be worth something in the region of the value lent. At the other, somewhat absurdly, a bank lends money so that borrower can place a huge bet on a horse. In this case the money lent has been 'sold' to the bookmaker, while the borrower has no title whatsoever to the horse. The only value in the whole arrangement was the fool's hope the horse might win; the entire adventure was utterly risky.

Hyman Minsky,[3] following John Maynard Keynes,[4] developed a typology of three phases of investment which neatly illustrate these risks from a macroeconomic perspective. The explanations are tailored to a debt finance context.

- During a *hedging phase*, market participants are cautious about whether financial transactions will be successful.
  - Debtor borrows and Bank lends to finance the acquisition of a machine to be used in debtor's factory. The parties proceed on the basis that the capital invested in the machine will generate sufficient income to repay both interest and capital of the loan. At term, the loan is repaid, and debtor is now debt-free.
- During a *speculative phase*, market participants are confident in the financial markets and particularly that, should money be needed, it can be borrowed easily in in the market at a tolerable interest rate.
  - Debtor borrows and Bank lends to finance the acquisition of a machine to be used in debtor's factory. The parties proceed on the basis that the capital invested in the machine will generate sufficient income to pay interest on the loan *but not capital*. At term, debtor borrows new money and uses that to repay the existing loan, i.e. the debtor refinances its debt, remaining a debtor.
- During a *Ponzi phase*, market participants are overconfident in the financial markets, believing that assets prices will rise considerably. Here banks will lend to anyone purchasing assets because the assets will 'always' be worth more going forward. There is competition to lend into assets, and so interest rates fall. Borrowers are able to obtain cheap credit.
  - Debtor borrows and Bank lends to finance the acquisition of a machine to be used in debtor's factory. The debtor proceeds on the basis that the capital invested in the machine will *not* generate sufficient income either to pay interest or capital. The bank lends because it believes the machine will still increase in value over the term. To service the debt, the debtor borrows even more to pay interest and capital as they fall due, becoming overleveraged.

---

3 Hyman P Minsky, 'The Financial Instability Hypothesis' (1992) The Jerome Levy Economics Institute of Bard College Working Paper No. 74, 6–8 <https://papers.ssrn.com/sol3/papers.cfm?abstract_id=161024> accessed 31 July 2024.

4 Hyman P Minsky, *John Maynard Keynes* (first published 1975, McGraw-Hill Professional 2008).

> At some point—a so-called Minsky moment—confidence collapses and lenders demand repayment. Unable to borrow, debtors sell their assets at any price. The price of our machine collapses, leaving bank holding a non-performing loan backed by a worthless asset.

Our interest here is less in the financial bubble which inflates during the Ponzi phase, and more in the parties' attitude to risk insofar as driven by the current value of the asset financed (taking into account its income generating potential) versus the sums loaned. During the *Ponzi phase* that link all but becomes uncoupled.

In finance law terms the relative endogenous riskiness is primarily indicated by the financial covenants (which we examined in Chapter 2). Particularly relevant is the Loan-to-Value covenant (sometimes called leverage). To return to our asset finance example, the value of the gold is hopefully more than the loan given. We can assess the precise value by reference to the price of gold on the market. The value in the betting example is much less easy to quantify, although common sense tells us the bet is likely worthless. If we wanted to be precise we could ask a bookmaker about the probability of success and use that to calculate the value of the bet up until the race is decided. One thing we can be confident of is that the value must be low compared to the money lent, given the risks of losing it all.

The reason for labouring the horseracing example is that some financings are much closer to lending on hope that value will be created, as we shall see.

7.2.1 Asset finance

As the name suggests, asset finance is lending of capital for the purchase of some (moveable) asset. This asset is usually a single, extremely valuable tangible chose in possession which will depreciate in value as its income generating potential is extracted. Examples of such assets include:

(1) ships;
(2) aircraft;
(3) rail stock;
(4) plant.

The obvious way to finance an asset purchase is for Lender to lend the purchase price to Borrower, who then acquires the asset and grants security to Lender. To be certain of ring-fencing the asset, Borrower might set up a 100% subsidiary SPV the sole function of which is to own the asset. Lender would the take security over both the asset and shares in the SPV. This kind of plain vanilla financing is not common, however.

Much more common is one of the following:

(1) finance lease;
(2) operating lease; or
(3) off-balance sheet lease.

In these cases, an SPV is incorporated by a third party to acquire the asset and lease it to the ultimate user.

Notice that under a vanilla loan structure, the user becomes owner of the capital asset. The owner-user can set off asset depreciation against earnings, but the asset still appears on its balance sheet. Under the lease, the user is not the owner but expends rent. This expense may be deducted from earnings, thereby reducing taxable income, and the asset does not appear on the balance sheet.

ENRON

The balance sheet treatment of finance leases and the like is highly problematic. The collapse of Enron is closely linked to this idea: Enron wished to conceal excessive debt financing and did so by creating SPVs. In one such arrangement it used an SPV called Whitewing to acquire Enron stock (shares) in a rising market. The SPV then used this stock as collateral for loans which it used to buy Enron assets. Enron guaranteed these loans and continued to use the assets on a leased basis. The effect was that Enron appeared to have sold assets (apparently increasing revenues), but in fact had indirectly borrowed via Whitewing, and was still liable under a guarantee of Whitewing's borrowing. In accordance with accounting standards, that guarantee did not appear on the balance sheet.

The result: the ostensible cash appearing on Enron's balance sheet was secretly negated by a contingent liability to Whitewing's creditors.

When the asset prices fell so did the stock value, and Whitewing could not repay the loans. Enron's guarantee was called and Enron, without assets, was bankrupted.

In 2016 the FASB changed the rules on accounting for off-balance sheet finance leases to make them more transparent.

In aircraft financing, one common method is the standard Cayman SPV structure. In this structure a Cayman law firm sets up, via a trustee company, a Cayman SPV. The SPV is administered under an agreement with the trustee company and the trustee company grants a mortgage of shares in favour of the lenders. The lenders, on receipt of a parent comfort letter from the law firm and the meeting of other conditions precedent, lend to SPV which uses this sum to acquire an aircraft from manufacturer. The aircraft is registered and security is granted to the lenders. Insurance is also taken out. The aircraft is leased to the airline, with the rent matching the amortization schedule of the loan, i.e. the rent payable to the SPV is at least equal in amount and timing to the interest payable by the SPV to the bank.

If you have carefully studied the chapter on security, you should be able to see several risk mitigations afforded by this structuring. The asset is not owned by the user but by a third party located in a creditor-friendly jurisdiction, isolating the asset from the user's creditors (even from

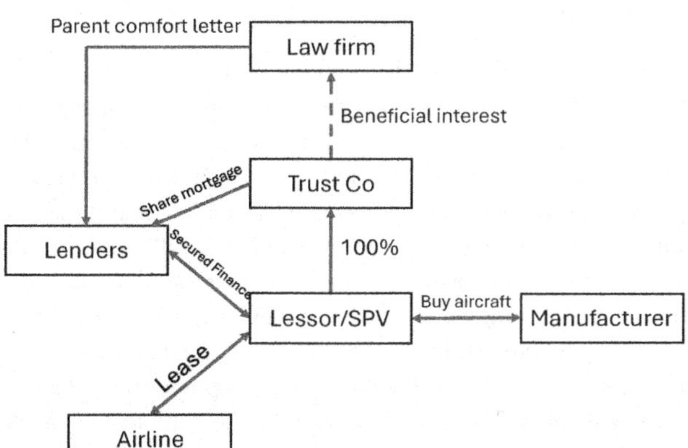

Figure 7.1 A typical aircraft financing structure

floating chargeholders). The SPV is standalone, so to speak, and through execution of the stock transfer form to perfect the mortgage and enforce, the lender can take control of the company and so both the aircraft and the receivables (the claim on the user for rent). This security is 'doubled' by a direct mortgage of the aircraft itself, registered on the appropriate aircraft register. Being set up solely to lease the aircraft in line with standard aviation industry practice, the SPV and aircraft are ready to be leased to a new airline. The entire value against which the lender is lending is kept ring-fenced, providing considerable risk mitigation. Destruction of the asset is mitigated by the insurance policy.

Of course, there are still risks. All tangible assets must be somewhere, but especially with aircraft and planes they tend not to be where they are registered but in other jurisdictions or international airspace/on the high seas. These risks raise important technical issues of public and private international law which go beyond the scope of this work (and indeed many asset finance departments, such matters tending to fall to (re)insurance and dispute resolution teams).

7.2.2 Real estate finance

Real estate finance is a special case of asset finance, with the added benefit of an immoveable asset. We have already encountered this kind of financing in our discussion of security. The structuring of real estate financing will depend on the ultimate purpose of acquisition: if the borrower will use the asset, we may well see an SPV incorporated to set up a sale and leaseback structure with its attendant accounting and tax benefits. If the borrower intends to lease to others, it will likely incorporate a subsidiary to hold the real estate and retain greater management control. Once again lenders prefer both security over the asset *and* security over the shares of an SPV which owns the asset, for enforcing share security is a swift paper exercise which also permits quick onward sale.

Real estate is both capital and a source of income as rent. As we saw with our discussion of taking security over receivables, control over a borrower-chargor's receivables requires careful drafting should the chargee be seeking a fixed charge which ranks prior to other creditors on insolvency. The reader is referred to Chapter 4 for details.

Real estate finance CFAs make use of financial covenants and maintenance undertakings tailored to the nature of the asset. Particular importance is placed on the Loan-to-Value covenant to ensure that the capital value of the land does not drop below an acceptable level relative to the debt incurred.

7.2.3 Project finance

In the previous examples of asset finance, the lender could be fairly happy that the money it had loaned was going directly into the acquisition (or refinancing) of a valuable asset. If anything goes wrong the lender has recourse to the asset/and or the SPV holding the asset. All things being equal, the margin payable on an asset financing should be relatively low compared, say, to a corporate financing. A trading corporate may well have some assets (land, plant and machinery, stock-in-trade), but a good proportion of its value consists in assets which are still be realized, either by producing goods or services, or by payment of debts from suppliers. Looking to the term of any corporate loan, the lender is thinking about the long-term economic performance of the borrower corporate—its ability not just earn so as to pay interest, but also to grow its capital base allowing it to repay the principal and reduce the loan-to-value. In short, lending to a corporate involves lending into a proposal for the future, into a business plan. The asset value is not there yet, but the business plan credibly sets out how it will be. The risk that the plan fails should mean margin is higher than for asset finance.

In project finance there are no existing assets; the financing is entirely focused on creation of assets and income streams in the future. Project finance lends to a *project*, typically a project to build infrastructure, develop a power generation facility, or extract natural resources such as oil and gas.[5] Risk, and therefore margin, on projects tends to be higher than an investment grade corporate loan, all things being equal, because of the following finance concerns:

(1) Apart from the finance capital, for a long time there will be little of capital value in the project company. Broadly speaking, the only asset will be intangible: the project itself as instantiated by obligations on various parties to perform certain tasks with a view to bringing the project to completion. These obligations as choses in action will be the only asset available to secure significant initial capital outlay.
(2) Likewise, the project will not produce income for some time, perhaps until it is completed. It therefore makes little sense to demand payment of interest—there is no income available to pay it.
(3) Worse, the initial outgoings of the project will be substantial. Cashflows will be negative for quite a period as concessions (licences) and materials are acquired, and contractors are paid, thus reducing the finance capital lent to the project company. There is a point in the lifetime of a project when a great deal of money has been spent, and cashflow is negative, but there is very little value to show for it.

In some respects, therefore, a project resembles a corporate start-up in that initial capital is spent attempting to develop a business proposition that will generate growth at some future date. Yet in the case of start-ups, we tend not to find advanced debt finance common to projects precisely because the risks are so great. Start-ups tend to be funded by equity investment and perhaps some development debt provided by private equity houses.

Projects financiers mitigate risks by the usual methods (security, guarantees, covenants), but in addition engage in novel techniques based around spreading risk and planning for the worst-case scenario. For example, in a typical project therefore we see a number of parties and agreements in

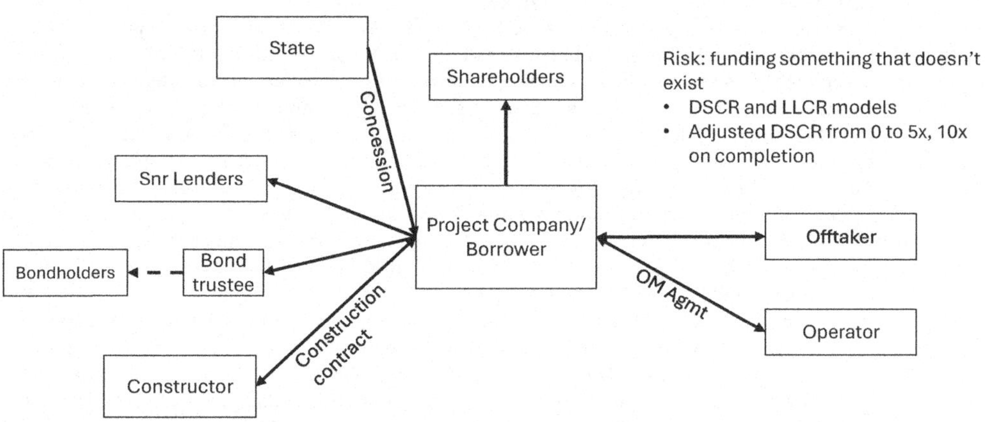

Figure 7.2 A typical project structure

play as indicated in the typical project finance structure illustrated below:

5 On extractivism as a concept, see Sylvia Federici, *Caliban and the Witch: Women, the Body and Primitive Accumulation* (Autonomedia 2014); for its application in projects context, see Jenny Lander, *Transnational Law and State Transformation: The Case of Extractive Development in Mongolia* (Routledge 2020).

By engaging multiple parties, the risk of failure is shared somewhat. This goes beyond syndication, for even as multiple banks will lend into a project, other project sponsors bear also bear risks. Often chief among them will be a public body:

(1) *The concession grantor:* this is commonly a (quasi-)public body which has both the rights and power to initiate and protect the project. Its interests may include revenue generation, economic development, or geopolitical advantage. It also may wash its hands of the concession or be the principal beneficiary of the completed project.
(2) The grantor will have a legal relationship with the project company through a concession agreement. The grantor may also be a shareholder/sponsor, operator, off-taker, and lender.

The other potential parties sharing the risk include:

(3) *Sponsors/shareholders:* not the government but the private parties interested in profit extraction via distributions and fees for construction/operating. They may well be the know-how behind the project and will looking not just for financial backing but risk sharing (risk minimization for them).
(4) The sponsors/shareholders will sometimes be expected to provide a form of limited guarantee to the lenders. The purpose here is not so much to seek payment from the guarantors but rather to create a subordinated debt obligation which is secured by the taking of a mortgage of the shares in the project company.
(5) *The concessionaire/project company:* in a way not dissimilar to acquisition and real estate finance it is critical that the object to be financed is placed in a corporate shell to ease enforcement against it on acceleration. Thus, the project will be held within an SPV: the project company.
(6) *The private lenders*: whereas the sponsors wish to make profit, the primary concern of the lenders is repayment, and this drives the very tight control over the SPV and its assets, both in terms of covenants and security.
(7) The private lenders will lend into the SPV which has the benefit of the project contracts, being the contracts containing promises to bring the projected result into existence. You can hopefully see why security over these promises is essential, for absent a concrete capital asset that can serve as security, the binding obligations to create such an asset are the next best thing. If the SPV defaults, the security taken over these choses in action—e.g. by equitable assignment of the benefit of the contracts—may be enforced and the Security Agent may swiftly take over the entirety of the project, ensuring no break in construction work. The definition of Secured Liabilities must be such as to capture all future assets of the project company. As in asset finance, the SPV also has the advantage that it separates the project from the sponsors and, through limited liability, limits recourse to them for liabilities arising from the project.[6]
    (a) *The contractor* i.e. the person which will be responsible for building the project, and thus risks failing to satisfy its contractual obligations. From a finance perspective, we have noted already that the finance parties will want security over the benefit of the contractual obligations of the contractor. As this is usually structured by means of an equitable assignment of the rights, notice of any assignment will be essential when the security is enforced through transfer of full legal title to the rights to the security agent. In fact, given the initially consensual nature of this multiparty transaction, the contractor will be fully aware that the equitable assignment is in place and should not be surprised, legally speaking, if the security agent now claims the benefit of the obligations. Yet in practice, this form of security has been deemed insufficient. In addition, the finance parties via the security agent and the contractor will enter into a **direct agreement**—a somewhat literal name for a contract which

6 Sponsors should be careful, however, to remember that the project is the SPV's 'business,' not their own, and contract accordingly. For a classic example of insuring the wrong person's loss, see *Macaura v Northern Assurance Co Ltd.* [1925] AC 619.

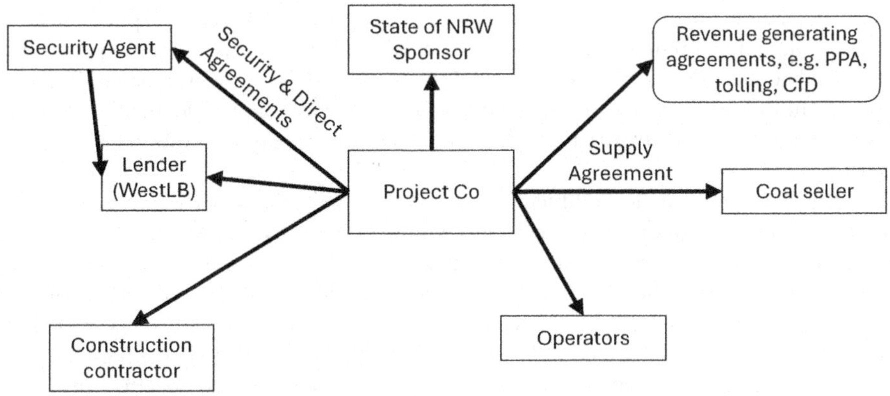

Figure 7.3 Simplified structure of the Trianel coal power station project

makes absolutely explicit that should the SPV and/or other obligors' default, the contractor will now take orders ('directions') from the security agent on behalf of the finance parties.

(b) The operator and the off-taker: these parties bear risk later down the line but the finance parties, grantor and sponsors will certainly want the operator (and where appropriate off-taker) ready to go. Their role makes sense through an example of a power production project, such the construction of the Trianel coal-fired power station in North-Rhein Westphalia, Germany (see Figure 7.3).[7] In this context the operator will manage the power station when it is built, and the off-taker will be available to purchase its product: electricity. If the constructor converts the projects plans and materials into a capital asset (the power station), the operator turns the capital asset into an income producing one. It may well be that the product (here, electricity) is sold on the open energy market on a 'merchant' basis, but the more common practice is for an obligated off-taker to be put in place to buy the product. For example, his could be via power-purchase agreement (**PPA**), where the off-taker effectively rents the power-generating sets of the power station to produce the electricity it requires, or via a 'tolling' agreement, where the off-taker supplies the raw material (coal) and pays for it to be turned into electricity.[8] Observe again that the finance parties will also wish to take security over the SPV's benefit of these contracts.

We have spent some time discussing how project finance spreads the risk between multiple parties because a similar multiplicity of parties arises LBOs. There are two further features of project finance which, while superficially particular to projects, also speak to LBO practice and so are worth covering in brief: A/B subordination between lenders and 'dynamic' financial covenants.

Our Trianel example was fairly simple in that the sponsor was the state of North-Rhein Westphalia, Germany, and the principal lender was that state's main public bank: West Landesbank ('WestLB'). Often, though, large development projects will see multiple lenders some of which will be Multilateral Agencies and development banks such as the European Bank for Restructuring and

7 Chosen because the author worked on it.

8 Many other possible arrangements exist. One pertinent one, which should be considered after studying the next chapter on derivatives, is a Contract for Differences arrangement where the SPV sells into the market its counterparty (a notional off-taker) pays or receives the difference between a pre-agreed price and the market price on the day. I.e. the counterparty pays SPV the shortfall if the market price is lower than the pre-agreed price; the SPV pays the counterparty if the price received from the market sale exceeds the pre-agreed price.

Development, European Investment Bank (**EIB**), or International Finance Corporation (to name just a few). These development banks expect seniority, i.e. if the SPV is unable to pay its debts as they fall due because of some delay or failure of the project, MLAs and development banks expect to be repaid in full first *before* the commercial lenders (and where applicable, bondholders) receive anything. This is achieved in part through an intercreditor agreement (ICA) such as we saw in Chapter 6.

The ICA in a project is more difficult to negotiate because the wider interests of the finance parties. MLAs and ECAs for example may be less willing to step-in to a failing project, and will seek a larger amount of debt subordination, including guarantees of breakage costs, enforcement costs and fees for cancellation. The ICA may contain conditionalities, such as the meeting of environmental requirements and coverage of a percentage of project costs. Stricter Events of Default may be put in place when defaults directly affect an MLA (e.g. any non-payment; any breach of 'special' CPs such as illegality, environmental issues). Finally, a threshold may be specified in the project guarantee coverage, below which the majority commercial lenders cease to control, and decision-making passes to the MLA alone.

The EIB operates financial covenants which determine when funds and/or guarantees are to be released. An **Adjusted Debt Service Covenant Ratio (ADSCR)** attempts to model the revenue generation of the project. Essentially, the ratio begins at 0 (because the project if anything will lose money initially) and as the project ramps up to operation it could rise to 5x to 10x debt service on completion of construction. This may trigger a first release of certain guarantees as the project moves into operation. Depending on whether operation will still require intensive capex or opex,[9] the ADSCR will continue to expand up to, say, 30 times at handback of the completed project, when the second release of guarantees will occur. This dynamic form of financial covenant is driven by the risks inherent in a project which on day 1 is merely in the minds of its architects, and it ratchets up as project milestones are met in reality. Although leveraged finance does not use the ADSCR specifically, one will find adjustable covenants in leveraged finance CFAs which may determine the drawdown of funds or the level of margin payable.

7.2.4 Leveraged buyouts

With this survey of specialist finance and its risk mitigation concerns and techniques in mind, let us return to the main subject of this chapter: LBOs. In this subsection, we consider LBOs in the abstract, before turning to our case study to flesh out some of the key legal principles at work.

Notice that LBOs share some of the risk profile of project finance: both transactions require debt capital to be invested to fund not a capital asset but simply a plan in the mind of its sponsors. In the case of the LBO, that plan is the acquisition of a target business. Yet LBOs also present additional risks:

(1) Projects are generally consensual, with all parties providing support to bring the project to fruition. In principle, one would expect risks from the project to arise exogenously (e.g. as political or environmental risks). LBOs can lack consensus. As its name suggests, a hostile takeover means that the directors of the target and/or a significant percentage of its shareholders are opposed to the acquisition. LBO lenders may be lending into a transaction which fails on day one because the takeover is fought off.

(2) Projects ought to have a fully informed vision of what is to be achieved. Again, the only unknowns should be exogenous and inherently unpredictable (e.g. war, market for electricity collapses). There is a certain leap of faith in a LBO, especially when hostile. The

9 Capital and operating expenditure.

sponsors will have done their homework on the target, but they will likely know no more than any other investment analyst; they will not know what the target's management knows. A great risk in an LBO is that the SPV set up to acquire the shares of the target (**Bidco**), buys 'a lemon.' That is, Bidco acquires a business which is not worth as much as it appeared to be from the outside.

All this comes back to the principal financial risk of the LBO in that the finance parties are lending considerable capital to an SPV which itself is worthless, all for the purposes of a takeover project which is inherently speculative. *LBOs are risky.*

Given the high level of risk, you might wonder why anyone would even suggest an LBO, and why in particular the subordinated creditors and shareholders involved—who could easily get wiped out—would be the instigators. The answer is a function of return on invested capital. Consider the following scenarios:

THE ECONOMIC ADVANTAGE OF AN LBO TO EQUITY INVESTORS

Targetco makes an annual profit of GBP10m. Its entire share capital can be acquired for GBP60m i.e. 6x annual profit. In Scenario (1) this acquisition is financed by GBP60m of equity. In Scenario (2) there is an LBO financed by GBP20m of equity and GBP40m of debt i.e. equity is one-third of invested capital.

Following the Venture Capital Method, let us imagine that after five years Targetco has grown by 10% compounding, such that its annual profit is GBP16m (i.e. 60% bigger). Assume also that Targetco's share can now be sold at 6x profit, so that investors receive GBP97m in consideration.

In (1) the shareholders thus receive 60% more back for each GBP1 they invested = GBP1.60.

In (2) the creditors are repaid their principal of GBP40m, leaving GBP57m for equity. The shareholders thus receive 185% more back for each GBP1 they invested = GBP2.85.

Now clearly the creditors did not lend for free; they would have received regular interest payments. Yet even with these payments (which are potentially tax deductible), and numerous other costs, LBOs is still more profitable than taking over a company with one's own capital. The problem is, the structure relies not only on the predicted growth actually occurring, but that it happens predictably such that the interest payment obligations each IPD are met.

The core structure of an LBO is set out in the following extremely simplified diagram. Do not worry, we will complicate things shortly. At its heart, an LBO involves equity and debt finance invested into a company (**Bidco**) incorporated for the principal purpose of bidding for and acquiring 100% of the issued share capital of a **target** company. The target may well be public listed on a regulated stock exchange, and so the takeover will involve convincing the directors of the target to recommend to the shareholders to accept to sell their shares to Bidco, failing which convincing sufficient shareholders to sell to gain effective control of the target. You may remember from company law that one of the magic numbers for control is 75% of the voting rights of the company, which allows one to pass a special resolution, but in fact Bidco is looking for more. If it acquires shares worth 90% of the whole bid's value and representing 90% of the voting rights, Bidco can expropriate the remaining 10% of shareholders.[10] This is called a **squeeze out**. Total control permits Bidco

10 s 979 Companies Act 2006. The 10% may, reciprocally, force the Bidco to acquire their shares—called a 'set-out.'

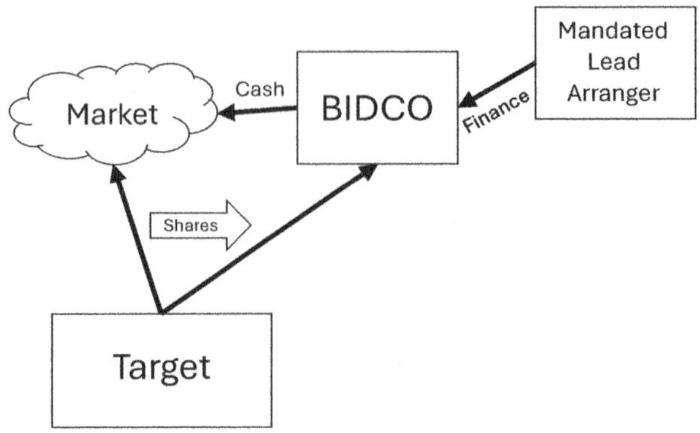

Figure 7.4 Highly simplified LBO structure

to restructure as the sponsors and finance parties see fit, including taking the target private (i.e. off the stock market, potentially reregistering as a private limited company).

Such is the basic structural idea. However, given the high risks of failure involved, the various capital providers (equity and debt) must mitigate that risk in some way. Starting from the position that the target is yet to be acquired, the principal mechanisms of mitigation must centre around the relationship between the capital providers among themselves. What this means is that some capital providers will mitigate their risk by subordinating others, just like in structured finance. These are then reinforced by mitigations should the takeover prove successful.

The first differentiation between capital providers is provided by company law itself: the difference between shareholders and creditors. We examine the legal technicalities of the difference later in this chapter. For now, just observe that as in project finance we have the sponsors and the debt financers injecting capital as equity and debt, respectively. Even in the basic LBO diagram we have this distinction. As we shall see later, simply as a function of company and insolvency law, the legal effect of incorporating a company and designating capital providers as shareholders and creditors respectively is that, on a winding up, the creditors must be paid in full first, before any capital is returned to shareholders. Result: the shareholder-sponsors are automatically subordinated to all the lenders into Bidco.

The second differentiation is between the lenders themselves. As in structured finance, different debt providers will have different risk appetites, being willing to risk losing more capital later in consideration of receiving more income (margin) now. In the language of LBOs, these differing lenders have special names:

(1) **Senior lenders**. This name is fairly self-explanatory: the senior lenders bear the least risk. The expect to be repaid first on default; in consideration they receive lower margin on the loan compared to junior lender.

(2) **Mezzanine lenders** (the 'mezz'). Literally, the lenders of middle rank, junior to the senior lenders, but still ranking prior to any shareholder loans put into the deal. When we looked at syndication and structured finance, the general practice was that all lenders were parties to the same loan agreement; it was only in the intercreditor agreement (**ICA**) that they were differentiated inter se as e.g. A Lenders and B Lenders. This is not the practice in LBOs. In buyouts two separate loan agreements are drafted, helpfully called the senior credit agreement and the mezzanine credit agreement. The debts created by these agreements are then regulated by an ICA. The reason for a distinct mezzanine credit agreement is that this contract is doing several things differently from the senior credit agreement. For example, the mezzanine credit agreement can provide for the conversion of the debt into equity, normally delays repayment after the senior debt is repaid, and critically from the senior lenders' perspective, it will be unsecured (we do not want out definition of 'Secured Liabilities' accidentally extending to the 'mezz debt.'

(3) **Second lien debt** (aka 'D' tranche debt). This is an import from New York practice, explaining the confusing name, and is not so common in Europe. Essentially, second lien lenders rank after senior lenders but before mezz lenders *and* are, as the US name suggests, also secured on a second-ranking basis. The ICA and security documents therefore need to ensure that both the contractual and security rankings reflect the priority of the senior lenders and posteriority of the mezz lenders. As it is less common, we will not discuss second lien debt further.

Appreciate that the actual capital structure of the bid may be more complicated even than this. The sponsors may, and often do, also inject shareholder loans into Topco. Where private equity is involved, they are likely also to have invested equity capital. In each case the debt capital will be subordinated by means of contractual agreements: named subordination agreements when the shareholders are being subordinated; called intercreditor agreements for other lenders.

The following diagram illustrates the corporate structuring for what was a Management Buyout of C Ltd. (it happened to be a truck company). Deutsche Bank were senior lenders; Rothschild mezz lenders. A venture capital (**VC**) firm provided equity capital (the shareholder-sponsors are not shown but would have sat alongside the VC firm as shareholders of Newco).

This MBO shares very similar, though simpler, structuring to that of an LBO. Deutsche and Rothschild lent under separate senior and mezz credit agreements, governed by an ICA inter se. Shareholder loans were covered by a subordination agreement. Notice also we have included a new company into the equation: Newco Ltd., which is the 100% shareholder of Bidco Ltd., its subsidiary. Deutsche as senior lends into Bidco; Rothschild as mezzanine lends into Newco. The effect of this is to replicate the relationship between the lenders and shareholder-sponsors: as between Deutsche and Newco, Newco is the shareholder of Bidco. As shareholder, Newco will only receive a return of capital when Deutsche is repaid what is owed by Bidco. Only when the capital is returned will Newco be able to repay Rothschild. This arrangement, to which we will return to in great detail, makes the subordination effected contractual by the ICA rock solid.

These corporate and finance structuring mechanisms are supported by a raft of further contractual techniques to mitigate the high risks, including:

(1) Ensuring Bidco (and related companies) are able to service debt given that before takeover they are empty shells. Ignoring the Target's economic capacity to repay the loans, we focus on the legal mechanism that connects Target EBITDA to Bidco debt service. The two principal mechanisms are:
    (a) Intercompany loans from Target to Bidco. These create issues of financial assistance and tax (see below), and of corporate benefit (ss 39, 172 CA 2006).

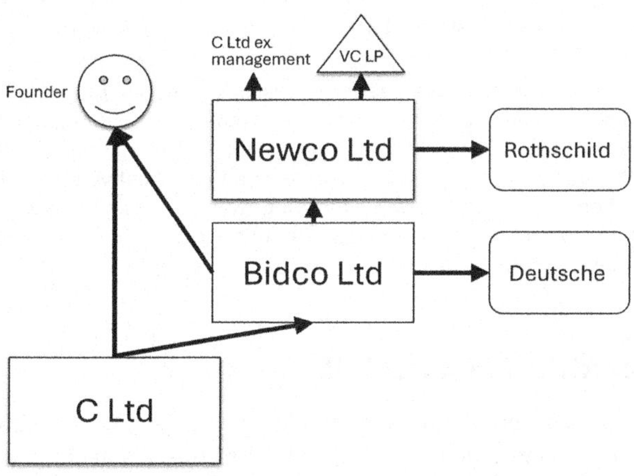

Figure 7.5 Corporate structure of an MBO

(b) Dividends. Apart from financial assistance and tax issues (see below), dividends must be declared in accordance with s 830ff CA 2006. We thus need to ensure that distributions are reliable and match the repayment dates under the Finance Documents.

(2) Ensuring cost/tax efficiency: debt service comes entirely from Target's cash flow, but how is that cash actually flowing to Bidco? Either as dividends or as repayments of loans from Bidco to Target. Interest is deductible before tax; dividends are payable from earnings after interest, tax, depreciation, and amortization, i.e. from profits. To reduce this effect, on acquisition an LBO may provide for a **debt push-down**. Essentially, the existing Senior CFA with Bidco is replaced with a facility from the Senior Lenders to the Target directly (by way of novation of the senior credit agreement).
   (a) The debt-push down creates several technical problems:
      (i) intra-day exposures.
      (ii) withholding tax liabilities. The latter issue relates to thin-capitalization rules: where a corporate is thinly capitalized the providers of debt may be deemed 'shadow' providers of equity, with the result that repayment of loans is a deemed dividend, subject to a withholding tax (see, e.g., Switzerland).
      (iii) financial assistance—a special topic in LBOs discussed separately below.

(3) Ensuring the senior lenders are able to access security/assets. Apart from the practical issues of identifying suitable assets to secure before one has taken over the target, corporate benefit, thin capitalization, and financial assistance may intervene to undo security granted. For example, a guarantee or security granted by a German subsidiary of the Target group may be voided. These concerns also speak in favour of a debt push-down which lends directly to this subsidiary.

(4) Maximizing ability to enforce on default, even and especially if the takeover fails. In terms of structuring, we need to consider the following:
   (a) Maximizing enforcement options over assets and particularly shares.
   (b) Use of a 'golden share pledge' (again the nomenclature is unhelpful) which forces redemption of equity by return of capital at a specified time; or
   (c) Being able to cut off the Mezz and equity by enforcing security over shares (but also ensuring upstream security and guarantees to the Mezz are released—pre-agreed in the ICA).

(5) Planning for exit: sale or IPO? A plan for exit will also affect the degree of integration of the SPV structure and the Target (debt pushdowns).

The nature of an LBO as a potentially hostile takeover of a corporate means that a huge amount of planning must be done to ensure that when D-Day—the takeover day—arrives, funds are ready to pay the acquisition price. Banks do not give GBP10s of millions to thinly capitalized SPVs on the off chance they *might* acquire some value. To minimize lender risk, the time between lending and acquisition must be the smallest possible. This determines the legal timing of an LBO.

(1) *Commitment/underwriting letter/term sheet*—in the initial planning stage the **mandated lead arranger** will be approached to arrange and underwrite financing on indicative terms and subject to specified conditions being satisfied. The mandated lead arranger will then pull together the syndicate of lenders based on the indicative term sheet.
   (a) The borrower countersigns, agreeing to pay fees and expenses, provide support, and to indemnify the arrangers. The letter may contain exclusivity and market flex clauses, like the following.

EXAMPLE MARKET FLEX CLAUSE

[6.1] During the period from the date of [this letter/the Term Sheet] to the date, following close of primary syndication, on which all the Lenders subject to such syndication become party to the Facility Documents, any Mandated Lead Arranger or Underwriter shall be entitled after consultation with the [(other)] Mandated Lead Arranger(s) and (other) Underwriter(s) [and the Company] [for a maximum period of [x] days] to change the pricing, terms and/or structure [(but not the total amount)] of the Facility/ies if that Mandated Lead Arranger or Underwriter determines that such changes are advisable in order to enhance the prospects of a successful syndication of the Facility/ies.

The Company agrees to, and shall ensure that each other Obligor shall, amend the Facility Documents to reflect any changes made under paragraph [6.1].

For the purposes of this paragraph [6], 'successful syndication' means the Underwriters each reduce their participation in the Facility/ies to a final hold of not more than [x].

The term sheet itself can be simple or quite detailed. Before the GFC, the boom became so intense that banks would **fund term sheets**—they couldn't wait for proper facility documentation. However, detail could well be required to convince the vendor-shareholders that the bid is serious.

(2) Mezzanine and Senior CFAs—although these CFAs are in the London Form, they are much more restrictive thanks to the high risk involved. Notable additional features include:
  (a) Mandatory prepayments on change of control (the Target is acquired by a third party), or on claims under the acquisition documents or engagement letters with report providers.
  (b) Heavy financial covenants, which are built to require the borrower to reduce leverage over the term and to not make capital expenditure.
  (c) A margin ratchet to follow changes in risk and/or financial covenants which model or track the expected EBITDA of the target.

These clauses are related to the dynamic financial covenants we saw in project finance in that the obligations under the CFAs vary as real-world events vary.

(3) **Certain funds** provisions. These are required under r 2.7(a) Takeover Code for public bids. Essentially the provision suspends the effect of many types of default (particularly draw-stop) for a specified certain funds period. Major defaults (e.g. non-payment) override this.

Supporting the CFAs, ICAs, shareholder subordination agreements, guarantees, and security documentation, as discussed above, will be prepared.

(4) Conditions Precedent (**CPs**) are doubly crucial—the lenders need to be sure everything is in place before binding themselves to provide certain funds for a takeover that may still fail. Thus, after the bid is accepted but before completion (and so funding), CPs beyond evidence that the equity and subordinated debt is in place revolve around provision of reports, a model, a business plan, a structure memo, a funds flow model, acquisition documents, accession deeds, and evidence that the Target group is free of all financial indebtedness not permitted under the CFAs.

If the takeover provers successful, post-closing matters include:

- New CFAs directly with the target to help it with day-to-day operations e.g. an RCF for working capital, an overdraft, a currency exchange facility. These are necessary because the **change of control** instituted by the takeover will almost always constitute a trigger event under the target's existing credit facilities agreement. In all likelihood, a change of control will have triggered a mandatory prepayment of all loans under the CFA, rendering immediately refinancing critical.
- Syndication documentation, such as transfer certifications, for lenders joining after the takeover is successful.
- Putting in place and registering the planned target security.
- Hedging to cover interest rate and currency fluctuations (see Chapter 8).

- Corporate and listing documentation, including resolutions, which will to work replace the board, terminate listing of the target's shares and ultimately take the company private, possibly re-registering as a private limited company.
- Finding out what Bidco has just bought, and if necessary, restructuring the target e.g. via a scheme of arrangement.[11]

There is much more that can be said about the intricacies of LBOs and the variety of market practices in the area which, especially in a boom, can stretch legal principles beyond what can be borne (see term sheet funding, above).[12] At this stage you just need to have a sense of what an LBO is trying to achieve (and acquisition), the kinds of risks the LBO presents compared to other specialist finance, and the key parties involved in an LBO. Some of the buyout's contractual features are not new to you—the basic structure of a CFA and the structuring of the finance in terms of contractual subordination has already been covered in earlier chapters. What is new is the use of company law to achieve structural subordination. To put flesh on the bones of LBOs and to build to utilise an achievable bridge from your studies of company, we are now going to focus on why, legally, this structural subordination works in the context of a case study.

7.3 Case study introduction: Manchester United plc

Manchester United Football Club is an English football club based in Old Trafford, Greater Manchester. The club was formed as Newton Heath LYR Football Club, the works team of the Lancashire and Yorkshire Railway depot in Newton Heath, in 1878. The club split from the railway company in 1892 and remained under private share ownership for almost 100 years, changing its name to Manchester United after being saved from insolvency in 1902.

The club was the subject of takeover bids from media tycoon Robert Maxwell in 1984 and property trader Michael Knighton in 1989, before going public in 1991 as Manchester United plc. Manchester United's shareholders received another takeover bid from Rupert Murdoch's BSkyB corporation in 1998 before Malcolm Glazer's stake was announced in September 2003.

In policy terms, and following Singer, we might classify the investors as property holders of the following kinds:[13]

(1) Loyal fans of the club, whose shareholding is often minimal, but who regard that share as unique i.e. a Manchester United fan would not swap one Manchester United share for one or even many Manchester City shares.

The shareholders regard their property as having value because it is subjectively useful to them. Like the proverbial 'Englishman's castle,' interference with the property's use should be prohibited in any case.

(2) Of institutional investors, who regard one Manchester United share as an investment perfectly substitutable with one Manchester City share, subject to a financial calculation.

These shareholders take a pure 'investment' view, seeing through what the share uniquely represents to its exchange value, determined 'objectively' by the market.

(3) Of investors who value control—they are less concerned with which club they invest in provided that they are able to dominate that club. Once so heavily invested they will not easily give up their control.

---

11 Parts 26 and 26A Companies Act 2006.

12 Shane McDonald and others, 'Recent Trends in Leveraged Financing: The Ever More Borrower Friendly Market' (2022) 7 JIBFL 489.

13 JW Singer, 'The Ownership Society and Takings of Property: Castles, Investments, and Just Obligations' (2006) 30 The Harvard Environmental Law Review 309.

The shares do have a use value, however: control. Twenty-nine percent of Manchester United shares does not aggregate with 1% of Manchester City shares; only Manchester United shares are needed for the immediate purpose of monopolizing Manchester United.

Keep in mind these constituencies as we work through how Malcolm Glazer and his brother managed to take over Manchester United plc. Ask yourself: does the law deployed in an LBO balance these interests justly?

To continue our overview: by the end of 2003, Glazer had increased his shareholding from 3.17% to around 15%, which he almost doubled in the year up to October 2004. His acquisition of John Magnier and JP McManus' 28.7% stake in May 2005 pushed his own up to around 57%, well over the 30% threshold that would force him to launch a takeover bid under what is now the Takeover Code. A few days later, he took control of 75% of the club's shares, allowing him to delist the company from the stock exchange, and within a month, the Glazers took 98% ownership of the club via their Red Football parent company, forcing a squeeze-out of the remaining 2%. The final purchase price of the club totalled almost GBP800 million.

Our question now is, how, legally, was this achieved? You will not be surprised to learn that a leveraged buyout was involved. Yet how did the Glazers convince lenders to fund the LBO of a football club?

7.4 Debt versus equity—capital maintenance

Although the Glazers likely did not realize it, the company law doctrine of capital maintenance played a critical role in the legal structuring of the Manchester United plc buyout. Let us work through the doctrine again, though we are going to put a modern spin on it.

The company law doctrine that capital must be maintained is usually stated by accountants as follows.

TRADITIONAL FORMULATION OF CAPITAL MAINTENANCE DOCTRINE

The capital of a company at the end of an accounting period should be equal to or more than the capital of that company at the beginning of that accounting period.

The merit of this formulation is that tells you what a company should do with its capital, but the shortcoming is that it fails to tell you why that should be the case, especially in the modern world. Therefore, let us reframe the doctrine of capital maintenance as the 'Fundamental Norm of Corporate Finance.'

ESSENTIAL: THE FUNDAMENTAL NORM OF CORPORATE FINANCE

On a return of capital, debt must be repaid before equity (shares).

The traditional justification for the doctrine should be fairly apparent: capital maintenance is about protecting creditors because it maintains a reserve of capital to meet their claims:

(1) Voluntary creditors, because they are deemed to have notice of the stated share capital of the company in the Register, and thus are entitled to expect that the company will indeed have available that capital to meet claims on insolvency.
(2) Involuntary creditors, for here the capital operates as a kind of public insurance fund against corporate externalities.

Yet in a world of limited liability companies with minimum capital of GBP1, this 'insurance fund' approach is a little misleading. Even when the company is public, a minimum capital of GBP50,000 will not even pay the liquidator's fees let alone meet creditor claims. Even if this was the nineteenth-century justification given in the cases, it seems an irrelevance now. As John Armour has observed, the modern capital maintenance doctrine is not as prohibitive as the traditional formulation makes out. Rather than ban returns of capital to shareholders, the better framing, and one which reflects the modern law, is that returns of capital to shareholders are permitted in certain restricted circumstances. My personal view is that after the Companies Act 2006, which is quite permissive on capital maintenance, we can go as far as the formulation of the FNCF, for it expresses the reality. Of course, capital can be returned to shareholders, it is just that they cannot have it until all other claims on the company's capital have been met. Why? Because built into company and insolvency law is a basic structural subordination: creditors rank senior to shareholders:

STRUCTURAL SUBORDINATION IN THE INSOLVENCY ACT 1986[14]

S.107 Distribution of company's property. [solvent company]

Subject to the provisions of this Act as to preferential payments, the company's property in a voluntary winding up shall on the winding up be applied in satisfaction of the company's liabilities pari passu and, subject to that application, shall (unless the articles otherwise provide) be distributed among the members according to their rights and interests in the company.

S.143 General functions in winding up by the court. [insolvent company]

(1) The functions of the liquidator of a company which is being wound up by the court are to secure that the assets of the company are got in, realised and distributed to the company's creditors and, if there is a surplus, to the persons entitled to it.

As John Armour rightly notes in his discussion of capital maintenance, it is as if the legislature has taken a contractual term from a subordination agreement whereby shareholders consent to subordinate their claims on capital to those of lenders, and made it a mandatory term implied by law.[15] And just like contractual subordination, Armour continues, there are provisions permitting junior investors to receive capital earlier in certain defined and limited circumstances. These limited permissions on distribution we also find in the Companies Acts. For example, just as junior creditors are likely to receive the benefit of increased income (interest) should a company perform well, so shareholders will be permitted to receive income as a distribution of dividends from profits. Other rights, such as the junior investor's rights to

14 Do note that these sections of the Insolvency Act were previously included in the Companies Acts.

15 John Armour, 'Share Capital and Creditor Protection: Efficient Rules for a Modern Company Law' (2000) 63 MLR 355. Note this article was written prospectively of the Companies Act 2006.

control the company, likewise read across from subordination between lenders to the basic subordination of shareholders in statute.

In essence the FNCF is trying to capture just what is important about the capital maintenance rule today: it provides for a statutorily backed subordination; it is not a moral prohibition on any distribution ever. Any given provider of GBP1 of capital is much the same as another, until one provider is classed as a provider of equity capital, the other as a provider of debt capital. The FNCF is, to labour the point, an implied intercreditor agreement in every corporate financing.

This is where our discussion of company law leads back to LBOs and structural subordination. The parties to the LBO proceed on the basis that what we are calling the FNCF will hold because it is stated in statute, and therefore this is virtually zero recharacterization risk compared to the contractual and trust-based subordinations we have examined. If one investor is a shareholder relative to another creditor, that creditor can be assured of their seniority—of their right to receive capital first—subject to the exceptions provided for in law. The LBO of Manchester United plc provides ample opportunity to examine the FNCF and the exceptions to the capital maintenance doctrine in practice.

7.5 Manchester United: structural subordination

To acquire all the shares of Manchester United plc, the Glazers incorporated a number of companies for the purposes of achieving structural subordination of the debt: Red Football JV Ltd. (RFJV), the 100% subsidiary of Red Football Shareholder Ltd. (RFSh), which in turn was the 100% subsidiary of Red Football Holding Ltd, as shown below. The Glazers were the only shareholders of the ultimate parent, Red Football Holding Ltd. The connected 'RF' companies and their creditors are the pre-LBO structure the Glazers had created.

This structure, common to LBOs, was developed to take advantage of the FNCF, i.e. of the statutory subordination of debt to equity. Let us step back and work through some simple examples to illustrate how this subordination works.

First, let's consider the solvent winding up of a company, the capital of which is constituted of debt and equity. How would the assets be distributed on the winding up?

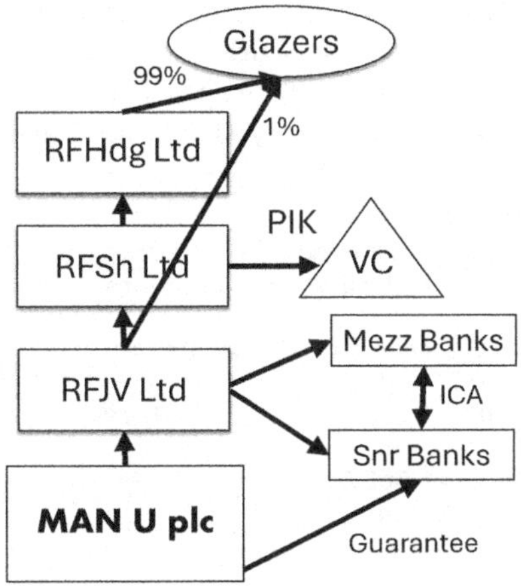

Figure 7.6 Structural subordination in the Manchester United LBO (post-acquisition)

STRUCTURAL SUBORDINATION CASE 1: WINDING UP A SOLVENT COMPANY

Zeno Limited has share cap 1m fully paid up £1 ordinary shares, of which the four members own one-quarter of the shares each. The balance sheet states it has £1.25m assets (land and stock) and a £200k debt owing to Deutsche Bank. The members resolve to effect a members' voluntary liquidation. They cause Zeno Ltd. to:

(i) realize the assets;
(ii) repay Deutsche £1.25*m* - £200*k* = £1.05*m*;
(iii) declare and distribute a final dividend of £50k, or 5p/share;
(iv) return the capital to shareholders ($\frac{£1m}{4} = £250{,}000$ to each member under s 107 IA 1986).

Zeno Ltd. is then dissolved (ceases to be as a legal person).

Notice the **waterfall** operating at the heart of this winding up. *Only* when the creditors are paid in full will whatever remains be distributed to the shareholders of the company. Compare it with the contractual waterfalls put in place in structured finance, or even the rent account waterfall and sweep we saw when discussing fixed charges of receivables. The same logic is at work here in company law (arguably, it originates here).

You might be unimpressed by Case 1. After all, every investor saw their capital returned. We could have paid everyone back in any order and it would have made no economic difference, though to do so would have breached the rules on capital maintenance. Yet it really matters, most of all when there is not enough money to go around.

STRUCTURAL SUBORDINATION CASE 2: WINDING UP AN INSOLVENT SOLVENT COMPANY

Diogenes Limited has share cap 1m fully paid up £1 ordinary shares, of which the four members own one-quarter each. The balance sheet states it has £1.3m assets (land and stock) and a £1.5m unsecured debt owing as follows: (1) £850k to Deutsche Bank; and (2) 650k to 'Supplier.' Neither creditor is secured.

Diogenes Ltd. defaults on its loan. Satisfied the company is unable to pay its debts as they fall due,[16] the court orders a compulsory winding up. The liquidator:

(i) gets in and realizes the assets;
(ii) pays £50k liquidation expenses;
(iii) repays the equal ranked unsecured creditors on a *pari passu* basis—for every £1 debt owned by a creditor, the creditor receives $\frac{£1.25m}{£1.5m} = 83\frac{1}{3}p$. Thus (a) Deutsche recoups $83\frac{1}{3}p \times £850k = £708{,}333.33$; and (b) Supplier recoups $83\frac{1}{3}p \times £650k = £541{,}666.67$.

16 s 123(1)(e) Insolvency Act 1986.

(iv) The creditors having used up all the assets, nothing remains for lower ranked creditors and nothing is returned to shareholders (they lose their entire investment).

Diogenes Limited is then dissolved.

The key thing to notice with Case 2 is the criticality of the doctrine of capital maintenance when formulated as the FNCF. Only when the creditors are paid in full can capital be returned to shareholders. Here the creditors could not be paid in full, so the shareholders received nothing. In finance terms, the shareholders are subordinated.

Let us look at one further example which sits in-between the last two because the shareholders do at least get something. In this case we also emphasize the role of limited liability. You will remember that limited liability means the members of a company (here shareholders) need only contribute a pre-agreed determinate amount to the capital of the company on a winding up. If, for example, shareholder acquired a GBP1 ordinary share (nominal value), that shareholder is liable to pay GBP1 to the company *and no more*. In finance terms, this means that the equity investor, like the debt investor, only ever risks the capital they provide to the company.

STRUCTURAL SUBORDINATION CASE 3: WINDING UP AN INSOLVENT SOLVENT COMPANY, PARTIALLY CAPITALIZED

Chrysippus Limited has share cap 1m £1 ordinary shares, four members owning one-quarter each. All shares are partly paid, 50p each (i.e. the shareholders still owe 50p on each share they own). The balance sheet states it has £750k assets (land and stock) and an unsecured £850k debt owing to Deutsche Bank.

The court is satisfied the company is balance sheet insolvent orders a compulsory winding up.[17] The liquidator:

(i) gets in and realizes the assets;
(ii) determines that debts exceed liabilities to the tune of £750*k* – £850*m* = –£100*k*;
(iii) calls for contributions on the unpaid shares, technically the whole sum then due (£500k) and no more;
(iv) pays liquidation expenses of £50k;
(v) repays Deutsche leaving [(*assets* £750*k* + *call* £500*k*) – £50*k*] – £850*k* = £350*k*;
(vi) returns the surplus to the members, such that each shareholder recoups $\frac{£350k}{£1m} = 35p$ for every £1 share.

Chrysippus Limited is then dissolved.

Once again, the statutory waterfall kicks in to subordinate shareholders *until* creditors are repaid in full. A useful analogy here is a pyramid of champagne glasses. Each tier of glasses in the pyramid represents a set of equally ranked capital providers, the most senior being at the apex of

17 s 123(2) Insolvency Act 1986. Winding up due to balance sheet insolvency is much less common in the UK (and New York) than in other jurisdictions, the general view being that as long as creditors are paid when debts fall due, the company is to be given time to trade itself out of balance sheet insolvency.

the pyramid. The liquidator gets in the assets, turns them into cash (champagne) and starts pouring from above. Only when the highest row of glasses is full does the surplus champagne overflow and start filling the next highest row, and so on. When the champagne runs out, the glasses of whichever rank we have reached stop filling and the glasses on the ranks below get nothing.

This subordination applies to every UK company by statute, and only in extremely unusual circumstances (fraud) would a court deviate from its strict application. What is different about structural subordination in the LBO context is that this it is being used deliberately to achieve results the parties would otherwise have achieved by contract.

Study again the diagram of the Manchester United plc LBO corporate structure, now paying attention both to the identity of the shareholders of each 'Red Football' company (in orange) and the parties on the right who provided debt finance. The senior and mezzanine lenders all lent into the same company; their respective subordination was achieved contractually, so let us just treat these two lenders as one (senior lenders) for our present purposes. We need to focus on the Venture Capital funds ('VC' i.e. private equity) which is lending into RFSh Ltd., for relative to the senior lenders, VC is structurally subordinated. Let us explain how.

CASE STUDY: STRUCTURAL SUBORDINATION OF VC's DEBT

RFJV Ltd. (aka Bidco) is the 100% direct subsidiary of RFSH Ltd. The only assets of RFJV will be the shares of Manchester United plc (when acquired), and the cash to be lent by the senior lenders. RFJV also has the corresponding liability to these senior lenders. The only assets of RFSh are the shares of RFJV, acquired using the cash lent by VC. It has the corresponding liability to VC.

Suppose we now wind up RFJV and RFSh.

Winding up RFJV, we apply the FNCF: on realizing any assets (e.g. selling the Manchester United plc shares, if acquired), the fund is distributed:

First, to RFJV's creditors, the senior lenders, until they are repaid in full; and
Second, if anything remains, this capital is returned to RFJV's sole shareholder: VC.

We now wind up RFSh: at this point RFSh's only asset is the capital returned on winding up RFJV. This fund is distributed:

First, to RFSh's creditor, VC, until it is repaid in full; and
Second, if anything remains, this capital is returned to RFSh's sole shareholder, RFHdg Ltd.

Try and work out for yourself what happens if we now wind up RFHdg Ltd.

Through this structural subordination it will be clear to the adequately advised VC lender that it is taking considerably more capital risk than the senior lenders. If Manchester United plc turns out to be worth as much as the various LBO funders put into this transaction, everyone will see a return of all their capital on a D-Day + 1 winding up. If Manchester United plc is worth less, on a winding up its value always goes first to repaying the senior lenders. Only when repaid in full will any remainder go to the VC lenders. This can helpfully be looked at from the converse perspective, in which we work out how a distribution of capital would play out and focus on who *loses* capital. By the FNCF the shareholders always *lose* capital before creditors. Applying this to the Red Football LBO structure, we can say for example that the VC lenders will *lose* capital before the senior lenders, and only when the VC lenders have lost all their capital will the senior lenders start losing their respective capital.

AN ASIDE: PIK DEBT

In our case study, private equity (VC) lent money to RFSh. This debt illustrates a controversial feature of LBOs, because it took the form of PIK debt.

PIK (Payment In Kind) debt is compounding debt. It is compounding because PIK means that when one pays for the delivery of some commodity, one pays using that commodity. If seller delivers debt, buyer pays with . . . debt. What this means is that when interest falls due on PIK debt, the borrower does not pay cash; rather it adds the amount owed as interest to the principal debt. The principal debt increases and the amount if interest payable next time also increases. This is called compounding. Observe that the interest payments will grow exponentially because the principal is always increasing by ever larger amounts. PIK debt feels usurious, even if not legally so.

The particular concern in LBOs is that PIK debt is created internally to the LBO structure; the same humans offering and accepting a PIK loan contract in a way which stretches the boundaries of an 'arm's-length' transaction. This is bad enough, but as we shall see later, once the target is acquired, the target can be made liable for the PIK debt e.g. by way guarantee. The Bidco can do this because it now controls the target. Yet the target would surely never have agreed to exponentially growing debt had it freely and independently considered such a transaction for its own corporate benefit.

This issue raises further capital maintenance issues to be explored in the following sections.

Where a junior lender starts losing capital (having regard to a hypothetical winding up), it is common to speak of the junior lender being **under water**. The image here, which somewhat contradicts the champagne example, is of water rising to harm the shareholders, then junior lenders who stand on their shoulders, then the senior lenders. Here each rank is only harmed when the rank below is completely under water. When a creditor is completely under water, this is called being **wiped out**. Under an LBO intercreditor agreement, being under water may trigger certain junior creditor rights such as the option to take control of the LBO or target, or to make payment to cure any default that could trigger insolvency proceedings. The intercreditor agreement will also in all likelihood provide that these rights are cancelled when the junior creditor is under water, for now the capital of the next more senior creditor is at risk and they may now exercise cure rights and so forth.

The FNCF—that capital must be returned to creditors before it is returned to shareholders—is designed to express the reality of the modern approach to the capital maintenance doctrine as exemplified in the corporate structuring of LBOs. Capital maintenance is not a prohibition on equity ever seeing a return of its capital, but a mandatory capital-provider ranking mechanism implied by law. Of course, shareholders may receive back their capital, but they must accept their structural subordination to creditors before they do.

The company law of capital maintenance has more to say on the matter. Just as in intercreditor agreements, junior creditors benefit from certain exceptions to the general subordination (control rights, right to interest), so shareholders can exert control until insolvency is upon the company, and receive capital back in certain restricted cases, such as from profits. These limited exceptions to the capital maintenance doctrine (or FNCF, if you prefer) also played an important role in the Manchester United plc LBO. We examine these in the remaining part of this chapter.

7.6 Permitted exceptions to the fundamental norm

It is a recurrent theme of the Companies Act 2006 that many things may be prohibited—the return of capital to shareholders—but there is usually a procedure which allows the prohibited thing to take place in restricted circumstances. This is not a cynical ploy: modern company law places considerable emphasis procedural transparency. Rather than guess the infinitely many situations in which a share transaction should or should not be allowed, company law requires the company and related parties to follow a procedure which publicizes the proposed act, and then allows interested parties to vote for/object to the proposal (if appropriate, in court).

In the context of capital maintenance, the doctrine of capital maintenance is the prohibition, but there are several share transactions which are allowed if a procedure prescribed in the Companies Act 2006 is followed. These include:

(1) repurchases of shares (buybacks and redemptions);
(2) reduction of capital;
(3) financial assistance in very limited circumstances; and
(4) the distribution of profits as dividends (cash) or in kind (as shares).

All of these can feature in an LBO, and three of them played a part in our Manchester United plc case study. We have already briefly mentioned how dividends can be used in an LBO to upstream profits from the target to Bidco, allowing Bidco to pay interest on the senior debt. The plan is not to go much deeper on this, especially as the Glazers ultimately effected a debt pushdown, making Manchester United directly liable for the senior debt. Rather, we will now focus share buybacks—which provide the classical case on capital maintenance—and the particularly controversial area of financial assistance.

7.6.1 Buybacks

Share buybacks were a technique considered by the existing board of Manchester United plc to defend the target from the Glazer-led LBO. Let us examine how they work and why they offend the doctrine of capital maintenance.

The leading case for the doctrine of capital maintenance is a share buyback case.

TREVOR v WHITWORTH (1887) 12 App Cas 409 (HL)

A company's constitution permitted the company to buy back its shares from shareholders. All to the good, but the shareholders, fearing insolvency, caused the company to buy back one-quarter of their shares. The company could not pay for this (as they knew), but the point was that now they were owed a debt by the company, and so ranked as creditors, not shareholders, when it came to a winding up.

Held per Lord Herschell:

> If the claim under consideration can be supported, the result would seem to be this, that the whole of the shareholders, with the exception of those holding seven individual shares, might now be claiming payment of the sums paid upon their shares as against the creditors, who had a right to look to the moneys subscribed as the source out of which the company's liabilities to them were to be met. And

the stringent precautions to prevent the reduction of the capital of a limited company, without due notice and judicial sanction, would be idle if the company might purchase its own shares wholesale, and so effect the desired result . . . I cannot think that the employment of the company's money in the purchase of shares for any such purpose was legitimate.

The public policy considerations for capital maintenance were stated by their Lordships, but they also specifically raised the following grounds:

(i) That returning capital to shareholders (first) is ultra vires the company even if the constitution provides for it, because a company cannot do what is prohibited by the Companies Acts (the prohibition is now s 658 CA 2006).

That such an improper transaction amounts to the company becoming a member of itself, which is 'inconsistent with the essential nature of a company.'

One might observe that the facts of the case lend themselves readily to the FNCF-interpretation we have been advancing. The mischief here was not that the shareholders caused the company to buy back shares, but that they did so to reconstitute the shareholders as sham creditors and so subvert the statutory priority ranking of creditors over shareholders.

If you are comfortable with balance sheets, you can also think about this problem in purely accounting terms, for this mischief is clear.

EXAMPLE: UNLAWFUL REPURCHASE

TVW plc has cash assets of £200 and debts to Bank of £50. It has £150 of shares in issue. Total assets £150 = total capital £150. Observe that on winding up at this point, Bank would comfortably recover its £50.

TVW hits some economic turbulence, losing £150 so that it now only has £50 cash. Worried for their own capital, the shareholders direct the company to buy back £50 of their shares at par.

The result: with no cash left, TVW has net liabilities of (£50) an amount which does not balance with capital of £100. Bank will recover nothing on winding up.

Notice how a correctly stated balance sheet tells us something is not quite right. In this case the liquidator, on behalf of Bank, would be looking to unravel the buyback and bring claims against the shareholders and directors.

The Companies Act 2006 now allows for share buybacks in two general circumstances:

(1) Where the shares are redeemable i.e. the constitution clearly provides that the shares are two be bought back on certain conditions: ss 684–689.
(2) Where the court approves the buy-back transaction under ss 690–708.

So, having stated exceptions to the general prohibition, how does CA 2006 deal with the other two concerns highlighted in *Trevor v Whitworth* (self-membership and creditor protection)?

(1) The self-membership problem:
   (a) A company cannot only issue redeemable shares.
   (b) A company cannot repurchase all its shares.
   (c) Any redeemed shares are cancelled. Any bought back shares can be held 'in treasury' but cannot be voted by the company (s 724). If they are not re-issued, they must be cancelled.
(2) Creditor protection:
   (a) Buybacks must be funded first from available profits (and any new share issuance to recapitalize the company). In *Trevor v Whitworth* the company was insolvent and so could not pay for the buyback.
   (b) A company can always accept back shares for free, as this does not reduce capital (s 659(1)).
   (c) Buy backs must be supported by special resolutions, directors' statement, auditor's report, and creditors' right to object (ss 709–723). All this is designed to ensure transparency, so creditors constructively know their rights relative to other capital providers.

Why would a company ever consider repurchasing its own shares? Why on earth, given the difficulty of attracting capital in the first place, would a company want to give it back? Again, the reasons are linked to the demands of the capital markets and appropriate capital structure:

(1) A company may have excess capital which it cannot invest. This reduces earnings per share (or ROIC if you prefer) and makes the company look a comparatively unattractive investment in the secondary market. Through a buyback earnings/share is increased.
(2) Existing share capital may be expensive compared to newly available forms of corporate finance (such as debt, or shares with fewer rights). A repurchase is a classic optimization of cost of funds.
(3) As a special case of the above, the company may wish to go private (i.e. the cost of funds is the 'irritation' of public investors).
(4) The board may feel that current shareholders have undervalued the company, reducing the secondary market price and making the company a target for takeover. Supply and demand calculations lead the directors to reduce the number of shares in circulation. It is precisely this motivation which features when boards are concerned about a potential hostile LBO.

CASE STUDY: FIGHTING OFF THE GLAZER TAKEOVER

That last justification for buybacks is what excised the directors of Manchester United plc when the Glazers started showing an interest in the company in the early 2000s. Partly in order to support the secondary market price of Manchester United plc shares, members of the company voted:

On 23 November 2001 to give the directors authority [under what is now s 701] to buy back up to 25,976,804 of the 350m Ordinary Shares (time limited to 15 months);

On 14 November 2003 to give the directors [s 701] authority to buy back up to 25,976,804 Ordinary Shares (time limited to 15 months).

Manchester United plc's board were thus primed to buy back shares, boosting the price both by making the offer and, on buy back, restricting market supply.

The Manchester United plc board prepared its takeover defences, but ultimately concluded that its share price did not need to be boosted by an offer which restricted supply. Rather, it deployed a different defensive technique in which its Employee Share Ownership Plan (ESOP) would buy the shares instead, financed by the company. This was lawful under what is now s693 CA 2006.

This ESOP defence mechanism had been developed in the US in the 1980s. For example, in 1988, Polaroid had used it to fight off a takeover by Disney[18]—an act which ended up in court because Disney (via subsidiaries called 'Shamrock') had excluded the ESOP shareholders from its bid, claiming the shares were improperly issued. The advantage of using the ESOP is that the board in each case regarded the ESOP as managed by persons loyal to the board (sharing directors) and therefore forming a bloc of votes which could be relied on to reject any bid. Polaroid won the court case and Disney abandoned the bid in 1989. As we know, Manchester United plc's use of the ESOP failed to stop the glazers.

7.6.2 Financial assistance

We have seen that the basic idea behind capital maintenance is that capital should not be returned to shareholders (before creditors). If share buybacks involve returning capital to shareholders, at least in consideration the company receives back its shares. Providing unlawful financial assistance does not even do that: the shareholders receive capital and get to have their shares too. This would happen, for example, if the company gifted capital to a non-shareholder for the purposes of that shareholder using the capital to acquire the company's shares, whether from the company or another shareholder. In this case you can hopefully see that:

(1) Company capital has been diverted away from creditors (and existing shareholders for that matter) to pay a shareholder.
(2) That the financially assisted person is not injecting fresh capital into the company.
(3) That the financially assisted person is acquiring rights 'for free,' and in particular diluting the claims of other shareholders ranked pari passu on winding up/return of capital.

It must be stressed that with the Companies Act 2006, the force of the prohibition on financial assistance is aimed at *public* companies.

An example might help.

EXAMPLE: FINANCIAL ASSISTANCE

B Plc has three shareholders b, c, and d and GBP1 x 750,000 of share capital, and GBP750,000 cash. It has authority to allot and issue 250,000 more shares to new members.

B Plc renders FA by giving GBP250,000 to a to buy shares in B Plc. At that point B Plc has £500,000 cash, having suffered a capital loss of £250,000 which should be reflected by a cancellation on the equity side. Shareholder a buys the shares and £250,000 is reinjected into the company.

The balance sheet now shows £750,000 assets and £1,000,000 of equity capital—it does not balance. The equity capital should be reduced to reflect this reality i.e. each £1 share should bear a loss of 25p (each share should be re-based at 75p (1,000,000 shares at 75p = £750,000).

18 Joseph Kershenbaum, 'Corporate Law—A Snapshot of the Takeover Decade: *Polaroid Corp. v Disney*—Whether a Target Corporation has Third Party Standing to Assert a Violation of the All-Holders Rule' (1991) 13 Western New England Law Review 63.

The above example focused on the problems for shareholders but consider this: B Plc has debts of GBP1,000,000 to X Bank. X Bank is entitled to expect that the issuance of 250,000 shares to a should have been for consideration of GBP250,000, and that B Ltd. should have had GBP1,000,000 of assets to meet its claims. This is particularly egregious if X Bank lent to B Ltd. on the basis of a balance sheet that showed equity capital of GBP1,000,000 (perhaps suggesting that the 'missing' GBP250,000 was unpaid).

The financial assistance need not be provided before the shares are acquired; the company can lend aid afterwards too.

EXAMPLE: POST HOC FINANCIAL ASSISTANCE

James borrows £500k from a third-party Bank to purchase the shares of Target plc. Bank would like some protection for its loan and asks that James arrange a suitable guarantor within one month of drawing down the loan. James acquires the Target plc shares and then a week later Target plc issues a guarantee to Bank declaring Target plc will act as surety for James' debt. This too would be financial assistance.

So, financial assistance can be simply thought of as a public company giving someone material assistance at any time to acquire shares in that public company. The enforcement problem with financial assistance is that normally no company is so inept as to offer financial assistance in such an obvious way. Various ingenious forms of financial assistance developed, and the prohibition of financial assistance has been extended to catch them all. Indeed, the courts have also developed the principle that financial assistance is not a legal concept (like the definition of theft) but rather signifies a commercial reality to which the court should be sensitive (*Charterhouse Investment v Tempest Diesels*).[19] Furthermore, the penal nature of the prohibition should mean that it should not extend to transactions which do not fairly fall within it (see further the leading case of *Brady v Brady*).[20]

Before 2006's Companies Act, LBO practices fell squarely within the ambit of the prohibition of financial assistance. Pushing the acquisition debt down into the target or requiring the target to guarantee that debt look very much like financial assistance. It was still just about possible for the sponsors and the acquired target to escape sanction—a so-called whitewash procedure existed which LBO specialists used to, if not sanctify their transaction, at least ward off the authorities most of the time. It was still possible to fall foul of the prohibition, though.

CHASTON v SWP GROUP PLC [2002] EWCA Civ 1999, [2003] BCC 140

SWP sought to acquire the entire share capital of DRC. C was a director and majority shareholder of C. SWP were advised in the takeover by Deloitte & Touche (as it then was). To aid the takeover, which would be profitable for C, C as director caused DRC to accept liability for Deloitte & Touche's fees.

The deal turned out to be a lemon for SWP, who sued C and DRC. As part of the litigation, DRC sued C in his role as director for breach of fiduciary duty in causing DRC to provide unlawful financial assistance.

19 *Charterhouse Investment v Tempest Diesels* [1986] BCLC 1.

20 *Brady v Brady* [1988] 2 All ER 617 (HL).

Held: Confirming that C had caused DRC to provide unlawful financial assistance, the Court of Appeal (led by Arden LJ) issued a stern reminder of the law that would send a chill down every LBO sponsor:

> The general mischief [is] . . . that the resources of the target company and its subsidiaries should not be used directly or indirectly to assist the purchaser financially to make the acquisition. This may prejudice the interests of the creditors of the target or its group, and the interests of any shareholders who do not accept the offer to acquire their shares or to whom the offer is not made.

In 2006, the legal regime was modified. Pay attention to the exceptions contained in ss 678–682, and most relevantly, s 678.

S 678 COMPANIES ACT 2006

(1) Where a person is acquiring or proposing to acquire shares in a public company, it is not lawful for that company, or a company that is a subsidiary of that company, to give financial assistance directly or indirectly for the purpose of the acquisition before or at the same time as the acquisition takes place.

. . .

(3) Where—

(a) a person has acquired shares in a company, and

(b) a liability has been incurred (by that or another person) for the purpose of the acquisition,

it is not lawful for that company, or a company that is a subsidiary of that company, to give financial assistance directly or indirectly for the purpose of reducing or discharging the liability if, **at the time the assistance is given**, the company in which the shares were acquired is a public company. [*my emphasis*]

Can you see the gaping loophole? A common post-2006 route around the prohibition of financial assistance is to take a plc private (re-register it as a limited company) because if you read carefully, there is no prohibition on a plc granting financial for the purchase of its shares *after* it has become private company: s 678 only covers 'before or at the same time as the acquisition!'

Given the structure of an LBO, in which of necessity the target will not be granting financial assistance until after takeover, it is a simple task for the acquirer to re-register the target as a private company and *then* have it take on the liabilities for the financing of the acquisition of its own shares. There is a research paper to be written documenting the legislative origins of the highlighted subclause.

The Manchester United LBO occurred just before Companies Act 2006 came in and so the older whitewash procedure was deployed (no doubt with one eye on the forthcoming legislative change of heart).

CASE STUDY: FINANCIAL ASSISTANCE FOR TAKING OVER MANCHESTER UTD PLC

When the Glazers took over Manchester United plc they financed the purchase by . . . getting Manchester United plc to pay for it. Well, not directly; the banks and other lenders paid for most of Manchester United plc's shares, with the Glazers providing the rest. But all of these people only did so because they knew that once they controlled Manchester United, they could make the football club pay them back.

By 13 May 2005 the Glazers, via RFJV Ltd. owned or controlled 74.81% of the shares of Manchester United plc, just shy of the 75% needed to trigger a formal takeover (under the City Takeover Code 8.3). They passed this threshold three days later, having issued a formal offer for Manchester United plc's entire remaining share capital in issue.

The net result was that by 22 June the Glazers' share in the club had hit 98%, permitting them to squeeze out the remaining shareholders (i.e. forcibly expropriate their shares—this is now a 90% threshold under s 979 CA 2006).

Having taken control, Manchester United plc was re-registered as a private limited company. Being a private limited company it was easier, and much easier under CA 2006, to follow a special procedure for permitting financial assistance. This was undertaken in stages through 2005, but the net result was that Manchester United **Ltd.** was made to guarantee the debts of RFJV to the Senior banks.

In other words, but for this future assumption of liability by Manchester United, the banks would not have given money to RFJV to acquire the shares of Manchester United plc. But for the exceptions, this would be a fairly obvious case of financial assistance under what is now s 677(1)(b).

In 2005 the financial assistance whitewash procedure was more complicated for lawyers to document, but still achievable enough. These days, as noted above, the re-registered would have sufficed to achieve automatic exemption from the prohibition on financial assistance thanks to s 678(3). The prohibition only applies if the financial assistance occurs when the company giving the financial assistance is a PLC. But Manchester United had reregistered as private *before* it gave the guarantee, so it was not a PLC at the relevant time.

Having been taken private, Manchester United Ltd, under Glazer control, signed a guarantee of all the debt that had been incurred by the Red Football companies to finance the LBO, secured on its assets worth over £200m. Its dividends were paid upstream to meet interest payments.

It is remarkable that a company should pay for the privilege of someone else taking control of it. And pay Manchester United did[21]—it ended up guaranteeing (and actually just paying) debt of GBP660m and interest payments of GBP62m per annum.[22] The PIK debt alone compounded to extraordinary levels, it grew to some GBP207m on its own,[23] driving the total debt to GBP716m in January 2010.[24] That year Manchester United was used to refinance the debt by means of a USD500m bond issue on the New York securities market.[25] The interest rate (coupon) payable on the bonds came in at an aggregate of USD46m per annum. It seemed that Manchester United's debt profile had become more famous than its football stars, and there was considerable supporter

21 David Bond, 'Manchester United Owners Hit by Debt Payment Rise' (*BBC Sport*, 20 August 2010) <http://news.bbc.co.uk/sport2/hi/football/teams/m/man_utd/8931026.stm> accessed 1 July 2011.

22 'Man Utd Play Down Fears After £660m Refinancing' (*ESPN*, 18 July 2006). Archived from the original on 27 May 2012 <https://archive.ph/20120527041225/http://soccernet.espn.go.com/news/story?id=374009&cc=5739> accessed 20 September 2024.

23 'The Full Details on the Terms of the PIKs' (*The Andersred Blog*, 16 November 2010) <https://andersred.blogspot.com/2010/11/full-details-on-terms-of-piks.html> accessed 1 August 2024.

24 'Manchester United Debt Hits £716m' (*BBC News*, 20 January 2010) accessed 1 August 2024.

25 'Manchester United to Raise £500m' (*BBC News*, 11 January 2010) accessed 1 August 2024.

disenchantment.[26] In 2024, after almost 20 years, the Glazers relinquished control of the club, selling a 25% plus stake to British industrialist Sir Jim Radcliffe.

7.7 Conclusion

Think back to our three kinds of Manchester United investors. Do you think finance and company law adequately balances their respective interests? As a supporter of the club, to be squeezed out is one thing (one can still support the club from the stands), but to be squeezed out using the money you put into the club, along with the investments of countless others, must seem galling. To watch a great club struggle under the weight of a debt it is paying for no other reason than someone several thousand miles away decided to invest in UK sports surely contradicts our intuitions about fairness and ownership of common property (albeit mediated via the form of the limited liability company). The leveraged buyout is a complex and powerful legal structure, yet is the legal regulation of buyouts pitched correctly so that all stakeholders are fairly treated?

Hopefully our case study has provided you not only with an opportunity to see some of the more technical aspects of company and finance law in action, from subordination to capital maintenance, but it has also motivated you to think about the effects of financial transactions on 'Main Street' (the real world).

26 Owen Gibson and Daniel Taylor, 'Manchester United Fans Want Answers as Glazers Prepare to Pay Off Debt' (*The Guardian*, 16 November 2010) accessed 8 September 2012.

Chapter 8

Securities and securitization

Chapter contents

DOI: 10.4324/9781003457220-8

8.1 Terminological troubles

When US Supreme Court Justice Potter Stewart was asked to describe his test for obscenity in 1964, he responded: 'I know it when I see it.'[1] Strikingly, a similar approach appears to apply to securities: a strict common law definition is lacking, but everyone knows securities when they see them. Securities are the product of mercantile and then financial practice, a pseudo-legal terminology being used by analogy and not in any conceptually rigorous way.

Legislative and judicial working definitions of 'securities' have arisen in contexts in which breadth has been justified. Parliament has sought to catch as much financial activity as possible in a regulatory statute; courts have interpreted a contract or will to determine a party's or executor's power of investment. The Regulated Activities Order 2001 defines 'security' to include company shares, bonds and debentures, rights under alternative finance investment bonds, and government and public securities (such as loan stock, bonds, or other instruments acknowledging indebtedness). The definition also extends to warrants or other instruments entitling the holder to subscribe for any of the above, and certificates giving contractual or property rights in respect of them. In addition, a unit representing the right or interest held in a collective investment scheme is a security and even an interest in a private pension scheme can come within the definition for certain purposes. Rights and interests in any of the above and in most options and futures contracts, contracts for differences and even in certain insurance contracts can all represent securities in their own right so that derivatives are regulated.[2]

This catch-all definition is far too wide for anyone seeking a handle on what securities are; it is much closer in sense to 'investment.' Our intuition, from market practice, is that the term 'securities' would principally cover shares, bonds (government and private) and debentures. If we hold that rather rough set of instruments in our mind, we have a practical sense of what is meant by securities with which to begin.

We might, however, attempt a more refined definition than a list which isolates the legal characteristics in which we are interested. In 1904, Vaughan Williams LJ commented obiter that the term 'securities' in the popular sense:

> is applied habitually by those who have to deal with *property transferable by the assignment of indicia of property*, be they commercial men or non-commercial men, lawyers or laymen; and a sense in which it has been used daily in The Times since the year 1886, and in divers Acts of Parliament.[3]

This statement captures key features common to securities:

(1) Securities relate to claims for the (re)payment of money. In bonds and debentures, this is a debt claim; with company shares it is a claim on the capital of the company on winding up. As such, securities relate to choses in action (see Chapter 6).

(2) Yet securities add an additional feature beyond a mere chose in action—they are transferred not by a legal or equitable assignment, but by transfer of some indicia or token of title to the chose in action.

(3) This index or token is called an 'instrument,' i.e. any bill of exchange caught by the 1882 Act, such as a promissory note, or any share or debenture issued by a company under the Companies Acts.

---

1 *Jacobellis v Ohio*, 378 U.S. 184 (1964) at 197.

2 As a further catchall, anything which has been or can be admitted to the Official List under s 102A of FSMA 2000 is also within the definition of a security. See the Financial Services and Markets Act 2000 (Regulated Activities) Order 2001 SI 2001/544, arts 3, 76–82, 89.

3 *in re Rayner* [1904] 1 Ch 176 (CA) 187. My emphasis.

It is this interaction between the indicating instrument and the underlying chose in action which leads to some of the confusion around securities. Merchants and financiers who traded in debts owed by third-party debtors wrongly came to regard not the intangible chose in action as the property they were buying and selling, but rather the physical document evidencing that title which was handed over when the title was bought and sold. It seems the word 'security' tries to capture this duality of chose in action and instrument. These observations suggest the following working definition.

ESSENTIAL DEFINITION: A SECURITY

A security is:

(a) a claim in debt or for the return of capital,
(b) title to and transfer of which is indicated by an instrument.

A security's instrument may either constitute proof of title and transfer, or merely represent title and transfer, proof of this being located in a central register. A security's instrument may be physical or dematerialized.

The security may also bear further rights, such as voting rights.

Thus, a debt arising from a contract is not itself a security without more, because the contract is not an instrument indicating title. An IOU, such as we saw in Chapter 2, is a security because the debt is indicated by a bill of exchange called a promissory note.

In what follows we focus solely on debt securities, that is, debt claims evidenced by instruments. For more information on shares and debenture stock issued by companies, please refer to any company law book.

8.1.1 Security versus securities

Why, though, do we use the same word—security—for two legally very distinct things? In Chapter 3 we saw that 'security' meant a kind of property right, whereas now 'security' is being used to describe an instrument representing with a property right in a chose in action. We saw Vaughan Williams LJ grappling with the potential confusion above.[4] The following judgment, which was affirmed in the House of Lords, provides an explanation of the homonymy.

***NATIONAL TELEPHONE COMPANY LIMITED v COMMISSIONERS OF INLAND REVENUE* [1899] 1 QB 250 (CA)**

For the purposes of a tax act, the question arose whether an instrument indicating an obligation to pay (i.e. a debt instrument) fell within the definition of documents subject to stamp duty. The relevant statutory schedule made reference to 'security,' and the appellant sought to argue that 'security' meant some collateral right over property which secured

4 ibid.

a separate obligation to pay, *not* the obligation to pay itself. On this view, an instrument evidencing an obligation to pay could not in itself be 'security.'

Held: an instrument evidencing an obligation to pay was a 'security' within the meaning of the tax act. Rigby LJ provided this helpful clarification:

> The phrase 'personal security' is almost as common as 'real security.' The latter is associated with property, but 'personal security' refers to something which has not property at the back of it, but is a mere personal obligation. I also agree that the words of the schedule in question include securities by which the obligation to pay money is originally created. [259]

Affirmed: *National Telephone Company Limited v Commissioners of Inland Revenue* [1900] AC 1.

In crude terms, Rigby LJ's point is this. 'Real security' (as he terms it) refers to security in the sense lawyers mean it i.e. some obligor promises to do or pay *x*, and the obligee has a property right over some asset (the 'security') which, if the obligor fails to repay, permits the obligee to enforce against the asset, sell it, and extract its value to satisfy the obligation (see Chapter 3). Rigby LJ informs us that 'personal security' is distinct from 'real security' because the risk mitigation does not derive from a property interest in an asset but from a personal claim against an individual. In this case the obligee, to enforce, simply claims payment of the debt owed by the person giving the personal security. The risk mitigation derives from the 'quality' of the individual granting 'personal security,' which in practical terms means how wealthy they are and how easy it is to enforce against them.

Observe that in more modern literature, the singular noun 'security' has indeed been limited to what Rigby LJ calls 'real security' to mark a clearer distinction. On this view, 'personal security' might at best be called a 'quasi-security' just because it does not create property rights in some asset. This practice does however occlude the reason why we still give securities—instruments evidencing personal security—the name we do.

EXAMPLE 1: WHY ONE SHOULD NOT CONFUSE SECURITIES WITH SECURITY

Arrow Ltd. owes £1,000 to Barbara, secured by way of floating charge over a named savings account Arrow Ltd. holds with Caerphilly Bank. Arrow Ltd. also has £100 in a separate deposit account which is not subject to the security. Arrow Ltd. is unable to pay its debts as they fall due and enters insolvency proceedings. Barbara enforces by taking control of the bank account. She finds £600 there and in virtue of her priority is able to use the entire sum in repayment. Barbara is still owed £400 but, having exhausted the security, is unsecured and must prove for the remaining amount in the insolvency proceedings, sharing losses with other unsecured creditors. She has no special recourse to the £100 in the deposit account.

Arrow Ltd. also owes £600 to Danielle, proof of which evidenced by a security (here a promissory note). Arrow Ltd. defaults and is bankrupted. Despite the name 'security,'

Danielle is an unsecured creditor. She must prove in the bankruptcy for the total £600 owing, evidenced by the IOU she holds.

Arrow Ltd.'s remaining assets are the £100 in the deposit account, to be distributed by the trustee in bankruptcy pari passu and pro rata to the unsecured creditors. Given the respective amounts now owed to Barbara and Danielle, Barbara will recover 40p for every pound she is owed; Danielle 60p in the pound.

In total, Barbara recovers £640; Danielle, £60.

If you found example 1 difficult, review Chapter 3. If not, reflect on the following further example.

EXAMPLE 2: WHY ONE SHOULD NOT CONFUSE SECURITIES WITH SECURITY

Eshun makes two promissory notes (a kind of security in the sense of this chapter) under each of which he promises 'to pay Freddie or bearer £500 on demand.' He hands both promissory notes to Freddie.

Freddie happens to owe £1,000 to Gareth. Gareth asks for security by way of charge for this debt. Freddie therefore grants a charge over both promissory notes in favour of Gareth.

Notice that Gareth has taken security over the securities.

Freddie defaults on his debt to Gareth. Gareth enforces against the promissory notes, takes possession and presents them to Eshun, demanding payment. As Gareth is bearer of the notes, Eshun must pay Gareth on demand.

Two subtle questions arise from example 2 here. First, just what is being secured? The law of bills of exchange operates a kind of legal fiction whereby taking security over the physical notes stands for taking security over what they really represent: choses in action, namely the debt claims against Eshun. This leads to a second question: did Freddie create a fixed and floating charge? In *Siebe Gorman & Co Ltd v Barclays Bank Ltd*,[5] it was held (1) that a charge over bills of exchange was a charge over book debts; and (2) that such a charge was a fixed charge. Judgment (1) is not to be doubted—despite the legal fiction the notes stand for the claim in debt and should not be confused with them. The notes themselves are just bits of paper. Judgment (2), however, is now incorrect, following *re Spectrum Plus Ltd*.[6] If promissory notes are evidence of book debts, then by simply presenting them the charger can convert them into cash. A fixed charge would fail because it has nothing determinate to fix upon, so if any charge subsists it must be floating charge which 'hovers over' the available fund as it transforms from debt to cash.

8.1.2 Instruments: bonds and bills of exchange

Our working definition of securities makes clear that we are dealing with rights to payment/debt claims which are in some way indicated by an instrument. **Instrument** just means a written

5 [1979] 2 Lloyd's Rep 142 (ChD).

6 [2005] UKHL 41, [2005] 2 AC 680. See Chapter 4.

document which, being in a legally specified form, of itself has a legal effect. The key here is the formality—some rule of law or statute specifies that if writing meets certain formal requirements, it will have a legal effect.

Of relevance for our purposes are two kinds of instrument:

- the deed; and
- the instrument under hand only.

At common law, the formal requirements of a *deed* are that it being in writing, and be signed, witnessed, (if required sealed), and delivered as a deed. The deed is of itself proof of the enforceability of any legal obligation or property transfer provided[7] for therein. As a deed is enforceable just if it meets the formal requirements of being a deed, one can make enforceable many things which would not otherwise be so.

An illustration from Chapter 2 suffices to underline the point: a variation of the CFA may fall foul of the rule in *Foakes v Beer*, for the creditor will receive no fresh consideration if the debt is reduced or repayment delayed—the variation therefore fails for want of consideration. The lawyer's simple workaround is to record the variation in a deed which renders its enforceable in virtue solely of being a deed.

As another example, you will also know that a bare promise without consideration (i.e. the promisee has not given or promised anything in return to 'buy' the promise) is unenforceable. Generally, unilateral promises are difficult to enforce. Yet if the unilateral promise is placed in the form of a deed, it is enforceable because deeds are of themselves enforceable. Deeds containing unilateral acts are called deeds poll because to indicate the unilateral nature of the instrument, a notary would cut off (*pollard*) all the teeth from a blank indenture document. By contrast, deeds containing bilateral agreements are sometimes called indentures because in older times triangular indents or 'teeth' (*dents*) were cut into the document so it could be easily recognized as bilateral by solicitors and notaries who kept rolls and rolls of these instruments in shelves and trunks.

Instruments under hand only are signed documents in writing meeting formal legal requirements which are less onerous than the formal requirements for a deed.[8] The IOU we saw in Chapter 2 is an instrument under hand only—it meets what are now the requirements of the Bills of Exchange Act 1882 for a promissory note.

You might ask, by way of contrast, how bills of exchange fare when it comes to the requirement of consideration. Imagine Andrew has made a bill of exchange expressing his indebtedness of GBP100 to Bob, payable on demand. Is this not just a gift and unenforceable? The first thing (to remember) is the bill is not any underlying contract. The bill is an instrument indicating a debt which may have arisen under an underlying contract. The second, very useful feature of bills of exchange is that there is a (now statutory) rebuttable presumption that value was given for the debt indicated in the bill (whether it was by way of consideration or simply an advance).[9]

The distinction between deeds and instruments under hand only helps us explain some further securities terminology.

---

7 The Latin for 'that which provides for' is *instrumentum*; hence 'instrument.'

8 *Chadwick v Clarke* (1845) 1 CB 700, 707–8.

9 Bills of Exchange Act 1882, ss 30(1), 89.

ESSENTIAL DEFINITIONS: BONDS AND BILLS OF EXCHANGE

A **bond** is an instrument under seal, usually a deed poll, whereby one person (an obligor) binds themselves to another (the obligee) for the payment of a certain sum of money either immediately or at a fixed future date.[10]

A **debenture** in this context means a bond issued by a company secured on the company's assets by way of fixed and floating charge.[11] Confusingly, however, 'debenture' is very often used in a loose sense to mean any document creating the fixed and floating charge.[12]

A **public/government bond** [*sic*] is an instrument (not necessarily a deed) issued by a public body under a relevant (statutory) power whereby that public body binds themselves to another (the obligee) for the payment of a certain sum of money either immediately or at a fixed future date.[13]

A **bill** or **note** in the general sense is defined by statute[14] as an unconditional instrument under hand only, addressed by one person to another, signed by the person giving it (the 'maker'), requiring the person to whom it is addressed (the 'payer') to pay on demand or at a fixed or determinable future time a sum certain in money to or to the order of a person (be it a specified person or to bearer) known as the holder and payee. No further conditions may attach to the bill. We differentiate between:

- a bill which orders another named individual to pay a person: a **bill of exchange** in the precise sense;
- a bill which orders a *bank* to pay a person from a specified account: a **cheque**; and
- a note which is the maker's own promise to pay a person: a **promissory note** (colloquially an 'IOU').

The point of highlighting this distinction is the confusion that arises when faced with multiple terminology relating to securities. Sometimes, when speaking of debt securities, one will find the term 'bonds'[15] used interchangeably for 'securities' given bonds' prevalence in modern financial contexts. Yet many of the classic cases around securities involve bills and notes. The reason for this is that a bill or note is much easier to create (you just need pen and paper) than a deed, and that facility was a product of the development of bills of exchange in the mercantile context as a means of payment. The use of bills as payment is a matter to which we return in the chapter on payments systems, but for present purposes we continue our focus on bills in their role as kinds of securities.

---

10 *National Telephone Co v Commissioners of Inland Revenue* [1900] AC 1 (HL); *British India Steam Navigation Co v Inland Revenue Commissioners* (1881) 7 QBD 165, 173, DC (J Lindley).

11 As opposed to 'debenture stock,' being the name for a divisible share security issued under the Companies Acts.

12 *Levy v Abercorris Slate and Slab* [1886–90] All ER Rep 509 (ChD).

13 Where the instrument is not a deed, strictly speaking it cannot be a bond but is rather a bill. Yet in the UK the term 'bond' has been used interchangeably with bill in practice. UK Government 'bonds' are also called 'gilts.' In the US, legal orthodoxy has won the day, which is why US federal government bonds (sic) are commonly called Treasury Bills ('T-Bills' for short). See further Exchequer Bills and Bonds Act 1866 (now repealed) and the Finance Act 1963.

14 Bills of Exchange Act 1882, which codified the law merchant on such bills.

15 One tangential problem with equating bonds with securities is that some bonds are arguably not securities in the modern sense. Bonds given by order of the Court (bail bonds and security for costs) are certainly bonds, certainly are 'personal security' in the traditional sense, and are even assignable. Yet they are not securities in the sense used in financial markets and regulation.

Given the relatively greater number of bills in circulation well into the twentieth century, the likelihood of cases arising around them was greatly increased. Bonds are now far more common thanks to several innovations which mitigated the practical hindrances resulting from the formal requirements of deed-making.

8.1.3 Coupon

As noted earlier, one of the requirements of negotiability is that the promise or order to pay should specify no more than the drawer, payee and time of payment. As soon as an instrument is subject to additional conditions it ceases to be a negotiable bill. The advantage of bonds is that they may specify further conditions as between issuer and holder and between the holders inter se. One of the most important conditions which clearly demarcates bills, with their quasi-monetary nature, from bonds, is that bonds very often obligate the issuer to pay interest.

In the nineteenth century, when bearer securities were far more popular, the possessory nature of bearer bonds was notionally extended to the right to interest. Imagine a company issues a number of bearer bonds of GBP100 each payable five years hence. The debt represented by the bond is stated on its face to attract interest of 5% per annum, payable in two instalments, on 1 April and 1 October. Down one side of the physical bond there would be inscribed 10 'coupons,' one for the sum of interest due on each interest payment date. To receive the interest, the bearer would tear off the relevant coupon and present it to the company, which would make the due payment (or default). This practice is archaic, but it does explain why today in the bond markets all interest on such securities, bearer, registered and so on, is referred to as **coupon**.

8.1.4 Negotiability, bearer, and registered securities

The fallback position of the law is that a debt, being a chose in action, has only been transferrable since 1925 by virtue of s 136 Law of Property Act legal assignment. Yet the law merchant, seeking to avoid the historical ban on such assignments, developed its own exceptions for bills of exchange to support the practice of buying and selling mercantile debts. A creditor could transfer certain kinds of debt to a third party where the debt was indicated in an instrument which was **negotiable.**

Negotiation means the transfer for value of a bill of exchange (including a cheque or promissory note) to a person, who thereupon becomes entitled to hold it, and is capable of suing on it in his own name. Negotiation is achieved:

(1) In the case of a bill which is made payable to order (i.e. to a named person), by indorsement and delivery of the bill. Practically, this means that the holder of the bill signs ('indorses') the bill and delivers it over to the new holder.
(2) In the case of a bill which is made payable to bearer, even the requirement of indorsement is forgone—the holder simply delivers the bill to a third party who immediately becomes owner and can sue on it.

Earlier we saw that securities refer to a financial practice which is somewhat at odds with legal thinking: financiers tend to confuse the instrument indicating the debt with the debt itself. With **bearer securities** this confusion is given legal sanction by means of a legal fiction: physical possession of the instrument is proof of title to the debt, and delivery of the instrument to a third party has the effect of transferring that title.

Not all negotiable instruments are bearer securities in this sense; only those marked 'payable to bearer.' If a bill of exchange specifies a named payee, or states that it is payable to someone indicated by that holder ('payable to x or to his order'), then irrespective of who else simply possesses the bill it is only payable to those persons. This does not prevent the holder from indorsing the bill over to someone else, but this necessarily requires writing on the bill (something not required with a bearer instrument).[16]

Observe how close a bearer instrument or security is to money. Indeed, because the sole determinant of title to the debt is possession of a physical instrument, as with money bearer security instruments should be made in a manner which precludes forgery. In the case of occasional, small-denomination bills, merchants (who in earlier times formed a closed group) were happy to accept physical signature/indorsement as a proof of genuineness. In the case of large denomination bills issued into retail markets, however, the temptation for forgery is great and so issuers of bearer securities will sequentially number each bearer security in an issue and add other security features, much like central bank issued currency.

With bearer securities, possession is everything. If you doubt this, Keith Cheeseman provides a salutary tale.

UNITED STATES v CHEESEMAN (1993) Southern District of New York (unreported)

At 9.00am on 2 May 1990, John Goddard, a 58-year-old messenger for brokerage firm Sheppards was walking through the City of London to make a delivery. A man of habit, he took the same route he always took, which, as a veteran of the City, involved several shortcuts through lost alleyways. It was not unusual for Goddard to be carrying financial documents for delivery, but that day the messenger was holding 301 particularly special documents: HM Treasury bills 'payable to bearer' in denominations of about £1,000,000 each (called 'Giants' in the trade).[17] The total market value Goddard held in his hands was £291.9 million.[18]

Goddard's movements had been monitored by what turned out to be a sophisticated criminal operation. In a quiet City side street—Nicholas Lane, near Monument—Goddard was waylaid by a man with a knife—believed to be Patrick Thomas—and robbed. The 'City Bonds Robbery' was one of the biggest in history, with Thomas making off with assets worth £840m in 2023 prices.

The bills were passed to Keith Cheeseman, a convicted fraudster and expert on laundering money and securities. He was instructed to negotiate the bills for the benefit of the IRA and subsequently Colombian drug cartels. Cheeseman had primed a contact in Switzerland ready to launder the bills but ran into trouble.

Sheppards had immediately informed the police and the Bank of England. The Bank publicly announced that the bills were worthless but behind the scenes transmitted the bills' security numbers to banks across Europe. The Swiss contact realized that the bills were now on a watchlist and would not be accepted for payment; Cheeseman needed a plan B. One of his co-conspirators, John Traynor, managed to obtain £200,000 as an advance

16 For a limit case where alteration of the writing was ineffective, see *Meyer & Co v Decroix, Verley et Cie* [1891] AC 520 (HL) (deleting words 'or to order' did not affect negotiability).

17 Technically some of the bearer securities were *certificates of deposit*. A certificate of deposit is a security made by a bank which declares that a certain sum has been deposited with the bank and will be paid out to bearer on demand. Their legal nature has yet to be formally considered—they are not promissory notes because they contain no promise to pay, only a statement that bearer has the right to the deposited funds. Being negotiable and underwritten by a deposit, they seem closer to private bank money (though even bank money, including modern Bank of England notes, contain promises to pay bearer on demand: the Bank Charter Act 1844 s 11; Currency and Bank Notes Act 1954 s 3).

18 This may sound crazy to you, but sending couriers and trainee solicitors to walk around the City with valuable financial instruments and bags full of cash was pretty standard practice well into the 2000s.

from a Swiss bank by altering the security numbers on some of the bills and using them as collateral, but even then the UK police were informed. Cheeseman made contact with the New York mafia and later, via Traynor's IRA contacts, the infamous US arms dealer Oliver North,[19] and, separately, South American drug cartels. In the months that followed the bills were recovered in luggage at airports in the UK, Tenerife, Singapore, New York and Florida, and in Cyprus, as Cheeseman and Traynor endeavoured to launder the bills.

In December 1991, Patrick Thomas was shot dead on his doorstep. A few months earlier Cheeseman had been arrested and sentenced to six and half years in absentia—he had absconded while on bail. In October 1991 a headless and handless body was found in Bolney, Sussex, and was initially believed to be that of Cheeseman. By 1992, however, Cheeseman had resurfaced in Spain where he was rearrested and extradited to the US to face money laundering charges. The identity of the Bolney body has never been established. Cheeseman claimed he had fled the UK in fear of his life, pleading guilty to the US federal charges.

Held: Cheeseman was candid about what he had done and admitted laundering £16m in bills. For our purposes, his most telling comments concerned why bearer securities were targeted:

> 'I could shift it now, US$200 million, US$300 million,' Cheeseman boasted, sitting in Manhattan's bleak Metropolitan Correctional Center. 'It's so easy to put them down. You can get 60 per cent as collateral for loans. You can't believe what I've been offered in here.' (quoted by *The Observer*)[20]

Cheeseman was sentenced to six and half years in federal prison. The UK police recovered all but two of the bills.

Originally negotiability of bearer securities was limited to bills of exchange, but observing that the law had developed from the law merchant and codified its practice, the English courts did not take too long to extend the notion to other kinds of securities which financiers de facto transferred as bearer securities. The principal extensions were to bearer bonds and bearer shares.

BECHUANALAND EXPLORATION CO v LONDON TRADING BANK [1898] 2 QB 658

B was in possession of certain English law bearer bonds issued by a UK company. B's company secretary fraudulently removed the bearer bonds from the company safe. The secretary approached LTB and negotiated the bonds for cash, before disappearing. B now sued LTB claiming that the bonds, not being bills of exchange, were not negotiable and consequently the transfer was void. B drew attention to the many conditions applicable to the bonds—conditions which meant the bonds could not be bills of exchange within the meaning of the 1882 Act.

19 See further the 'Iran-Contra' scandal, e.g. Peter Kornbluh and Malcolm Byrne, *The Iran–Contra Scandal: The Declassified History* (New Press 1993).

20 Michael Gillard, 'My Role in the World's Biggest Robbery' *The Observer* (London, 11 April 1993) 2–27.

Held: In virtue of extensive mercantile practice, imported from the US, that negotiability was a product of the law merchant, and the clear terms on the face of the bond that they were negotiable securities payable to bearer, it was legally possible for the secretary to negotiate the bonds. The usual rules on acquisition of title therefore applied: LTB was a bona fide purchaser for value without notice and so had absolute and valid title to the bonds. B's claim would fail.

The case was followed in the leading case of *Edelstein v Schuler & Co* [1902] 2 KB 144, which reinforced the finding by declaring that the court would take judicial notice that a bond stated to be payable to bearer was negotiable. In other words, there was no need to prove this each time.

Notice how easy it was for Bechuanaland Exploration Co.'s secretary to steal the bearer bonds, not simply because he had access to them—company officers and employees have access to all kinds of documents—but because he could move them and dispose of them for value at a respectable financial institution, no questions asked. This money-like quality made bearer bonds (and bearer shares) particularly suited to misuse in criminal financing and money laundering during the twentieth century when they were in most widespread use.

1980s ACTION MOVIES

Bearer bonds were the unsung financial stars of 1980s and 1990s action flicks. In films such as *Die Hard, Pure Heat*, and *Beverly Hills Cop*, criminal gangs could be found demanding ransoms or shifting ill-gotten gains across borders in the form of 'negotiable, non-sequential bearer bonds.' Their nature, it is true, greatly facilitate money laundering and tax evasion.

Bearer securities can be transferred by delivering possession; other negotiable instruments by indorsing the instrument and delivering it. Non-negotiable instruments must be transferred by other means, chief of which is through entering the transfer of title on a centralized register.

A **registered security** is a security, title to which is proven by entry of the name of the titleholder on such a centralized register. The titleholder may well receive a document stating that they hold the security, but this document is no more than a 'certificate,' having no legal effect in itself and therefore not an instrument. Delivering the certificate to a third party will not transfer title. Rather, to transfer title, the holder must complete a form of transfer to a named third party and deliver this and (where required by the terms of the issuance) the certificate to the centralized register holder. This holder will amend the register by deleting and inserting the names of the transferor and transferee against their modified holdings, and then send certification of the same to the transferee. The following leading case concerned registered shares but is of general application to registered securities.

SOCIÉTÉ GÉNÉRALE DE PARIS AND COLLADON v WALKER (1885) 11 App Cas 20 (HL)

W has a shareholder of a company ('Tramways Union Co. Ltd.') that issued registered shares. The company's articles of association provided that no transfer would be registered by the Company Secretary until a duly completed stock transfer form *and* the relevant certificates were delivered to the company.

W borrowed money from a third party using the shares as security. The third party sensibly required W to sign but not date a stock transfer form and deliver this and the share certificates into the third party's possession. Note that the third party had not become legal owner; it had an equitable mortgage of the shares (see Chapter 3).

W then fraudulently approached SG and attempted to borrow further monies using the same shares as collateral. He provided another signed but undated stock transfer form but told SG he had 'lost' the share certificates. When W defaulted, SG dated the stock transfer form and delivered this to Tramways Union Co. Ltd. The Company Secretary refused to effect the transfer for want of the certificates.

Held: SG had no legal (or here even equitable) title in the registered securities, nor any right to be registered as shareholders. Any equitable interest SG had was second in priority to and could not displace the prior equitable interest of the third-party mortgagee.

As noted earlier, one of the requirements of negotiability under the Bills of Exchange Act 1882 is that the promise or order to pay should, apart from specifying the drawer, payee, and time of payment, be otherwise unconditional.[21] Any additional conditionality renders the bill non-negotiable, which in practical terms means that a holder cannot simply deliver title to the instrument to a third party by handing it over. Observe that registered securities necessarily are subject to an additional condition: transfer must be initiated by delivery of signed and dated transfer form and certificate to the registrar and is only effective when the registrar amends (or ought to have amended) the register. The result is that registered securities are not negotiable. This appears confusing, but it underscores the difference of negotiability from transferability. Negotiability means that a holder may simply transfer title by delivery (with indorsement as required) and the new holder takes absolute title. Even if the old holder's title is questionable, as in the case of a rogue, the new holder's title is unquestionably absolute. Not so with mere transfer of registered securities. A third party, the registrar/company secretary/intermediary, must take steps to validate the transfer. A comparable observation may be made with choses in action, where transfer is only valid on giving of written notice to the obligor. In such cases, therefore, the acquiring holder's title may be defective.

One might ask: if the certificates are not instruments representing debt, but representations of those instruments which represent the underlying debt, just where are these instruments to be located? These too are held centrally: for bonds, as a central trust deed constituting the indebtedness; for bills, as a centrally held set of notes. All registrations are with respect of these documents. This leads to a practical follow-up question. If the instruments are held in one place, could the issuer/maker simplify matters by reducing many securities to a single one?

8.1.5 (Un)divided securities and the fungibility problem

The answer to the previous question is 'yes': rather than hold an aggregate of individually numbered securities worth together the total nominal amount of the issue, it is open to the issuer of securities

21 *Mortgage Insurance Corpn v Commissioners of Inland Revenue* (1888) 21 QBD 352 (CA); *Akbar Khan v Attar Singh* [1936] 2 All ER 545 (PC) 550; *Claydon v Bradley* [1987] 1 WLR 521, [1987] 1 All ER 522 (CA). So, for example, where a bill of exchange was only payable on condition that a bill of lading attached to it be genuine, it was held not to be a negotiable instrument: *Guaranty Trust Co of New York v Hannay & Co* [1918] 1 KB 43.

to make a single **global note** or bond held by itself or, more commonly, a securities trustee, and representing the value of the entire issue.

Thus, where a person holds bearer securities in a certain amount (e.g. bearer bonds of GBP100), we say they hold **divided** securities because they hold an aliquot of the whole issuance. On the other hand, a registered holder of some part of a global note has an interest in **undivided** securities.

The practical notion of undivided securities is not particularly new: when merchants came together to invest in common enterprise, their capital would be instrumentalized by purchasing stock-in-trade. No one thought a particular investor was acquiring 15 shoes (or whatever the business traded); rather the investor had an interest in the whole stock as it varied (and hopefully grew) from time to time. Just as instruments came to be confused with the debts they represent, so instruments representing the investors' interests in the stock came to be confused with the stock itself: the instruments were called 'stock,' the holders 'stockholders,' and the businesses issuing the instruments 'joint stock companies'—indeed they still are in the United States. It was only in 1837 that the English courts recognized that the interest in the stock security was separate from any purported equitable interest in in the stock-in-trade.[22] It is worth noting that the predecessor of the share in the UK—stock—is divisible in any fashion the holder sees fit, whereas the more modern 'equity' security—the share—may only be transferred in pre-agreed nominal amounts, such as 1p or GBP1. Nevertheless, even registered shares are certificates of an undivided security in the capital of the company. One share does not represent a specific bit of the company's capital (these 15 shoes); it represents a proportion of the whole, undivided capital as it varies through time.

It is far more common these days for issuers of debt securities to issue an undivided security, i.e. a global note. Interests in the global note may only be transferable in preset 'portions' (not a technical term), such as multiples of GBP100.

The notion of (un)divided assets is linked to another legal concept with a less helpful name: **fungibility**. Fungibility arises in the context of a common practical problem. If a merchant delivers one tonne of grain to a bailee to be stored in a grain warehouse with other grain, and the grain is mixed, lawyers know that some grain belongs to our merchant, but which grain? Must we require the merchant to mark each kernel of grain with the merchant's name and then go sifting through the bulk to recover all those belonging to a particular merchant? On the other hand, the whole of the grain in the warehouse seems divisible, for the merchant can deposit and withdraw one tonne of grain from the whole. The problem is particularly pressing in the following scenario:

Merchant A deposits 1 tonne of grain with Warehouse keeper W; W mixes the grain with 3 tonnes of the same species of grain in his warehouse. A contracts to sell one-half tonne of 'my grain held by W' to Merchant B, who pays the price. A is then bankrupted.

In this situation B has a personal claim in breach of contract against A, but that may not be particularly valuable if A is bankrupt. As ever, B would much prefer to have a property claim over the grain itself. Had A's grain been 'identified' and had half of it been further identified and allocated to the contract with B, the Sale of Goods Act 1979 (SGA 1979) tells us that (without any contrary contractual stipulation) the property in the goods transferred to B on the making of the contract.[23] B would thus have a proprietary claim on his one-half tonne of grain. Yet before 1995 the courts disagreed that in this scenario the goods were identifiable and allocated to the contract. They asked: just which one-half tonne in the warehouse belonged to B? If the total 4 tonnes held by W has been reduced (by rot, fire, or whatever), has A borne a proportionate loss, and if so, ought B only be able

22 *Bligh v Brent* (1837) 160 ER 397. See further Paddy Ireland, 'Capitalism Without the Capitalist: The Joint Stock Company Share and the Emergence of the Modern Doctrine of Separate Corporate Personality' (1996) 17 The Journal of Legal History 41.

23 Sales of Goods Act 1979, ss 16, 17, 18. r 1 and r 5.

to recover a proportionately reduced amount? What if the rot had been present in the other grain only, A's being of excellent quality? The courts, faced with the impossibility of ascertaining which grain was whose, took the view that the goods were not identifiable and thus not allocated to the contract. The result was no property had transferred; it could only transfer when one-half tonne be actually segregated from the whole. As this had not happened before breach, B had no proprietary claim to legal title in the one-half tonne of grain.

Faced with this, lawyers advanced a second argument highly pertinent to the way securities are held. They argued that though SGA 1979 denied a legal property right in unidentified goods, B had acquired an *equitable* interest in the grain. The Court of Appeal in *re Wait* (which had broadly these facts)[24] was having none of it:

> The total sum of legal relations (meaning by the word 'legal' existing in equity as well as in the common law) arising out of the contract for the sale of goods may well be regarded as defined by the Code. [The courts below held there had been an equitable assignment of a portion of the grain.] I feel bound to repel the disastrous innovations which in my opinion the judgments under review would introduce into well settled commercial relations. [640-641 (Atkins LJ)]

It is worth noting for later that Atkins LJ, as he then was, did not take the whole Court of Appeal with him; Sargent LJ fundamentally dissented on grounds of commercial practicality.

A sale of goods contract to transfer an undivided share in an identified bulk mixed with others did not create an equitable interest in that part which the seller promised to transfer. The decision was followed in an investment context in the following case.

IN RE GOLDCORP EXCHANGE LTD (IN RECEIVERSHIP) [1995] 1 AC 74 (PC)

G was in the business of buying and selling gold for itself and for clients. It held itself out as buying individual amounts of bullion and coin on behalf of clients and holding the gold for them as custodian. It further promised that it would hold sufficient bullion to meet all claims. However, G did none of these things, mixing all the gold, buying and selling amounts at will, and holding insufficient amounts. G collapsed and the clients claimed they had property rights in the gold.

Held: Despite G's representations and promises, individual amounts of gold were never appropriated and allocated to particular clients' contracts. Legally, following SGA 1979 and re *Wait*, property had never transferred to them. As to the question of a trust, settlement of a trust required three certainties, of which certainty of the subject matter was one. This observation took the court back to the identification and allocation problem, where it again concluded that there was no way to ascertain which bullion from the bulk belonged to which clients or any. There was accordingly no trust for want of certainty of subject matter. The clients only had personal claims sounding in damages.

24 [1927] 1 Ch 606 (CA), LJ Sargent dissenting.

Goldcorp followed *re Wait* and a Chancery Division case from a decade earlier: *re London Wine Co (Shippers) Ltd*.[25] The facts were quite similar, save that here clients invested in fine wines. When the wine merchant collapsed, the clients sought to argue that the wine bottles were held on trust for them and so they had an equitable interest in some very valuable wines. Following *re Wait*, the court found that individual wine bottles had not been allocated to individual clients but remained part of a bulk. Moreover, wanting of certainty of subject matter, no trust in favour of the clients had been created either. No property right, legal or equitable, had transferred to the clients.

In light if the difficult results if these cases, the Law Commission launched a review, reporting in 1995, which led to the introduction that year of ss 20A, 20B Sale of Goods Act 1979.[26] Now a depositing merchant becomes co-owner (tenant in common) of a share of the undivided but identifiable bulk of tangible goods, title to which may be transferred under contract. This is deemed possible just where all the grain is in material respects of the same kind, for in such a case the merchant should not care which tonne of grain he receives back as it is all the same.

Where does this leave sales of securities from an undivided bulk? There was some fear following *re Wait* that if Shareholder contracted to transfer to T a portion of her holding in undivided registered shares, T would have no legal nor equitable interest in the shares until identified shares were appropriated to the contract—something extremely impractical in the context of intangible property such as shares. The 1995 amendment to the SGA 1979 was of no help because it only applied to sales of tangible goods.

HUNTER v MOSS [1994] 1 WLR 452, [1994] 3 All ER 215 (CA)

M was registered holder of 950 the 1,000 shares in a company. H claimed that a benefit of his employment was that he be given 5% (i.e. 50) of the shares in the company. M refused to transfer the shares. H argued that he had an equitable interest in the shares because M held them on oral trust for him. M argued that there could be no trust because the subject matter of the trust was uncertain, for which 50 shares of the bulk of 950 were to be held on trust?

Held: The reasoning is somewhat murky, but seems to have turned on the complete indistinguishability of the shares held and that the holding was only ever divisible in nominal terms (i.e. x number or percentage of shares). This sufficed to distinguish the case from those discussed above, and accordingly the 50 shares were held on trust for H, who had a corresponding equitable interest in them.

The decision attracted severe criticism because, though it considered some of the bulk cases, it seemed completely at odds with *re Wait*, *re London Wine* and others, with those gift cases expressing similar thoughts.[27] Yet such criticism is misplaced, for the principal policy motivation behind

---

25 [1986] PCC 121. Being an English court, *London Wine* is the authority, but I chose to highlight the later Privy Council decision in *re Goldcorp* for reasons of relevance.

26 And a qualification of s 18 r 5 with new paras (3) and (4).

27 Notably, D Hayton, *Underhill and Hayton: Law Relating to Trusts and Trustees* (15th edn, Butterworths 1995) 61; Sarah Worthington, 'Sorting Out Ownership Interests in a Bulk: Gifts, Sales and Trusts' [1999] Journal of Business Law 1.

re Wait and subsequent authorities was the defence of the SGA 1979 as a complete code for the sale of *goods*. The SGA 1979 has nothing to say about gifts or sales of intangible assets. The one transferrable lesson from *re Wait* was the need to uphold commercial practicality, and by admitting that it was impractical to segregate a part of an intangible shareholding to a trust, the Court of Appeal in *Hunter v Moss* was giving effect to common sense in the context of a very different class of moveable property. Moreover, the decision prefigures the 1995 changes to the SGA 1979 by in effect stating that because shares are completely fungible—an ordinary share no. 12445 in Faco plc is legally equivalent to and interchangeable with ordinary share no. 12446 in that company—there are absolutely no concerns about who should bear the risk that one part of the shares be damaged, shares of the same class bear all capital loss rateably. Sir Roy Goode has subsequently written that *Hunter v Moss* was correctly decided.[28] Any criticisms are likely more a function of the somewhat weak judicial reasoning in the case. It remains, grudgingly in the eyes of the court, good law—a point we will pick up in the next section.

From the discussion of 'bulk' and 'shares' you may well have guessed how this reasoning transposes to the field of securities. Broadly:

(1) Bearer securities and bills generally, which are of necessity each unique and physical, are divided securities of the maker/issuer and in no way fungible. A possessor owns just *this* bearer bond, for example, and no other.

(2) Registered securities are considered fungible,[29] certificates representing an interest in the undivided bulk of the identified[30] debt (or equity capital) of the issuer. A holder of registered securities can transfer her title in the usual way, and it matters not that the central registrar issue fresh certificates with different serial numbers to the transferee than those returned by the transferor because the transferee takes an interest in a share, which is priced in nominal value of the undivided security—remember, the certificates are merely symbolic. An unexecuted contract to sell, gift of, or declaration of trust over shares can confer on the transferee/donee/beneficiary an equitable interest in the securities.

This deals with the property rights as between holders and maker/issuer *directly*. Yet in modern securities markets the majority of investors do not directly hold registered securities. Rather, they hold them *indirectly* through intermediaries. Here English law has tied itself up in knots.

8.2 Securities and indirect interests in securities

Modern securities markets use intermediaries. A company will issue a single global note to a trustee, and investors will all invest in that single note. Retail investors, who lack direct access to the market, may also need to use an intermediary who is an admitted market member to gain indirect access to securities. This intermediary may well buy a large interest in the global note on behalf of multiple clients. That interest may change as the intermediary increases or decreases its position, reflecting client orders, and it may even stay the same as the clients change, with these clients selling their interests to incoming third parties. This intermediation can be represented as follows.

28 Sir Roy Goode, *Commercial Law in the Next Millennium* (Sweet & Maxwell 1998) 73.

29 *re The International Contract Co (Ind's Case)* (1872) LR 7 Ch 485, *Platt v Rowe* (1909) 26 TLR 49.

30 e.g. the debt constituted by a specific issue of notes, bonds, or a class of shares.

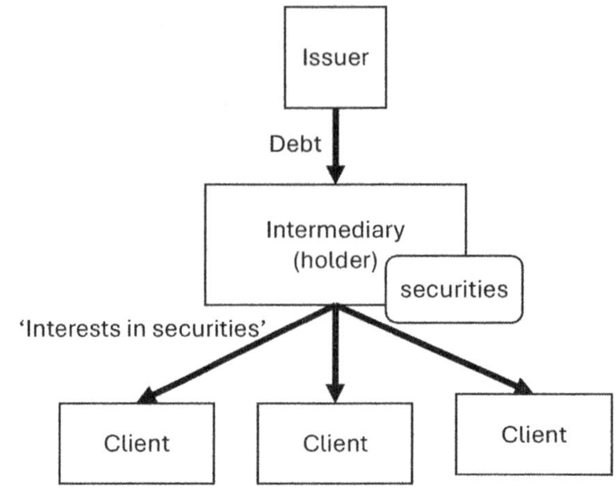

Figure 8.1 Holding of securities by an intermediary

We are now dealing with a distinct situation from that considered in the previous section. Our attention turns to scenarios of the following type:

Anil and Beth each give £1,000 to Intermediary for the purposes of acquiring securities issued by Issuer plc. Intermediary acquires these securities which are worth £2,000.

The legal nature of the Intermediary, as direct holder of the securities, can be dealt with using our analysis from the previous section. What, though, is the nature of the legal interest of each of Anil and Beth? Is it simply contractual, or proprietary also, and if proprietary, legal or merely equitable? Consider these additional facts:

Beth contracts to sell '£50's worth of my securities held with Intermediary' to Colm. Before she can instruct Intermediary to effect the transfer, she is bankrupted.

What is the nature of Colm's interest (if any) in the GBP50 worth of securities? If Beth has a proprietary interest in the securities, has Colm acquired a proprietary interest which he can enforce against the Intermediary and Beth's other creditors? These questions lead to the core problems we encountered in the previous section: division and fungibility. If Beth points to GBP50's worth of securities, *which* (part of the) securities does she mean and so on which securities does Colm have a claim?

Let us break these arrangements down. If the Issuer's securities were in bearer form, provided Intermediary had rightfully taken possession of them, Intermediary would be legal owner of the securities. If the securities are registered, Intermediary is legal owner if it has been duly registered as holder, and equitable owner if it has acquired the right to be registered as such. This first link in the chain discloses nothing new.

PAUSE FOR THOUGHT

The Intermediary holds property for Beth and Anil. Using your existing legal knowledge (review the previous section) propose how the courts might characterize this arrangement and how as a consequence they would classify Beth and Anil's rights with respect to the Intermediary.

Legally, the precise nature of the rights between Anil, Beth, and the Intermediary is more complicated than it perhaps need be. Broadly, there are two positions: (1) what appears to be the current law, which is conceptually unsatisfactory; (2) Joanna Benjamin's 'equitable interest' account,[31] which is cleaner and fits fairly well with a long history of financial practice. These are set out below. I have put the legal position first because authority demands it, but you may prefer to reading Benjamin's account first as it is easier to grasp.

8.2.1 The law

As you may have guessed, the current law on interests in securities follows *Hunter v Moss* (see previous section). That is, it is possible for one person, a trustee or nominee, to hold some as yet unappropriated part of a 'bulk' of registered shares and by extension any other registered security on trust or as nominee for some other person, called a beneficiary. Why this should be so and why securities should be treated differently is not really explained in the cases, which have preferred rather to simply accept *Hunter*'s authority and not delve much deeper.

RE HARVARD SECURITIES LTD (IN LIQUIDATION); HOLLAND v NEWBURY [1997] 2 BCLC 369 (ChD)

Harvard was a securities broker. He bought and sold securities, including shares, for his clients. More particularly, Harvard would appoint a nominee who would own the securities to its order for the benefit of named clients. The main issue was whether the clients had a beneficial (i.e. equitable) interest in the securities.

Held: *Hunter v Moss* was binding—it was possible to declare a trust of unidentified and unallocated parts of a bulk of a class[32] of shares for the benefit of others.

Neuberger J (as he then was), said:

> While I am not particularly convinced by the distinction [between *re Wait* and *Hunter*], it appears to me that a more satisfactory way of distinguishing Hunter from the other cases is that it was concerned with shares, and not with chattels. First, that is a ground which is consistent with Dillon LJ's reliance on re *Rose* (a case concerned with shares) and his ground for distinguishing *re London Wine Co (Shippers) Ltd.* (and, by implication, *re Wait*) which, it will be remembered, he described as being 'concerned with the appropriation of chattels and when property in chattels passes.' Second, it is on this basis that the editors of Underhill and Hayton believe that Hunter is explained (although they regard it on an unsatisfactory basis). Third, the observations of Atkin LJ in *re Wait* [1927] 1 Ch 606, 630 . . . referring to the 'ordinary operations of buying and selling goods'

31 Joanna Benjamin, *Interests in Securities: A Proprietary Law Analysis of the International Securities Market* (OUP 2000).

32 For share classes, see s 629ff Companies Act 2006.

could be said to provide a policy ground for there being one rule for chattels and another for shares.

In the following Hong Kong case, *Hunter v Moss* was followed much more enthusiastically.

RE CA PACIFIC FINANCE LTD (IN LIQUIDATION) [1999] 2 HKLRD 1; [2000] 1 BCLC 494 (Hong Kong CFI)

CAPF operated in tandem with a sister company CA Pacific Securities Ltd. (CAPS). CAPF would face retail customers, and where these wished to invest, it would take their money and pass it to CAPS for the purpose of buying, holding and selling securities on each client's respective behalf, to the order of CAPF. As such, CAPS acted as intermediary.

CAPS would buy and sell securities through the Hong Kong Central Clearing & Settlement System (CCASS), operated by Hong Kong Securities Co Ltd. (HKSCC). HKSCC would match trades between buyers and sellers, but legally it would then create two new contracts, one buying the securities from a selling trader, one selling the securities on to the buying trader. In effect, HKSCC itself was an intermediary between e.g. CAPS and relevant issuers.

When the companies became insolvent, the liquidator sought directions as to the nature of the clients' proprietary interests (if any).

Held: Noting *Hunter v Moss* and informally distinguishing *re Wait*, Yuen J said:

> What is required is not segregation for the sake of segregation. What is required is certainty of the property over which it is intended there should be a disposal of the beneficial interest. What is necessary is the means of identifying or distinguishing the subject matter of the trust.
>
> How one identifies or distinguishes things must depend on the nature of the thing. For tangible goods, that is done by segregating one parcel from the rest of a bulk. Each parcel has its own characteristics and would be subject to its own risks (eg corking of the wine in *re London Wine Co (Shippers) Ltd*). But for intangible things such as fungible shares ranking pari passu—which enjoy exactly the same rights, which have no separate characteristics and no inherent risks (as HKSCC takes responsibility for replacing any defective securities in CCASS: CCASS, r 815)—it is difficult to see why segregation is necessary, so long as one knows **the quantity of the shares which are to form the subject matter of the trust**. [my emphasis]

Yuen J went on to tackle the open question of the nature of the proprietary interest in the shares:

> I find it difficult to infer a tenancy-in-common of a pool of securities (which may change in quantity from day to day) when the language of the client agreement is in terms of an individual proprietary interest. And as recognized by Oliver J in *re London Wine Co (Shippers) Ltd.*, where the numerical whole is unknown because

> of its ever-changing nature, it would be even more difficult to infer an intention of the client that his interest would be that of a tenant-in-common of an ever-changing proportion of an unknown quantity. . . .
>
> I conclude therefore that the specified client . . . have acquired and retained proprietary interests in the securities so purchased, and that they hold their proprietary interests as individual beneficiaries.

The case is suggestive (though not more) of two thoughts for the English law position:

(1) Sufficient appropriation of securities from a bulk to one person will occur where the quantity of securities is known. This is different from identification by market value (which can and does change very often). On the one hand, if Beth declares she holds '50 Faco plc securities in my account with Intermediary' on trust for Colm, we have sufficient certainty as to which securities she means, even if Intermediary holds other Faco plc securities because of their perfect fungibility (interchangeability). On the other hand, it seems that if Beth declares a trust over GBP50 of her Faco plc securities, things are uncertain because the market price of the securities fluctuates (and they may become worthless).

(2) This leads to the second point: on the facts the client agreement spoke of *individual* proprietary interests. This led the judge to find a proposed tenancy in common of a fund of all the CAPS securities was inappropriate at least in the case. A fund may well fluctuate in number, kind and value of securities, with the key result that those interested in the fund would bear gains and losses proportionate to their interest. That could not apply here because of the individual, severable interest defined in terms of number of securities. Beth has 50 securities which bear gains and losses themselves but are in no way affected by the gains, losses, and trading activity of the other persons with interests in the intermediary's securities holdings.

There are difficulties, however. If we think back to the way these issues were resolved for comixed bulk goods by amending SGA 1979, the analysis is that owners and their transferees have and obtain a proprietary interest, but this interest is as equitable tenant-in-common. Yet neither *Hunter*, *re Harvard*, nor *CA Pacific Finance* come to that conclusion, at least explicitly. In these cases the courts really seem to think that the client (and then transferee) have a proprietary interest just of their own *separate* from other possible clients, just as they have an individual account with the intermediary just recording their shares.

Yet nor can we conclude with certainty from all this that a tenancy in common is not the correct analysis; all we know is the CAPS/CAPF arrangements expressly and impliedly excluded such an arrangement in favour of individual interests. By way of comparison, take a unit trust which invests the collective capital of members in a range of financial instruments. Here the unit holders (beneficiaries of the trust) are benefitted in proportion to their unit holding valued by the overall performance of the fund. It is then one technical step from a unit trust to an Open Ended Investment Company (OIEC) where the shareholders invest capital in exchange for shares, and therefore the *Bligh v Brent* analysis applies: the shareholders have no property right to what the capital is invested in; they only have rights in the capital on a winding up (including any redemption or buy back of their shares). What is clear from the cases is that the clients using the intermediaries did not want to participate in a fund; they wanted the intermediary to buy, hold and sell specific securities just for them unaffected by the investment decisions of others. The modern position for sale of bulk goods—tenancy in common at best—seems unhelpful and unjust if applied by analogy to intermediation of securities. *Hunter v Moss* provides some relief from that position, but the disdain with which the judgment is regarded casts a shadow over any intermediated registered securities transaction where the securities are comingled (as is inevitable in global note issues).

8.2.2 Benjamin's 'interests in securities' account

Joanna Benjamin breaks down intermediated securities transactions to argue that clients who instruct intermediaries to hold securities for them have a specific proprietary right she calls an 'interest in securities.'[33] The essence of this arrangement is one of trust: the intermediary holds legal title to the securities (be they bearer or registered, divided or not); the clients are beneficiaries of the intermediary and have an equitable interest in the securities held as against third parties.[34] As with any trust relationship, the beneficiary clients also have personal claims (breach of contract, breach of fiduciary duty) against the intermediary as trustee.[35] As a result, the clients have no direct claim in contract or property against an issuer of securities; only claims against the intermediary and rights versus third parties asserting claims against the intermediary.[36]

As you may know from your study of real property or trusts, equitable interests can be defeated. This places the clients in a weaker position that legal title holders of securities. For example, the clients' equities may be defeated if the property is transferred to a bona fide purchaser for value without notice, and may rank junior to any prior equitable interest, such as a charge over the securities in favour of a third party made by the intermediary prior to the creation of the client's interest. Conversely, equitable interests are non-negotiable (see section 8.1.4), meaning that purchasers of such interests do not have prima facie protection against possible equitable claims of third parties (even if defeasible, being open to a claim is unwelcome). One might add that these equitable interests also face hurdles of recognition in jurisdictions which reject the trust concept.

Benjamin admits the allocation problem creates problems for this analysis. Where an intermediary acquires a bulk interest in securities on behalf of multiple clients, the law's tendency is to see a joint trust fund held for the benefit of all. Moreover, the traditional unallocated bulk cases discussed above treat the clients' interests in a non-segregated bulk of assets as an equitable tenancy in common. The result, as we mentioned, is that the clients bear losses and gains in the bulk rateably. If that was what was intended, no one would be particularly concerned, but intermediary arrangements are principally of the type where one client is led to believe that if they instruct intermediary to buy and hold 50 Faco plc bonds, or some equivalent position, those interests in those bonds are the client's alone to the exclusion of others.

In view of this, and the *Hunter v Moss* line of cases, Benjamin argues that interests in securities should developed so that the interest of the client is an outright interest and not a co-ownership interest, even in the absence of allocation.[37] On this view, interests in securities are to be treated much as we treat a shareholder's interest in registered shares: there is a register specifying a nominal set of securities against that named shareholder and no other person. This is for all practical purposes what an intermediary does: it keeps client accounts recording client orders. One feature of the post–*Hunter v Moss* cases seems to have been that the court had no trouble identifying the securities in which the client was interested even if they were not formally segregated.

Benjamin's general thrust is that English property law has been too physicalist, meaning it is too wedded to the paradigm that property means property in a defined, tangible thing.[38] Such a paradigm struggles with bulks of grain, not least because physical grain can vary or be lost to the elements. A grain merchant may well be unhappy if 'her' grain is comixed with rotten grain. Yet none of these concerns bear on intangible property defined only nominally. One (interest in a) security of Faco plc is as good as another. By way of example, Benjamin points us to the vernacular

33 Benjamin (n 31).
34 ibid ch 2.
35 ibid chs 2, 13.
36 ibid.
37 ibid ch 14, 18.
38 ibid ch 13F.

statement 'my money is in the bank.'[39] As we have seen, there is no 'my money' in the bank even if I placed specific coins there. I have a debt claim on the bank which may be met by delivering to me money of the same type *but not exactly the same money*. Furthermore, if I wish to pay a third party, the bank simply cancels its debt to me and creates a debt to third party. Given the attendant contractual rights associated with account holding, this is all accompanied by a cancellation of my contract with bank, and the creation of a new contract with third party. In short, we have a novation,[40] and novation is just how intermediaries, custodians, and central securities depositories have been handling securities intermediation transactions for years.

This view is compelling though there remain questions around 'difficult cases.' Benjamin should place more stress, for example, on Yuen J's explicit reference to the *quantity* of securities held.[41] The analogy from registered shares works because a shareholder of 10,000 1p shares in Faco plc can point to a members' register stating as much, and when the rights of the shareholders are considered inter se and as against third parties, a definite if interchangeable 10,000 shares of Faco plc are just the shares of the named shareholder, no more, no less. What happens, though, when a client takes up not a nominal position (10,000 Faco plc securities) but an 'economic' position ('buy for me GBP100 of Faco plc securities')? The price paid will likely not reflect nominal but market value even for a primary issuance of securities. If intermediary buys in bulk for multiple clients, even if he records their name against the market value paid, how do we deal with variations in market value thereafter? Do the clients bear gains and losses rateably? And if the client now wishes to sell their interests in securities, are they permitted to sell them for GBP100 even if the market price has fallen to GBP90? If so, Benjamin's analysis fails in this case at least, for she denied distribution of rateable gains/losses between clients. One possible solution is to read this transaction through a legal lens: the client and intermediary may have commonly thought to acquire GBP100 of Faco plc securities, but legally it was an instruction to buy as many Faco plc securities in nominal terms as GBP100 would manage to buy. Once the transaction is cleared, the client then becomes in the law's view equitably interested in just that nominal amount of the relevant securities *not* in their fluctuating market value.

Somewhere between the extremes of nominal and market value lies the global note. Here there is but one note, so reference to x number of securities greater than one is meaningless. Rather, must use a monetary value to quantify their desired interest in the intermediary's holding of the global note. The solution again seems to be to legally characterize the situation: the global note has a nominal value on its face (e.g. the debt it represents) and in naming a value to be acquired, we examine what respective portion of that nominal face value is acquired by the intermediary for the client by means of the sum actually paid to the market. One does feel, however, that such clients may be disappointed and surprised if such a judicial recharacterization of their position is carried out to their disadvantage.

8.3 Securities and interests in securities as collateral

In Chapters 3 and 4 we examined the forms of English law consensual security, and already had occasion to touch on security over securities (namely shares). Given our discussion of intermediation and interests in securities, we are now presented with the problem of analysing how such

39 ibid ch 14, 26.

40 ibid ch 3.27ff. There is a question mark whether novation does occur, as Benjamin concludes, or whether there is, in the absence of an explicit novation, an assignment of an equitable interest (not to be confused with an equitable assignment of one's legal rights e.g. an equitable mortgage).

41 *re CA Pacific Finance Ltd. (In Liquidation)* [1999] 2 HKLRD 1; [2000] 1 BCLC 494 (Hong Kong CFI), see above.

interests can constitute security. In the securities market, securities as representations of rights to claim a debt against a *person* have, as the nomenclature suggests, long been associated with the more traditional sense of *real* security (i.e. rights over a thing) with potentially confusing results.

We have noted already (section 8.1) that securities derived their name from *personal* security in the sense that a debt claim against someone offered security-like risk mitigation of some value to the creditor—it just did not offer real rights over property. Yet if you think through how real security works what we have in practical terms is less a sharp distinction between the personal and the real, and more of a spectrum. Ask yourself what a chargee wants from security: to enforce against it should the debtor fail to pay. Enforcement here means seizing the asset, selling it, and thus liquidating it into money to be used to repay the debt (excess returned to debtor). What though is money but a promissory note issued by the state, negotiable in the hands of bearer, and, critically, utterly liquid in that an immediate 'buyer' of money can always be found. Imagine if the chargee could not obtain money but a cash equivalent. This would not be ideal, but other government bills are also highly liquid at least in financial markets, and so our chargee might well accept T-bills as the 'next best thing.' Compare this level of liquidity to a security interest in land, where realizing the value as cash through sale may take months. Thus, at the one end of our spectrum we have highly illiquid assets which the chargee attempts to convert into liquid assets (money), and at the other end money and cash equivalents like T-bills and then notes and bills from other makers and issuers. Where everything converges is in the securities market. You might imagine someone taking real security over money. In such a case enforcement just means asserting title over the cash for there is no need to realize the money, it is already in the desired form. If you paid a deposit for a flat tenancy, you could be said to grant security over the cash by way of mortgage (you transferred the credits to your bank account to the landlord). We are very close to this in the securities market, for when one person grants real security over securities, they can be offering in affect property which is very close to being cash, especially in a market where buyers for the securities are readily found. At this point, one can understand why market participants have long equated personal securities with real security have, for granting real security in security tends to result in simply delivering securities as cash equivalents to the 'secured' party.

For this reason, the market has developed different terminology to describe just when securities are used as real security. Where a person offers (personal) securities as (real) security, perhaps for a loan, this is called offering **collateral**. Just to add to the confusion, often collateral is also called **margin** though it has nothing to do with margin in the Chapter 2 sense of the contractually agreed profit on lending money.

ESSENTIAL DEFINITIONS: COLLATERAL AND MARGIN

Collateral means, in the context of securities markets, real security rights over securities.

The terms, however, are used *as if* the securities were the collateral i.e. no practical distinction is made between the security interest in the securities and the securities themselves. In the context of negotiable bearer securities, such as bills, this makes sense, because they are all but equivalent to money and so holding them is little different from holding the monetary proceeds of enforcing 'normal' security.

The amount of collateral a secured party requires in this context—effectively the risk 'margin of error' should the provider of collateral fail to meet its current of future obligations—is called **margin**.

Warning: you already encountered the same word 'margin' being used in a different sense (as profit on lending) in Chapter 2. Be clear which one is meant in a given context.

Margin lending is a form of credit facility secured by collateral in the sense above. The margin is normally variable, indexed to financial covenants measuring borrower leverage (Loan to Value (**LTV**)) and/or the Value at Risk (**VaR**) as a result of the investment positions the borrower takes from time to time. Primarily, margin loans fund securities trading, but such loans can also be used e.g. by private equity houses to monetize their portfolio securities holdings for the purposes of further private equity investing.

A **margin call** is a contractual right of a creditor under margin lending to require the borrower to rectify a breached financial covenant by any of:

(i) Prepayment of (all or part of) the loan;
(ii) Disposal of investment positions e.g. selling shares until LTV is no longer breached;
(iii) Delivery pre-agreed collateral not yet held by the creditor;
(iv) Provision of additional collateral to mitigate additional risk.

Margin calls look harmless enough: who could complain from a policy perspective when creditors mitigate risk in a readily enforceable manner i.e. by taking and realizing highly liquid assets? Yet margin calls, when they become systemic, have proved to be one of the ways in which financial crises intensify.

Brunnermeier and Pedersen explain how margin calls were a key feature of the 2008 Credit Crunch.[42] First observe that the margin will reflect a financial institution's view of a borrower's creditworthiness with particular reference to the positions the borrower is taking in the securities markets (broadly, what securities they are holding, shorting, etc.). This view, often assessed by reference to a VaR and/or leverage ratio, is dynamic such that as the borrower's situation improves or worsens, so the margin requirements fall or rise reciprocally. Some event may occur affecting securities that impinges on our borrower. For example, their investments go bad, or even the collateral they have provided—securities themselves—have fallen in value. Notice that events affecting particular securities will touch every market participant interested in those securities, not just one borrower. In the light of this, the VaR changes for each such borrower, leading to one or more responses:

(1) Each borrower fears that it will breach the terms of margin lending, and so
  (a) unwinds its position in the affected securities; and/or
  (b) sells further securities to reduce overall VaR and to be able to meet any margin call.
(2) The creditor institution issues a proportionate margin call to the borrowers to offset the risk.

This has knock-on effects: the aggregate effect of the borrowers unwinding their positions to meet margin calls is to drive down the price of affected securities. This though means that any residual positions in securities of that type are now worth less, so responses A and B above are repeated, further driving down the price of affected securities and spreading to other securities as borrowers are forced to unwind unrelated positions just to deleverage and meet margin calls. Very quickly (we are talking a few days, if not hours), all parties are locked into a spiral in which creditors force borrowers to sell into a crashing securities market, exacerbating losses on positions, ramping up risk,

42 Markus K Brunnermeier and Lasse Heje Pedersen, 'Market Liquidity and Funding Liquidity' (2009) 22 The Review of Financial Studies 2201.

and provoking greater and greater margin calls. Against this background creditors refuse to engage in further margin lending, or only at very expensive rates, and try to close existing arrangements. Liquidity 'disappears down a black hole.'[43]

> ### *MARGIN CALL* (2009)
>
> JC Chandor's film is one of the best representations of what it was like to be involved in the 2008 Credit Crunch. The eponymous margin call refers to a situation a fictional Wall Street Bank found itself in when it discovered it was severely over-leveraged due to its huge investments in securities backed by US residential mortgages. Essentially, these securities were worthless, and as soon as the margin lenders found out, they would be calling for new margin even as a margin spiral occurred. Given the size of the bank's position in these securities, it faced destruction. *Spoiler alert*: ultimately the bank's bosses decide the only way forward is to unwind the banks positions as quickly as possible before the margin spiral picks up pace. A team of sellers is brought together with strict instructions to clear the books of the offending securities at any price, even if a loss. As the trading day progresses, counterparties buying the securities begin to smell something rotten, and as realization sets in there is great anger, but the bank, having still made significant losses on the day, does survive.

8.3.1 Taking collateral

8.3.1.1 Bearer securities

Title to bearer securities derives from possession of the physical securities as chattels. This results in a rather metaphysical collapse of two distinct kinds of security into one. In practice, the markets for bearer securities have spoken of a pledge of shares, granted like any pledge by delivering the physical property into the hands of the secured creditor. Yet a moment's thought indicates a confusion: the secured creditor, now holding the bearer securities, is the absolute title holder to the securities. What has actually been achieved is a legal mortgage, i.e. a transfer of title to the mortgagee to secure a debt and capable of redemption.

Consider the traditional statement of the nature of the pledge:

> The contract [of pledge] is to be distinguished from the contract of hypothecation by the transfer of possession, or the actual delivery, of the thing intended to be charged to the creditor, and from the contract of mortgage by the absence of a transfer of the ownership or right of property thereof to the pawnee during the continuance of the trust. [*Bristol and West of England Bank v Midland Railway Co* [1891] 2 QB 653 (CA)][44]

In short, for bearer securities, pledge and legal mortgage seem indistinguishable, though the market has proceeded as if pledge is the appropriate term. The following case demonstrates that a purported pledgee of bearer securities and any third party which deals with the pledgee are in a stronger position than is usually the case for pledges.

---

43 Avinash Persaud, 'Liquidity Black Holes' (2002) UNU/Wider Discussion Paper No. 2002/31 <wider.unu.edu/sites/default/files/dp2002-31.pdf> accessed 4 August 2024.

44 See also *North Western Bank v John Poynter & MacDonalds* [1895] AC 56 (HL); *Blundell-Leigh v Attenborough* [1921] 3 KB 235 (CA); *re David Allester Ltd.* [1922] 2 Ch 211.

LONDON JOINT STOCK BANK v SIMMONS [1892] AC 201 (HL)

S left certain of his bearer bonds in custody with a stockbrokers at which D was a partner. D then, without any authority from S, converted the bonds to his own use. First, D sold the bonds and used the proceeds for his own trading, and with the profits bought back equivalent bonds which he registered in the firm's accounts as belong to S. Second, he took the replacement bonds and pledged them to LJSB (who knew nothing of D's wrongdoing) as security for a loan. The stockbrokers, and so D, became insolvent. With D's default, LJSB sold the bonds and applied the cash to repay the loan.

On discovering what had happened and realizing D was impecunious, S sued LJSB for return of the bonds.

Held: The bearer bonds were inherently negotiable and title transferred immediately to whomever held them. When LJSB took the bonds in pledge, and in the absence of any notice of S's interest, LJSB acquired absolute legal title for value. Accordingly, S's action would be dismissed.

The House of Lords were unconcerned as to the use of the term 'pledge' even if it was essential to their opinions that legal title had transferred. Again, cash notes provide a useful extremum: is it possible to pledge cash (however absurd that sounds)? Once again, title vests in the bearer of bank notes. Nor could a pledgor seriously complain if the pledgee used the notes and replaced them with others. And were the pledgee to deposit the bank notes with a third party by way of collateral for some investment position, it would be difficult to argue that the third party, absent knowledge, is now to turn over cash to the pledgor. Of course, nothing prevents a legal mortgagor from converting assets to his use either. Fraudulent behaviour is not the key issue here; the key issue is that legal title has transferred, and that seems contrary to the nature of pledge as traditionally defined. Surely as lawyers we should now speak only of the legal mortgage of bearer securities.

8.3.1.2 Registered securities

Being intangible, registered securities cannot be subject to possessory security. Rather, security must be granted by means of some form of title transfer or charge. In simple, off-market transactions where share security has been somewhat ancillary to the main deal, the traditional preference has been to take a mortgage of the securities. Legal mortgage is achieved by agreeing to transfer by way of mortgage, completing the necessary transfer form and delivering certificates to the relevant registrar, all with a view that the mortgagee become legal titleholder to the securities.

Legal mortgages can have undesirable side effects, however. Taking legal title to shares, for example, means the mortgagee becomes a member of the company and benefits from all attendant rights and obligations. So be it—after all it is easy enough for the parties to agree that the mortgagee exercise these rights as the mortgagor directs, provided the latter is not in default and holds the mortgagee harmless for any attendant losses.[45] Yet these concerns are as nothing to the regulatory significance of a financial institution becoming shareholder. If the shareholding is relatively large in the context of the company, the mortgagee may have to register as a Person with Significant Control, and even account for the company because it has inadvertently become a subsidiary. For example, if

45 e.g. there is a rights issue in which the mortgagor wishes to participate but in virtue of the mortgage has no rights.

a bank took legal mortgages of shares as a matter of course, in aggregate it may inadvertently exceed the percentage limits for takeover shareholding notifications and even bids under the UK Takeover Code. If the shares are in another financial institution, prudential and competition concerns may be raised. Even in the case of debt securities, situations may arise, such as issuer insolvency, where the bank finds itself in an embarrassing, possibly conflicted, position of having to vote at a creditors' meeting in which it is, wearing another, otherwise interested.

In short, then, the legal mortgage may be perfect security, but it comes at a price which few financial institutions wish to pay. For this reason, again in cases where taking security over securities is a small part of a wider transaction, a creditor will prefer to take an equitable mortgage of certificated shares. Relying on the maxim that equity regards as done that which ought to be done, here the mortgagor does everything he would have done for the legal mortgage, save that having signed the stock transfer form he does not date it, and he delivers this and any relevant certificates to the mortgagee, who puts them in a safe. Should the mortgagor default, it is enough for the mortgagee to pull the documents from its safe, date the stock transfer form, and deliver them to the company's registrar to complete transfer for legal title. As the mortgagee controls any certificates, third parties can be deemed as having notice of something untoward should the mortgagor attempt transfer to shares without them.

Such are the traditional methods of taking security over shares, but there are hardly appropriate for collateral arrangements in modern securities markets. The simplest reason for this is that these days registered securities of the kind having the requisite liquidity for use as collateral will be in dematerialized (i.e. uncertificated) form. This is another way of saying that (certificated) securities have been issued to a custodian/intermediary to hold, and everyone else trades interests in securities through that custodian using a clearing system such as CREST/Euroclear. Each notional holder will have an account with the clearing system, and title will be transferred by crediting a person's account with the number of securities they now hold.

Dematerialization presents benefits for legal mortgages: transfer of title by way of mortgage, and retransfer on redemption, is a swift matter of debit and crediting the relevant accounts with the securities in question, pursuant to a security agreement.[46]

Some rethinking is required for equitable mortgages. There are no certificates or incomplete stock transfer forms for the equitable mortgagee to hold, and the clearing system may not be minded to set up 'halfway house' holdings which would undermine settlement finality (see Chapter 10). Faced with the practical impossibility of creating an equitable mortgage of securities, and possessory security already ruled out, lawyers turned to the fixed charge for a solution. The charge, as we have seen, does not confer title but merely encumbers the owner's asset, thereby avoiding the problems of the legal mortgage. Yet not all clearing houses run an obvious system, equivalent to the charges register of the Land Registry, to record charges. The solution was to use an old trick known to lawyers: if one cannot take security over an object, one takes security over a container and then places the object in it. In clearing system terms, this means opening an escrow account in the chargor's or security nominee's name over which the chargee has sole signing rights, and having the chargor instruct the clearing house to transfer the registered shares into this escrow account. By locking the shares in the escrow account, the chargee attains the requisite control over the securities to assert a fixed charge, but title does not transfer to the chargee. On enforcement, the chargee need only use its signing rights to have the securities transferred to an account in its own name or to its order.

---

46 Uncertificated Securities Regulations 2001 SI 2001/3755, reg 34.

EUROCLEAR BANK'S AND CLEARSTREAM'S 'PLEDGED ACCOUNTS'

Two clearing houses that do run a kind of 'charges register' for securities are Belgium's Euroclear and Luxembourg's Clearstream. Here market participants open a 'pledge account' into which may be transferred securities by way of collateral for margin lending. To facilitate this, these clearing houses offer a Triparty Collateral Management Service so that all parties have sufficient control to achieve certainty and security.

Yet wait, what is this talk of *pledging* registered securities? Confusingly for English lawyers, in civilian jurisdictions like Belgium, Luxembourg, and Germany, it is quite possible to grant a 'pledge' of intangible securities (*nantissement, Verpfändung*). The legal translation as 'pledge' is unhelpful, as while civilian pledges are usually highly formal affairs involving a notary, they are not true parallels of the English concept of pledge, which relates solely to tangibles.

8.3.2 Rehypothecation and the financial collateral regulations

Constantly holding in one's mind how securities, particularly T-bills, approach money in their liquidity explains (though does necessarily not excuse) many strange legal aberrances encountered in the securities market. Perhaps the single practice most likely to horrify the private lawyer is called *rehypothecation*.

ESSENTIAL DEFINITION: REHYPOTHECATION

Let creditor C1 take collateral from debtor D as security for D's debt to C1. Further, let C1 owe a debt to some third-party creditor C2. Then rehypothecation is the act of C1 taking the collateral provided by D and using it as collateral for C1's debt to C2 i.e. as if C1 owned the collateral outright.

Replace the collateral with money proper and think through the consequences. D may have taken a loan from bank C1 and may also have deposited cash in an account at C1. The express and implied terms of that whole relationship include an obligation of bank C1 to pay out money to D or to D's order. Critically, it need not be the same money D deposited; any money will do. C1 also has a right to set off the money D deposited (or more precisely the credit) against the debt D owes, if he defaults. In the meantime, bank C1 can use the money as it sees fit, perhaps to lend to a third party, or it could deposit the cash with a third party as collateral for some debt C1 owes to C2, perhaps as part of its money market or securities trading operations (as was the case in the *City Bonds Theft*).[47] If banks had to keep exactly the same coinage and notes in bank vault, ready to be returned only to their depositor, banking would be reduced to simple custody.

Now if we accept that T-bills and other securities lie on a spectrum of cash equivalence, one can understand why securities market participants would regard taking deposits of securities, even as collateral, as subject not to a requirement to return exactly the same securities to the depositor or collateral provider, but as subject to a requirement to provide equivalent securities when the time

47 See section 8.1.4, where the bearer T-bills were being delivered to collateralize various financial institutions' borrowings from the Bank of England and others for the day.

comes. In other words, a right to the (re)delivery of a GBP100 T-bill is no different to the right to (re) delivery of GBP100 cash—both being perfectly fungible, any T-bill or note will do.

Rehypothecation potentially offends several basic tenets of English property law, chiefly the equities that attend any mortgage (see further Chapter 3): the equity or redemption, the maxim 'once a mortgage, always a mortgage,' and rule against unconscionable collateral advantages.[48] In the context of rehypothecation of securities, if a debtor grants security over certain assets to creditor, we might interpret these equitable rules as follows:

(1) The debtor is entitled to redelivery of just those securities on discharge of the debt. Generally, no secured party should be allowed to sell the securities and then redeliver other securities on discharge.
(2) The creditor cannot treat the security arrangement as a true sale, entitling it to alienate the securities as if the creditor were absolute legal owner.
(3) The creditor ought not unfairly and unconscionably to use the securities (and put them at risk) to make profits from them.[49]

Rehypothecation seems clearly to run afoul of A and B, and one could argue C just where the creditor fraudulently holds himself out to others as the legal owner to obtain profits for himself.

One would think, therefore, that the English courts would have struck down rehypothecation at the first opportunity. In fact, already in the 1920s the court found a way to tolerate the practice based on the quasi-monetary analysis discussed above. As an aside, you should note that the judge in the following case was Sargent J, the Lord Justice of Appeal who dissented from the majority led by Lord Atkins in *re Wait*.[50]

ELLIS AND CO's TRUSTEE v DIXON-JOHNSON [1924] 2 Ch 451 (CA)

Ellis & Co were a stockbroker partnership which traded securities on their own account and on behalf of clients such as the respondent DJ. To demonstrate that DJ would be able to underwrite any trading losses he made through E, DJ provided security to E. Specifically, DJ transferred certain shares by way of legal mortgage, and provided signed but undated stock transfer forms and share certificates by way of equitable mortgage. It was clear from the contract between them that DJ could demand redelivery of the same subject to certain conditions.

E collapsed and a trustee in bankruptcy was appointed. DJ at this point owed money to E's estate, having made trading losses. Yet it was also revealed that E had rehypothecated DJ's securities i.e. it had transferred the shares to third parties as collateral for its own positions with them.

E's trustee calculated the face value of DJ's shares provided as collateral and found that they were worth less than the amount DJ owed to E. E's trustee therefore sued DJ for the balance in E's estate's favour. DJ responded inter alia that the market value of the shares was now greater than any debt owed by DJ to E, E ought to have held the collateral but absent that it ought to have acquired equivalent securities, DJ was entitled to any increase in value in the collateral or indeed the equivalent securities, for in either

48 *Noakes v Rice* [1902] AC 24 (HL), per Lord Macnaghten; *Marquess of Northampton v Pollock* (1890) 45 ChD 190 (CA) 215 (Bowen LJ).
49 *Vernon v Bethell* (1761) 28 ER 838, but cf *Santley v Wilde* [1889] 2 Ch 474 (CA) 478–79 (MR Lindley).
50 See section 8.1.5.

case E could have enforced against the securities to satisfy the debt in full—thus DJ owed nothing.

Held per Sargent LJ:

> In a case like the present, where the security that has been wrongly disposed of in part by the mortgagees consisted of freely marketable shares which can readily be replaced by others of precisely similar value, there is no necessity for insisting on the restoration of the particular shares charged. The obligation of the mortgagee can be sufficiently performed by the replacement of the shares by others of the same denomination, or even by furnishing the mortgagor with funds sufficient to enable him so to replace the shares. But I see no reason for further relaxing the clear general principle, that, as a condition of recovering his debt or the balance of it, the mortgagee must perform the reciprocal obligation of restoring the security, or so much of it as has not been properly disposed of by him. [473]

On this point, Warrington LJ concurred:

> It would be absurd to insist on a retransfer of the identical shares mortgaged when other shares of the same nature are available, and so also, I think, the judge is right in substituting for the actual shares the value thereof, inasmuch as the money representing the value could, if the mortgagor so pleases, be at once invested in the purchase of shares. [471]

Pollock MR sidestepped the point, seemingly preferring the view that any mortgagee could wrongfully (and probably fraudulently) convert security to his own use, and that in such a case equity would try to assist by tracing the assets. Ultimately, however, the wronged party would have to accept that the law of property can only do so much and all that remained was a damages claim, on which Pollock MR's discussion focused.

We must be careful with this case. Sargent and Warrington LJJ are not saying the equity of redemption does not apply to securities; they are not giving licence to collateral-takers to deal with collateral as if it were their own property; they are clear that breach of contract and a tort (of conversion) has been committed and the collateral provider has been wronged. The Lord Justices' decision is much narrower: if collateral which is readily interchangeable in the securities market is wrongfully converted to the use of the secured party (by rehypothecation), then it seems the collateral provider has a right to delivery of equivalent securities rather than cash, even if those equivalent securities are now more valuable and thus more costly for the secured party to acquire. Where the collateral provider has defaulted, he is entitled to ask the secured party to find equivalent securities and enforce against those *as* if they were the original collateral. The result for common law, then, is that the negative common law view of rehypothecation remains.

The problem for lawyers is that rehypothecation is common practice, it was in the 1920s and it probably was in the 1820s too. Even the Lord Justices in *Ellis & Co.* could see how the practice flowed from the quasi-money nature of securities. As with derivatives (another financial practice that was until fairly recently, legally questionable (see Chapter 9)), the UK used its then-leading role in EU financial law and policy to bring in the Financial Collateral Regulations (**FCRs**) in the early 2000s. The provision relevant for our purposes is set out below.

THE FINANCIAL COLLATERAL ARRANGEMENTS (NO.2) REGULATIONS 2003 SI 2003/3226

Right of use under a security financial collateral arrangement

16.—(1) If a security financial collateral arrangement provides for the collateral-taker to use and dispose of any financial collateral provided under the arrangement, as if it were the owner of it, the collateral-taker may do so in accordance with the terms of the arrangement.

(2) If a collateral-taker exercises such a right of use, it is obliged to replace the original financial collateral by transferring equivalent financial collateral on or before the due date for the performance of the relevant financial obligations covered by the arrangement or, if the arrangement so provides, it may set off the value of the equivalent financial collateral against or apply it in discharge of the relevant financial obligations in accordance with the terms of the arrangement.

The FCRs provide a blanket approval for various activities which would otherwise run into trouble under local law. The FCRs' general regulatory stance is one preferring information symmetry in a market of sophisticated investors.[51] Provided the collateral-taker informs the provider that the collateral-taker asserts the right to rehypothecate, the provider is taken to have granted consent to seeing its property disappearing off, of being only able to redeem equivalent securities, and of running the counterparty risk that there be no property rights left to assert against third parties in case of collateral-taker insolvency. Notice that the FCRs do not change the basic property law position in England—there is no statutorily constituted property right in equivalent assets as this is entirely about permitting rehypothecation and the collateral-taker side.

It is at this point that one must ask whether the lawyers are really alone? Concerns about the property law analysis of rehypothecation are not merely theoretical; there is a very real concern that a collateral provider should lose their property, and thus suddenly discover their balance sheet less valuable than it was minutes before. Transposed into the financial context, in which millions in collateral may be held with and rehypothecated by a single investment bank and one could foresee a serious crisis in which collateral providers suddenly discover they are left only with damages claims against an insolvent entity. Deryugina argues that permitting rehypothecation creates huge systemic risks,[52] only mitigated to date by other structural factors of securities markets: principally, the holding of securities by intermediaries and the close-out netting of reciprocal positions by market participants, now also expressly permitted in insolvency by Reg 12 FCRs.

8.4 Securitization

8.4.1 What is securitization?

Securitization combines much of what you have learnt in this and the proceeding chapters, particularly concerning the legal nature of debt, security, structured finance, and securities. At its heart,

51 Financial Conduct Authority, *Client Assets Sourcebook* (March 2011), CASS 9.2.1R (c) (updated 2 August 2024). See also Regulation (EU) 2015/2365 of the European Parliament and of the Council of 25 November 2015 on transparency of securities financing transactions and of reuse, which came in in light of Lehman Bros.' collapse.

52 M Deryugina, 'Standardization of Securities Regulation: Rehypothecation and Securities Commingling in the United States and the United Kingdom' (2009) 29 Review of Banking Law 253.

the word indicates the transformation of choses in action (due debts or obligations to pay at some future date) into securities. Yet this 'securities' perspective alone does not explain *why* anyone would securitize, beyond the advantages of negotiability offered by promissory notes and the like.

To understand why, think back to syndication and structured finance. In those transactions the size of the debt was deemed simply too great to be borne by a single lender, and so they shared the risk, sometimes even subordinating some syndicate members to mitigate the risk of others. Securitization arises partly for similar reasons, partly for converse ones. The similar reasons are that again the size of the aggregate debt in a securitization (we are talking GBP1bn plus potentially) is again too great for one lender to be happy to bear alone. For this reason, it initiates a structure in which many investors on securities markets can take on a portion of that risk, thereby spreading the burden. Notice how this opens up syndication-style investment to a greater number of market actors who are able to take relatively smaller portions of the total risk than would be expected in a syndication.

The 'converse reasons' are much more interesting. The debts in a securitization are not a few facilities provided to a single corporate or project, they are thousands of small retail debts which are sufficiently similar in profile to be aggregated and considered as a whole. By retail debts we mean the kind of credit banks and the like grant to consumers and small businesses, such as mortgage loans, credit cards, and finance leases for vehicles. For one debtor we may be talking a few hundred pounds being owed monthly on their credit card, but take 5,000 such credit card holders and the bank can expect several million in owed credit card repayments every month as a relatively stable income stream. What securitization does is bundle together multiple such income streams from credit into a sizable aggregate debt, then transform that debt into securities in which very many market participants can invest.

There is another key driver for securitization which is determinate of its structure: the originate to distribute model which is designed to do two things: (1) decouple the bank which gave the retail credit from the aggregate risk of non-payment of the debt; and (2) turn those debts, due later, into cash paid by investors now. Securitization thus has significant balance sheet and liquidity advantages for the bank. Provided it can remove the debts from its balance sheet, it no longer must reserve as much capital against the risk of default on those loans. And provided investors wish to buy securities linked to these debts, the bank has fresh cash available for its own further investment, principally in granting further credit to retail customers.

So, we have three key features of securitization which might provide a non-legal definition of the practice.

ESSENTIAL DEFINITION: SECURITIZATION

1. The process of turning multiple debt income streams of a similar kind into securities and selling these into the market.
2. A means of permitting securities market investors, as a whole, to invest in and so bear the risk of, the retail (personal and business) lending of banks, building societies, and similar financial institutions.
3. A means of decoupling of the originating lender from the risk of non-payment of the debts that are securitized.

Let us expand on this with a naïve discussion of a securitization with an example linked to 'residential mortgages' (i.e. home finance loans secured by way of statutory charge of land). Banks lend to homeowners. A lot. In fact, a given bank may lend several billion GBP to homeowners, each loan secured by way of mortgage of their residencies. These borrowers are all different kinds of people, some rich, some middling, some poor. They live in different areas, some well-to-do, some being gentrified, some the other side of the tracks. Some borrowers are sacked, some are divorced, some die, some win the lottery.

Every month each borrower-homeowner is required to make a payment of interest and perhaps of capital. The precise amounts vary, but Bank knows this:

(1) It can expect to receive most repayments on the monthly interest payment date.
(2) It thus expects most borrowers not to default.
(3) It also expects that is some borrowers default, most will either remedy the default or, if their home is foreclosed against, Bank will recoup a reasonable amount of capital.

In other words, 'overall' Bank receives significant sums of income every month backed or secured overall by a significant portfolio of mortgages of residential property.

Bank would like to make more such loans, but it has lent its existing capital and must either wait until the home loans are repaid before it can make more loans or raise capital in the market. What Bank wants to do is **transform** illiquidity into liquidity by releasing capital. If only it could find some to acquire these debt obligations, thus reimbursing capital to Bank for new lending. Other bank purchasers are not available (they have their own loan books) but, if enough smaller investors could group together, then together they would be able to buy out the debt obligations. The problem is however that one cannot simply assign individual debts to individual investors. For a start, individual investors not only do not want to be mortgage lenders, but financial services regulations prevent them.

The solution is to securitize the loans: to turn them from home loans into a legal form in which investors can invest. Broadly, this involves the interposition of an SPV. The mortgage-backed debt obligations of the homeowners are then assigned to the SPV. The SPV then issues securities (usually notes (medium term bonds)) in the capital market. The securities are acquired for capital and the aggregate of the capital paid by investors is used by SPV to acquire the mortgage-backed debt obligations from Bank. The securities offer investors a coupon (interest) which in aggregate matches the income paid by homeowners to SPV. In this way the securities reflect the economic value of the mortgage-backed debt obligations but are not themselves such obligations. We call these securities Residential Mortgage-Backed Securities (**RMBS**).

Let us examine a common type of securitization structure—the 'true sale'[53] securitization—in some detail.

By way of example, consider Figure 8.2, which presents a simplified true sale securitization. The numerals indicate notional phases of the securitization structure, though most are simultaneous:

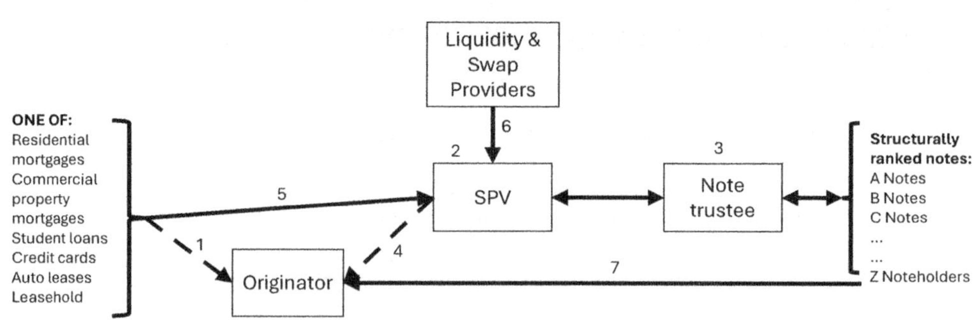

Figure 8.2 A simplified true sale securitization structure

53 The term 'true sale' is examined in section 8.4.2.

(1) In the first phase, which is the longest, a financial institution such as a bank originates loans of broadly similar characteristics. For example, let us say our originator makes loans to purchasers of residential property secured by way of statutory charge over that property. One such loan might be worth GBP400,000 (which would not cover the professional fees of a securitization), but the originator bank will aim to make loans with a target in mind—perhaps GBP1bn of loans of the same kind i.e. to residential purchasers in the UK providing security over the land, and on the bank's standard terms of business. Slowly but surely, the bank will build up a loan book of (secured) debts owed to it with fairly homogeneous interest payment and capital repayment schedules.

The plan to securitize is developed before the loans are made, just so the employees of the bank no just what parameters they need to operate in (e.g. sterling-only loans in the UK). These parameters are cascaded down from the bank's City office where the securitization has been developed. If you have ever heard people complain that when they sought finance from a high street bank they were denied because the employee effectively said 'computer says no,' this is the reason: the lending criteria are set centrally, often with a view to securitization.

(2) Originator arranges for a Special Purpose Vehicle (**SPV**, more accurately called a Securitization Special Purpose Entity or **SSPE**) to be incorporated, the shares of which are held by a nominee *not* the originator. The SPV is an empty shell whose sole purpose will be to facilitate the securitization. It is not uncommon for the SPV to be incorporated in a jurisdiction offering insolvency and/or tax advantages to the future investors, such as Jersey, the Isle of Man, or the Cayman Islands.

Sometimes the originator to assign its loan book to the SPV from an early stage, in consideration of the SPV owing the market value of the debt to originator. This will not be done loan-by-loan but in chunks, especially where a set of loans all come from the same transaction (e.g. the purchase of a third party's loan book, or a lending drive in a particular construction development). This practice of 'storing' loans in an SPV in advance of a planned securitization is called **warehousing**. The securitization may never happen, in which case the SPV may syndicate its loans, or its shares will be sold to a third party.

(3) Aided by the originator as a managing agent, the SPV prepares for securitization. It develops a prospectus meeting the usual regulatory requirements which proposes to raise capital from the securities market for the purposes of purchasing a loan book from the originator. The prospectus makes an invitation to treat: if the potential investors offer money, in consideration they will receive debt securities (usually notes) having a certain capital value and paying a coupon. Critically, (a) the value and coupon reflect the capital and interest payments of the underlying loan book; and (b) the payment of capital and coupon on the securities will be backed by those loans, which themselves are secured. Investors will not receive notes directly, but a global note (or notes) will be held by a note trustee on trust for the investors as beneficiaries. All enforcement will be undertaken by the note trustee on the investors' behalf.

Having read the prospectus, investors make an offer on its terms, usually by completing the relevant forms electronic via a clearing house. A book is run of all interested subscribers and once the minimum amount in aggregate is reached to complete the acquisition of the originator's loan book, notes are issued to the note trustee (investors acquiring interests in securities), and the consideration is paid to the SPV.

It is important to realize that noteholders have no divided, allocated interest in any particular loan. Noteholder Smith has no claim whatsoever on Mr and Mrs Jones for repayment of their residential mortgage. All the interest payments and capital repayments are owed to SPV; Noteholders' claims are entirely against the SPV for repayment of their respective notes, these claims being paid out, on insolvency, of the SPV's assets as a whole, i.e. the aggregate debt owed under the loan book. If you remember your company law, this is just an application of the principle of separate corporate personality in a debt context.[54]

As these securities are backed by residential loans, and better, those loans are secured by statutory charges, they are called **RMBS**. Were they backed by secured commercial property loans, they would be CMBS; by other kinds of assets generally, ABS.

54 *Salomon v A Salomon & Co Ltd.* [1896] UKHL 1, [1897] AC 22.

Provided one has a sizable set of similar income streams (receivables), securitization is possible.

Usually, the transaction will not involve issuance of securities of a single class or rank. Using techniques we have encountered in structured finance and syndication, the interest payments and repayments will be 'tranched,' i.e. certain creditors will receive higher and/or prior payments compared to other creditors, all of whom have consented to this subordination. The ranking is identified using the nomenclature of the notes. For example, on an insolvency of the SPV, the holder of (interests in) A Notes will receive a return of capital prior to a holder of (interests in) B Notes, with the B Noteholder only receiving its return once the A Noteholder is repaid in full. To compensate for this risk, it will be agreed that the B Notes bear a higher coupon than the A Notes, which means that the total interest payments to SPV are not distributed equally to noteholders, but a greater percentage of the total is diverted by the Note Trustee (or a paying agent) to the B Noteholders. An example of tranching from a RMBS prospectus is given in Figures 8.3 and 8.4. Notice the subordination structure and differential coupon payable.

	Class of Notes				
	Class A1a notes	**Class A1b notes**	**Class A2 notes**	**Class M notes**	**Class Z notes**
Currency	Sterling	Euro	Sterling	Sterling	Sterling
Initial principal amount	£200,000,000	EUR450,000,000	£546,100,000	£38,400,000	£102,500,000
Note credit enhancements	Subordination of class M and class Z notes	Subordination of class M and class Z notes	Subordination of class M and class Z notes	Subordination of class Z notes	N/A
Reserve credit enhancements	Reserve fund	Reserve fund	Reserve fund	Reserve fund	N/A
Interest reference rate	3 month GBP LIBOR [*Nb. This example comes from 2016.*]	3 month GBP LIBOR	3 month GBP LIBOR	3 month GBP LIBOR	3 month GBP LIBOR

Figure 8.3 Prospectus excerpt summarizing the tranched structure of securitization notes

	Class of Notes				
	Class A1a notes	**Class A1b notes**	**Class A2 notes**	**Class M notes**	**Class Z notes**
Relevant margin	Up to and excluding the Step-Up Date, 1.30%	Up to and excluding the Step-Up Date, 1.30%	Up to and excluding the Step-Up Date, 1.45%	Up to and excluding the Step-Up Date, 2.00%	Up to and excluding the Step-Up Date, 2.00%
Step-Up Margin	From and including the Step-Up Date, 2.60%	From and including the Step-Up Date, 2.60%	From and including the Step-Up Date, 2.90%	From and including the Step-Up Date, 4.00%	N/A
Payment Dates	Interest and Principal will be payable quarterly in arrears on the Payment Dates falling 24 January, 24 April. 24 July and 24 October in each year				
Call Option/ Step-Up Date	24 April 2016	24 April 2016	24 April 2016	24 April 2016	N/A
Final Redemption Date	24 April 2047	24 April 2047	24 April 2047	24 April 2047	24 April 2047
Form of Notes	Bearer	Bearer	Bearer	Bearer	Bearer

Figure 8.4 Prospectus excerpt summarizing the differential coupon on securitization notes

(1) Originator assigns (or novates) its RMBS loan book debt to SPV in consideration of SPV paying the price. As you have guessed, SPV is now able to pay because it has been put in funds by the Noteholders.

(2) The result now is that the debtors under the loan book owe money to the SPV and the Originator drops out of the picture (or at least it should do).

Remark A: Originator takes the proceeds of selling its loan book and . . . starts lending it out again into the residential loan market, with a view to securitization. Notice that this process is infinitely repeatable on the originator's side. The problem is there is not an infinite number of creditworthy residential mortgagors out there. This contradiction lay at the heart of the Global Financial Crisis.

Remark B: The residential mortgagors will have no clue this is happening unless the read the small print. If they do they will have found a term of their mortgage contract giving the lender express consent to securitize the loan. The relative opacity is ensured by originator agreeing to continue to facilitate borrower payments as agent for the SPV (for a fee). Thus the borrower still thinks she is dealing with her old bank, unless and until this facilitation arrangement changes. This can happen, for example when TSB was forcibly split from Lloyds Bank in the UK and half the loan book went with them.

(3) A consequence of the structure is the income and capital streams from the borrowers are aggregated in the SPV and then paid out as coupon and capital repayment to the noteholders according to a predetermined schedule. A risk here is that this schedule ceases to match the sums received from borrowers, producing a liquidity mismatch. Given the sheer number of borrowers backing a RMBS structure, it is inevitable some will default, and so a certain tolerance is built into the structure for non-performing loans. Yet it remains possible that even this tolerance is exceeded, and the SPV finds it lacks cash to meet its obligations on a given payment date. To mitigate this risk, the SPV will usually contract with one or more financial institutions to in effect 'insure' against any liquidity shortfall. This could either be by means of a (possibly syndicated) **swing-line credit facility agreement** which permits drawdown to cover shortfalls; a swap in which the counterparty tops up any shortfall in exchange for receiving any excess borrower payments in a given month (see further Chapter 9 on derivatives); or even a true insurance policy called **monoline insurance** which pays out if there is a shortfall (though these were notably failures during the Global Financial Crisis). These credit protection devices are marketed as beneficial risk mitigations in the prospectus, and hence have the nickname **sweeteners**.

(4) Although in a true sale securitization, the originator is supposed to cease to have any legal interest in the underlying loans, there are multiple ways in which the originator involves itself in the structure. We have already seen that it acts as agent for the SPV in receiving borrower payments, but it may also offer management services to the SPV, or provide the swingline facility or swap, all for fees. One might query just how arm's length all this is—for the SPV is de facto a creature of the originator, even if de jure regulators are happy the SPV's liabilities will not revert onto the originator. One continued relationship between the two, however, seems to be popular: the originator acquiring subordination notes in the securitization, called having **skin in the game**. Consider the similarity to corporate financing, where shareholders invest equity capital which, in virtue of company and insolvency law, bears losses before debt. Such willingness to bear losses indicates confidence in the company's future and offers a capital 'cushion' for other creditors with which losses are absorbed. The same principle extends to securitizations, with, as in the example, the originator taking the lowest ranked 'Z' notes and so bearing capital losses first. Doing so presents a further sweetener to potential investors, though the originator is not being charitable—the coupon payable on super-subordinated notes could well be significant. Indeed, the coupon on the originator's notes can be marketed as paying a kind of originator and/or management fee over the term of the notes.

JINGLE MAIL[55]

Securitizations were at the heart of the Global Financial Crisis, channelling defaults on residential loans into the securities market and into liquidity and swap providers. In 2006 it was already becoming clear to some that the mid-2000s US residential property bubble was coming to an abrupt end, with US house prices falling rapidly. This often left borrowers paying mortgages on houses worth much less that the debt owed to the bank to fund the original purchase price (so-called negative equity). The mortgages in question tended to be made on a limited-recourse basis: the lender had recourse to the house as security but no further recourse to the borrower personally. This, and differing cultural approaches to bankruptcy in the US, favoured what Paul Krugman calls[56] 'strategic default'—the rational conclusion that in case of negative equity and limited recourse, it was far better to default now and abandon the real estate than be tied into a long-term deal which would see one lose even more money in interest and capital payments.

Thus borrowers began putting their housekeys into envelopes and posting them to the lender banks, indicating that they were abandoning the property to the banks. The jingle of the envelope as it arrived gave rise to the name **jingle mail**.

Lenders were soon swamped by jingle mail, but it was not them that were running the risk; the lenders had securitized the loans in RMBS structures and so it was the SPVs, liquidity and swap providers, and securities holders who now ultimately bore the risk. The structures had factored in some default, but by 2007–08 over 38% of residential loans were in default—losses across multiple RMBS securitizations which could not be mitigated by liquidity and swap providers. Soon monoline insurers, for example, were insolvent because they could not meet their obligations. Some of the originating banks so things coming and had already been dumping loans and any residual securities into the market, and very quickly all securities investors were doing the same. Tranching of the securities quickly became notional, because whole deals were in trouble, and even if the most senior notes were protected, there was no market for the notes as no one was buying RMBS.

Securities investors' positions quickly went sour, triggering VaR and similar leverage covenants and so precipitating margin calls. Unable to ditch RMBS at any price, a margin spiral ensued, and investors began unwinding positions in any securitization to improve their balance sheets, and because all faith has been lost in securitization as a financial structure.

All investors also looked to their investments in others with exposure to securitizations. This went beyond calls in margin lending to those who financed financial institutions by way of securities, be they notes or shares. Any whiff of exposure to RMBS (or soon any securitization) saw investors dumping bank shares and/or withdrawing deposits.

One problem was that the exposure was not at all transparent; it seemed that a great deal of banking was going on beyond the official balance sheets of banks (a form of **shadow-banking**). Investors and depositors only now realized the consequences of originators' attempts to transfer risk onto SPVs. Sometimes the transfer was incomplete (because the origination was still ongoing); sometimes the originator was still

55 For a detailed journalistic account, see John Bellamy Foster and Fred Magdoff, *The Great Financial Crisis: Causes and Consequences* (New York UP 2009).

56 Paul Krugman, 'One to the Left' *New York Times* (12 August 2008) <https://archive.nytimes.com/krugman.blogs.nytimes.com/2008/02/12/one-to-the-left/> accessed 16 September 2024.

residually liable for losses (by means of guarantees, Z notes, or liquidity provision); sometimes the 'true sale' of the debts to the SPV was questionable and ran the risk of recharacterization as a secured lending in which the originator remained liable as a debtor of the SPV.

Investors dumped their bank securities; depositors queued to withdraw their funds. For example, the overexposed British residential lender Northern Rock saw a terminal bank run (September 2007) and its loan book was forcibly sold. Then, in the heart of securitization, New York, Bear Stearns (forcibly acquired by JPMorgan in March 2008) and, most cataclysmically, Lehman Bros, which collapsed on 15 September 2008.

In the US alone, the Federal Deposit Insurance Corporation dealt with 485 bank failures/forced acquisitions as a result of the 2007–08 financial crisis.[57]

As you are likely aware, the excesses of securitization up to 2008 led to significant regulation of the area. As this work focuses on the private law of finance, not the fast-changing field of financial regulation, it is out of scope to examine the raft of regulatory measures put in place after the Credit Crunch. As a first port of call for those wishing to look more deeply, post-Brexit UK initially retained the relevant EU regulations, of which the Securitization Regulation is the core. As part its plan for a Capital Markets Union, the European Commission concluded it would be better to provide a safe harbour for securitizations which they deemed simple, transparent, and standardized (**STS**), rather than attempt a wholly negative control of the practice. As such, STS securitizations benefit from reduced due diligence burdens and more appropriate prudential requirements for banks' and insurers' investments into STS products.

The relevant EU regulations, in force from 2019, are:

- The Securitisation Regulation (EU) 2017/2402 (EU Securitisation Regulation) which applies to all EU securitizations and includes due diligence, risk retention, and transparency rules together with the criteria for STS securitizations; and
- Regulation (EU) 2017/2401 (the EU CRR Amendment Regulation), which makes the capital treatment of securitizations for banks and investment firms under the Capital Requirements Regulation (EU) 575/2013 (EU CRR) more risk-sensitive and able to reflect properly the specific features of STS securitizations

The UK retained these as its Assimilated Regulation (EU) 2017/2402 (as amended)[58] but quickly began consultation to reform (and relax) the rules for the UK. This process has led to the Securitisation Regulations 2024 SI 2024/102, and attendant amendments to prudential requirements, which shifted the regulatory dial back from hard rules to a more 'principles-based approach' to oversight. The concern is that principles-based regulation had been all the rage in the period leading up to 2007–08, being but another term for deregulation. The reform process remains unfinished—the 2024 SI is just the first phase of a process envisaged by HM Treasury.

57 'Failed Bank List' *fidc.gov* <https://www.fdic.gov/resources/resolutions/bank-failures/failed-bank-list/> accessed 1 August 2024.

58 Amended by the Securitisation (Amendment) (EU Exit) Regulations 2019 SI 2019/660 (Securitisation Exit Regulations) and the Securities Financing Transactions, Securitisation and Miscellaneous Amendments (EU Exit) Regulations 2020 SI 2020/1385.

8.4.2 True sale securitizations and re-characterization risk

As noted above, two advantages of securitization for the originator are (1) it removes the assets (debts) from the originator's balance sheet in exchange for cash, improving its capital structure and particularly liquidity; and (2) CRAs usually require the securitization to be entirely isolated from the originator in a such a way that the originator has no claim on the SPV to recover any of the assets. A chief object of the true sale securitization is to achieve this isolation by doing everything legally possible to effect a final transfer of absolute legal title in the securitization assets to the SPV. **True sale** is not a legally defined term but is taken to mean just this: the transfer of the securitization assets has finality i.e. is as irreversible as a sale of absolute legal title to a bona fide party purchaser for value without notice under an enforceable contract. More particularly:

(1) The originator must have no liability for the asset once sold (e.g. if there is a non-payment)—if it does, then it is still an owner.
(2) The SPV must have exclusive control and dominion—but note this can be tricky in e.g. consumer mortgages, where the originator we be appointed agent to continue dealing with unwitting mortgagors.
(3) The sale must be non-revocable on bankruptcy of originator, e.g. because SPV considered part of originator group, or because assignments were not publicized to third parties, or because sale is a voidable preference.
(4) There must be no possibility that originator has a security interest, express or implied, in any securitization asset—the main feature of security is the chargor's right to redeem. If the originator has some right to call back the sale, or re-purchase it, it may be re-characterized. Usually, the originator does have the right to purchase the rump to take the junior risk, but tricky. In the US, UCC Art 9 is notably problematic, as it treats an interest as security according to effect, regardless of form.

Any adequately advised originator will ensure that the securitization transaction document will explicitly rule out any rights or obligations which contravene the above and so suggest the transaction was not a 'true sale.' The problem is that parties never have absolute control over the objective legal meaning of the language they employ, nor are they the final arbiters of the legal effect of their actions; only the court is the final arbiter. There is always a risk that a court examine a securitization and legally **recharacterize** what has occurred as something other than a true sale, e.g. it is really a loan by the SPV secured on the assets.

Recharacterization has a long pedigree. In the 1895 case of *McEntire v Crossley*, the House of Lords recharacterized a leasing arrangement for goods as a true sale.[59] Crossley had provided a gas engine to one Peel under a contract which used the terms 'lessor' 'hire' and 'rent.' Peel was then bankrupted; his trustees sought to claim that Peel owned the engine. The House of Lords had little trouble looking at the contract 'as a whole' and concluding that in its substance it was a contract for sale—Peel would take ownership of the engine when, and only when, he had paid a series of instalments purporting to be rent. As Peel had not paid, the engine was Crossley's property still and unavailable to Peel's creditors.

The House of Lords' approach to looking 'in the round' at substance over form was followed in the Court of Appeal in *re George Inglefield*. For this case and those we examine subsequently, it is important to remember from Chapter 3 that a charge of a company's assets (the fixed and floating charge, sometimes called a debenture) is void if not registered at Companies House within 21 days.

---

59 *McEntire and Another v Crossley Bros Ltd.* [1895] AC 457, [1895–99] All ER Rep 829 (HL).

RE GEORGE INGLEFIELD LTD [1933] Ch 1, [1932] All ER Rep 244 (CA)

The company GI was in the business of selling furniture on a hire-purchase basis. Observe that this meant GI would have to wait to recoup the full value of its sales, and ran the risk of buyer default. To improve its liquidity, it arranged sales and then 'sold' them to a finance company, Finance Discount Co Ltd. (F). More particularly, GI would assign its rights under a given sales contract to F, and then transfer to F the furniture needed to satisfy the seller's obligations under that contract. In consideration, F would pay 75% of the purchase price upfront, less fees.

GI became insolvent. Its liquidators sought to argue that the arrangement with F was not a true sale of the contractual rights and furniture. Rather, it was substantively a financing agreement and the assignments and transfers were done by way of security. As the security had not been registered it was void and so the contractual rights and furniture properly belonged to GI and were available to its creditors.

Held: The arrangement was a true sale. There was nothing in the arrangement to suggest that GI could redeem its debt and demand return of its property; these were outright and irreversible sales to F. Moreover, if furniture buyers defaulted, F ran the risk of the loss (and conversely would keep any gains). All economic risk fell on F—something inconsistent with being a lender who would expect payment of any debt by GI whether customers paid or not.

Romer LJ provided some policy for the court's liberal position:

> If a man so conducts his affairs that he proves himself outside the operation of an Act of Parliament, and he may be said either to be evading it, or defeating it, all I can say is that he has done nothing that is unlawful, and he has done nothing that calls for adverse comment from the court. [256]

In other words, provided the transaction was otherwise lawful and its terms consistent with its intended legal effect (such as sale), the fact that the arrangement *avoided* some statutory provision was no reason for the court to cut the arrangement down.

How do these classic recharacterization cases apply to securitizations? Consider the following scenario: originator agrees to sell its rights to cinema ticket receivables (book debts generated from their sales) to SPV but also to continue to manage the contracts creating those receivables including collecting debts as SPV's agent and passing them through to SPV. In consideration for transfer of this income stream SPV agrees to pay a sum of money upfront (financed by issuance of securities). Subsequently, the originator becomes insolvent, and administrators are appointed. The administrators refuse to pass through the receivables payments to SPV. They argue the relationship with SPV is not one of sale but of loan. First, they contend SPV is not in the business running or even financing cinemas, being but a shell company designed to engage with securities market, demonstrated by its leaving management to originator. Second, being uninvolved in the business, SPV is much more like a finance house making a loan to originator, which originator had been repaying even if the payments were dressed up as passing through cinema ticket receipts. Third, the loan was secured on the receivables i.e. if originator failed to pass through payments, SPV regarded itself as entitled to have the books debts assigned to it as secured party.

The administrators' line of reasoning, they claim, leads to the following conclusions: (1) if the originator company's book debts/receivables were secured in favour of SPV, then the charge ought to have been registered under the Companies Acts; (2) the charge was not registered in time or at all, and so is void; (3) therefore SPV has no proprietary interest in the book debts which properly and absolutely belong to the originator, and are thus available for liquidation to meet the claims of all originator's creditors.

Were the court to support the administrator's line of reasoning, this would be potentially disastrous for true sale securitizations. We now examine the relevant case law to see if the courts agree. One reason for this lengthy lead-in to the cases is that the facts do not touch directly on a modern securitization. Nevertheless, you should be able to draw the parallel from them to the hypothetical example given above.[60]

WELSH DEVELOPMENT AGENCY v EXPORT FINANCE CO LTD [1990] BCC 393 (ChD)

Parrot Ltd. (P) was in the business of manufacturing and selling computer discs. WDA provided credit to P, secured by way of a duly registered fixed and floating charge over all of P's assets (aka a 'debenture'). The credit agreement contained a negative pledge which inter alia prohibited P from granting security over its book debts to third parties. These book debts included the debts of customers who had purchased computer discs.

P also sought to export its discs. To facilitate these international sales the Export Finance Co (Exfinco) would normally provide suitable credit support, such as letters of credit and guarantees. In this case, however, a financing was unsuitable because Exfinco could not take security over P's assets due to the negative pledge. Partly to circumvent this, Exfinco and P entered into the following arrangement:

(i) P would set up export sales to customers as agent for Exfinco. The result was a series of contracts directly between Exfinco and each customer.
(ii) P would then *sell* the discs to Exfinco so that it could perform the contracts.
(iii) P would draw up invoices to customers ordering payment to a named P account controlled exclusively by Exfinco. Exfinco would remove any agreed sums before releasing the balance to P.
(iv) The export advantage was that customers now dealt with a UK Government-backed counterparty and so could rely on its creditworthiness.

To emphasize: P *sold* the discs to E in consideration of the required credit support guaranteeing its performance to third-party customers and the balance of sales receipts.

Subsequently, P became insolvent, defaulting on its debt to WDA. WDA benefited from an old-style debenture which enabled it to appoint an all-powerful administrative receiver, capable of taking over the running of P in its entirety. These receivers discovered the arrangement with Exfinco and immediately wrote to all export customers instructing them to make payment to P's own account and neither to the Exfinco controlled account nor Exfinco directly.

The receivers argued inter alia that:

(a) The arrangement with Exfinco was a sham. It was not a sale of computer discs but clearly an advance of money by Exfinco (the credit guarantees) dressed up as one, not least to circumvent the negative pledge. Exfinco had no business interest

60 The following selection of cases draws on Nicholas Grandage and Daniel Franks, *The Law & Practice of True Sale* (Butterworths 2015).

in selling computer discs but was a financial institution. Any proprietary interests it had in the discs or book debts were properly understood as security interests, securing the credit advanced.

(b) The security was a registrable charge over company assets which was void for want of registration.

(c) Therefore, Exfinco had no right to the book debts and the receivers were right to direct customers to make payments directly to P.

Held at first instance by Browne-Wilkinson VC: the only purpose of the arrangement was for the advance of money:

> The first point to note is that the transaction is a highly artificial one. Exfinco had no need for the floppy discs it was buying. Nor, save through the medium of the master agreement, was it trading in floppy discs. The manifest purpose of the document was to clothe the advance of money in the legal form of a sale of goods and that was the only purpose of the sale. That is no reason for holding that it is not a sale: but it is a proper ground for looking at the master agreement 'very narrowly' to find whether the legal substance of the transaction is in fact a sale. [406]

Browne-Wilkinson VC reviewed the terms of the arrangement and concluded that while there had been a sale of goods, there had not been a 'true sale' of them:

> It was a transfer of the property in the goods as security for the repayment of sums advanced by Exfinco to Parrot. Although expressed as a discount, there was no once and for all discount but Exfinco was in substance entitled to interest at its daily rate for the period during which it was out of its money. The anticipated source of the repayment of the loan in the ordinary course of events was payment by the overseas buyers. But Parrot could at any time, on three months' notice, pay off the debt and recover both the goods and the benefit of the contracts with the overseas buyers. In my judgment, the advances made by Exfinco were in substance loans secured on the goods 'sold' and the contracts made with the overseas buyers. [409]

The receivers were thus right to direct all customer payments to P.

Exfinco appealed.

***WELSH DEVELOPMENT AGENCY v EXPORT FINANCE CO LTD* [1992] BCLC 148 (CA)**

Facts as above.

Held: The parties were entitled lawfully to arrange their legal affairs as they saw fit, even if the resulting transaction had the same economic effect as another. This would be subject to two qualifications:

(a) The *external test:* The transaction was not a 'sham' having regard to the substance of the agreement and not the labels the parties placed on it.
(b) The *internal test*: The terms of the transaction, having regard to the whole and not discounting the express use of particular words such as 'sale,' were not such as to be inconsistent with the intended legal effect of the parties.

Dhillon LJ quoted dicta from *Lloyds & Scottish Finance v Cyril Lord Carpet Sales Ltd.*[61] with approval:

> To suppose . . . that the assignments were made not by way of sale but by way of security, would be to impose upon the parties a form of transaction totally different from that which they had selected namely one of sale—and which there is no evidence that either of them desired. Indeed there was evidence—uncontradicted—. . . accepted by both courts below that the respondents 'had no intention of creating any charge over book debts or merely making a series of loans.' It would be a strange doctrine of 'looking for the substance' or 'looking through the documents' which would produce a contractual intention so clearly negated by the documents and by . . . the evidence. [615]

Having examined the stipulations of the agreement between P and Exfinco, the CA concluded that the arrangement was truly on of a sale of goods. As such the receivers of P had wrongfully caused P to direct customers to make payments to P otherwise than in accordance with P's contract with Exfinco, and Exfinco had a corresponding claim for breach of that contract against P.

The policy standpoints at first instance and in the CA are very different: at first instance, Browne-Wilkinson VC starts from the position that elaborate legal arrangements are inherently suspect, especially where they appear to avoid contractual obligations to third parties; the CA is much more liberal, arguing parties may arrange their affairs as they see fit provided there is no sham or contradiction with basic legal requirements.[62] The CA's judgment was followed in *in re Cimex Tissues Ltd.*[63] two years later.

Think back to the securitization example given at the start of this section. The result of *WDA v Exfinco* is that provided a securitization structure satisfies the usual private law requirements and is not a sham, the courts will uphold the parties' intentions unless the terms of the contractual documentation, taken as a whole, are inconsistent with that claimed intention. The fact that an arrangement produces a result which is economically equivalent to some other legal arrangement is unimportant, however frustrating that might be to a third party.

61 *Lloyds & Scottish Finance v Cyril Lord Carpet Sales Ltd.* [1992] BCLC 609, 129 NLJ 366 (HL).

62 A discussion of the meaning of 'sham' would take us too far off topic into some very difficult case law. Company lawyers may recognize the term from the veil piercing cases. The essential policy idea is to strike down otherwise lawful arrangements the principal purpose of which is to evade the acquired (or sometimes to be acquired) rights of another person. The classic example is a person who contracts to sell land, but then wishes to back out. He fears an order for specific performance of transfer, so instead transfers the land to a nominee company which he hopes will escape the order. The arrangement is lawful but clearly designed to deny the buyer's rights and so a sham: *Jones v Lipman* [1962] 1 WLR 832 (ChD), but for current scepticism see now *Hurstwood Properties (A) Ltd. v Rossendale Borough Council* [2021] UKSC 16, [2020] All ER 93.

63 *in re Cimex Tissues Ltd.* [1994] BCC 626.

WDA v Exfinco remains the authority on which securitization lawyers rely to support the 'true sale' nature of their transactions. There has been no English securitization-specific case which has specifically called into question the character of an otherwise lawful transaction. Yet is it all plain sailing? Is recharacterization simply a non-issue in a much more liberal judicial environment. The answer is no—it is still possible for a sale to be 'untrue' and recharacterized as something else, as the next case, which readily applied *WDA v Exfinco* illustrates.

ORION FINANCE v CROWN FINANCIAL MANAGEMENT [1996] 2 BCLC 78 (CA)

Atlantic bought and leased out computers, including to Crown. To fund the purchase of the computers to be leased out to Crown, Atlantic agreed with a specialist financer, Orion, to a 'hire-purchase' arrangement whereby Orion would provide cash upfront to Atlantic on provision of conforming documents to Orion, including:

- a signed lease to Crown;
- an assignment of the rents (book debts) payable by Crown under the lease; and
- a copy of the notice of the assignment as sent to Crown.

Notably, the assignment agreement did not perfectly mirror the sums payable by Crown. Crown would always pay the same rental amount; but the amount due to Orion varied with an interest rate schedule, and the assignment of the rental payments was said to be 'by way of security' for these varying amounts. Thus, Orion could sue Atlantic personally for any shortfall in 'interest' payable but also, and crucially, it had recourse to the rents directly if Atlantic could not pay.

Atlantic became insolvent and Crown terminated its lease of the computers. Orion now demanded that Crown make rental payments directly to Orion, which Crown refused to do. In court, Crown's lawyers contended that the 'hire-purchase' of the lease receivables was not a true sale to Orion but on its face an assignment by way of security of company assets for the money advanced. Not being registered, the security was void: Orion had no proprietary rights in the rental payments and so no claim against Crown.

Held: The transaction documents were quite a mess of hire-purchase and security language but they clearly stated inter alia that the assignment of the lease receivables was 'by way of security' for the monies advanced. Applying *WDA v Exfinco*, the various clear statements creating a security interest were inconsistent with the avowed intention of the parties to create a hire-purchase arrangement. This security, being unregistered, was void and so Orion had no claim against Crown.

Millett LJ is always worth quoting at length:

> The proper approach which the court adopts in order to determine the legal category into which a transaction falls is well established. The most recent case on the subject is *Welsh Development Agency v Export Finance Co Ltd*. The first task is to determine whether the documents are a sham intended to mask the true agreement between the parties. If so, the court must disregard the deceptive language by which the parties have attempted to conceal the true nature of the transaction into which they have entered and must attempt by extrinsic evidence to discover what the real transaction was. There is no suggestion in the present

> case that any of the documents was a sham. Nor is it suggested that the parties departed from what they had agreed in the documents, so that they should be treated as having by their conduct replaced it by some other agreement.
>
> Once the documents are accepted as genuinely representing the transaction into which the parties have entered, its proper legal categorisation is a matter of construction of the documents. This does not mean that the terms which the parties have adopted are necessarily determinative. The substance of the parties' agreement must be found in the language they have used; but the categorisation of a document is determined by the legal effect which it is intended to have, and if when properly construed the effect of the document as a whole is inconsistent with the terminology which the parties have used, then their ill-chosen language must yield to the substance.
>
> The legal classification of a transaction is not, therefore, approached by the court *in vacuo*. The question is not what the transaction is but whether it is in truth what it purports to be. Unless the documents taken as a whole compel a different conclusion, the transaction which they embody should be categorized in conformity with the intention which the parties have expressed in them. [84]

Perhaps it feels so obvious it goes without saying, but the English court is not so liberal as to allow English lawyers to get away with sloppy drafting. Securitization documentation must be careful to effect a true sale in form *and* substance.

8.5 Case study: securitizing student loans

To the student, securitization can seem highly abstract—even the retail aspects, such as residential loans, might seem practically remote. Yet even students are part of the securitization world. In the UK and US, for example, governments have seen fit to have students pay for their tertiary education, shelling out for fees using finance in the form of student loans. Indeed, there is an argument that getting into debt *is* the education this structure is promoting. Each individual loan is insignificant in grand scheme of the financial markets, but each student loan is sufficiently similar to the next and offers a fairly predictable repayment profile. In short, student loans can be and are securitized.

When we looked at the theory of money and debt in Chapter 1, creditworthiness was one of the important social factors in play. People evaluated the trustworthiness of potential borrowers; bankers turned this skill into a business. Yet it was always a case of assessing the creditworthiness of a given individual or corporate. With securitization what we see is something remarkable: the socialization of creditworthiness. As Donatella Alessandrini has remarked in a discussion of financial risk and derivatives, credit systems have moved increasingly beyond the evaluation of individual credit risk to the evaluation of credit risk of social 'types.'[64] This is the culmination of a process which began with the mortality tables of Hudde and de Witt in the seventeenth century, used to calculate life insurance premia, and develops with the refinement of sociological, particularly

64 Donatella Alessandrini, *Value Making in International Economic Law and Regulation: Alternative Possibilities* (Routledge 2016). See in particular the chapter on derivatives.

statistical techniques from the late nineteenth century onwards.[65] Heretofore, creditors have lent to individuals based on each individual's circumstance; whereas now securitization investors de facto lend to types and classes of people.

This is all facilitated by the legal techniques at work. The investor is not lending to an individual; the investor is not even a party to any legal arrangement with that individual. The individual's debt has been aggregated with thousands of others, sold to an SPV, and then the SPV has issued notes tranched to reflect the risk profile of that aggregate. The investor is 'lending' into that sociological whole, taking a risk on its objective make up, i.e. that on average, *x* number of persons of such and such a type will default. Borrowers, who will likely knowing of securitization, will only vaguely be aware of this process of socialization through the 'computer-says-no' responses of retail lenders who categorize potential borrowers according to the sociological type-structure developed to market the securitization to investors.

PAUSE FOR THOUGHT

As a student, what do you think are the generalizable factors about students and their loans which could be used to classify them into different risk types for investors? Think about the common kinds of things which would make a student loan a safer or riskier investment for a lender.

To put meat on these theoretical bones, let us look at how UK student loans are securitized. Now that you have encountered a true sale structure, we can move quite quickly to present student loan securitization in diagrammatic form. In Figure 8.5 we present an overview of one of the first securitizations of student loans by the UK Government.

Notice how groups of student loans are 'warehoused' into SPV subsidiaries of the Share Trustee, allowing for replication across multiple series of loans. The loans are described as 'income contingent'

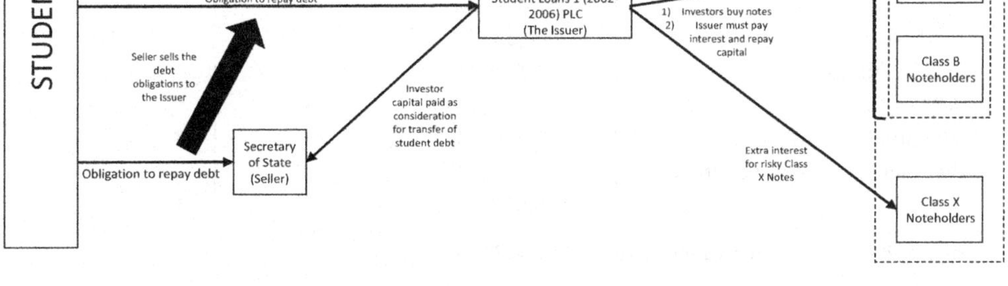

Figure 8.5 Structure of the 2016 UK student loan securitization

65 See Theodore M Porter, *The Rise of Statistical Thinking 1820–1900* (Princeton UP 1986).

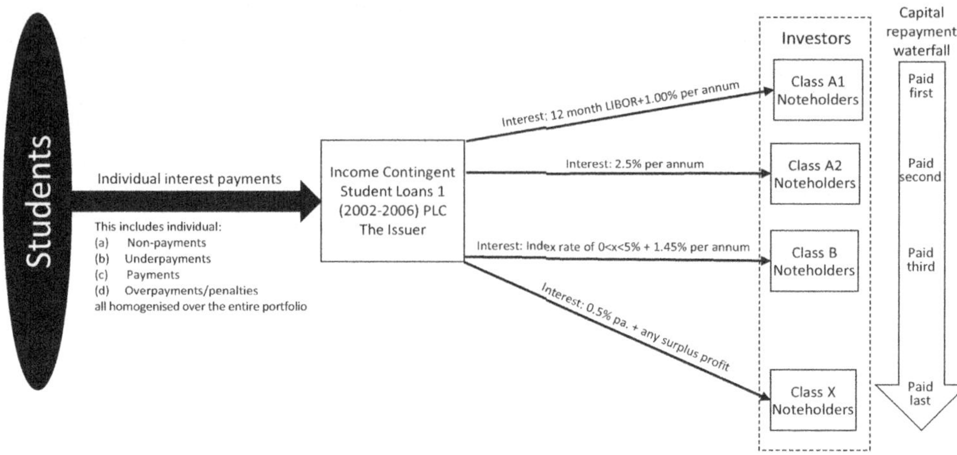

Figure 8.6 Tranching of notes in student loan securitization

because, as you know, students will only start repaying the loans when a certain personal income threshold is met—until then investors must wait for payments of coupon. You might also observe how the Student Loans Company acts as selling agent for the UK Government, which itself sells the debt obligations to the SPV—a doubling up of the true sale problematic discussed in the previous subsection.

Figure 8.6 illustrates how the aggregate of student loans are tranched into risk classes effected by subordination and differential coupon.

Thus, as with most securitizations, investors purchase the notes that best reflect their risk appetite based on their evaluation of the underlying assets (debt) as a whole. It is here that the sociological aspect comes in. There is no hiding it here: the student loan prospectus is open about the risk factors pertaining to the *types* of students whose debt makes up the loan book. Remember, from the investors' perspective, the question is: will these students earn enough to pay back their loan and pay it back?

For example (and these are all drawn directly from the prospectus), the type of degree obtained (or not!) is considered a relevant risk factor:

Course type	Aggregate current balance (£)	% of total
BA/BSc degree	955,814,083	86.50%
BA Law	10,606,479	1.00%
BA/BSc Medicine	1,689,294	0.20%
HND/HNC	40,539,111	3.70%
PGCE or equivalent	55,908,866	5.10%
MA/MSc	13,689,229	1.20%
Foundation degree	12,025,133	1.10%
Other (certificates and diplomas)	15,301,030	1.40%
	1,105,573,224	**100.00%**

Figure 8.7 2016 student loan securitization assets by course type

Why is this relevant to an investment decision? One might guess (this is left to the investor) that one would expect students with bachelor's degrees to go on to earn above the threshold required to repay the debt—which is broadly true. Notice how law and medicine degrees are differentiated from the other bachelor's degrees, the suggestion seemingly that here earnings will be excellent and the risk lower. Further data in the prospectus highlights that 9% of the students on the loan book did not complete their course.

If type of degree is considered an important investment consideration, so is type of university.

University ranking	Aggregate current balance (£)
Top 20	368,915,663
Top 21–30	153,103,697
Top 31–40	284,422,345
Top 41–50	234,589,848
Not in top 50	2,184,684,667
Other	500,800,668
	3,726,516,887

Figure 8.8 2016 student loan securitization assets by university ranking

The Oxbridge and the Russell Group are alive and kicking, for evidently their relative ranking is a critical consideration for the would-be investor. Remember, the investor does not invest in 'Warwick University' debt but in the aggregate debt; it is just that in so doing the investor is aware that some of the debt represents law-ranking universities where, one assumes, the risk of default on the student loan could be higher. This is the implication of the sociological data provided to the investor; nothing is stated explicitly.

So much for the degree, but what of the borrowers? Are their characteristics relevant? Of course: the investors wish to gauge the chances that the students will go on to earn sufficient to repay the loans. In effect, they wish to know about student careers, as separating out law students already indicated. Again, a little thought from your own experience suggests that students who gravitate towards London are likely to earn more. The prospectus is ahead of you.

	2006 Cohort			
Region or residence	Aggregate current balance (£)	% of total	Number of borrowers	% of total
Greater London	194,026,325	17.5%	20,069	16.7%
North West	160,794,713	14.5%	17,705	14.7%
South East	143,765,110	13.0%	16,392	13.6%
Yorkshire and Humberside	119,774,023	10.8%	13,415	11.1%
South West	113,944,609	10.3%	12,222	10.1%
West Midlands	107,558,393	9.7%	11,815	9.8%
East Anglia	87,214,422	7.9%	9,893	8.2%
East Midlands	74,664,493	6.8%	8,284	6.9%
North East	39,362,112	3.6%	4,496	3.7%
Scotland	8,439,428	0.8%	826	0.7%
Wales	9,083,989	0.8%	911	0.8%
Northern Ireland	1,217,966	0.1%	117	0.1%
Channel Islands	131,358	0.0%	11	0.0%
Isle of Man	75,921	0.0%	9	0.0%
not available	45,520,362	4.1%	4,275	3.5%
	1,105,573,224	**100.00%**	**120,440**	**100%**

Figure 8.9 2016 student loan securitization assets by residence of borrower

Over 30% of the 2006 loan book are in Southeast England, of which 17.5% are in London. In terms of assumptions, however, this is as nothing, for the risk profiles are also explicitly gendered.66 It is well-known that women still end up earning less than male counterparts over the medium to long term. The prospectus turns this sociological fact into a risk factor: investing in female students is riskier than investing male students.

	Full Pool			
Income bracket (for borrowers who made repayment in last receipts period)	Aggregate current balance (£)	% of total	Number of borrowers	% of total
< £10,000	96,148,011	8.8%	10,929	7.7%
>= £10,000 and < £13,000	61,807,920	5.7%	7,190	5.1%
>= £13,000 and < £17,775	183,146,441	16.7%	21,173	14.9%
>= £17,775 and < £20,000	118,643,387	10.8%	13,717	9.7%
>= £20,000 and < £22,000	103,368,515	9.5%	12,358	8.7%
>= £22,000 and < £25,000	127,997,253	11.7%	15,777	11.1%
>= £25,000 and < £28,000	108,639,776	9.9%	14,259	10.1%
>= £28,000 and < £32,000	114,281,800	10.4%	16,578	11.7%
>= £32,000 and < £36,000	79,090,271	7.2%	12,582	8.9%
>= £36,000	100,562,873	9.2%	17,252	12.2%
	1,093,686,249	**100.00%**	**141,815**	**100.00%**
Male borrowers	**Aggregate current balance (£)**	**% of total**	**Number of borrowers**	**% of total**
< £10,000	79,178,044	8.5%	8,599	7.2%
>= £10,000 and < £13,000	30,081,773	3.2%	3,204	2.7%
>= £13,000 and < £17,775	102,115,244	11.0%	10,827	9.1%
>= £17,775 and < £20,000	86,128,209	9.3%	9,333	7.9%
>= £20,000 and < £22,000	80,409,695	8.7%	9,178	7.7%
>= £22,000 and < £25,000	113,807,767	12.3%	13,639	11.5%
>= £25,000 and < £28,000	101,007,325	10.9%	12,979	10.9%
>= £28,000 and < £32,000	118,866,157	12.8%	16,475	13.9%
>= £32,000 and < £36,000	85,217,958	9.2%	13,138	11.1%
>= £36,000	130,428,477	14.1%	21,335	18.0%
	927,240,649	**100.00%**	**118,707**	**100.00%**

Figure 8.10 2016 student loan securitization assets by gender and actual earnings over time

Again, it must be stressed that the investor does not choose to invest in male versus female students' loans; the investor is choosing to invest in a pool of both kinds of loan. Nevertheless, that choice of investing or not is, the prospectus suggests, to be determined having regard to risk factors such as the gender or a portion of the asset pool.

What to make of all this (and there is much more in the prospectus)? While tranching does not relate one-to-one to the risks posed by particular (types of) students, it is clear that investors

66 On the gendered economy, see Ann Stewart, *Gender, Law and Justice in a Global Market* (CUP 2011); Serena Natile, 'Regulating Exclusions? Gender, Development and the Limits of Inclusionary Financial Platforms' (2019) 15 International Journal of Law in Context 461.

in subordinated notes will bear the losses which flow from defaults by, in all probability, students of certain types indicated in the prospectus. The investment decision therefore involves consideration of whether one is prepared to risk backing students who may default, because if one does, one will choose to by subordinated X Notes, whereas if one wants a fairly sure bet, A1 Notes are the safest option. And A1 Notes are the safest option not least because the other notes will bear the losses deriving from, statistically, the riskier students. In other words, the other noteholders provide a capital cushion by accepting the risk of default by, statistically, female students living in the north of England who have completed foundational degrees or not completed a qualification at all. Conversely, whole X Notes are risky, the increased coupon payable is in effect the profit the X Noteholder makes on the structural inequalities of British society.

This is financialization writ large: one invests in the very structure of society, from its gendered workplaces to its unequal geographic wealth distribution, to the lack of equality within the UK university system. Building on Alessandrini[67] and the work of Paddy Ireland,[68] we might say society itself gains a capital structure; capital becomes socialized in the field of consumption.

67 Alessandrini (n 64).

68 Paddy Ireland, 'Company Law and the Myth of Shareholder Ownership' (1999) 62 MLR 32, 55–57.

Chapter 9

Derivatives

Chapter contents

DOI: 10.4324/9781003457220-9

9.1 Introduction

Derivatives contracts are a fascinating topic at the heart of finance law, but they also present two basic problems for the student and teacher: the law of derivatives alone could fill a ten-week module but learning the law of derivatives is a really bad way to understand derivatives. Here, more than anywhere else in finance, the gap between legal principles and financial practice feels the most strained. At times the *law* of derivatives seems to share much of the technical complexity, ingenuity, and moralizing of the Ptolemaic account of the cosmos: it can certainly be made to work, with enough qualifications and caveats, to describe its object of study, but a Copernican system that admitted financial practice was the centre of these things would be far more revelatory.

In view of these difficulties, this chapter has two main goals: (1) provide a naïve account of what a derivative contract is by means of explaining what it does, with a focus on its role in supporting the transactions you have already examined in this book; and (2) examine in detail one legal problem for the law of derivatives: the validity of the 'close-out netting' clause in derivatives contract in light of the anti-deprivation rules. As ever, these choices are motivated by a desire to build on what you already know from this book and your foundational legal studies.

This chapter opens with some examples of legal definitions of derivatives, but do not stumble at this first hurdle: read the definitions and do not be concerned that you are none the wiser as a result. In the sections that follow, this chapter seeks to explain the component parts of a derivatives contract, at each stage explaining the motivation for its elements in financial practice. The derivatives contract is not one legal concept, like 'debt,' but is constructed from multiple smaller legal concepts such as the 'option' and 'future.' Sometimes it is better to speak of a derivative contract as one would of a corporate group or global value chain i.e. as something built from smaller legal 'units.' We then briefly highlight some key areas of legal contention in the field, pausing to examine cases where public bodies have sought to argue their entry into a derivatives contract was ultra vires. The cases provide useful context as to the older judicial attitude to derivatives, and tie neatly back to our discussion of authority when we looked at sovereign debt. The remaining third of the chapter then focuses, as trailed, on just one legal topic as a case study: the validity of close-out netting.

9.2 The problem of a definition

Commonly, when a lawyer is asked what a word means, they will reach for a statute, code, or case to locate an authoritative definition. If that fails, they might turn to academic commentary. The problem with the word **derivative** is that positive law is less than helpful, and academic commentary generally accepts that finding a satisfactory, all-encompassing definition is difficult. Everyone involved with derivatives knows one when they see one, but 'derivative' is said in many ways, covering all kinds of financial transaction. The Court of Appeal, for its part, adopted[1] the following proposal by Simon Firth in his work on derivatives:

> [a **derivative** is a] transaction under which the future obligations of one or more of the parties are linked in some specified way to another asset or index, whether involving the delivery of the asset or the payment of an amount calculated by reference to its value or the value of the index. The transaction is therefore treated as having a value which is separate (although derived) from the values of the underlying asset or index. As a result, the parties' rights and obligations under the transaction can be treated as if they constituted a separate asset and are typically traded accordingly.

1 *Lomas v JFB Firth Rixson* [2012] EWCA Civ 419 (CA) [2].

The definition is quite correct, but hardly revelatory to the neophyte. Moreover, it could apply as much to betting on a horse.

An attempt to define 'derivative' was made by the EU's Market in Financial Instruments Regulation[2] (**MiFIR**) and its implementing directive, called MiFID II.[3] This definition was transposed into UK law when the UK was an EU Member State and then **onshored** by various Brexit-related enactments in 2017–18.[4]

DEFINITION: DERIVATIVES

Article 2(1)(29) MiFIR: 'derivatives' mean 'those financial instruments defined in point (44)(c) of Article 4(1) of Directive 2014/65/EU [i.e. MiFID II]; and referred to in Annex I, Section C (4) to (10) thereto' [namely:]

[MiFID II] (4) Options, futures, swaps, forward rate agreements and any other derivative contracts relating to securities, currencies, interest rates or yields, emission allowances or other derivatives instruments, financial indices or financial measures which may be settled physically or in cash;

(5) Options, futures, swaps, forwards and any other derivative contracts relating to commodities that must be settled in cash or may be settled in cash at the option of one of the parties other than by reason of default or other termination event;

(6) Options, futures, swaps, and any other derivative contract relating to commodities that can be physically settled provided that they are traded on a regulated market, a MTF, or an OTF, except for wholesale energy products traded on an OTF that must be physically settled;

(7) Options, futures, swaps, forwards and any other derivative contracts relating to commodities, that can be physically settled not otherwise mentioned in point 6 of this Section and not being for commercial purposes, which have the characteristics of other derivative financial instruments;

(8) Derivative instruments for the transfer of credit risk;

(9) Financial contracts for differences;

(10) Options, futures, swaps, forward rate agreements and any other derivative contracts relating to climatic variables, freight rates or inflation rates or other official economic statistics that must be settled in cash or may be settled in cash at the option of one of the parties other than by reason of default or other termination event, as well as any other derivative contracts relating to assets, rights, obligations, indices and measures not otherwise mentioned in this Section, which have the characteristics of other derivative financial instruments, having regard to whether, inter alia, they are traded on a regulated market, OTF, or an MTF[.].

In the UK, a version of the text in paragraphs (4)–(10) of MiFID II is now to be found in the amended Schedule 2, Part 1 of The Financial Services and Markets Act 2000 (Regulated Activities) Order 2001 (the **RAO**).[5] The UK's HM Treasury evidently concluded that MiFIR's attempt to define 'derivative' was unsatisfactory, and so when they transposed MiFIR and MiFID II into UK law they

2 Regulation (EU) No 600/2014 of the European Parliament and of the Council of 15 May 2014 on markets in financial instruments, and amending Regulation (EU) No 648/2012.

3 Directive 2014/65/EU of the European Parliament and of the Council of 15 May 2014 on markets in financial instruments and amending Directive 2002/92/EC and Directive 2011/61/EU (recast).

4 The Financial Services and Markets Act 2000 (Regulated Activities) (Amendment) Order 2017 SI 2017/488; The Markets in Financial Instruments (Amendment) (EU Exit) Regulations 2018 SI 2018/1403 (with savings in SI 2019/680, reg 11); 2020 cl 1, sch 5, para 1(1).

5 The Financial Services and Markets Act 2000 (Regulated Activities) Order 2001 SI 2001/544, as amended.

deleted any reference to paragraphs (4)–(10) being a definition of 'derivative' and left the question open.6 It seems the transactions in paragraphs (4)–(10) are financial instruments which happen to be derivatives, but other transactions could be (and are) derivatives too.

If you are new to derivatives, then I suspect that at this point you are none the wiser as to what a derivative actually is. All we have at the moment is a non-exhaustive list full of technical jargon and circular definitions, such as (7) which refers us back to 'derivatives contracts.' To learn, we need to approach from a different angle—one which appreciates that some derivatives contracts are actually built up out of simpler derivatives, and that the definition above is trying to capture all these kinds of derivatives.

9.3 Building up a derivatives contract

To understand what derivatives are, we are going to focus on a subset of these instruments called **swaps**. These are built out of smaller derivative components, so understanding these components and how they come together in a swap will give you a good sense of the kind of transaction we mean when we speak of derivatives. There is a further reason for choosing to focus on the swap: swap transactions often occur in relation to credit facilities agreements, securitizations, and several other of the transactions we have already encountered in this book.

Following Schuyler K Henderson,[7] it might be reasonable to regard the option as the basic form of the derivative and build up other kinds developed by the market from this. Let us follow this suggestion.

- Traditionally an option is the right of one party (**P**) to demand transfer of property to or from a counterparty (**CP**). The option may be either:
  - a **call**—CP must transfer property to P when P calls for it; or
  - a **put**—CP must take transfer of P's property from.

EXAMPLE OF A PHYSICALLY SETTLED CALL OPTION

CP offers to sell a call option on BAT plc shares for 5p per share at a strike price of 60p per share. The strike date is in one month and the current BAT share price is 50p. P buys one call option for 5p and waits . . .

1. On the strike date BAT plc shares are at 70p. P exercises the call, pays 60p and receives one share, which he immediately sells for 70p. Less the 5p he paid for the call, he makes a profit of 5p.
2. On the strike date BAT plc shares are at 50p. P abandons his call. Had he exercised it he would have paid 60p for a share worth less. Combined with the option price, P would have made a loss of 15p.
3. On the strike date BAT plc shares are at 62p. P exercises the call, pays 60p and receives one share, which he immediately sells for 62p. Although P paid in total 60p + 5p, and so made a loss, his loss is only 3p. Had he not exercised the option at all, his loss would have been 5p.

6 Instead, the RAO definitions in Article 3(1) (*Interpretation*) only refer to the entirety of sch 2 part I as listing the kind of financial instruments to which the RAO applies. The Financial Conduct Authority's *Perimeter Guidance* provides a further gloss: PERG13.4 (QQ30–34).

7 Schuyler K Henderson, *Henderson on Derivatives* (2nd edn, Butterworths 2010) 1.3.

In the derivatives markets the term **option** has an abstract meaning in which the option is derived from a notional transfer of property. P and CP contract to pay the difference between (1) the price at which P and CP agreed in advance the option could be exercised (the **strike price**) and (2) the then value of the property in the market (the **settlement price**). Because this contract is for the difference of price, the UK legislature has sometimes called derivatives **contracts for differences** (**CfDs**).

In the case that the option is completed simply by payment of the difference, we say the option is **cash settled**. Where, as in example 1 above, completion involves transfer of some non-cash asset, we say the option is **physically settled**.

The CP writes the option for the benefit of P, but CP does not do this gratuitously: on the day the option is written and becomes effective P must pay for the privilege of acquiring the option. This is called a **premium** and the day the **Premium Payment Date**. The premium is the main source of income for the option writer. This payment is what marks out an option: one side of the contract is performed at the beginning of the contract; the other side is performed in the future.

Consider the following example: P1 pays a premium to enter into a cash settled equity call option with CP with a strike price of GBP100. P2 pays a premium to enter into a cash settled equity call option with CP for the same shares with a strike price of GBP150. On the given valuation date, the settlement price in the market is GBP145.

- P1 calls—P1 owes GBP100 to CP and CP owes GBP145 to P1, so CP pays GBP45 to P1. On this date we say P1's option is **in-the-money**.
- P2 calls—P2 owes GBP150 to CP and CP owes GBP145 to P2, so P2 must pay GBP5 to P2. On this date we say P2's option is **out-of-the-money**.

Where more than one asset of a kind is part of the option, we call this a basket. Commonly the settlement price for the basket is valued by reference to an index. E.g. a FTSE100 **index option** contains one of each share in the index, and so the basket's settlement price is the value of the index on valuation day.

A **forward** is an option in which both sides of the contract must be performed not today but at some time in the future. Options are rights to buy/sell; forwards are obligations to buy/sell. Again, taking the example of an equity derivative, P and CP agree that on a specified date, P will pay an agreed **forward price** to CP in consideration of delivery on that date of either (1) specified shares; (2) the cash equivalent of such shares; or (3) the value of an index of such shares. In cases of cash/index settlement P will receive/pay an amount = (forward price—the settlement price) × the number of shares.

It is quite possible to prepay the forward price, conditions being specified in the confirmation. Forwards may be subject to caps, floors, and collars which limit risk. We come back to these later.

A **swap** might then be considered as a series of options and forwards which settle over an agreed time period. It is essentially a series of mutual payments or delivery flows taking place, say, every month by reference to some underlying market value such as the value of a basket of equities. As swaps are a significant feature of the transactions we are examining, let us focus on their rationale.

9.4 What does a swap do?

The swap arose as a reaction to wild currency fluctuations following the 1970s abandonment of the gold standard and the **First Oil Shock**. Thus, it makes sense to begin our look at rationale with currency swaps.

THE FIRST OIL SHOCK FX

By the October 1973 Yom Kippur War, oil-producing countries had come to realize the oligopoly power they held. By simply altering output they could dramatically alter oil prices, which, as a fundamental input of Western industry, would have significant macroeconomic consequences. Saudi Arabia was particularly aware of this: while it did not participate militarily in the war, King Faisal spoke to Egyptian envoys of his willingness to use the 'oil weapon.'[8]

This weapon was deployed by agreement of the original Oil-Producing and Export Countries on 16–17 October 1973. An oil embargo was called which initially included countries such as the USA, Canada and UK and soon extended to others, notably South Africa and Rhodesia. Unable to access oil from the main producers, oil-importers scrambled for limited alternative sources. The oil price rocketed by 300%.

The result was macroeconomic downturns across the Global North, but what interests us were three important financial effects:[9]

1. The balance of payments to oil exporters once the embargo was released grow considerably in their favour. In short, a huge amount of money (US dollars) began flowing to the OPEC countries to pay for oil at the new price levels.
2. People who profited from oil production in the OPEC countries became exceptionally rich but needed to find a home in which to invest their capital.
3. Western central banks dropped interest rates, aiming to boost growth, making holding their currencies less desirable.

A hangover of empire had been that capital tended to flow back to the metropolis. Money made in East Africa or India was invested in London, in West Africa, in Paris, and so forth. South American money tended to flow to New York. Capital was divided according to spheres of interest. The OPEC capital was not tied in this way; it flowed to whichever financial capital offered the best rates of return.

What now occurred further disrupted the macroeconomic landscape. Petrodollars remitted from OPEC countries looked for returns where they could be found; central banks competed to attract the capital; the capital could shift from Frankfurt to London at the drop of a hat; deutschmarks were bought in bulk, only to be quickly sold as sterling was seen as a better home; petrodollars were converted into gold, and the gold moved country at previously unknown rate of turnover. Suddenly the gold and currency markets, and interest rates, became highly volatile as they reacted to these movements of capital.[10]

Against this background, industrial companies sought to export/import, buy raw materials abroad, and borrow money, all in a world where the price of doing so could fluctuate wildly. Chief financial officers asked how they could insure against these risks.

Currency and then interest rate swaps were the financial market's answer.

With this background, we can illustrate just what the first swaps were trying to achieve.

8 Rüdiger Graf, 'Making Use of the "Oil Weapon": Western Industrialized Countries and Arab Petropolitics in 1971–1974' (2012) 36 Diplomatic History 185.

9 Pavlos Masouros, *Corporate Law and Economic Stagnation: How Shareholder Value and Short-termism Contribute to the Decline of the Western Economies* (Eleven International Publishing 2013).

10 One notable result of the currency volatility was the collapse of Bank Herstatt. We examine this case study in the context of payment settlement in Chapter 10.

9.4.1 The currency swap

P is a US auto manufacturer that plans to buy parts from subcontractors in the UK. For this it needs 30m of sterling, but on entering the currency markets it finds that financial institutions are wary of lending GBP to P because of the inherent currency risk in its activities. If GBP rises significantly, then P will not acquire sufficient parts and may make a loss, causing it to struggle to repay the loan. The market will lend but will charge a high 9% margin to cover this risk—high compared to the rate P would be paying if it just borrowed USD at home: 5%.

CP is a bank with operations in London. CP borrows GBP all the time and is in good standing, such that it would be charged a rate of 6% to borrow the same amount of sterling P needs. P approaches CP and effectively asks CP to borrow GBP in P's stead. That way GBP will be borrowed at 3% less than if P had borrowed it directly. In exchange P agrees to transfer the USD equivalent of GBP30m to CP (let's say USD50m). In this way each party benefits from the other's credit rating.

So, in short, the bank (CP) borrows pounds sterling in London at 6% and hands it over to the auto manufacturer (P); the auto manufacturer borrowers US dollars in Michigan at 5% and hands this money to the London bank.

The difficulty is that P is still the debtor for those USD, and is still contractually obliged to pay interest. Likewise, the London bank CP is liable for the GBP—each of P and CP must pay interest on money they are not using because they handed it over to the other party to the transaction. The solution: P agrees that when the London bank CP must pay interest on the sterling CP borrowed (say, every quarter), P will send to CP just enough money so that CP can pay that interest. Likewise, when P must pay interest on the USD, CP will send to P just enough money to make that interest payment.

But why have P send all that money to CP to help make the interest payment, only for CP to send some (or even all of it back)? Instead, P and CP agree not to send the full amounts needed to make the interest payments to each other; rather they **net off** the amounts they owe each other for the respective interest payments and the party that owes the greater of the two amounts pays the difference (hence the language of **Contract for Difference**). This arrangement is illustrated in Figure 9.1.

Now let us look at that again in slightly more detail. The currency swap is effected as follows:

(1) Having borrowed the respective amounts, on the Effective Date the Initial Exchange Amounts are swapped: P transfers USD50m to CP; CP transfers GBP30m, for a term of three years.
(2) As agreed, on each periodic Payment Date (say, every three months), P pays an agreed amount to CP for the privilege of using the GBP30m and CP pays P an agreed amount for the privilege of using the USD50m. This amount could be:
    (a) A fixed margin, say 6% of GBP30m from P to CP and 5% of USD50m from CP to P.
    (b) A mixed margin: say 6% of GBP30m from P to CP and LIBOR on USD50m from CP to P.
    (c) A floating rate: say the respective LIBOR on each amount.
        (i) Notice that both amounts are paid in the respective currency. They have to, to match the corresponding repayment obligation of each party to their lender.
(3) On the Termination Date (Final Exchange Date), the parties re-exchange the currency.

Notice the following: it is not actually necessary for the Initial Exchange physically to occur. Where P and CP can just as easily borrow the amount to be delivered themselves (e.g. they are both international banks), they can just do this directly and pretend the capital has been borrowed and swapped. The only exchange then is of the periodic amounts—the parties simply swap the cost of funds (which incidentally reduces counterparty risk on return of capital).

The economic effect of the swap is as if P was able to borrow GBP in the currency markets like a bank. The legal structure of the swap recreates that effect as if it were the case. For this reason, we call such transactions **synthetic** i.e. artificial constructs.

Given that the currency swap effectively swaps interest rates, it is not surprising that the interest rate swap should have developed out of it.

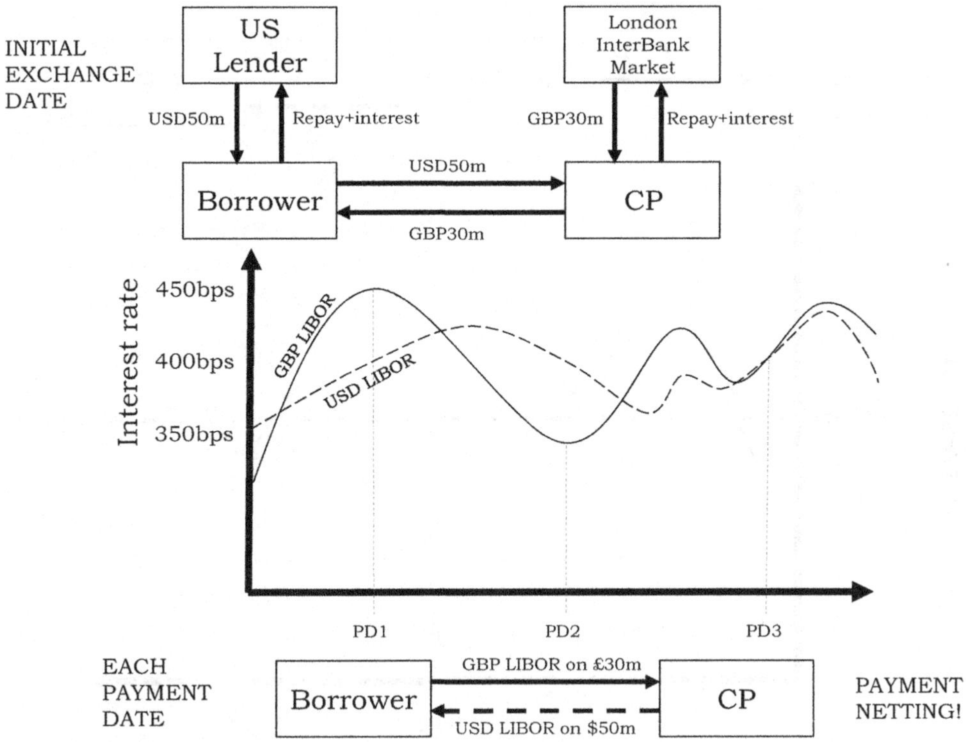

Figure 9.1 A 'classic' currency swap

9.4.2 Interest rate swap

An interest rate swap might be regarded as a natural evolution of the currency swap: take a currency swap, forget about swapping the actual currency and focus only on the interest rates payable on the Interest Payment Dates.

For example, P is a borrower from Bank under a London Form CFA. The GBP100m term facility is fully drawn, and P is obligated to pay floating interest of LIBOR + Margin every three months (in this paragraph, the IPD). P is concerned that LIBOR could rise and wishes to fix the interest rate.

P agrees with CP to pay CP an amount equal to, say, 4% of GBP100m every. In consideration CP agrees to pay to P an amount equal to the relevant LIBOR on GBP100m. Synthetically, P swaps its obligation to pay floating rate interest for one to pay a fixed rate (see Figure 9.2).

Careful! P must pay Bank floating interest and does pay floating interest. What actually happens is this:

(1) If LIBOR > 4%, say 4.5%, then P pays 4.5% (+ Margin) to Bank. Simultaneously, P notionally pays 4% to CP and CP notionally pays 4.5% to P. The two notional payments are netted off and so CP just pays 0.5% to P. The economic effect of this is that while P has paid 4.5% to Bank, it has received 0.5%, and so its cash balance is only reduced in the last analysis to 4% as if it were paying a fixed rate.

(2) If LIBOR < 4%, e.g. 3.5%, then P pays 3.5% (+ Margin) to Bank as per the terms of the floating rate CFA. Simultaneously, P notionally pays 4% to CP and CP notionally pays 3.5% to P. The two notional payments are netted off and so P must pay 0.5% to CP. The economic effect of this is that while P has paid 3.5% to Bank, it has also paid 0.5% to CP, and so its cash balance is reduced in the last analysis to 4% as if it were paying a fixed rate.

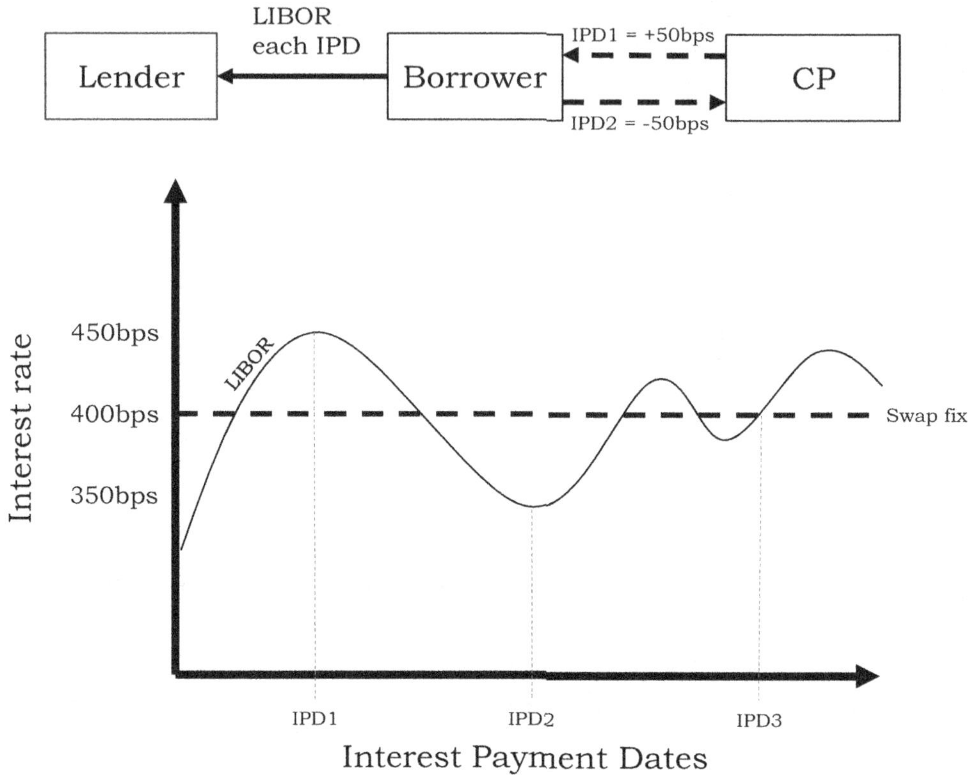

Figure 9.2 An interest rate swap

(3) If LIBOR = 4% the P pays 4% (+ Margin) to Bank as per the terms of the floating rate CFA. As the notional payment obligations under the swap are equal but opposite they cancel each other out and no payment is made.

In other words, the interest rate swap smooths out the interest rate payments of the borrower: the borrower's CFO knows that each IPD the corporate must pay a fixed sum, whatever the market interest rate is from time to time. This certainty helps manage corporate liquidity, and is often more desirable than any speculative benefit that could be obtained by allowing the interest to float.

9.4.3 Caps, floors, and collars

Under these kinds of swaps, reference values (such as an interest rate) are permitted to float within certain predetermined parameters. They are illustrated in Figure 9.3.

Under a cap, a Cap Buyer sets an upper limit to the floating rate it will pay. Let P from 9.4.2 above be a Cap Buyer with respect to the loan from Bank. P agrees to buy a cap of 4.7% from CP, and on the Effective Date agrees to pay a premium to CP for this privilege. Provided always that LIBOR is less than or equal to 4.7%, then P bears the risk of the fluctuation and CP pays nothing to P. If on a given maturity date LIBOR > 4.7%, then CP pays to P an amount equal to the difference between LIBOR and 4.7%. In this way P fixes rate rises at 4.7% because CP will always provide any excess interest it must pay, and benefits from any falls in LIBOR because P will pay whatever LIBOR is less than 4.7% and need not pass through that fall to CP.

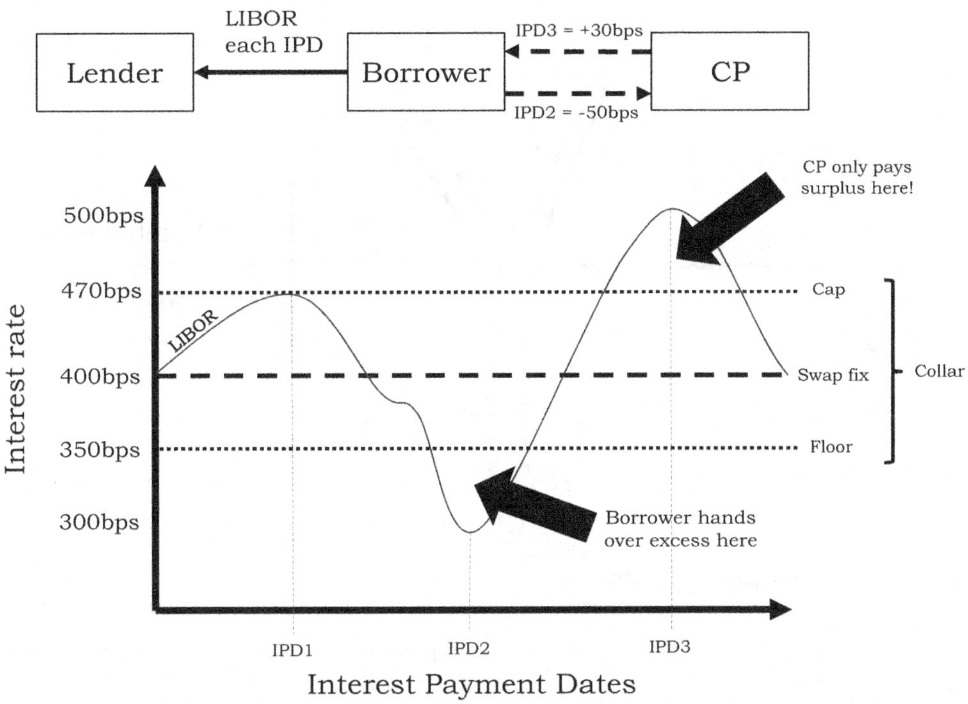

Figure 9.3 A cap, a floor, and a collar

Observe how a cap is really just a series of automatic call options, called **caplets**. As each caplet matures, P calls for cash settlement at the strike rate for that caplet.

A floor is simply the inverse of a cap: a Floor Purchaser obtains, for a premium, the obligation on Floor Seller to pay to Purchaser the difference between LIBOR and, if greater, the specified Floor Rate. Again, the swap is just a series of call options, called **floorlets**. A floor can be desirable for pension and insurance funds which seek to protect expected interest flows from investments, usually because a certain minimum rate of return has been promised to fund investors.

A collar is best understood as a combination of a cap and a floor—the Cap Purchaser sells the Floor. Because both parties could benefit from interest rates fluctuating without the collar the parties might forgo an initial premium, transforming the collar into a series of forwards. A collar is attractive because with a cap P benefits from all the downside of the interest rate because the lower rate means it pays less to Bank. By selling a Floor to CP, CP can benefit from the lowest bounds of any downside. In this way assumption of the risk of high rights is mitigated by assumption of the benefits of extremely low rates.

9.5 Swaps in special financial settings

We have already encountered swaps in a number of other settings. Consider for example securitization. Here SPV receives many mortgage payments from borrowers and this stream is used to fund fixed coupon payments on RMBS. The risk however is that the floating rate paid by the borrowers will be less than the fixed rate due to the noteholders. Additionally, the currency of the borrowers may not all be the same, and the SPV may have to convert EUR into GBP before paying noteholders. To reduce these risks SPV enters into:

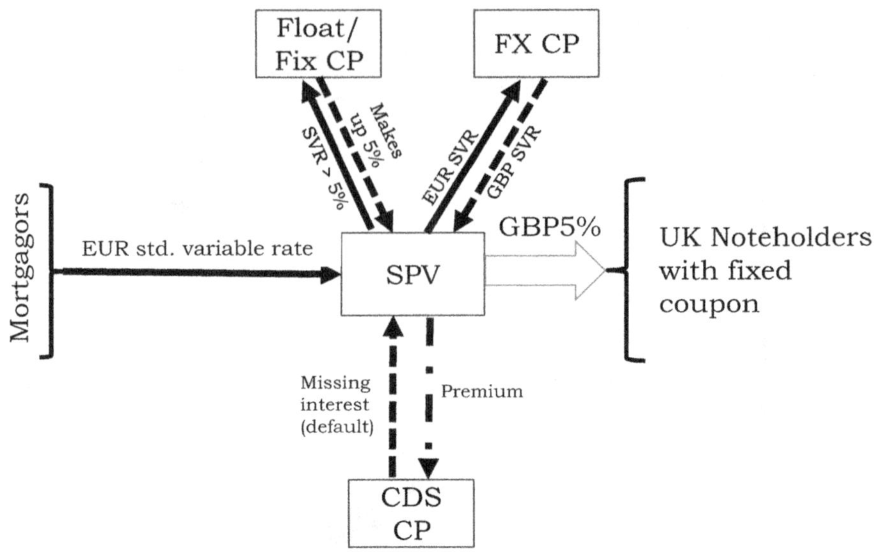

Figure 9.4 Use of swaps in a securitization

(1) An interest rate swap in which CP agrees to pay a fixed rate to SPV and SPV pays the floating rate to CP. Only the net is paid and SPV finds it has transformed a floating into a fixed rate to meet its note obligations.
(2) A notional currency swap in which CP synthetically lends a EUR equivalent amount of the euro-based underlying value and requires SPV to pay periodic EUR interest to CP. SPV notionally lends the GBP equivalent to CP and CP pays the GBP interest rate to SPV. In this way SPV receives a set income in a currency which matches the currency of the payment obligation owed to noteholders.

Things get even more abstract when we deal with synthetic securitizations. If we consider again a European-style securitization from Chapter 8, we remember the necessary true sale of the assets from Originator to SPV. In a synthetic securitization there is no sale. Rather:

(1) SPV agrees that if there is any default (a credit event) by an underlying borrower in Originator's credit pool, SPV will bear that risk i.e. pay to Originator an amount equivalent to the loss on the non-performing loan.
(2) In consideration, Originator agrees to pay to SPV a premium on a periodic basis for this protection. The combination of this premium and credit risk protection is called a Credit Default Swap (**CDS**).
(3) SPV issues Credit-Linked Notes (**CLNs**) to the market. A CLN basically states that provided a credit event does not occur in the reference obligation (the CDS), the holder will receive par on maturity (e.g. EUR 100 a year later on a one-year EUR 100 note) and periodic coupon payments. If the credit event does occur, the holder receives nothing or perhaps a pre-agreed recovery rate amount.
(4) Notice that under a CDS, the seller does not initially transfer anything to the buyer (but does so only on a credit event); under a CLN the noteholder loans capital upfront.
(5) SPV uses the proceeds of CLN issuance to acquire AAA-rated securities. The income from these third-party securities services the coupon on the CLNs and meets calls under the CDS.

Appreciate that the economic effect of all this is that the CLN holders have synthetically written a CDS for Originator i.e. they have provided a swap without actually signing one, in which case we say there is a CDS 'embedded' in the notes.

PARMALAT[11]

The Italian dairy giant was a huge fan of CLNs, as investors discovered to their cost in 2003. Parmalat, working with *inter alios* Bank of America and Grant Thornton in 1999, set up an offshore SPV which sold a CDS to Parmalat. The SPV also issued CLNs which would become worthless if a credit event occurred in the underlying (Parmalat).

The problem was that the chief investor in the CLNs was . . . Parmalat. It was effectively betting on its own creditworthiness.

Parmalat had done this because Parmalat's balance sheet showed the benefit of both the CDS *and* the CLNs, appearing to double the value of its assets and so defrauding its other investors.[12]

Various members of Parmalat's financial team, who had kept the arrangement secret, were arrested, and management was replaced as Parmalat went through an insolvency process. The new management team caused Parmalat to bring claims against the former advisers behind the CLN scheme, ultimately recouping some US$700m in settlement payments.[13]

Commodity swaps are not uncommon in project finance. Interest rate and currency swaps may be in play, but it serves no purpose to repeat their mechanics. More interesting are those swaps pertaining to the project itself:

(1) A commodity swap: e.g. in an oil and gas project the oil-producing SPV may sell oil at the market spot price into the market. This is risky: the income is variable, and SPV must interest and capital on its loan according to a fixed schedule. Thus, SPV enters into a commodity swap with a specialized dealer under which:
   (a) Dealer agrees to pay a fixed price (say USD55) per barrel to SPV.
   (b) SPV agrees to pay a floating price based on the notional value of x number of barrels produced.
   (c) Dealer enters into a corresponding swap with the end user, who likewise seeks to fix the costs of his energy usage.

(2) Note this is notional—SPV and user both actually acquire oil in the market. The end result is that after netting if the floating price is less than USD55, SPV still receives USD55 (the market price actually paid + the difference from netting with the Dealer). If floating price greater than USD55 SPV pays the difference to Dealer who receives benefit of the upside. These amounts are passed through to end user—end user ends up paying USD55 (being either compensated if the floating price is high; having to pay if too low).

(3) In project finance, power producers must match their loan obligations to the price they receive for the power produced. A PPA may offer a fixed price, but in many cases the SPV power producer (or off-taker) will be paid at the market sport rate. To smooth out price fluctuations SPV could enter in a synthetic PPA which offers a collar on price. SPV sells into the market as usual but where the price falls below a pre-agreed amount, the counterparty makes good the difference; conversely any upside above the cap is passed to the counterparty.

11 'Skimming Off the Cream' (*The Economist*, 22 January 2004) <https://www.economist.com/finance-and-economics/2004/01/22/skimming-off-the-cream> accessed 1 September 2024.

12 Had the arrangement been governed by English law, further problems with it included (1) it was a transaction at an undervalue (no value was really given) and a preference, both prior to insolvency (ss 238, 239 Insolvency Act 1986); and (2) insider trading to the extent the notes had been listed, Insider Trading Act 1986 and Market Abuse Regulation (Assimilated Regulation) (EU) 596/2014.

13 Adrian Michaels, 'Deloitte to settle Parmalat lawsuit' (*Financial Times*, 12 January 2007) <https://www.ft.com/content/728aa3c2-a28b-11db-a187-0000779e2340> accessed 29 September 2019.

These example swaps are clearly non-exhaustive. Moreover, individual types of swap can all be combined into more complicated products, just as options and futures were combined into a swap. These combinations are all achieved using a framework contract which allows counterparties to weld together multiple swap arrangements quickly and conveniently without having to negotiate a lengthy contract every time.

9.6 The International Swaps and Derivatives Association (ISDA) master agreement

Now that we understand the economic rationale for swaps, how are they contracted and what legal issues do they come up against? As we shall see, a key issue for swaps is the avoidance of 'cherry picking,' which is an insolvency officials attempt to cancel or defer swap liabilities while upholding swap claims of the insolvent. Most swaps, like other treasury transactions such as forward FX contracts, were initially documented by email or fax sent by one party to the other confirming and occasionally supplementing terms agreed by telephone. The other party normally responded by fax or telex confirming the agreement.

Under English and New York law (thanks to an amendment made in 1994 to the Statute of Frauds), the written confirmations merely evidence an oral agreement which is binding on both parties from the time the swap transaction is concluded by telephone, assuming agreement was reached on all essential terms of the transaction.

Because swaps, unlike some other treasury instruments, often involve a significant degree of credit risk over an extended period (they can have maturities of 1 to 5, to even 15 years) the above exchange of confirmations is not generally considered to be sufficiently complete to provide adequate protection to the parties.

Interest rate and currency swaps developed out of the market in parallel and back-to-back loans in the 1970s. This, coupled with the credit risk mentioned above, resulted in early swap documents bearing a strong resemblance to loan documents and current documentation continues to bear the stamp of this origin. Two practices developed regarding the use and reuse of agreements of up to 25 pages:

(1) The separate transaction approach, in which a set of standard terms would be drawn up which would be incorporated into each individual standalone swap agreement.
(2) The single agreement approach in which a **master agreement (MA)** was agreed setting out details of every term to be incorporated into each transaction. All subsequent transactions would form part of the single MA and together constitute a single contract.

One of the principal reasons why the single agreement approach prevailed was that it was relatively successful at stopping the cherry-picking problem. You will remember the term 'cherry picking' refers to a power that insolvency officials have under the insolvency laws of certain jurisdictions to reject certain contracts burdensome to the insolvent company while affirming contracts beneficial to the insolvent company. If a counterparty has a number of swaps with an insolvent company, 'cherry picking' results in those swaps which are liabilities to the insolvent company being rejected and those swaps which are assets being affirmed. Assuming the swaps are unsecured, the counterparty is in the disastrous position of being forced to pay full value in respect of the swaps which are liabilities to itself while likely to receive only part value (if any) in respect of the swaps which are assets to itself.

MAs attempt to overcome this problem by making it clear that the MA and all swap transactions entered into under it constitute a single agreement between the parties which must therefore be affirmed or rejected by the insolvency official as a whole (see, e.g., the first paragraph of the 2002

ISDA MA). The most important standard form MAs for our purposes are those prepared by the International Securities and Derivatives Association (**ISDA**).

Normally, upon termination of a MA by reason of an insolvency default, all swap transactions are terminated and a value is determined for each one. Some of these swaps may be assets and some liabilities of the non-defaulting party. The ISDA MA envisages that the values for the transactions are converted to a single currency and netted against each other to produce a single 'close-out.' Netting of swap values on termination is often important to the treatment of swaps under the insolvency laws applicable to the defaulting party and for capital adequacy purposes.

IMPORTANT!

The last point is worth spelling out—there are now **two** lots of netting occurring: (1) one under each individual swap governed by the MA; and (2) one as between all the swaps governed by the MA on close-out.

For example, A plc and Bank enter into various interest rate swaps governed by an ISDA Master Agreement:

- Under one swap relating to a loan of euros, on a given reference date A notionally pays fixed interest of EUR100, B notionally pays a floating rate calculated to come to EUR110. Thus, B actually owes a net EUR10 to A.
- Under another swap, perhaps relating to a notional sterling loan, A notionally pays a fixed rate sterling amount, which we will say is equal to EUR105 on the reference day. On the same day, B notionally pays a floating rate amount equivalent to EUR90 to A. The swapped amounts again are netted, and this time A owes a net EUR15 to B.
- If close-out occurs at that point, the EUR10 B owes to A is now netted against the EUR15 A owes to B, producing the close-out amount of EUR5 payable by A to B.

It is this second order close-out netting which will prove central to the cases we examine later in this chapter.

It should be noted that although by the 1980s the single agreement approach had become standard, leading dealers in different markets used different forms of MA, each contractually dealing with matters including close-out netting in their own way, e.g.:

(1) The 1992 and 2002 **ISDA** MA which uses the method of valuation, conversion, netting, termination of existing obligations and creation of a new obligation equivalent to the netted amount which is called the close-out amount.
(2) The current International Foreign Exchange MA (**IFEMA**) which uses a similar mechanism, netting off all current swaps and then super-adding a new obligation to pay an amount equal to the sums then due.
(3) The Global Master Repurchase Agreement (**GMRA**) which simply accelerates all obligations into one immediately payable amount.

During the 1980s many more standard forms or 'codes' were used, but in 1992 the International Swaps and Derivatives Association introduced the 1992 ISDA Master Agreement (Multicurrency Cross Border) which became the most widely used MA in the market. ISDA introduced a 2002 MA, but it took several years for market participants to move over to this revised document.

The 1992 and 2002 ISDA MAs are MAs composed of two parts: a printed form of about 18 pages and a Schedule. The Schedule (included by ISDA only after it was clear that agreement would not be reached among the members of ISDA on all credit points) permits counterparties to tailor the printed form to their specific credit, tax and other policy requirements. Most negotiations of the ISDA MA concern the provisions of Parts 1 (Termination Provisions), 2 (Tax Representations) and 5 (Other Provisions) of the Schedule. For example, it is frequently necessary or desirable to include special provision in art 5 of the Schedule dealing with special counterparties, such as UK building societies and insurance companies.

It is important to remember that the ISDA Agreement does not include details of any specific transaction. Each transaction is evidenced by a separate document called a Confirmation which is incorporated into the ISDA Agreement. Although ISDA provides a form of Confirmation (in the 2000 ISDA Definitions) most parties use their own form, commonly set out as a letter. Section 2(a)(i) of the ISDA MA simply provides that each party is required to make those payments specified in each Confirmation. This makes the MA extremely flexible.

Since none of the economic terms relating to specific transactions are included in the ISDA MA, all such detail (e.g. regarding rate sources and settings, calculation of fixed and floating amounts, business day conventions, and so on) must be included separately in each Confirmation. In order to keep the Confirmations to a reasonable length, ISDA has, over the years, published a number of product specific definitions booklets such as the 2003 ISDA Credit Derivatives Definitions and the 2000 ISDA Definitions (**Definitions**, the latter of which provides the basic framework for the documentation of privately negotiated interest rate and currency derivative transactions).

Thus, we have the following structure:

(1) the MA (printed form and Schedule);
(2) a Confirmation; and
(3) the 2000 ISDA Definitions (incorporated into the Confirmation by reference).

This structure means that different types of swap (e.g. a weather swap and a currency hedge) can be separately confirmed and still be governed by a single MA. Notice that any given swap, or all, may be fully performed and so discharged, but the MA will continue to bind, permitting confirmation of further swaps as much as sustaining any secondary obligations (such as governing law for disputes).

9.7 Some legal issues with derivatives

The legal issues raised by swaps and similar transactions will vary from jurisdiction to jurisdiction. However, many issues are similar or analogous in the jurisdictions where the principal swaps markets are located. Here are some key issues arising frequently under English law, with some reference to other jurisdictions:

(1) **Capacity**: swaps are complicated transactions with potentially limitless liabilities. It is thus not unusual for an out-of-the-money party to claim that they did not have the capacity to enter into the swap contract in the first place. This is a particular issue with bodies corporate, whose powers are constitutionally limited. While ss 33 and 39 CA 2006 arguably alleviate any risks when contracting with 'vanilla' post-2006 companies in the UK, the old ultra vires rules apply to corporations not incorporated under CA 2006, such as chartered corporations and municipalities. As you will have studied ultra vires in a public law course, and come across it as a slightly outmoded topic of the company law syllabus, let us review a couple of key cases. The first is the leading authority.[14]

14 Mark Hsiao, 'Recent developments on the ultra vires in the UK courts and the relationship with the representation of power to execute in the ISDA 2002 Master Agreement' (2023) 38 JIBLR 79.

HAZELL v LONDON BOROUGH OF HAMMERSMITH & FULHAM [1992] 2 AC 1 (HL)

Many public bodies enter into swaps. A university, for example, may have borrowed money on a floating rate basis, thus running the risk that the interest rate will increase. It might hedge that risk with a fixed/floating swap as discussed above. Hammersmith & Fulham (H&F), a public municipal entity, also entered into swaps, but not in a way ancillary to core cash management. Through the 1980s, H&F were speculating in the derivatives market, hoping to generate profits which would fund other activities.

H&F entered into all kinds of interest rate swap arrangements, often as seller of the floating side i.e. it would pay the floating rate to the counterparty; the counterparty would pay a fixed rate. There were swaps with floors, caps and collars, and even forward rate agreements and options on cash and gilts.

Up to 1989, H&F had not done too badly: it had recouped as much as it had paid out. Yet now, following Black Wednesday when the United Kingdom was humiliatingly forced to abandon the European Exchange Rate Mechanism to defend sterling, H&F was in trouble. Bank of England base rate shot up over 10%, which meant that sellers of floating rates like H&F were paying huge amounts to counterparties versus fixed rates agreed during the 'good times.' On marking H&F's positions to market to determine how much H&F was due to pay out in the coming months and years, accountants calculated H&F would owe some £100m.

H&F began unwinding positions but, being a public body, they were also required to call in an auditor in investigate its finances and make recommendations. The auditor took one look at the swap positions and called in counsel, who opined that many of swap contracts were void because they were ultra vires (exceeded the legal powers of) H&F as a public body.[15]

The auditor sought a declaration to this effect from the court. Were the court to agree, the contracts would simply never have subsisted and H&F could not be liable under them.

Held: The core of the case turned on the precise ambit of certain laws regulating the finances of local authorities. Nevertheless, there are generalizable elements, of which the most striking is the House of Lords' moralizing approach to swaps:

> For the banks it was argued that swap transactions are akin to insurance which enables provision to be made for possible risks. By insurance, an assured sacrifices a premium which when aggregated with premiums from other assured, will form a pool from which the insurer will indemnify the unfortunate victim (if any) who suffers from the risk insured against. A swap contract based on a notional principal sum of £1m. under which the local authority promises to pay the bank US$600m if LIBOR rises by one per cent. and the bank promises to pay the local authority £10,000 if LIBOR falls by one per cent. **is more akin to gambling than insurance**. [34–35, my emphasis)]

This view seems to lie behind a critical distinction the House of Lords made. The bank counterparties had argued that the swaps were ancillary features of H&F's borrowing activity, or, alternatively, that at the very least entering into these swaps fell within the genus of activities of any finance office performing 'debt management.' The House of

15 See Part I of sch 13 to the Local Government Act 1972.

Lords disagreed: borrowing was the sort of thing the local authority was expected to do, but entering into these kinds of swap arrangements was a wholly separate activity of a purely speculative nature. Lord Templeman said:

> Debt management is not a function. Debt management is a phrase which has been coined in this case to describe the activities of a person who enters the swap market for the purpose of making profits which can be employed in the payment of interest on borrowings. . . . [34]
>
> Although the phrase 'debt management' may be a convenient one, swap transactions in fact leave the debt wholly unmanaged. [46]

As such, they were ultra vires they capacity of H&F and, for that matter, any other local authority.

Hammersmith & Fulham is stronger on the public law aspects of the case than it is on understanding the world of derivatives. As Henderson notes,[16] their Lordships evidently struggled to grasp these new financial arrangements, their common usage, or even why a counterparty would seek to hedge its existing financial obligations rather than simply prepay[17] its loans and borrow again on better terms. Compare this attitude to that of the Court of Appeal in 2023, where Sir Julian Flaux C, an experienced judge of derivatives cases, gave the only judgment.

This case involved an English law-governed ISDA master agreement, one of the counterparties to which was an Italian *comune* (municipality). The question of capacity was therefore referred to Italian law, but if Italian law said that the municipality lacked capacity, the English law of contract and agency would, on that premise, conclude that the master agreement were void.[18] Note this is a special case of the ultra vires in sovereign debt concerns we examined in Chapter 5.

BANCA INTESA SANPAOLO SPA; DEXIA CREDIT LOCAL SA v COMUNE DI VENEZIA [2023] EWCA Civ 1482

In December 2002, the city of Venice issued a 20-year bond with an interest rate (coupon) which floated with EURIBOR (see Chapter 2). To hedge this floating rate, Venice entered into a fixed/floating swap with US investment bank, Bear Stearns, derived from a notional loan amount equal to the bonds in issue.

When Bear Stearns collapsed during the GFC and was forcibly taken over, restructuring talks relating to the swap were pursued and ultimately the two appellant Italian banks to 68% and 32% of Bear Stearns' position, respectively. This was achieved by way of novation of the master agreement. At this time, Venice was severely out of the money, and took legal advice, which opined that the swap was ultra vires. It was only in 2019, however, that Venice sought a declaration that the novated contract was void for want of capacity

16 Henderson (n 7) 13.6.

17 Because prepayment is not 'free,' and the borrower has calculated a swap is a cheaper way forward.

18 *Haugesund Kommune v Depfa ACS Bank* [2010] EWCA Civ 579, [2012] QB 549.

and for restitution of monies paid over. In particular, Venice argued that the novated swap was speculative because it assumed *from the outset* (i.e. because the novated contract was legally a new, standalone contract) Venice was out of the money.

The High Court agreed that the swap was a purely 'speculative' investment, ultra vires the city of Venice, and thus the novated contract was void ab initio.

Held by the Court of Appeal: The judge in the high court had made several errors, including imputing his theories about what is speculative for the purposes of Italian law rather than relying on local experts as would have been procedurally correct.

On the substance, the High Court judge had erred both in regarding the novated swap in isolation from the original Bear Stearns swap (which was valid),[19] and in recharacterizing it as unrelated to bond interest rates it continued to hedge.

On the first point, assuming Venice was out of the money was not wild speculation on the part of the novated swap but simply an appreciation of the truth of the current mark to market value of the Bear Stearns swap. The novated swap was simply structured accurately to reflect the economic history of the arrangement.

On the second, it remained the case that the novated swap only existed to hedge the interest rate payable on the bonds and was part and parcel of Venice's debt management strategy. The novated swap was valid.

The *Comune di Venezia* decision demonstrates significantly greater nuance in the understanding of swaps in day-to-day financial management. It looks beyond the agreement in issue (the novated swap) to the context in which it was agreed, to determine the purpose of the swap in light of its context. The case does not directly overrule *Hammersmith & Fulham*, however. The Venetian's swap was squarely a hedging arrangement closely tied to a financial transaction undertaken by municipalities all over the world: the issuance of debt instruments. This still feels far from what appeared to be the running of a wholly separate derivatives desk at a local authority, as was the case in *Hammersmith & Fulham*. Nevertheless, were an H&F-type scenario to come before the Court of Appeal today, one would expect a detailed fact-finding mission to determine the function of particular swap arrangements, likely starting from an implicit presumption that they did fulfil a purpose subordinate to the objects of the local authority. As in the sovereign debt cases on capacity, the general trend seems to be judicial negativity to public body attempts to extricate themselves from bad deals on capacity grounds. Indeed, on an interim application by the claimants in *Banca Nazionale Del Lavoro SpA and others v Provincia di Catanzaro* (2023),[20] following in the wake of *Comune di Venezia*, the court struck out those parts of the municipality's defence which relied on want of capacity.

(2) **Recharacterization as an insurance contract**: because it is difficult to classify a swap transaction, they can fall foul of re-characterization as a transaction which is subject to illegality, or at least regulatory restrictions. One view of swaps, at least those made by reference to a third-party event such as index fluctuations, is that they are an illegal form of insurance. The Marine Insurance Acts[21] require that the insured must have an interest in the subject matter insured, a rule which derives from a time in the 18th

19 Venice had never sought to argue that the Bear Stearns swap was speculative; rather it had tried a wholly different argument based on want of authority, alleging that the swap had not been approved by the City Council. This argument had failed in the Italian courts and the High Court judge ought to have concluded therefore that Venice accepted the Bear Stearns swap was valid—yet he failed to consider its bearing on the novated swap at all.

20 [2023] EWHC 3309 (Comm).

21 Marine Insurance Act 1906 ss 4–5 and the MI (Gaming Policies) Act 1909, s 1.

century when London coffee house investors would take bets on which British admiral would die next in battle. To the uninitiated, a swap like a CDS does fell like insurance, and where the counterparties use a third party's default as merely a reference, the counterparties' lack of legal interest in the underlying is manifest. More precision is required. Here is the classic definition of an insurance contract from *Lucena v Crauford* (1806):

> insurance is a contract by which the one party in consideration of a price paid to him adequate to the risk, becomes security to the other that he shall not suffer loss, damage, or prejudice by the happening of the perils specified to certain things which may be exposed to them. If this be the general nature of the contract of insurance, it follows that it is applicable to protect men against uncertain events which may in any wise be of disadvantage to them; not only those persons to whom positive loss may arise by such events, occasioning the deprivation of that which they may possess, but those also who in consequence of such events may have intercepted from them the advantage or profit, which but for such events they would acquire according to the ordinary and probable course of things.[22] [Laurence J, my emphasis]

Under a contract of insurance a party must suffer loss, damage or prejudice, at which point the insurer pays out to meet that loss etc.; under a derivatives contract neither party need suffer loss, damage or prejudice—all that is required is that some event occur, and that one party or another will be obligated to the other in some amount.[23] As such, derivatives contracts are not contracts of insurance.

(3) **Recharacterization as a wagering contract**: another view is that swaps are what the common law calls 'wagering contracts' due to the lack of the counterparties' legal interest in the event hedged by the swap.[24] The classic definition provides you with a dose of nostalgia:

> [A] wagering contract is one by which two persons, professing to hold opposite views touching the issue of a future uncertain event, mutually agree that, dependent upon the determination of that event, one shall win from the other, and that other shall pay or hand over to him, a sum of money or other stake; neither of the contracting parties having any other interest in that contract than the sum or stake he will so win or lose, there being no other real consideration for the making of such contract by either of the parties. *Carlill v Carbolic Smoke Ball Co* [1892] 2 QB. [Hawkins J][25]

'Gaming' and 'betting' are now regulated by the Gambling Act 2005, which defines the 'betting' as making or accepting a bet[26] on (1) the outcome of a race, competition, or other event or process; (2) the likelihood of anything occurring or not occurring; or (3) whether anything is or is not true. So, the question is: are swaps a form of betting, to be regulated and even voided as such? The matter was considered extensively in the following case.

---

22 (1806) 2 Bosanquet and Puller (New Reports) 269; 127 ER 630.

23 See also *Wilson v Jones* (1867) 2 Ex 150; *Prudential Assurance v IRC* [1904] 2 KB 658, 633 (J Channel).

24 This lack of interest is the critical distinction from an insurance contract: *Belmont Park Investments Pty Ltd. v BNY Corporate Trustee Services Ltd.* [2011] UKSC 38 [135].

25 Carbolic Smokeball Co. (CSC) had sought to argue at first instance that even if there had been a (unilateral) contract with Mrs Carlill, then it was void and unenforceable because it was a wagering contract (a bet on Mrs Carlill's continued illness?!). It was no such thing: there was no mutuality in the wager, for if CSC would win nothing if Mrs Carlill recovered.

26 It is bizarrely circular in its definition.

WW PROPERTY INVESTMENTS LTD v NATIONAL WESTMINSTER BANK PLC [2016] EWCA Civ 1142

WW had entered into various LIBOR rate collar swaps with NatWest. Out of the money, WW commenced proceedings arguing inter alia that the swaps were void wagering contracts. The first instance judge was unimpressed and had granted NatWest summary judgment. WW appealed, giving the Court of Appeal chance to lay down precedent.

In the background, note that up to 2005 the law controlling wagering contracts was governed by the Gaming Acts of 1848 and 1842, which were subject to a carve out permission for swaps under old s 412 FSMA 2000. The new Gambling Act of 2005 had rendered s 412 redundant because it only referenced the old and now repealed Gaming Acts. WW sought to argue that either (1) there was now no applicable carve out; and/or (2) the common law of wagering contracts applied, and under the old common law such contracts were void as *contra bones mores* (against public morality).

Held per Briggs and Clarke LJJ: swaps were expressly excepted from the Gambling Act 2005 under s 10 which covered all activities regulated by the regime of FSMA 2000 (which they did not offend).

It seems to me that, in the light of the comprehensive regime established under the Gambling Act and the FSMA 2000 there is now no room for any common law rule (if there ever was one) that wagering contracts in which there is unequal knowledge are invalid. A contract such as the Swap contracts in the present case (even if it is a wagering contract) does not fall within the Gambling Act: section 10. But it does fall within FSMA 2000 and the Regulations made thereunder. ([67])

(1) **Insolvency**: this goes to the cherry-picking issue, but also to the related problem that an innocent party that owed a net amount to the insolvent party could just 'walk away.' We examine this in detail below.

(2) **Tax**: payments under the swap could be subject to withholding taxes, which mean that an amount net tax is received by a counterparty—much less than expected. UK tax law[27] has a specific regime for qualifying derivatives contracts which ensures are payments are not subject to withholding tax. A question also arises about how each party writes off losses under the swap. It is quite possible to draft a swap which ensures artificial losses are incurred, thus reducing taxable income or gains to zero. There are lengthy anti-avoidance rules to ensure only swaps entered into on an arm's-length basis benefit from this tax treatment.

(3) **Relation to CFAs**: swaps may be used to hedge the floating interest rate under a loan agreement. Commonly a floating-to-fixed swap will be sold to a borrower corporate by the arranging bank, usually as a 'soft' condition of the deal. The swap must exactly mirror the payment obligations under the CFA. The swap creates a significant form of financial indebtedness for the borrower, and its fluctuations may dramatically affect its financial statements and so covenant ratios. It is not uncommon for CFOs to have serious arguments with banks about how corporate swaps are to feature in financial calculations.

While swap counterparties are not parties to the CFA, if they are linked to the syndicate banks it is again common for the 'Hedge Counterparties' as they are called to enter into an ICA and to rank as senior debt. This is not so much about favouring the Hedge Counterparties as about controlling them on Default (which will cross-trigger the ISDA MA). Significant termination losses owed by the borrower could allow the Hedge

27 Part 7, Corporation Tax Act 2009 as amended.

Counterparties to drive the borrower into insolvency and claim a large slice of any distribution. The creditor control clauses of the ICA ensure that the Hedge Counterparties agree to behave and support a restructuring or orderly default.

(4) **Other issues**: the GFC and the involvement of CDS swaps in spreading losses which could bring down key institutions led to calls for OTC derivatives to become more transparent and for them to be traded through central market structures which would act as contagion firebreaks. This leads us into the issue of clearing and settlement infrastructure, and so Central Counterparties (**CCPs**), to which we will return in the next chapter.

9.8 Case study: close-out netting and the anti-deprivation rule

Close-out netting is a derivative-specific mechanism which can easily be confused with the more general legal concepts of set-off and netting. Close-out netting is not a set-off. By way of refresher, and so to reduce flipping between pages (which is tiresome with e-books), here is a brief summary of these concepts here. For the key cases on the interaction between set-off and the pari passu rule, see Chapter 6.

Set-off is a legal doctrine which allows the claim of party A against party B to be used to reduce the claim of B against A to the extent the claims are worth the same amount, leaving any excess claim outstanding. Thus, if A owes B 100 and B owes A 90, then after set-off A owes just 10 to B, but this 10 is still the same legal liability as the 100; it is just the value that has reduced. Set-off comes in several flavours:

- **Independent (statutory) set-off**—essentially this is a procedural device parties use in a court case where A claims a money debt from B relating to one transaction and B counterclaims a money debt from A that arises under a completely unrelated transaction. Here the court will allow the two unrelated claims to be set-off.
- **Transaction set-off**—this is far more common as many parties now govern their whole relationship through contractual frameworks. This set-off arises under the same transaction in which debts have arisen on both sides. If the transaction fails then it is more likely that if A sues B then B will counterclaim for some alleged default of A, hoping thereby to set-off against substantial damages.
- **Contractual set-off**—this is not set-off that parties may use in court relating to the same contract; rather this is a set-off right that parties have expressly drafted into that contract. You will find such set-off rights in the ICA (and also prohibitions of setting-off in the CFA).
- **Current account set-off**—this is a customary right of banks to set-off debits and credits of multiple bank accounts held in the name of the same bank client.
- **Insolvency set-off**—this important form of set-off can be found in the UK's Insolvency Rules r 4.90. It exemplifies why set-off is such an important issue, for the rule provides that on insolvency the innocent party may set off its liabilities to the insolvent against its claims, and then prove for any surplus owed to it, the innocent party, or leave the liquidator to decide to pursue any claim for the reduced amount against it.

  > [A]n account must be taken as at the date of the notice of what is due from the company and a creditor to each other in respect of their mutual dealings and the sums due from the one must be set off against the sums due from the other.[28]

28 re Nortel Networks UK Ltd. [2018] Bus LR 206 [5]–[6].

- That said, the innocent party cannot claim for more than the balance—this helps the liquidator. Now it prevents some of the cherry-picking mentioned above, for solvent parties do not want their rights being disclaimed just as the liquidator pursues them for the gross amounts owing. Observe that the cherry-picking issue is one of the drivers for drafting for contractual set-off.

(**Payment**) **netting**: this is a contractual agreement whereby if A owes B money and B owes A money of the same currency and payable at the same time, then the two amounts will be treated as inverses (x and $(x + a)$) and summed such that to the extent they are equal the amounts owing will be cancelled and any surplus (a) will become payable (from A to B or vice versa as the case may be). You encountered this when we looked at *British Eagle*.

Close-out netting: this is a contractual agreement specific to swaps. On termination all the various confirmations under an MA are closed out and valued. The values are then netted across the whole MA leaving a single net amount owing. Evidently the liabilities could be in different forms or currencies, until termination due at different times; the MA contains provisions to convert the liabilities into one currency for netting purposes. It is my view that the closed-out amount owing is a new liability created by the agreement and equivalent to the net amount, which is cancelled.

We will focus on one particular legal issue around close-out netting which relates several important matters. It centres on the old cl 2(a) 1992 ISDA MA, which reads:

CL 2(a) and (c) 1992 ISDA MASTER AGREEMENT

(a) General conditions

(i) Each party will make each payment or delivery specified in each Confirmation to be made by it, subject to the other provisions of this Agreement.

(ii) Payments under this Agreement will be made on the due date for value on that date in the place of the account specified in the relevant Confirmation or otherwise pursuant to this Agreement, . . .

(iii) Each obligation of each party under Section 2(a)(i) is subject to (1) the condition precedent that no Event of Default or Potential Event of Default with respect to the other party has occurred and is continuing, (2) the condition precedent that no Early Termination Date in respect of the relevant transaction has occurred or been effectively designated and (3) each other applicable condition precedent specified in this Agreement.

(c) Netting

If on any date amounts would otherwise be payable:

(i) in the same currency; and
(ii) in respect of [two or more Transactions],

by each party to the other, then, on such date, each party's obligation to make payment of any such amount will be automatically satisfied and discharged and, if the aggregate amount that would otherwise have been payable by one party exceeds the aggregate amount that would otherwise have been payable by the other party, replaced by an obligation upon the party by whom the larger aggregate amount would have been payable to pay to the other party the excess of the larger aggregate amount over the smaller aggregate amount.

You will remember from contract law that if one party has breached a condition of the contract (fundamental breach), the other party may either:

(1) terminate the contract from that moment such that:
   (a) all obligations of the parties accrued to that point would still be enforceable. In particular, if the innocent party owes money, it would still owe it;
   (b) the parties would be released from all further primary obligations;
   (c) the innocent party could sue for breach.
(2) Affirm the contract, with the result that:
   (a) the contractual obligations continue to bind both parties;
   (b) the innocent party may also reserve its rights to sue for damages.

The first problem with cl 2(a)(iii) is that it wants to have its cake and eat it—it allows the innocent party to affirm the contract for the time being but releases it from both its accrued and forthcoming payment obligations. If the innocent party terminates it must pay anything it owes, so many innocent parties decided the better course of action was to not terminate and not pay, even as it expected the defaulting party to make payments to it. In practical terms, especially where the defaulting party is being liquidated, this all means the innocent party can suspend and walk away, because on dissolution the defaulting party and so its contractual rights will simply cease to subsist.

In an insolvency context—which is highly likely as the main default is a failure to pay a debt—this all leads to a second and critical problem. As we saw in Chapter 6, the insolvency policy considerations included, in outline:

- The **anti-deprivation rule** (i.e. the parties *intentionally* agree that the insolvent's property be reduced on insolvency, leaving less for distribution to creditors, see *ex p Jay* (1880) 14 Ch D 19).[29]
- the (no contracting out of) **pari passu rule** (i.e. the insolvent's property is left untouched but a contractual arrangement objectively results in the debtor repaying one creditor ahead of other creditors who are not party to that contractual arrangement: see *British Eagle International Airlines Ltd v Compagnie Nationale Air France* [1975] 1 WLR 758 (HL);

Cl 2(a)(iii) allows the innocent party to suspend its payment obligations even as the contract continues to bind. A liquidator would feel that the insolvent's counterparty owes money into the insolvent's estate, but is seemingly able to withhold it, depriving the other creditors of that value on distribution and giving the counterparty a preference. A liquidator could argue the contractual clause offends insolvency policy because:

- The various events of default included insolvency-linked events which then triggered this payment suspension clause. This looks like just the kind of clause identified in the cases which expressly and intentionally deprived the insolvent's estate on the occurrence of on insolvency—the primary mischief targeted by the anti-deprivation rule.
- The payment suspension clause also appears to contract out of the usual ranking of creditors, because it allows the counterparty withhold funds and still prove for any remaining debt from the reduced estate. For example, a liquidator might (as it turns out, incorrectly) argue,

29 Sarah Worthington argues for a difference between naturally time-limited property rights (such as rights to receive regular payments) and all other property rights. In the latter case the recipient of the property obtains title forever, and so a condition in the transfer that the property be returned on insolvency is a deprivation of her assets. In the former case the nature of the right is such that it could terminate at any specifiable time, and if that be insolvency so be it, for here the insolvent loses no asset (they simply did not acquire an asset forever). S Worthington, 'Insolvency Deprivation, Public Policy and Priority Flip Clauses' (2011) 7 International Corporate Rescue 26.

let insolvent party A have GBP45 of assets, of which a debt of GBP25 owed by CP. A also owes GBP65 to CP and a further GBP40 to B. CP withholds the GBP25 it owes, *seemingly* reducing A's estate to GBP20 for distribution, and then proves for the remainder it is owed (i.e. GBP40). As CP is now owed the same amount as B, CP and B share what remains as a distribution of GBP10 each. CP thus recovers GBP35; B GBP10 all as a result of cl 2(a)(iii). The clause offends the pari passu rule.

Variations on these policy driven arguments were advanced by insolvent counterparties' liquidators across the globe. Let us examine a clutch of cases in which they were put to the test.

9.8.1 The international legal context

The English law cases did not arise in a vacuum; given the widespread use of the standard form 1992 ISDA master agreement, cl 2(a)(iii) was appearing everywhere long before things came to a head in the High Court of England and Wales. It is worth examining a couple of these as many of the arguments prefigure those of English law counsel. Our first case comes from New South Wales, Australia.[30]

ENRON AUSTRALIA v TXU ELECTRICITY LTD [2003] NSWSC 1169 (Aus)

The plaintiff and defendant entered into an electricity swap master agreement which covered multiple positions on electricity prices. On some positions, Enron would 'pay' a fixed amount to TXU, TXU a floating amount to Enron; on other positions the roles were reversed. As usual, a net amount was calculated on each payment date and that sum would be payable. At the relevant time, Enron was 'in the money' to the tune of AU$3.3m when its parent company collapsed due to an accounting scandal at its Texas parent (the reasons are not material, but it is discussed in Chapter [7]).

The master agreement was the 1992 ISDA MA which included cl 2(a)(iii) modified by additional language to make absolutely clear that on insolvency, TXU was

> the party entitled to give the notice under Section 6(b)(iv) designating the Early Termination Date for the foregoing Termination Event.

TXU noted an insolvency event of default had occurred and was continuing, so suspended payments but did not terminate the contract.

Enron Australia's liquidator sought to disclaim the contract and claimed for payment of the net amount then owing by TXU as an 'asset' of the insolvent's estate.

Held: The court gave literal effect to cl 2(a)(iii) as drafted, thus respecting its 'commercial purpose.' TXU could withhold payment even as it refused to terminate the contract. It seems that the modification to clause gave impetus to the court's finding, but also limited the potential utility of the decision beyond cases with just this wording.

With hindsight, the most interesting feature of the judgment was a comment that parties should take care with the term 'asset,' for a merely contingent amount which could be the subject of a legally enforceable right to payment was not yet legally enforceable

30 See also Skye Watson, 'Australia: Bad News for Insolvent Counterparties' (2004) 4 JIBFL 141.

and so was not yet an 'asset' (a chose in action) in the legal sense. This thought drives the decision in *Lomas*.

Schuyler Henderson has noted that to the extent section 2(a)(iii) is enforceable as set forth in *Enron v TXU*,[31] it constitutes a 'walk away' clause permitting an out-of-the-money counterparty to retain its net value in the derivatives positions it has with an insolvent counterparty.

The implications of this, he writes, are illustrated by considering an insolvent bank like Lehman Bros, which carried on its balance sheet a net positive value of USD21 billion for its derivatives portfolio. Do the accounts provide a true and fair view of Lehman's assets if, legally, even its net positions are not assets at all but unenforceable notional amounts? Surely this creates a significant policy concern and hazard both for regulators and other creditors.

At the danger of oversimplifying, consider the following contract: Jane lends to Kieran the sum of GBP10,000, principal repayable and interest payable 'at such time as Kieran, in his absolute discretion, deems fit.' If we look at Jane's personal balance sheet, what should it show? An asset (Kieran's debt) of GBP10,000. But this asset is entirely contingent and may never be realized. Kieran may pass away, and Jane remain unpaid. If Jane is bankrupted in the interim, what should her trustee in bankruptcy do with this debt? The trustee can hardly force Kieran to pay, it seems, and so Jane's other creditors will not have the benefit of it. Should we be clear sighted about the debt: it is not an asset worth GBP10,000 at all, but a debt which may never be repaid. What would a third party pay to acquire the right only to be possibly paid? Significantly less than GBP10,000, one would think.

There was a very different outcome, perhaps surprisingly, in the Southern District of New York (home to ISDA).

METAVANTE v LEHMAN (SUB NOM. IN RE LEHMAN BROTHERS HOLDINGS INC.), (2009) Case No. 08-13555 (JMP) (Bankr. SD NY Sept. 15, 2009)

Metavante and one of the Lehman Bros entities, Lehman Bros Special Finance (**LBSF**), had agreed a fixed-floating interest rate swap linked to a notional principal amount of US$600m. Metavante would pay fixed interest payments on quarterly dates; LBSF would pay floating rate interest payments. The reciprocal payments on each date would be netted. The contract was documented with the 1992 ISDA master agreement, including cl 2(a)(iii) in standard form.

Lehman Bros had collapsed and, in the US, entered bankruptcy. Under the US Bankruptcy Code, a stay on enforcement of claims came into force (a moratorium). Metavante exercised its alleged right under cl 2(a)(iii) to suspend payment but neither affirm nor terminate[32] the contract.

31 Henderson (n 7) 11.4.

32 In New York law, 'assume or reject' the contract.

LBSF's New York liquidator argued that the effect of the clause was to drive the bankrupt's estate of what was owing, and moreover amounted to enforcement of a claim contrary to the bankruptcy stay.

Held: Judge Peck held LBSF was entitled to continued receipt of payments from Metavante under the Agreement. He said:

> Metavante's attempts to control LBSF's right to receive payment under the Agreement constitute, in effect, an attempt to control property of the estate

in violation of the Bankruptcy Code's automatic stay, meaning cl 2(a)(iii) was ineffective on grounds of insolvency policy.

Accordingly, the court ordered Metavante to perform under the Agreement until such time as LBSF determined whether to affirm or reject the contract.[33]

The stage was thus set for the English court's consideration of cl 2(a)(iii) and whether it contravened insolvency law and policy. We are going to look at these cases in great detail.

9.8.2 *Marine Trade SA v Pioneer Freight Futures Co Ltd BVI* (2009)[34]

Marine Trade and Pioneer entered into 14 forward freight agreements (**FFAs**) between May 2007 and September 2008, just before the Global Financial Crisis initiated a global trade downturn that hit freight rates in Q4 2008. The FFAs were governed by the FFA Brokers Association's 2007 Terms and, per those Terms, were constituted as a single agreement through use of a 1992 ISDA Master Agreement. Net payments were payable on a monthly basis.

EXPLANATION: FORWARD FREIGHT AGREEMENT (FFA)

A freight agreement is simply an agreement to ship goods from one port to another. The cost of shipping (i.e. freight) will vary over time depending on fuel costs, ship availability, and so on.

A charterer seeking to ship goods in the future will be concerned that when the time comes to ship the goods, the actual price of freight will have risen considerably compared to the merchant's expectations (thus eating into his profits of sale). The merchant will thus want to fix the price of freight now, if he thinks the price will rise later. This is a forward contract much like any other.

For its part, the shipowner will want to fix the price of freight now if it thinks that price will fall in the future.

33 cf the Michigan case of in *re Lucre, Inc.*, 339 BR 648 (Bankr. W.D. Mich. 2006), which held that a non-material breach by debtor justified non-debtor in withholding performance.

34 [2009] EWHC 2656 (Comm), [2009] 2 CLC 657.

> If charterer and shipowner agree a charterparty contract to ship the goods in the future, whatever price is agreed is *the* price for freight. This charterparty is *not* an FFA.
>
> Rather, a FFA is a separate contract which hedges the risk that the price in the charterparty does not reflect the market price on the day of shipping.
>
> The FFA between charterer and shipowner could agree that:
>
> - charter will pay to shipowner a fixed price on the reference date;
> - shipowner will pay merchant the floating index price on that date; but
> - actually, the two amounts will be netted off so that only the difference will be paid by the party owing the greater amount.
>
> Let the fixed price be equal to the charterparty price at £100. On the reference date (a month later, say) the relevant index prices freightage at £90. Charterer owes £100 to shipowner; shipowner owes £90 to charterer, but we net these off such that charterer pays £10 to shipowner.
>
> In a market where a fall in the freight index is expected, the shipowners tend to the **sellers** of FFAs to charterer-**buyers**. The shipowners are looking to fix the price now because they fully expect they would be paid less later for shipping.
>
> The above example involves counterparties actually interested in the underlying freightage, but no one need be. The parties to the swap could create an entirely derivative trade based on the shipping of notional goods, purely for speculative purposes.
>
> Many FFAs are brokered in London via the Baltic Exchange.

The explanation provides an example which helps us understand what happened in *Marine Trade*. The FFAs were agreed going into a period when the freight price indices fell, and so the seller would receive a net hedge against a fall, paid by its counterparty who had bought the fixed price at the earlier, higher market rate.

In fact, things in *Marine Trade* were slightly more complicated. The Master Agreement covered multiple individual FFAs as noted above, but under some Marine Trade was the seller; under others Pioneer was the seller. Marine Trade had made money on its sell-side FFAs; Pioneer had made money on the others, which it had sold. By January 2009 the respective FFA sellers were significantly in the money, and as both parties were alternately sellers under FFAs, the result was that:

(1) Marine Trade was owed *gross* ca. USD7m for the FFAs under which it was seller;
(2) Pioneer was owed *gross* ca. USD12m for its sell-side FFAs; and
(3) *net*, Pioneer was owed ca. USD5m by Marine Trade.

In January 2009, Marine Trade took the view—for reasons unclear from the judgment—that a cl 5(a)(vii)(2) Event of Default (unable to pay debts as they fall due) had occurred and was continuing with respect to Pioneer and demanded payment of the USD7m *gross*. As it turned out, Pioneer's counsel conceded on the last day of the trial that Marine Trade were probably right about Pioneer. It was a strategic move because it meant the subsequent judgment could simply take the point as agreed without publicising Pioneer's detailed payment history to the world.

Returning to January 2009, Pioneer responded to Marine Trade's demand by itself demanding payment of the *net* USD5m. When Marine Trade failed to pay, Pioneer served notice under cl 5(a)(i) commencing the three-day grace period for payment defaults. After failing to obtain an injunction, Marine Trade paid the net balance of USD5m under protest and sued Pioneer for the gross USD7m Marine Trade was owed.

The High Court held that Pioneer had indeed been unable to pay its debts as they fell due and that an Event of Default was continuing. This entitled Marine Trade to trigger cl 2(a)(iii), but what was the effect of triggering the clause?

Flaux J first considered whether cl 2(a)(iii) applied to each individual payment governed by the FFA, or whether it applied to the net amount only. Strangely the court adopted the former view. Flaux J placed *literal* emphasis on the word 'payable' in cl 2(c), which he interpretated as providing netting only applied to amounts payable on a given date. As the amounts were not 'payable' on the relevant dates because events of default had occurred and were continuing, there was nothing to net. No netting meant the amounts must be considered gross. Flaux J determined to ignore the net USD5m that Pioneer claimed in favour of 'gross' amounts of USD7m owed by Pioneer and USD12m owed by Marine.

The effect of this was that Marine could use cl 2(a)(iii) to deny that it was obligated under s 2(a)(i) to make any of its USD12m of payments to Pioneer, the implication being however that Pioneer could still be obligated under s 2(a)(i) to make its gross USD7m payments to Marine.

Flaux J then considered whether Pioneer remedying the Event of Default (so that it was no longer continuing) had the effect of resurrecting the liabilities cancelled by cl 2(a)(iii), such that Pioneer could now claim payment from Marine. The court held that on a literal interpretation of the clause, the liability arose only on the payment date stated in the Confirmation, provided that the conditions precedent were met. If they were not met *on that date alone*, then that was final; no payment was due, and it could not unexpectedly become due to the innocent party at a later date. Flaux J reached this view despite an intervention by ISDA that the liability must be considered as outstanding 'forever.'

As a result:

(1) Pioneer did owe a gross amount of USD7m to Marine Trade.
(2) Marine Trade did not owe anything to Pioneer because no obligation to pay had arisen at the relevant time.
(3) But Marine Trade was not entitled to restitution of the USD5m net balance it had paid. This was due to technical reasons involving the law of unilateral mistake: the court found that Marine Trade had not paid under a mistake, but had primarily been motivated to assume the risk of making a payment which may not have been due in order to prevent Pioneer declaring a default and perhaps triggering Marine Trade's insolvency.[35]

If you find this decision a little strange, you are not alone.

Finally, it is worth noting, that although Pioneer and Marine Trade were both subject to a Bankruptcy Event of Default within the meaning of the master agreement, neither party was subject to formal insolvency proceedings and so there was no question of Section 2(a)(iii) falling foul of the anti-deprivation rule. But what if one party *had* been in liquidation?

Imagine if Pioneer was now in liquidation. Pioneer's liquidator has received USD5m already, but Marine Trade owed Pioneer USD12m, and so there is USD7m 'missing.' If we follow Flaux J, it seems Pioneer for its part owes USD7m to Marine Trade, but Marine Trade owes nothing to Pioneer. The result is that Marine Trade could prove for that debt of USD7m in the insolvency, arguably reducing distributions to other creditors (1) by having not paid the full USD12m, but only USD5m; and (2) then proving for a debt of USD7m which would be paid from the fund available to all unsecured creditors.

35 See ibid [69]ff, and *Brendon International Ltd. v Water Plus Ltd.* [2024] EWCA Civ 220, [2024] 1 WLR 2434; *Deutsche Morgan Grenfell Group plc v IRC* [2006] UKHL 49, [2007] 1 AC 558.

However, in the case neither party had entered into formal insolvency proceedings. Perhaps Flaux J's analysis would have changed if one or both of them had been. The next case considers just this point.

9.8.3 *Lomas v JFB Firth Rixson, Inc* (2012)[36]

This appeal conjoined four cases from the commercial court. The first two arose from the fallout of Lehman Bros' collapse. Lomas, with others, was the UK liquidator of Lehman Bros International Europe Ltd. (**LBIE**) and Lehman Bros Special Financing, Inc. (**LBSF**) which had entered into GBP and USD interest rate swaps with a number of parties joined in appeal, including JFB. When Lehman Bros. had collapsed, JFB was in-the-money and so decided not to terminate and close-out, but to wait and see how things panned out. Two payment dates came but LBIE failed to pay, prompting JFB to issue a notice under cl 2 declaring events of default linked to non-payment and insolvency. Over the next couple of years, however, the swaps moved in LBIE's favour and now JFB was out-of-the-money to the tune of approximately GBP8m and USD53.5m. When LBIE's liquidator, Mr Lomas, demanded payment, JFB refused claiming that on a true construction of cl 2(a)(iii) JFB's payment obligation was suspended.

In light of the decision in *Marine Park* all the parties sought judicial clarification of their respective rights under cl 2(a)(iii) 1992 ISDA MA, and specifically whether the innocent counterparty's payment obligation falling due when an Event of Default has occurred and is continuing is suspended, and, if it is still continuing, when the 'natural' term of the obligation expires, whether the payment obligation is extinguished. The Court of Appeal did its best to lay concerns to rest. Note that of the four conjoined cases, in two there had been no early termination, but in the other two there had been an automatic early termination. ISDA itself intervened on the first two.

The two remaining conjoined cases on appeal involved FFAs, and one of them featured none other than Pioneer Freight. To the extent that these two cases considered matters additional to the validity and effect of cl 2(a) ISDA 1992, we will not cover them here. One might note though, for additional flavour, that in parallel with these cases a fifth case on cl 2(a)(iii) interpreting, *Pioneer Freight v TMT Asia*,[37] had given rise to two further judgments handed down by Gloster J.

The Court of Appeal, led by Longmore LJ, grounded their interpretation of cl 2(a)(iii) on a fundamental distinction between:

(1) a debt obligation which is **due**; and
(2) a debt obligation which is **payable**.

Framed in this way, the distinction was nothing new—it is common to all debts. To take an example from negotiable securities, a note which states 'I promise to pay bearer GBP100 on 1 March 2075' creates a debt that is due to bearer, but the drawer of the note is not obligated to pay bearer until 1 March 2075. Likewise, a note payable on demand to John Smith creates a debt due to John Smith but it is only payable when John Smith demands payment. John Smith may well choose not to make demand, but to indorse the note in favour of a third party for value. What would the third party be acquiring if the debt were not due? Admittedly, some of the confusion that arises here is in the evolution of the meaning of 'due.' In the vernacular, we have a tendency to say a debt is due when it is time for payment, conflating two different concepts. Yet 'due' derives from French *dû* (past participle of *devoir* = to owe) and so from *debitus*, and really should only apply to the normative fact that there subsists a debt at all even if not currently payable.

36 [2012] EWCA Civ 419, [2012] 1 CLC 713.

37 *Pioneer Freight v TMT Asia* [2011] EWHC 1888 (Comm), [2011] 2 Lloyds Rep 96.

Longmore LJ noted that Gloster J had considered this matter in the parallel in *Pioneer Freight Co Ltd v TMT Asia Ltd* (2011).[38] She had said:

> Once one approaches the analysis on the basis that, under Section 2(a)(iii), one is only looking at the payment obligation, rather than the debt obligation, the whole machinery makes sense. Thus, the wording of Section 2(a)(iii) makes it clear that the payment obligation is subject to the condition precedent that no Event of Default or Potential Event of Default has occurred '. . . and is continuing.' The natural reading of those words envisages that once a condition precedent is fulfilled, the obligation to pay revives. There is no need for any further creation of the debt obligation itself, as [counsel] seeks to suggest. [91]

The Court of Appeal respectfully adopted these observations of Gloster J,[39] holding that the underlying debt obligation was undisturbed by the Event of Default; it was merely the payment obligation which was barred if there was an Event of Default. The effect of cl 2(a)(iii) was to suspend and even extinguish the obligation to *pay* on the date stated in a given confirmation, but it did not extinguish the underlying debt which continued to be *due* and could, for example, be used to determine a close-out netting value.

The Court of Appeal also upheld Gloster J's view in a second judgment arising from *Pioneer Freight v TMT Asia*[40] (so-called *TMT 2*) that cl 2(a)(iii), combined with cl 2(c) should apply to netted, not individual gross, amounts. Remember, Flaux J had held netting only applied if a payment obligation arose under cl 2(a)(iii); where it did not, he decided, there was no netting and so the gross amounts must be due. The Court of Appeal explicitly stated Flaux J's interpretation was 'wrong.'[41] It was clearly the intention that netting should occur automatically on a daily basis and it was absurd to suggest one party could claim gross amounts from the other while ignoring its own obligations.

In short, on a given reference date the only amount that could be payable was the net amount calculated by reference to the respective positions of the parties, and that net amount would only be payable if certain conditions precedent were met—namely that no events of default had occurred and were continuing.

This part of the decision was germane to the two conjoined cases where automatic early termination had not been built into the master agreements, because it permitted the non-defaulting counterparties to suspend performance and walk away even if they would have had to pay a net amount had the conditions precedent been met at the given time.

Such was the commercial interpretation of the cl 2 ISDA 1992, but now the question was whether this clause was vitiated as a matter of public policy—did it offend against insolvency law? When it came to the anti-deprivation and pari passu rules the Court of Appeal followed the recently decided Supreme Court case of *Belmont Park* (see Chapter 6)—the validity of provisions triggered on bankruptcy should be considered on a case-by-case basis to determine if the shift if interests to the creditor could be regarded as a genuine and justifiable response to the onset of the debtor's insolvency. On this basis, Longmore LJ said:

> If this [principle] is the touchstone then it is difficult to see how [Clause] 2(a)(iii) of the Master Agreement can be said to offend against the anti-deprivation principle. The suspension of the payment obligations of the non-defaulting party for the duration of the insolvency does no more than to prevent [the innocent counterparty] from having to make payments under

38 ibid, which had been decided after Briggs J's judgment at first instance in the conjoined *Lomas v JFB Firth Rixson* (n 1).

39 ibid [28].

40 [2011] EWHC 1888 (Comm); [2011] 2 Lloyd's Rep 565.

41 [2012] EWCA Civ 419, [2012] 1 CLC (n 36) [78].

> a hedging arrangement with a bankrupt counterparty. There is no suggestion that it is formulated in order to avoid the effect of any insolvency law or to give to the non-defaulting party a greater or disproportionate return as a creditor of the bankrupt estate. [87])

A further key factor in finding that cl 2(a)(iii) did not deprive LBIE's other creditors was that the insolvency event as defined was a cross-default–style clause which could have been triggered by Lehman Bros' bankruptcy in New York. The clause could not be said to be motivated simply by depriving creditors of the separate Lehman entities LBIE and LBSF.

The Court of Appeal also heard argument on the pari passu principle. It was alleged that the operation of section 2(a)(iii) breached rule because it suspended the recoverability (and therefore the distribution) of an asset of the bankrupt estate amongst its creditors. If this were right then questions of whether the contractual arrangements were entered into for bona fide commercial reasons were irrelevant—as we have seen, the application of the rule is mandatory.[42] Longmore LJ agreed the pari passu rule did not require consideration of the intent and good faith of the parties, but it did only concern the correct distribution of assets during the insolvency process. As the obligations to *pay* did not subsist due to cl 2(a)(iii), there were no sums payable for the non-defaulting counterparties to 'hold back' from LBIE's and LBSF's liquidators and creditors. Compare with *British Eagle*, where the sums owed by Air France and others were payable and the multilateral netting was designed to simplify what was payable to whom.

From these observations, Longmore LJ concluded:

> The anti-deprivation principle therefore protects the value of the estate from attempts to evade the insolvency laws and, as a consequence, facilitates the application of the pari passu rule. But their areas of operation are distinct and it is clear that the pari passu rule is only engaged in respect of assets of the estate as at the commencement of the bankruptcy or liquidation. This was why in *British Eagle* the decisive issue was whether a debt was owed to the company when the resolution for voluntary liquidation was passed.
>
> In this case there was no debt payable to LBSF when its bankruptcy commenced. The obligation to pay was subject to a condition precedent that there should be no continuing Event of Default. In the event there were at least two. It follows that [Clause] 2(a)(iii) does not infringe the pari passu rule because it operates at most to prevent the relevant debt ever becoming payable. There is therefore no property which is capable of being distributed.

The idea that an insolvent estate is said to be owed a debt which it can never recover remains a difficult one to parse. Indeed, Longmore LJ described the operation of the clause as 'imperfect,'[43] but he added that it remained commercially justifiable. This was because the main purpose of the clause was to protect the innocent counterparty from being put in a position (as Marine Trade had been) of having to perform its gross obligations even as the defaulting party did not. If the risk of the clause was to fall somewhere, it made sense that it fell on the side of the defaulting party. In the conjoined appeals the Lehman Bros entities were the one's seeking relief from the consequences of their own insolvencies.

While the standard form drafting had survived potential judicial recharacterization, obiter dicta clearly found the cl 2(a)(iii) and (c) imperfect. In light of this, in 2014, ISDA published[44] a standard

42 See Chapter 6, *British Eagle International Airlines Ltd. v Compagnie Nationale Air France* [1975] 1 WLR 758 (HL).

43 [2012] EWCA Civ 419, [2012] 1 CLC (n 36) [92].

44 Catherine Gurney, 'Calling Time on Section 2(a)(iii) of the ISDA Master Agreement: ISDA Publishes an Amendment' [2014] JIBFL 520–21.

amendment to its Master Agreements allowing contracting parties to insert an agreed time limit on the operation of the condition precedent in Section 2(a)(iii), thereby avoiding a 'walkaway.'[45]

9.8.4 Sometimes payment demands are a dish best served cold

In 2010, the contract between LBIE and JFB Firth Rixson came to its originally planned conclusion through effluxion of time, though any accrued rights remained in force, namely the debt JFB owed to LBIE. No further swaps were confirmed under the master agreement. JFB found themselves in a good position: cl 2(a)(iii) did indeed mean that JFB could suspend payments to LBIE, the underlying debt being owing but not payable for as long as an event of default was continuing. With LBIE deep in an insolvency process, JFB could just walk away and, in the background, LBIE would be wound up, its rights dissolved with it.[46] JFB needed only to be patient.

LBIE's liquidators had other ideas, however. Over the next decade they worked incredibly hard to find a route out of the Lehman Bros mess and, by 2018, were in a position to agree a Companies Act 2006, Part 26 Scheme of Arrangement with the requisite majority of creditors. Debts received haircuts, distributions were made, and remarkably, LBIE came out the other side having settled its outstanding liabilities. The administration was closed and LBIE transitioned to a distribution administration which was also confirmed in the US.[47] LBIE was now solvent, and the first thing Mr Lomas' successor, Mr Grant, did was send a demand to JFB for payment of the ca. USD60m due under the old swap from 2009 which, he claimed, was *now* payable. On receipt of the demand, JFB's managers must have choked on their morning coffee.

GRANT v JFB FR ACQUISITIONS CORPORATION (EUROPE) LTD [2022] EWHC 2352 (Ch)

In the face of the demand for payment, JFB now argued *inter alia*:

(1) back in 2009, LBIE had failed to make two payments to JFB and had never subsequently made those payments—a non-payment event of default under cl 5(a)(i) was therefore continuing; and, or alternatively,

(2) an insolvency process event of default within the meaning of cl 5(a)(vii) was continuing in virtue of, alternatively, the distribution administration, the scheme of arrangement, the US order enforcing the scheme there, or all of them being part of the same original insolvency process.

For any of these reasons, an event of default was still continuing and, thanks to cl 2(a)(iii), JFB's debt remained due but not payable.

Held: Hildyard J placed great weight on the finding in *Lomas* that:

> the purpose of [clause] 2(a)(iii) is to protect the Non-defaulting Party from the **additional credit risk** involved in performing its own obligations whilst the defaulting counterparty remains unable to meet its own. [my emphasis]

45 Subsequent applications of *Lomas* include *Lehman Brothers Finance S.A. (in Liquidation) v Sal Oppenheim Jr & Cie KGAA* [2014] EWHC 2627 (Comm); *Monde Petroleum S.A. v WesternZagros Ltd.* [2016] EWHC 1472 (Comm), [2017] All ER (Comm) 1009.

46 *Grant v JFB FR Acquisitions Corporation (Europe) Ltd.* [2022] EWHC 2352 (Ch) [6].

47 By a Bankruptcy Code ch 15 order.

Circumstances had now changed in such a way that this purpose was no longer relevant in the following ways:

- The commercial arrangement had ended over a decade before. Cl 2(a)(iii) was aimed at risks affecting upcoming payment dates under swap arrangements. There were no such upcoming dates—no 'live' counterparty risk in an ongoing transaction where JFB would have to perform only to discover suddenly LBIE could not.
- LBIE was now in surplus and able to pay creditors. It was solvent and so the risk LBIE could not pay by reason of insolvency had dissipated. Yes, *other* creditors had taken haircuts, but it was precisely because of that that LBIE had become solvent.
- Moreover, whereas JFB had been right to call an insolvency event of default back in 2008–09, in exiting the administration on a solvent basis, the liquidators had brought that event to an end.

Through this line of argument, Hildyard J was consistent: if an event of default had occurred and had continued thereafter, it was necessary to assess if at any point the underlying event had ceased to continue. JFB could not argue 'once continuing, always continuing' as they seemed to be. If the underlying mischief aimed at by an event of default was cured, then the event of default ceased to be continuing. LBIE's insolvency had been cured by the liquidators' efforts.

This was LBIE's route to victory even on the non-payment point. While LBIE had failed to pay in 2008, in 2009 LBIE's liquidators had noted the greater amount JFB now owed to LBIE and deployed mandatory insolvency set off[48] to reduce LBIE's liability to JFB using JFB's liability to LBIE. LBIE's liability had been reduced to zero and JFB had been given credit for it. This was as good as payment of LBIE's debt and, importantly for the instant case, it cured the non-payment event of default such that it was no longer continuing.

In summary, all events of default that had occurred had been cured, and none of the additional events since, such as the (solvent) scheme of arrangement, had qualified as events of default on Hildyard's interpretation of the master agreement. The suspension of JFB's payment obligation under cl 2(a)(i) was lifted, and JFB had to now pay LBIE the outstanding debt.

Justice was done in the end but only on the facts. LBIE had managed to regain solvency; many companies do not. Had JFB been luckier in its counterparty it would have been strategically justified in simply holding out until the counterparty's dissolution. Is this really the most desirable outcome? One response to this, already trailed, is that focusing on the total debt is to start from the wrong position. The asset we are examining is a chose in action arising from a contract, and therefore the contract precisely delimits the nature of the asset. If the contract provides that in certain circumstances a debtor may suspend payment, the creditor is not being denied an asset because they never owned the asset in the first place—they were never owed x amount in all circumstances. Were a

48 r 4.19, Insolvency Rules 1986, discussed above.

third party to acquire the JFB debt from LBIE, they would not sensibly price acquisition at par, but based on the chances of recovery (which seemed small in 2010).

More generally, while there is an underlying consistency in the approach to cl 2(a)(iii) now—Hildyard J following the reading in *Lomas* closely—the overriding rule (*Belmont*) requires a case-by-case analysis. The Court of Appeal expressly disapproved of Flaux J's interpretation of Cl 2(c), but they left it open for continued deviations, especially where drafting has been tweaked. *Marine Trade* seems to have been heavily influenced by Pioneer Freight's approach to business, which had given rise to much court work, and this might explain the difference in judicial attitude compared to *Lomas*, where the problems were very much the fault of the Lehman Bros business.

And then there is the fundamental conceptual conundrum: the possibility contractually to create a debt payment of which is suspended indefinitely. *Lomas* seems to suggest that such a clause could fall foul of either limb of the anti-deprivation rule, and we know cl 2(a)(iii) alone does not, but where should the line be drawn, if only roughly? Might it not be easier to create a statutory power of liquidators to terminate netting arrangements of this sort early, so as to force an end to suspension, subject to court sanction based on fairness to the counterparty. This would surely aid the insolvency process by closing out a live issue and augmenting the distribution fund, and moreover discourage debtors who feel all they have to do is to outlast an ailing company. And indeed, some jurisdictions do enable insolvency officials to terminate open derivatives transactions in a way which overrides the express provisions of the ISDA Master Agreement. The most notable are EU members who enforce the provisions of article 49 and article 64 of the European Bank Recovery and Resolution Directive (BRRD).[49] In particular, article 49(4) of the BRRD empowers a bank resolution authority to calculate the close-out amount contrary to the terms of the transaction, whilst article 64(1)(f) of the BRRD empowers a resolution authority to cancel or modify the terms of certain contracts in order to cancel, reduce, or defer liabilities.

49 Directive 2014/59/EU.

Chapter 10

Payment systems and CCPs

Chapter contents

DOI: 10.4324/9781003457220-10

10.1 Introduction

In this chapter we come full circle, revisiting the nature of money (as name, credit, or concept) now at a technical legal level. Having studied modern financial practices, such as setoff and its survival (or not) in insolvency, multilateral netting, close-out netting, securities, and derivatives, we are now in a position to examine that most simple of things: using 'money' to make payment. Our first step will be to examine some important moments from the development of modern payment systems examples, which should make much more sense now we know more about negotiable instruments and netting arrangements. This allows us to tackle today's payment systems which, as we demonstrate with one line of cases, inherit thinking already developed in the nineteenth century. As you can imagine, this is a highly regulated area, but keeping with the focus of this book, such prudential regulation will continue to occupy a supporting role. More important is to understand what is going on when payments are settled as a matter of private law, based on all the things you have learnt up to this point. Hopefully once you have worked through, you will recognize structures and legal risks you have seen elsewhere, in cases like *British Eagle*.

Once we regard payments systems as grounded on private law principles and concerns, it becomes easier to see further parallels with other private law arrangements. The guiding thread of the second half of this chapter is the legal-structural similarity between multilateral payment settlement systems and both centralized clearing of securities and of derivatives. All three clearing structures deploy a Central Counterparty (**CCP**) and a series of 'client members' who intermediate between the CCP and other investors/paying parties. Our aim will be to understand how these structures work to mitigate risks and why most recently, regulators have forced OTC derivatives contracts to be cleared through CCPs. As we shall see, the idea of deploying CCPs in this way derives from their use in payment and settlement systems, and so it makes sense to understand these in this before examining mandatory clearing. Nevertheless, in finance there is no 'silver bullet'—there is always a risk of crisis which cannot be regulated away. We examine one relatively recent crisis which almost brought down a commodities exchange, and ask whether current regulation is adequate.

10.2 Looking at bank money again

Remember how Mitchell-Innes (Chapter 1) used a Hobbesian story to explain the way a money system could operate on the basis of debts only, simply by interposition of a banker? The banker had a bench in a village, and he took in deposits of debt instruments (e.g. tally sticks) and issued instruments of indebtedness against himself. At the end of each day, he looked at what he owed a depositor A, and he looked at what A now owed him, and he cancelled or 'netted off' the corresponding debits and credits. He does this for everyone with whom he has debit and credit relations, and this process is called clearing. Its principal advantage is to reduce the number of obligations in the system, freeing people up to engage in further activity.

Mitchell-Innes was writing at a time (ca. 1913) and in a place (the USA) where such a characterization of the monetary system as a clearing system for debt instruments would not have seemed so far-fetched (as we will explain in the historical account that follows). You may still be unconvinced that 'money' is nothing more than a transferrable debt obligation between persons—in your heart you still need some fixed point (money) by reference to which you can say *x* is worth GBP*y*, and perhaps even more importantly, 'buyer concludes their part of the transaction when they deliver GBP*y*.' You have an urge that the transaction 'clears' and is 'final.' Mitchell-Innes is perhaps too strong in his claim that money and debt are identical, but there is some utility in it: you really need to regard money as 'just another' debt instrument, and then work from there in terms of distinguishing it as money from other private debt instruments. Why is it that of all the instruments, payment is taken primarily to mean the delivery of a certain number of money instruments?

Now that we have studied such topics as securities, derivatives, setoff, and netting, we have the legal tools to engage in some more detailed legal and economic history which will help clarify the link between money, payment, and debt instruments. This topic is vast and so there can be no hope of covering it adequately. Rather, we propose a picaresque of moments in the history of money and payment systems which show, using our newly acquired knowledge, the link between money and debt. The examples are in thematic order rather than date order. The general trend is towards increasingly modern systems for clearing the respective payment obligations of banks and bank customers. A first look at clearing a cheque payment permits examination of a simple bilateral 'clearing' agreement between banks. We then consider clearing of bank (promissory) notes, before looking at the early bank note and cheque clearing houses. The final example is in fact the earliest in time but perhaps more demanding of one's understanding: it deals with the use of bills of exchange to solve the problem of remitting payment across borders and into a different currency. We trace this example into the nineteenth century when bills as means of payment relating to specific sales of goods metamorphose into a means of payment tout court, i.e. they circulate as cash equivalents.

10.2.1 Cheques

The cheque is certainly not the earliest financial instrument, but it is a feature of the rise of modern banking, and it helps illustrate the relationship between payment in the market and clearing. Remember from our discussion of bills of exchange: a cheque is an instruction by the drawer of the cheque to a third party to pay someone,[1] the drawee, a specified sum of money. If you have encountered a cheque at all, it is likely to be a bank cheque: a special form issued by the bank which you as depositor complete, which instructs the bank to draw a definite amount of funds from your account and pay them to the person stated. The bank is obligated to follow this instruction not because the cheque creates the obligation, but because the contract between client and customer obligates the bank to honour any cheque drawn by the customer provided its account is in funds.[2]

In the following example, we use cheques to illustrate how they are used to make payment and how they are 'cleared' at the end of the business day. Imagine we have someone we call buyer who banks with Bank II. Yesterday buyer deposited GBP10 of currency with Bank II and now has a debt claim against Bank II; Bank II owes the corresponding obligation to deliver GBP10 in demand. As part of its service, Bank II issues a cheque book to buyer for buyer's use.

We introduce a grocer, who happens to bank with Bank I instead, but whose current account balance is GBP0. Buyer and grocer enter into a contract to buy and sell certain fruit and vegetables. Buyer promises to pay GBP10 for the goods but he does not pay with cash. Rather, he pays with a debt instrument: the cheque. Assume the grocer is happy with this (people used to be). Now the grocer has a cheque for GBP10. This cheque states that he, the grocer, is the payee, not bearer, so it is seemingly worthless in anyone else's hands. Were they to present the cheque at a bank, the bank would just pay the grocer as instructed. The cheque in this form is a 'one-shot' mode of payment. The grocer therefore ought to use the cheque as intended: take the instruction to Bank II to pay, and present it at Bank II so that Bank II pays monies out of buyer's account. The problem is the grocer does not want to go all the way to the other side of town to present the cheque at Bank II. His bank—Bank I—trades just on the market square (it is why he banks with them). Therefore, grocer

1 Even if 'bearer,' though standard form cheques are crossed 'a/c payee only' and so assume a named payee.

2 *Hopkinson v Forster* (1874–75) LR 19 Eq 74, 76, (Jessel MR).

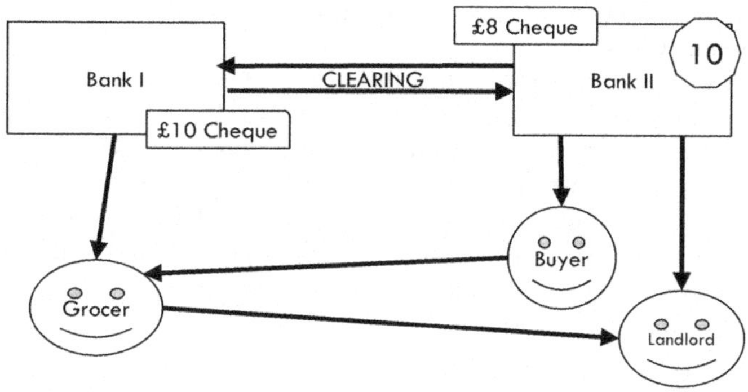

Figure 10.1 Clearing of cheques

deposits the cheque with Bank I which, remarkably, accepts it and credits grocer's account with GBP10.[3] Why Bank I accepted a Bank II cheque will become clear (*pun intended*).

Later in the day, grocer receives a visit from his landlord who requests due payment for the day of GBP8 (the values reflect the age of the cheque usage). Bank I happens also to have issued its own cheque book to grocer, so grocer writes out a cheque to the landlord for GBP8 which the latter accepts in payment. As chance should have it, landlord banks with Bank II, and deposits the GBP8 cheque there before close of business.

The net result of all this trading activity is illustrated in the diagram. Note in particular that Bank I is holding a Bank II cheque for GBP10, while Bank II is holding GBP10 of cash and a Bank I cheque for GBP8.

At this point, Bank I could send a junior clerk to Bank II and present the buyer's cheque on grocer's behalf, and likewise Bank II could send its own clerk the other way to present grocer's cheque to the landlord to Bank I. Apart from the impracticality, this runs the risk of loss of the cheques before presentation. Far better for the banks to take each other on trust and communicate a list of each other's cheques and the gross amount payable at the end of the day. In the above example, Bank I would debit grocer's account and send GBP8 to Bank II (allowing Bank II to confirm the credit to the landlord's account), and Bank II would debit buyer's account and send GBP10 to Bank I (allowing the latter to credit the grocer's account). If either debited account's balance is insufficient, the cheque is dishonoured ('bounces') and the corresponding payee account will not receive benefit of the payment. All things being well, the cheques have **cleared** by means of **gross settlement**.

Yet all things are not quite well: how could Bank I send GBP8 cash to Bank II? Bank I does not have GBP8 cash. It needs to wait for Bank II to pay GBP10 to it, deduct GBP2 to hold, and send the GBP8 back. And why should Bank II send the GBP10 to Bank I if Bank I is not yet sending the GBP8 the other way? What if, between Bank II sending GBP10 and Bank II sending GBP8, Bank I collapses into insolvency? This is also a severe risk.

The solution should be obvious to you after studying the previous chapters: Bank I and Bank II agree to net off their respective obligations to pay out on the cheques. In the example, Bank II owes GBP2 more to Bank I than Bank I owes to Bank II, so netting the respective payment obligations off produces a net liability of Bank II to deliver GBP2 of cash to Bank I. If we follow this through, we find everything cashes out correctly: given the day's transactions, our grocer has a credit of just GBP2 in his Bank I bank account, and happily Bank I is now holding GBP2 cash; the buyer's bank

3 Crediting grocer's account now is a business decision by the bank, based on its confidence the drawee bank will honour the cheque on presentation. If we go back in time banks were more likely not to credit the account *until* payment had been made by the drawee (see e.g. the discussion in *Hare v Henty* (1861) 10 CBNS 65; 142 ER 374).

account balance is GBP0 and the landlord's bank account balance is GBP8, which is just as well as Bank II is now holding GBP8 cash.

The major advantage of netting, though, is that identified in the post-*British Eagle* cases: if Bank II were to collapse and only gross settlement were permitted, Bank I would need to prove for an unsecured debt of GBP10 in Bank II's insolvency even as Bank II's liquidator demanded it pay in GBP8 to Bank II's estate. With payment netting, provided it is respected by local insolvency law and so final, Bank I is free from Bank II's claim for GBP8 and need only prove for a quarter of the debt owed to it (GBP2). In this way a bank's exposure to counterparty insolvency can be dramatically reduced, and significant liquidity, which otherwise would have been caught up in an insolvency process, is freed up to circulate in the financial system.

10.2.2 Scottish 'private money'

You will remember from the chapter on securities that the UK Bills of Exchange Act 1882 classified three kinds of negotiable debt instrument: the cheque, the promissory note, and the bill of exchange proper. Bearer notes—promises to pay x to bearer on demand—form the next crucial step in our story. It is exemplified by eighteenth-century Scottish banking.[4]

Observe first that until the Bank of England obtained its monopoly over the issuance of bank notes, any bank in England could privately issue its own bank notes. Following Scotland's de facto bankruptcy resulting from a failed colonial endeavour (the Dorian expedition), its main creditor—England—suggested what we might regard as a restructuring plan whereby Scotland merged with England as the United Kingdom in 1707. Under this plan the Scottish banks, including Bank of Scotland, retained greater independence from London, and in particular continued to be able to issue their own private bank notes. The Bank of Scotland had been granted a 21-year monopoly on note issuance in 1695, but with its loss of status, loss of government, and perhaps at the behest of the Bank of England which coveted a national monopoly, the Bank of Scotland monopoly was not renewed. In 1728, the Royal Bank of Scotland began issuing its own bank notes, followed by the British Linen Bank in 1746.[5]

A private bank note is 'just' a promissory note payable to bearer. Ignore the pretty pictures and security features and the sheet of special paper is just a promise to pay signed by the director of the issuing bank. It is a security and can be traded as such. The Scottish economy today still has private bank notes circulating, much as England had before the Bank of England obtained its monopoly.

If someone issues a promissory note to bearer, payable on demand, what is in their interest? Well, provided they do not mind being in debt on moral grounds, they would hope that the current bearer does not present the note and make the demand for payment, because then issuer would be required to meet the demand (let us suppose by finding some gold of the stated value). Indeed, issuer would hope that no bearer demands payment for as long as possible, and perhaps never. In such a case, issuer would be able to use its reserves of gold for other investments. If the issuer circulated many such notes, they would observe how often demands are made, and for how much, and compare this to the daily demands on gold from its reserves. It might find only 10% of reserves are called on any day, freeing up the other 90% for investment. This is just what the Scottish banks were

---

4 For a detailed account of what follows, and on which we draw, see Lawrence White, *Free Banking in Britain: Theory, Experience and Debate, 1800–1845* (IEA 1995); Randall Kroszner, *Free Banking: the Scottish Experience as a Model for Emerging Economies* (Mimeo, Columbia University 1995); Cornelia Holthausen and Cyril Monnet, *Money and Payments: A Modern Perspective* (2003) ECB Working Paper No. 245 <https://papers.ssrn.com/sol3/papers.cfm?abstract_id=457317> accessed 19 August 2024.

5 The British Linen Bank, somewhat like the South Sea Company, was not chartered with the principal purpose of acting as a financial institution but rather migrated into it thanks to a widely drafted constitution which also permitted banking. The British Linen Bank was amalgamated with Bank of Scotland in 1969.

doing—issuing 'bank' promissory notes, or just 'bank notes,' in great number, and hoping that the bearers would not demand repayment simultaneously.

Now think back to the cheque scenario but replace the drawee's presentation of the cheque with a bearer's presentation of a bank note for payment. Our bearer has still engaged in the same economic activity, it is just that he was 'paid' using bank notes, not cheques, and is now seeking to convert these into (let us say) gold. These bank notes might have been issued by his bank, in which case the bank ought to have factored them into its calculation of intraday demands for payment. Yet in the Scottish system there is no reason why the presented notes should have been issued by our bearer's bank, they could just as easily have been issued by another bank. Provided our bearer is happy to be 'paid' in other bank notes instead of those issued by 'his' bank, 'his' bank can expect bearer and many others to turn up with other bank notes, hoping that like cheques the bank will 'clear' them. In other words, the bank will collect together all the 'other' bank notes at the close of business and present them to whichever bank issued them for payment to bearer in gross. The other banks will do the same with any notes they receive, and as with cheques, they are likely to agree not to process gross payments, but to net off the gross payments to create a single net amount payable (in gold, for argument's sake).

So far so good, but remember, it is in the interests of the issuer of promissory notes payable to bearer on demand that bearer does not demand any time soon. The timing of the demand is impossible to control if the bearer is an unknown person 'out there' somewhere in the market. Now, however, we have a small number of Scottish banks who at the end of each day are all holding bank notes payable to bearer on demand, and all sharing the same interest: that bearer does *not* demand. It was with some inevitability then that first bilaterally, and then trilaterally, RBS, BoS and the British Linen Bank tacitly agreed to hold and *not* demand payment of each other's notes. Rather, when a depositor sought to withdraw notes for payment in the market, the respective bank would deliver the requisite notes either as issued by itself *or* by the other banks. A BoS GBP10 note was as a good as an RBS GBP10 note for payment in the market (and it still is). Depositors consented to this arrangement because payment was always honoured by the three banks. This payment system with 'suspended' clearing expanded as the three banks acquired or merged with other Scottish banks through the eighteenth century.

The Scottish 'private money' system stood on the most ephemeral of threads. It relied both on no bank demanding payment of all notes at any one time, and on customers accepting delivery of notes issued by other banks, either when withdrawing or as payment in the market. In 1772, the system faced collapse when the mismanaged Douglas, Heron & Company (known as 'Ayr Bank') ran into trouble. It had been issuing notes to finance unsuccessful infrastructure and, facing a shortage of funds, borrowed heavily from a correspondent London bank—Ayr Bank received correspondent bank notes and bills and used these as payment to Scottish banks, even as it continued to force more of its own notes into circulation. When the correspondent bank failed, the Scottish banks demanded payment on outstanding notes, but Ayr Bank had no means to settle. Panic spread and, with clients rejecting Air Bank notes, all other private bank notes were called into question.

Faced with collapse, the big three Scottish banks acted, they bought outstanding Ayr Bank notes, effectively redeeming the worthless paper by exchanging them for their own issue bank notes, and relying on depositors' confidence that the bigger banks had sufficient reserves to meet demands for payment. We had in a sense a 'bailout' of noteholders by the private banking system in order to restore confidence. The bailout was aided by the unlimited liability status of the bank, which meant that its liquidator could pursue unlimited claims against its members who were drawn from the Scottish landowning gentry, all to make the company's estate whole and so meet creditor claims. A dozen or more Scottish lairds were totally ruined and faced debtor's prison. Evaluating the debacle, AW Kerr wrote:

> The essential errors of the Ayr Bank were trading beyond their means; divided control by permitting branches to act independently; **forcing the circulation of their notes**; giving credit too easily; ignorance of the principles of business; and carelessness or iniquity of officers.[6] [my emphasis]

The key lesson of this private money system for our purposes is the obvious duality of the bank notes in circulation: on the one hand, they were money used to make payment, the notes of different banks being equivalent for this purpose; on the other hand, they very much remained securities being used to evidence indebtedness, capable of being convertible into the reserve stated, and capable of being used as settlement or collateral for liabilities. This is particularly clear when Ayr Bank started using London bank notes to settle what were effectively 'margin calls' being made on it in Scotland.[7]

10.2.3 The banking system of Suffolk, Massachusetts

From 1825 to 1858, a private money system in Massachusetts gave rise to something akin to a modern centralized multilateral netting system.[8] You have already encountered one of these in a non-payment systems context: the system operated by IATA for airlines in *British Eagle* was a multilateral netting system. If you review that case, you will be able to see the parallels here.

Like Scottish private money, the 'Suffolk banking system' was a product of no little collusion between a cartel of banks, this time based in Boston, Massachusetts, and ultimately including the eponymous Suffolk Bank. It arose because New England had inherited from England the practice of allowing banks to issue promissory notes to bearer, payable on demand, which bank notes were used as a means of payment in trade. By 1800, Massachusetts was awash with notes from all kinds of banks and, given the distances involved between issuing banks and traders in the Northeast United States, the notes did not trade at par. Were a seller in Boston to be paid with notes issued by a Williamstown Bank (hundreds of miles away), he or his banker would need to travel to obtain settlement. If the note was accepted at all, it would be taken at a discount to face value to factor in all the risks of settling the thing. These bank notes issued by banks outside of Boston came to be called 'country notes' and, even more parochially, 'foreign money.'

The practical problems were one thing, but there was also a business problem for the banks. Remember, ideally an issuer of bank notes wants to delay demand for payment for as long as possible, while still attracting as many people as possible to acquire the notes (thus providing debt capital to the issuer). The sheer volume of country notes circulating both (1) proportionately reduced the capital available to individual banks as they competed for custom and (2) encouraged holders to cash in their notes (i.e. demand repayment of capital) so they could acquire other bank notes to settle their own trade debts across the state. In Boston the local city banks had enough: they colluded in 1803 to issue a joint ban on accepting country notes, hoping that by so doing, the people of Boston at least would only use Boston bank notes.

The ban had the opposite effect, for brokers set up shop as *bureaux des change*, exchanging merchant country notes for Boston bank notes for a fee (a discount to face value). This fee paid for

6 Andrew W Kerr, *History of Banking in Scotland* (2nd edn, A&C Black 1908) 109.

7 For a discussion of English local bank monies during this period, see Iain Frame, '"Country Rag Merchants" and English Local Currencies in the Late Eighteenth and Early Nineteenth Century' [2015] Journal of Law and Society 588.

8 This account relies on Arthur J Rolnick, Bruce D Smith, and Warren E Weber, 'Lessons from a Laissez-Faire Payments System: The Suffolk Banking System (1825–58)' [1998] Federal Reserve of St. Louis Review 105.

the wholesale (and consequently cheaper) transport of country notes to their home banks, and the broker made a healthy profit. So good was business, indeed, that the brokers even encouraged the use of country notes such that through 1812–1844, over half of all notes in circulation were country notes.

The Boston banks began to realise their plan had backfired, and some even set up brokerage arms themselves. Suffolk Bank began buying every country note it could lay its hands on. Its first aim was undercut the other brokers by offering a lower fee (discount to face value), and it soon halved the discount, driving many smaller brokers out of business. This did mean Suffolk Bank was operating at cost, at best, so it then developed a new strategy. It formed a cartel with six other Boston banks to buy up every country note on the street with a view to driving them out of circulation. This too failed.

The third plan, implemented in 1825, proved a turning point. The cartel agreed to an arrangement with the country banks whereby Suffolk Bank would accept country notes at par and simply clear them *as if they were Suffolk Bank notes.* Rather than wait to ship the country notes around Massachusetts, it would make a record of the sums owing by each country bank. It asked the country banks to make their own records of the sums Suffolk Bank owed to them because Suffolk Bank notes has been presented to them, and a record of all the gross sums owing between the country banks themselves. Suffolk Bank then netted off the respective debts to create a single, or as appropriate a series, of net debt(s), which were then debited to the relevant accounts of participating banks. To meet the net demands for payment into the system, each participating bank was expected to maintain a reserve for this purpose with Suffolk Bank—USD2,000 worth of assets (e.g. gold) for each USD100,000 of capital the bank possessed.

The advantage of the Suffolk Banking System to the Boston Banks was that country notes stayed in Suffolk Bank; when it came to customers presenting country notes at Suffolk Bank, which offered payment at par so they would not go elsewhere, Suffolk Bank would always issue Boston Bank money. Already in 1825, Suffolk Bank was clearing half the notes in circulation in Boston. By 1848 it was clearing 100% of them with the result that Boston bank money achieved the desired pre-eminence as currency. More importantly, the clearing system with its payment-at-par basis ensured that even where notes were issued by different banks, all notes were economically equivalent: a one-dollar denominated bill issued by Suffolk Bank was worth the same as a one-dollar denominated bill issued by any other member of the Suffolk Banking System. The clearing mechanism achieved a uniformity of currency.

The Suffolk Banking System ultimately ended because Suffolk Bank too greatly enjoyed the privilege of its monopoly of the clearing system. It foisted much of the costs of handling clearing onto members, set restrictive conditions for clearing (no presentation after noon) to save its own costs, and made the most of the way it had been set up as sole profit-taker from the system, refusing to share these profits with system members. Suffolk Bank, for its part, claimed it ran the risk of country bank default, which occasionally occurred. Challenger clearing houses arose but faced a sitting monopoly which could threaten simply to stop clearing, forcing notes to be cleared by tiny competitors who had no hope of handling the volumes Suffolk Bank processed. And indeed, Suffolk Bank did halt all clearing operations in 1858 when a new clearing house—the Bank of Mutual Redemption (BMR)—forced its way into the market by offering to share clearing profits with member country banks. Suffolk Bank was encouraged back into clearing but refused to clear country notes save for a monopolistic fee. The country banks refused and by the end of 1858 the Suffolk Banking System was over, superseded by BMR's system, which however proved unprofitable and had too ended by 1860.

The Suffolk Banking System presents us with an early example of a multilateral netting system created for the express purpose of clearing payments. Its structure, and many of the policy issues it raises (especially around clearing house monopolies, reserve liabilities, and settlement finality) will recur as we look to more modern clearing systems.[9]

10.2.4 Country clearing houses for cheques, England

Clearing houses also expanded in the UK, and in the late 1850s the traditional bilateral netting of presented cheques began to be superseded by new 'country' clearing houses operating for the benefit of local banks. The rules of clearing were issued by the clearing houses themselves, but this gave rise to legal questions. What was the status of these clearing house rules and, if clearing of a cheque failed for some reason internal to the clearing house (such as bureaucratic error, delay or loss of the instrument), what bearing did the rules have on the drawer and payee of the cheque who sat 'outside' of the bank-only clearing house? In 1861 the very question came before the courts.

HARE v HENTY (1861) 10 CBNS 65, 142 ER 374

A bank's customer (C) had sold goods to a firm: John Kidd & Son, who paid for them by a cheque for £245 drawn on their account with what we will call 'Lewes Bank.' Of Sussex, C deposited the cheque with his bank (let us call it Worthing Bank) in his hometown of Worthing, Sussex.

Until recently, banks had simply cleared cheques between themselves, the presenting bank rushing to present the cheque on the same day as its deposit by a customer.

Now, however, both Lewes Bank and Worthing Bank were members of a country clearing house for cheques. The practice of that clearing house was that cheques deposited on one day should be presented via the clearing house by no later than the next day. Worthing Bank complied with this practice, presenting the cheque the day after C had deposited it with them.

C, however, had assumed based on previous experience that his account would be credited with payment the same day of deposit, but when certain demands on his account were made he found himself unable to pay, causing loss and no little commercial embarrassment.

C sued Worthing Bank for breach of contract and professional negligence in delaying presentation of the cheque. There was no explicit term of the contract between C and Worthing Bank as to the latest time by which Worthing Bank could present client cheques.

Held: The Worthing Bank had met its obligation to diligent present the cheque in time, having regard to bankers' usage.

9 A further interest US example of a clearing house is the New York Clearing House Association established in 1853. Like the Suffolk Banking System, it cleared private bank notes for member banks, who all paid in a reserve to back their liabilities and also to meet the obligations of an insolvent member. The notable innovation of the NYCHA was that though it was not itself a bank, it began to issue its own 'clearing house money' (Clearing House Loan Certificates (CHLCs)) for use solely by member banks within the exchange. The members bought the CHLCs on credit and used them to settle net debts to other members. The significant advantage of these CHLCs was that it mitigated member bank illiquidity—if the member could not settle debts on a given day, it could borrow CHLCs and create a replacement debt to the clearing house, repayable later when funds became available. It seems to have helped: the NYCHA is still operating, now as The Clearing House Association LL. For more, see Richard H Timberlake, 'The Central Banking Role of Clearinghouse Associations' (1984) 16 Journal of Money, Credit and Banking 1.

Willes J commented in argument:

> A man who employs a banker is bound by the usage of bankers. [379]

Erle CJ gave the court's judgment, saying:

> Lord Ellenborough says the rule which convenience requires must be adopted [*Rickford v Ridge* (1810) 2 Campb 537, 170 ER 1243]. The decision has been recognized and acted on, and establishes the general rule in all cases between parties to the cheque. And we think the rule applies not only as between the parties to the cheque, but as between banker and customer, unless circumstances exist from which a contract or duty on the part of the banker to present earlier, or to defer presentment to a later period, can be inferred. No such circumstances existed here; for, it was admitted that the alleged usage [that existed prior to the creation of the country clearing house] did not exist at the time [C presented his cheque]. [383]

The underlying policy rationale seems to have been convenience: cheques should be presented swiftly, but that meant at the earliest convenience, not immediately. Convenience was assessed by reference to the needs of all involved, and bankers had determined that the clearing house rules struck the right balance between swift settlement of cheque payments and facilitating multilateral clearing between banks over medium to long distances.

This case is more significant than it first appears, especially for payment systems. It implied by custom the mere rules of a clearing house (and indeed any other bankers' usages and customs) into the contracts both between client and bank, and as between banks themselves *even when* the clearing house is not a party to any of these contracts. *Hare v Henty* will return later in this chapter.

10.2.5 Use of 'correspondents' in Renaissance exchange trade and Victorian fictitious capital

Although this section begins with the earliest illustration of a payments system, it involves cross-border transfers of funds for the purposes of payment settlement and so is more complicated. It introduces some additional features into our analysis: the notion of a correspondent (representative or bank) which will settle demands for payment on behalf of the drawer of a bill. The previous examples worked on the basis that the various banks would pay out on presentation of cheques or notes because they could net this off against claims by other banks in a clearing system. Technically, such a clearing system is not present here, it relies either on the correspondent being part of the same business, or on underlying merchant transactions effecting the netting. This is easier to see with an example provided by Eileen Power.[10]

In the fifteenth century, there was a booming wool trade between England, which produced excellent wool, and Flanders in the Low Countries, where resided northern Europe's finest textile weavers. The trade was carried on by *staplers* (wool merchants) and *mercers* (textile merchants) across the North Sea. These merchants faced a practical problem: remitting home the money acquired

10 Eileen Power, *The Wool Trade in English Medieval History* (first published 1941, OUP 1955) 68.

from selling their goods abroad without losing it to robbery, piracy, or shipwreck, and then converting it into usable currency.

Imagine, for example, that an English stapler had travelled to Bruges with a cargo of wool and had successfully sold the lot for a good price. How should this cash be remitted? At the same time, a Flemish mercer was looking to buy textiles and ship these to London where there was a good market for high-quality Flemish craftsmanship. In the absence of liquid cash, mercer would need to borrow. Why not 'borrow' from the cash-rich stapler? This benefits both mercer and stapler because as a result the mercer has local currency he needs, and stapler has converted that local currency into a debt. Now the clever bit: rather than record the loan relationship as a matter entirely local to Bruges, the mercer would draw up a bill of exchange directing its representative (or correspondent) in London to pay the stapler on presentation of the bill. The correspondent would have the cash because it was selling the textiles bought by the mercer in London, and by selling it in London the correspondent would have local currency available to meet payment.[11] Our stapler could now return to London carrying just the bill of exchange, and there draw local currency in satisfaction, with which to buy more wool. As the bill was made in one jurisdiction to be presented in another, it is called a **foreign bill** of exchange, as opposed to a bill made and presented in the same jurisdiction, like a cheque, which is then called an **inland bill** of exchange.[12]

Observe that this arrangement works the other way: stapler can also 'borrow' money in London on a bill of exchange it draws in favour of our mercer, to be drawn on the stapler's correspondent in Bruges. If both merchants are effectively exchanging multiple bills on either side of the North Sea, they can now net off those in their favour against those drawn on them. reducing gross liabilities to net liabilities (or assets), freeing up the remainder for further purchases of stock. JS Rogers provides the following illustrative case:

BURTON v DAVY (1437) 49 Selden Soc. 117, London Mayor's Court[13]

John Audeley was the Bruges representative of a London-based mercer named Elias Davy. To acquire textiles, Audeley had the Bruges representative of a Norwich wool merchant, John Burton, 'make over' £30 by way of exchange. Audeley drew up the following bill of exchange and handed it to Burton's representative:

> To my very honoured master Elias Davy, mercer, at London, let this be given: Very honoured sir, please it you to know that I have received here of John Burton, by exchange, £30 payable at London to the aforesaid John or to the bearer of this letter of payment on the 14th day of March next coming, by this my first and second letter of payment. And I pray you that it may be well paid at the day. Written at Bruges, the 10th day of December, by your attorney.
>
> John Audeley, etc.

As it was payable to bearer, Burton sent another of his men, John Walden, to present the bill to Davy in London. Davy refused to pay.

11 Medieval merchants seem to have deployed complicated exchange rate tables which factored in the costs of the transaction, all to determine the 'price' of drawing various bills.

12 See now s 4, Bills of Exchange Act 1882.

13 Cited by James S Rogers, *The Early History of the Law of Bills and Notes: A Study of the Origins of Anglo-American Commercial Law* (CUP 1995) 46. From Hubert Hall, *Select Cases Law Merchant*, vol I (Bernard Quaritch 1931) 49, ss 117.

Held: In the trial, Davy admitted that Audeley was his man, that the bill had been drawn up, the £30 received in Bruges and that, having purchased textiles with it, those textiles had arrived at Davy's premises in London for his use. The court therefore found Davy liable to pay on presentation of the bill.

Again, the stress here is on the use of correspondents located abroad to facilitate exchange, rather than the precise legal nature of the bill which at that time, despite the name, had not taken on all its formal legal characteristics as a security. As JS Rogers has noted,[14] this exchange arrangement bears greater similarity with modern cross-border bilateral payment settlement due to the function of correspondent banks.[15] One might also add that similar thinking seems to underpin the 1970s currency swap structures we examined in the chapter on derivatives. It is for this reason we are discussing these early bill of exchange transactions as examples of payment systems rather than under the heading of securities.

Burton v Davy and the example preceding focus on mercantile practice, but early banking families were very much involved also, using family representatives from Florence to London and Leipzig to make over monies and present or pay out on bills of exchange. The profit here consisted purely in the fee payable on the loan and the difference in that fee depending on the currency of repayment (the exchange rate). The fee was reflected in the bill of exchange itself: if a stapler's representative had borrowed GBP100 English in London from the Tolomei family of bankers, the bill of exchange would record e.g. GBP110 in equivalent Flemish currency so that it could be presented in Bruges by another Tolomei representative. Here the additional GBP10 represented a price of GBP1 for every GBP10 English lent *and* the conversion of that debt into Flemish currency (so loan interest *and* exchange fee).[16] Again, for our purposes just observe how cross-border multicurrency payments are effected using correspondents and communication via bills.

Through the early modern period, the negotiability of bills of exchange permitted their evolution in much the same way as promissory notes and cheques payable to bearer. That is, though bills of exchange originally were tied to specific sales of goods, and though it was expected that a bearer be in some way related to the seller of goods, by the early nineteenth century bills of exchange circulated among merchants like bank notes—as cash equivalents. Identifying when this separation of the bill from its underlying trade occurred is difficult, but by the 1840s many, including Parliament,[17] had become sufficiently concerned to investigate the massive expansion in the capital value of the bills circulating compared to the value of trade supposedly subtending it. In 1847, one Charles Turner—head of one of the leading 'East Indian' houses in Liverpool—wrote:

> We are all aware of the events which have taken place as regards the Mauritius trade, and other trades of that kind. The brokers have been in the habit . . . not only of advancing upon goods after their arrival to meet the bills drawn against those goods, which is perfectly legitimate, and upon the bills of lading . . . but . . . they have advanced upon produce before

14 Rogers (n 13) ch 2.

15 Rogers cautions that modern correspondent payments differ because they involve *sending* money abroad, whereas the medieval merchants were concerned with remitting money home. Yet sending money home remains a concern not just for businesses concerned about exchange rate variations, but also hundreds of thousands of migrant workers.

16 Rogers (n 13) 40ff, noting that the UK Crown became so concerned about exchange pricing it initiated a Royal Commission in 1564 to investigate the matter.

17 See the *Reports of the Committees of Commercial Distress 1847–48*, debated in the Commons: HC Deb 30 November 1847, vol 95, cols 374–477.

> it was shipped, and in some cases before it was manufactured. Now, to speak of my own individual instance: I have bought bills in Calcutta to the extent of six or seven thousand pounds in one particular instance; the proceeds of the bills went down to the Mauritius, to help in the growth of sugar; those bills came to England, and above half of them were protested; for when the shipments of sugar came forward, instead of being held to pay those bills, it had been mortgaged to third parties . . . before it was shipped, in fact almost before it was boiled. [*Swindling in the East Indian and Chinese Market* (1847) (78)][18]

In short, drawees (the finance houses and brokers)[19] were paying out on bills of exchange drawn by merchants to 'pay for' goods which did not even exist yet.[20] The bills were being sold at a discount for cash, and it seemed acceptable to the discounter that the bills were not backed by any underlying trade of goods, just the credit of a drawee finance house. Turner continues:

> There is one house which failed in London the other day, and in examining their affairs, a transaction of this sort was proved to have taken place; there is a house of business at Manchester, and another at Calcutta; they opened a credit account with a house in London to the extent of £200,000; that is to say, the friends of this house in Manchester, who consigned goods to the East India House from Glasgow and from Manchester, had the power of drawing upon the house in London to the extent of £200,000; at the same time, there was an understanding that the corresponding house in Calcutta were to draw upon the London house to the extent of £200,000; with the proceeds of those bills sold in Calcutta, they were to buy other bills, and remit them to the house in London, to take up the first bills drawn from Glasgow . . . There would have been £600,000 of bills created upon that transaction. [79][21]

Turner's point is that because bills had become separated from the underlying trade, there was nothing stopping the drawer from multiplying the number of bills he drew up off the back of one trade (or none). All he had to do was be sure that when time came to settle accounts, he had access at that moment to enough cash to settle. Yet it seems that provided the drawer's credit was good, he would simply 'pay' again by drawing another bill of exchange. One W Leatham—a Yorkshire banker writing in 1840—foresaw the risks of this untethered expansion of circulating bills:

> This enormous superstructure of bills of exchange rests upon the base formed by the amount of bank-notes and gold, and when, by events, this base becomes too much narrowed, its solidity and very existence is endangered. . . . If I estimate the whole [of this pseudo-currency] and the amount of the liabilities of the Bank and country bankers, payable on demand, I find a sum of 153 million [pounds], which, by law, can be converted into gold . . . and the amount of gold to meet this demand only 14 million [pounds]. . . . The bills of exchange are not . . . placed under any control, except by preventing the abundance of money, excessive and low rates of interest or discount, which create a part of them, and encourage their great and dangerous expansion. It is impossible to decide what part arises out of real *bonâ fide* transactions, such as actual bargain and sale, or what part is fictitious

---

18 Quoted in Karl Marx, *Capital: A Critique of Political Economy*, vol 3 (David Fernbach tr, Penguin 1981) 539–40.

19 For a legal historical analysis of one such house, Overend and Gurney, in the context of the 1840s, see Iain Frame, 'Between the "Bank Screw" and "Affording Assistance": Rules, Standards and the Bank Charter Act of 1844' (2020) 83 Modern Law Review 64.

20 This looks very much like a futures contract, but there was nothing new in a futures contract for commodities (see Chapter 9); what is novel is the use of a bill of exchange, with its in-built negotiability, for this purpose.

21 Quoted in Marx (n 18) 540.

> and mere accommodation paper, that is, where one bill of exchange is drawn to take up another running, in order to raise a **fictitious capital**, by creating so much currency. In times of abundance and cheap money this I know reaches an enormous amount. [*Letters on Currency* (1840); my emphasis][22]

Leatham sees the system of fictitious capital as an inverted triangle, with a finite reserve (of gold here) at the bottom, and an expanding or contracting upper side linked to the expansion of the number of notes and bills in circulation acting as money. Were payment of all those debts to be demanded on the same day, the system must collapse. Karl Marx found all this fascinating and jotted down these examples for use in the incomplete Volume III of *Das Kapital* in the middle of the nineteenth century.[23] It was his friend and editor, Friedrich Engels, who was so struck by Leatham's turn of phrase—fictitious capital—that he used it as the title for this chapter of Marx's edited notes.[24]

For our purposes, it suffices to note that along with cheques and bank (promissory) notes, bills of exchange proper had also by the nineteenth century taken on something akin to the character of money, being a means of payment whose value bore an increasingly tenuous relation to some underlying commodities acting as a reserve, such value rather being determined by the current willingness of another to accept the bill in payment (i.e. the pure exchange value). In view of this, we cannot restrict our understanding of a 'payment system' to simply a means of managing the physical transfer of coins, or even of central bank monies. The range of possible payment systems extends just as widely as the range of that dangerously flexible term 'cash equivalent.' Accordingly, our notion of payment system blends seamlessly, in times of credit growth, into systems for the exchange of securities and contracts for difference. It is only when credit contracts dramatically is there a sudden rush to payment only in central bank monies, or, in the severest crises, gold. It is for this reason that we will examine the structure of payment settlement systems together with the structure of securities clearing and derivatives clearing.

10.3 Payment settlement

With the foregoing historical tour, combined with the legal knowledge garnered from previous chapters, you are hopefully in a position to appreciate why modern payment systems operate as they do, especially in terms of (multilateral) netting and the use of correspondents and perhaps a central clearing house. We open this discussion by focusing on payment settlement.

ESSENTIAL DEFINITION: (PAYMENT) SETTLEMENT

Settlement in a payment context means the act of discharging one or more payment obligations between two or more parties.

Settlement may refer to each individual payment obligation (**gross settlement**), or if agreed may refer to the netting off of obligations and payment of the net (**net settlement**).

22 ibid 526.

23 For a discussion of the modern significance of this, see Carolina Alves, 'Fictitious Capital, the Credit System, and the Particular Case of Government Bonds in Marx' (2022) 28 New Political Economy 398.

24 Only Engels seems to have expressly the term, see Marx (n 18) ch 25, and his gloss at 537.

> **Settlement finality** is settlement which is irrevocable and unconditional. In particular, the settlement should not normally be capable of being questioned by a court.

One can extend this definition by speaking not of payment (delivery of monies) but of 'delivery of securities.' Hopefully by now you appreciate the fluid boundary between bank money, bank (promissory notes), and cash equivalents like liquid securities.

In the last section we looked at payment by various negotiable instruments (the cheque, the (bank) promissory note, the bill of exchange). A could pay with tally sticks or gold, or he could pay by drawing up an instruction to Bank I to hand over to the presenter of this instruction a specified amount. Alternatively, Bank I could completely standardize this instruction in a denominated form i.e. it could issue bank notes of, say, USD50 or USD100 which, if presented, entitle the presenter to the specified amount (e.g. in gold or tally sticks). As another alternative, this standardized instruction could be by means of instantaneous communication to the bank e.g. A uses a debit card to tell Bank I to make payment to some C.

In an 'on us' payment settlement, Bank I deals with a situation in which payer and payee are both account holders with Bank I. Thus, if A pays C USD50 by debit card, the following happens (see Figure 10.1):

(1) A sends an instruction to Bank I to pay C USD50.
(2) Bank I debits A's account by USD50. Bank I now owes A less.
(3) Bank I credits C's account USD50. Bank I now owes C more.
(4) Bank I's vault of gold (its reserves) remains untouched. Its overall liabilities are the same.

'On us' payment settlements still occur today in smaller banks. The next step is to consider two different banks. The simplified version of this is unusual these days but is a useful steppingstone for our learning. Here A pays D USD70. D banks with Bank II. Payment settlement proceeds as follows (see Figure 10.2):

(1) A sends an instruction to Bank I to pay D USD70.
(2) Bank I debits A's account USD70.
(3) Bank I instructs Bank II to credit D with USD70.
(4) Bank II will only do this if Bank I credits Bank II with USD70 i.e. Bank I promises to transfer USD70 to Bank II by close of business.
(5) Bank II credits C's account with USD70.

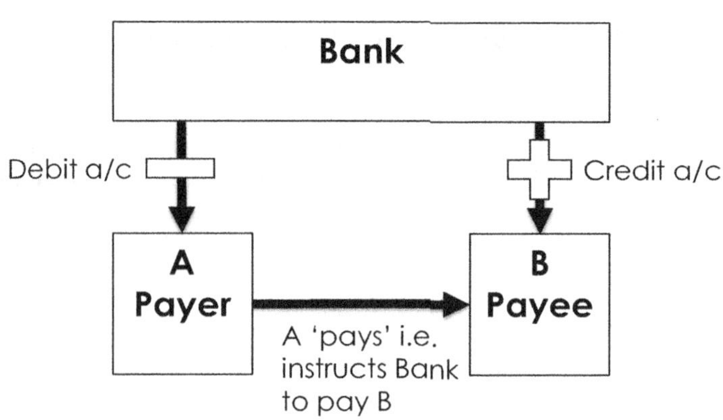

Figure 10.2 'On us' clearing

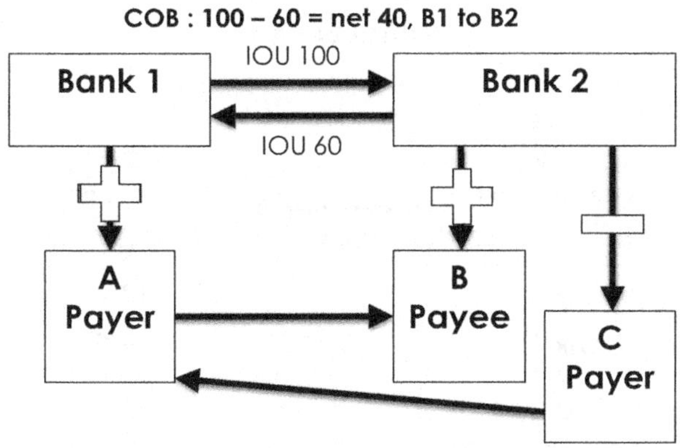

Figure 10.3a Classic clearing (which clears at close of business each day)

At close of business Bank I and Bank II look at all transfers due that day between themselves and net them off. Any remaining liability is then transferred between banks. Here there is just one transaction so USD70 (e.g. in the form of gold) leaves Bank I's vault and arrives in Bank II's vault.

But what happens if at the end of the day Bank I has collapsed into insolvency? This system suffers from a significant counterparty risk. See the Bank Herstatt Crisis discussed below.

The 'on us' payment settlement system described above is somewhat archaic but reflects our analysis of negotiable instruments during the eighteenth century. These days payment settlement tends to take two more advanced forms:

(1) Correspondent bank arrangements; or
(2) Multilateral or 'interbank' payment systems.

The common feature of both is how they deal with counterparty risk by interposing one or more financial institutions as 'buffers.'

In a **correspondent bank arrangement:** the payer and payee banks interpose one or more agreed third-party banks which they regard as creditworthy such that, should a payer/payee bank default, the correspondent bank(s) will nevertheless meet settlement payments at least long enough to ensure liquidity. Why would such banks regard a designated correspondent bank as more creditworthy? Well, in many cases the correspondent bank is sufficiently large and sophisticated so as to have a direct link to its own Lender of Last Resort—a central bank. So, we could have Bank I and Bank II using the same correspondent bank (**CBank**) or using different CBanks which latter both use the central bank. This could create the following payment architecture (Figure 10.3b).

Payment settlement then proceeds as follows:

(1) A sends an instruction to Bank I to pay E USD90.
(2) Bank I debits A's account USD90.
(3) Bank I has a 'nostro a/c with CBank I. CBank I calls it a 'vostro a/c.'
(4) CBank I debit's Bank I's Vostro a/c USD90.
(5) CBank I agrees with CBank III to be liable to CBank III for USD90—a USD90 which it holds on account with the central bank.
(6) Central bank debits CBank I's account with it and credits CBank III's account. This is 'central bank money.' I underline that CBank III will only accept in payment claims on the central bank.
(7) CBank III credits Bank III's Vostro a/c.
(8) Bank III credits E's account.

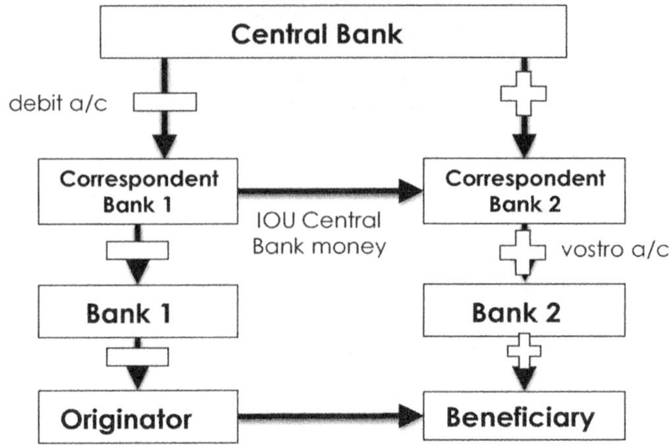

Figure 10.3b Correspondent bank clearing arrangement

The above assumed that all payments were made in real time, but it may be that payment settlement only occurs, for example, at the end of day. Indeed, different institutions in the same chain could settle immediately or at the end of the day. This is possible because each link promises to be liable to make payment at the end of the day and it is this promise which is the requisite (central) bank money.

The correspondent bank arrangement is subject to at least two criticisms:

(1) As with letters of credit arrangements in international sale of goods, it leads to a proliferation of bilateral arrangements for every two banks—arrangements which are specifically negotiated and so lack standardization.
(2) It relies on the creditworthiness of correspondent banks, which after Lehman cannot be taken as given. Yes, Central Banks pay only using claims on a central bank, but this is still predicated on the Central Bank actually functioning.

BANK HERSTATT RISK

Bank Herstatt was a German bank which in 1974 became bankrupt and in so doing illustrated the risks that had emerged in the post-oil shock global economy. Due to the petrodollars sloshing around the financial system between northern states, FX trading was highly volatile. BH became heavily involved in FX positions and rapidly accumulated DM470m of losses. On 26 June 1974 BH agreed to deliver several million USDs to counterparties in New York by the end of the trading day. In consideration these counterparties released equivalent value Deutschmarks to BH. Due to the time difference the DMs were released in Frankfurt before close of business there. At close of business (16:30 Frankfurt time) the German authorities forced BH into bankruptcy. But it was only 10:30 in New York and so the USD had not been delivered—the counterparties did not receive their payments leading to corresponding losses and loss of faith in the FX trading system.

As Charles Goodhart has noted,[25] the Bank Herstatt debacle brought to the financial world's attention the changing, internationalized nature of finance and the stresses this

25 Charles Goodhart, *The Basel Committee on Banking Supervision: A History of the Early Years 1974–1997* (CUP 2011) ch 1.

could place on nation-focused banking supervision. It can be seen as the origin of several key modern developments in international finance:

A. The German authorities acted unilaterally, leading to severe disruption in the US. From now on central banks would set up processes for talking to each other on an increasingly regular basis so that they could deal with systemic risks in international financial. Initially central bankers from the Benelux countries and then Germany met, and soon France and then the UK became involved in monthly meetings to coordinate. Eventually this group would expand to the G10 and form the Basel Committee on Banking Supervision under the auspices of the BIS. Bank Herstatt was thus the origin of the Basel Accords.

B. Banks themselves altered their bilateral and multilateral settlement arrangements and over the next 30 years developed Real Time Gross Settlement systems to avoid settlement risk i.e. a counterparty failing to settle (see below). This covered most of the risk, but not all, as there remained the residual problem of any net balances. This dealt with payment as such but not with the attendant cross-border currency risk. For that purpose, the Continuous Link System (**CLS**) was created to provide timely FX pricing for payments.

The alternative to correspondent bank arrangements is a multilateral payment system or interbank funds transfer system. To understand such a system, some terminological distinctions are relevant:

(1) Payment vs settlement: as we have seen, payment can be understood merely as an assumption of liability or assignment of an existing liability e.g. when a central bank creates **central bank money**. Settlement is the discharging of those obligations. In this context, given that an underlying obligation such as bank money is being transferred, settlement refers to discharging of obligations to transfer as between the members of the payment system.

(2) **Settlement finality** means payment which is irrevocable and unconditional. It is particularly relevant in insolvency as bar to a liquidator attempting to overturn transactions.

(3) **Gross vs net settlement**: under gross settlement each payment is transferred in its entirety, so that a payment system member may have gross assets and liabilities outstanding at any one time (allowing a liquidator to disclaim liabilities and claim assets). Under net settlement all payment instructions to or from a payment system member are netted off leaving a single asset/liability to be enforced.

(4) **Designated time vs real time settlement**: designated time settlement such as end of day settlement means that all payment instructions outstanding at a designated time are at that time executed gross or net. Real-time settlement, possible with modern computing, means payments occur on a continuous basis.

(5) The most common forms of large-value payment system (**LVPS**) are designated time net settlement systems (**DNS**) and real-time gross settlement systems (**RTGS**). Both TARGET2 and CHAPS are RTGS; BACS (now VOCA) is a DNS.

Taking a DNS first, the basic idea is that a clearing house may stand as an intermediary counterparty for all the LVPS member banks. In payment systems this clearing house commonly is the central bank. Consider by way of example the following three member LVPS (Figure 10.4), which should remind you of the structure deployed in *British Eagle*.

The advantages[26] of such a system are that netting via the CCP clearing house reduces counterparty risk (especially if the central bank is exposed). Also the liquidity demand on members

26 Nicholas Garvin, 'Central Counterparty Interoperability' (June 2012) Reserve Bank of Australia Bulletin, 59–68 <https://www.rba.gov.au/publications/bulletin/2012/jun/7.html> accessed 19 August 2024.

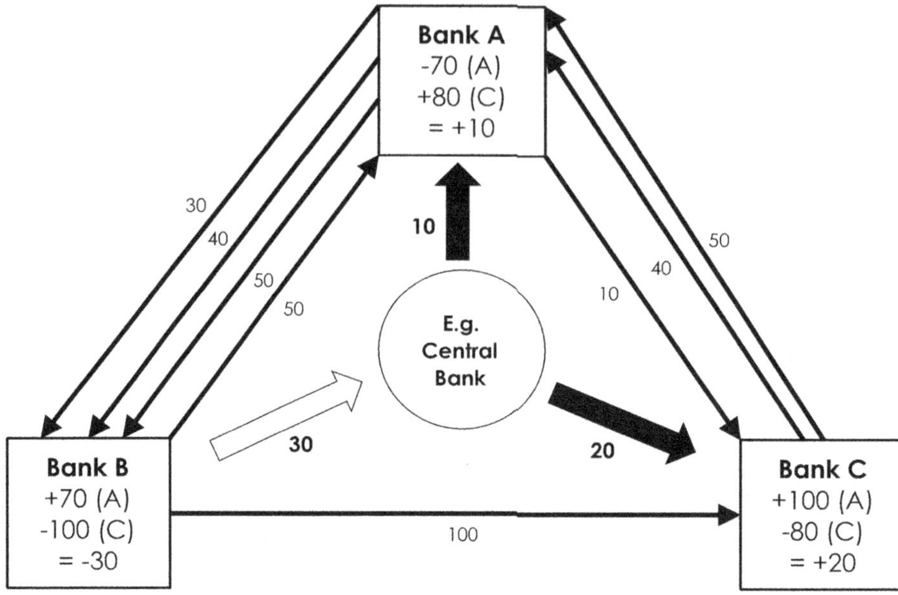

Figure 10.4 Payments settled in a multilateral settlement system, here operated by a central bank (adapted from Kokkola, ECB, 2010)

is comparatively low—a net amount is due at the designated time rather than each gross liability needing to be met through the day. A key disadvantage (in the absence of supervening statute) is that settlement finality may be delayed until the designated time and so payments may be clawed back or attached by liquidators or third parties.

By comparison an RTGS will be a foreshortened version of the correspondent bank structure, with the central bank standing as the direct intermediary between the originator and beneficiary banks (see Figure 10.5).

The reality is slightly more complicated than the simple diagram above. In the UK, for example, several clearing houses have created interfaces through which client members can place payments into the RTGS system.

These clearing houses include BACS (Bank Automated Clearing System), FPS (Faster Payments Service), CREST (Certificateless Registry for Electronic Share Transfer)[27] and CHAPS (Clearing House Automated Payment System). The Bank of England, in its Prudential Regulation Authority guise, regards these payment clearing houses as Financial Market Infrastructures (**FMIs**) and subjects them to additional prudential regulation.[28] In particular, pursuant to s.188 Banking Act 2009, the Bank of England adopted and published the *Principles for Financial Market Infrastructures* (**PFMIs**) issued by the Bank of International Settlements, and the International Organization of Securities Commissions (IOSCO).

It is worth emphasizing the clearing houses do not become parties to the payments, they simply provide a means inputting payment instructions into the RTGS system and communicating the output payment information to the payee bank. The banks are still, ultimately, engaging directly to

27 A securities intermediate we encountered in the chapter on securities. It features here because it also processes the payments for shares and other securities.

28 Part 5, Banking Act 2009, particularly ss 188–89.

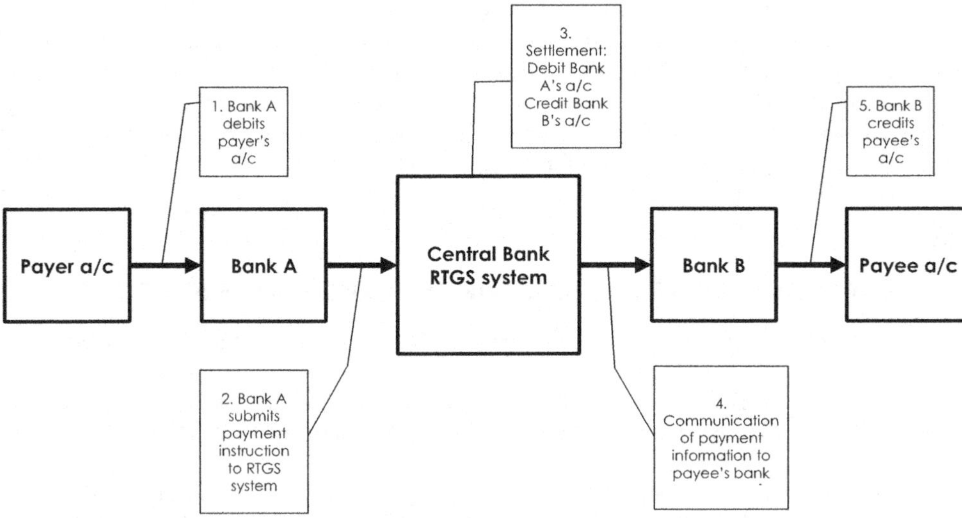

Figure 10.5 Payments settled via an RTGS system.

Source: ECB (adapted from *Payment Systems in Denmark*, Danmarks Nationalbank, Copenhagen, 2005)

pay between each other on a bilateral basis. The net result is the same, provided the RTGS system is working. The following case confirmed the bilateral nature of the client members' relation in any payment by clarifying the status of the rules promulgated by clearing houses such as CHAPS.

TIDAL ENERGY LTD v BANK OF SCOTLAND PLC [2014] EWCA Civ 1107

The payer was the victim of fraud. It had been provided with the payee's name, bank account number and sort code, but on seeing the name to be correct had failed to verify the other account details. It had passed all these details to its bank, BoS, which executed the payment. In fact, the fraudster had worked out that the CHAPS clearing interface only ever asked for the account number and sort code, never the payee's name, to construct a SWIFT number that uniquely identified the bank and payee account. The account and sort code number were those of the fraudster, who, on the crediting of his account via CHAPS, withdrew the money and disappeared.

The payer, with no other recourse, sued BoS for failing to act on its *full* instructions by crediting the *named* account.

Held: CHAPS clearing was governed by a set of rules issued by CHAPS (the CHAPS Rules). These provided that client members should only input payee account numbers and sort codes (for the purposes of SWIFT). Following *Hare v Henty* (1861)[29] a person who employs a banker is bound by the usage of bankers. The CHAPS Rules constituted such a usage and thus were implied by custom into the contract between the payer and bank. The bank had accordingly performed its obligation correctly and the payer's account would not be re-credited.

29 *Hare v Henty* (n 3) and analysed above. For a case which acts as a bridge between the two, see *Barclays Bank plc and others v Bank of England* [1985] 1 All ER 385, which involved the time for presentation of cheques through a modern interbank clearing system.

The key advantage of such an RTGS system is immediate settlement finality, reducing intraday exposures to a defaulting originator bank and giving each member and the central bank and immediate view of payment flows. The disadvantage is that each member must keep its mirror account with the central bank in funds at all times so that it can meet settlement in real time. This is a huge liquidity demand which only major banks can satisfy. Moreover, modern RTGS systems can fail *even* if they are operated by banks, because ultimately, they rely on information technology. This happened in the UK in 2014.

THE 2014 OUTAGE OF THE BANK OF ENGLAND'S RTGS SYSTEM[30]

These things happen: on Monday, 20 October 2014, the Bank of England's technology behind its RTGS fell over and was out of action for eight hours on a business day.

The result was that during this period the various UK payment clearing houses could not settle payments through the RTGS system. This affected them in different ways:

- BACS and FPS were DNS systems—settlement was 'Deferred Net.' In effect, though these clearing houses used a real-time system, they only used it at intervals and their client members accepted as much. BACS and FPS would net off all the transactions during the interval and only at the end process the net payments through the Bank of England RTGS system. For these clearing houses, broadly speaking, they could simply wait until the RTGS system came back online.
- CREST did clear settlements in real time, but it had it operated two systems in parallel. On the one hand, it used the RTGS system; on the other, it had agreed with the Bank of England that certain central bank reserves would stand behind payments. Thus, if a payer client member of CREST failed to settle, the payee client member did not look to the payer (or even CREST) but to the earmarked central bank funds. Thanks to this reserve client members could tolerate the RTGS system going down temporarily—even if payer funds did not reach them, they knew the payee had central bank funds with the payee's 'name on it' and could trade by reference to that reserve.
- CHAPS cleared settlements in real time but did not have a parallel system as back up. It was in trouble.

The question on 20 October 2014 was: if CHAPS in particular could not fulfil its clients' payment instructions, who was liable for any consequential loss? What if Mega Bank could not buy shares which subsequently rose in value? What if Mr Singh could not complete on his house purchase?

Was the Bank of England (BoE) liable?

This was one of those situations when an organization's words would come back to haunt it (if not render it legally liable). Back in 2011, the International Monetary Fund had analysed the role of CHAPS and the BoE's role in supervising it. Its report had found[31] that the

30 This account relies on Roger Jones and Raymond Cox, 'Implications of the Failure of the Bank of England RTGS System' (2015) 2 JIBFL 69. Note that Roger Jones was the head of TARGET payment system working group for the European banking industry.

31 International Monetary Fund, 'United Kingdom Observance by CHAPS of CPSS Core Principles for Systemically Important Payment Systems: Detailed Assessment of Observance' (2011) IMF Country Report No. 11/237, 12 <https://www.imf.org/external/pubs/ft/scr/2011/cr11237.pdf> accessed 19 August 2024.

BoE had only 'broadly observed' its responsibility to ensure MFIs comply with the PFMIs and that:

> [t]he BoE assesses the RTGS infrastructure against the Core Principles in an indirect and fragmented manner through its oversight of CHAPS (and other recognized systems that use it, such as CREST, FPS, and Bacs). However, not all activity in the RTGS is undertaken in regard to these recognized systems, and, given the importance of the RTGS infrastructure to the U.K. financial system, a direct and unified assessment would be beneficial.[32]

To this, the BoE's response, recorded in the report, was:

> **RTGS is not an interbank payment system but an accounting infrastructure that supports some payment systems.** It would therefore not be appropriate to assess RTGS against the CPSS Core Principles as they apply to Payment Systems [the predecessor to the PFMIs]. The Bank will, however, this year conduct a unified assessment of RTGS based on its existing internal risk assessment, monitoring and management framework. That will be done at arms' length as well as by line management.[33] [my emphasis]

The highlighted statement was a confirmation of its and the UK Government's legal position on the matter: when ss 188-189 Banking Act 2009 were enacted, HM Treasury had made clear they placed no legal liability whatsoever on the Bank of England for oversight of these payment systems.

This position was drafted explicitly into the standard Terms 7 Conditions of the contractual relationship between the BoE and clearing houses uses of its RTGS system. Clause 6.1(b) provided that:

> [The Account Holder agrees and acknowledges that] the [BoE], and its representatives and agents shall not be liable, save in the case of wilful default or reckless disregard of the Bank's obligations, for any Loss arising directly or indirectly from the operation by the Bank of the RTGS Central System . . . or any interruption or loss of the RTGS Central Systems . . . or loss of business, loss of profit or other consequential damage or any damage whatsoever and howsoever caused (including but without prejudice to the foregoing by reason of machine or computer malfunction or error and also any suspension or variation pursuant to clause 6.1(a) above).

Any claim by CHAPS against the BoE was going to struggle against such an exclusion clause—the RTGS outage fell squarely and expressly within it. Even if one could read wriggle room into this clause, the fact that the majority of clearing houses had put in place systems or workarounds which could tolerate an RTGS system outage suggested CHAPS' predicament was down to its own level of preparedness.

32 ibid.
33 ibid. 15.

Was CHAPS liable?

Let us turn to the contractual relationship between CHAPS and its client members. Could these client members sue CHAPS for any losses caused by CHAPS failure to ensure settlement of payments?

Remember how we introduced this clearing houses. They do not enter into any given payment as a party, they have simply created computer interfaces which facilitate the input and output of payments into and from the BoE RTGS system. To the extent that two client members wish to effect payment, they enter into a legal relationship with each other on a bilateral basis. Insofar as any individual payment failed to settle, CHAPS was not a party to a contract whereby it promised to settle payment. The CHAPS interface was not as resilient as some other clearing house interfaces, but it was the client members who had chosen to contract using it.

Was each paying client member liable to customers for failure of settlement?

The rule in *Hare v Henty* affirmed in *Tidal Energy Ltd. v Bank of Scotland* (see above) applies. Remember, when it comes to payment systems the usages of bankers, including the clearing house rules, are implied by custom into the contract between bank and customer.

Under CHAPS Rule 2.2, the client members must for the purposes of making payments through the CHAPS system:

> accept and give same day value to all Payments [through CHAPS] denominated in sterling received within the timeframes set out in the CHAPS Timetable in the CHAPS Procedural Documentation.

This does not say the client member must use the BoE's RTGS system, only that payment must be effected in line with the CHAPS timetable. The implication is that any lawful means is permitted, but payment must be settled.

Here the rule about bankers' usage works in the customers' favour. One might well argue that implied into the customer contract is just this time frame. We have a case like *Hare v Henty* when a time frame is customarily agreed between bankers for settlement; the difference here is that CHAPS might not have met it in any individual case.

All in all, then, the risk of failure of the BoE's RTGS system fell on the client members of CHAPS and any similar clearing house.

The outage of the Bank of England's RTGS demonstrated some very specific flaws—CHAPS was particularly affected just because it was solely reliant on the system. These systems, however, raise problems of more general application which tie in with long-running themes from this book. Let us illustrate some of the above principles and risks by reference to two key events—the insolvency of Bank Herstatt and the *British Eagle* case already familiar to you.

10.4 Payment settlement with cryptocurrency

How would a cryptocurrency like bitcoin fit into the payment systems just described? The claim made by supporters is that crypto-payments do not fit within these systems at all, though we will see that the reality is different. Note that we cannot hope to cover the minutiae of this topic here—we just propose to account for payment settlement of cryptocurrencies, taking bitcoin as our focus.

The Financial Stability Board defines **crypto-assets** (including cryptocurrency) as type of private sector digital asset that depends primarily on cryptography and distributed ledger or similar technology. The crypto-asset markets have various segments, including unbacked crypto-assets (such as bitcoin), so-called stablecoins, and decentralized finance (DeFi). A **distributed ledger technology (DLT)** may be contrasted with any system which centrally holds a record (ledger) of who holds how much currency, or who owes what to whom (a better understanding of public and private bank monies). A CCP would hold such a centralized ledger. In a DLT system all members of the system hold an electronic version of the ledger. In a **permissionless DLT** system every person holds and authenticates the ledger as valid—all have equal authority. In a **permissioned DLT** system, a select few have this validation role. The disintermediation of payment by removing banks, who traditionally hold the ledgers, from the equation, was claimed to be a liberatory innovation of bitcoin by its founder.[34]

We must further distinguish between **unbacked** and **backed** cryptocurrencies. A backed cryptocurrency is constituted by tokens which represent a claim on an underlying asset. In this, backed cryptocurrencies are much closer to electronic monies with which crypto should not be confused. Electronic money is simply the recording of a claim for money against an issuer on some device, such as a transit card.[35] Backed cryptocurrency can approach this functionally but it depends on the rules of the cryptocurrency e.g. are the claims on a single (variable, bulk) global asset, on assets allocated to the holder of cryptocurrency, or to monies held on the individual's account with some centralized provider (thus defeating the aim of disintermediation). Backed cryptocurrencies of this kind tend to call themselves **stablecoins**.

Unbacked cryptocurrencies, such as bitcoin, are entirely fiat currencies. Their value is only that which the next person will provide in exchange for one unit of the cryptocurrency. The bitcoin price, for example, is highly unstable, rendering the cryptocurrency a poor store of value and much more a purely speculative asset class.

At one level, payment settlement with bitcoin is decided simple.[36] Let us assume Kate has acquired some bitcoin, either by purchasing it for central bank money via a broker, or by 'mining' it herself using bitcoin's method of generating interest in the cryptocurrency by rewarding people for applying themselves to validating transactions and otherwise supporting the system's liquidity. Kate has identified a vendor of goods who will accept bitcoin in payment. Kate therefore effects transfer of the bitcoin, which is debited from her wallet and credited to the vendor's wallet by amending the distributed ledger. No CCP or other intermediary ought to be involved; the recording is distributed and the only legal liabilities arising are as between the parties to the sale.

There are still risks. Apart from the exogenous risks that Kate refuses to pay or vendor refuses to provide the goods, there is the instability of the coin itself: vendor's wallet may be credited with the correct amount of bitcoin, but its value to vendor may have collapsed. Vendor may have priced the goods in central bank money because he must use that to produce them with input materials, but just before payment the bitcoin price has collapsed, and our vendor has in effect made a loss. Then there is technological risk: bitcoin's proof-of-work validation system is pushing on two-decades old and is outdated in terms of security and the slowness with which it works. As time goes on, the chances of failure or security breach must increase. Nabilou summarizes the problem:

34 Satoshi Nakamoto, *Bitcoin: A Peer-to-Peer Electronic Cash System* (Bitcoin Foundation 2008) <https://www.ussc.gov/sites/default/files/pdf/training/annual-national-training-seminar/2018/Emerging_Tech_Bitcoin_Crypto.pdf> accessed 19 August 2024.

35 See e.g. Art 2(2) of the EU e-money Directive 2009/110/EC, 'electronic money' means 'electronically, including magnetically, stored monetary value as represented by a claim on the issuer which is issued on receipt of funds for the purpose of making payment transactions . . . and which is accepted by a natural or legal person other than the electronic money issuer.'

36 I draw here on Ulrich Bindseil and George Pantelopoulos, *Introduction to Payments and Financial Market Infrastructures* (Springer 2023) ch 9.

> Rather than opt for fast and efficient payments, Bitcoin goes a long way to create extreme inefficiencies by introducing a distributed ledger that should be maintained, updated and validated by all fully validating nodes, only to make sure that no single or a small group of participants violate the rules of the Bitcoin protocol, modify the ledger arbitrarily or censor other stakeholders from participating in the Bitcoin network. Such a trade-off has been made because the unique value proposition of Bitcoin and blockchain technology is not to replicate the functions of centralized technologies in a faster or cheaper fashion. Indeed, as blockchain technology is one of the least efficient technologies for payments and data storage, and as virtually everything that can be done on blockchain can also be performed on a network that uses a client-server or master-slave architecture, the very use of blockchain technology creates inefficiencies that do not apply to centralized systems. As the client-server architecture uses a centralized coordination mechanism, it is much faster, cheaper and efficient than the systems relying on blockchain technology. . . . Since Bitcoin is designed to operate outside the legal framework . . ., it assumes an adversarial environment and prepares to defend itself against various attack vectors using a variety of ex-ante built-in mechanisms within the Bitcoin network rather than rely on the external legal system for ex-post remedies.[37]

Add to this the inevitable specialization of certain entrepreneurs in terms of mining and in offering simplified interfaces for 'retail' users of bitcoin, identified by Poon and Dryja[38] as real problems for cryptocurrencies. The sheer environmental cost of electricity usage for mining and validation is enormous and increasing with every unit mined and transaction undertaken. The impact seems wholly unjustifiable. As for offering 'retail' interfaces—**Crypto-Asset Service Providers (CASPs)**—all these have done is recreate intermediation and clearing houses for bitcoin, defeating the very reason for its creation.

As a result, the 'simple' payment settlement structure we just illustrated has in many cases been replaced by models much closer to the modern payment settlement systems examined in this chapter (absent a central bank). For example, consider a cross-border payment effected between two CASPs, which may be part of the same business but for legal and regulatory purposes are separate and located in the respective jurisdictions. Then if retail service user A wishes to transfer bitcoin to retail service user B, she inputs the instruction with her CASP A. CASP A communicates the same to B's provider CASP B, which credits the account of B. Many other service users may be making payments in the day, so CASP A and CASP B will net off the debits and credits to minimize risk. With this you have traditional bank clearing. Add in an underlying reference asset as the store of value 'stabilizing' the coin, held by a central depository for this purpose, and we are approaching a correspondent bank arrangement with a central reserve behind it. In fact, we will see such a model is proximate to securities clearing using a CCP and client members.

All this has not stopped central banks investigating the possibility of establishing their own Central Bank Digital Currency (**CBDC**). As the currency would electronically represent a liability of the central bank, we are very far from the ideological underpinnings that framed bitcoin's creation. Here one must distinguish between wholesale CBDCs (which may only be used by selected banks in their dealings with the central bank) and a retail CBDC which could be used by anyone. The technical difference has one immediate import: wholesale CBDCs have been around for years. Think back to a RTGS system backed by a central bank. In this system the client members of the system are confident of settlement finality because each payment is underpinned by a claim

37 Hossein Nabilou, 'Bitcoin Governance as a Decentralized Financial Market Infrastructure' (2020) 4 Stanford Journal of Blockchain Law and Policy 177, 191.

38 Joseph Poon and Thaddeus Dryja, *The Bitcoin Lightning Network: Scalable Off-Chain Instant Payments* (independently published 2023).

on an earmarked reserve held by the central bank (see CREST or the Danish central bank RTGS). That claim is simply represented by an electronic ledger entry held within the RTGS system, and it may be used with confidence by member banks to back further transactions. As between the central bank and the client banks, this is a CBDC; it is just closed to everyone else. As for retail CBDCs, a full analysis of the debate on offering this form of currency to the public would take us too far off track.[39] It raises questions about overreach by public institutions in occupying a market already serviced by a niche private sector, and by developing a currency which, unlike traditional cash and bank notes, is a central record of every citizen's payment history. Some worry that a retail CBDC will compete with and potentially drive out cash, or conversely it will be an expensive failure precisely because it is aiming for a market which is ideologically opposed to central bank money.

For our purposes, it has been enough to understand the how cryptocurrencies payment settlement sits within the wider scheme of bank clearing and payment settlement systems. Through the hype, some very familiar structures have once again emerged.

10.5 Clearing of securities

It might seem strange to move now to consider the clearing of securities, but we do so for two reasons: (1) our understanding of money as claims on a bank, or the central bank, helps us understand the genetic similarities between Large Value Payment Systems and securities clearing; and (2) securities clearing is a historical step to derivatives clearing.

When we looked for example at correspondent bank arrangements, we notice the role played by a clearing house such as the central bank. The bank made both sides of the transaction work because even if the originator bank failed it could simply meet the demand of the beneficiary bank by making payment by means of issuing a claim on the central bank. This is central bank money.

In the last analysis all the originators and beneficiaries are doing is transferring claims on the central bank, we just happen to call this payment. Currency is just a special case where originator has access directly to a claim on the central bank, rather than through a chain of bank and settlement bank.

Securities clearing applies a similar logic, but whereas the claims in a payment system relate to a central bank, claims in a security clearing system relate to a specific security (such as a bond or share) backed by a corporate or sovereign.

Having studied securities in Chapter 8, you should know by now that we need to forget about old-fashioned share trading where shareholder A transfers shares in PLC to B by means of a stock transfer form, such that B now takes delivery of share certificates. That method is valid, but a bit like communicating by post. These days PLC will issue a single global security to a (International) Central Securities Depositary (**(I)CSD**). Think of this note as gold in a bank reserve. It is not going to go anywhere. Rather it will stand behind a whole system of transfers of interests in that global security. To ease your reading, let us briefly rehearse some findings from Chapter 8 which will be relevant to our discussion of CCPs:

KEY LEGAL BIT I: By way of reminder, we face a technical problem. If the global note amounts to a debt of 100 and A is the owner of an interest in 10 of that debt obligation, in which 10 does A have an interest? Critically, if A wishes to transfer 5 of his interest in 10, how can he meet the usual sales requirements that he must identify the property he is transferring?

---

39 For a survey, see Bindseil and Pantelopoulos (n 36) 138ff.

Luckily, it seems English law allows allocation of an interest in securities by reference to a bulk of securities because two parts of a debt obligation are indistinguishable (being negotiable), does not also require the usual segregation condition that applies where one is selling from a physical bulk of goods (such as grain). This means, as Philip Wood says, that:

(1) a sale or trust of 100 bonds of PLC would be invalid because which and whose bonds are being identified; but
(2) a sale or trust of 100 bonds from my holding of PLC bonds is valid; and, crucially . . .
(3) a sale or trust of 100 PLC bonds from my PLC bonds holding account with Central Securities Depositary or other intermediary is valid.

As we have seen, in cases such as *re Harvard Securities Ltd.* [1997] 2 BCLC 369, declarations of trust over assets identified in the manner stated in (3) have been held to be sufficiently certain.

KEY LEGAL BIT II: Now observe what is being transferred in case (c) above. A has a holding of PLC bonds with CSD and decides to transfer what? Well not the bonds because we do not know which 100 bonds he is trying to transfer, and really there is only one global note in issue. A is transferring '100 PLC bonds from my PLC bonds holding a/c with CSD.' That's not the same. What A is transferring is his interest in the global note which CSD is holding for him as trustee. A has a beneficial interest in that legal title measured by his investment. B, the transferee, receives an interest in '100 PLC bonds' held on trust by CSD. To effect the transfer CSD simply debits A's account—its proportionate obligation to A as beneficiary—and credits B's accounts with an obligation to deliver PLC 100 bonds (Figure 10.6).

In short, A is not transferring bonds, or the global note, or a part of the global note. These transfers are legally impossible here. **A is transferring its equitable interest in the global security**.

Do you notice a structural similarity between the diagram above and the correspondent bank settlement structure examined in section 10.3? In a sense the CSD acts like a passive central bank

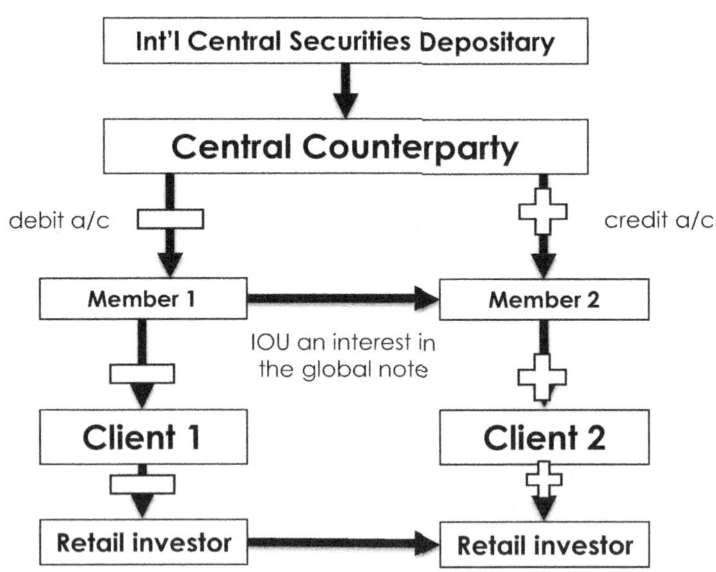

Figure 10.6 CCP 'hub and spoke' clearing

in securities clearing. While it cannot create new interests—the global note is worth what it is worth—it stands as a determinate and limited reserve to meet the claims of bondholders should they demand final settlement.

Risks are further mitigated by counterparties demanding margin (in its 'securities as collateral' sense, see Chapter 8). For example, client 1 may demand that an investor provide a certain percentage of **initial margin** as collateral just in case the investor's deal sours, and investor is required to pay its ultimate counterparty. Their contract may further provide for the payment of further agreed margin if the trade goes far worse than expected—**variation margin**—and there may even be provision for top ups of as yet unspecified amounts in case of a really disastrous trade (sometimes called 'additional margin,' but this is occasionally used interchangeably with variation margin). These dynamic forms of margin are more commonly used in the derivatives context, it depends on who a particular trade is structured. Note that the CCP can also ask its Members to provide margin, both for trades on Member's own account and for the positions the Member is clearing through the system, not least where there is a risk that the Member itself could collapse mid-trade (as in the case of Lehman Bros, where LCH, the London Clearing House, demanded variation margin from the ailing bank of up to USD2bn in the weeks leading up to its collapse—a wise move given that LCH was able to close out Lehman's outstanding positions with investors and counterparties using the margin obtained).

In reality, and not dissimilar to correspondent banking, investors do not interact directly with the (I)CSD. (I)CSDs merely act as silent custodians of global securities. Rather (I)CSDs deal either with a small number of **member** financial institutions which act like settlement banks, or with one **central counterparty** clearing agent which itself has members. The members—banks, brokers, funds—then act for their clients who buy and sell interests in securities. Hence you might see this clearing structure: with this sort of structure in play we can see similarities with payment settlement. Yet securities clearing has also proved innovative in the field of multilateral netting, as we shall now see.

10.6 Clearing and CCPs

Where a clearing system deploys multilateral netting, we may find one of the following transfer structures in play, which also feature in transfers of OTC derivatives:

(1) Buyer and seller agree to trade 100 bonds. These mutual obligations to pay versus deliver are really instructions to various clearing system members to credit and debit their respective buyer and seller accounts. These respective obligations are the replaced with two new contracts between a CCP and the clearing house members: CCP will deliver bonds to the buyer side on payment (credit interests in the global security; debit cash) and CCP will deliver case to seller on delivery (credit cash; debit interests in the global security). This replacement of the buyer-seller contract with two buyer-CCP and CCP-seller contracts is called novation. You might also see the concept of 'dropping' a trade into a CCP.

(2) Alternatively, you might see an open offer system. Here buyer and seller make open offers to market to trade and where a match is found, and certain conditions are met, both offers are accepted by the CCP. Thus, no buyer-seller contract is made. Rather, CCP initiates original contracts with each of buyer and seller.

As trades drop into the clearing system the CCP is able to net corresponding delivery and payment obligations and account for the balance, thus reducing the contractual exposures of members (and their clients).

BRITISH EAGLE AGAIN

You will remember that *British Eagle International Air Lines Ltd v Compagnie Nationale Air France* [1975] 1 WLR 758 also involved a crude payment settlement system between air lines that was administered by IATA. Critically this system was a designated time gross settlement system with no central clearing house—each member ran up liabilities with the others directly and all IATA did was at the end of each week tally up the net assets and liabilities of each member and submit invoices to the invoices demanding settlement of the net amounts.

When a member (British Eagle) entered insolvency proceedings it was open to its liquidator to disclaim each British Eagle liability to the other members and claim gross payments from those members (here Air France). Insolvency set off is allowed where debts are mutual (Air France owes British Eagle, and British Eagle owes Air France), but under this system it might be that (1) British Eagle owed British Airways but (2) Air France owed British Eagle—debts (1) and (2) could not be set off despite the contractual netting arrangement.

The point here is that had IATA been a central clearing house such that all payment obligations were due to or by it, then all BE's assets and liabilities relating to the IATA clearing scheme would be mutual with IATA and netting would have been respected. In other words, all British Eagle would only ever owe money to IATA as CCP, and only IATA as CCP would owe money to British Eagle, thus providing the desired mutuality permitting insolvency set off.

The harsh lesson of *British Eagle* provided further impetus for financial institutions to pursue multilateral netting involving a central clearing house.

For all the advantages of deploying a CCP, however, there remain risks. There is still a counterparty and so counterparty risk. In a central bank multilateral payment system, the counterparty is, or is backed by, the central bank. The central bank ensures settlement, standing behind payments with its reserves and so promoting confidence. A CSD is not a central bank and a CCP is thus more exposed. Particular risks include:

(1) Neither CCP nor CSD can print money. If payment fails to occur after delivery, CCP risks illiquidity. This risk has been reduced by Payment versus Delivery (**PvD**) models.
(2) Nor can they print securities. If delivery fails to occur, CCP must find replacement securities and buy these, possibly at a premium, to meet its obligations to the non-defaulting member.
(3) A clearing house member may default, leaving both CCP and client exposed on either side.

To combat these risks, CCPs are not passive but (should) actively regulate clearing house members to ensure payments and deliveries are timely. The four main risk mitigation techniques are:

(1) Restriction of clearing house membership to only then most creditworthy financial institutions (think central bank and settlement bank).
(2) Requirements that members post collateral to back their payment and delivery exposures from time to time. Collateral in this context is confusingly called **margin** and comprises:
    (a) Initial Margin for the privilege of membership, being cash and/or collateral.
    (b) Variation Margin, which varies with exposures.
(3) Requirements that members make contributions to a CCP administered default fund which exists to pay out once initial and variation margin are exhausted.
(4) Porting—a system that allows clients of defaulting clearing house members to be transferred to solvent client members so that trading continuity can be maintained.

10.7 Mandatory clearing

We have been building up to deal with the mandatory clearing of OTC derivatives through CCPs but this would imply that derivatives are new to the clearing game. Actually, they are not. The simplest derivatives—options and futures—were actually traded through CCPs 300 years before other securities on exchanges such as Chicago Mercantile Exchange (**CME**) or the London Metal Exchange.

So, for example, Farmer is worried pork belly prices will fall from the current level of USD5 in six months so enters into a forward with Bank obliging it to deliver pork bellies (or cash settlement) in six months at USD5. Bank agrees to take at that price. In six months, the price has in fact risen to USD6. Farmer sells the pork bellies in the market and cash settles by delivering USD1 to bank.

How was this cleared? Well, Farmer phones broker-member who places an open offer into the CME for a forward. Bank has an open offer on matching terms in the CME as well. In this instance broker may well match the offers and execute a contract with Bank agreeing to clear the forward through the clearing system. When the contract is accepted for clearing CCP (here CME) novates the contract into two new contracts: Farmer-to-CCP and CCP-to-Bank. Confirmations are sent to Bank and Farmer (see Figure 10.7).

The point about long form, specifically negotiated derivatives, is that lacking standardization they were not normally cleared but remained bilateral agreements. These derivatives were thus called 'over-the-counter' (**OTC**). Being bilateral trades, OTC derivatives do not benefit from the risk mitigation advantages of using multilateral netting through a CCP. This is partly why OTC derivatives developed as master agreements with several trade confirmations—OTC derivatives mirrored netting at least as between the parties to the master agreement (see Chapter 9).

Following the subprime and the collapse of Lehman Bros, the risks of OTC derivatives were brutally exposed on a number of fronts.

(1) Counterparty risk: an insolvent counterparty is unable to meet contractual payment obligations. Not unusual on its own, but when key players like Lehman collapsed, thousands of swaps were effected and stalled.

(2) Re-characterization risk: liquidators refusing to respect (close-out) netting provisions and claiming gross amounts as due.

(3) Transparency risk: bilateral trades OTC were practically invisible to regulators because they were off-market. It was difficult to gauge the systemic effects of a key OTC market player collapsing because the value at risk in all its trades was opaque.

(4) Credibility risk: likewise, banks could not assess each other's exposures to OTC derivatives and thus refused to deal with each other.

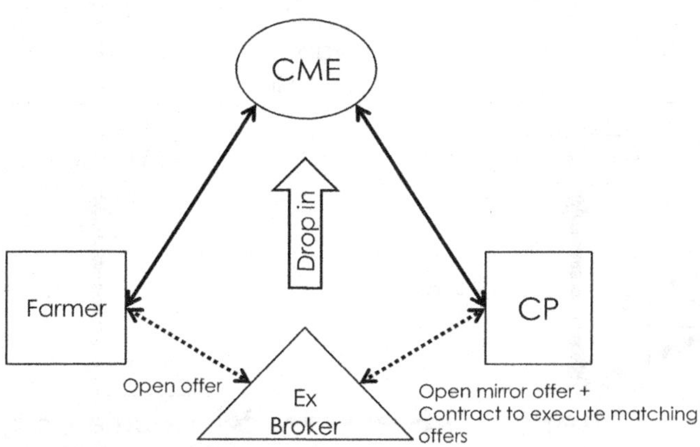

Figure 10.7 Exchange clearing by broker novation

By 2010 there was broad consensus in the G20 that to reduce these risks OTC derivatives meeting certain criteria **must be cleared through a CCP**. In the EU these requirements are principally set out in the European Market Infrastructure Regulation of 2012 (**EMIR**) and mart of the Markets in Financial Instruments Regulation (**MiFIR** (see Chapter 9)).

To begin with, in much the same way as when one previously entered into an uncleared OTC derivative, Client would enter into a transaction (**C-EB Trade**) with an executing broker (**EB**). As part of the C-EB Trade, you would need to agree the matching facility through which both parties will be submitting the trade details (the 'Affirmation Platform') and the CCP through which the transaction will be cleared.

A number of steps must be taken before a cleared transaction is established (see Figure 10.8):

(1) once the C-EB Trade is entered into, its details must be submitted by both parties and checked via the Affirmation Platform (either manually, or automatically if the C-EB Trade is executed on an Affirmation Platform which automatically matches and submits the trade details to the relevant CCP);
(2) C-EB needs to submit the identity of its Client Member of the CCP (**CM**) so that it can be checked and confirmed by the CCP;
(3) the CCP and the CM for each party need to accept the trade for clearing. If each accepts, then the following cleared transactions are automatically put in place:
    (a) a transaction between your CM and the CCP on terms identical to the C-EB Trade but with the CM taking your position and the CCP taking the EB's position (**CM-CCP Trade**);
    (b) a transaction between you and your CM on terms mirroring the terms of the CM-CCP Trade (**C-CM Trade**);
    (c) a transaction between the EB (assuming it is also a CM) and the CCP on terms identical to the C-EB Trade but with the CCP taking your position (**EB-CCP Trade**).

So, whereas before there was a bilateral contract between Client and Exchange Broker, now that contract is mirrored by one between CM and CCP. Client is related to CM by a contract whereby Client makes CM good for its side of the underlying contract. EB is related to CCP by a contract whereby EB makes CCP good for its side of the contract. This assumes EB is a member of the clearing system.

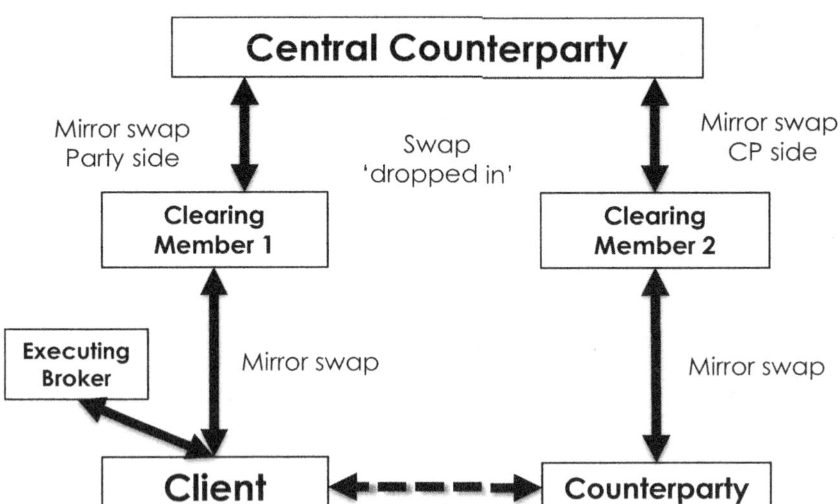

Figure 10.8 EU-style mandatory clearing

As with securities clearing, the whole system is backed by initial and variation margin, a default reserve fund, porting, and careful selection of client members. Furthermore, CCPs are supervised by regulators as Systemically Important (Financial) Market Infrastructure and are required inter alia to keep appropriate capital reserves.[40]

So, does this nullify risks? The following case study warns us not to be complacent.

10.8 Case study: the Einar Aas affair (2018)

Einar Aas was a Norwegian commodities trader specializing in Scandinavian energy markets.[41] He had left his employer brokerage firm in 2005 with USD30k and with this had managed to amass of fortune of USD245m by 2016 through trading on his own account from his home in the small Norwegian fishing town of Grimstad.

Aas traded in the energy segment of the Nasdaq Nordic Exchange: 'Nord Pool' or 'Nordic AS.' Norway is not a member of the European Union, but through a memorandum of understanding with the European Securities and Markets Authority, it was understood that the Norwegian government would enact equivalent markets regulation laws to those of the EU, such as MiFiD.[42] The Norwegian regulator (*Finanstilsynet*) has a presence at ESMA, and together they may investigate such matters as market abuse on Norwegian exchanges. One wonders whether the not-quite-in but not-quite-out status of Norwegian securities regulation contributed to the problems that arose.

Einar Aas brought about his own downfall, but it was the context that allowed him to do so and potentially take the entire Nordic Exchange with him that are interesting. If one thinks back to the Suffolk Banking System, one will remember that exchanges and clearing houses which are also private businesses face a potential conflict between maintaining stability for members and the profit motive of the business (for its shareholders). This conflict arises as much in a monopoly (Suffolk Bank price gouging) as in free competition (Suffolk Bank causing a clearing crisis by downing tools in the face of BMR's entry onto the market). Nasdaq Nordic faced competition from numerous other small European exchanges, competition which had intensified in light of the UK's vote for Brexit and the 'Brexodus' of euro-denominated financial services from the City of London to an as yet undetermined European financial hub. Exchanges across Europe were vying for market share. In broad terms they needed to demonstrate two things to potential investors: sufficient market capitalization on the exchange (i.e. it was a big market) and, even more importantly, sufficient liquidity on the exchange (i.e. if a trader needed to sell securities, it could find a buyer at a truly competitive price). It is what City-types call 'deep and broad markets.' Market capitalization is relative. For an energy or metals exchange, the size need not be great compared to a share exchange, it just needs to be large relative to the commodities in the world/region available to trade. Given Norway's extensive oil and gas fields, and successes with hydroelectric power, Nasdaq Nordic could certainly boast significance for Scandinavia.

Liquidity was more difficult, and this is where Einar Aas comes in. Our model of 'hub-and-spoke' clearing by a CCP relies on the financial solidity of the CCP *and* of the Client Members. The

---

40 The European Market Infrastructure Regulation (EU) 648/2012 (EU EMIR), the Dodd-Frank Wall Street Reform and Consumer Protection Act 2010 (Dodd-Frank Act), and similar legislation. The UK assimilated the EU's EMIR as UK EMIR in 2020: Assimilated Regulation (EU) 648/2012. See also, for the UK, UK MiFIR Assimilated Regulation (EU) 600/2014 and UK CRR Assimilated Regulation (EU) 575/2013. Amendments to the Financial Services and Markets Act 2000, in 2023, gave the Bank of England broad rulemaking and resolution powers for CCPs (see e.g. new ss 55L–55M, s 57).

41 The case study draws on my own minor consultancy on the affair for the *Financial Times*. See: Philip Stafford and David Sheppard, 'Trader Blows EUR100m Hole in Nasdaq's Nordic Power Market' (*Financial Times*, 13 September 2018); Philip Stafford, 'Regulators Probe Nasdaq's Derivatives Market Safeguards' (*Financial Times*, 14 September 2018) and Philip Stafford's explanatory 'How clearing houses aim to avert market disasters' in the same edition.

42 See Norway's Securities Trading Act 2007 (as amended to integrate EU norms), for example.

system is designed to cope if a CM becomes insolvent, but CMs are selected so that insolvency is likely to be a rare occurrence. CMs are large investment banks[43] with deep pockets, to fall over something bigger than a problem on a single clearing house/exchange must be happening. So why, then, was Mr Einar Aas of Grimstad, Norway, a Client Member of the Nasdaq Nordic?

The answer appears to be twofold. First, Einar Aas provided liquidity—though he was physically absent from the exchange, never attending committee meetings or events, from his home in Grimstad he was in the market daily trading and so making markets for everyone else. Second, Einar Aas had always provided liquidity—he had been in the market since before the 2007 EU-inspired law reforms and before Nasdaq had taken over the Norwegian exchange. Einar Aas had attained the status of a fixture and fitting—he came with the light fittings and no one had thought to revisit his presence given the markets he made.

From 2005 to August 2018, Einar Aas had largely got it right, but in September 2018, he got it spectacularly wrong. Aas had been examining northern European energy markets and had concluded that German power prices, which had been having rough time, would decline in the future. If a person promised to *sell* German power in the future at *today's* price, they would earn more than if they sold it later at the predicted lower price. He also concluded that Norwegian power prices would rise due to shortages. If a person promised to *buy* in the future at *today's* price, they would earn more by then on-selling the power because in the future the power would be more expensive than the price paid today.

Einar Aas could have just made two futures contracts at this point: one selling German power in the future at today's price; one buying Norwegian power in the future. He did something more complicated, however, and created a kind of derivative contract known as an index spread. Under this contract, Aas did not need to enter into the actual German and Nordic futures contracts. Rather, he bet with a counterparty that the difference (or 'spread') in the price of German and Nordic power would decrease. This makes more sense if you imagine a line graph in which the price of German power is greater on the *y*-axis over time than the price of Nordic power. Crudely speaking, Aas was betting that the 'gap' between the German power price and the Nordic power price would decrease.[44]

More particularly:

- If the spread between the two prices *decreased*, Aas' counterparty would pay to Einar Aas a sum calculated by reference to that decrease, such that the greater the decrease, the greater sum Aas would receive.
- If the spread *increased*, Aas was required to pay a sum to the counterparty calculated by reference to the increase, such that the greater the increase, the greater sum Einar Aas would be paying.

Notice that in principle, there is nothing stopping the spread between the two prices increasing to infinity. This is why spread betting is a particularly risky and destructive mode of speculation.

In early September 2018, two things happened: (1) carbon emissions trading went on a bull run, and Germany, which largely avoided nuclear in favour of carbon-emitting power production, had to pay more for permission to burn coal and gas, driving up the power price; and (2) the Norwegian summer was unusually wet, pushing Norway's hydroelectric plants to produce a massive surplus which depressed the price of Nordic power. The spread between the German and

43 In commodities exchanges they will also be major corporates trading in the commodity, e.g. mining companies and automotive manufacturers on metals exchanges.

44 Aas was likely betting on the ratio between the two prices, rather than the brute difference, but this is much more complicated than we need.

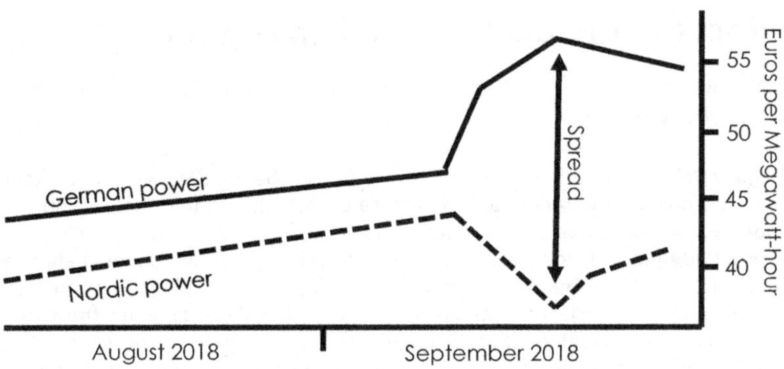

Figure 10.9 Simplified chart of German-Nordic power price spread through August–September 2018

Source: Bloomberg.

Nordic power prices opened to 17 times the normal difference. Einar Aas would have to pay the counterparty. A lot.

The trade started burning through the exchange's prudential systems:

- Note that such a risky bet may never have been allowed in the first place, and certainly not without significant collateral in place. But Einar Aas was not a broker seeking permission from a Client Member—he was his own Client Member and was clearing his own trades. There was no oversight on his side of the transaction.
- Aas had put some initial and variation margin down, but the sum was burnt through quickly.[45]
- Aas then put in additional margin of USD36m; it also was used up within hours.
- At this point a Client Member should have stepped in to support the trade, transfer it, or unwind it, but again the Client Member was Einar Aas, who had already been wiped out.
- Therefore, the next reserve available to meet the counterparty's claims was the regulatory capital of the exchange itself: Nasdaq Nordic. It is at this point one sees the enormity of what Einar Aas had done: the counterparty was still owed USD114,000,000; the regulatory capital of Nasdaq Nordic was just USD7,000,000.
- The exchange could not meet the counterparty's claims but had put in place a Mutual Default Fund to supplement reserves in case of default, capitalized by Client Members. This was able to provide a further USD166m to meet the counterparty's claims and stave off complete collapse of the exchange. All reserves were reduced to USD59m. One more bad trade could have finished the Nasdaq Nordic completely.

The Nasdaq Nordic had not been destroyed, but within 48 hours it had come close with 68% of its reserve and default fund eaten up by a single trade. Other Client Members no doubt fumed at seeing their capital lost in this way, questioning how Aas' trade had been allowed to clear. Investors more generally looked at how easily the exchange came to disaster, and how undercapitalized it was as a result. Nasdaq Nordic immediately launched a recapitalization round, asking its Client Members for a further USD166m, which no doubt added to their sense of goodwill to current management. To be fair, Nasdaq itself increased the exchange's capital by USD19m.

As for Einar Aas, he was kicked out of the exchange with immediate effect.

45 The exact figures are not publicly known.

10.9 Defects in the CCP and bail-in regime

The literature[46] identifies several defects in the current mandatory CCP structure, some of which are highlighted in the Einar Aas Affair.

(1) **Legacy CMs**: the problem here is that existing exchange CMs who are no longer suitable to play a quasi-settlement bank role were grandfathered into the CCP structure without thought. Einar Aas was a key example.

(2) **Capital adequacy**: a key feature of payment systems is that standing behind every transaction is a central bank that can always print bank money. Behind securities settlement systems we find a CSD with a global security which will meet claims, the remaining losses being borne by investors. Where in the OTC derivative clearing structure is this final resort? The CCP? Albuquerque et al. (2016) have criticized the capital adequacy requirements as 'inappropriately low' for the size of liabilities in play.

(3) **Conflicts of interest**: several key CCPs began life as mutual organizations owned by client members and acting for their interests. However, increasingly they have become corporates with obligations to shareholders.

   (a) Share capital is at risk and so it is in the interests of shareholders to deflect that risk onto CMs in a manner which creates systemic risk. This can happen by voting for the CCP to increase default fund contributions from CMs.

   (b) Shareholders seeks profits, and they may push the CCP to increase IM and VM requirements, and exchange fees, ostensibly for risk purposes but really to generate income.

   (c) Likewise, shareholders may push the CCP to trade on its own account (skin in the game is sometimes encouraged), tying the CCP into exacerbating risks, or at least suffering losses.

(4) **Collateral is only as good as its value when you realize it**: this is a classic problem which played a big role in the GFC. Just because CMs are required to post IM and VM does not automatically mean that this collateral will always meet losses. Where an asset price downward spiral occurs the value of the collateral will also fall (a crash) leaving the CCP holding worthless paper.

(5) **Moral hazard**: once private actors, now deemed systemically important market infrastructure, the feeling is that a CCP facing insolvency will not be allowed to fail. Does this encourage risk-taking by CCPs? Would it not be better to mutualize or nationalize them—make them 'boring'?

(6) **Why mandatory?** Singh argues[47] that the mandatory clearing rules in EMIR are arbitrary and should be made flexible at least on CCP default. If a CCP is seen to fail, authorities such as ESMA should be able to suspend mandatory clearing for affected trades, returning to an OTC position to permit market continuity while a replacement CCP is identified.

(7) **What about cl 2(a)(iii) of the 1992 ISDA Master Agreement**? Remember what happened in *Lomas*? To the extent that the parties are still using the original wording of cl 2(a) and not the amended Condition End Date version, if CM defaults would Client be able to withhold its payment? CCP? Would porting override the cl 2(a)(iii) rights because the replacement CM is able to settle? The question remains moot because lawyers now draft around it in line with ISDA's advice, but the legal issue has not vanished and could still catch out older master agreements.

(8) **Collateral versus novation**: for example, LCH's Rulebook r.8 explicitly provides that if a CM defaults then Client and its collateral would be ported to a new CM by novation. What happens here depends on whether Client collateral was charged to CCP directly or to CM.

---

46 Mark J Roe, 'Clearinghouse Overconfidence' (2013) 101 Cal L Rev 1641; Dermot Turing, *Clearing & Settlement* (Bloomsbury 2021) 10.7ff; Stephen Connelly and Saveethika Leesurakarn, 'Tis Said They Ate Each Other? The Interaction Between OTC Clearing Requirements and the BRRD' (2017) 4 JIBFL 205.

47 Manmohan Singh and Dermot Turing, 'CCPs Resolution—An Unresolved Problem' IMF Working Paper No. WP/18/65 <https://www.imf.org/-/media/Files/Publications/WP/2018/wp1865.ashx> accessed 5 February 2018. See more generally: Jens-Hinrich Binder and Dalvinder Singh (eds), *Bank Resolution: The European Regime* (OUP 2016).

If the former, a novation may release the collateral although in practice CCP should make porting conditional on immediate re-grant of security as a condition precedent. In the latter case there is a mismatch risk: Client granted collateral to CM which on-charged it to CCP. CCP could enforce against CM due to its default, but port client to a new CM with the same collateral (!) or require new collateral, imposing additional burdens on Client.

(9) **Auction of defaulting positions may fail**: When the CCP calls on CMs to take over a defaulter's book positions it does so by auction, with each CM bidding the lowest price at which it would accept the out-of-the-money positions. There are risks that the auction fails (no CM would reasonably take a seriously loss-making provision) and CCP bears the loss.

(10) **Breakdown of CCP mirroring**: Unless CCP has been shut down entirely, while it is porting one side of trades to new CMs it is still having to pay out on the other counterparty side of each cleared transaction e.g. by providing variation margin (which before it would be passing through).

(11) **Bail-in and respect of security**: where a resolution authority initiates a bail-in—effectively asking solvent parties to take a haircut by extinguishing liabilities to the resolution entity (CM or CCP)—they are prohibited from bailing in liabilities in 'so far as secured' (s 48B(8)(d), Banking Act 2009). The problem in this context is once again that collateral value and swap liabilities may radically diverge in a financial crisis. If liabilities are collateralized, but not 100%, should the whole liability be protected, or should the excess over the value of collateral be open to bail-in?

All these issues place significant liquidity strains on the CCP which may become legally insolvent, as almost happened to Nasdaq Nordic.

In addition to the above, the requirement for mandatory clearing has had some wider, unforeseen consequences for the financial markets which may prove problematic:

(1) **Economic rent**: by mandating OTC derivatives clearing through a CCP, governments have handed a monopoly to key CCPs. The profit potential has seemingly changed the attitude of key market players which have in recent years moved from clubs or mutual of CMs to private businesses driven by shareholders. Should the economic benefits to CCPs of mandatory clearing be counterbalanced by significantly greater controls over how they are operated? Should this kind of monopoly not be state operated?

(2) **The scramble for monopoly is fostering risks**: as the Einar Aas debacle showed, as clearing houses battle to consolidate their control over OTC clearing, smaller exchanges are being pushed to take bigger risks to remain viable. It seems that one reason Aas remained a CM was that his presence in the Norwegian exchange maintained liquidity/trading levels. Losing him to another exchange would have meant the end. Is this the right attitude for systemically important infrastructure administrators?

(3) **Tie up between CCPs and data miners**: a side effect of the need for transparency has been that exchanges now have huge amounts of new information about what OTC derivative parties are doing. An interesting result of this is that CCPs are finding profit in monetizing this data and selling the information to banks, who trade accordingly. The effects of this are not yet clear.

The complexity is greater, and the assets traded more complicated, but many of these concerns and risks can be discerned in the historical examples with which we opened this chapter. The tension CCPs face between providing market stability and making a profit; counterparty risk; the cornering of service provision by specialists which sets off efficiency gains against concerns over control and anticompetitive practices; and beguiling notion that one can simply structure oneself out of financial crises. These features continue to appear as modern payment settlement systems and their brethren, securities and derivatives clearing systems, move into a world of cryptocurrencies, possible even issued by central banks.

Index

Made in the USA
Monee, IL
13 September 2026

62980171R00240